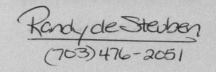
5-39 Budgeted ending finished goods inventory 72,000 units
5-40 Ending finished goods inventory at Quarter 4 24,000 units
5-41 September cash disbursements $543,300
5-42 Cash disbursements $383,100
5-43 June ending cash balance $35,603
5-44 July ending cash balance $2,400
5-45 (c) Budgeted income $118,008
5-46 (a) Ending cash balance $4,875
5-47 (b) Total required purchases $315,480
　　　(e) Budgeted net income $53,250
5-48 (d) Ending cash balance in September $20,100
　　　(f) Budgeted total assets $885,700
5-49 Cost of goods sold, September quarter $590,496
5-50 (a) Units to produce in January 32,000
5-51 Raw materials for quarter 796,200 ounces
5-52 (d) Budgeted net income $260,000
5-53 (e) Total overhead for itemtwo $164,000
5-BDC Budgeted net income $1,137,500

6-22 No key figure
6-23 (b) Rent revenue in 19X2 $6,000
6-24 (b) 19X2 Interest receivable = Interest revenue = $0
6-25 (b) 19X2 Prepaid insurance expense $0
6-26 (b) 19X1 Wages payable $10,000
6-27 (f) Total cash sales $80,000
6-28 (f) Cash cost of goods sold $115,000
6-29 (d) Cash from operating activities $95,700
6-30 Net decrease of cash $(10,000)
6-31 Cash from operating activities $42,000
6-32 Cash from operating activities $17,000
6-33 Cash from operating activities $70,000
6-34 Net increase in cash $5,000
6-35 Net increase in cash $15
6-36 Net decrease in cash $(25)
6-37 Cash from operating activities $(45,000)
6-38 Net increase in cash $30,000
6-39 Net income $110
6-40 Cash from operating activities $(30,000)
6-41 No key figure
6-42 No key figure

7-21 (b) Labor rate variance $(1,260)
7-22 (b) Actual labor cost per hour $3.95
7-23 (a) Direct labor cost should have been $120,000
7-24 (a) Direct labor efficiency variance $250
7-25 (a) Material quantity variance $(5,625)
7-26 (b) Variable overhead efficiency variance is $(1,200)
7-27 (b) Labor efficiency variance $(350)
7-28 (a) Variable manufacturing overhead spending variance $(275)
7-29 Indirect labor efficiency variance $(3,300)
7-30 Variable overhead efficiency variance $(1,680)
7-31 Variable overhead spending variance $3,000
7-32 Materials quantity variance $(4,000)
7-33 August labor efficiency variance $(7,700)
7-34 (b) Variable overhead efficiency variance $1,500
7-35 (b) Helmit standard cost per pound $.3908
7-36 Standard variable cost $6.12

7-37 (b) Material quantity variance $(1,000)
　　　(d) Labor efficiency variance $3,000
7-38 Direct labor rate variance $500
7-BDC Standard cost per carton using greasocide $4.1677

8-26 Machining department overhead rate = $.50 per machine hour
8-27 (b) Volume variance $20,000
8-28 Actual cost of goods sold $131,800
8-29 Fixed overhead is underapplied by $10,000
8-30 Volume variance $5,000
8-31 Budget variance $15,000
8-32 Volume variance $1,000,000
8-33 Budget variance $(400,000)
8-34 Manufacturing overhead variance $1,200,000
8-35 (c) Cost of Wright $24,000
8-36 September production costs $105,000
8-37 Cost per unit of TAC $48
8-38 Budget variance $181,000
8-39 (a) Overhead rate $9.03
8-40 (d) Direct labor hours 1,600 hours
8-41 Volume variance $21,700
8-42 Budget variance $(181,744.19)
8-43 (b) Budget variance $261,500
8-44 (a) Volume variance $16,000
8-45 (b) Volume variance $2,500
8-46 Volume variance $(4,500)
8-47 Budget variance $(4,650)
8-BDC (c) Cost of overhead per cooler = $5.75

9-24 At 180,000 units, total cost $3,580,000
9-25 At 400,000 machine hours, total cost $19,000,000
9-26 At 90,000 units, net income $3,020,000
9-27 No key figure
9-28 Sales variance $0
9-29 At sales of $540,000, net income $170,000
9-30 (a) Material quantity variance $(98,000)
9-31 Total labor variance $(760)
9-32 Total variable overhead variance $(10,000)
9-33 Volume variance $(80,000)
9-34 (a) Cost formula for maintenance $.10 per direct labor hour
9-35 At 250,000 stylings, net income $1,168,000
9-36 (b) At 1,200 units, net income $40,000
9-37 (a) Breakeven point 150,000 calculators
9-38 (b) At 24,000 robot hours, net income $1,200,000
9-39 No key figure
9-40 (c) Flexible budget variance $(11,000)
9-41 (b) At 42,000 machine hours, sales variance $(20,000)
9-42 (b) Regression line is cost = $-120 + 11 \times$ machine hours
9-43 (a) Projected cost of variable overhead $10,560
9-44 (a) Projected cost of fixed overhead $31,000
9-BDC (b) Activity variance $(38,000)

10-21 Total materials cost $5,600
10-22 Cost per unit of Job 432 $24.50
10-23 Cost per unit
10-24 Balance of wo
10-25 Work in proce
10-26 (b) Labor rate

MANAGEMENT ACCOUNTING

The HBJ Accounting Series

MANAGEMENT ACCOUNTING

J. Edward Ketz

Deloitte and Touche Faculty Fellow
Pennsylvania State University

Terry L. Campbell, CPA, CMA

Pennsylvania State University
International Institute for
Management Development
(Lausanne, Switzerland)

Sidney J. Baxendale, CPA, CMA

University of Louisville

HARCOURT BRACE JOVANOVICH, PUBLISHERS
San Diego   New York   Chicago   Austin   Washington, D.C.
London   Sydney   Tokyo   Toronto

To

John Joseph Ketz,

Kyle Bradley Heyne, Chad Michael Heyne, and Kelsey Marie Heyne

and

Sidney and Thelma Baxendale

ISBN: 0-15-554667-8

Library of Congress Catalog Card Number: 90-084805

Printed in the United States of America

Lotus® and 1-2-3® are registered trademarks of Lotus Development Corporation.

Symphony™ is a trademark of Lotus Development Corporation.

IFPS® and Interactive Financial Planning Systems are registered trademarks of Execucom Systems Corporation.

We are grateful to the National Knitwear and Sportswear Association for its permission to adapt Ephraim Dworetsky's "The Concept of 'Book Value'" from *Knitting Times*, October 1988, p. 71, on p. 42.

Preface

Management Accounting has been written for a one-term course in management accounting and assumes no prior knowledge of this area of study. We assume that the student has had one prior course in financial accounting, but the instructor can overcome this by treating the review material in Chapters 1 and 2 as new material and by omitting the journal entries in Chapters 6, 10, and 11 or by teaching journal entries.

The emphasis of this textbook is on the use of accounting data by managers in making decisions. The general approach is to discuss a given type of decision that a manager faces, then to describe the information needed by the manager to make the decision, and finally to specify how a management accountant can provide that information. Thus, we present the management accountant as a team player who assists managers in decision-making activities.

In addition, we explain that decision making in the real world is a messy process. The available data may be incomplete and may contain errors. Moreover, because it is difficult to predict the future, managers should investigate various scenarios. In this way we introduce the idea of decision support systems.

While we do not emphasize the accounting bookkeeping and technical aspects, neither do we ignore them. These techniques and methods are fully discussed but in their role as an aid to decision making. The technical side of management accounting is explained as a means to an end.

Many recent changes in the business world affect management accounting, among them the automation of the manufacturing process and the adoption of a "just-in-time" philosophy. These changes and their impact on management accounting are fully articulated in Chapter 17, but they are also explained where appropriate throughout the textbook. We adopt this integrated approach because we believe that it is easier for a student to understand this impact by contrasting the traditional approaches and techniques with those brought about by automation and by the just-in-time philosophy.

Another major change in the economy is a decrease in manufacturing activities coupled with an increase in the service sectors. We provide not only for the management accounting for manufacturing firms but also for merchandising and service organizations.

Yet another major impact on businesses is the effect of changing prices. At this writing Iraq has invaded Kuwait and American troops are in the Middle East to prevent Iraq from invading Saudi Arabia. All three of these countries are major producers of the world's oil, and gasoline and oil prices have been volatile since the invasion. While increases in the price of petroleum products have obvious negative consequences for consumers, they have complex effects on all businesses. Management accountants should understand the effects of such price swings on the firm so that they can convey the relevant information to managers, who must make informed decisions based on that knowledge.

PEDAGOGICAL FEATURES

Management Accounting is organized in a flexible manner and contains pedagogical features designed to involve students in the material. After Chapters 1 and 2, the remaining chapters can be taken up in many different orders. **Learning objectives** at the beginning of each chapter, with page references, state explicitly what is expected of the student. **Boxed inserts,** one per chapter, extract from professional magazines real-world examples of topics discussed in the chapter. **Key terms** are boldfaced in text and appear in an end-of-chapter **glossary** that defines the major terms clearly and concisely. These glossaries have also been combined into one main glossary at the back of the book and the terms cross-referenced to the chapters in which they appear. (Minor terms are italicized where they are mentioned in the text.) A **review of chapter objectives** summarizes the chapter in terms of its learning objectives. **Review questions** ask the student to describe the key concepts of the chapter. **Discussion questions** ask the student to extend the concepts discussed in the chapter; these require thought and analysis by the students. **Exercises** and **problems** allow students to practice the major concepts and techniques of the chapter. These items are referenced by chapter objective. **Business decision cases,** one per chapter, ask the student to apply the accounting methods in a decision-making situation. Further, a **Demonstration Problem and Solution** immediately following the text of each chapter applies that chapter's material to solving problems and also previews for students the test items that follow.

ANCILLARIES

A full range of integrated *ancillaries for the instructor* are available with *Management Accounting.* The **Instructor's Manual,** by David E. Jensen (Bucknell University), includes chapter review, lecture notes and illustrations, overviews of exercises and problems, and ethics cases. These cases identify ethical dilemmas to start discussion rather than provide simplistic resolution. The Instructor's Manual also contains solutions to the Practice Set.

The **Solutions Manual,** by the textbook authors, provides complete solutions to all assignment material. Also available are **Transparencies** of the solutions for all Exercises, Problems, and Business Decision Cases, as well as 85 two-color **teaching transparencies** of key exhibits from the textbook. The **Test Resource Manual,** by Sidney Baxendale, contains over 600 multiple-choice questions and short examination problems. Many of the multiple-choice questions involve computations. Most of the questions have been used by Baxendale in the examinations he has administered. As a result, the questions have been purged of ambiguities and errors. All items in the test resource manual are cross-referenced to the learning objectives for each chapter. The entire test is available in SOPH-TEST™ software format, for use on most DOS-based or Macintosh personal computers.

Software includes an **instructor's manual and master disk** for Baxendale's *What If? Electronic Spreadsheet Templates for Decision Making.* This software can be assigned to the student or used with proper display technology for classroom lecture. To supplement the Practice Set (see following), a **master spreadsheet disk** allows instructors to provide a spreadsheet option for students if desired.

Ancillaries for the student include a **Study Guide** by Alan Reinstein (Wayne State University), with chapter reviews, equation reviews, demonstration problems, and a wealth of objective questions and problem material, with worked solutions, cross-referenced to chapter objectives and textbook discussions. **Working Papers** provide customized worksheets and accounting forms for all exercises, problems, and business decision cases in the textbook. A **Practice Set,** "Leisure Equipment, Inc.," by Gary L. Saunders (Marshall University) and Ruth E. Saunders (Integrated Business

Systems of Ohio), covers cost decisions and flexible budgeting for a manufacturing firm. (A spreadsheet option allows integration of computers with portions of the Practice Set at the instructor's discretion.)

Two software ancillaries are free to the student (in the form of a master disk to the instructor): *What If? Electronic Spreadsheet Templates for Decision Making* by Baxendale, and *MicroStudy Plus* by Delta Software. Brief instructions for both appear as appendixes to the textbook. The *What If?* software introduces spreadsheet templates as a decision-making tool. The computer exercises are designed to be increasingly challenging and instructive as the student progresses through the book. It is through the use of these computer exercises that students gain an appreciation of the decision support systems aspect of management accounting. Problems that can be worked using the *What If?* software are identified by a small computer logo. *MicroStudy Plus* is a computerized study guide that helps students consolidate their understanding of the chapters in the book. (An electronic spreadsheet template, free on adoption of the Practice Set, is also available.)

Finally, a **Checklist of Key Figures** is printed on the endpapers, allowing students to check the accuracy of their homework solutions.

ACKNOWLEDGMENTS

We gratefully acknowledge the assistance and constructive advice of the following instructors who reviewed this book in manuscript or in page proof:

Ronald S. Barden, Georgia State University
Wayne G. Bremser, Villanova University
Thomas B. Clevenger, Washburn University
Richard Coppage, University of Louisville
David E. Jensen, Bucknell University
Alan Reinstein, Wayne State University
Mostafa H. Sarhan, The University of Akron

We wish to thank Laura Ahrens and Jan Pollard at the University of Louisville, and Barb Apaliski, Deanna Rudy, Judy Sartore, and Tammy Snook at Pennsylvania State University, for their help in typing the manuscript.

We are also grateful to the following at Harcourt Brace Jovanovich: Ken Rethmeier, executive editor; Bill Teague, acquisitions editor; Paul Raymond, associate editor; Craig Avery, manuscript editor; Eleanor Garner, permissions editor; Judi McClellan, production editor; Don Fujimoto, Ann Smith, and Lyn Knipe, designers; Karen DeLeo, art editor; and Mary Kay Yearin, production manager.

We also wish to thank those at HBJ who worked on the ancillary package: Ken Fine, software editor; Lori McThomas, designer; Tracey Engel and Jennifer Johnson, production editors; and Jacqui Parker, production manager.

J. Edward Ketz
Terry L. Campbell
Sidney J. Baxendale

Contents

Part III Product Costing: Planning and Control

MANAGEMENT
ACCOUNTING

INTRODUCTION

Introduction to Management Accounting

CHAPTER OBJECTIVES

After reading Chapter 1, you should be able to:

1. Describe and explain the information needs of different types of organizations (pp. 3–9).

2. Compare and contrast strategic planning, management planning and control, and operational control (pp. 3–4).

3. Distinguish between data and information (pp. 4–5).

4. Discuss centralization and decentralization (pp. 5–7).

5. Explain the six types of tasks performed by managers (pp. 7–9).

6. Describe management accounting and differentiate it from financial accounting (pp. 9–14).

7. Explain decision support systems and what-if, goal-seeking, and analysis of the variables operations (pp. 14–17).

8. Recognize the behavioral aspects of management accounting for managers (pp. 17–18).

*A*ccounting is the information system used by external parties and internal management to report on and control profit-oriented and nonprofit organizations alike. (This textbook concentrates on profit-oriented entities.) External reporting is referred to as *financial accounting;* internal reporting is referred to as *management accounting.* Decisions such as entering a new market, raising or lowering prices, how to finance an investment, and whether to make or buy a product, among many others, are usually made based on management accounting precepts.

Although all organizations need information, not all need the same management accounting information system. The primary difference in many situations is one of degree, not of concept. All organizations need information regarding the relative profitability of items and segments, but not all need to obtain it through a complex management accounting system. Usually the larger the organization is, the more complex the management accounting information system must be. The corner grocery store manager may determine that a certain candy is more profitable and expand the offerings; a larger organization may decide to add a second shift to produce this candy. Each organization has made a decision using management accounting information.

ORGANIZATIONS AND MANAGEMENT: THE NEED FOR INFORMATION

CHAPTER
OBJECTIVE 1
Information needs of organizations

An organization is composed of individuals grouped by choice or self-selection to achieve common goals. The individuals perform tasks and make decisions that enhance or help achieve these goals. Decision makers must interpret the organization's goals, and their own roles in reaching them, as a basis for selecting which decisions to make. They need information about their tasks and those of others, and about the goals themselves. Decision making in organizations is not necessarily profit-centered, but it is always goal-centered.

Decisions and Planning

A decision is a choice among alternatives on some given issue. The choice is based on the judgment of the manager. Managers at all levels, from top management to first-line supervisors, must make decisions as part of their roles in establishing or carrying out the organization's goals. Each level requires different types of information because of the different types of decisions they must make.

CHAPTER
OBJECTIVE 2
*Levels of planning
and control*

Top management, consisting of the president or chief executive officer and other upper-level managers, undertakes strategic planning to define the organization's overall objectives or focus. Management at this level must scan the business environment, consider present economic and political conditions, and predict future conditions in order to direct the company toward its goals. Examples of such goals are: (1) to provide mass-produced wall clocks through numerous outlets; (2) to provide complex accounting, auditing, and consulting services to client firms; and (3) to provide financial services to individuals whose net worth is greater than $1,000,000. Such goals are much more complex than can be depicted here. The point is that strategic planning is the process of setting objectives for the firm.

Middle management makes decisions that implement the strategic plan and increase its specificity. For example, to implement the three goals above, middle managers could (1) devise the marketing, production, and financial plans for selling the wall clocks through specific outlets; (2) devise detailed plans for developing the personnel, resources, and business practices for the corporate accounting, auditing, and consulting services the firm wishes to provide; and (3) develop a package of financial services and investment options that would meet the needs of potential clients with the required net worth. These types of decisions, called management planning and control, move the organization closer to actually producing the product or providing the service. Periodically middle managers evaluate the progress toward meeting the goals. Where needed, amendments or corrections are then made to the plans. Middle managers are concerned with carrying out the strategic objectives successfully (a measure of their effectiveness) and with a minimum amount of resources (a measure of their efficiency). Thus management planning and control activities focus on the effective and efficient implementation of strategic goals.

The decisions of *first-line supervisors* implement top management's strategic plan and middle management's interpretation of the plan. In terms of our ongoing example, first-line supervisors would: (1) oversee the materials, production, marketing, and short-term financing of the wall clocks and their components; (2) hire and develop the personnel and control the flow of services to the client firms; and (3) sell and monitor investments for qualified individual clients. Decisions at this level are made continually; many are made daily or even more frequently. Thus operational control is concerned with carrying out specific tasks effectively and efficiently. At this level, as at all management levels, managers must make sure that their decisions are consistent with the overall strategy of the organization.

The Characteristics of Business Information

CHAPTER OBJECTIVE 3
Data and information

Data are symbols that represent something. Information is data processed to yield useful insights for a decision maker. For example, a firm engages in hundreds of transactions every day. Knowledge about each of these transactions does not help an upper-level manager perform his or her job; therefore, the transactions (data) are collated and summarized in monthly, quarterly, or annual financial reports (information). The manager can then analyze these reports for purposes of planning and control.

The characteristics of information used for strategic planning, management planning and control, and operational control are different. Strategic planning involves scanning the industry, the nation, and even the world to unearth new business opportunities. Strategic information originates largely outside the organization (such as economic statistics of the nation or a foreign country or region) and covers many diverse topics. This information is highly generalized to give top management an overall perspective, and it tends to look for future trends that could help in the assessment of upcoming opportunities. The information used in strategic planning is usually relatively old because the data are collected over a long period. Additionally, it must be summarized to be of use. The accuracy of such information is relatively low; pinpoint accuracy and absolute certainty are not achievable in generalized information used to forecast the future. Since organizations tend not to change their mission very often, they make infrequent use of strategic information.

By contrast, strategic information differs markedly from information developed for operational control, which involves line supervision of specific tasks. The source of

EXHIBIT 1-1

THE CHARACTERISTICS OF BUSINESS INFORMATION BY DECISION CATEGORY

	Strategic Planning	Management Planning and Control	Operational Control
Source	External	External and internal	Internal
Scope	Very wide	Wide	Narrow
Level of aggregation	Highly aggregate	Medium	Low; detailed
Time horizon	Future	Future and past	Past
Currency	Quite old	Somewhat current	Highly current
Required accuracy	Low	Medium	High
Frequency of use	Infrequent	Frequent	Very frequent

operational information is internal rather than external, and its scope is limited to specific tasks. Operational information tends to be detailed and is usually based on historical data, since the information is designed to help managers ask whether specific tasks are working as planned. Further, operational information must be up to date and highly accurate, as it is used often as the basis for decisions affecting detailed costs and operations.

The characteristics of information used for management planning and control fall between those of strategic planning and operational control. The source of information is both external and internal, the scope is wide, and the level of aggregation is medium. This information can be either projections of the future or based on historical data. The information is somewhat current and the required level of accuracy is medium. This information is used frequently. Information used for management planning and control takes on some of the features of information for strategic planning and some of the traits of information for operational control, since middle managers need to communicate both with top managers and with first-line supervisors. The characteristics of business information are summarized in Exhibit 1-1.

Centralization and Decentralization

CHAPTER OBJECTIVE 4
Centralization and decentralization

In the previous section we discussed how the type of decisions affects the kinds of information gathered and disseminated. These in turn affect the way entities are structured. Some organizations are highly structured and are said to have a centralized organization, in which authority is maintained by a few people in top management. Other entities have loosely structured segments. They are referred to as decentralized organizations; in them authority is delegated downward—for example, to divisions.

Each perspective has its merits, and both are often used in the same organization. The focus of centralization is usually on efficiency (accomplishing goals using the least resources); the focus of decentralization is usually on effectiveness (accomplishing the

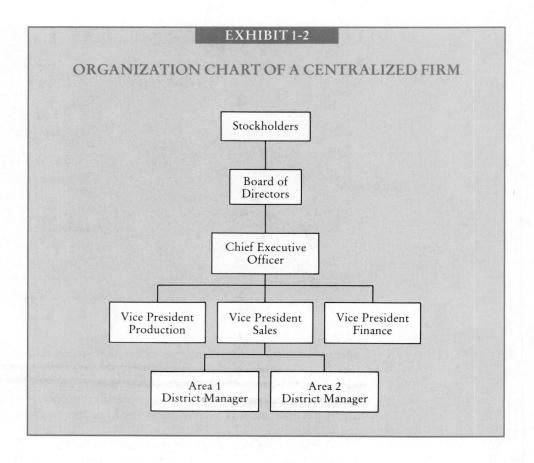

EXHIBIT 1-2

ORGANIZATION CHART OF A CENTRALIZED FIRM

goal successfully). Both centralization and decentralization require accurate, relevant, and timely management accounting information in order to function. This is because both management styles depend on a number of individuals to get things done. No one person could undertake all of an organization's activities. Therefore, the workload must be spread out to accomplish goals in a timely manner, and each individual carries his or her share of the overall load. In order to establish some system of managing the large amount of work that must be delegated, the organization requires some way of communicating and evaluating goals and plans from one level or subentity to another. Most organizations create an organization chart to depict these formal relationships.

A typical organization chart would include the board of directors representing the owners, various management levels, and other key personnel. (We are assuming that the firm is large enough to organize into these components and that the firm is a corporation.) Although the stockholders provide the capital for the organization, few of them wish to manage the day-to-day operations of the organization. Therefore, they delegate the organizational oversight to a *board of directors,* which selects a top manager or top management team and guides the organizational strategy. The top management team, usually led by a *chief executive officer* or president, is the primary strategic planning and goal-setting group for the organization. The top management team oversees others who represent a broad range of management specialties in production, marketing, and finance—and who focus their energies on creating and managing a subgroup of lower-level managers within the organization.

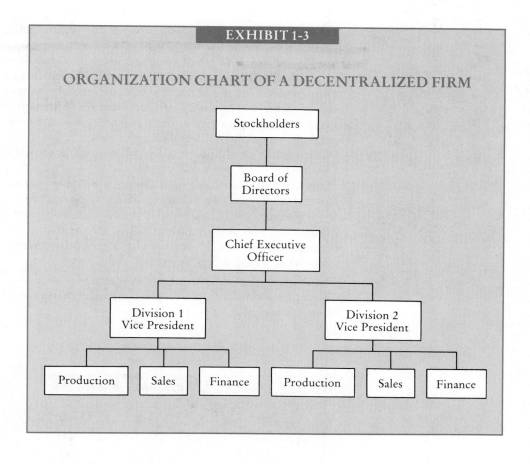

EXHIBIT 1-3

ORGANIZATION CHART OF A DECENTRALIZED FIRM

These reporting responsibilities identify the formal communication links for reporting, advising, changing, monitoring, and other management tasks. In essence, the organization chart officially mandates the chain of command.

The organization chart of a typical centralized firm is depicted in Exhibit 1-2. The chart for a typical decentralized organization is shown in Exhibit 1-3. Both charts encompass the major functions of the corporation but each does so differently. The centralized firm has one production group, one sales group, and one finance group. The decentralized company organizes the firm into divisions, possibly by product line. Each division has its own functional groups. Some corporations are hybrids in the sense that they centralize some functions but decentralize others.

In addition to the formal lines of communication mandated by the management structure, organizations also rely on informal communication links, generally termed "the grapevine." They allow information to pass quickly and efficiently around the organization to reinforce particular goals.

Management Tasks

CHAPTER OBJECTIVE 5
Management's six tasks

Members of an organization perform many tasks, some of them typical and similar to one another, others unique in character and in aim. In this respect managers' tasks are no different, except that they have the larger responsibility to direct the activities of the employees under their leadership toward the organization's goals. Their similar tasks may be grouped into six categories: planning, organizing, staffing, directing, controlling, and reporting. (Each of these tasks is defined and discussed next.) Managers may be involved in all of these tasks simultaneously. Further, the tasks are integral to each management level and are carried out continuously, subject to the constraints of authority and the responsibility of each manager. Although decision making takes effort and consumes much of a manager's time, it is not considered a separate task because decision making is integral to each of these tasks.

Management's six tasks form a decision process, as shown in Exhibit 1-4.

1. **Planning** is the identification of a future position or goal and the determination of the necessary steps to reaching it. Planning predetermines organizational action and is the cause of it. Once a goal is identified, management communicates the plan in more detail by way of a *budget*. Plans are the central thread around which the organization functions. They are also a means of communication to employees about what is expected of them.

2. **Organizing** is the determination of the structure needed to achieve a goal. Organizing can be considered the creation of a skeletal structure needed for achievement of organizational goals.

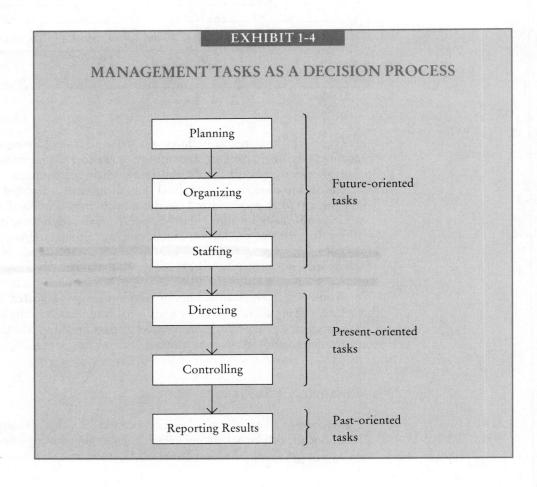

EXHIBIT 1-4

MANAGEMENT TASKS AS A DECISION PROCESS

Planning → Organizing → Staffing } Future-oriented tasks

Directing → Controlling } Present-oriented tasks

Reporting Results } Past-oriented tasks

3. **Staffing** is the selection of personnel to perform the organization's tasks. It is closely related to organizing. Staffing can be considered the initial fleshing out of the skeletal organizational structure. Whereas organizing is the establishment of structures such as committees and departments, staffing is filling these structures with employees.

4. **Directing** is leading the organization toward the achievement of its goals. Directing involves managing events and requiring employees to perform certain tasks in a prescribed fashion.

5. **Controlling** is the review of performance and progress toward goals, and reinforcing or taking corrective action where necessary. It involves comparing activities that have occurred (or are expected to occur) against expectations. Information gathered in the control function can be used to create new plans, new organization, new staffing, and new direction.

6. **Reporting** is receiving and transmitting information about performance and progress toward goals. Further, reporting involves action in the form of requests or mandates for changes in performance based on that performance. Reports provide formal communication across the organization about how effectively and efficiently operations are being carried out.

Regardless of management level and task, managers make decisions based on available information. The continuity, survival, and success of the organization depend on the availability of accurate information.

These tasks occur in this order only in a logical sense. In practice, managers can easily jump from one task to another seemingly out of sequence. For example, while controlling an operation, a manager might want to move some fatigued employees to a different task and add freshly trained employees to speed up or improve the segment. The manager could jump from controlling an assignment back to staffing the operation. Thus the sequencing is only a general tendency.

THE ROLE OF THE MANAGEMENT ACCOUNTANT

CHAPTER OBJECTIVE 6
Management accounting

The management accountant may have a variety of titles. Among them are chief financial officer (CFO) and *controller* (or *comptroller*). (Decentralized firms also have CFOs, although this is not shown in Exhibit 1-3.) Regardless of title, however, the function in all firms is similar.

As the organization chart in Exhibit 1-2 shows, the vice president of finance (or CFO) reports to the chief executive officer. The role of the management accountant is to support management as it is engaged in the primary activity of the business: to provide goods, services, and information to customers and clients. Such roles are referred to as *staff* positions. Actually producing and selling the goods, services, or information—along with their management—are *line* activities. Thus management accountants provide support services to the organization by analyzing, interpreting, and communicating accounting information to management. This in no way diminishes the importance of the management accountant's role, as the CFO is a member of the top-management team.

The management accountant makes decisions about what, how, when, where, to whom, and why accounting information is presented using a technique called *information evaluation,* in which the costs and benefits of alternatives are estimated and evaluated. Information evaluation is similar to cost-benefit analyses (as discussed further in Chapter 4). The management accountant also helps design and operate the accounting information system, which is a subsystem of the computerized management information system that supplies managers with information of many kinds.

A Definition of Management Accounting

The definition of management accounting developed by the National Association of Accountants (NAA) in its *Statement No. 1A,* "Definition of Management Accounting" (1981), is the main source of the functions of management accounting:

> The process of identification, measurement, accumulation, analysis, preparation, interpretation, and communication of financial information used by management to plan, evaluate, and control within an organization and to assure appropriate use of and accountability for its resources. Management accounting also comprises the preparation of financial reports for non-management groups such as shareholders, creditors, regulatory agencies, and tax authorities.

This definition fits well with the earlier discussion of the characteristics of management information, except that it includes preparation of reports to shareholders and other external users of the firm's information among the management accountant's duties. (The next section details the distinctions between financial accounting, which is chiefly concerned with such external reporting, and management accounting.)

In addition, the management accountant must be able to operate effectively in two other distinct but overlapping accounting perspectives:

1. Cost accounting is the accumulation and determination of the cost of a project, process, or activity. It is undertaken by most entities as a basic tool for planning, monitoring, analyzing, and controlling costs. (Cost terms and their definitions, the building blocks of cost accounting, are discussed in Chapter 2, and cost accounting is discussed throughout the book, especially in Chapters 3 and 7–11.) Cost is determined by direct measurement, arbitrary assignment, or systematic and rational allocation.

2. Responsibility accounting is a reporting system in which costs and revenues are assigned to the level of the organization having responsibility for them. Its emphasis is on reporting the *performance* of the level based on these assigned costs and revenues.

Cost accounting and responsibility accounting differ in their focus. Cost accounting looks at the project, process, or activity regardless of department or level it passes through on the way to completion. (A product may pass through a number of departments before being sold, accumulating costs in each.) Responsibility accounting, on the other hand, reports on the entity (the whole organization), the subentity (a subunit of the organization, such as sales), or the individual responsible for generating costs and revenues. (This idea is developed throughout the textbook, including discussions in Chapters 5, 12, and 13.)

To provide reports under responsibility accounting, a budget is required. A budget is a financial plan that provides the basis for performance appraisal as well as a blueprint for future resource organization and general management decisions. A budget depicts a goal in measurable or quantifiable terms. This is because it contains estimates of the expected (or *standard*) costs of items or activities. The reliance on standard costs and budgets allows achievement of goals and forecasts to be measured objectively. *Performance reports* highlight deviations from the budget called **variances.** Static budgets is the subject of Chapters 5 and 6, flexible budgets are covered in Chapter 9, and capital budgets are the focus of Chapter 14. Standard costs are discussed in Chapters 7, 8, and 9. Managers are evaluated externally by financial statements, and their analysis is covered in Chapter 15. Finally, the impact of inflation on management accounting is the topic of Chapter 16.

Management Accounting and Financial Accounting Compared

The definition of management accounting presented in the previous section included the preparation of financial reports to external users, which is usually considered the role of financial accounting. **Financial accounting** is geared to producing financial statements to be read by those outside the firm. Nevertheless, there are differences between these two areas of accounting, which are discussed next and summarized in Exhibit 1-5 (page 13). (Aspects of financial accounting that are relevant to management accountants are pointed out in Chapters 2, 6, 15, and 16.)

Management accounting focuses primarily on future performance and decisions affecting upcoming events, whereas financial accounting focuses on reporting historical results. Management accountants do not evaluate past goals that have been met; rather, they concentrate on how to learn from past results in order to achieve future goals. Management accounting is primarily aimed at internal users; financial accounting is carried out to provide information to outside parties. In this regard, management accounting is largely voluntary, as no external agency mandates a particular report. Of course, management may demand certain internal reports. Users of external financial reports include investors, creditors, government agencies, labor unions, suppliers, and the general public.

Management accounting rules are imposed by management and not usually mandated by an external agency. The numbers generated in financial accounting statements must conform to *generally accepted accounting principles* (GAAP). These rules are generated by agencies such as the Securities Exchange Commission (SEC) and the Financial Accounting Standards Board (FASB). Management accountants sometimes rely on GAAP, but this is usually a mistake. Management accountants must be attuned to their managers' information needs and not to rules that ignore the needs of managers.

Management accounting reports and analyses may include monetary data and nonmonetary information; financial accounting includes only monetary data with explanatory footnotes. For example, financial reports rarely report how many labor hours it takes to make a product—information that may be crucial to management.

Management accounting includes each subentity that can be reasonably measured in a responsibility accounting setting and includes the overall entity; financial accounting usually focuses only on the overall entity unless mandated to report a segment. Management accounting draws on extensive interdisciplinary activity, including economics, finance, psychology, sociology, and speech communication. Financial accounting is interdisciplinary (it includes concepts from finance and economics), but not to the extent that management accounting is.

Technology is changing the way corporations do business. Increasing automation and the use of robotics and other advanced manufacturing techniques, discussed

STANDARDS OF ETHICAL CONDUCT
FOR MANAGEMENT ACCOUNTANTS

Management accountants have an obligation to the organizations they serve, their profession, the public, and themselves to maintain the highest standards of ethical conduct. In recognition of this obligation, the National Association of Accountants has promulgated the following standards of ethical conduct for management accountants. Adherence to these standards is integral to achieving the *Objectives of Management Accounting.* * Management accountants shall not commit acts contrary to these standards nor shall they condone the commission of such acts by others within their organizations.

COMPETENCE

Management accountants have a responsibility to:
- Maintain an appropriate level of professional competence by ongoing development of their knowledge and skills.
- Perform their professional duties in accordance with relevant laws, regulations, and technical standards.
- Prepare complete and clear reports and recommendations after appropriate analyses of relevant and reliable information.

CONFIDENTIALITY

Management accountants have a responsibility to:
- Refrain from disclosing confidential information acquired in the course of their work except when authorized, unless legally obligated to do so.
- Inform subordinates as appropriate regarding the confidentiality of information acquired in the course of their work and monitor their activities to assure the maintenance of that confidentiality.
- Refrain from using or appearing to use confidential information acquired in the course of their work for unethical or illegal advantage either personally or through third parties.

INTEGRITY

Management accountants have a responsibility to:
- Avoid actual or apparent conflicts of interest and advise all appropriate parties of any potential conflict.

*National Association of Accountants, *Statements on Management Accounting: Objectives of Management Accounting,* Statement No. 1B, New York, N.Y., June 17, 1982.

- Refrain from engaging in any activity that would prejudice their ability to carry out their duties ethically.
- Refuse any gift, favor, or hospitality that would influence or would appear to influence their actions.
- Refrain from either actively or passively subverting the attainment of the organization's legitimate and ethical objectives.
- Recognize and communicate professional limitations or other constraints that would preclude responsible judgment or successful performance of an activity.
- Communicate unfavorable as well as favorable information and professional judgments or opinions.
- Refrain from engaging in or supporting any activity that would discredit the profession.

OBJECTIVITY

Management accountants have a responsibility to:
- Communicate information fairly and objectively.
- Disclose fully all relevant information that could reasonably be expected to influence an intended user's understanding of the reports, comments, and recommendations presented.

RESOLUTION OF ETHICAL CONDUCT

In applying the standards of ethical conduct, management accountants may encounter problems in identifying unethical behavior or in resolving an ethical conflict. When faced with significant ethical issues, management accountants should follow the established policies of the organization bearing on the resolution of such conflict. If these policies do not resolve the ethical conflict, management accountants should consider the following course of action:

- Discuss such problems with the immediate superior except when it appears that the superior is involved, in which case the problem should be presented initially to the next higher managerial level. If satisfactory resolution cannot be achieved when the problem is initially presented, submit the issues to the next higher managerial level.

  If the immediate superior is the chief executive officer, or equivalent, the acceptable reviewing authority may be a group such as the audit committee, executive committee, board of directors, board of trustees, or owners. Contact with levels above the immediate superior should be initiated only with the superior's knowledge, assuming the superior is not involved.

■ Clarify relevant concepts by confidential discussion with an objective advisor to obtain an understanding of possible courses of action.

■ If the ethical conflict still exists after exhausting all levels of internal review, the management accountant may have no other recourse on significant matters than to resign from the organization and to submit an informative memorandum to an appropriate representative of the organization.

Except where legally prescribed, communication of such problems to authorities or individuals not employed or engaged by the organization is not considered appropriate.

SOURCE: *Management Accounting* (August 1986), p. 63. Copyright © 1986 by the National Association of Accountants. Reprinted by permission.

further in Chapters 8, 10, 11, and 17, are changing the manufacturing process. Some of these changes are altering what the management accountant does. As new concepts and principles are introduced in the textbook, we will describe the impact of technology on these concepts and principles. Technology is also changing how firms gather and process information. One aspect of this change, decision support systems, is introduced later in this chapter. Other facets of information technology are presented in Chapter 17.

Management Accounting as a Career

We encourage you to consider the information needs of management and to recognize the expanding role of the management accountant. We believe that this role is critical in all organizations. First, management accountants are an integral part of the top-management team. Without this recognition, management accounting could not participate in top-management decisions.

EXHIBIT 1-5

FINANCIAL ACCOUNTING AND MANAGEMENT ACCOUNTING COMPARED

Focus	Financial Accounting	Management Accounting
Time	Emphasis on the past	Emphasis on the future
User	External	Internal
Rules	Generally accepted accounting principles	Emphasis on relevance to managements' information demands
Measurement	Monetary	Monetary and nonmonetary
Entity level	Usually overall entity	Subentity and overall entity
Domain	Some interdisciplinary activity	Extensive interdisciplinary activity

Second, the National Association of Accountants (NAA) in 1972 originated professional certification of the management accountant by sponsoring the Certified Management Accounting (CMA) examination. Increasing recognition of the CMA by industry has provided substantial support for those interested in professional management accounting certification. The NAA states:

> The CMA program requires candidates to pass a series of uniform examinations and meet specific educational and professional standards to qualify for and maintain the Certificate in Management Accounting. NAA has established the Institute of Management Accounting to administer the program, conduct the examinations, and grant certificates to those who qualify.
>
> The objectives of the program are threefold: (1) to establish management accounting as a recognized profession by identifying the role of the management accountant and the underlying body of knowledge, and by outlining a course of study by which such knowledge can be acquired; (2) to foster higher educational standards in the field of management accounting; and (3) to assist employers, educators and students by establishing objective measurement of an individual's knowledge and competence in the field of management accounting.

A CMA certificate gives management accountants increased recognition, job mobility, and opportunities for higher salaries.

DECISION SUPPORT SYSTEMS

CHAPTER OBJECTIVE 7
DSS

The most significant contribution to management accounting during the 1960s was the development and use of mathematical and statistical models such as regression analysis. Most significant to management accounting during the 1980s was the recognition that there were limitations to applying these models in actual businesses. The result was a new approach to applying these principles called decision support systems.

Decision support systems (DSS) are computer programs designed to support the decision-making process of managers by providing information from data and models. In contrast to the earlier approaches, in which models were used to obtain the *correct answer*, under the current approach the model's result is considered additional information useful for making the *decision*. In other words, the model's answer is not the final word. Data may be measured with error, models may be misspecified and incomplete, and some variables and functions are not susceptible to mathematical manipulation. Because of these inherent problems, no model can give the single correct answer. Thus, managers must use the model's solution as an approximation; they must still use their expertise to make a sound decision.

Three common functions of decision support systems are what-if analysis, goal-seeking, and displaying how variables were calculated via analysis. (Other operations, such as simulation and optimization, can be used in decision support systems. They are described in Chapter 4.) All three functions manipulate the data to provide some insights but leave the decision making to managers.

A simple example of a decision support system program is shown in the computer display in Exhibit 1-6. A four-year planning model covers 19X0–19X3. First-year sales are $1,000,000 and they grow at a 10% rate. Cost of sales is assumed to be 40% of sales. Salaries are $100,000 in 19X0 and grow at the rate of 6%. Taxes are 35% of income before taxes. Net income equals sales minus the expenses of cost of sales, salaries, and taxes. Finally, return on sales is calculated as net income divided by sales.

In practice a manager or a management accountant or a computer operator would be running the software package. The data would come from files based on transactions and other historical data or on future projections such as the budget. The models could be developed already by others or be built by the user. Thereafter the user could manipulate the DSS however desired.

The screen display shows two parts or windows, the model and the solution. The model depicts the parameters of the variables and the relationships among the variables. The solution gives the numerical results for each of the variables. The solution window is displayed so that the manager can observe the values of the financial variables.

By their nature, all forecasts contain errors. One way of examining the solution's sensitivity to errors in the data is to try new values and ascertain their impact. This process is called what-if analysis. For example, a what-if analysis is depicted in Exhibit 1-7. In this case, the manager assumes that sales grow at 8% instead of 10% and that salaries grow at 8% rather than 6%. All other parameters are assumed to be the same (for example, the tax rate remains 35%), and all other relationships are unchanged (for example, the same formula is used for return on sales). The solution for the what-if analysis is displayed in the bottom half of Exhibit 1-7. (The numbers may be verified by computation, but this takes longer—compared to the speed of DSS programming.)

A second dimension of decision support systems is goal-seeking, in which a manager sets some numerical goal and specifies which variable to change in an attempt to

---

EXHIBIT 1-6

DECISION SUPPORT SYSTEM MODEL AND SOLUTION

Model

Years 19X0–19X3

Sales	$= \$1,000,000$, previous $\times 1.1$
Cost of Sales	$= .40 \times$ Sales
Salaries	$= \$100,000$, previous $\times 1.06$
Taxes	$= .35 \times ($Sales $-$ Cost of Sales $-$ Salaries$)$
Net Income	$=$ Sales $-$ Cost of Sales $-$ Salaries $-$ Taxes
Return on Sales	$=$ Net Income/Sales

Solution

	19X0	19X1	19X2	19X3
Sales	$1,000,000	$1,100,000	$1,210,000	$1,331,000
Cost of Sales	400,000	440,000	484,000	532,400
Salaries	100,000	106,000	112,360	119,102
Taxes	175,000	193,900	214,774	237,824
Net Income	325,000	360,100	398,866	441,674
Return on Sales	.325	.327	.330	.332

EXHIBIT 1-7

DECISION SUPPORT SYSTEM USING WHAT-IF ANALYSIS

What-if

Sales   = $1,000,000, previous × 1.08
Salaries = $100,000, previous × 1.08

What-if Solution

	19X0	19X1	19X2	19X3
Sales	$1,000,000	$1,080,000	$1,166,400	$1,259,712
Cost of Sales	400,000	432,000	466,560	503,885
Salaries	100,000	108,000	116,640	125,971
Taxes	175,000	189,000	204,120	220,450
Net Income	325,000	351,000	379,080	409,406
Return on Sales	.325	.325	.325	.325

EXHIBIT 1-8

DECISION SUPPORT SYSTEM USING GOAL-SEEKING

Goal

Variable (goal): Net Income = $400,000
Variable to Adjust: Sales

Solution

	19X0	19X1	19X2	19X3
Sales	$1,192,308	$1,202,308	$1,212,908	$1,224,144
Cost of Sales	476,923	480,923	485,163	489,658
Salaries	100,000	106,000	112,360	119,102
Taxes	215,385	215,385	215,385	215,385
Net Income	400,000	400,000	400,000	400,000
Return on Sales	.335	.333	.330	.327

reach the goal. Exhibit 1-8 is an example. Suppose we return to the original example in Exhibit 1-6 but here the manager has a goal of $400,000 net income. The manager specifies that sales are to change to accomplish this goal. (Computer programs do not allow several changes to occur simultaneously because an infinite number of solutions could occur.)

EXHIBIT 1-9

DECISION SUPPORT SYSTEM: ANALYSIS OF THE VARIABLES

Analyze

Variable: Return on Sales

Model

Return on Sales = Net Income/Sales

Solution

	19X0	19X1	19X2	19X3
Sales	$1,000,000	$1,100,000	$1,210,000	$1,331,000
Net Income	325,000	360,100	398,866	441,674
Return on Sales	.325	.327	.330	.332

The solution window displays how the goal is achieved. Notice that the net income in each year is $400,000, as requested. Notice also that the other aspects of the modeling (such as salaries and tax rate) are the same as in the original specification shown in Exhibit 1-6.

A third function of decision support systems is an **analysis of the variables.** This function asks the system to display how the variable is calculated and the numerical values. In the example in Exhibit 1-9, the user has requested the system to analyze the return on sales ratio. The system responds with the modeling statement or formula that tells how the variable is computed. Then the variables that make up the ratio are tabulated along with their values so that the user can see the components of the analyzed variable. This step could be important, for example, if return on sales becomes unacceptably low.

Decision support systems allow managers to interrogate the model and the values. It allows a manager to perform what-if analysis and goal-seeking, and to analyze a variable. In this way, the manager can see how sensitive the solutions are to changes in the data and to the various modeling relationships.

BEHAVIORAL ASPECTS OF MANAGEMENT ACCOUNTING

CHAPTER OBJECTIVE 8
Impact of management accounting on behavior

This introductory chapter makes it clear that we believe management accounting to be behaviorally based. In fact, without an understanding of the behavioral implications of management accounting, it is difficult to define and use management accounting concepts. It is not just the numbers that must be collected, aggregated, and reported; the underlying assumptions about each decision and decision maker must also be reviewed continually.

For example, management wishes to adopt a new strategy or revise its current strategy. Management accountants are provided the assumptions and asked to extrapolate them into long-term financial and other results (such as market share). Thus, the management accountant is intimately involved in strategic planning and can affect the decision with the reports.

Another possibility is that members of middle management wish to evaluate the performance of their subordinates. They request the management accountant to prepare performance reports on these employees. Thus, the management accountant is intimately involved in the middle management performance evaluation process.

Also, consider line-level supervisors who wish to monitor the efficiency (measured as the relationship between inputs and outputs) of a certain process. They request the management accountant to prepare a report comparing daily inputs and outputs. Thus, the management accountant is intimately involved in the day-to-day operations.

The management accountant must be able to take the perspective of the manager, gather the appropriate data, evaluate it with the appropriate analytical tools, and communicate the results in a way that helps the decision maker achieve the organization's goals.

In future chapters, where appropriate, behavioral aspects of management accounting will be addressed. For example, we will discuss budget slack in Chapter 5, the construction of performance measures and their impact on managers in Chapter 12, and the problems of management in the face of technological change in Chapter 17. Thus, management accounting is not only a quantitative discipline, but one that also affects the way people act and behave.

Review of Chapter Objectives

1. Describe and explain the information needs of different types of organizations (pp. 3–9).

   ■ Accounting is the pervasive form of information in organizations. Organizations of all types and sizes need information to survive, compete, and succeed. More complex organizations need more complex management accounting information systems. Management uses information evaluation and cost-benefit concepts to assess the system needed.

   ■ The importance of information is that it helps managers in their decision making. A decision is a choice among alternatives on some given issue. Information can assist the manager by improving the decision-making process.

2. Compare and contrast strategic planning, management planning and control, and operational control (pp. 3–4).

   ■ Management makes different types of decisions, to some extent dependent on their level within the organizational structure. Top management usually makes long-term strategic decisions. Middle management's decisions implement the strategic plan. The first-line management's decisions are oriented to day-to-day operations. These activities are referred to respectively as strategic planning, management planning and control, and operational control.

3. Distinguish between data and information (pp. 4–5).

   ■ Data are symbols that represent something. Information is processed data. Data is processed into information so that it can assist managers in making decisions.

A good information system will allow managers to make the best decisions possible.

4. Discuss centralization and decentralization (pp. 5–7).

- Organizational structures may be centralized or decentralized. A centralized organization maintains authority centrally. An organization is decentralized when authority is not maintained centrally but is delegated downward in the organization.

- An organization chart is a graphic depiction of the organization. It shows the formal relationships among the managers and other employees of the firm. An organization chart shows the major functions of the organization and indicates whether the organization is centralized or decentralized.

- Regardless of the degree of centralization chosen, management must have accurate, relevant, and timely information. Management levels differ in the characteristics of the information they must receive. Top management usually prefers generalized information at relatively long frequencies. First-line supervisors prefer detailed information at relatively short intervals. Middle managers' information needs are between these extremes.

5. Explain the six types of tasks performed by managers (pp. 7–9).

- Management's decision process involves planning, organizing, staffing, directing, controlling, and reporting. Planning embraces the identification of future positions or goals. Organizing comprises the determination of the structure needed to achieve the goals. Staffing incorporates the selection of personnel to perform the organization's tasks. Directing involves leading the organization toward achievement of its goal. Controlling encompasses the review of performance and progress and taking appropriate reinforcement or corrective action where necessary. Reporting includes receiving and transmitting information about performance and progress toward goals.

6. Describe management accounting and differentiate it from financial accounting (pp. 9–14).

- Management accounting is the process of identification, measurement, accumulation, analysis, preparation, interpretation, and communication of financial information used by management to plan, evaluate, and control within an organization and to assure appropriate use of and accountability for its resources. Management accounting also comprises cost accounting and responsibility accounting. Cost accounting is a method for accumulating the cost of a project, process, or product. Responsibility accounting is a system in which costs and revenues are reported at the level having the related responsibility within the organization.

- Management accounting and financial accounting are alike in several ways. They both produce information so that users might make better decisions. Financial and management accounting also use some similar terms and some similar reports. However, management accounting reports are geared toward internal users such as managers, whereas financial accounting reports are directed to external users such as creditors and investors. The primary differences are that management accounting is more oriented to the future, to internal reporting, to relevance, to monetary and nonmonetary measurements, to subentity evaluation, and to extensive interdisciplinary activity.

- The management accounting profession is becoming increasingly visible. The professional certification designation (CMA) is an indicator of this. The increasing linkage between top management and management accounting is another indicator.

7. Explain decision support systems and what-if, goal-seeking, and analysis of the variables operations (pp. 14–17).

- Decision support systems are computer systems designed to support the decision-making process of managers by providing information from data and models. Because data are measured with error and models are never completely accurate, managers must be able to test the sensitivity of the model's answers. This can be done using what-if analysis, goal-seeking, and analysis of the variables. What-if analysis tries different sets of data and calculates solutions for each set. Goal-seeking ascertains the value a variable needs to have to achieve a pre-specified goal. Analysis of the variables simply asks the computer system how a variable is calculated and also gives numerical values.

8. Recognize the behavioral aspects of management accounting for managers (pp. 17–18).

- Management accounting primarily focuses on quantitative calculations, which serve as information for managers in decision making. However, these numbers and data have an impact on people. For example, it is natural for managers to use those numbers that make them appear effective and efficient and criticize those numbers that make them appear inadequate. Managers and management accountants must understand these behavioral phenomena so that they are prepared to overcome them as they arise in practice. Specific examples of these behavioral aspects will be given throughout the rest of this textbook.

Glossary of Key Terms

analysis of the variables   With respect to decision support systems, a request to know how a variable is calculated.

budget   A financial plan that provides the basis for performance appraisal as well as a blueprint for future resource, organization, and general management decisions.

centralization   An organizational approach in which a supervising function maintains significant direction and authority over operations and policies relating to a number of identifiable, separate activities and operations.

Certified Management Accountant (CMA)   A professional designation awarded by the Institute of Management Accounting to an accountant who has met the requirements of the institute, including satisfactory completion of a comprehensive examination.

chief financial officer (CFO)   Usually the chief management accountant, in some organizations referred to as the chief information officer, controller (or comptroller), or management accountant.

control   The review of performance and progress toward goals, and reinforcing or taking corrective action where necessary.

cost accounting   The process of accumulating and determining the cost of a project, process, or activity.

data   Symbols that represent something.

decentralization   An organizational approach in which a supervising function does not maintain significant direction and authority over operations and policies relating to a number of identifiable, separate activities and operations. Rather, it allows decentralized divisions to have that authority.

decision   A choice among alternatives on a given issue.

decision support systems (DSS)   Computer systems designed to support the decision-making process of managers by providing information from data and models.

directing   Leading the organization toward the achievement of its goals.

effectiveness   The degree to which a goal or objective is accomplished.

efficiency   The degree to which a limited amount of resources (input) are expended to achieve a certain output.

financial accounting   Accounting for purposes of financial reporting to external users via the financial statements.

goal-seeking   With respect to decision support systems, setting some goal and specifying some variable to change in an attempt to reach the goal.

information   Data processed to yield useful insights for a decision maker.

management accounting   "The process of identification, measurement, accumulation, analysis, preparation, interpretation, and communication of information used by management to plan, evaluate, and control within an organization and to assure appropriate use of and accountability for its resources." (*NAA Statement No. 1A*, 1981)

management planning and control   The process of implementing the strategic goals of the firm effectively and efficiently.

operational control   The process of carrying out specific tasks effectively and efficiently.

organization   A group of individuals united to achieve common goals.

organizing   The determination of the structure needed to achieve a goal.

planning   The identification of a future position or goal and the determination of the necessary steps to reaching it.

reporting   Receiving and transmitting information about performance and progress toward goals.

responsibility accounting   A reporting system in which costs and revenues are assigned to the level of the organization having responsibility for them.

staffing   The selection of personnel to perform the organization's tasks.

strategic planning   The process of summarizing and articulating the basic objectives and goals for the organization.

variance   The difference between actual and planned results.

what-if analysis   With respect to decision support systems, the altering of certain parameters and variable relationships to assess the sensitivity of the solution to these changes.

Review Questions

1-1   What is an organization?

1-2   What is a decision?

1-3   What is strategic planning?

1-4   What is management planning and control?

1-5   What is operational control?

1-6   Differentiate between data and information.

1-7   Compare and contrast the information characteristics of strategic planning, management planning and control, and operational control.

1-8   What is a centralized organization? A decentralized organization?

1-9   How is the organization chart different between centralized and decentralized organizations?

1-10   "Complete decentralization is the most appropriate way to manage." Comment.

1-11   What are the major tasks of a manager? Define each of them.

1-12   What is the role of the management accountant?

1-13   What is management accounting?

1-14   Define *cost accounting*.

1-15   Define *responsibility accounting*.

1-16   Contrast management accounting with financial accounting.

1-17   How do budgets enhance responsibility accounting?

1-18   What is a CMA?

1-19   What are decision support systems?

1-20   Name and explain three operations a user can invoke with decision support systems.

1-21   Discuss the behavioral aspects of management accounting.

Discussion Questions

1-22   Information needs of managers differ depending on the organizations they manage. (a) Describe the information needs of a local pizza store, a national grocery chain, and an international conglomerate. (b) Describe the similarities and differences of the information needs among these three organizations.

1-23   Identify the strategic plan of your university, of the place of your employment, of your former employer, or of your prospective employer.

1-24   Differentiate between the primary focus of top management, middle management, and first-line supervisors. Identify an organization from which you purchase a product or service and describe its management levels.

1-25   A friend of yours recently commented that her family's business has been reasonably successful since its founding ten years ago. Her family now realizes that the business requires more professional management expertise than they can give it. Your friend knows your educational background and has asked you to comment on what they might do to: (a) identify strategic opportunities; (b) develop plans to capitalize on these opportunities; and (c) maintain and improve profitability. As a parting comment, the friend mentions that profits seem to have declined recently, although sales revenues are still the same.

1-26   Sally Firth has decided to re-enter the business world after an absence of more than 15 years. John Cravens, a long-time friend of Sally's, has had a reasonable business sales career. Sally and John dislike managing by the numbers but do not want to fail in their new business venture. They feel that Sally's technical expertise and John's sales know-how make for an excellent team to market a high-technology item developed by Sally. Yet they are hesitant to proceed without a better understanding of management accounting and how it fits with their goals. Explain to them how management accounting would help them.

1-27   Gorgeous George Ice Cream (GGIC) is attempting to expand its operations in two ways. One, GGIC has considered expanding its line of flavors from 18 to 36. Two, GGIC has considered increasing the number of its stores from 21 to 36 over three years to penetrate the market in surrounding states. GGIC manufactures, distributes, markets, and retails ice cream in company facilities. At present GGIC has a CEO, CFO, vice president for production, vice president for sales, three area sales managers, a plant superintendent, five supervisors, three truck drivers, and one store manager for each store. Briefly sketch an organization chart. Under the proposed expansion, three more area sales managers, two more supervisors, three more truck drivers, and store managers for the new stores would be needed. Outline the role management accounting would have. Identify some of GGIC's potential difficulties and opportunities.

Exercises

CO 7

1-28 WHAT-IF ANALYSIS Burwell, Inc., has an asset for which it paid $44,000. The asset has a life of five years and a salvage value of $4,000. Burwell uses the straight-line method of depreciation.

a. Given these facts, how much is the depreciation expense?

b. If the salvage value is $14,000, how much is the depreciation expense?

c. What is it if the salvage value is zero?

CO 7

1-29 WHAT-IF ANALYSIS Goldenrod Company has an asset for which it paid $120,000 and it has zero salvage value. Goldenrod uses the straight-line method of depreciation. How much is the depreciation expense if the life of the asset is (**a**) 4 years? (**b**) 6 years? (**c**) 10 years?

CO 7

1-30 WHAT-IF ANALYSIS Fremont Corporation has beginning inventory of $12,000, net purchases of $534,000, and ending inventory of $16,000.

a. What is the cost of goods sold?

b. Suppose net purchases were $565,000 instead. Then how much is cost of goods sold?

CO 7

1-31 WHAT-IF ANALYSIS McCook has net purchases of $600,000 and inventory increased by $16,000.

a. How much is cost of goods sold?

b. Suppose inventory decreased by $9,000. Then how much is cost of goods sold?

CO 7

1-32 GOAL-SEEKING Sidney, Inc., has sales of $1,000,000, cost of goods sold of $540,000, wages expense of $80,000, rent expense of $140,000, and depreciation expense of $50,000.

a. How much is net income?

b. Suppose the firm desired an income of $300,000. Assuming that expenses are unchanged, how much must sales be to achieve the income goal of $300,000?

CO 7

1-33 GOAL-SEEKING AND ANALYSIS OF THE VARIABLES Chadron has an income of $400,000, a cash balance of $76,000, sales of $4,000,000, and owners' equity of $2,000,000.

a. Compute the return on sales and the return on equity.

b. Suppose that a return on sales of 12% is desired. What is the minimum sales that yields a 12% return on sales?

c. Suppose a manager wants to investigate the return on equity number. Show how to analyze by indicating the variables and numbers used to obtain the answer.

Problems

CO 7

1-34 WHAT-IF ANALYSIS Solve the following model and do the additional analysis requested:

Years 19X1–19X4

Sales = $500,000, previous $\times 1.2$

Costs of Sales = $.50 \times$ Sales

Depreciation = $10,000, $10,000, $10,000, $10,000

Taxes = $.30 \times$ (Sales $-$ Cost of Sales $-$ Depreciation)

Net Income = Sales $-$ Cost of Sales $-$ Depreciation $-$ Taxes

REQUIRED

a. Solve the model.

b. Show results if sales grow at 10% instead of 20%.

c. Show results if cost of sales were 55% of sales instead of 50%.

d. Show results if both requirements b and c occur at the same time.

1-35   WHAT-IF ANALYSIS AND GOAL-SEEKING Suppose you have the following model:

CO 7

Years 19X1–19X3

Net Income	= $10,000, $12,000, $15,000
Sales	= $100,000, previous × 1.2
Equity	= $40,000, $40,000, $40,000, $40,000
Return on Sales	= Net Income/Sales
Return on Equity	= Net Income/Equity

REQUIRED

a. Solve the model.

b. Solve the model if net income changes to $9,000 each year.

c. Suppose a manager wants to achieve a return on equity of $33\frac{1}{3}\%$. Show what the net income must be to provide this return on equity.

1-36   WHAT-IF ANALYSIS A company forecasts its cost of goods sold in the following manner:

CO 7

Years 19X2–19X4

Beginning Inventory	= $20,000, previous Ending Inventory
Net Purchases	= $200,000, $225,000, $250,000
Ending Inventory	= .1 × (Beginning Inventory + Net Purchases)
Cost of Goods Sold	= Beginning Inventory + Net Purchases − Ending Inventory

REQUIRED

a. Solve the model.

b. Show the results if net purchases equaled $200,000 every year.

c. Show the results if net purchases were $200,000, $250,000, and $300,000.

1-37   WHAT-IF ANALYSIS Xelta Company is filling out a depreciation schedule. It is as follows.

CO 7

Years 19X1–19X5

Cost	= $100,000
Life	= 5 years
Salvage Value	= $20,000
Depreciation	= (Cost − Salvage Value)/Life
Accumulated Depreciation	= Depreciation + Previous Accumulated Depreciation

REQUIRED

a. Solve the model.
b. Show the results if the life is 8 years.
c. Show the results if the salvage value is zero.

Business Decision Case

Barbara and George are preparing a family budget. They arrive at the following:

Barbara's salary	$30,000	
George's salary	30,000	
Interest on bank account	1,000	
Total family revenues		$61,000
Taxes and other salary deductions	$24,000	
Mortgage	$18,000	
Food	8,000	
Utilities	6,000	
Clothing	2,000	
Miscellaneous	3,000	
Total family expenses		61,000
Net family income		$ –0–

REQUIRED

a. Explain whether this information is helpful in making decisions.
b. Explain what happens when food costs go up 10%.
c. Explain what Barbara and George must do to save $1,000 per year.
d. Suppose that the revenues are as predicted but that they spend $62,500. Further assume that most of the clothing costs are for Barbara's office wardrobe and that most of the miscellaneous costs are for George's fishing and hunting trips. Predict how they will discuss the overspending.
e. Some family counselors say that the best thing from preparing a family budget is that it forces the family to communicate. Discuss.

2

COST TERMS, COST BEHAVIOR, AND DECISION MAKING

Cost Terms for Business Organizations

CHAPTER OBJECTIVES

After reading Chapter 2, you should be able to:

1. List and discuss the three types of business organizations (p. 29).

2. Define *selling costs* and *administrative costs* (pp. 29–30).

3. Prepare the income statement and the balance sheet for a service organization (pp. 30–32).

4. Differentiate between period costs and product costs (p. 30).

5. Prepare the income statement (including the cost of goods sold section) and the balance sheet for a merchandising organization (pp. 32–35).

6. Define *direct materials, direct labor,* and *manufacturing overhead* (p. 35).

7. Prepare the income statement (including the calculation of cost of raw materials used, cost of goods manufactured, and cost of goods sold) and the balance sheet for a manufacturing organization (pp. 36–41).

8. Describe variable and fixed costs, direct and indirect costs, controllable and noncontrollable costs, incremental costs, sunk costs, and opportunity costs (pp. 41–45).

9. Identify the behavioral aspects of cost terms for management (pp. 45–46).

*M*anagement accountants assist their firms by providing managers with information organized to help them make better and more timely decisions. Usually this information is based on cost. Before discussing further how management accounting enhances management's decision-making activities, however, we must establish a foundation of cost definitions and concepts.

A cost is the amount paid or charged for something. Usually "paid or charged" means that the firm has given up or will give up cash or some other asset. Sometimes, as in the term *opportunity cost* (discussed later), "paid or charged" means the sacrifice of other potentially good courses of action. In all cases, *cost* refers to the firm's sacrifice of something to obtain something else. For example, the company might give up cash to buy materials so that a product can be made and sold to customers.

TYPES OF BUSINESS ORGANIZATIONS

CHAPTER OBJECTIVE 1
Types of business organizations

There are three types of business entities, based on the forms of value exchanged for the customer's money and the process used to produce that value: service, merchandising, and manufacturing. Unlike merchandisers and manufacturers, service organizations do not sell a tangible product; instead, they sell a service. Examples of service organizations include accounting firms, law firms, banks, insurance companies, and consulting firms.

Merchandising organizations buy products from other businesses and in turn resell them to their customers. Grocery stores and department stores are merchandisers. Manufacturing organizations make a product and sell it to customers. Typical manufacturing organizations are automobile parts manufacturers, steel companies, and paper mills.

Besides these three types of business organizations, there are other entities that are not profit oriented. *Nonprofit* organizations try to achieve some social goal rather than earn profits for the owners. Examples of nonprofit entities include public universities, charitable organizations, and government agencies. Accounting for nonprofit entities is somewhat similar to accounting for service organizations because both groups are providing services rather than goods to their clientele. This textbook focuses on profit-oriented organizations rather than nonprofit entities.

COST TERMS FOR SERVICE ORGANIZATIONS

CHAPTER OBJECTIVE 2
Cost terms for service firms

Costs for service organizations are relatively straightforward compared to those for manufacturers, for example. Selling costs are simply costs incurred to sell their services. They include costs for advertising, promotion, and such costs as depreciation on delivery trucks and on automobiles used by the sales staff. Costs associated with the general management of the business are often called *general and administrative costs,* or simply administrative costs. Wages, insurance, computer costs, the president's salary,

EXHIBIT 2-1

INCOME STATEMENT FOR A SERVICE ORGANIZATION

Deanna Family Counseling
Income Statement
For the Year Ended December 31, 19X1

Revenues		
Billings to Clients	$200,000	
Interest Earned	10,000	
Total Revenues		$210,000
Expenses		
Rent Expense	$ 50,000	
Wages Expense	40,000	
Insurance Expense	10,000	
Utilities Expense	10,000	
Marketing Expense	5,000	
Miscellaneous Expenses	10,000	
Total Expenses		$125,000
Net Income		$ 85,000

CHAPTER
OBJECTIVE 3
*Statements for
service organizations*

CHAPTER
OBJECTIVE 4
*Period vs.
product costs*

depreciation on office equipment, interest charges, taxes, and utilities are all administrative costs.

Service companies make a profit by selling their services for a price that more than covers their selling and administrative costs. For example, the income statement for Deanna Family Counseling, a service organization, is shown in Exhibit 2-1. Deanna received $210,000 in total revenues in 19X1, which was more than its expenses of $125,000 for that year. Note that marketing expense is a selling cost; the other expenses on Deanna's income statement are administrative costs.

Costs incurred by Deanna Family Counseling for 19X1 have been matched with the revenues for the same period on its income statement. This raises the distinction, important for all three organization types, between period costs, which are costs matched against revenues on a period basis (such as by month, quarter, or year), and product costs, which are costs associated with the purchase or manufacture of a product in whatever period the costs are incurred. That is, period costs are costs expensed in the period, whereas product costs are costs accumulated for or during the manufacture of a specific product and are thus carried as part of inventory, regardless of period, until that product is sold. Before sale, product costs are shown in the current assets section of the balance sheet. At the end of the period in which the item is sold, the product costs are moved from the balance sheet to the income statement as an expense. Of course, service organizations, which do not have products for which to accumulate product costs, incur only

EXHIBIT 2-2

BALANCE SHEET FOR A SERVICE ORGANIZATION

Deanna Family Counseling
Balance Sheet
December 31, 19X1

ASSETS

Current Assets

Cash	$10,000	
Accounts Receivable	25,000	
Total Current Assets		$ 35,000

Long-term Assets

Land		$60,000	
Building	$150,000		
Less: Accumulated Depreciation	70,000	80,000	
Total Long-term Assets			140,000
Total Assets			$175,000

LIABILITIES AND STOCKHOLDERS' EQUITY

Liabilities

Accounts Payable	$25,000	
Mortgage Payable	75,000	
Total Liabilities		$100,000

Stockholders' Equity

Common Stock	$25,000	
Retained Earnings	50,000	
Total Stockholders' Equity		75,000
Total Liabilities and Stockholders' Equity		$175,000

period costs. Since Deanna Family Counseling does not have a product to sell, it does not show a product inventory in the current assets section of its balance sheet (see Exhibit 2-2).

Accounting for long-term assets is the same for all types of organizations and we will not explore this issue. Similarly, accounting for liabilities and common stock or owner's equity is not a concern of this chapter. Students interested in these topics should consult a textbook on financial accounting.

In summary, the cost flows in a service organization are period costs (see Exhibit 2-3). They can be categorized as either selling costs or administrative costs and are

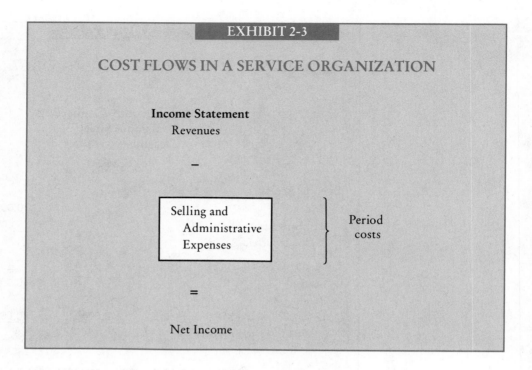

expensed immediately. Thus, the costs are placed on the income statement and subtracted from revenues to yield net income.

COST TERMS FOR MERCHANDISING ORGANIZATIONS

Merchandising organizations buy products and then sell them to customers. Gross profit arises from selling the product at a higher price than the cost of acquiring the merchandise for sale. Net income is derived by achieving a gross profit greater than the selling and administrative costs (including taxes).

Besides selling and administrative costs, merchandisers also incur product costs. These include the cost of purchasing items to resell and the cost of transportation, which would be netted against any discounts or returns and allowances. As long as the product is unsold, its cost is shown on the balance sheet as merchandise inventory. During the period in which the product is sold, its cost is transferred to cost of goods sold and shown as an expense on the income statement.

An income statement for Tammy's Candy Store, a merchandising organization, is given in Exhibit 2-4. Cost of goods sold is computed as beginning merchandise inventory plus net purchases minus ending merchandise inventory. Beginning inventory plus net purchases is often called, as here, *cost of goods available for sale*. Net purchases is equal to gross purchases plus the cost of transportation in minus purchase discounts given by the supplier and purchase returns and allowances (for goods sent back to the supplier).

The income statement is structured as sales (revenues) minus cost of goods sold minus selling and administrative expenses equals net income. Sales minus cost of goods sold is termed gross margin or gross profit.

CHAPTER
OBJECTIVE 5
*Statements for
merchandising
organizations*

EXHIBIT 2-4

INCOME STATEMENT FOR A MERCHANDISING ORGANIZATION

Tammy's Candy Store
Income Statement
For the Year Ended December 31, 19X1

Sales			$200,000
Cost of Goods Sold			
Beginning Inventory		$10,000	
Gross Purchases	$75,000		
Transportation In	1,000		
Purchases	$76,000		
Purchases Discounts	$1,000		
Purchases Returns			
and Allowances	1,000	2,000	
Net Purchases		74,000	
Cost of Goods			
Available for Sale		$84,000	
Ending Inventory		14,000	
Cost of Goods Sold			70,000
Gross Margin			$130,000
Selling and Administrative			
Expenses			50,000
Net Income			$ 80,000

Note that the only difference between the income statements of service and merchandising organizations is the cost of goods sold section for merchandisers. The structure of the income statement for manufacturing companies is the same as that for merchandising firms. However, as we will see, the computation of cost of goods sold is somewhat different for manufacturers.

A balance sheet for Tammy's Candy Store is depicted in Exhibit 2-5. The only essential difference between the balance sheets of service organizations and merchandisers is that merchandisers have merchandise inventory as a current asset, whereas service organizations have no merchandise, hence no inventory. (Compare Exhibits 2-2 and 2-5.) The Merchandise Inventory account shows the cost of unsold inventory.

The cost flows in a merchandising organization may be depicted as in Exhibit 2-6. Like service organizations, merchandisers put selling and administrative costs directly into the income statement as an expense. Merchandisers also carry product costs in inventory. The product costs are kept on the balance sheet until they can be matched with the revenues brought in by selling the product. Thus, the cost of the unsold goods is shown on the balance sheet as merchandise inventory. The cost of goods sold is placed on the income statement as an expense.

EXHIBIT 2-5

BALANCE SHEET FOR A MERCHANDISING ORGANIZATION

Tammy's Candy Store
Balance Sheet
December 31, 19X1

ASSETS

Current Assets		
Cash	$10,000	
Accounts Receivable	25,000	
Merchandise Inventory	14,000	
Total Current Assets		$ 49,000
Long-term Assets		
Land		$60,000
Building	$150,000	
Less: Accumulated Depreciation	70,000	80,000
Total Long-term Assets		140,000
Total Assets		$189,000

LIABILITIES AND STOCKHOLDERS' EQUITY

Liabilities		
Accounts Payable	$25,000	
Mortgage Payable	75,000	
Total Liabilities		$100,000
Stockholders' Equity		
Common Stock	$25,000	
Retained Earnings	64,000	
Total Stockholders' Equity		89,000
Total Liabilities and Stockholders' Equity		$189,000

COST TERMS FOR MANUFACTURING ORGANIZATIONS

Manufacturers make products and sell them to their customers. Gross profit arises from selling the product at a higher price than the cost of making the product. Net income is achieved by attaining a gross profit that more than covers the selling and administrative costs (including taxes).

The structure of the income statement for a manufacturer is similar to that for a merchandiser but is more complicated to compute because cost of goods sold for a manufacturing organization depends on the cost of goods manufactured. This cost depends in turn on the cost of raw materials used in production, as well as the cost of labor and other manufacturing costs called *overhead* costs.

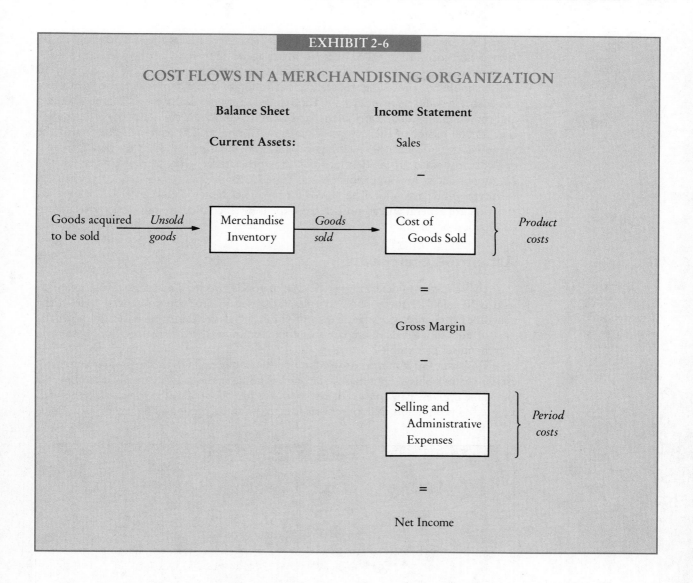

EXHIBIT 2-6

COST FLOWS IN A MERCHANDISING ORGANIZATION

Balance Sheet   **Income Statement**

Current Assets: Sales

−

Goods acquired to be sold → *Unsold goods* → | Merchandise Inventory | → *Goods sold* → | Cost of Goods Sold | } *Product costs*

=

Gross Margin

−

| Selling and Administrative Expenses | } *Period costs*

=

Net Income

Manufacturing Costs

CHAPTER OBJECTIVE 6
Definitions of manufacturing cost terms

There are three manufacturing costs: direct materials, direct labor, and overhead. Direct materials consists of the raw materials that are used in the manufacture of a product. The direct materials for an automobile manufacturer, for example, include steel, glass, plastic, and tires. Direct labor refers to the wages of the workers who actually make a product. For an automaker direct labor costs would consist of the salaries or wages of the workers along the assembly line. Manufacturing overhead or factory overhead, or simply overhead, is any other production cost. Some overhead costs for an automaker are factory utilities, factory insurance, depreciation on the factory building, and depreciation on equipment used in the production process. In some entities, the cost of direct materials is combined with that of direct labor and the sum referred to as prime costs. In other entities, the cost of direct labor is combined with the cost of manufacturing overhead and termed conversion costs. Prime costs refer to what were traditionally the two largest manufacturing costs. In today's computerized and automated plants, direct materials and direct labor are often not the largest manufacturing costs. Conversion costs are so called because direct labor and manufacturing overhead are the costs incurred to convert the direct materials into a product to be sold.

It should be pointed out that the classification of a cost depends on the purpose of the cost. Consider an insurance bill for $10,000. Suppose that the cost can be analyzed and shown that $4,000 relates to the factory building, $3,000 relates to the office building, $2,000 relates to the cars of the sales staff, and $1,000 relates to the cars of the executive staff. The $4,000 relating to the factory building is factory overhead, since it is a cost related to production facilities. The other three items are not part of factory operations and so are not product costs. The $2,000 insurance is a selling cost because it relates to selling activities. The $2,000 for the office building and the $1,000 for executive cars are general and administrative expenses, since they are not directly related to production or sales.

Accounting Statements

**CHAPTER
OBJECTIVE 7**
*Statements for
manufacturing
organizations*

The first step in determining the cost of goods sold for a manufacturing organization is to calculate the cost of raw materials used in production, as was done in the schedule for Diane's Manufacturing in Exhibit 2-7. This calculation basically shows the cost of direct materials. Compare this computation to that of cost of goods sold for a merchandiser in Exhibit 2-4.

The cost of raw materials used in production is equal to the beginning raw materials inventory plus net purchases of materials minus ending raw materials inventory. As the name implies, raw materials inventory is just the stock of raw materials that will be used in production. Net purchases is equal to gross purchases of raw materials plus

---

EXHIBIT 2-7

COST OF RAW MATERIALS USED IN PRODUCTION

Diane's Manufacturing
Schedule of Cost of Raw Materials Used in Production
For the Year Ended December 31, 19X1

Beginning Raw Materials Inventory			$ 3,000
Gross Purchases		$126,000	
Transportation In		2,000	
Purchases		$128,000	
Purchases Discounts	$500		
Purchases Returns and Allowances	500	1,000	
Net Purchases			127,000
Cost of Raw Materials Available for Manufacturing			$130,000
Ending Raw Materials Inventory			4,000
Cost of Raw Materials Used in Production			$126,000

transportation in minus purchase discounts minus purchase returns and allowances. The cost of raw materials used in production will be employed in the calculation of cost of goods manufactured.

The schedule of cost of goods manufactured for Diane's Manufacturing, in Exhibit 2-8, discloses the three production costs: direct materials, direct labor, and manufacturing overhead. The cost of goods manufactured equals the cost of direct materials plus the cost of direct labor plus the cost of manufacturing overhead plus beginning work in process inventory minus ending work in process inventory. Work in process inventory is the cost of goods placed into production but not yet complete. When the goods are completed, their costs are referred to as finished goods inventory. Note that the balance of direct materials in Exhibit 2-8 has the same cost value as that computed in Exhibit 2-7. Some firms combine the two schedules into one schedule.

Diane's cost of goods manufactured schedule contains several items included in manufacturing overhead. *Indirect materials* are small items of material, such as nails and screws, that are part of the product but are not separately accounted for (because it is too difficult or uneconomical to account for them). *Indirect labor* is labor not directly associated with the production process, such as production supervisors, crew chiefs, superintendents, and engineers. *Factory depreciation* is depreciation on the factory building and its equipment. *Factory insurance* is insurance on the factory facilities. *Factory utilities* are utilities consumed by the factory.

Now that we have determined the cost of goods manufactured, we are in a position to compute cost of goods sold and prepare the rest of the income statement. An income

---

EXHIBIT 2-8

COST OF GOODS MANUFACTURED

Diane's Manufacturing
Schedule of Cost of Goods Manufactured
For the Year Ended December 31, 19X1

Direct Materials		$126,000
Direct Labor		30,000
Manufacturing Overhead		
Factory Utilities	$26,000	
Factory Depreciation	23,000	
Indirect Materials	14,000	
Indirect Labor	11,000	
Factory Insurance	2,000	
Total Manufacturing Overhead		76,000
Total Manufacturing Costs		$232,000
Beginning Work in Process Inventory		10,000
		$242,000
Ending Work in Process Inventory		12,000
Cost of Goods Manufactured		$230,000

EXHIBIT 2-9

INCOME STATEMENT FOR A MANUFACTURING ORGANIZATION

Diane's Manufacturing
Income Statement
For the Year Ended December 31, 19X1

Sales		$400,000
Cost of Goods Sold:		
Beginning Finished Goods Inventory	$ 20,000	
Cost of Goods Manufactured	230,000	
Cost of Goods Available for Sale	$250,000	
Ending Finished Goods Inventory	25,000	
Cost of Goods Sold		225,000
Gross Margin		$175,000
Selling and Administrative Expenses		95,000
Net Income		$ 80,000

---

statement for Diane's Manufacturing is displayed in Exhibit 2-9. As with merchandisers, the structure of the income statement for manufacturers is sales minus cost of goods sold minus selling and administrative expenses equals net income. Sales minus cost of goods sold is called *gross margin* or *gross profit.* For a manufacturer, cost of goods sold equals beginning finished goods inventory plus cost of goods manufactured minus ending finished goods inventory. Finished goods inventory consists of manufactured goods that are ready for sale. Beginning finished goods inventory plus cost of goods manufactured equals cost of goods available for sale. Note that the cost of goods manufactured shown in the income statement in Exhibit 2-9 comes from the schedule in Exhibit 2-8.

Balance sheets for manufacturing organizations differ from those for service and merchandising organizations because manufacturers have three inventories: raw materials, work in process, and finished goods. These are classified as current assets on the balance sheet.

These three inventory accounts are in the current assets section of the balance sheet for Diane's Manufacturing in Exhibit 2-10. There are no accounting differences among the organization types for long-term assets, liabilities, and stockholders' equity.

The cost flows in a manufacturing organization are summarized in Exhibit 2-11 (page 40). Like service organizations, manufacturers put selling and administrative costs directly into the income statement as expenses. Like merchandising organizations, manufacturers also have product costs, which are not put into the income statement as expenses until the product is sold. Also like merchandisers, manufacturers place the cost of unsold products in the balance sheet as inventory. Merchandisers, however, have only one inventory—merchandise inventory—whereas manufacturers have inventories for raw materials, work in process, and finished goods.

As summarized in Exhibit 2-11, manufacturers have production costs for direct materials, direct labor, and overhead. The cost of direct materials flows into the cost of

EXHIBIT 2-10

BALANCE SHEET FOR A MANUFACTURING ORGANIZATION

Diane's Manufacturing
Balance Sheet
December 31, 19X1

ASSETS

Current Assets

Cash	$10,000	
Accounts Receivable	25,000	
Raw Materials Inventory	4,000	
Work in Process Inventory	12,000	
Finished Goods Inventory	25,000	
Total Current Assets		$ 76,000

Long-term Assets

Land		$60,000	
Building	$150,000		
Less: Accumulated Depreciation	70,000	80,000	
Total Long-term Assets			140,000
Total Assets			$216,000

LIABILITIES AND STOCKHOLDERS' EQUITY

Liabilities

Accounts Payable	$25,000	
Mortgage Payable	75,000	
Total Liabilities		$100,000

Stockholders' Equity

Common Stock	$25,000	
Retained Earnings	91,000	
Total Stockholders' Equity		116,000
Total Liabilities and Stockholders' Equity		$216,000

raw materials inventory. This inventory, plus direct labor and overhead, flow into work in process inventory. As the goods are completed, the costs flow from work in process inventory into finished goods inventory. When the goods are sold, the costs flow from finished goods inventory into cost of goods sold.

The resulting income statement shows the relationship typical of all organization types: sales less cost of sales (goods sold) equals gross margin; gross margin less selling and administrative expenses equals net income.

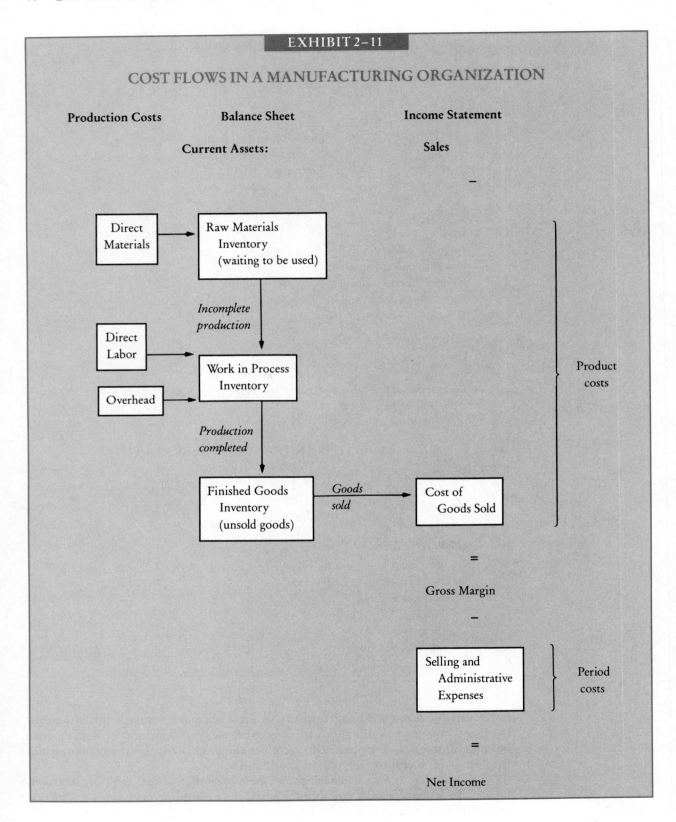

EXHIBIT 2–11

COST FLOWS IN A MANUFACTURING ORGANIZATION

Technological changes such as robotics and computers have greatly altered the manufacturing process. As a result, inventory levels, especially work in process inventory, may be greatly reduced. It is also possible for direct labor to be reduced, in some cases to practically zero. These changes simplify financial statements and schedules, but the concepts remain the same.

OTHER COST CLASSIFICATIONS

**CHAPTER
OBJECTIVE 8**
Other cost terms

Up to this point, we have defined and illustrated cost terms used by the three business organization types: service, merchandising, and manufacturing. Other definitions of cost are appropriate for certain types of decisions.

Further, different cost definitions may apply for different purposes. That is, a particular cost will be relevant from one vantage point and a different cost may be relevant from another vantage point. The decision context determines which cost term is appropriate.

Six different cost definitions and classifications are examined in this section: variable and fixed costs, direct and indirect costs, controllable and noncontrollable costs, incremental costs, sunk costs, and opportunity costs. They are explained here and will be used in the rest of the textbook.

Variable and Fixed Costs

For planning and control purposes, it is useful to be able to understand how costs behave in relation to business activity. As the level of business activity changes, does the cost stay the same or does it change also? The answer to this question determines whether the cost is variable or fixed.

A variable cost is a cost that varies in proportion with changes in activity level. For example, consider a car that gets 40 miles per gallon and assume that gasoline costs $2 per gallon. The car expends $.05 per mile on gasoline. The following table shows the cost of gasoline at several activity levels:

Miles Driven	Gasoline Cost
100	$ 5
200	10
500	25
1,000	50

Gasoline is a variable cost relative to the activity measure "miles driven." Note that the cost per unit, here gasoline cost per mile driven, is fixed at $.05.

Fixed costs do not change as the level of activity varies. For example, straight-line depreciation on an automobile would not vary by the miles driven. If the depreciation is computed as $2,000 per year, then it will remain that amount despite changes in the level of the activity:

Miles Driven	Depreciation Cost
100	$2,000
200	2,000
500	2,000
1,000	2,000

THE CONCEPT OF "BOOK VALUE"

In the course of a recent inquiry, a question was posed relating to the significance of a mill's net value, and the terms "net worth," "net equity," and "book value" assumed a prominent position in the discussion.

Doesn't the financial statement reflect the net worth of the firm's ownership? Isn't the book value of a mill's equity indicative of the owners' or stockholders' interests?

The inquiry continued with reference to the methods employed by certified public accountants to determine the book value of a mill. Realistically, this information is warranted for setting out and selecting proper options in buy/sell agreements, profit sharing and pension plans, inception and liquidation agreements, subscriptions to life insurance contracts, and income and estate tax planning and procedures.

From an accounting and economic viewpoint, the equity of a firm is universally accepted as a concept of residual values, representing the owner's interests. The balance sheet clearly states the "total assets" of the firm and its component categories as "current assets," "plant and equipment," and "investments and intangibles."

Correspondingly, the "total liabilities" consisting of "short-term obligations," "long-term obligations," "accruals," and "deferrals," normally show the creditors' interests in the firm. Therefore, the net equity of the firm is an expression of total assets less total liabilities.

To attribute a more meaningful and useful purpose to the interpretation of values on the balance sheet, it is important to reflect on the terminology of expressions used in the financial statements. Important definitions have been promulgated by the Financial Accounting Standards Board, "Elements of Financial Statements of Business Enterprises," *Statement of Financial Accounting Concepts No. 3* (FASB, Stamford, Conn. 1980), p. XI.

ASSETS: Probable future economic benefits obtained or controlled by a particular entity as a result of past transactions or events.

LIABILITIES: Probable future sacrifices of economic benefits arising from present obligations of a particular entity to transfer assets to other entities in the future as a result of past transactions or events.

EQUITY: Residual interest in the assets of an entity that remains after deducting its liabilities. In a business enterprise, the equity is the ownership interest.

A practical analysis suggests that a firm's net value, as reported in its financial statements, results from assigning values to resources and liabilities, determined from information involving past transactions or events. In this context, current and liquidation values are reserved for specialized evaluation procedures.

"Book value" of a mill may be defined as "original historical cost less any accumulated depreciation, depletion, or amortization."

Caution is to be exercised in relying solely on book value analysis in evaluating a mill's performance and worth. The guidelines often suggested by financial analysts—"find assets worth a dollar and buy them for 50 cents," and "search out companies with stocks selling below book value"—do not specify the accounting principles exercised in the computation.

John Lisco, in his article (*Barron's*, July 25, 1988, p. 16), compiles a list of two dozen plus companies selling below book value. Among these is Beeba's Creations, Inc., a women's cotton sportswear manufacturer, with a stock value of $7 as of July 20, 1988, and reported ratio of price to book value of 72%.

Similarly, *Barron's* (July 25, 1988, p. 44) quotes Oppenheimer & Co.'s research that Fieldcrest-Cannon's stock—selling at a level 21% discounted to estimated 1988 book value—is a premium accorded mostly textile stocks.

The reliance of the concept of book value determination for mill valuation in the structure of the stock market price leaves much to be desired. Numerous variables, including economic forecasts, tax consequences, alternative accounting valuation procedures, need to be studied in depth. This is a subject requiring further investigation.

SOURCE: Adapted from Ephraim D. Dworetsky, "The Concept of 'Book Value'," *Knitting Times* (October 1988), p. 71.

Depreciation is a fixed cost relative to miles driven. However, the cost per unit, here depreciation cost per mile driven, is variable (respectively, $20, $10, $4, and $2).

Of the selling and administrative costs, rent, insurance, utilities, and advertising are fixed. Salaries are fixed, whereas commissions to salespersons are variable because they depend on the amount the salesperson sells. Cost of goods sold for a merchandiser is a variable cost (varying by amount of goods sold, hence merchandise inventory). Cost of goods sold for a manufacturer is a mixture of variable and fixed costs. Specifically, direct materials and direct labor are variable costs. Manufacturing overhead is partly fixed and partly variable. In general, indirect materials and indirect labor are variable costs. Increases in production level generally require more indirect materials and more indirect labor. Factory depreciation and factory insurance are usually fixed costs. Increases in production level will not affect straight-line depreciation or how much is paid for property insurance.

Direct and Indirect Costs

Another way to classify costs is whether they are direct or indirect. Given a particular activity, a direct cost is a cost that can be traced easily and unambiguously to that activity. An indirect cost is a cost that cannot be traced easily or unambiguously to an activity. Indirect costs are often allocated to various activities.

Assume that a firm manufactures two products in two different plants. Direct costs are those that can be traced easily to one product or the other (or perhaps to one plant or the other). Direct materials, direct labor, factory supervision, factory depreciation, and factory utilities can be traced to one or the other plant and therefore are direct costs. The president's salary is indirect because it applies to both plants and will be allocated to them (that is, a portion of the president's salary is charged against each plant's operations).

In a more realistic example, a plant would manufacture several products. Thus, factory supervision, factory depreciation, and factory utilities would be indirect costs charged proportionately to each of the products made in the plant. (How indirect costs are allocated is discussed in Chapters 7 and 8.)

Controllable and Noncontrollable Costs

In Chapter 1 we described *responsibility accounting* as a system of reporting in an organizational structure so that costs and revenues are reported at the level having the related responsibility within the organization. Thus managers report only costs and revenues that they can control and are responsible for.

A plant manager or superintendent is responsible for the activities at a particular plant. He or she is responsible for the costs incurred at the plant, such as costs of materials and labor. These are controllable costs to the plant manager. On the other hand, he or she has no control over costs incurred at other plants, or over the corporate issuance of bonds (hence no control over bond interest expense). A portion of bond interest expense might be allocated to the plant, but since the plant manager has no authority to issue or retire bonds, the bond interest expense is a noncontrollable cost at that level.

The importance of controllable and noncontrollable costs comes into focus most clearly in evaluations of managerial performance. Performance evaluations are better and fairer when the manager is evaluated on the aspects of the firm over which he or she has authority and responsibility and thus can control.

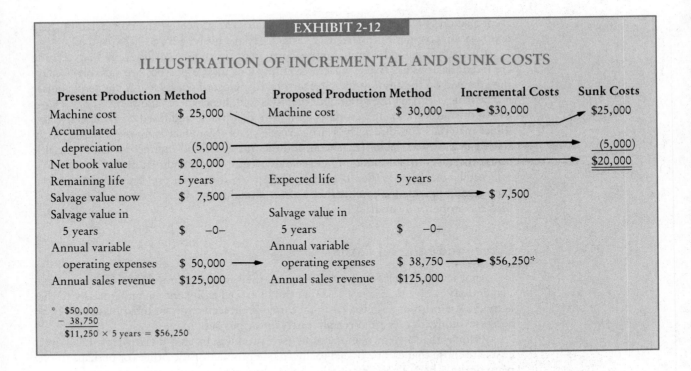

EXHIBIT 2-12

ILLUSTRATION OF INCREMENTAL AND SUNK COSTS

Present Production Method		Proposed Production Method		Incremental Costs	Sunk Costs
Machine cost	$ 25,000	Machine cost	$ 30,000	$30,000	$25,000
Accumulated depreciation	(5,000)				(5,000)
Net book value	$ 20,000				$20,000
Remaining life	5 years	Expected life	5 years		
Salvage value now	$ 7,500			$ 7,500	
Salvage value in 5 years	$ –0–	Salvage value in 5 years	$ –0–		
Annual variable operating expenses	$ 50,000	Annual variable operating expenses	$ 38,750	$56,250*	
Annual sales revenue	$125,000	Annual sales revenue	$125,000		

```
*   $50,000
  – 38,750
   $11,250 × 5 years = $56,250
```

Incremental Costs

When managers make business decisions they choose from among several alternatives. A cost that appears in one alternative but not in another in a decision-making context is called an **incremental** (or *differential*) **cost.** Incremental costs are important in that they indicate the differences among various alternatives.

Linda Lomax, Inc., currently has a machine that cost $25,000 and has a remaining life of five years and an accumulated depreciation of $5,000. Currently its annual variable operating expenses are $50,000. (See Exhibit 2-12.)

Management is considering purchasing a new machine, requiring a new production process, that costs $30,000 and has an expected life of five years. It is more efficient than the old machine with its process and has annual variable operating expenses of $38,750. If the new machine is bought, the old one can be traded in for $7,500. What are the incremental costs?

Annual variable operating expenses are different by $11,250. Over five years this incremental cost is $56,250. The depreciation on the new machine will be $30,000 and that cost is incremental. The $7,500 trade-in on the old machine is also incremental.

The $20,000 remaining depreciation on the old machine (its net book value) is *not* incremental, because it will be written off as depreciation if the asset is kept or written off as a loss on the trade-in if it is sold. If the new machine is purchased, this gross loss of $20,000 is netted against the old machine's trade-in value of $7,500 to give a loss on the trade of $12,500.

We will examine this example in greater detail in Chapter 4.

Sunk Costs

A sunk cost is a cost that has already been incurred. The relevance of sunk costs is that they have no bearing on any future decision, because the manager cannot undo the past. What has been incurred cannot be changed under any alternative.

In Exhibit 2-12, the cost of the old machine is a sunk cost. The $25,000 to buy the machine has already been incurred and is irrelevant to the decision whether to acquire the new machine. Another way of viewing this is to consider the two alternatives. If Linda Lomax, Inc., keeps the old machine, its cost remains $25,000. If it decides to obtain the new machine, it still incurred the $25,000 cost of the old machine. Looking at the proposal in this manner shows that sunk costs are never incremental costs.

Opportunity Costs

An opportunity cost is the potential benefits sacrificed by the selection of a particular action over another. By choosing one alternative, the decision maker gives up the potential benefits provided by other alternatives.

For example, if two favorite activities, a basketball game and an opera, begin at the same time in different places, then one would have to make a choice. If one chooses to attend the basketball game, then one cannot attend the opera. The opportunity cost of viewing the basketball game is the missed chance of seeing the opera. Alternatively, if one decides to go to the opera, one would have to miss the basketball game.

Another example concerns the choice of going to college. Attending college not only requires outlays of cash for tuition, books, and the like, but it requires an opportunity cost of not taking on a full-time job (unless you do not need any sleep!). The missed wages over a four-year period is the opportunity cost of attending college.

In the Linda Lomax example above, the opportunity cost of keeping the old machine is the lost benefits derived from the new machine, namely the lower operating costs. The opportunity cost of obtaining the new machine is the lost benefits that the $30,000 cost could have provided.

DECISION SUPPORT SYSTEMS AND BEHAVIORAL ASPECTS OF COST TERMS

CHAPTER OBJECTIVE 9
Behavioral aspects of cost terms

Decision support systems use models that require the user to specify relationships among the variables, as illustrated in Chapter 1. For example, a manufacturer would specify the following relationships:

Cost of Raw Materials Used = Beginning Raw Materials Inventory
+ Net Purchases
− Ending Raw Materials Inventory

Cost of Goods Manufactured = Direct Materials
+ Direct Labor
+ Manufacturing Overhead
+ Beginning Work in Process Inventory
− Ending Work in Process Inventory

$$\text{Cost of Goods Sold} = \text{Beginning Finished Goods Inventory}$$
$$+ \text{Cost of Goods Manufactured}$$
$$- \text{Ending Finished Goods Inventory}$$

The importance of this chapter is that these terms have been defined so that the student understands what they mean and that these relationships have been explored.

Decision support systems also use such operations as "what-if" analysis and goal-seeking. Recall from Chapter 1 that each of these operations manipulates certain variables chosen by the user. The changes in the values of the variables are controlled by such relationships specified for the manufacturer. For example, if the ending work in process inventory is lowered, we can determine that the cost of goods manufactured is increased and, accordingly, that cost of goods sold is increased.

The behavioral aspects of using well-defined cost terms is straightforward. To the extent that the key terms are understood and the relationships are clear, the manager is capable of thinking more clearly and making better decisions. If these terms are imprecise or the relationships among them unknown, the manager is more apt to make faulty decisions.

Demonstration Problem

Following is a list of selected accounts and their balances for Pressler Piano, Inc., as of December 31, 19X2, the end of its fiscal year:

Cash	$ 12,000
Direct Labor	250,000
Factory Depreciation	65,000
Factory Rent	120,000
Finished Goods Inventory (beginning)	25,000
Finished Goods Inventory (ending)	20,000
Gross Purchases	200,000
Indirect Labor	30,000
Indirect Materials	20,000
Notes Receivable	50,000
Purchases Discounts	3,000
Purchase Returns and Allowances	1,000
Raw Materials Inventory (beginning)	1,000
Raw Materials Inventory (ending)	4,000
Retained Earnings	180,000
Transportation In	5,000
Work in Process Inventory (beginning)	11,000
Work in Process Inventory (ending)	14,000

REQUIRED

From the preceding accounts, compute the cost of goods sold as of the end of the fiscal year by preparing schedules of cost of raw materials used in production, cost of goods manufactured, and cost of goods sold.

SOLUTION TO DEMONSTRATION PROBLEM

The problem uses almost all of the accounts employed earlier in the discussion of manufacturers. The only trick to the problem is to realize that three of the accounts—Cash, Notes Receivable, and Retained Earnings—are balance sheet accounts and thus irrelevant for computing cost of goods sold.

Pressler Piano, Inc.
Schedule of Cost of Raw Materials Used in Production
For the Year Ended December 31, 19X2

Beginning Raw Materials Inventory			$ 1,000
Gross Purchases		$200,000	
Transportation In		5,000	
Purchases		$205,000	
Purchase Discounts	$3,000		
Purchase Returns and Allowances	$1,000	4,000	
Net Purchases			$201,000
Cost of Raw Materials Available for Manufacturing			$202,000
Ending Raw Materials Inventory			4,000
Cost of Raw Materials Used in Production			$198,000

Pressler Piano, Inc.
Schedule of Cost of Goods Manufactured
For the Year Ended December 31, 19X2

Direct Materials		$198,000
Direct Labor		250,000
Manufacturing Overhead		
Factory Depreciation	$ 65,000	
Factory Rent	120,000	
Indirect Labor	30,000	
Indirect Materials	20,000	
Total Manufacturing Overhead		235,000
Total Manufacturing Costs		$683,000
Beginning Work in Proess		11,000
		$694,000
Ending Work in Process		14,000
Cost of Goods Manufactured		$680,000

Pressler Piano, Inc.
Schedule of Cost of Goods Sold
For the Year Ended December 31, 19X2

Beginning Finished Goods Inventory	$ 25,000
Cost of Goods Manufactured	680,000
Cost of Goods Available for Sale	$705,000
Ending Finished Goods Inventory	20,000
Cost of Goods Sold	$685,000

Review of Chapter Objectives

1. List and discuss the three types of business organizations (p. 29).

   ■ Service organizations do not sell a product but instead sell a service. Merchandising organizations buy products from other businesses and in turn sell them to their customers. Manufacturing organizations make a product and sell it to their customers. (Nonprofit entities, whose aim is to provide a needed service rather than generate profits, are not included in this group.)

2. Define *selling costs* and *administrative costs* (pp. 29–30).

   ■ Selling costs are costs incurred to sell the organization's service or product. Administrative costs are costs associated with the general management of the organization. Service, merchandising, and manufacturing organizations all have selling and administrative costs.

3. Prepare the income statement and the balance sheet for a service organization (pp. 30–32).

   ■ The income statement of a service company shows that net income equals revenues minus selling and administrative costs.

   ■ The balance sheet of a service firm depicts the firm's assets, liabilities, and shareholders' equity.

4. Differentiate between period costs and product costs (p. 30).

   ■ Period costs are costs matched against revenues for a period. Product costs are costs associated with the purchase or manufacture of a product in whatever period the costs are incurred. Selling costs and administrative costs are period costs. Service organizations do not have product costs since they do not sell products. Product costs for a merchandiser are the costs of buying the merchandise inventory and the transportation costs of obtaining it. Product costs for a manufacturer are the costs for making the product and include the costs of materials, labor, and manufacturing overhead.

5. Prepare the income statement (including the cost of goods sold section) and the balance sheet for a merchandising organization (pp. 32–35).

   ■ The income statement for a merchandiser shows that net income equals revenues minus cost of goods sold minus selling and administrative costs. Cost of goods sold equals beginning merchandise inventory plus net purchases minus ending merchandise inventory.

   ■ The balance sheet for merchandisers is like that for service organizations except that merchandisers have a current asset "merchandise inventory," which shows the cost of unsold inventory.

6. Define *direct materials, direct labor,* and *manufacturing overhead* (p. 35).

   ■ Manufacturers have three manufacturing costs. Direct materials consists of the raw materials that go into the manufacture of a product. Direct labor refers to the cost of the workers who make a product. Manufacturing overhead, or simply overhead, is any other production cost.

7. Prepare the income statement (including the calculation of cost of raw materials used, cost of goods manufactured, and cost of goods sold) and the balance sheet for a manufacturing organization (pp. 36–41).

   ■ The income statement is more complicated for manufacturers than for other forms of business organizations. The cost of raw materials used in production is equal to beginning raw materials inventory plus net purchases of materials minus ending raw materials inventory. The cost of goods manufactured equals direct materials plus direct labor plus manufacturing overhead plus beginning work in process inventory minus ending work in process inventory. The cost of goods sold is equal to beginning finished goods inventory plus cost of goods manufactured minus ending finished goods inventory. Once these items are determined, one can prepare the income statement for the manufacturing organization. Net income equals revenues less cost of goods sold less selling and administrative expenses.

- The balance sheet for a manufacturer displays the entity's assets, liabilities, and stockholders' equity, as do the balance sheets for service organizations and for merchandisers. However, unlike the other two, manufacturers have three types of inventory in the current assets section of the balance sheet. Raw materials inventory consists of direct materials to be used in production. Work in process inventory consists of goods placed in production but not yet complete. Finished goods inventory is completed but unsold goods.

8. Describe variable and fixed costs, direct and indirect costs, controllable and noncontrollable costs, incremental costs, sunk costs, and opportunity costs (pp. 41–45).

- Variable costs vary in proportion with changes in the activity level. Fixed costs do not change as the activity level changes.

- Given a particular activity, product, or organizational unit, a direct cost is one that can be traced easily and unambiguously to it. An indirect cost is one that cannot be traced easily or unambiguously to an activity, product, or organizational unit.

- Controllable costs are costs that managers influence and for which they are responsible. Noncontrollable costs are costs that managers cannot influence and for which they are not responsible.

- Incremental costs are costs in one alternative but not in another alternative in a particular decision-making context.

- A sunk cost is a cost that has already been incurred.

- An opportunity cost is the potential benefits sacrificed by the selection of a particular action over another.

9. Identify the behavioral aspects of cost terms for management (p. 46).

- When key cost terms are understood and thus the relationships among costs are known, the manager can think more clearly and make better decisions. When cost terms are imprecisely defined, the manager is more apt to make faulty decisions.

Glossary of Key Terms

administrative cost   Cost associated with the general management of the organization.

controllable cost   Cost that managers can influence and for which they are responsible.

conversion cost   Direct labor cost plus manufacturing overhead costs.

cost   The amount paid or charged for something. Usually "paid or charged" means that the firm has given up or will give up cash or some other asset. Sometimes "paid or charged" means the sacrifice of other potentially good courses of action. In all cases, *cost* refers to the firm's sacrifice of something to obtain something else.

cost of goods manufactured   The cost of the product made by the manufacturing firm. It is equal to direct materials plus direct labor plus overhead plus beginning work in process inventory minus ending work in process inventory.

cost of goods sold   The cost of the product sold to the firm's customers. For a merchandiser, it is equal to beginning merchandise inventory plus net purchases minus ending merchandise inventory. For a manufacturer, it is equal to beginning finished goods inventory plus cost of goods manufactured minus ending finished goods inventory.

cost of raw materials used in production   The cost of direct materials placed in the production process. It is equal to beginning raw materials inventory plus net purchases minus ending raw materials inventory.

direct cost   Given a particular activity, product, or organizational unit, a cost that can be traced easily and unambiguously to it.

direct labor   The workers who make a product; the cost in wages of these workers.

direct materials   Raw materials that are used in the manufacture of a product; the cost of these materials.

finished goods inventory   Completed but unsold goods; the cost of such goods.

fixed costs   Cost that does not vary as the activity level changes.

gross margin or **gross profit**   Sales minus cost of goods sold.

incremental cost   A cost that appears in one alternative but not in another in a particular decision-making context.

indirect cost   Given a particular activity, product, or organizational unit, a cost that cannot be traced easily or unambiguously to it.

manufacturing organization   A firm that makes a product and sells it to its customers.

merchandise inventory   Goods awaiting sale that were acquired from another organization; the cost of such goods.

merchandising organization   A firm that buys a product and then sells it to its customers.

noncontrollable cost   Cost that a manager cannot influence and for which he or she is not responsible.

opportunity cost   The potential benefits sacrificed by the selection of one particular action over another.

overhead   Any production cost except direct materials and direct labor.

period cost   Cost matched against revenues on a period basis.

prime cost   A term for direct materials plus direct labor.

product cost   Cost associated with the purchase or manufacture of a product in whatever period the costs are incurred.

raw materials inventory   The stock of raw materials that will be used in the production process; the cost of these materials.

selling cost   Cost incurred in order to sell a service or a product.

service organization   A firm that sells a service (as opposed to a product) to its customers.

sunk cost   A cost that has already been incurred.

variable cost   A cost that varies in proportion with changes in activity level.

work in process inventory   Goods that have been placed in production but are not yet complete; the cost of such goods.

Review Questions

2-1 Distinguish service, merchandising, and manufacturing organizations.

2-2 Define *selling costs*. Define *administrative costs*.

2-3 Contrast period costs and product costs.

2-4 Depreciation can be a selling cost, an administrative cost, or a product cost. Explain.

2-5 The format of the balance sheet for service, merchandising, and manufacturing organizations is the same. Explain.

2-6 What is the format of a typical income statement for a service organization?

2-7 Give the formula for cost of goods sold for a merchandiser.

2-8 What is the format of a typical income statement for a merchandising organization?

2-9 What are the three manufacturing costs? Define them.

2-10 What three types of inventory does a manufacturer have? Define them.

2-11 Give the formula for cost of raw materials used in production for a manufacturer.

2-12 State the computation for cost of goods manufactured.

2-13 Give the formula for cost of goods sold for a manufacturer.

2-14 Are there any differences on the balance sheet for service, merchandising, and manufacturing organizations?

2-15 What is meant by variable cost? fixed cost?

2-16 Contrast direct and indirect costs.

2-17 Why is overhead an indirect cost of a product?

2-18 When is it necessary to decide whether a cost is controllable or noncontrollable?

2-19 What are incremental costs? Can a fixed cost be an incremental cost?

2-20 What is a sunk cost?

2-21 What is an opportunity cost?

2-22 Why are definitions of cost important for decision support systems and for behavioral considerations?

Discussion Questions

2-23 Discussion of business organizations as either service, merchandising, or manufacturing assumes that the firm is a profit-oriented business. Accounting for a nonprofit organization is similar to which type of business organization? How would the "income statement" look?

(Nonprofit organizations often use different terms from those used by business entities. For example, many nonprofit organizations do not use *revenue* or *income*. For the purpose of answering this question, ignore this fact. If you are interested in pursuing this issue, see a textbook on nonprofit accounting.)

2-24 Years ago manufacturing involved a high degree of direct labor. Also, due to uncertainties of demand, firms would hold large work in process inventories. In today's manufacturing environment with the aid of computers and robots, it is possible to have only a small amount of direct labor and very little work in process inventory. (We will explore these topics in detail in Chapter 17.)

Assume for practical purposes that such a firm has no direct labor and carries no work in process inventory. To account for this type of firm, revise the formulas for (a) the cost of raw materials used in production, (b) the cost of goods manufactured, and (c) the cost of goods sold. Also indicate what is different about such a firm's balance sheet.

Exercises

2-25   ORGANIZATION TYPE   Identify the following businesses as either service, merchandising, or manufacturing organizations.

CO 1

a. A hot dog stand.

b. A baseball team.

c. A restaurant.

d. A farmer.

e. A home builder.

f. A hair stylist.

g. A paper mill.

2-26   ORGANIZATION TYPE   A company that deals with computers might be a service firm, a merchandiser, or manufacturer. Explain.

CO 1

2-27   ACCOUNTING FOR SERVICE ORGANIZATIONS   Following are accounts for A. Bealing, Consultant. Prepare the income statement and the balance sheet for March 19X5 for this firm, replacing the question mark with the amount that should appear.

CO 3

Accounts Payable	$ 25,000
Accounts Receivable	20,000
Accumulated Depreciation—Building	20,000
Advertising	5,000
Building	100,000
Cash	10,000
Common Stock	50,000
Depreciation Expense—Building	10,000
Land	40,000
Retained Earnings	?
Revenues	100,000
Salaries	50,000
Supplies Expense	15,000

2-28   MERCHANDISER COST OF GOODS SOLD   In the following independent cases, replace the question marks with the amounts that should appear in the computations of merchandisers' cost of goods sold:

CO 5

	A	B	C
Beginning Merchandise Inventory	$ 10,000	$?	$ 25,000
Gross Purchases	120,000	100,000	?
Transportation In	10,000	5,000	10,000
Purchases Discounts	1,000	?	3,000
Purchases Returns and Allowances	1,000	2,000	2,000
Net Purchases	?	100,000	205,000
Cost of Goods Available for Sale	?	120,000	?
Ending Merchandise Inventory	12,000	?	?
Cost of Goods Sold	?	105,000	190,000

2-29 **MERCHANDISER INCOME STATEMENT** Prepare the income statement for Kalber's, Inc., for January 19X3 from the following list of selected accounts:

CO 2, 4, 5

Administrative Expenses	$ 95,000
Merchandise Inventory (beginning)	5,000
Merchandise Inventory (ending)	10,000
Purchases	250,000
Purchases Discounts	5,000
Purchases Returns and Allowances	5,000
Sales	500,000
Selling Expenses	115,000
Transportation In	20,000

2-30 **MERCHANDISER BALANCE SHEET** Following are the balance sheet accounts for Basu, Inc. Prepare the firm's balance sheet for December 31, 19X2.

CO 5

Building (net)	$150,000
Cash	10,000
Common Stock	150,000
Equipment (net)	100,000
Land	100,000
Merchandise Inventory	30,000
Notes Payable	40,000
Prepaid Expenses	20,000
Retained Earnings	160,000
Wages Payable	60,000

2-31 **COST OF RAW MATERIALS USED** For the following independent cases, replace the question marks with amounts that should appear in the computations of cost of raw materials used in production.

CO 6, 7

	A	B	C
Beginning Raw Materials Inventory	$ 20,000	$?	$ 30,000
Gross Purchases	140,000	100,000	?
Transportation In	20,000	5,000	10,000
Purchases Discounts	2,000	?	3,000
Purchases Returns and Allowances	2,000	2,000	1,000
Net Purchases	?	100,000	250,000
Cost of Raw Materials Available for Manufacturing	?	120,000	?
Ending Raw Materials Inventory	24,000	?	?
Cost of Raw Materials Used in Production	?	105,000	260,000

2-32 **COST OF RAW MATERIALS USED** Following are selected accounts and their balances for Doogar, Inc. Prepare a schedule to show the cost of raw materials used in production.

CO 6, 7

Raw Materials Inventory (beginning)	$ 50,000
Raw Materials Inventory (ending)	60,000

Gross Purchases	680,000
Purchases Discounts	25,000
Purchases Returns and Allowances	10,000
Transportation In	45,000

2-33 MANUFACTURER COST OF GOODS SOLD For the following independent cases, replace question marks with amounts that should appear in the computations of cost of goods manufactured.

CO 6, 7

	A	B	C
Direct Materials	$30,000	$?	$ 20,000
Direct Labor	80,000	150,000	?
Indirect Materials	5,000	10,000	1,000
Indirect Labor	10,000	10,000	4,000
Factory Depreciation	5,000	?	20,000
Factory Rent	50,000	50,000	100,000
Factory Utilities	20,000	40,000	?
Total Overhead	?	150,000	150,000
Total Manufacturing Costs	?	350,000	250,000
Beginning Work in Process Inventory	20,000	?	40,000
Ending Work in Process Inventory	25,000	25,000	?
Cost of Goods Manufactured	?	350,000	275,000

2-34 COST OF GOODS MANUFACTURED Following are selected accounts and their balances for McClure Company. Prepare a schedule that shows the cost of goods manufactured.

CO 6, 7

Work in Process Inventory (beginning)	$ 25,000
Direct Labor	150,000
Direct Materials	100,000
Work in Process Inventory (ending)	20,000
Factory Depreciation	10,000
Factory Insurance	10,000
Factory Rent	60,000
Factory Utilities	20,000
Indirect Labor	10,000
Indirect Materials	5,000

2-35 MANUFACTURER COST OF GOODS SOLD For the following independent situations, replace the question marks with amounts that should appear in computations for cost of goods sold.

CO 7

	A	B	C
Beginning Finished Goods Inventory	$ 50,000	$?	$ 75,000
Cost of Goods Manufactured	600,000	800,000	?
Ending Finished Goods Inventory	75,000	50,000	60,000
Cost of Goods Sold	?	800,000	780,000

2-36 **MANUFACTURER COST OF GOODS SOLD** Following are selected accounts for Keating, Inc. Prepare the schedule of cost of goods sold.

CO 7

Finished Goods Inventory (beginning)	$ 120,000
Cost of Goods Manufactured	2,000,000
Finished Goods Inventory (ending)	200,000

2-37 **MANUFACTURER INCOME STATEMENT** From the following accounts for Wartick, Inc., prepare the income statement for the year ended June 30, 19X2.

CO 2, 4, 7

Administrative Expenses	$ 900,000
Direct Labor	750,000
Direct Materials	500,000
Factory Overhead	1,500,000
Finished Goods Inventory (beginning)	25,000
Finished Goods Inventory (ending)	65,000
Sales	5,000,000
Selling Expenses	800,000
Work in Process Inventory (beginning)	30,000
Work in Process Inventory (ending)	40,000

2-38 **MANUFACTURER BALANCE SHEET** Following are selected accounts for Lubich, Inc. Prepare the firm's balance sheet as of June 30, 19X3.

CO 6, 7

Building (net)	$200,000
Cash	10,000
Common Stock	100,000
Equipment (net)	50,000
Finished Goods Inventory	25,000
Land	100,000
Notes Payable	80,000
Prepaid Expenses	20,000
Raw Materials Inventory	15,000
Retained Earnings	?
Taxes Payable	20,000
Work in Process Inventory	10,000

2-39 **VARIABLE AND FIXED COSTS** Fischer and Fischer, Inc., is planning for future electrical costs. Electricity cost is partly fixed and partly variable. The fixed portion is $6,000. The variable portion is estimated to be $2,000 at 10% of plant capacity, $4,000 at 20% of capacity, $6,000 at 30% of capacity, and so on up to $20,000 at 100% of plant capacity. Estimate the total cost of electricity from 0% to 100% of plant capacity at 10% intervals.

CO 8

2-40 **CONTROLLABLE COSTS** Mindy's parents have proposed to pay her $X for each A on her report card and $Y for each B on her report card. Evaluate this reward system.

CO 8

2-41 **INCREMENTAL, SUNK, AND OPPORTUNITY COSTS** Joella owns a five-year-old car that cost $15,000 and is worth $6,000 today. She is thinking of buying a new car for

CO 8 $20,000 with a $6,000 trade-in. She also has to pay $25 to renew her driver's license. What are the incremental costs of the new car? What are the sunk costs? If she decides to keep the old car, what is the opportunity cost?

Problems

2-42   ACCOUNTING FOR SERVICE ORGANIZATIONS   Following is a list of the accounts and their balances for Denise's Dating Service:

CO 3

Accounts Payable	$ 10,000
Accounts Receivable	15,000
Accumulated Depreciation—Building	60,000
Billings to Clients	300,000
Building	300,000
Cash	20,000
Common Stock	50,000
Computer Rental Expense	20,000
Electricity Expense	4,000
Insurance Expense	10,000
Land	200,000
Marketing Expense	3,000
Mortgage Payable	160,000
Rent Revenue	40,000
Retained Earnings	?
Telephone Expense	3,000
Wages Expense	50,000

REQUIRED

Prepare (a) the income statement and (b) the balance sheet for the fiscal year ended June 30, 19X2.

2-43   ACCOUNTING FOR MERCHANDISERS   Following is a list of accounts and their balances of Sean's Sports Shop.

CO 5

Accounts Receivable	$ 143,000
Accounts Payable	90,000
Accumulated Depreciation—Building	80,000
Administrative Expense	800,000
Building	500,000
Cash	20,000
Common Stock	100,000
Gross Purchases	2,800,000
Land	400,000
Merchandise Inventory (beginning)	60,000
Merchandise Inventory (ending)	61,000
Notes Payable	320,000
Purchases Discounts	12,000
Purchases Returns and Allowances	2,000

Retained Earnings	?
Sales	5,000,000
Selling Expense	1,000,000
Transportation In	15,000

REQUIRED

Prepare (a) the income statement for the year ended October 31, 19X2, and (b) the balance sheet as of October 31, 19X2.

2-44   ACCOUNTING FOR MANUFACTURERS   The following is a list of accounts and their balances for Charles H. Smith Publishing.

CO 7

Accounts Receivable	$ 90,000
Accounts Payable	85,000
Accumulated Depreciation—Building	600,000
Accumulated Depreciation—Equipment	900,000
Administrative Expense	640,000
Building	2,000,000
Cash	70,000
Common Stock	600,000
Direct Labor	200,000
Equipment	1,500,000
Equipment Depreciation	70,000
Factory Building Depreciation	80,000
Factory Insurance	40,000
Factory Utilities	70,000
Finished Goods Inventory (beginning)	76,000
Finished Goods Inventory (ending)	60,000
Gross Purchases	500,000
Indirect Labor	50,000
Indirect Materials	50,000
Land	800,000
Mortgage Payable	1,100,000
Purchases Discounts	25,000
Purchases Returns and Allowances	15,000
Raw Materials Inventory (beginning)	6,000
Raw Materials Inventory (ending)	20,000
Retained Earnings	1,300,000
Sales	4,000,000
Selling Expense	830,000
Transportation In	30,000
Work in Process Inventory (beginning)	37,000
Work in Process Inventory (ending)	45,000

REQUIRED

Prepare the following as of December 31, 19X1: a schedule of cost of raw materials used in production; a schedule of cost of goods manufactured; an income statement; and a balance sheet.

2-45   COST CLASSIFICATION   The following is a list of costs for a merchandiser:

CO 3, 8

a. Merchandise is acquired at a gross cost of $75,000.

b. Transportation in of $1,000 is paid.

c. Purchase discounts of $1,000 are recorded.

d. Salaries of the sales clerks total $60,000.

e. Salary of the company president is $70,000.

f. Rental of the building costs $60,000.

g. Advertising cost $20,000 per year.

h. Depreciation of company car is $2,000.

i. The owner has been offered $500,000 for the business.

REQUIRED

For each cost, identify whether it is fixed or variable, whether it is a period cost or a product cost, and whether it is a sunk cost or an opportunity cost. Not all cost categories apply to each cost.

2-46   COST CLASSIFICATION   The following is a list of costs for a company that constructs earth-moving equipment.

CO 4, 6, 8

a. Steel used per piece built costs $10,000.

b. Labor to assemble pieces is $40 per machine.

c. Depreciation of factory building is $25,000 per year.

d. The president's salary is $1,200,000.

e. Depreciation of office building is $20,000 per year.

f. Electricity in factory is $60,000 per year plus $100 per machine built.

g. Electricity in office building is $5,000 per year.

h. Cost of screws and nuts is $500 per year.

i. Janitor in factory earns $15,000 per year.

j. Commissions to salespeople are $1,000 per machine sold.

REQUIRED

For each cost, identify whether it is fixed or variable; a period or product cost; if a product cost, whether it is direct materials, direct labor, or manufacturing overhead; and whether it is a direct or indirect cost. Not all cost categories apply to each cost, and one of the costs has both fixed and variable components.

**Business
Decision Case**

You are employed by a bank and your supervisor asks you to examine the following income statement of Needcashnow Company. She wants to know whether the bank should grant a loan to Needcashnow and, if it does, what interest rate to charge.

Needcashnow Company
Income Statement
For the Year Ended June 30, 19X1

Sales		$3,000,000
Cost of Goods Sold		1,800,000
Gross Margin		$1,200,000
Administrative Expenses	$600,000	
Selling Expenses	500,000	1,100,000
Income before Taxes		$ 100,000
Taxes		40,000
Net Income		$ 60,000

REQUIRED

a. What type of firm is this?

b. Why would you need to know the nature of this firm's business?

c. Suppose you wanted to run a "what-if" analysis. For example, you would like to see what the income statement would look like if sales increased or decreased by 10%. What impedes your running this analysis?

d. What additional information would you need before you could answer this question?

Chapter

3

Cost Behavior and Cost–Volume–Profit Analysis

CHAPTER OBJECTIVES

After reading Chapter 3, you should be able to:

1. Summarize the basic assumptions of cost–volume–profit analysis (pp. 61–63).

2. Understand and evaluate the behavior of fixed costs, variable costs, and mixed costs at different levels of operating activity and their effect on the cost–volume–profit analysis (pp. 63–68).

3. Apply cost–volume–profit relationships graphically and analytically to find the breakeven point and the activity level necessary to earn a target net income (pp. 68–74).

4. Describe how cost–volume–profit analysis is used in decision support

for proposed changes to selling price, to variable costs, to fixed costs, and to multiple variables (pp. 75–77).

5. Prepare contribution margin income statements and describe their use in cost–volume–profit analysis and incremental decision making (pp. 77–82).

6. Explain the contribution margin approach to multiple products (pp. 79–80).

7. Discuss the behavioral aspects of cost–volume–profit analysis for managerial performance (p. 82).

*M*anagers of all organizations must understand the fundamental relationships of sales (revenues), costs (expenses), and net income (profit or residual). The primary method of studying these relationships is usually called *cost–volume–profit analysis*. Its emphasis is on relatively short-term decisions, although it may be applied to longer-term and strategic decisions. An especially important aspect of cost–volume–profit analysis is its use in answering "what if?" questions, such as "What if sales decline?" "What if costs increase?" "What if we introduce a new product?" Cost–volume–profit analysis is a tool for answering such questions.

The use of cost–volume–profit analysis is an integral part of the management decision process. Managers at varying levels of responsibility rely on cost–volume–profit analysis to make both major and minor decisions concerning individual products as well as overall performance. Managers usually have a variety of decision models, or formal frameworks involving quantitative analysis, at hand for making a choice among alternatives. Cost–volume–profit analysis is one of the most useful decision models the management accountant can prepare for management.

THE BASIC ASSUMPTIONS OF COST–VOLUME–PROFIT ANALYSIS

CHAPTER
OBJECTIVE 1
*Cost–volume–profit
assumptions*

Cost–volume–profit (C–V–P) analysis is the study of the effects of changes in fixed costs, variable costs, sales quantities, sales prices, and sales mix on profit. It rests on a series of assumptions and is limited in its ability to contain all elements of the business environment. By recognizing the limitations these assumptions impose and providing additional complexity within the C–V–P model, management accountants can usually capture the essence of the decision ahead. The assumptions are listed in italics and then explained further.

1. *Each cost may be divided into variable and fixed components.* The activity level is the operating level (or *volume*) chosen for examination. In essence, this first assumption recognizes that certain cost components vary in total in relation to the activity level (variable costs) while other cost components do not vary in total (fixed costs). Two examples of variable costs are direct materials and direct labor. *Direct materials* consists of the raw materials that go into the manufacturing of a product, or the cost of those materials. *Direct labor* refers to the workers who actually make a product, or their cost in wages. *Overhead costs* are any costs other than direct materials and direct labor. Overhead is composed of variable overhead and fixed overhead. We will describe direct materials, direct labor, and overhead in much greater detail in later chapters. For now, it is sufficient to note that direct materials and direct labor are variable costs and that overhead has both variable and fixed components.

2. *The relationship of sales and costs has been estimated and is assumed to be linear over the relevant range.* The relevant range consists of the activity levels over which the cost–volume–profit assumptions hold. The activity level may be measured in a variety of ways, among them the number of units produced and the number of direct labor hours needed to produce the items.

> ## EXHIBIT 3-1
>
> ## THE BASIC ASSUMPTIONS OF
> ## COST–VOLUME–PROFIT ANALYSIS
>
> 1. Each cost may be divided into variable and fixed components.
>
> 2. The relationship of sales and costs has been estimated and is assumed to be linear over the relevant range.
>
> 3. Total fixed costs remain the same over the relevant range.
>
> 4. Total variable costs are proportional to volume.
>
> 5. The sales price does not change over the relevant range.
>
> 6. No change in efficiency occurs.
>
> 7. Either one product is analyzed or a given sales mix of multiple products is analyzed.
>
> 8. Sales and production are equal.
>
> 9. All relevant factors and data are known.

Stating that sales is linear means that sales at a particular activity level (such as the number of units produced and sold) equals the selling price per unit times the activity level. Similarly, variable costs equals variable cost per unit multiplied by the activity level.

3. *Total fixed costs remain the same over the relevant range.* This statement is the first corollary to assumption 1 that each cost may be divided into variable and fixed components. Total fixed costs are assumed to be a fixed amount and remain at that amount over the relevant range of activity.

4. *Total variable costs are proportional to volume; in other words, unit variable costs are the same for each unit of output within the relevant range.* In essence, this proposition is the second corollary to assumption 1 that each cost may be divided into variable and fixed components. That is, variable costs are the same for each unit of output within a certain activity level. Exceptions to this assumption may occur when there are step variable costs, which are costs for items purchased in lump sums at various stages.

5. *The sales price does not change over the relevant range.* This is the corollary to assumption 2 for the linear relationship of sales and costs.

6. *No change in efficiency occurs.* In other words, productivity holds constant over the relevant range. That is, there is no gain or loss in productivity from producing more or less of the product or service.

In fact, change in efficiency does occur when a learning effect takes place. Workers learn a new process with the production of the first few items. Once they have learned the process, they can work more efficiently and more quickly, and costs of production go down. However, we assume here that *no* learning effects occur. (Techniques exist to describe and plot learning effects, but they are covered in more advanced textbooks.)

7. *Either one product is analyzed or a given sales mix of multiple products is analyzed.* Given our limiting assumptions, we must recognize that to try to analyze multiple

products in a dynamic environment can be virtually impossible. Changing this assumption would allow analysis of a particular sales mix result compared to a variety of sales mix results—producing an absurd analysis.

8. *Sales and production are equal.* We assume that the number of items sold is the same as the number of items produced, in order to eliminate any effect that an inventory costing method (FIFO, LIFO, or weighted average) would have on our analysis.

9. *All relevant factors and data are known.* We assume that the C–V–P model is deterministic and perform the analysis as though we knew all the numbers and their relationships.

These assumptions constrain C–V–P analysis to a relatively simple level. The manager must keep the assumptions clearly in mind when using C–V–P analysis as a decision-making aid. These assumptions are summarized in Exhibit 3-1 (page 62).

COST BEHAVIOR

Fixed Costs

CHAPTER OBJECTIVE 2
Fixed, variable, and mixed costs

Chapter 2 introduced *fixed costs,* which are costs that in total do not change within the relevant range for a given period of time. They are usually costs that cannot be altered in the short run, such as executive salaries, depreciation, and a portion of utilities. Fixed costs are in effect capacity costs; that is, if the organization continues to operate as a going concern, these costs will continue to be incurred and will not change over the entity's relevant range.

Note that it is total fixed costs that do not change at various activity levels; fixed cost per unit changes with each change of activity level. For example, a firm with $100,000 total fixed costs and a relevant range of 40,000–100,000 units per month has the same total fixed costs at any activity level within the relevant range but has varying fixed costs per unit. These relationships are depicted analytically in Exhibit 3-2 and graphically in Exhibit 3-3. (We will refer to this firm and its data throughout the chapter.)

If 40,000 units were the chosen activity level, fixed costs per unit would be $2.50, whereas if 100,000 units were the activity level chosen, fixed costs per unit would be $1. In all cases, in the relevant range between 40,000 units and 100,000 units, the total fixed

---

EXHIBIT 3-2

TOTAL FIXED COSTS AND FIXED COST PER UNIT AT DIFFERENT ACTIVITY LEVELS

Activity level in units	40,000	50,000	80,000	100,000
Unit fixed cost	$2.50	$2.00	$1.25	$1.00
Total fixed cost	$100,000	$100,000	$100,000	$100,000

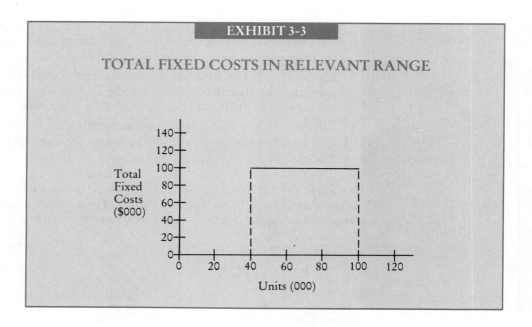

costs would be $100,000. But if the activity level is outside the relevant range, what kind of an analysis of fixed costs at those levels is necessary? For example, if the activity level is expected to drop to 20,000 units per month for a prolonged period, management might decide to sell some of the equipment to reduce the depreciation charges and make other adjustments in their fixed costs. Such a response to production planning necessitates an analysis of fixed costs to determine the magnitude of change made by an activity level of 20,000 units per month. Conversely, if management felt that the activity level would increase significantly from the 100,000 units on a regular basis, and in fact the relevant range for future decisions was 80,000–140,000 units, then a separate C–V–P analysis would be necessary. Again, keep in mind that total fixed costs remain the same over the relevant range but fixed cost per unit is different at each activity level.

Variable Costs

Variable costs change proportionately in total within the relevant range for a given period of time. These are costs such as direct materials and direct labor required for each unit of output, as well as other items required on a per-unit basis. To determine total variable costs, it is necessary to multiply the variable costs per unit by the activity level. Conversely, if an item is identified as a variable cost and the total variable costs are known at a particular activity level, the total variable cost is divided by the activity level to obtain the variable cost per unit. For example, assume that the activity levels between 40,000 units and 100,000 units have a variable cost per unit of $5. As Exhibits 3-4 and 3-5 indicate, the total variable cost would vary between $200,000 and $500,000 depending on the activity level chosen.

In fact, the total variable costs increase in a linear rate in the relevant range, as shown in Exhibit 3-5. Outside the relevant range, further analysis would be necessary. For example, if the activity level is expected to drop significantly for a continued period of time, a reevaluation of the variable costs would be necessary. Perhaps the

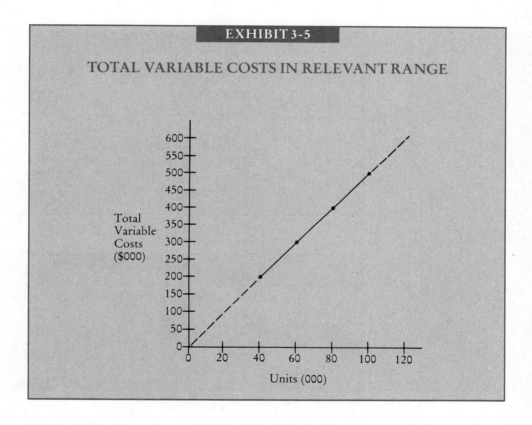

EXHIBIT 3-4

TOTAL VARIABLE COSTS AND VARIABLE COST PER UNIT AT DIFFERENT ACTIVITY LEVELS

Activity level in units	40,000	60,000	80,000	100,000
Unit variable cost	$5.00	$5.00	$5.00	$5.00
Total variable costs	$200,000	$300,000	$400,000	$500,000

EXHIBIT 3-5

TOTAL VARIABLE COSTS IN RELEVANT RANGE

organization is able to take advantage of quantity discounts to some extent in the range of 40,000–100,000 units, whereas it would be unable to do so under 40,000 units. Once above the upper limit of the relevant range, management would consider that variable costs might be reduced with the increase in activity level.

Mixed Costs

Some costs have both fixed and variable components. Such costs are called **mixed costs.** Recall from the previous section that assumption 1 of cost–volume–profit analysis is that we can divide each cost into fixed and variable components. In addition, we noted that a portion of the cost of utilities is a fixed cost; the other portion of utilities must be a variable cost because it is a function of activity level. Thus, to properly analyze a mixed cost, we must first determine its fixed and variable components. One method of charting these components is the high–low method. (Regression analysis, a more sophisticated technique, is covered in Appendix A following this chapter.) In the high–low method, two costs are selected, one at the high side and another at the low side of the relevant range, and transferred to a graph scaled for cost and units of production. If these points are representative of activity in the relevant range, a line connecting them should be a close estimate of the cost pattern for the entire relevant range of activity. For example, assume that the total utilities cost is $30,000 at 50,000 units and $45,000 at 80,000 units of production output. These relationships are depicted analytically in Exhibit 3-6 and graphically in Exhibit 3-7.

EXHIBIT 3-6

MIXED COSTS SELECTED FOR THE HIGH–LOW METHOD

Utilities

Activity Level (units)	Total Costs
80,000	$45,000
50,000	30,000

EXHIBIT 3-7

RELATION BETWEEN COST AND UNITS

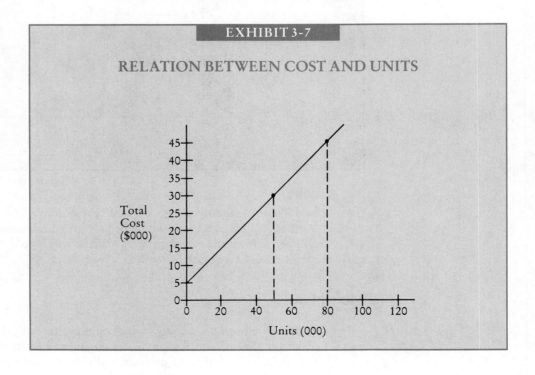

By extending the line to zero volume, we find that $5,000 is the estimated fixed cost component of utilities. That is, at zero volume utilities costs do not fall to zero but remain $5,000. The more usual method of determining the fixed and variable components of a mixed cost under the high–low method is to use algebra to calculate the fixed and variable portions of the total fixed costs. The algebraic method is based on the reasoning that only the variable cost causes total costs to change when the activity level changes. Accordingly, variable costs cause total costs to change from $30,000 to $45,000 when the activity level changes from 50,000 units per month to 80,000 units per month. Once the variable cost per unit is determined, the fixed portion of total costs may be calculated using the following equations. Assume that there are two activity levels (L_1 and L_2) with respective total costs (TC_1 and TC_2).

$$\text{Variable Cost per Unit (VC):} \quad VC = \frac{TC_2 - TC_1}{L_2 - L_1}$$

$$\text{Total Fixed Costs (FC):} \quad FC = TC_1 - (VC \times L_1)$$
or
$$FC = TC_2 - (VC \times L_2)$$

For this example, the two activity levels and their total costs are as follows:

Activity Level (units)	Cost
80,000	$45,000
− 50,000	− 30,000
30,000	$15,000

As the equation states, the variable cost per unit is equal to the change in costs divided by the change in activity level. Thus for this example:

Variable cost per unit = $15,000/30,000 units = $.50

Once the variable cost per unit is known, we solve for total fixed costs. For either the high point or the low point, total fixed costs equal total costs minus the product of variable cost per unit times the activity level. Thus for this example we obtain:

$45,000 − ($.50 × 80,000 units) = $5,000 total fixed costs

or:

$30,000 − ($.50 × 50,000 units) = $5,000 total fixed costs

Therefore, the utilities cost formula within the relevant range is estimated as $5,000 fixed cost per month plus $.50 per unit. In essence, the formula states that utilities are incurred at the rate of $.50 per unit of activity, with the fixed component of $5,000 per month regardless of the activity level.

Let us quickly review these three cost patterns:

1. Fixed costs remain constant in total over the relevant range and variable costs change proportionately in total over the relevant range.
2. Fixed cost per unit changes over the relevant range and variable cost per unit is constant over the relevant range.
3. Mixed costs have components of a fixed cost and variable costs. They must be separated into their respective components prior to the C–V–P analysis. As we examine further the use of C–V–P analysis, we assume that the mixed costs have been analyzed and are appropriately included in the fixed costs and variable costs.

Since we can now analyze all costs at various levels of activity, we can also estimate total costs in any activity level within the relevant range by summing all the variable costs per unit and summing all the fixed costs in total to arrive at the total cost. The formula then would be:

$$\text{Total Cost} = \text{Total Fixed Cost} + (\text{Variable Cost per Unit} \times \text{Activity Level})$$

APPLICATIONS OF COST–VOLUME–PROFIT ANALYSIS

CHAPTER OBJECTIVE 3
Breakeven analysis

Even though the cost patterns in an organization may be identified as such by the high–low method just discussed, they have little usefulness for decision making until they are placed in a decision context. Once we have determined the sales price and the revenue, we can analyze the relationships of cost, volume, and profit (or residual). A primary use of cost–volume–profit analysis is breakeven analysis. Often a manager must determine a production activity level at which total revenues (inflows) equal total costs (outflows). Income statements are usually stated as in the following manner (we substitute *costs* for *expenses* to make our upcoming explanations easier to understand):

$$\text{Revenue} - \text{Costs} = \text{Net Income}$$

or as:

$$\text{Revenue} - \text{Fixed Costs} - \text{Variable Costs} = \text{Net Income}$$

Rearranging, we find that:

$$\text{Revenue} = \text{Fixed Costs} + \text{Variable Costs} + \text{Net Income}$$

This last equation is the most general form for performing breakeven analysis.

Breakeven Point

The breakeven point is the activity level at which neither profit nor loss occurs. A manager may want to know the breakeven point to assess the probability of not achieving that point or higher. Thus the analysis will help the manager to assess the riskiness of a project.

Assume that an organization has $100,000 in total fixed costs, $5 in variable costs per unit, and a sales price of $7 per unit. The manager is searching for the breakeven point—the activity level that equates revenues and costs. One of the C–V–P

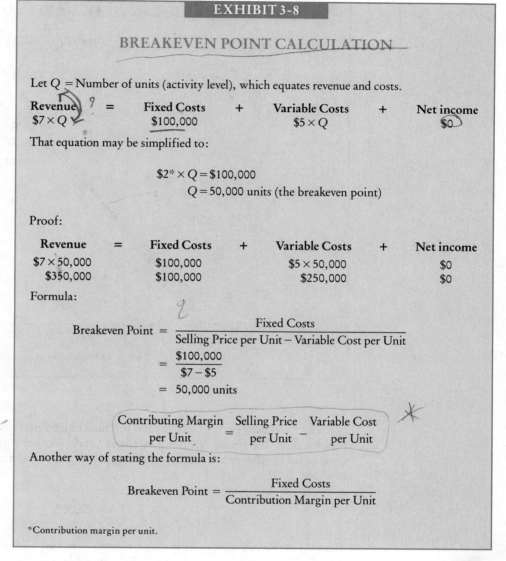

EXHIBIT 3-8

BREAKEVEN POINT CALCULATION

Let Q = Number of units (activity level), which equates revenue and costs.

Revenue	=	Fixed Costs	+	Variable Costs	+	Net income
$7 × Q$		$100,000		$5 × Q$		$0

That equation may be simplified to:

$$\$2^* × Q = \$100,000$$
$$Q = 50,000 \text{ units (the breakeven point)}$$

Proof:

Revenue	=	Fixed Costs	+	Variable Costs	+	Net income
$7 × 50,000$		$100,000		$5 × 50,000$		$0
$350,000		$100,000		$250,000		$0

Formula:

$$\text{Breakeven Point} = \frac{\text{Fixed Costs}}{\text{Selling Price per Unit} - \text{Variable Cost per Unit}}$$

$$= \frac{\$100,000}{\$7 - \$5}$$

$$= 50,000 \text{ units}$$

$$\frac{\text{Contributing Margin}}{\text{per Unit}} = \frac{\text{Selling Price}}{\text{per Unit}} - \frac{\text{Variable Cost}}{\text{per Unit}}$$

Another way of stating the formula is:

$$\text{Breakeven Point} = \frac{\text{Fixed Costs}}{\text{Contribution Margin per Unit}}$$

*Contribution margin per unit.

[handwritten margin note: Contribution margin = Total Revs − Variable Costs]

assumptions is that production is equal to sales. Thus, the number of units sold times the selling price per unit should equal total fixed costs plus total variable costs. These relationships are depicted analytically in Exhibit 3-8 and graphically in Exhibit 3-9.

If Q is the number of units produced and sold, then the total revenues are $7 × Q$ and the variable costs are $5 × Q$. The *contribution margin* is the total revenues minus variable costs, and the *contribution margin per unit* is the contribution margin divided by the number of units produced and sold. (Contribution margin analysis is discussed on pages 77–79.) In this example, the contribution margin is

$$(\$7 × Q) - (\$5 × Q) = \$2 × Q$$

and the contribution margin per unit is $2.

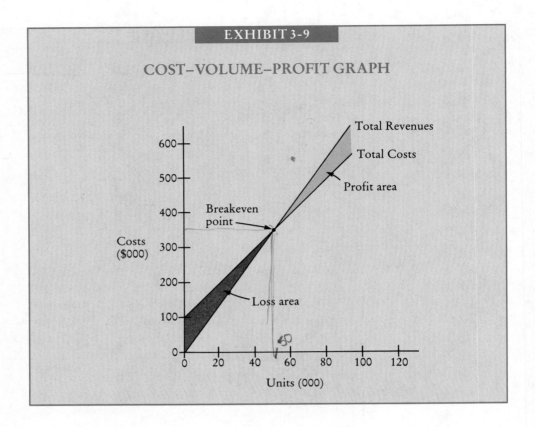

The breakeven point is where total revenues equal fixed costs plus variable costs. In other words, the breakeven point is where total revenues minus variable costs equal fixed costs or where the contribution margin is equal to fixed costs. In this problem, it is where

$$\$2 \times Q = \$100,000$$

Thus Q is 50,000 units. This can be easily verified. Total revenues are $350,000 ($7 × 50,000). Fixed costs are $100,000. Variable costs are $250,000 ($5 × 50,000). Total costs are $350,000. Therefore, total revenues and total costs are both $350,000.

The breakeven point in units may be calculated using the formula in Exhibit 3-8, as follows:

$$\text{Breakeven Point} = \frac{\text{Total Fixed Costs}}{\text{Selling Price per Unit} - \text{Variable Cost per Unit}}$$

Thus, in this example,

$$\text{Breakeven Point} = \frac{\$100,000}{\$7 - \$5}$$
$$= 50,000 \text{ units}$$

Using the cost–volume–profit graph allows us to evaluate profit or loss over the relevant range as well as locate the breakeven point (see Exhibit 3-9). The recognition of profit or loss at various activity levels is the primary advantage of the C–V–P graph. Profit or loss is measured by the distance between the total revenues line and the total costs line for any activity level within the relevant range. At the breakeven point there is no difference between these two lines and neither profit nor loss exists.

Before leaving this section, note the limitations that the relevant range places on cost–volume–profit predictions. For example, one cannot conclude that the breakeven graph predicts a loss of $100,000 at the zero-unit activity level or a loss of $60,000 at the 20,000-unit activity level ($2 \times 20,000 - \$100,000$). These activity levels are not within the relevant range; therefore, the analysis is not appropriate for these levels.

Target Net Income

Although C–V–P graphs are an important descriptive tool to display the relationships of cost, volume, and profit, the formula approach to C–V–P analysis may be more useful in decision making. An example of this increased usefulness arises when C–V–P analysis is used to answer the question, "What activity level is necessary to earn a desired or target net income?" (In Chapter 1 we called such questions and their analysis *goal-seeking*.) Target net income is inserted in the basic income equation (expressed using *costs*) as follows:

$$\text{Revenues} = \text{Fixed Costs} + \text{Variable Costs} + \text{Target Net Income}$$

(Note that target net income in the breakeven analysis is zero.) The solution to this equation reveals the activity level required to generate the target net income under the cost–volume–profit assumptions listed earlier. Assume that in our continuing example $20,000 is the target net income per month. The solution to the basic equation will reveal the activity level necessary to cover all costs, fixed and variable, and leave a net income (residual) equal to the $20,000 target net income.

$$\$7 \times Q = \$100,000 + (\$5 \times Q) + \$20,000$$
$$\$2 \times Q = \$120,000$$
$$Q = 60,000 \text{ units}$$

The proof calculation of 60,000 units would appear as follows:

Revenue (60,000 × $7)	=		$420,000
Fixed costs	=	$100,000	
Variable costs (60,000 × $5)	=	300,000	
Total costs			400,000
Target net income *or* net income			$ 20,000

The breakeven formula becomes:

$$\text{Breakeven Point} = \frac{\text{Total Fixed Cost} + \text{Target Net Income}}{\text{Selling Price per Unit} - \text{Variable Cost per Unit}}$$

MULTIDIMENSIONAL BREAKEVEN ANALYSIS

We are all familiar with break-even analysis that takes a two-dimensional approach and determines the sales quantity at which total revenues equal total costs. In this article, Roger A. Camp *illustrates a "multidimensional" break-even approach used in profit analysis of his company's trucking operations. The author is the CFO of The Motor Convoy, Inc., a Georgia-based common carrier operating primarily in the southeastern United States.*

The chart below illustrates a typical break-even analysis at The Motor Convoy for a relevant range of trips—from about 100 to 450 miles. The rate and cost per pound are graphed along the Y axis, while the length of the trip (in miles) is charted along the X axis. The following curves are plotted:

- Motor Convoy's rate curve.
- A competitor's rate curve.
- Motor Convoy's cost curves at various volumes.

Graphing the rates charged by each competitor illustrates the competitive forces that the company must confront and the competitive constraints affecting analysis of profit margins. (Information for plotting this curve is obtained from the marketing department.)

Within the range of the chart, the fixed costs per unit increase or decrease while the variable costs per unit remain constant. The slope of the cost curves stays the same, producing a series of curves at different volumes parallel to each other. As volume increases, total costs per pound decrease by the reduction in fixed costs per unit.

In the chart the cost curve is plotted for volumes of 2,000, 2,500, 3,000 and 3,500 pounds. Motor Convoy's break-even points for the above volumes are trip lengths of approximately 190, 260, 320 and 410 miles, respectively.

The interrelationship of such factors as volume, trip length and competitors' rates are extremely important, requiring careful study so that strategies for increasing profits can be developed. To examine these interrelationships, let's discuss four cases at Motor Convoy, which are charted on the opposite page. In each case, volume is 2,000 pounds for the range of trips illustrated.

Case 1. The competitor's rate curve is parallel to Motor Convoy's cost curve and both rate curves cross at 110 miles. At this volume Motor Convoy's business should be concentrated on trips between 110 and 190 miles. On shorter trips, the competition is cheaper than Motor Convoy, while on longer trips Motor Convoy is losing money.

Case 2. The competitor's rate curve is parallel to and above Motor Convoy's rate curve. Motor Convoy's cost curve crosses its rate curve at 190 miles (the break-even point at this volume). Although Motor Convoy is more competitive at all levels, it should direct its sales effort toward obtaining shorter trips of less than 190 miles, since it is unprofitable above this level.

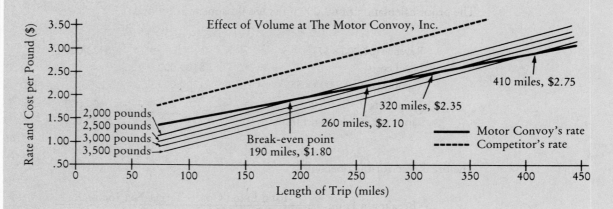

Case 3. Motor Convoy's rate and cost curves are parallel. The competitor's rate curve crosses Motor Convoy's rate curve at 135 miles. Although Motor Convoy is profitable at all levels, it should probably place more effort on obtaining trips greater than 135 miles, since below that level the competition has lower rates.

Moreover, in this case, if Motor Convoy obtains its competitor's short business, it could probably eliminate that competition—not an unhappy scenario.

Case 4. Although highly unlikely, this is the ideal environment to operate in because the competitor's rate curve is parallel to and above Motor Convoy's rate and cost curves. There is no competition at any point and Motor Convoy is profitable at all levels.

In each of the above cases, volume changes and trip lengths outside the illustrated range could significantly alter strategies. Furthermore, such analysis can highlight those areas in which a company is not competitive and provide guidance for changing the company's rate structure to improve its performance and competitive position.

A MUST FOR SURVIVAL

Financial analysis of profit margins must take into consideration underlying cost and rate structures, competitors' rate structures, volume and patterns of business. This type of analysis is a must for survival because of the tight profit margins in most industries.

SOURCE: Roger A. Camp, "Multidimensional Break-even Analysis," *Journal of Accountancy* (January 1987), pp. 132–33. Reprinted by permission.

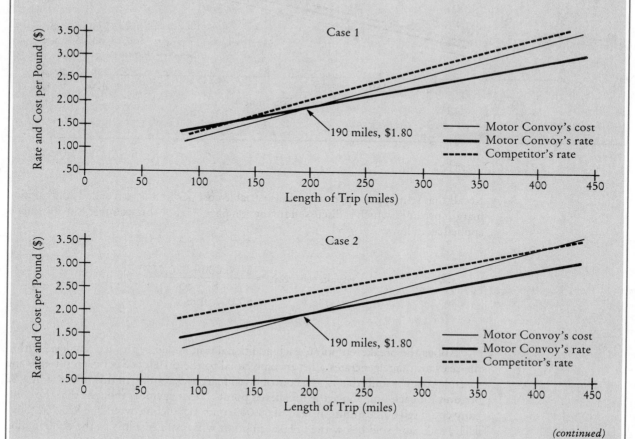

(continued)

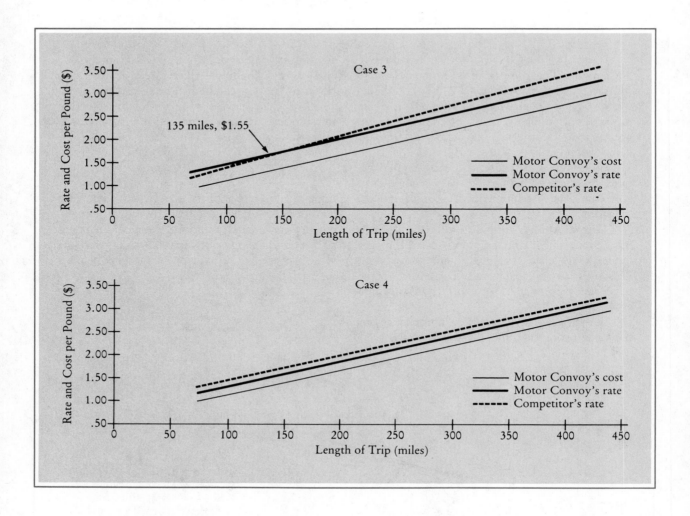

Recall that selling price per unit minus variable cost per unit is also called contribution margin per unit, which is discussed further on page 77. For this example, the formula is applied as follows:

$$\text{Breakeven Point} = \frac{\$100,000 + \$20,000}{\$7 - \$5}$$
$$= 60,000 \text{ units}$$

Above the breakeven point, each additional unit added to the activity level within the relevant range generates a net income equal to the difference between revenue and variable cost per unit (that is, the contribution margin per unit). In this instance, it is $2 per unit for each unit above the breakeven point. If management thought that the company could sell 60,001 units instead of 60,000 units, net income would be $20,002. Similarly, each unit sold below the breakeven point will result in a loss of the contribution margin per unit. If sales were 59,999 units, net income would be $19,998.

COST–VOLUME–PROFIT ANALYSIS AND DECISION SUPPORT SYSTEMS

CHAPTER OBJECTIVE 4
Cost–volume–profit analysis in decision support

The assumptions and the data gathered for breakeven analysis are subject to change. Managers must assess this possibility by examining the impact of various changes on the terms in the equation. What if fixed costs were different? What if variable cost per unit is different? What if selling price per unit is different? The impact of these changes should be assessed before making a decision.

This section examines how the formula approach to cost–volume–profit analysis is used to aid management in assessing the impact of changes in the variables to affect net income.

In each of the examples, we introduce no value judgment regarding the desirability of the changing variables. Management accounting in general, and C–V–P analysis in particular, provides managers with quantitative information for decision making but does not provide the decision itself. C–V–P analysis is only one of many tools the manager uses to make decisions.

Change of Selling Price

If we assume the sales price is decreased from $7 to $6, the breakeven point equation now appears as follows:

$$\$6.00 \times Q = \$100,000 + (\$5 \times Q) + \$0$$
$$\$1.00 \times Q = \$100,000$$
$$Q = 100,000 \text{ units to break even, or } \$600,000 \text{ total revenue}$$

Other factors being equal, a decrease in the sales price will increase the breakeven point from the original analysis. Further, the price of $6 and the resulting breakeven point are at the limit of the relevant range. Therefore, this price is so low that we would not be able to generate a targeted net income if our assumptions about the relevant range are correct.

Conversely, if we assume that the sales price is increased to $7.50, the breakeven point equation now appears as follows:

$$\$7.50 \times Q = \$100,000 + (\$5.00 \times Q) + \$0$$
$$\$2.50 \times Q = \$100,000$$
$$Q = 40,000 \text{ units to break even, or } \$300,000 \text{ total revenue}$$

Other factors being equal, an increase in the sales price will decrease the breakeven point. This price is at the lowest activity level in the relevant range; any increase in activity level from this point will generate a net income equal to $2.50 per unit for each unit above this breakeven point.

Change of Variable Cost

Management may feel that it can do nothing about the selling price but that it can lower the variable cost. If we assume that the variable cost per unit decreases from $5 to $4.50, the breakeven point equation now appears as follows:

$$\$7 \times Q = \$100,000 + (\$4.50 \times Q) + \$0$$
$$\$2.50 \times Q = \$100,000$$
$$Q = 40,000 \text{ units to break even, or } \$280,000 \text{ total revenue}$$

Other factors being equal, a reduction in the variable cost per unit decreases the breakeven point.

Conversely, if management were to find that variable cost per unit had increased from $5 to $6, the breakeven point equation would appear as follows:

$$\$7 \times Q = \$100,000 + (\$6 \times Q) + \$0$$
$$\$1 \times Q = \$100,000$$
$$Q = 100,000 \text{ units to break even, or } \$700,000 \text{ total revenue}$$

Other factors being equal, an increase in the variable cost per unit raises the breakeven point.

Change of Fixed Costs

Management may find that fixed costs had increased above the estimated level. Assuming that fixed costs increased to $120,000, the breakeven point equation now appears as follows:

$$\$7 \times Q = \$120,000 + (\$5 \times Q) + \$0$$
$$\$2 \times Q = \$120,000$$
$$Q = 60,000 \text{ units to break even, or } \$420,000 \text{ total revenue}$$

Other factors being equal, an increase in total fixed costs increases the breakeven point.

Conversely, management may have the opportunity to decrease fixed costs. If we assume that fixed costs decrease to $80,000, the breakeven point equation now appears as follows:

$$\$7 \times Q = \$80,000 + (\$5 \times Q) + \$0$$
$$\$2 \times Q = \$80,000$$
$$Q = 40,000 \text{ units to break even, or } \$280,000 \text{ total revenue}$$

Other factors being equal, a decrease in total fixed costs decreases the breakeven point.

Change of Multiple Variables

Changing multiple variables to examine the results is more common in business than changing one variable at a time. Assuming that the sales price increases to $8, variable costs increase to $5.50, and total fixed costs increase to $150,000, the breakeven point equation now appears as follows:

$$\$8 \times Q = \$150,000 + (\$5.50 \times Q) + \$0$$
$$\$2.50 \times Q = \$150,000$$
$$Q = 60,000 \text{ units, or } \$480,000 \text{ total revenue}$$

> ### EXHIBIT 3-10
>
> ## CONTRIBUTION MARGIN FORMAT FOR THE INCOME STATEMENT
>
> **Rethmeier, Inc.**
> **Contribution Margin Income Statement**
> **For the Year Ended December 31, 19X1**
>
> | | Units | Price | Total |
> |---|---|---|---|
> | Revenue | 50,000 | $7 | $350,000 |
> | Variable Costs | 50,000 | 5 | 250,000 |
> | Contribution Margin | 50,000 | 2 | $100,000 |
> | Fixed Costs | | | 100,000 |
> | Net Income | | | $ –0– |

By changing multiple variables we create new terms for the equation and new scenarios or alternatives for management to evaluate. Note also that no general statement about the breakeven point can be made when several variables change.

CONTRIBUTION MARGIN

CHAPTER OBJECTIVE 5
Contribution margin income statements

Another way to solve cost–volume–profit problems is through contribution margin analysis. Recall that contribution margin is equal to sales price minus variable cost and that contribution margin per unit is equal to revenues per unit minus variable costs per unit. In the preceding breakeven analysis, it was shown that the breakeven point is equal to fixed costs divided by the difference between selling price per unit and variable costs per unit. Thus, the breakeven point is equal to fixed costs divided by the contribution margin per unit. If the selling price per unit is $7 and the variable cost per unit is $5, then the contribution margin is $2 per unit. If fixed costs are $100,000, the breakeven point is $100,000/$2, or 50,000 units.

These relationships are sometimes depicted in an income statement prepared in a contribution margin format, such as the one shown in Exhibit 3-10. Essentially, variable costs are subtracted from revenues to obtain the contribution margin. From this number is subtracted fixed costs, and the result is net income. Of course, in this breakeven analysis, net income is zero.

The contribution margin approach simply states that each unit sold contributes something toward fixed costs and profit. The revenue from each unit sold must help cover variable costs; fixed costs and profits will be recovered from the contribution margin. The contribution margin is applied to fixed costs until they are completely covered and then to net income. The breakeven concept then focuses on the number of unit contribution margins required to cover fixed costs. In the above example, when 50,000 units are sold, the fixed costs of $100,000 are covered by the total contribution margin of $100,000 (50,000 × $2). Each additional unit sold would generate $2 in unit contribution margin, which would be applied as $2 in net income because the fixed costs have been covered. A key element of C-V-P analysis is that beyond the breakeven point, the unit contribution margin has no fixed costs to cover and is, therefore, net income per unit. Conversely, if only 49,999 units are sold, the net loss would be $2:

Revenue	$49,999 \times \$7 = \$349,993$
Variable costs	$49,999 \times \$5 = \underline{249,995}$
Contribution margin	$\$99,998$
Fixed costs	$\underline{100,000}$
Net income (loss)	$\$(2)$

Assuming that the activity level is in the relevant range, the shortfall of unit sales below the breakeven point results in a loss equal to the number of units in the shortfall times the unit contribution margin.

Thus far we have considered the breakeven point and the target net income amount in terms of the required activity level expressed in units. If a related revenue level were desired, we could merely multiply the number of units times the selling price per unit. However, there is a more direct way to calculate the breakeven point for the target net income sales dollars. This method makes use of the contribution margin ratio. Contribution margin ratio is the percentage of contribution margin to sales price—that is, contribution margin per unit divided by selling price per unit. To find the breakeven point in sales dollars, we divide the fixed costs by the contribution margin ratio. For the example problem, the contribution margin ratio is $2/$7, or 2/7. The breakeven point in sales dollars is $100,000/(2/7), or $350,000.

Note that when fixed costs are divided by the contribution margin ratio, the result is breakeven sales dollars. When fixed costs are divided by the unit contribution margin, the result is units. This is expressed in the following two general equations:

$$\text{Breakeven Point in Dollars} = \frac{\text{Fixed Costs}}{\text{Contribution Margin Ratio}}$$

$$\text{Breakeven Point in Units} = \frac{\text{Fixed Costs}}{\text{Contribution Margin per Unit}}$$

A manager can use this technique to explore a desired or targeted net income. Assume the manager expects a net income of $20,000. Thus:

$$\text{Breakeven Point in Dollars} = \frac{\text{Fixed Costs} + \text{Target Income}}{\text{Contribution Margin Ratio}}$$

$$= \frac{\$100,000 + \$20,000}{2/7}$$

$$= \frac{\$120,000}{2/7}$$

$$= \$420,000$$

Contribution Margin and Decision Support Systems

In a previous section, we discussed how to assess the impact of changes in the data when performing breakeven analysis. We return to this issue but now focus on contribution margin. The principles are the same, but here they are stated in terms of the contribution margin—that is, other factors being equal, an increase in the contribution margin per unit will decrease the breakeven point. Conversely, other factors being equal, a decrease in the contribution margin per unit will increase the breakeven point.

COST–VOLUME–PROFIT ANALYSIS WITH MULTIPLE PRODUCTS

CHAPTER OBJECTIVE 6
Multiple products

Few firms have only one product. Therefore, to use C–V–P analysis in a multiple-product setting, we assume a given **sales mix** of products, or the relative quantities of all products sold. This sales mix may be based strictly on historical data or it may be an estimate of future activity. Regardless, once the sales mix is estimated, the ratio of each product in the mix of products is assumed to be constant at all activity levels within the relevant range. That is, at 10,000 units or at 90,000 units, the sales mix does not change. This constant ratio permits the use of composite units. Each **composite unit** contains the constant proportion of each product as originally assumed.

For example, the sales managers expect that two units of Product A will be sold for every three units of Product B sold. Product A has a selling price of $10 per unit and variable costs of $6 per unit, and Product B has a selling price of $20 per unit and variable costs of $17 per unit. If fixed costs are expected to be $200,000 per year, we can calculate the expected breakeven point in dollars as follows:

Sales Price					Percent of Composite Unit Sales Price
Product A	2 units @ $10	= $20			
Product B	3 units @ $20	= 60			
Composite unit sales price				$80	100%
Variable Costs					
Product A	2 units @ $6	= $12			
Product B	3 units @ $17	= 51			
Composite unit variable costs				63	78.75%
√ Composite unit contribution margin				$17	21.25%

$$\text{Breakeven Point in Dollars} = \frac{\$200,000}{.2125} = \$941,176.47$$

$$\text{Breakeven Point in Composite Units} = \frac{\$200,000}{\$17} = 11,764.7$$

One composite unit consists of two units of Product A and three units of Product B. The breakeven point is 23,530 units ($2 \times 11,764.7$ units) of Product A and 35,294 units ($3 \times 11,764.7$ units) of Product B (rounded). Essentially, we are weighting the sales price and the variable costs by the proportion of relative sales of these items. Based on this assumed product mix (two units of Product A to three units of Product B), we can determine the proportion of the breakeven point of total dollars to be generated by each product in order to break even. If Q is the total number of units sold, the calculation is as follows:

$$\$941,176.47 = (\tfrac{2}{5}Q \times \$10) + (\tfrac{3}{5}Q \times \$20)$$

This says that 2/5 of the quantity will be sold at $10 per unit and 3/5 of the quantity will be sold at $20 per unit. Solving:

$$\$941,176.47 = (\$4 \times Q) + (\$12 \times Q)$$
$$= \$16 \times Q$$
$$Q = 58,823.52 \text{ units}$$

Because 40% of the total units are Product A, 23,530 units (40% of 58,824 units) of Product A must be sold to break even. Using the same reasoning, 35,294 units of Product B (or 60% of 58,824 units) must be sold in addition to the 23,530 units of Product A, in order to break even.

The income statement in the breakeven format for this illustration is prepared in Exhibit 3-11. Although there is more work involved in the contribution margin approach for multiple products, conceptually the income statement is similar to that for a single product in Exhibit 3-10.

EXHIBIT 3-11

MULTIPLE-PRODUCT BREAKEVEN FORMAT FOR THE INCOME STATEMENT

Teague Company
Breakeven Income Statement
For the Year Ended December 31, 19X1

| | Product A (23,530 units) | | Product B (35,294 units) | | |
	Unit	Total	Unit	Total	Total
Sales	$10	$235,300	$20	$705,880	$941,180
Variable Costs	6	141,180	17	599,998	741,178
Contribution Margin	$ 4	$ 94,120	$ 3	$105,882	$200,002
Fixed Costs					200,000
Net Income					$ 2*

*Rounding error; net income should be zero.

INCREMENTAL ANALYSIS

CHAPTER OBJECTIVE 5
Contribution margin and incremental analysis

The contribution margin approach is an important tool for evaluating alternative choices for strategic and operational decisions. Regardless of whether a manager elects to change price, variable expenses, fixed expenses, or a combination of all three, the examples in the previous section reveal the major role of contribution margin analysis in decision making.

The most important factor in business decision making is determining an alternative's effect on contribution margin. In fact, once the breakeven point is known, we can determine the effects of alternative decisions merely by observing the change or effect relative to the contribution margin ratio. This approach is known as incremental analysis or *differential analysis*. Chapter 2 explained that incremental costs are costs that differ among decision alternatives. Here incremental items include both revenues and costs that change from one set of alternatives to another. Incremental analysis is simply the examination of only these differing items. The three most important characteristics of incremental analysis are as follows:

1. Incremental analysis requires an examination of *only* the items that change; we may ignore the items that do not change.

2. Incremental analysis requires estimates of the future in the form of alternatives; therefore, we are involved in projecting the future and estimating its impact on the organization through C–V–P analysis or other appropriate techniques.

3. Incremental analysis requires compilation of data from sources other than historical-cost financial records. We may use such records, but we also gather data from whatever source yields the best information.

Recall the data for the original example on page 69:

Sales price	$7 per unit
Variable costs	5 per unit
Contribution margin	$2 per unit
Fixed costs	$100,000
Breakeven point	50,000 units; or revenues of $350,000

We may use incremental analysis to answer the following questions about this data, as opposed to solving equations and performing other types of calculations.

● *How many additional units must be sold to attain a target net income of $20,000?* Recall that above the breakeven point, each unit or dollar of contribution margin goes to net income. Thus, 10,000 additional units (the increment) above the breakeven point must be sold, each with a $2 contribution margin, to realize a target net income. The only relevant numbers are incremental revenue, incremental costs, and thus incremental contribution margin. Fixed costs are not relevant to this decision because they do not change.

● *How many additional units must be sold to break even if fixed costs increase by $30,000?* With a $2 unit contribution margin, 15,000 additional units (the increment) must be sold in order to break even. That is, the new breakeven point equals the old breakeven point (50,000 units) plus the incremental units (15,000), or 65,000 units at the new breakeven point.

● *If fixed costs increase by $40,000 and variable costs per unit decrease by $1, will the breakeven point increase or decline?* Many industries in the United States and the world economy must evaluate the extent to which items should be automated and labor and other variable components reduced, thus increasing fixed costs and decreasing variable costs per unit. In this example, the extent of the reduction is determined when the new fixed costs of $140,000 are divided by the new contribution margin per unit of $3 ($7 − $4) to get 46,667 units. The overall breakeven point would decline from 50,000 units to 46,667 units.

We do not intend by this example to state that in every case of increasing fixed costs and decreasing variable costs the breakeven point would move down. We merely point out that a choice to increase fixed costs is a function of the estimate that variable costs will decline and volume will increase to cover the increase in total costs.

Incremental analysis permits examination of many alternatives in an efficient manner. These results may be interpreted by management in order to decide among alternative courses of action based on the overall strategy of the firm. Again, management accounting techniques such as this are only tools to aid in decision making.

BEHAVIORAL ASPECTS OF COST–VOLUME–PROFIT ANALYSIS

CHAPTER OBJECTIVE 7
Behavioral aspects

It should be clear that profits can be maximized by raising the contribution margin ratio and lowering fixed costs. Managers under pressure from higher-level managers or shareholders to increase earnings have been known to take actions similar to the following to maximize the contribution margin ratio and minimize fixed costs: (1) cut back on the preventative maintenance staff to trim fixed costs; (2) make a product component rather than purchase it in order to substitute a fixed cost for a variable cost; (3) purchase components that are of lower cost and inferior quality in order to reduce the cost per unit and improve the contribution margin ratio; and (4) emphasize only the products with a high contribution margin ratio.

Each of these actions is the result of shortsightedness. The greatest danger in using C–V–P analysis is that it can cause the manager to place too much emphasis on short-term actions to improve profits. *C–V–P analysis should be used to make decisions consistent with the overall strategy of the firm.*

Another danger, especially in substitutions of fixed costs for variable costs, is the possibility that funds will be committed to purchase the equipment to manufacture a component without proper consideration of the long- and short-term costs of buying and maintaining the equipment. Analyses for make-or-buy decisions, and for all cost–volume–profit decisions, should include all costs.

Demonstration Problem

Schwartz Corporation, a manufacturer of soccer balls, has fixed costs of $120,000 per year and variable costs of $3 per ball. The selling price is $8 per ball. Present sales are 90,000 units.

REQUIRED

a. Determine the breakeven point in units and in dollars.

b. Find the increase or decrease in profits resulting from (1) a 10% increase in volume and (2) a 10% decrease in volume.

c. Determine the effect of (1) a change in variable cost per unit to $4, (2) a change in selling price to $9, (3) both happening.

SOLUTION TO DEMONSTRATION PROBLEM

a. Breakeven point in units $= \dfrac{\$120,000}{\$8 - \$3} = 24,000$ units

Breakeven point in dollars $= \$8 \times 24,000 = \$192,000$

b. Contribution margin per unit $= \$8 - \$3 = \$5$

Present volume	90,000 units
Breakeven volume	24,000 units
Volume in excess of breakeven	66,000 units

Current profits $= \$5 \times 66,000 = \$330,000$

Volume increases by 10% $= 9,000$ units; profit $= \$5 \times (66,000 + 9,000) = \$375,000$

Volume decreases by 10% $= 9,000$ units; profit $= \$5 \times (66,000 - 9,000) = \$285,000$

c. 1. If variable cost per unit changes to $4, the contribution margin per unit is $4 ($8 − $4). The breakeven point in units is 30,000 units ($120,000/$4).

2. If selling price per unit changes to $9, the contribution margin per unit is $6 ($9 − $3). The breakeven point in units is 20,000 units ($120,000/$6).

3. If variable cost per unit is $4 and selling price per unit is $9, then the contribution margin per unit is $5 ($9 − $4), the original amount. The breakeven point in units is 24,000 units ($120,000/$5).

Review of Chapter Objectives

1. Summarize the basic assumptions of cost–volume–profit analysis (pp. 61–63).

   ■ There are nine assumptions invoked when cost–volume–profit analysis is used. We assume that: (1) each cost may be divided into variable and fixed components; (2) the relationship of sales and costs has been estimated and is assumed to be linear over the relevant range; (3) total fixed costs remain the same over the relevant range; (4) total variable costs are proportional to volume; (5) the sales price does not change over the relevant range; (6) no change in efficiency occurs; (7) either one product is analyzed or a given sales mix of multiple products is analyzed; (8) sales and production are equal; and (9) all relevant factors and data are known.

2. Understand and evaluate the behavior of fixed costs, variable costs, and mixed costs at different levels of operating activity and their effect on the cost–volume–profit analysis (pp. 63–68).

   ■ To carry out cost–volume–profit analysis, a clear understanding of cost behavior is needed. Costs need to be studied to determine whether they are fixed, variable, or mixed. This can be done with the high–low method (or regression analysis, presented in Appendix A).

3. Apply cost–volume–profit relationships graphically and analytically to find the breakeven point and the activity level necessary to earn a target net income (pp. 68–74).

- The most basic use of cost–volume–profit analysis is breakeven analysis. The contribution margin per unit is the selling price per unit minus the variable cost per unit. The breakeven point can then be found as the fixed costs divided by the contribution margin per unit. This relationship can also be graphed and is referred to as the cost–volume–profit graph. The breakeven point is where total revenues equal total costs.

- The cost–volume–profit model can be extended to consider the activity level needed to reach target net income. The formula becomes: breakeven point equals the sum of total fixed costs plus target net income divided by the contribution margin per unit.

4. Describe how cost–volume–profit analysis is used in decision support for proposed changes to selling price, to variable costs, to fixed costs, and to multiple variables (pp. 75–77).

- Another useful feature of the cost–volume–profit model is that it allows management to assess how sensitive the breakeven point is to other considerations. One can raise or lower revenues or costs and recalculate the breakeven point. This helps managers understand the cost, volume, and profit relationships better and thus make better decisions. For example, it allows managers to assess the effects of substituting fixed costs for variable costs.

5. Prepare contribution margin income statements and describe their use in cost–volume–profit analysis and incremental decision making (pp. 77–82).

- The relationships developed in this chapter can be used to reorient the income statement in a manner that can be more helpful to managers. The income statement then appears in the following format: Revenue minus variable costs equals contribution margin; contribution margin minus fixed costs equals net income.

- Another useful formulation involves the contribution margin ratio. It is the contribution margin per unit divided by the selling price per unit. Then the breakeven point—now in dollars, whereas the previous formula gave the answer in units—is equal to the fixed costs divided by the contribution margin ratio.

6. Explain the contribution margin approach to multiple products (pp. 79–80).

- Incremental costs were discussed in Chapter 2. The concept is extended in this chapter to include incremental revenues and called incremental analysis. It is the examination of only the revenues and costs that change from one alternative to another. Often incremental decisions can be couched in terms of fixed and variable costs so cost–volume–profit analysis can be used to solve the problem.

7. Discuss the behavioral aspects of cost–volume–profit analysis for managerial performance (p. 82).

- One danger of using cost–volume–profit analysis is that managers might place too much emphasis on short-term actions to improve profits. For example, they might be tempted to cut back on the preventative maintenance staff to trim fixed costs. This, of course, could lead to equipment failures sooner than desired and larger expenditures in the future to fix the equipment. Cost–volume–profit analysis should be used to make decisions that are consistent with the overall strategy of the firm.

Glossary of Key Terms

activity level   The operating level or volume chosen for examination, stated in either units or dollars.

breakeven analysis   Analysis of sales, variable costs, and fixed costs to determine the breakeven point.

breakeven point   The point at which total revenues equal total costs. (The formula can be amended to include target net income.)

capacity cost   The fixed cost of an entity resulting from the need to provide operating facilities to process material and services.

composite unit   A production cost unit that describes the fixed proportions of a sales mix in a multiple-product organization.

contribution margin   Sales price minus variable cost; also referred to as marginal income. It may be expressed as a total, as a ratio, or on a per-unit basis.

contribution margin ratio   The contribution margin divided by the sales price.

cost–volume–profit analysis   The study of the effects of changes in fixed costs, variable costs, sales quantities, sales prices, and sales mix on profit.

cost–volume–profit graph   A graph depicting the relationships between variable costs, fixed costs, total costs, and total revenue.

high–low method   A rudimentary approach to separating fixed and variable components of total cost by selecting a high and a low activity level and corresponding cost within the relevant range of activity, drawing the points on a cost–volume–profit graph, and extending a line through the points.

incremental analysis   The examination of only the cost and revenue items that differ among decision alternatives. (Also known as differential analysis.)

mixed cost   A cost composed of fixed and variable components over various relevant ranges of operation.

regression analysis   A statistical method that determines the best straight line that represents a data set (Appendix A).

relevant range   The range of economic activity within which estimates and predictions are valid. The range of activity levels (volume) over which fixed costs remain fixed in total and variable costs are proportional in total to the volume. Cost–volume–profit analysis assumptions are valid within the relevant range.

sales mix   The relative combination of quantities of the various products that make up the total sales of a company.

target net income   A desired level of profit or contribution management establishes as a goal.

APPENDIX A

Regression Analysis

In the chapter the high–low method was used to estimate the relationship between the activity level and the total costs for utilities. A more sophisticated approach to this estimate is regression analysis. The idea behind **regression analysis** (also called the *least squares method*) is to fit the best line possible to the data by means of statistical analysis. The objective of this approach is to determine this best straight line:

$$Y = a + bX$$

where:

$$Y = \text{the dependent variable}$$
$$X = \text{the independent variable}$$
$$a = \text{the intercept}$$
$$b = \text{the slope of the line}$$

X is called the *independent variable* because it can take on any reasonable value. Once X is determined, Y can be calculated. Since the value of Y depends on the value of X, Y is called the *dependent variable*.

When regression analysis is used in estimating a cost function, the intercept is interpreted to be the fixed cost. The slope is interpreted to be the variable cost per unit of activity as measured by X. Thus, in the equation $Y = a + bX$, a represents the fixed cost and b represents the variable cost per unit.

Suppose that instead of only the high and low point as on page 66, the following data for the continuing example are available to the cost accountant:

Activity Level (units) X	Total Utility Costs Y
50,000	$30,000
60,000	36,000
70,000	42,000
80,000	45,000

The goal is to discover the relationship between the activity level (X) and the total utility cost (Y).

From the data, two equations can be developed simultaneously. From them we solve them for a and b. The two equations are:

$$\Sigma XY = a\Sigma X + b\Sigma X^2$$
$$\Sigma Y = na + b\Sigma X$$

where:

$$\Sigma = \text{summation over the values}$$
$$n = \text{number of observations}$$

These values are illustrated for the sample data in Exhibit 3-12. After conducting the analysis, it is determined that $a = \$5,100$ and $b = \$.51$ per unit. Thus, the cost estimation equation is:

$$Y = \$5,100 + \$.51X$$

The fixed portion of the utilities cost is $5,100 and the variable portion is $.51 per unit of activity.

The graph of these data and the regression line are given in Exhibit 3-13 (page 88). Notice that the four points do not lie on the regression line. Most points do not lie exactly on a regression line derived in practice. But note that the regression line is

---

EXHIBIT 3-12

SAMPLE REGRESSION ANALYSIS

Activity Level (X)	Total Utility Cost (Y)	X^2	XY	Y^2
50,000	$ 30,000	2,500,000,000	$ 1,500,000,000	$ 900,000,000
60,000	36,000	3,600,000,000	2,160,000,000	1,296,000,000
70,000	42,000	4,900,000,000	2,940,000,000	1,764,000,000
80,000	45,000	6,400,000,000	3,600,000,000	2,025,000,000
260,000	$153,000	17,400,000,000	$10,200,000,000	$5,985,000,000

$$\$10,200,000,000 = a(260,000) + b(\$17,400,000,000)$$
$$\$153,000 = 4a + b(260,000)$$

Multiply both sides of the second equation by 65,000. Then subtract the second equation from the first:

$$\$10,200,000,000 = 260,000a + \$17,400,000,000b$$
$$9,945,000,000 = 260,000a + 16,900,000,000b$$
$$\$\quad 255,000,000 = \qquad \$\quad 500,000,000b$$

Therefore, $b = \$.51$ per unit. Substituting b into the first equation yields:

$$\$10,200,000,000 = 260,000a + \$17,400,000,000(\$.51)$$

or

$$\$10,200,000,000 = 260,000a + \$8,874,000,000$$

so that

$$260,000a = \$1,326,000,000$$

Therefore, $a = \$5,100$.

---

relatively close to the points. This is what regression analysis does: it finds the line closest to all the data points.

There are statistical methods to assess how well the regression line fits the data. We can compute the closeness of the actual Y values to the values of Y predicted by the regression equation.

The predicted values of Y are computed by substituting X into the regression equation. For example, for the first data point, X equals 50,000. Then, $Y = \$5,100 + \$.51(\$50,000) = \$30,600$. This number is the predicted value of Y.

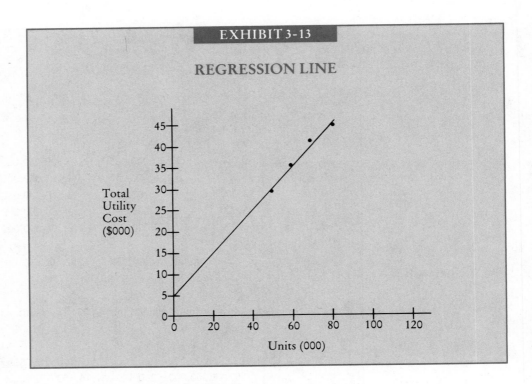

EXHIBIT 3-13

REGRESSION LINE

EXHIBIT 3-14

COMPUTATION OF REGRESSION RESIDUALS

Actual Y	Predicted Y $(Y = \$5,100 \times \$.51X)$	Residual	Residual^2
$30,000	$30,600	$ – 600	$ 360,000
36,000	35,700	300	90,000
42,000	40,800	1,200	1,440,000
45,000	45,900	– 900	810,000
		$ –0–	$2,700,000

The errors or residuals of the regression analysis are defined as the actual value of Y minus the predicted value of Y. These residuals are calculated in Exhibit 3-14. (As a computational guide, note that the sum of the residuals is zero. This fact can be a useful check that you have performed the arithmetic correctly.)

Probably the most popular statistic for seeing how well the regression line fits the data is R^2. To obtain this we need two more calculations. The first is to square each of the residuals and then add them together, as in the last column of Exhibit 3-14. The sum of the squared residuals is $2,700,000. Also we need to compute the total variation in Y, which is:

$$\Sigma Y^2 - \frac{(\Sigma Y)^2}{n} = \$5,985,000,000 - \frac{\$23,409,000,000}{4}$$
$$= \$132,750,000$$

The data is given in Exhibit 3-12. R^2 is defined as:

$$1 - \frac{\text{Sum of the Squared Residuals}}{\text{Total Variation in } Y}$$

For our example, this is:

$$1 - \frac{\$2,700,000}{\$132,750,000} = .979$$

Interpret the number this way. When R^2 is close to one, then the regression line represents the data points very well. When it *is* one, the points lie exactly on the regression line. When R^2 is close to zero, the regression line is poor. If it is exactly zero, it says that the relationship between X and Y is random.

   Once the management accountant has determined the regression equation, he or she can use it in cost–volume–profit analysis. Regression analysis is considered superior to the high–low method because it uses all the data, not just two points. Also, the high–low method might use extreme, unrepresentative data. If the data are not representative, the resulting equation might be distorted.

Review Questions

3-1   What types of questions does C–V–P analysis help answer?

3-2   List the assumptions that limit C–V–P analysis and explain them.

3-3   How do fixed costs behave over the relevant range? Fixed costs per unit?

3-4   How do variable costs behave over the relevant range? Variable costs per unit?

3-5   Define *mixed costs* and provide a simple method of analyzing their behavior.

3-6   Why is the concept of relevant range critical to C–V–P analysis?

3-7   Define *breakeven point* in terms of dollars and units.

3-8   Does the breakeven point assume that profit must be zero?

3-9   How does a cost–volume–profit graph help management understand the relationship of cost–volume–profit?

3-10   Given a particular situation and assuming that all other things are equal, what is the effect of an increase in the sales price on the breakeven point? An increase in variable costs? An increase in fixed costs?

3-11   "Management accounting and C–V–P analysis make the decision for the manager." Do you agree or disagree? Explain.

3-12   Define *contribution margin*.

3-13   Define *contribution margin ratio*.

3-14   What are the general equations for contribution margin and contribution margin ratio that allow almost all types of cost–volume–profit analysis?

3-15   Explain unit contribution margin as the amount of profit per unit above the breakeven point.

3-16   Why does targeted net income act as an addition to fixed expenses in the calculation of targeted sales revenue?

3-17   Explain the composite unit approach to breakeven and targeted profit levels. Why must the relationship of the product units remain the same?

3-18   Decision making under pressure often requires a rapid review of alternatives. How can incremental analysis help in making decisions under time pressure?

3-19   A firm is confronted with the possibility of substituting fixed costs for variable costs. How may it analyze this approach to determine its effectiveness?

3-20   Give examples of how cost–volume–profit analysis might have (a) a positive impact and (b) a negative impact on management's behavior.

Discussion Questions

3-21   The following is a graph of a cost function. Use C–V–P analysis by drawing a straight line to estimate cost. What is the relevant range for using this straight-line estimation of the cost function?

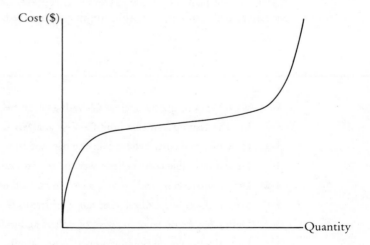

3-22   An electric utility considers building a nuclear power plant. The fixed costs of the new facility would be approximately $100 million. The selling price per kilowatt-hour is estimated at $1 and the variable cost per kilowatt-hour at $.60. Thus, the breakeven point is 250 million kilowatt-hours. If management feels that there is a high probability to achieve this much sales, should it go ahead with the project?

Exercises

3-23   **COST BEHAVIOR** The following cost relationships between direct labor hours and
CO 2   total maintenance cost pertain to the year's budgeted activity for Sartore Company:

Total Direct Labor Hours	Total Maintenance Cost
600,000	$387,000
800,000	487,000

Using the high–low method:

a. Calculate the variable maintenance cost per unit pertaining to the year's activity;

b. Calculate the budgeted fixed maintenance cost for the year;

c. Estimate the total maintenance cost for Sartore Company if 750,000 hours were chosen as the activity level.

(CPA adapted)

3-24   COST BEHAVIOR Round Corporation is attempting to estimate the fixed and variable portions of its utilities expense as measured against direct labor hours for the first quarter of the year. Information for the first quarter is as follows:

CO 2

	January	February	March
Direct labor hours	51,000	46,500	49,000
Utilities expense	$1,830	$1,755	$1,790

a. What is the fixed portion of Round's utility expense? Round to the nearest dollar.

b. What is the variable cost per unit of the utilities expense?

c. What would be the estimated utilities expense budget at 50,000 direct labor hours?

(CIA adapted)

3-25   BREAKEVEN ANALYSIS Turtle, Inc., wants you to perform a breakeven analysis on one of its products. The selling price is $10 per unit, the variable cost is $5 per unit, and the total fixed costs are $230,000. How many units must be sold to break even? Verify this by showing that at this activity level income is zero.

CO 3

3-26   BREAKEVEN ANALYSIS Murphy Company is considering dropping a product line. It currently produces a number of items, one of which is an eight-place flatware set. Variable costs amount to $12 per unit, fixed overhead costs amount to $7 per unit at the present production of 20,000 units. Unfortunately, the sales estimates for the next year indicate that sales will drop below 10,000 units. All of the fixed costs and variable costs are directly attributable to this particular product. How many units are necessary to break even and continue production of sales of this flatware set at a selling price of $20?

CO 3

(CMA adapted)

3-27   TARGET NET INCOME Pivek Company estimates that a new product can sell for $13 per unit. It will have variable cost per unit of $5 and fixed costs of $160,000. How many units must be sold in order to earn $40,000 in income from this product?

CO 3

3-28   DSS AND C–V–P Passionate Pizza, Inc. owns and operates a number of pizza parlors around a major city. The company has asked you to use the following annual budget data to compute the expected net income for each of the assumptions shown below.

CO 4

Sales	Variable Costs	Fixed Costs
$5,000,000	$4,000,000	$600,000

Consider each assumption independently.

a. Total revenue increases 5% and total variable expenses remain constant.

b. Total revenue decreases 5% and total variable expenses remain constant.

c. Total contribution margin increases 10% with no change in sales.

d. Total contribution margin decreases 10% with no change in sales.

e. Sales volume increases 12%.

f. Sales volume decreases 12%.

g. Fixed costs increase 8%.

h. Fixed costs decrease 8%.

i. Fixed costs increase 8% and sales volume increases 8%.

j. Fixed costs increase 8% and total variable costs decrease 8%.

3-29   CONTRIBUTION MARGIN RATIO Complete the calculations that would explain the unknown items in each of the four unrelated cases that follow.

CO 5

	Sales	Variable Costs	Fixed Costs	Total Costs	Net Profit	Contribution Margin Ratio
a.	$2,000	$1,000	$?	$1,800	$?	?
b.	$4,500	$?	$1,200	$?	$?	.40
c.	$?	$1,000	$?	$2,400	$4,800	?
d.	$3,000	$?	$900	$?	$400	?

3-30   BREAKEVEN ANALYSIS Pringle Company is planning to sell a product for $5 a unit. Variable costs are $3.50 per unit and fixed costs are $150,000.

CO 4

a. What are the total sales revenues to break even?

b. How many units must be sold to break even?

c. What would be the effect to the breakeven point, in dollars and units, if fixed costs increased to $200,000 and variable costs declined to $2.50?

3-31   CONTRIBUTION MARGIN INCOME STATEMENT White Company is considering marketing a new product. Marketing research indicates that it can sell 11,000 units in 19X1 at $3 per unit. Variable costs are estimated to be 40% of the unit selling price. Fixed costs are estimated to be $7,200.

CO 5

a. What is the breakeven point in units?

b. What is the breakeven point in dollars?

c. Management wants a contribution margin income statement for the expected sales and costs at the level that the market research has identified.

3-32   BREAKEVEN ANALYSIS Schrader Company is planning its annual operations based on a sales forecast of $9 million. It has prepared the following estimates of its variable and fixed costs for the upcoming year.

CO 3

	Variable Costs	Fixed Costs
Direct materials	$2,400,000	
Direct labor	2,100,000	
Factory overhead	900,000	$1,000,000
Selling expenses	360,000	400,000
Administrative expenses	90,000	200,000
	$5,850,000	$1,600,000

a. Calculate the sales revenue at the breakeven point.

b. Calculate the sales revenue necessary to generate $450,000 in net income.

(CPA adapted)

3-33   COMPOSITE UNITS Hunt Corporation sells two products, G and H, which are sold in the proportion of two units of Product G to three units of Product H. The contribution margin is $6 for Product G and $4 per unit for Product H. Hunt Corporation has fixed costs of $960,000.

CO 6

a. What would be the total units sold at the breakeven point?

b. Of the total units sold, how many units would be Product G?

c. Of the total units sold, how many units would be Product H?

3-34   COMPOSITE UNITS Assume that the sales ratio is three units of G to two units of H in Exercise 3-33. What is the new breakeven point in dollars and units of G and H?

CO 6

3-35   DSS AND C–V–P Malcolm Company sells one product for $105 per unit. The variable costs associated with this product are $84 per unit. If Malcolm Company thinks that a 20% increase in the selling price of its product is appropriate, by how much can the unit sales decline before net income will decline? That is, how will the increase in the contribution margin affect the breakeven point?

3-36   COST BEHAVIOR (Appendix A) The following cost relationships between direct labor hours and total utilities cost for Umanath Company are:

CO 2

Direct Labor Hours	Total Cost
3,000	$16,000
4,000	21,000

a. Determine the fixed and variable components of total cost by the high–low method.

b. Determine the fixed and variable components of total cost by regression analysis.

c. Comment on the results.

Problems

3-37   BREAKEVEN ANALYSIS Johnson Company is planning to produce and sell 300,000 units of a product. The fixed costs are estimated to be $520,000 and the variable cost ratio is 60%. Johnson Company wants to realize a profit of $200,000.

CO 2, 3

REQUIRED

a. Calculate the unit selling price to achieve the targeted profit.

b. Calculate the breakeven point in units (without the targeted profit).

c. Calculate the breakeven point in dollars (without the targeted profit).

d. Explain to management how it may assess differing sales levels and different marketing campaigns to achieve those levels, given the information you are providing them.

3-38   CONTRIBUTION MARGIN RATIO Phillips Company is planning to sell 400,000 units of Product O for $8 per unit. The contribution margin ratio is 25%. Phillips will break even at this level of sales.

CO 3

REQUIRED

a. Calculate the fixed costs.

b. Assuming Phillips wanted to earn 10% of the total revenue as net income, calculate the total sales in units and dollars to generate this.

3-39   BREAKEVEN ANALYSIS Fillem Purse Company operates a group of leased purse departments. These departments sell a number of different styles of ladies' purses with a series of identical variable costs and selling prices. The following data have been collected. The company asks you to consider each of the questions independently.

CO 3, 4

Selling price	$40.00
Variable data (per unit):	
Cost of purses	$22.50
Sales commissions	4.00
Total variable expenses	$26.50
Annual fixed expenses:	
Lease	$ 90,000
Salaries	210,000
Advertising	85,000
Other fixed expenses	20,000
	$405,000

REQUIRED

a. Find the annual breakeven point in dollars and in units.

b. Calculate the net income if 50,000 purses were sold.

c. Refer to the original assumptions. Assuming commissions were discontinued and replaced by an increase in fixed salaries of $150,000, find the breakeven point in dollars and units.

d. Management has decided that a targeted net income of $80,000 is appropriate. Calculate unit sales in units and dollars necessary to achieve this goal under the original assumptions in the data provided and the revised assumptions in requirement c.

3-40   C–V–P GRAPH   The following questions are based on X-Y-Z Company, which uses a *profit–volume* graph similar to the one depicted. The axes are identified as well as the various lines.

CO 3, 4

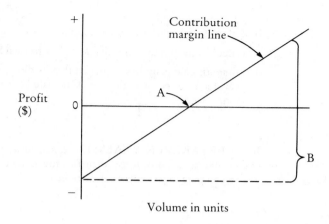

Volume in units

REQUIRED

a. Identify the breakeven point on this graph.

b. Identify the total contribution margin available to cover fixed costs and variable costs relative to selling units.

c. Sketch the line that would depict an increase in fixed costs.

d. Sketch the line that would indicate an increase in the unit contribution margin.

e. Explain how X-Y-Z Company might use the chart for further evaluation of alternatives.

(CMA adapted)

3-41 CONTRIBUTION MARGIN INCOME STATEMENT Dirsmith Company manufacturers and sells a single product. It has identified its revenue and cost relationships as

CO 3, 4, 5   follows:

Selling price per item	$50.00
Variable costs per unit:	
Raw materials	$14.00
Direct labor	6.00
Manufacturing overhead	3.80
Selling expenses	1.60
Total variable costs per unit	$25.40
Annual fixed costs:	
Manufacturing overhead	$ 824,200
Selling and administrative costs	1,205,300
Total fixed costs	$2,029,500
Forecast annual sales (@100,000 units)	$5,000,000

REQUIRED

a. Prepare a contribution margin income statement showing the budgeted annual income. Include per-unit, total, and percent columns.

b. Calculate the breakeven point in units.

c. Calculate the number of units necessary to earn $492,000 in net income.

d. Dirsmith Company has estimated that its direct labor costs will increase by $2 per unit next year due to a recent settlement. Calculate how many units must be sold next year to break even.

(CIA adapted)

3-42   **BREAKEVEN ANALYSIS** Management of Welker Company requested budget data for two products, A and B. It has identified the following price and cost relationships and would like you to compute independent calculations.

CO 3, 4, 6

| | Product | | |
	A	B	Total
Selling price	$5	$10	
Variable costs	2	5	
Contribution margin	$3	$ 5	
Total fixed costs	$84,000	$120,000	
Number of units to be sold to break even	?	?	?
Number of units expected to be sold	30,000	50,000	80,000

REQUIRED

a. Assume that the direct expenses are directly attributable to each product. Find the breakeven point for each product.

b. Disregarding the assumptions in (a), assume that Product A or B is discontinued or unavailable for sale and that sales of the other product must make up for the lost sales of the unavailable product. What breakeven point in units is necessary for either Product A or Product B to become the sole product of the organization with no change in fixed expenses of $204,000?

c. Assume that management has decided to market Products A and B by an approach in which the composite units are sold in a 1:1 ratio. Find what is the breakeven point for these assumptions.

d. Refer to the original assumptions. Calculate the net income for the organization as a whole under the estimated number of units expected to be sold.

3-43   **BREAKEVEN ANALYSIS** Mathews Company, producers of a high-quality rug, has experienced growth in sales for the previous five years. The competition has increased to a degree that Sarah Mathews, president of the organization, believes additional advertising will be necessary to maintain the company's market share. The following costs have been identified for the current year:

CO 3, 4

Variable costs (per rug)	
Direct labor	$12.00
Direct materials	6.50
Variable overhead	5.00
Total variable costs	$23.50

Fixed costs	
Manufacturing expenses	$110,000
Selling expenses	90,000
Administrative expenses	140,000
Total fixed costs	$340,000
Selling price, per rug	$40.00
Expected sales, 19XX (25,000 units)	$1,000,000
Tax rate: 40%	

REQUIRED

a. Calculate the breakeven point in units and dollars for Mathews Company for the current year.

b. Calculate the projected after-tax net income for the current year.

c. Mathews has set the sales target for the following year at $1,200,000. She believes that additional advertising of $40,000 with no increases in costs would be necessary to obtain this sales target. Find the after-tax net income if the additional $40,000 is spent and the sales target is met.

d. Calculate the breakeven point in dollars if the additional $40,000 is spent.

e. Assuming the $40,000 is spent for advertising, find the required total revenue to generate a net income equal to the current year's net income. Hint: First convert to pretax income.

f. At a sales level of 30,000 units, calculate the maximum that could be spent on incremental advertising to achieve an after-tax net income of $80,000.

3-44   DSS AND C–V–P The officers of Young Company are reviewing the profitability of the firm's operations and the potential effects of several proposals changing the product mix from the original four products. Each of the following scenarios should be considered independently. Therefore, consider only the changes stated in each proposal; the activity of the other products remains the same. The income taxes for the moment are irrelevant.

CO 4

	Product P	Product Q	Product R	Product S	Totals
Sales	$10,000	$18,000	$12,600	$22,000	$62,600
Less: Cost of goods sold	4,750	7,056	13,968	18,500	44,274
Gross profit	$ 5,250	$10,944	$(1,368)	$ 3,500	$18,326
Operating expenses	1,990	2,976	2,826	4,220	12,012
Income before income taxes	$ 3,260	$ 7,968	$(4,194)	$ (720)	$ 6,314
Units sold	1,000	1,200	1,800	2,000	
Sales price per unit	$10.00	$15.00	$7.00	$11.00	
Variable cost of goods sold					
per unit	2.50	3.00	6.50	6.00	
Variable operating expenses					
per unit	1.17	1.25	1.00	1.20	

REQUIRED

a. Calculate the effect on net income if Product R is discontinued.

b. Calculate the total effect on net income if Product R is discontinued and a consequent loss of customers causes a decrease in volume of 200 units in sales of Product Q.

c. Calculate the effect on net income if the sales price of Product R is increased to $8 with a decrease in the number of units sold to 1,500 due to the price increase.

d. The factory in which Product R is produced can be used to produce a substitute Product T. Total variable costs per unit are $8.05 for Product T, and 1,600 units can be sold at $9.50 each. Calculate the effect on net income if Product T is introduced and Product R is discontinued.

e. A portion of the factory in which Product P is produced can easily be modified to produce Product S. But changes in quantities may make changes in sales prices advisable. Calculate the total effect on net income if production of P is reduced to 500 units to be sold at $12 each and the production of S is increased to 2,500 units to be sold at $10.50 each.

f. The production of Product P could be doubled by adding a second shift. Higher wages for this shift would have to be paid, which would increase the variable cost of Product T to $3.50 for each additional unit. Calculate the total effect on net income if 1,000 additional units can be sold at $10 each.

(CPA adapted)

3-45   CONTRIBUTION INCOME STATEMENT Savage Company is planning its advertising budget for the next year and has prepared the following budget based on its understanding of the cost, volume, and profit relationships. Savage's owner believes that the company can sell the estimated quantity without any advertising at all.

CO 5

Normal plant capacity	400,000 units
Sales	250,000 units
Selling price	$35 per unit
Variable manufacturing costs	$29 per unit
Fixed manufacturing costs	$700,000
Fixed selling and administration expenses	$800,000

A friend of the owner claims that her marketing firm could increase Savage's unit sales by 40%.

REQUIRED

a. Calculate the most that Savage Company can pay for this marketing campaign and obtain an operating profit of $200,000. Assume that the relevant range is from 200,000 to 400,000 units.

b. Prepare contribution margin income statements in increments of 50,000 units.

c. Provide a brief memo to Savage's management explaining the contribution margin income statements and how it might determine the maximum amount Savage can pay for advertising on an ongoing basis in each of these scenarios.

(CPA adapted)

3-46   BREAKEVEN Bandy, Inc., produces a variety of cleaning compounds and solutions for industrial and household use. Although most of its products are processed independently, the processing for a few is related. "Grit 337" is a coarse cleaning powder with many industrial uses. It costs $1.60 per pound to make and has a selling price of $2 per pound. A small portion of the annual production of this product is retained for further processing with several other ingredients to form a paste that is marketed as a silver polish selling for $4 per jar.

CO 3

This further processing requires .25 pound of Grit 337 per jar. Other ingredients, labor, and variable overhead associated with this further processing cost $2.50 per jar. Variable selling costs amount to $.30 per jar.

REQUIRED

If the decision were made to cease production of the silver polish, $5,600 of fixed costs in the mixing department could be avoided. Find the minimum number of jars of silver polish that would have to be sold to justify further processing of Grit 337.

3-47 BREAKEVEN ANALYSIS Maxwell Company manufactures and sells a single product. Price and cost data regarding production and operations are:

CO 3, 4

Selling price per unit	$15
Variable costs per unit:	
Raw materials	$ 4
Direct labor	3
Manufacturing overhead	2
Selling expenses	1
Total variable costs per unit	$10
Annual fixed costs:	
Manufacturing overhead	$ 96,000
Selling and administrative	104,000
Total fixed costs	$200,000
Forecast annual sales (@ 50,000 units)	$750,000
Income tax rate	30%

REQUIRED

a. Calculate Maxwell's breakeven point in units.

b. Calculate the number of units Maxwell Company must sell in order to earn $168,000 after taxes. Hint: Convert $168,000 to a pretax target.

c. Maxwell Company estimates that its direct labor costs will increase 8% next year. Calculate the number of units Maxwell must sell next year to reach the breakeven point.

d. Assume Maxwell Company's direct labor costs increase 8%. Find the selling price per unit of product Maxwell must charge to maintain the same contribution margin ratio.

3-48 BREAKEVEN ANALYSIS The following is budgeted financial data from Burrowes Company for its Product X:

CO 3, 4

Burrowes Company
Budgeted Income Statement for Product X
For the Year Ended December 31, 19XX
($000)

Sales (200 units @ $150 per unit)		$30,000
Manufacturing Cost of Goods Sold:		
Direct Labor	$3,000	
Direct Materials Used	2,800	
Variable Factory Overhead	3,000	
Fixed Factory Overhead	3,200	
Total Manufacturing Cost of Goods Sold		12,000
Gross Profit		$18,000

(continued)

Selling Expenses:		
Variable	$3,000	
Fixed	4,000	
Administrative Expenses:		
Variable	2,500	
Fixed	5,500	
Total Selling and Administrative Expenses		15,000
Operating Income		$ 3,000

REQUIRED

a. Calculate the number of units of Product X Burrowes must sell to break even.

b. Find the operating income if projected sales increase by 25%.

c. Calculate the sales at the breakeven point if fixed factory overhead increases by $1,700.

3-49   COST BEHAVIOR (Appendix) The following cost relationships between direct labor hours and total utility cost for Tsenton, Inc., are:

Direct Labor Hours	Costs
1	$ 4
2	14
3	16
4	18
5	20
6	22
7	24
8	26
9	30
10	40

REQUIRED

a. Determine the fixed and variable components by the high–low method.

b. Determine the fixed and variable components by regression analysis.

c. Comment on the results.

d. Drop the two lowest and the two highest data points. Revise the regression analysis and comment on the results.

Business Decision Case

CO 3, 4

The income statement for Haggard Co. represents the operating results for the fiscal year ending December 31, 19X1, during which Haggard had sales of 1,800 tons of product. The manufacturing capacity of Haggard's facilities is 3,000 tons. Following is pertinent data concerning Haggard's operation:

Sales	$1,350,000
Variable costs:	
Manufacturing	630,000
Selling costs	369,000
Total variable costs	$ 999,000
Contribution margin	$ 351,000
Fixed costs:	
Manufacturing	98,000
Selling	101,000
Administration	52,000
Total fixed costs	$ 251,000
Net income before income taxes	$ 100,000
Income taxes (40%)	40,000
Net income after income taxes	$ 60,000

REQUIRED

Consider the following independent situations:

a. Calculate the breakeven volume in tons of product for 19X1.

b. The sales volume is estimated to be 2,100 tons in 19X2, and prices and costs are expected to stay at the same levels and amounts. Calculate the after-tax net income that Haggard can expect for 19X2.

c. Haggard has a potential foreign customer that has offered to buy 1,500 tons at $650 per ton in 19X2. Assume that all of Haggard's sales and costs would be at the same levels and rates as in 19X1. Calculate the net income after taxes Haggard would make if it accepted this order and rejected some business from regular customers so as not to exceed capacity.

d. Haggard plans to market its product in a new territory. It estimates that an advertising and promotion program costing $84,000 annually must be undertaken for the next two or three years. In addition, a sales commission of $30 per ton over and above the current commission to the sales force in the new territory would be required. Calculate the number of tons that would have to be sold in the new territory to maintain Haggard's current after-tax income of $60,000.

e. Haggard is considering replacing a highly labor-intensive process with an automatic machine. This change would result in an increase of $89,500 annually in manufacturing fixed costs. The variable manufacturing costs would decrease $40 per ton. Find the new breakeven volume in tons.

(CMA adapted)

Chapter

4

Business Decision Making

CHAPTER OBJECTIVES

After reading Chapter 4, you should be able to:

1. Explain relevant costs, sunk costs, and opportunity costs, and their use in decision making (pp. 103–8).

2. Analyze special sales orders and evaluate whether a business segment should be added or dropped (pp. 108–16).

3. Discuss sell-or-process-further decisions (pp. 116–18).

4. Explain make-or-buy decisions (pp. 118–20).

5. Describe decision making with scarce resources (pp. 120–22).

6. Explain linear programming and how to set up a linear programming problem (pp. 122–25).

7. Identify behavioral aspects of business decision making for the issues in Objectives 1–6 (pp. 107, 108, 116, 120, 122, 124, and 125).

*M*anagers make decisions about segments of an organization as well as for the entire organization. They get involved in making decisions regarding segments because segments make up the organization. By focusing on them, management may make decisions to increase the overall profit. These decisions are made in all types of organizations, profit-oriented and nonprofit alike; however, our focus is on profit-oriented organizations. These decisions usually involve choices from among a variety of alternatives. Therefore, due to constraints on managers' time, it is critical that only the necessary variables be considered and analyzed. From a management accounting view, these necessary variables are usually defined as *relevant costs.*

There are many types of business decisions, the most common of which are as follows:

1. Whether to accept special sales orders.
2. Whether to add or drop a business segment.
3. Whether to sell a particular product or process it further before selling it (sell-or-process-further decisions).
4. Whether to make a product or whether to buy it from a vendor (make-or-buy decisions).
5. How to allocate scarce resources to maximize profits.

Because the concept of relevant costs is important for all of these types of decisions, it is described first.

RELEVANT COSTS AND THE DECISION PROCESS

Accounting information has many uses in decision making, but each accounting number or ratio is not relevant for every decision. In other words, different costs are appropriate for different purposes. The attempt to include every accounting number or ratio into every decision is an example of the application of information overload (too much data) to the decision. Therefore, managers and management accountants must understand the *relevance*, or usefulness, of the accounting information selected for a decision. For example, the decision to institute a new production method would not necessarily require an analysis of selling expenses. Rather, the first task would be to identify those items directly related to the issue at hand—the new production method. In other words, managers need to identify the variables associated with the alternatives. Once this is done, costs that are unavoidable in either alternative need no further consideration.

The following list briefly summarizes the steps in determining relevance:

1. Identify the relevant variables associated with the alternative decisions.
2. Identify avoidable and unavoidable costs.
3. Omit the unavoidable costs from further consideration under the present assumptions.

When the alternatives under consideration change, the process must be restarted from the beginning.

Unavoidable costs are usually considered costs that have occurred or will occur. They generally take two forms: (1) They may be *sunk costs,* or costs that have been incurred and cannot be changed. (2) They may be expected future costs that do not differ among the alternative decisions. Unavoidable costs are irrelevant to the decision.

The relevant costs for a particular decision are costs that should be considered when choosing among alternatives. They frequently take either of two forms. One set of relevant costs are those expected to be incurred in the future. Another set are those that vary among alternatives (*incremental* or differential costs).

Therefore, future incremental costs are the only costs relevant to a decision. (This also applies in the case of incremental revenues.) The manager makes the decision by evaluating only the increment of relevant costs or revenues between alternatives.

The manager should include the following steps, expanding the earlier list, in deciding among alternative courses of action:

1. Identify variables associated with the alternative decisions.
2. Identify unavoidable costs, both sunk costs and future costs that do not differ.
3. Discard the unavoidable costs from the analysis.
4. Make a decision based on the remaining incremental costs. These costs, by definition, are the future costs that are relevant and that vary among alternatives.

An Example of Relevant Costs

We have outlined the concept of relevant costs in decision making. The purpose of the following example is to demonstrate the use of relevant costs in a specific decision. The time value of money is ignored at this time; it and capital budgeting are subjects reserved for Chapter 14. Assume the facts given in Exhibit 4-1 about a decision regarding a new production method requiring a new machine. Recall that this example was described in Exhibit 2-12. There we were concerned with the definitions of various types of costs. Here we will show how to use the concepts to make a decision.

A machine costing $25,000 with a remaining life of five years and an accumulated depreciation of $5,000 (thus a book value of $20,000) can be salvaged for $7,500 and replaced with a machine costing $30,000 with an expected life of five years. The new machine would have no expected salvage value. The annual variable operating expenses are $50,000 using the present method and would be $38,750 using the proposed method, annual sales revenues being equal for both alternatives. The issue for management is this: Should the company purchase the new machine and institute the new production method, or should it continue using the present machine? Keep in mind that we are going to search for the relevant costs and benefits that we defined conceptually in Chapter 2.

Note that purchase of the new machine would require selling the old machine at a financial accounting "loss" of $12,500, as follows:

Net book value	$20,000
Less salvage value	7,500
Financial accounting loss	$12,500

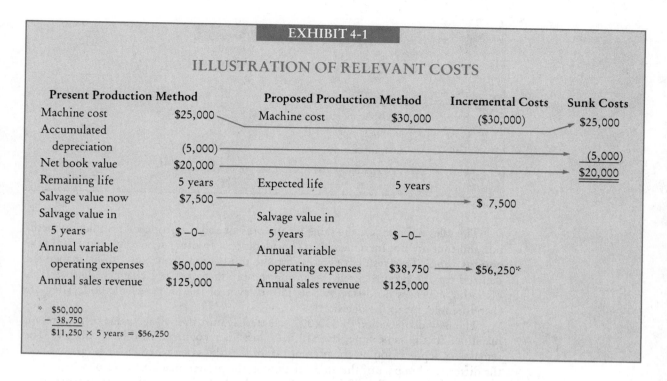

EXHIBIT 4-1

ILLUSTRATION OF RELEVANT COSTS

Present Production Method		Proposed Production Method		Incremental Costs	Sunk Costs
Machine cost	$25,000	Machine cost	$30,000	($30,000)	$25,000
Accumulated depreciation	(5,000)				(5,000)
Net book value	$20,000				$20,000
Remaining life	5 years	Expected life	5 years		
Salvage value now	$7,500			$ 7,500	
Salvage value in 5 years	$ –0–	Salvage value in 5 years	$ –0–		
Annual variable operating expenses	$50,000	Annual variable operating expenses	$38,750	$56,250*	
Annual sales revenue	$125,000	Annual sales revenue	$125,000		

```
*   $50,000
  – 38,750
    $11,250 × 5 years = $56,250
```

Regardless of management's inclination to continue using the present machine in order to avoid a "loss" from a salvage sale, the net book value represents a sunk cost (a cost established by a past decision) and therefore not relevant to future decisions. Thus the book loss is irrelevant here. We can demonstrate this by analyzing the totals projected for five years from the facts in Exhibit 4-1, as displayed in Exhibit 4-2. This is the *total cost method* of analyzing relevant costs.

EXHIBIT 4-2

RELEVANT COSTS: FIVE-YEAR ANALYSIS OF PROPOSED VERSUS PRESENT PRODUCTION METHOD

	Present Method	Proposed Method	Incremental Costs
Sales revenue	$625,000	$625,000	$ –0–
Variable operating expenses	(250,000)	(193,750)	56,250
Remaining depreciation	(20,000)	(20,000)*	–0–
New depreciation	–0–	(30,000)	(30,000)
Salvage value—present machine	–0–	7,500*	7,500
Contribution—five years	$355,000	$388,750	$33,750

*The net of these two amounts equals the $12,500 "loss."

EXHIBIT 4-3

RELEVANT COSTS: INCREMENTAL ANALYSIS

Reduction of variable operating expenses ($11,250 × 5 years)	$56,250
Cost of proposed machine	(30,000)
Salvage of present machine	7,500
Net increase in contribution by accepting proposed method	$33,750

The sales revenues are the same for the present and the proposed production methods and thus are not incremental to consideration. (In other words, incremental revenue is zero.) This result is typical, for the production process does not change the demand for the product itself (assuming the product does not change). The variable operating expenses do differ by $56,250 in favor of the proposed method. They are therefore relevant to the decision.

The new depreciation of $30,000 is netted against the salvage value of the present machine. At the same time, the $12,500 "loss" is recognized in this calculation. The remaining depreciation on the present machine is the same whether we keep it or not; the differential impact of this depreciation on the present machine is zero, which indicates that it is not a relevant cost. Moreover, the depreciation of the present machine is a sunk cost that has been incurred by the firm and cannot be changed.

On the other hand, the depreciation has a differential impact on the proposed machine. This is so because the cost can be avoided entirely (it is sometimes called an avoidable cost) by not acquiring the new asset. Therefore, it is a relevant cost. This makes sense because the depreciation is a result of the cash outlay for the new machine less the cash obtained from selling it (the salvage value, here zero).

These revenues and expenses result in a $33,750 favorable cost pattern for the proposed method. This cost pattern is *favorable* because it means that the firm would incur $33,750 *less* in costs by adopting the new production process. In turn, it implies a greater profit of $33,750. Subject to the assumptions that have been made, the firm will realize a greater net income over five years by purchasing the new machine. The net book value of the old machine must be charged to expense within the five-year period, regardless of whether this is a one-time disposal or continued amortization of the initial cost of the machine over the five years. This net book value represents a sunk cost; therefore, it is not relevant to this decision.

What are the relevant costs for this proposal? Earlier, we defined *relevant costs* as costs expected to be incurred in the future and expected to vary among alternatives. In the example, variable operating expenses were expected to differ by $11,250 annually ($50,000 − $38,750), the new machine was purchased and depreciated over five years, and the present machine was sold for $7,500. These facts are often handled differently than in Exhibit 4-2, in a manner called *incremental analysis,* in which only the costs that change are included, and then only their change is analyzed. Exhibit 4-3 consists of an incremental cost analysis of this proposal.

The incremental cost analysis shows only the relevant costs, yet we arrive at the same decision to undertake the proposed method. Incremental analysis proves to be beneficial from the standpoint of management efficiency. Decision makers must concentrate on multiple tasks under time pressure every day. Given this situation, management must make the decisions that are best for the organization using the least amount of scarce resources, especially management time. Incremental analysis highlights the changes that the manager must address and so helps him or her make a decision more efficiently.

Some managers or students immediately want to disregard all depreciation as a sunk cost. This is not correct, nor is it so depicted in this example. The $30,000 cost of the proposed machine would be expensed as depreciation over the next five years. (Some accountants prefer to refer to the $30,000 as the cost of the new investment.) The key to this delineation is that the present machine's book value is a committed historical cost, whereas the proposed machine's investment will occur in the future. Therefore, the cost of the proposed machine is avoidable and thus is included as a relevant cost in the analysis. It is critical that the decision maker identify the variables associated with the decision and classify them based on whether or not they are avoidable.

A Summary of Relevant Cost Methods

In the previous example, we demonstrated two methods of using relevant costs to make a decision. First, the total cost method requires an examination of detailed data that may not be available to the manager. For example, the manager may not have access to revenue data or other items that are not necessarily directly related to the decision at hand. Thus, the manager would be forced to use only information that is available and relevant to the particular decision, applying the second method by default.

Second, the incremental cost method requires the examination of only the future costs that vary among alternatives. The manager is more likely to have access to this type of information, based on his or her authority or responsibility. (Responsibility accounting dictates that the decision maker should know the controllable costs of his or her segment.)

Behavioral Aspects of Decision Making Using Relevant Costs

CHAPTER OBJECTIVE 7
Behavioral aspects

In spite of the fact that the book value of the current machine is not relevant, the "loss" or disposition may take on more relevance than is appropriate. If you were the manager of the division and your annual bonus depended on the profits of your division, would you be willing to take a $12,500 loss on the sale of equipment to save $11,250 in operating expenses for that first year? The decision to replace the current machine is even more difficult considering that if you report a large profit you might be promoted and move to a larger division or a new assignment. If you were to be promoted, some other manager would reap the benefits of your decision to reduce operating costs by $11,250 per year in future years. Hence, the goals of an individual manager may not align with those of the organization. Management theory refers to such conflicts as a lack of goal congruency.

Goal congruency simply means that the various people in the organization are working together. They have the same goals and objectives and so move together with the same purpose—a desirable scenario. **Goal incongruency** means that people are working to accomplish different goals and objectives. They may be working at cross purposes and hampering the efforts of one another. Moreover, they may not be advancing the organization's goals.

An example of goal incongruency is incentive compensation, which often results in sound management accounting theory being replaced by the pragmatic concern of how to satisfy managers' desires for more incentives. In the earlier example, the replacement

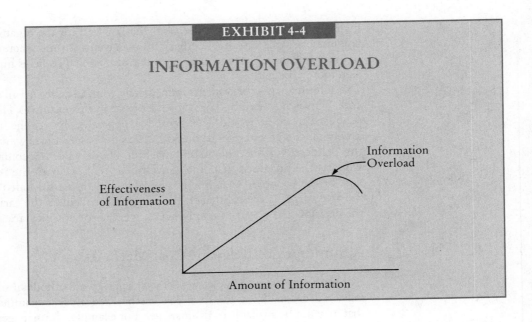

EXHIBIT 4-4

INFORMATION OVERLOAD

Effectiveness of Information

Information Overload

Amount of Information

of the current machine with the new one would be best for the organization. If a bonus is based on financial income, the manager's best option is to keep the current machine. The company needs to find a different bonus scheme to enhance goal congruency.

Another behavioral issue is that of information overload. The concept is graphed in Exhibit 4-4. When information is received, it provides benefits in terms of better decision making. However, at some point the maximum benefit of the information is achieved and additional information causes less effectiveness rather than greater effectiveness. This point is called *information overload*. It occurs because a person has limits on what he or she can process. With too much information, the manager spends too much time absorbing and analyzing the information, withholding decisions or making them too late to be useful. Even if his or her performance does not decline, the manager consumes excess time processing and analyzing the data, leaving less time for other management tasks. Eventually the expected benefits from making the decision are offset by the cost in time and lost efficiency arising from gaining the additional information.

Therefore, incremental cost analysis may be more useful than total cost analysis because it screens out irrelevant data (that is, unavoidable costs). Even though both forms of cost analysis result in the same answer when done correctly, incremental cost analysis presents the manager with only the information relevant to the decision at hand.

SPECIAL SALES ORDERS AND SEGMENT ANALYSIS

Special Sales Orders

CHAPTER OBJECTIVE 2
Analyze special sales orders

Companies are often confronted with the opportunity to sell in new geographic areas or markets where it normally does not sell to certain customers. Confronted with such situations, management must analyze the relevant costs and benefits of fulfilling the special order on a case-by-case basis. For example, suppose that we produce a line of

---

EXHIBIT 4-5

SPECIAL ORDER ANALYSIS

	Total		Per Pair	
Incremental revenue		$750,000		$37.50
Incremental costs				
Variable	$440,000		$22.00	
Fixed	60,000	500,000	3.00	25.00
Incremental income		$250,000		$12.50

Note: There are 20,000 pairs to be produced and sold.

---

shoes under the trade name Charlie's Designer Shoes. These shoes sell for $60 per pair, and management has been able to sell 100,000 pairs per year with seemingly level sales. However, a European organization has indicated that it would be willing to buy 20,000 pairs of these shoes for resale to its customers. Our cost structure is such that we could double production with only slight changes in manufacturing costs.

The current environment is as follows. Charlie's Designer Shoes produces and sells 100,000 pairs per year. The variable costs are $2,400,000, the fixed costs are $1,600,000, so the total cost is $4,000,000. Thus the variable costs per unit are $24, the fixed costs per unit are $16, and the total costs per unit are $40.

The full cost of production includes the variable costs and the fixed costs. When production of this line was initially considered, both variable costs and fixed costs were relevant because they were future costs to be borne should the alternative be pursued. We assume that decision was made in the past; this decision is whether to meet a special sales order. As described below, the relevant costs for this special sales order are the variable production costs. The initial fixed costs are sunk. Any additional fixed costs are also relevant costs.

Fixed costs of $1,600,000 will not be affected by this decision. The European firm has offered to purchase the 20,000 pairs of shoes from us for $37.50 per pair (for a total of $750,000). These shoes will not bear our trade name and will be resold only to European customers. None of these shoes will circulate back to the normal U.S. markets in which 100,000 pairs are sold. This special order would reduce some of the variable marketing costs by approximately $2 per unit, but an additional $60,000 of fixed costs would be incurred to produce a particular logo that the European organization has requested.

The decision management faces is whether or not the company should accept this offer. Exhibit 4-5 is a special-order analysis of this proposed sale. If the incremental income is positive, the special order should be accepted. If the incremental income is negative, it should be rejected. From an accounting standpoint, we are concerned with the $24 per unit in variable costs and the reduction of $2 per unit in variable marketing costs. We would also incur an additional $60,000 of fixed costs on the 20,000 pairs, or $3 per pair. The incremental revenue is $750,000. The incremental variable costs are $22 per pair × 20,000 pairs, or $440,000. The incremental fixed costs are $60,000. The

EXHIBIT 4-6

SEGMENT ANALYSIS

Oviedo Store
Income Statement
For the Year Ended January 31, 19X1

	Segment A	Segment B	Total
Sales revenue	$100,000	$200,000	$300,000
Variable expenses	60,000	100,000	160,000
Contribution margin	$ 40,000	$100,000	$140,000
Selling expenses:			
Advertising	$ 6,000	$ 9,000	$ 15,000
Delivery expenses	3,000	6,000	9,000
Salespersons' salaries	10,000	26,000	36,000
Depreciation of equipment	400	600	1,000
	$ 19,400	$ 41,600	$ 61,000
General expenses:			
Office salaries	$ 20,000	$ 40,000	$ 60,000
Bad debts	500	1,500	2,000
Rent, light, and heat	1,250	3,750	5,000
Building maintenance	2,250	6,750	9,000
	$ 24,000	$ 52,000	$ 76,000
Total expenses	$ 43,400	$ 93,600	$137,000
Net income (loss)	$ (3,400)	$ 6,400	$ 3,000

total incremental costs are $500,000. Therefore, management should accept the proposal, with the following justification. Since this is a one-time sale, the additional $3 per unit of fixed costs should not harm us. We are confronted with a cost structure of $24 − $2 + $3, resulting in a total cost of $25 per pair for the shoes in this special order. With an agreed-upon selling price of $37.50, it would seem feasible to generate $12.50 per pair in incremental income, or $250,000 incremental income in total, from this special order. Exhibit 4-5 also illustrates the analysis on a per-pair basis.

Determining Whether a Segment Should Be Added or Dropped

CHAPTER OBJECTIVE 2
Evaluate a business segment

How does an oil company know to discontinue its service stations and distribution in a certain state or states? How does an organization know to offer cherry-flavored soft drinks as well as apple-flavored soft drinks, as well as diet soft drinks and regular soft drinks? These decisions to add or drop a product line, or business segment, are typical of many management decisions. Although many nonaccounting factors may enter the decision process, eventually the decision rests on an analysis of the impact of dropping the segment on short-term operations—that is, net income. Such analyses are termed **segment analysis,** and the rest of this section provides an example. The incremental income will be computed. If it is negative, the segment should not be added or it should be dropped.

To help us focus on the concept of relevant costs in segment analysis, we assume that one segment of a company is apparently losing money. The manager of Oviedo Store is considering closing Segment A because it appears to be operating at a loss. The advisability of continuing Segment A was questioned when the income statement, shown in Exhibit 4-6, was submitted for the year just ended.

Oviedo Store has two segments, A and B. In practice, corporations may have many segments to evaluate. These segments could be product lines, departments, divisions, branches, or geographic markets. For this example, Segment A is the sales department and Segment B is the repair and maintenance department. Given this, the manager of the Oviedo Store has determined some means of allocating to both segments certain costs that are not directly attributable to either segment. The resulting income statement shows that Segment A generates $100,000 sales revenue and a net loss of $3,400. Segment B generates $200,000 in sales revenue and net income of $6,400. The overall income of Oviedo Store is $3,000. The manager, who understands that relevant cost concepts apply in issues of arbitrary allocation, examines in more detail her assumptions about the operation in Segment A and Segment B. Further investigation reveals the following information:

- Advertising is a direct cost of each department. The implication is that each department has control of its own advertising budget and advertises through a particular niche using selected media. (However, advertising in one segment might add to the name recognition to help increase revenues in another segment. Therefore, these direct costs may have indirect consequences for the other segment.)

- Delivery expenses are allocated to the two departments on the basis of sales revenue.

- Salespersons' salaries are direct costs of each department. The implication is that there is relatively little crossover of salespeople from one segment to the other.

- Rent, light, heat, and building maintenance costs are allocated to departments on the basis of floor area. Segment A and Segment B share the building. Thus, the manager has determined that the most appropriate allocation is based on floor area.

- Office salaries are allocated to the departments in relation to sales volume. The office staff works for both segments A and B. In essence, the office staff works for Oviedo Store in general rather than for any particular segment. It is expected that these office salaries will not be reduced if Segment A is discontinued.

- Losses from bad debts are direct department costs. The implication is that each segment approved its own credit and thus the bad debts are directly related to the sales within each department.

If Segment A is discontinued, it is estimated that total delivery expenses for the year can be reduced to $7,000. The implication is that the manager has assessed the delivery cost and determined that without Segment A the delivery expense would total $7,000. The equipment now in use in the department would be discarded at no salvage value. Any equipment used in Segment A is not usable in Segment B, nor does it have any salvage value on the open market.

EVALUATING A SPORTS PROGRAM

Goalposts vs. Test Tubes

Recently the football program at our Division IA institution, Utah State University (USU), came under attack. In a May 1987 University Faculty Senate meeting, we were given a report that revealed the athletic department accumulated an operating deficit of $800,000, which triggered a resolution calling for the elimination of the football program (the sport which, after six losing seasons, was singly most responsible for the deficit). The expected savings would be used to support the other athletics programs and possibly to rebate student activity fees.

Few resolutions have caused so much debate, controversy, and emotion. Proponents of dropping football argued that the missions of the university are to educate students, further knowledge through research, and provide service to the community. Supporting athletics to such a degree, they contended, is beyond those established missions.

Opponents of the resolution argued that recent coaching changes would help turn the program around and that winning football at USU would take care of the deficit problems. They pointed out that the most successful alumni events were held in conjunction with football games, even when regular football attendance was down. They also suggested that many intangible benefits accrue to campus and community, and they must be considered also.

We decided to conduct an objective analysis of intangible benefits resulting from a strong athletics program as well as tangible benefits and costs. We developed an accounting model that, by focusing on the tangible benefits and costs, could help the university decide whether to drop football or retain it. Our model meets current accounting and reporting guidelines for intercollegiate athletics departments, and it improves budgeting and control.

OUR ACCOUNTING MODEL

The athletics department accounting model we created is being used at Utah State University now. It requires the university to identify all revenues and expenditures that can be traced directly to each sport. It also identifies indirect revenues and expenditures that are allocated to each sport based on the amount that could be eliminated if the particular sport were dropped.

Indirect expenditures classified as nonprogram specific represent residual amounts that remained after we determined the amounts that could be saved through the independent elimination of each sport. Look at football, the single largest expenditure sport in our budget and in most other intercollegiate athletics departments' budgets. The budgeted direct expenditures for football amount to $1.267 million or 61% of the total direct expenditures. Little wonder that such expenditures are highly visible! They often are targeted as a potential source of funds for faculty salaries, library use, scholarships, and other important university requirements should the program be dropped.

The appropriate method for evaluating the cost of specific sports, however, is to examine the revenues and expenditures for the entire intercollegiate athletics program, both with and without the sport. In other words, we must ask precisely what revenues would be lost and what costs would be saved if a particular sport—here, football—were dropped.

Our model categorizes all revenues and all expenditures that can be traced directly to a specific sports program. Revenue items include ticket sales, revenue guarantees from away games, radio and television rights, concessions, parking, and program sales. Direct expenditures include the coaches' and other salaries, travel for the team and for recruiting, financial aid, guarantees to visiting teams, and equipment and other supplies.

Current funds general ledger accounts should be maintained separately for all direct revenues and direct expenditures for each sport. Although each head coach has primary control over these budget items, the college administration should prepare and review periodic control reports comparing budgeted and actual amounts.

Indirect revenues such as state appropriations, student activity fees, and booster-generated income (gifts, investment income, and endowment income) cannot be identified directly with a specific sports program because they are raised or provided for the athletics department in general.

Likewise, indirect expenditures are incurred by the athletics department for the benefit of all sports programs, but they are not caused directly by a specific program. Each of these items should be accounted for in total in the current funds general ledger in athletics department accounts classified as nonprogram specific. Although the athletic director has primary responsibility for these budget items, higher-level administrators should review them, too.

THE BASIS FOR ALLOCATING

To what extent should these indirect revenues and expenditures be allocated to a specific sport to determine its margin? The basis of an allocation should not be arbitrary or irrational, such as need for additional revenue or ability to bear additional expenditures. Such allocations distort the program margin and present program financial information that is misleading and of little decisionmaking value. Unfortunately, many cost and revenue allocations for athletics departments are done arbitrarily, including some previously done at Utah State.

State appropriations for the athletics department provide for salaries of the athletics department personnel. Board of regents members have suggested that some reduction in the appropriation would be likely if the football program, for example, were dropped. But the reduction, if any, would not be as great as the $563,510 state appropriation subsidy provided in the state-approved budget. Some regents have suggested that reduction in the appropriation equal to the direct salaries is reasonable to assume and that this amont could be used elsewhere in Utah's system of higher education.

Student activity fees designated for athletics carry no stipulation as to the amount that must be used for specific sports although student body officers have indicated they would expect a reduction in student activity fees if a sport were discontinued. The amounts allocated to each sports program as the line item titled student activity fees are the amounts that student officers anticipated they could expect student activity fees to be reduced should the sport be dropped.

We also analyzed boosters' revenues to identify probable reductions in gifts, investment income, and endowment income. For each indirect revenue item, the total revenue reduction to be realized by dropping individual sports totals less than the amount of revenues received. The difference is assigned to the nonprogram specific category.

We also reviewed the indirect expenditures on a sport-by-sport basis to determine costs that could be eliminated by dropping a sport. In the ticket office, the number of hours of part-time workers and supply costs could be reduced. For sports information, travel and publicity costs could be saved. Medical and training costs could be reduced for wages, supplies, and insurance premiums. General expenditures that could be reduced included travel, mailing, promotion, cheerleaders, awards, physical plant, insurance, and supplies. Also, the number of administrative personnel or their number of hours devoted to athletics department activities could be reduced.

Indirect revenue and expenditure amounts that could not be allocated to a specific program and were not avoidable are identified as nonprogram specific. These amounts are allocated to the various sports programs more realistically based on the service or support provided each sport by the general department operation. Therefore, the excess (or deficiency) of revenues over expenditures represents the net results of each program when all department revenues and expenditures have been allocated rationally.

THE RIGHT ACCOUNTING METHOD

With the high cost of intercollegiate athletics, other universities also may begin to think about eliminating those programs that are financially troubled, and, if necessary, replace them with programs that are less costly. Traditional accounting and reporting methods, even those recommended by the NCAA, do not allow insititutions to make a complete analysis of the financial considerations for such a decision. The model we developed for Utah State guides this decision process and improves general cost control in athletics departments.

Our model has shown that dropping the football program at Utah State probably would not have eliminated the athletics department's financial pressures. In fact, it would have led to *more* financial pressures. Other insitutions, with their

(continued)

own circumstances to consider, may, of course, derive different outcomes.

Critics of our outcome can find justification only in the allocation of indirect revenues and indirect expenditures that could be eliminated by discontinuing a sport. Therefore, as much accuracy as possible is essential.

Because of unknown variables, some figures may turn out different from the projection if the decision to discontinue is actually made. In our case, the state appropriation is the biggest question.

Institutional budgets are approved annually, and no one knows for sure how money ultimately will be appropriated. These uncertainties, as well as the probabilites of various outcomes for different institutions, must be kept in mind in interpreting the results. Only then can a university make a rational decision about a sport.

SOURCE: Adapted from Clifford R. Skousen and Frank A. Condie, "Evaluating a Sports Program: Goalposts vs. Test Tubes," *Management Accounting* (November 1988), pp. 43–49. Copyright ©1988 by the National Association of Accountants, Montvale, N.J.

If Segment A is closed, the space it now occupies will be used by Segment B. Segment B can use the space but the space may or may not generate any increase in revenue. In fact, the manager of Oviedo Store has asserted that there is no reason to believe that the sales volume of Segment B will be substantially increased.

Using the original information and the further assumptions provided by the store manager, we can tabulate the relevant costs as in Exhibit 4-7.

The avoidable expenses include variable expenses of $60,000, advertising of $6,000, delivery expenses of $2,000, salespersons' salaries of $10,000, and bad debts of $500. Thus, $78,500 in avoidable costs are relevant to our decision. The other costs within the total of $297,000 must be incurred whether or not Segment A is discontinued; therefore, these costs are not relevant.

EXHIBIT 4-7

RELEVANT COSTS FOR OVIEDO STORE

	Total Costs	Avoidable Costs (Relevant)	Unavoidable Costs (Not Relevant)
Variable expenses	$160,000	$60,000	$100,000
Fixed selling expenses:			
Advertising	15,000	6,000	9,000
Delivery expenses	9,000	2,000	7,000
Salespersons' salaries	36,000	10,000	26,000
Depreciation of equipment	1,000	–0–	1,000
Fixed general expenses:			
Office salaries	60,000	–0–	60,000
Bad debts	2,000	500	1,500
Rent, light, heat	5,000	–0–	5,000
Building maintenance	9,000	–0–	9,000
Total expenses	$297,000	$78,500	$218,500

EXHIBIT 4-8

Oviedo Store
Pro Forma Income Statement
(Segment B Only; Segment A Discontinued)
For the Year Ended January 31, 19X1

	Segment B	Unavoidable Costs of Segment A	Total
Sales Revenue	$200,000	$ –0–	$200,000
Variable Expenses	100,000	–0–	100,000
Contribution Margin	$100,000	–0–	100,000
Fixed Selling Expenses:			
Advertising	9,000	–0–	9,000
Delivery Expenses	6,000	1,000	7,000
Salespersons' Salaries	26,000	–0–	26,000
Depreciation of Equipment	600	400	1,000
Fixed General Expenses:			
Office Salaries	40,000	20,000	60,000
Bad Debts	1,500	–0–	1,500
Rent, Light, and Heat	3,750	1,250	5,000
Building Maintenance	6,750	2,250	9,000
Total Expenses	$ 93,600	$ 24,900	$118,500
Net Income (Loss)	$ 6,400	$ (24,900)	$(18,500)

The relevant costs for this decision are $78,500. These costs are avoidable if the decision is made to discontinue Segment A. Something else is avoidable if we discontinue Segment A—its sales revenue of $100,000. Therefore, a contribution of $21,500 to continuing fixed costs and net income will be lost if Segment A is discontinued. Based on the initial income statement, which showed a net income for both segments of $3,000, discontinuing Segment A would result in a net loss of $18,500, as proven in the pro forma income statement for Segment B in Exhibit 4-8.

In the proof, all the amounts for Segment B are as stated in the assumptions. Note also that the unavoidable costs of Segment A would then become costs of Segment B because they are not avoidable. Thus, the total costs for Segment B would increase by $24,900, resulting in a net loss of $18,500. Oviedo Store will be better off by continuing Segment A. Yet the initial income statement showed a net loss for Segment A. This apparent inconsistency is caused by the allocation of common fixed costs to segments. In essence, *common fixed costs* (discussed more fully later) are the costs of an organization or a group of segments that are incurred for the benefit of that group or the entire organization but are allocated according to some arbitrary formula to those segments. These allocated fixed costs are unavoidable and therefore should not affect the decision.

Opportunity cost is the maximum alternative earnings that might have been obtained if the next best alternative had been chosen instead of the alternative actually selected. In this decision, the opportunity cost of dropping Segment A is a reduction in profits from $3,000 to ($18,500), or an opportunity cost of $21,500.

OBJECTIVE 1
Explain opportunity costs

Behavioral Aspects of Segment Analysis

CHAPTER
OBJECTIVE 7
Behavioral aspects

Managers often note that other variables may influence segment decision making. For example, if management perceives that a low margin per item or segment is a necessary cost of offering customers a full complement of goods and services, managers may decide to keep the item or segment regardless of the cost analysis. Thus managers must recognize some subjective and intangible variables when making decisions. We find nothing inconsistent with good management principles in this recognition, but segment analysis at least reveals the contribution of the segment under review to net income in direct financial terms. The subjective conclusion that a full line may be needed then must be examined on its own merits.

Further, management would not discontinue an item or segment just because the historical avoidable costs are greater than the historical avoidable revenues. The decision to discontinue should be based on future expectations for the item or segment. The analyses of historical management accounting information is relevant only to the extent that the information indicates trends and alerts management to situations that require further analysis. Note again that the analysis of past data and experience is only useful if it helps us understand or estimate the future, for managers must always make decisions that are future oriented.

Because the compensation of managers is to some extent related to the size of the operations they manage, managers are frequently unwilling to view segment analysis objectively. Optimism frequently prevails as managers seek to protect their domains. A manager rarely takes the action necessary to terminate an item or segment, even though termination is clearly indicated. Those segment termination decisions are most often made by a higher echelon of management based on a combination of historical management accounting information and an assessment of future expectations. It takes historical management accounting information as well as an assessment of the future to create a management accounting analysis leading to an appropriate decision.

Dropping a segment may have many other effects besides those mentioned already. Plant closings during the past decade have brought unemployment—and in some cases stagnation of the local economy—to those regions affected by the loss in wages and business. Managers must be aware of these social concerns and of the corporation's responsibility to society.

SELL-OR-PROCESS-FURTHER DECISIONS

CHAPTER
OBJECTIVE 3
*Discuss sell-or-
process-further
decisions*

Another management decision arises when two or more separate products are produced through a common process from a common input. The outputs from the common process are called joint products. (If one of the joint products is considered relatively minor or unimportant, it is referred to as a *byproduct.*) The management problem involves the common costs of getting a product to a split-off point, the point at which these common inputs become separable into processes and costs for distinct products (shown schematically in Exhibit 4-9). The management problem is whether to sell a product at the split-off point or to process it further and sell it after the additional processing. This is called a sell-or-process-further decision. The question also arises whether the allocated joint costs are relevant for this decision. A typical example of this is petroleum refining, which involves several steps of processing to reach a split-off point for the production of various grades of fuel. The common costs of such processing are also referred to as *joint costs* because they are incurred to produce two or more products simultaneously by a single process or processes from a common raw material.

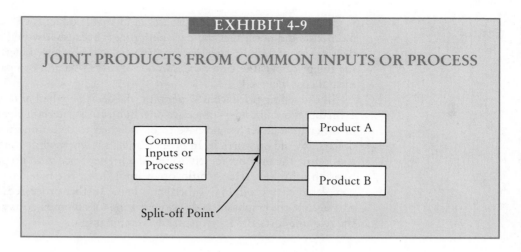

EXHIBIT 4-9

JOINT PRODUCTS FROM COMMON INPUTS OR PROCESS

Normally, we cannot identify these joint costs as belonging to any particular portion of the joint products. Thus, we are forced to allocate the costs arbitrarily to these products.

The *relative sales value method* is usually used to allocate the joint costs to the individual products. The relative sales value of each of the products is estimated by comparing the relative sales value of the product that can be sold at split-off with the total sales value of all the products. However, if any further processing is needed, the relative sales value can be approximated by subtracting the additional processing costs from the final sales value. The relative sales value method is simple and intuitively appealing. However, it ignores important economic factors such as the ability to sell one product given a change in price of another product.

A simple example of this cost allocation procedure is as follows. A joint process that makes products P and Q has total costs of $500,000. The P lot can be sold for $300,000 and the Q lot for $700,000. Then P would be allocated 30% ($300,000/$1,000,000) of the common (or joint) costs while Q would be allocated 70% ($700,000/$1,000,000). Thus P would be assigned costs of 30% of $500,000, or $150,000, and Q would be assigned a cost of 70% of $500,000, or $350,000.

Consider an example in which management needs to decide whether to sell a product at the split-off point or process further and then sell it. Assume that two products, Product E and Product F, are produced from a joint process. Using the relative sales value method, Product E has been allocated $5,000 of the total common costs of $40,000 for 1,000 pounds produced. Product E can be sold at the split-off point for $5 per pound, or it can be further processed with additional cost of $2,000. After this additional processing, Product E can be sold for $6 per pound. In identifying the relevant costs, the issue of common costs is immaterial. That is, Product E could be sold at the split-off point for revenues of $5,000 ($5 × 1,000 lbs.). If Product E is processed further, sales revenue would be $6,000 ($6 × 1,000 lbs.), but an additional cost of $2,000 would be incurred. From an incremental standpoint, the incremental revenue is simply $1 per pound [($6 − $5) × 1,000 lbs. to be sold] or $1,000; incremental cost is $2,000. The net effect on income from the additional process would be a $1,000 decrease. Thus, Product E should be sold at the point of split-off rather than processed further.

The general procedure is to compute incremental income from further processing. If it is positive, then the product should be processed further. If it is negative, then the product should not be processed further.

In reviewing this decision process, note that Product E's $5,000 share of total common costs did not affect the decision process because it would have no impact on the decision in total. Note also that the decision could be solved incrementally by multiplying the price per unit times the number of units sold and comparing that to the incremental cost incurred.

If the selling price were $7 per unit, the decision whether to sell or process Product E further would be a less objective one. Subjective criteria such as the opportunity cost or other intangibles would have to be weighed to determine whether or not "trading dollars" would be worth it. In other words, is it worthwhile to the organization to further refine the product merely to sell at a higher price with no prospect of profit? Perhaps this higher price would open up a different market segment or provide a complementary product to other items being further processed. Regardless of qualitative factors, the emphasis on decision making for common costs and joint products is on the relevant costs and incremental decision making.

Behavioral Aspects of Sell-or-Process-Further Decisions

CHAPTER OBJECTIVE 7
Behavioral aspects

In the sell-or-process-further decision for joint products, we avoid any arbitrary allocation cost that may hinder making a proper decision. All cost allocation is arbitrary, at least to some extent, for the purposes of making decisions. We avoid this arbitrary allocation and examine only those incremental costs beyond the split-off point. Thus, management's behavior may be affected by the concept of joint costs, just as it would be by depreciation for a fixed asset that is not fully depreciated yet.

Similar to the previous decision type, there is a tension between financial accounting and management accounting. However, it seems clear that common costs *are* irrelevant for the sell-or-process-further decision because they are unavoidable. Because this decision focuses on *relevant* costs, it is conceptually the same as all the other decisions discussed in this chapter.

MAKE-OR-BUY DECISIONS

CHAPTER OBJECTIVE 4
Explain make-or-buy decisions

The dilemma of the make-or-buy decision—whether to produce a component, product, or service internally or to purchase it from an outside supplier—frequently occurs in many organizations. An example is the data entry of credit card billing, or other types of massive data entry tasks, that has been exported to countries with lower wage rates. Certain firms have elected to move this part of their operations offshore, judging that they could more efficiently buy the services of a vendor than generate the services themselves. This is an example of management accounting analysis in an information-oriented society. In this section we consider a more concrete example.

Historically, the make-or-buy decision has been most common in manufacturing; however, the relevant cost principle as used in make-or-buy decisions applies to components in manufacturing, the service industries, and information processing alike. The decision process noted earlier is the same in each case: identify the variables, classify avoidable and unavoidable costs, and analyze only the relevant costs. Similar to previous decision types, the general procedure is to calculate the incremental income from making the item and the incremental income from buying the item. The action with the higher incremental income should be chosen.

A firm purchases 6,000 units monthly of a component that it could manufacture, paying a unit cost of $7.50. For the expected future, the firm estimates operations in the

EXHIBIT 4-10

DETERMINATION OF FIXED AND VARIABLE OVERHEAD (HIGH–LOW METHOD)

Let TOH = total overhead

FOH = fixed overhead

VOH = variable overhead per unit

DLH = number of direct labor hours

Because Total Overhead = Fixed Overhead + Variable Overhead,

$$TOH = FOH + (VOH \times DLH)$$

Thus,

$$64,000 = FOH + (VOH \times 16,000)$$
$$68,000 = FOH + (VOH \times 20,000)$$

Subtracting the first equation from the second equation yields:

$$4,000 = VOH \times 4,000$$

so:

$$VOH = 1$$

Also,

$$64,000 = FOH + (1 \times 16,000)$$
$$FOH = 64,000 - 16,000$$
$$= 48,000$$

Therefore,

$$FOH = \$48,000$$

and

$$VOH = \$1 \text{ per DLH}$$

Processing Department to be 80% of *normal capacity* (the capacity usually available under regular operating conditions), which is 20,000 direct labor hours. Since the organization is operating at 80% of normal capacity, there are 4,000 hours of excess capacity available for other operations, as follows:

Material	$3.50 per unit
Direct labor (½ hr. @ $4 per hr.)	$2 per unit
Factory overhead (@ 16,000 hrs.)	$64,000
Factory overhead (@ 20,000 hrs.)	$68,000

Identifying the fixed and variable portions of overhead is the first step in the decision process. We use the high–low method to calculate the variable overhead, as explained in Chapter 3, page 66. The variable overhead is $1 per direct labor hour, as shown in Exhibit 4-10. Fixed overhead is $48,000 per month and is not relevant to this decision as it will not change. To manufacture 6,000 units requires 3,000 hours of direct labor (6,000 units × ½ hour per unit), which is well within the excess capacity of 4,000 hours.

The relevant costs are $7.50 per unit if purchased and $6 per unit if made. The latter number is computed as follows:

Materials	$3.50
Direct labor	2.00
Overhead (½ hour × $1 per hour)	.50
	$6.00

If the company makes the product, the firm will save $1.50 per unit.

Managers must be aware of extenuating variables that may affect the make-or-buy decision. For example, the excess capacity may only be temporary (new future orders may reduce or eliminate the excess capacity). In that case, the risk of alienating a reliable supplier when normal capacity is used to produce the product at a lower rate becomes relevant to the decision process. Another variable to consider is the opportunity cost of the resources used. Perhaps the firm could produce an item with more cost savings or contribution margin using the same resources. In other words, perhaps there is a product that management has not considered making in those 4,000 hours of excess capacity, permitting the company to enter a new market, develop a new product, or gain some other competitive advantage. Few management decisions are made disregarding qualitative variables such as these.

Behavioral Aspects of Make-or-Buy Decisions

CHAPTER OBJECTIVE 7
Behavioral aspects

The example used above is a simplification of the typical make-versus-buy situation. More typically, the decision to make a part or component necessitates the acquisition of additional equipment—and a variable cost is replaced, at least in part, by a fixed cost. Recall the first example in the chapter (pp. 104–7) about the new production process. Such a replacement is advantageous if demand for the product containing the component is sufficiently high. However, if demand for the product were to drop off, results could be disastrous because the newly created fixed costs do not disappear as the variable costs did when the part or component was purchased. Thus, variability of product demand is a relevant consideration for managers faced with a make-or-buy decision—and a key concern of all managers, as the general trend toward increasing fixed costs results in costs that do not disappear (as former variable costs would have) when the part, component, or segment is discontinued.

SCARCE RESOURCES

CHAPTER OBJECTIVE 5
Decision making with scarce resources

Few managers operate with unlimited resources at their command; resources such as labor, raw materials, and processing capacity are always limited by factors such as the cost of labor, the availability of raw materials or suppliers, the age or size of the plant, or the speed of equipment. Scarce resources must be expended efficiently (gaining maximum output for the limited input) and at their highest and best use in order to best achieve the organization's goals. Therefore, managers must continually evaluate the contribution margin of their various products in light of the constraints of resources available to achieve that margin.

EXHIBIT 4-11

DATA FOR LIMITED CAPACITY EXAMPLE

	Product X	Product Y
Sales price	$20	$10
Material cost per unit	$4	$2
Labor cost per unit	$7	$2
Machine hours per unit	2	1
Maximum demand in sales dollars	$200,000	$80,000
Maximum available machine hours		20,000

EXHIBIT 4-12

FIRST STEP IN SOLVING LIMITED CAPACITY EXAMPLE

	Product X	Product Y	Total
Units	10,000	–0–	10,000
Machine hours required	20,000	–0–	20,000
Sales	$200,000	–0–	$200,000
Variable costs	110,000	–0–	110,000
Contribution margin	$ 90,000	–0–	$ 90,000

Let us examine a firm with only two products, X and Y. The goal of the firm is to maximize profits in the short run, but the firm only has 20,000 machine hours available. Therefore, its scarce resource is a *limited capacity*. Selected accounting data are shown in Exhibit 4-11.

The selling price of Product X is twice that of Product Y. The materials and labor are given as shown for each product. The maximum demand in sales dollars for these items is $200,000 for Product X and $80,000 for Product Y. Further investigation reveals that selling, general, and administrative expenses will not change over the relevant range. Management is confronted with scarce resources (here, machine hours available) by noting demand totals for Products X and Y that it cannot meet and the need to maximize profit. Which product should the managers produce? What combination of products would be most profitable?

At first glance, it appears that the entire demand for Product X should be satisfied because it has the larger contribution margin per unit ($20 – $4 – $7 = $9). Exhibit 4-12 examines what would happen if Product X were selected to fill the available machine hours. The contribution margin is $90,000 and all of the 20,000 hours were used producing the 10,000 units that happened to be the maximum demand in sales dollars for Product X.

The analysis in Exhibit 4-12 fails to fully consider that one of the constraints is machine hours, and that Product X requires two machine hours and Product Y requires one machine hour. Product X has a contribution margin of $4.50 per machine hour and Product Y has a contribution margin of $6 per machine hour ($10 − $2 − $2). When the constraining machine hours are fully considered, the emphasis is placed on producing as many of Product Y as demand will support. Thus Product Y is the most profitable, and maximum production consistent with the sales estimate should be planned. We might expect the firm to sell 8,000 units of Product Y, resulting in $80,000 worth of revenue and $48,000 in contribution margin. The remaining hours would be dedicated to Product X, which would permit the firm to produce 6,000 units, resulting in $54,000 in contribution margin. Thus, the contribution margin, focusing first on Product Y and then on Product X based on the scarce resource, is $102,000. This result is $12,000 higher than the $90,000 attained by concentrating on Product X alone. We can observe this in the summary calculation of Exhibit 4-13 (page 123).

Behavioral Aspects of Decision Making with Scarce Resources

CHAPTER OBJECTIVE 7
Behavioral aspects

Managers must be *consistently* alert to opportunities to maximize contribution margin dollars. They must also focus on constraints, because maximizing gross margin percent, contribution margin per unit, or some other alternative measure alone may not maximize contribution margin dollars. The key steps in this process are to identify the variables, classify them appropriately, and recognize the issue of scarce resources.

LINEAR PROGRAMMING

CHAPTER OBJECTIVE 6
Explain linear programming

Managers recognize that various quantitative tools are necessary to help them absorb the many factors necessary in analyzing various decision options. Because so many decisions involve multiple variables and resource constraints, management has recently focused on *optimization* techniques. One such technique is linear programming, a quantitative means of analyzing for maximum profit or minimum costs. Linear programming is used most frequently for product mix calculations, scarce resource calculations, selecting from distribution channels, and other resource allocation processes.

In order to demonstrate the concept of linear programming, we must introduce several terms. First, the *objective function* is the function that we are attempting to maximize or minimize. One example is to maximize profit. The objective function in this case is revenues minus variable costs minus fixed costs. Another example is that the firm may wish to minimize costs. The objective function is then variable costs plus fixed costs. (Linear programming addresses only one objective; more advanced techniques allow addressing two or more objectives.) We return to the firm and its data used in the preceding section on limited capacity, with the objective to maximize profit. That profit is recognized as contribution margin, or $9 for each unit of Product X and $6 for each unit of Product Y. The objective function to maximize is:

$$9X + 6Y$$

Recognizing that this objective has constraints on it, we must identify those limitations. The sales of Product X must be less than or equal to 10,000 units:

EXHIBIT 4-13

SOLUTION TO LIMITED CAPACITY EXAMPLE

	Product X		Product Y		
Sales price	$ 20.00		$ 10.00		
Variable costs:					
Material	$ 4.00		$ 2.00		
Labor	7.00		2.00		
	$ 11.00		$ 4.00		
Contribution margin per unit	$ 9.00		$ 6.00		
Machine hours required per unit	2		1		
Contribution margin per hour	$ 4.50		$ 6.00		
Maximum sales in units	6,000		8,000		
Machine hours required	12,000	+	8,000	=	20,000
Contribution margin	$54,000	+	$48,000	=	$102,000

$$X \leq 10,000$$

Sales of Product Y must be less than or equal to 8,000, its maximum sales demand:

$$Y \leq 8,000$$

The scarce resource to be allocated among these is two hours for each unit of Product X and one hour for each unit of Product Y, with a total of 20,000 hours available. Thus:

$$2X + Y \leq 20,000$$

X and Y cannot be negative. Thus:

$$X \geq 0$$
$$Y \geq 0$$

The constraints are graphed in Exhibit 4-14. The sales constraint of X at 10,000 units and the sales constraint of Y at 8,000 units form a rectangular *constraint area.* The point of intersection of these, R, where Y is 8,000 and X is 10,000, forms a boundary indicating the maximum sales of each at that particular point. Had we no other constraints, this rectangle would form the *feasible space.* That is, it would be feasible to sell at any point within this area. However, we are also constrained by machine hours. The line $2X + Y = 20,000$ machine hours forms a constraint eliminating the triangular portion of the top right corner of the rectangle. We have now redefined our feasible space to be the polygon of the origin (O); point A (10,000 units of X); point B (6,000 units of Y); and point C (8,000 units of Y). To maximize profit, we want to move as far out from the origin in that feasible space as the contribution margin would permit. This would

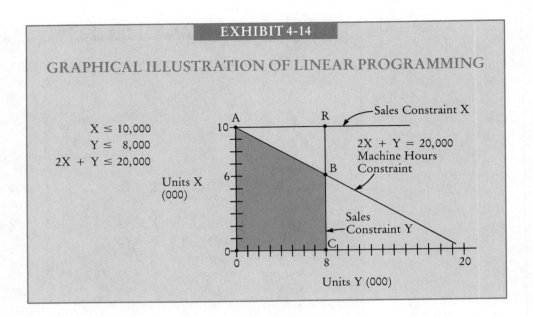

EXHIBIT 4-14

GRAPHICAL ILLUSTRATION OF LINEAR PROGRAMMING

$X \leq 10,000$
$Y \leq 8,000$
$2X + Y \leq 20,000$

Units X (000)

Sales Constraint X

$2X + Y = 20,000$
Machine Hours Constraint

Sales Constraint Y

Units Y (000)

take us to to the point of intersection of the $2X + Y$ machine-hour constraint and the 8,000 line or B. The point of intersection, then, is the 8,000 sales for Y, 6,000 for X, indicating that the graphic solution would be the same as the analytical solution in Exhibit 14-13.

The *feasible region* is the space containing the points that would satisfy all of the constraints. The feasible region for this problem is the shaded area in Exhibit 4-14 bounded by OABC. It should be intuitively obvious that the solution would lie somewhere on the ABC section because any other point could be improved upon by moving to the outer edge. In particular, it can be shown that A *or* B *or* C must be the solution. This fact can be used to find the correct answer. We simply solve the objective function at each of these points and choose the one with the highest value—here, the maximum profit—or the lowest if the problem is to find the minimum point. In this case, the objective function is maximize $9X + 6Y$. At point A, $X = 10,000$ and $Y = 0$, so the objective function has the value of $90,000. At point B, $X = 6,000$ and $Y = 8,000$, so the objective function equals $102,000. At point C, $X = 0$ and $Y = 8,000$. This makes the objective function equal to $48,000. Therefore, point B is the solution.

However, not all problems are this simple. Nor can they be solved in this manner. The computer can be used to solve these problems. Such problems are beyond the scope of this textbook, however.

Behavioral Aspects of Linear Programming

CHAPTER
OBJECTIVE 7
Behavioral aspects

Linear programming is one of the most quantitative techniques discussed in this book. Its description allows us an opportunity to point out that mathematical methods can offer managers effective tools that aid in the decision-making process. It does not mean that managers or management accountants must obtain a degree in mathematics, because persons with such backgrounds can be hired as members of the management team. Managers and management accountants must simply be aware of these tools so that they can use them in practice whenever appropriate.

Another reason for becoming familiar with these tools is that the manager or the accountant needs to assess the assumptions behind the analysis. For example, linear programming loses its utility if some constraints are not articulated or if some of the constraints are not linear. In other words, managers and accountants should not rely solely on mathematicians to carry out this analysis because they may not have sufficient expertise in business to understand how to set up the problem.

In practice, the greatest benefits usually accrue to management teams whose members have a varied background. However, the members of such a team must communicate with each other. This communication is enhanced if the members understand each other's jargon. The management accountant is often a valued member of this team because he or she brings an expertise in business and accounting and understands concepts like linear programming at least well enough to communicate with the more technical members of the management team.

DECISION SUPPORT SYSTEMS AND DECISION MAKING

Decision support systems (DSS), first mentioned in Chapter 1, are important tools for the decision maker involved in the types of decisions discussed in this chapter. The use of decision support systems permits the decision maker to focus on the relevant variables and assumptions. As noted in Chapter 1, the ability to perform what-if, goal-seeking, and analyses of the variables functions is a significant advantage to the decision maker. Regardless of the decision type, the decision maker must be free to focus on decision making and leave "number-crunching" and data manipulation to the DSS.

A decision support system may be designed to prompt the decision maker to enter the relevant data. The DSS responds with a suggested solution. As always, the decision maker is free to interrogate the DSS for further analysis. In addition, the DSS may even have built-in queries for certain types of decisions and automatically ask the decision maker about the assumptions. Finally, the DSS may incorporate *expert system* software, allowing it to provide decision advice upon request. (Expert systems are discussed further in Chapter 17.)

Demonstration Problem

Sexton, Inc., has an opportunity to sell 10,000 gadgets at $60 each. Sexton can buy the gadgets at $25 or it can make them. The firm has tested the manufacturing process at a cost of $30,000 and has found that it can make 10,000 gadgets at the following costs:

Direct material	$10 per unit
Direct labor	$1 per unit
Variable overhead	$3 per unit
Fixed overhead	$100,000

The testing also revealed that the gadget can be further processed. With additional fixed overhead of $10,000, Sexton could further process 5,000 units and sell them for $70 each.

REQUIRED

a. Determine whether Sexton should make or buy the gadgets.

b. Determine whether Sexton should sell or process further.

SOLUTION TO DEMONSTRATION PROBLEM

a. The testing cost is not relevant to this decision; the corporation has already incurred this $30,000 cost. No matter what decision Sexton makes, the testing has been undertaken and the cost paid. All other costs are incremental and so they are relevant to this decision.

The cost per unit of making the gadget is as follows:

Direct material	$10
Direct labor	1
Variable overhead	3
Fixed overhead ($100,000/10,000)	10
Product cost	$24

Therefore, Sexton should make the gadget for $24 per unit rather than buy it for $25.

b. The remaining question is whether Sexton should take 5,000 of the gadgets and process them further. This extra processing should be carried out if the incremental revenue is greater than the incremental expenses. In this case, the incremental revenue is $10 per unit. The incremental cost is $10,000/5,000, or $2 per unit. Sexton should process the gadgets further.

The total incremental revenues are as follows:

5,000 units sold @ $60	$300,000
5,000 units sold @ $70	350,000
Incremental revenues	$650,000

The incremental costs are:

5,000 units @ $24	$120,000
5,000 units @ $26 ($24 + $2)	130,000
Incremental costs	$250,000

The incremental profit is $400,000 ($650,000 − $250,000).

Review of Chapter Objectives

1. Explain relevant cost, sunk costs, and opportunity costs, and their use in decision making (pp. 103–8).

- Relevant costs for a particular decision are costs that should be considered when choosing among alternatives. These are costs that would occur in one scenario but not in another. Thus, only those costs yet to be incurred and that will differ among the alternatives are relevant in decision making.

- Sunk costs are costs that have already been incurred. They are never relevant costs. Since they have taken place, the different alternatives cannot be affected by them. Moreover, since they have occurred in the past, and since it is impossible to go back in time and change these items, sunk costs cannot be undone, erased, or modified. They are irrelevant to any decision-making activity.

- Opportunity costs are the sacrifices of potential benefits of selecting a particular action. When a manager chooses one action, other possibilities often become precluded. For instance, one of the costs of going to college is the income foregone from full-time employment.

2. Analyze special sales orders and evaluate whether a segment should be added or dropped (pp. 108–16).

   - These two types of business decisions are specific applications of the concepts of relevant costs and also relevant revenues. They are both solved by determining the relevant revenues and costs and seeing whether the activity is profitable.

   - Special sales orders are judged by analyzing the relevant items and then determining whether the special order should be accepted. The relevant revenue is the incremental revenue from the special order. The relevant costs are the incremental costs from the special order, including the variable costs and any incremental fixed costs. Incremental income equals incremental revenue less incremental costs. When incremental income is positive, the special order should be accepted.

   - Another decision managers sometimes face is whether to add or drop a segment. A segment of a business is just some part of the business, such as the selling activity and the service activity of a firm. The segment analysis proceeds in a manner similar to the special order decision. Determine the incremental revenue and the incremental costs. If the net amount, the incremental income, is greater than zero, then the segment should be added or not dropped. If the incremental income is negative, then the segment should not be added or it should be dropped.

3. Discuss sell-or-process-further decisions (pp. 116–18).

   - This decision arises when a firm produces joint products—that is, when there are several outputs produced by a common set of inputs. The production process reaches a point at which these joint products become separable, called the split-off point. The issue is whether any of the products should be processed further (to produce a modified product) or sold as they are.

   - The relative sales value method is often used to allocate the joint costs to the individual products. The relative sales value of each product is calculated and each product's proportion to the total relative sales value is determined. Costs are allocated to the products using these proportions. However, this allocated set of costs is irrelevant to the sell-or-process-further decision.

   - To consider whether to process further, determine the relevant costs and revenues and ask, What incremental revenues could be generated by further processing? What would be the incremental costs—those occurring after the split-off point? If the incremental income from further processing is greater than zero, then the product should be processed further.

4. Explain make-or-buy decisions (pp. 118–20).

   - Make-or-buy decisions come up often in business. The question is whether the firm should make an item it needs—for example, in the manufacturing process—or whether it should buy the item. Of course, the organization wants to choose the alternative that yields more income.

   - The decision process is similar to the other situations described in this chapter. Determine the incremental income from making the item. Determine the incremental income from buying the resource. Choose the action that generates the higher incremental income.

5. Describe decision making with scarce resources (pp. 120–22).

- "Scarce resources" simply means that management cannot use an unlimited amount of the resources available to it. They are finite; they are limited. In addition, there are constraints on what a business can achieve due to its production capacity. For example, at full capacity a plant can make only so much of a particular product. Such constraints must be accounted for when managers are planning what products and how much to produce.

6. Explain linear programming and how to set up a linear programming problem (pp. 122–25).

- Linear programming is a mathematical tool used to solve problems dealing with limited capacity. Although the technique is beyond the scope of this textbook, the essentials of linear programming should be understood so that the student can recognize when a problem of limited capacity arises and have a basic idea of how to solve it.

- In linear programming, a function to optimize is first stated—in this case, it is contribution margin. The constraints are then listed. The feasible area is the area bounded by these constraints. One way of solving for the maximum function is to compute the contribution margin for each of the corners along the uppermost and rightmost edges of the feasible region and choose the point that yields the highest answer.

7. Identify behavioral aspects of business decision making for issues in Objectives 1–6 (pp. 107, 108, 116, 120, 122, 124, and 125).

- One critical behavioral issue is the common discrepancy between correct decision making and how managers are evaluated. The section on relevant costs contains an example decision for an asset exchange despite the certainty of incurring a loss in financial accounting terms. If top managers include this financial loss in their performance evaluation of the responsible manager, overlooking the need for the asset exchange, in the future the manager will probably use the financial numbers as the primary standard for making decisions even though they may lead to an incorrect decision.

- Another behavioral issue is information overload, which means that information improves decision making only up to the point at which the manager becomes saturated with data, beyond which the extra information is really detrimental. Accountants therefore should try to screen information reports for the most important items, rather than trying to state everything in the report in the name of completeness.

- Finally, all of the decisions discussed in this chapter require the decision maker to focus on the relevant items and to ignore extraneous items. Specifically, incremental income should be computed for the various alternatives (add or drop a segment, sell or process further, make or buy). The manager should choose the action that produces the largest incremental income.

Glossary of Key Terms

avoidable cost   An ongoing cost that may be eliminated by ceasing to perform some economic activity or segment thereof or by improving the efficiency by which such activity is accomplished.

common cost A cost of resources used jointly in the production of two or more outputs; the cost cannot be directly assigned to those outputs. Customarily, assignment is made through a series of consistent allocation procedures. Also called joint cost.

constraint An activity, resource, or policy that limits or bounds the attainment of an objective.

goal congruency Various people in the organization working toward the organization's goals.

goal incongruency People in the organization working to accomplish different and conflicting goals that are at odds with the organization's goals.

incremental revenue The additional revenue, either as to amount or as to timing, that results from pursuing an alternative course of action.

joint products Two or more products so related that one cannot be produced without producing the others, each having relatively high substantial value and being produced simultaneously by the same process up to a split-off point.

linear programming A mathematical technique for allocating limited resources among activities for the attainment of goals. The measure of performance is a linear function of the controllable variables, and restrictions on the use of resources may be expressed as linear equations or inequalities.

make-or-buy decision The decision whether to produce a component, product, or service internally versus purchasing it from an outside supplier.

relevant cost A cost that should be considered when choosing among alternatives. Only those costs yet to be incurred (future costs) that will differ among the alternatives (the differential costs) are relevant in decision making.

scarce resources Resources limited in some way that hinders unlimited production and sales.

segment An identifiable collection of related resources and activities. Operationally it is a significant strategic or organizational component of an entity enterprise—a subsidiary, division, department, the entity itself, or other units—having distinctive resources and activities that can be treated as an entity for planning and control purposes.

segment analysis The examination of a portion of an entity, a product line, or any other subdivision of an entity.

sell-or-process-further decision The decision regarding joint products that may be sold or processed further at the split-off point.

split-off point The point in the production process for joint products, at which common inputs become separable, individual products become identifiable, and beyond which separate costs are recognized.

unavoidable costs Sunk costs that have been incurred and thus cannot be changed; future costs that do not differ among alternatives.

Review Questions

4-1 Why do managers get involved in making decisions about individual components or segments of the organization?

4-2 Define *relevant costs*.

4-3 Why is it true that not every accounting number or ratio is relevant for every decision?

4-4 Define *unavoidable costs*.

4-5 Define *avoidable costs*.

4-6 What are the steps in deciding among alternatives?

4-7 Why is the "loss" on a present machine or other asset not a relevant cost in a decision to acquire a new machine to engage in a new production method?

4-8   Why does the total cost method and the incremental cost analysis method arrive at the same answer?

4-9   Explain what is meant by *goal congruency* and *goal incongruency*.

4-10   What is information overload?

4-11   What is the decision rule regarding special sales orders?

4-12   What accounting and nonaccounting factors enter the decision process in identifying and deciding whether a segment should be discontinued?

4-13   Why are allocated fixed costs sometimes unavoidable? What impact should they have on a decision?

4-14   What is a typical example of a joint product and how does a manager decide whether to sell or process further individual products coming from a joint process?

4-15   What is a split-off point?

4-16   Should an organization desire to produce all components internally? Why or why not?

4-17   When organizations operate with scarce resources, what decision criteria should be used to allocate those scarce resources?

4-18   What quantitative technique would help us allocate scarce resources in order to minimize costs or maximize contribution margin?

Discussion Questions

4-19   You own a 10-year-old car and are considering trading it in for a new automobile. Identify some of the sunk costs and some of the costs that do not differ among alternatives. Also identify some of the differential costs.

4-20   Barry Cushing is a talented athlete in both basketball and skiing. He is trying to decide between a professional career in the two sports. Identify some of the quantitative and the qualitative factors he should consider.

Exercises

4-21   **RELEVANT COST** Bounceback Corporation manufactures boomerangs. Bounceback has capacity for 6,000 boomerangs per year at a variable cost of $15,000 and fixed costs of $9,000. Based on Bounceback's best estimates of the future, 4,800 boomerangs will be sold at the regular selling price of $6 each. A separate special order has been proposed to the management of Bounceback in which, under a special promotion, 1,000 boomerangs would be sold at 40% off the regular price. Determine the unit relevant cost for Bounceback's decision and calculate the effect on net income.

CO 1

4-22   **RELEVANT COST** Rowlinds Company manufactures footballs. It produces one type of football at very high quality level. Rowlinds' estimated income statement for the year, without inclusion of any special orders or discount orders, contains the following data:

CO 1

	Amount	Per Unit
Sales	$9,600,000	$24.00
Manufacturing cost of goods sold	7,680,000	19.20
Gross profit	$1,920,000	$ 4.80
Selling expenses	720,000	1.80
Operating income	$1,200,000	$ 3.00

Fixed costs included in the estimated income statement amount to $2,880,000 in manufacturing cost of good sold and $240,000 in selling expenses. Rowlinds has received a special promotional order offering to purchase 50,000 footballs for $18 each. The capacity is sufficient to absorb this increase in production with no change in the cost structure other than that previously mentioned.

a. Calculate the unit relevant cost for this decision.

b. Calculate the change to operating income by the acceptance of this decision.

c. Provide management a brief memo outlining the rationale for your decision.

4-23   SPECIAL SALES ORDER Milliron Company sells Product Z at $44 per unit. Milliron's cost per unit, based on full capacity of 300,000 units, is as follows:

CO 2

Direct materials	$ 8
Direct labor	12
Overhead (3/4 of which is fixed)	12
	$32

Although Milliron has estimated its pricing structure on Product Z and its cost structure on Product Z at full capacity of 300,000 units, Milliron is operating well under the full capacity and has sufficient existing capacity to manufacture any additional units required.

A special-order proposal to buy 30,000 units of Z has come to Milliron's attention. The only selling costs that would be incurred on this order are $5 additional cost per unit for shipping. Milliron Company is attempting to negotiate with customers for the special order.

a. What is the minimum selling price that Milliron can charge for this order?

b. If Milliron decides to sell these 30,000 additional units, they would want to have incremental increase in net income of $120,000. What price should Milliron charge?

(CPA adapted)

4-24   SELL OR PROCESS FURTHER A company uses a joint manufacturing process to produce two products at a joint cost of $800,000. These products may be sold at split-off or, when further processed at an additional cost, as more expensive items. Management has asked you to identify an appropriate allocation mechanism to assist in this sell-or-process-further decision relating to the $800,000 in cost. Provide management a brief memo.

CO 3

(CPA adapted)

4-25   SELL OR PROCESS FURTHER Maximax Corporation produces three products, X, Y, and Z, in a joint process. Each product may be sold at its split-off point or processed further. These additional processing costs are entirely variable and directly traceable to the particular products. Joint production costs for the past year were $90,000. When allocating joint costs, Maximax Corporation uses the relative sales value at split-off. The accounting data pertaining to this situation follows:

CO 3

		Sales	If Processed Further	
Product	Units Produced	Value at Split-off	Sales Value	Additional Costs
X	20,000	$ 81,000	$108,000	$36,000
Y	15,000	135,000	176,400	36,000
Z	15,000	54,000	111,600	32,400
		$270,000		

Which product or products should Maximax process further? Why? Write a memo to management including your calculations and explanation.

(CPA adapted)

4-26   MAKE OR BUY Ramsy is considering the purchase or manufacture of a certain component part for which it needs 20,000 units in its current production cycle. If Ramsy buys the part from Damsy instead of producing it internally, Ramsy could not use the excess capacity in any other activity. Sixty percent of the fixed overhead costs will continue regardless of what decision is made. The following data pertains to Ramsy Company:

CO 4

Cost to Ramsy to make the part:	
Direct materials	$ 12
Direct labor	48
Variable overhead	24
Fixed overhead applied	30
	$114
Cost to buy the part from Damsy Company	$108

a. Calculate Ramsy's total relevant cost to make the part.
b. Which alternative should Ramsy select?
c. Write a memo to management outlining your recommendations.

(CPA adapted)

4-27   MAKE OR BUY Puddin Company manufactures 10,000 units of a particular part that it uses in its own internal production. The following annual costs are reported to management:

CO 4

Direct materials	$ 30,000
Direct labor	82,500
Variable overhead	67,500
Fixed overhead	105,000
	$285,000

Tain Company has offered to sell Puddin these parts for $27 per unit. If Puddin accepts this offer, some of the facilities presently used to manufacture this part could be rented to an external organization for $15,000 per year. In addition, $6 per unit of fixed overhead applied to this part would be eliminated.

a. What is the relevant cost per unit to buy the part?
b. What is the relevant cost per unit to make the part?
c. Should Puddin accept Tain's offer?

4-28   LIMITED CAPACITY Using the graph on page 133 as depicted, provide management the following information:

CO 5   a. What do each of the lines on the graph mean?
b. Identify the feasible space and explain this concept to management.

(CIA adapted)

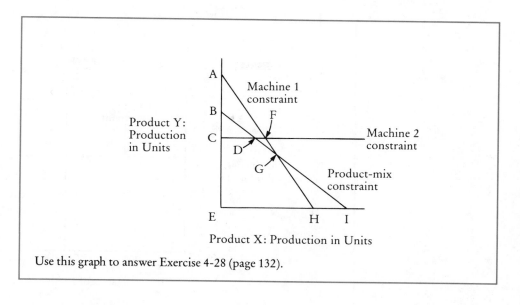

Use this graph to answer Exercise 4-28 (page 132).

4-29 LIMITED CAPACITY Sussnick Company manufactures Product R and Product S on two machines, as follows:

CO 5

	Type G Machine	Type H Machine
Product R	9 hours	6 hours
Product S	12 hours	10 hours

The contribution margin is $18 for Product R and $11 for Product S. The available time daily for processing the two products is 120 hours for Machine G and 80 hours for Machine H.

a. How would the restriction (constraint) for Machine H be expressed?

b. How would the constraint for Machine G be expressed?

c. How would the objective function be expressed?

(CPA adapted)

4-30 LINEAR PROGRAMMING Snerd Company manufactures Products G and H, each of which requires two processes: mixing and packing. The contribution margin is $4.50 for

CO 6 Product G and $6 for Product H. The graph on page 134 shows the maximum number of units of each product that may be processed in the mixing department and the packing department respectively.

a. Give the objective function for this equation.

b. Which combination of G and H provide the maximum profitability to the organization?

Problems

4-31 SPECIAL SALES ORDER Petovey Company, a manufacturer of end tables, budgeted

CO 1, 2 sales of $1,410,000 at $30 per unit for the year. Variable manufacturing costs were budgeted at $12 per unit, and fixed manufacturing costs at $8 per unit. In April Petovey received a special order

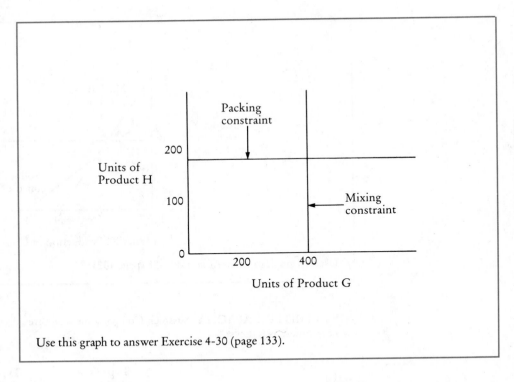

Use this graph to answer Exercise 4-30 (page 133).

offering to buy 14,000 end tables for $19.50 each. Petovey has sufficient plant capacity to manu-facture the additional quantity of end tables; however, the production would have to be done by the present work force on an overtime basis at an estimated additional cost of $1.50 per end table. Petovey will not incur any selling expenses as a result of the special order.

REQUIRED
a. Calculate the relevant cost per unit.
b. Calculate the effect on operating income if the special order could be accepted without affect-ing normal sales.

4-32   SEGMENT ANALYSIS General Wholesale Company (GWC) sells many products in each of its 18 different product lines. At various times a product or an entire product line is dropped because it ceases to be profitable. The company does not have a formalized program for reviewing its products on a regular basis to identify those products that should be eliminated.

CO 2, 7

At a recent meeting of top management, one person stated that there were several products, possibly a product line, that were unprofitable or producing an unsatisfactory profit. After dis-cussion, management decided that GWC should establish a formalized product discontinuance program. The purpose of the program would be to review the company's individual products and product lines on a regular and continuing basis to identify program areas.

The vice president of operations has proposed that a person be assigned to the program on a full-time basis. This person would work closely with the marketing and accounting departments to determine (1) the factors that indicate when a product's importance is declining and (2) the underlying data that would be required in evaluating a prospective discontinuance.

REQUIRED
a. List the benefits of GWC's formalized product discontinuance program.
b. List the factors that would indicate the diminishing importance of a product or product line.

c. Give examples of the accounting information that would be helpful to management in making segment analysis decisions.

(CMA adapted)

4-33 SPECIAL SALES ORDER Giddens and Sons build custom-made sailing craft that range in price from $30,000 to $750,000. For the past 30 years, Mr. Giddens, Sr., has determined the selling price of each boat by estimating the costs of material, labor, a prorated portion of overhead, and adding 1/3 to these estimated costs. For example, a recent price quotation was determined as follows:

CO 2, 7

Direct materials	$15,000
Direct labor	24,000
Overhead	6,000
	$45,000
Plus 1/3	15,000
Selling price	$60,000

The overhead figure was determined by estimating total overhead costs for the year and allocating them at 25% of direct labor.

If a customer rejected the price and business was slack, Mr. Giddens would often be willing to reduce his markup to as little as 5% over estimated costs. Average markup for the year is estimated at 15%.

Mr. Giddens, Jr., believes the firm could use the contribution margin approach to pricing, and he feels such an approach would be helpful in determining the selling prices of their custom-made boats.

Total overhead including selling and administrative expenses for the year has been estimated at $300,000, of which $150,000 is fixed and the remainder varies in direct proportion to direct labor.

REQUIRED

a. Calculate the proportion of variable overhead to total overhead.

b. Calculate the variable overhead rate as a percent of direct labor dollars. (Hint: Determine the total overhead rate by comparing total overhead to direct labor cost.)

c. Assuming Giddens and Sons accept an offer of $48,000 for the craft on which a price quotation was presented, calculate how much profit or loss will occur.

d. Find the minimum price that Giddens and Sons should accept on the craft for which a price quotation was presented if they allocate fixed costs to each project.

e. Explain which approach to pricing Giddens and Sons should take and why.

f. Name the major pitfall in the contribution margin approach to pricing.

4-34 MAKE OR BUY Hammer, Inc., has been manufacturing 5,000 units of Part 3845, which is used in the manufacture of one of its products. At this level of production, the cost per unit of manufacturing the part is as follows:

CO 4

Direct materials	$ 6
Direct labor	24
Variable overhead	12
Fixed overhead applied	18
	$60

Colt Company has offered to sell Hammer 5,000 units of the part for $57 a unit. Hammer has determined that it could use the facilities currently used to manufacture this part to manufacture Product 357 and generate an operating profit of $32,000. Hammer has determined that two-thirds of the fixed overhead applied will continue even if Part 3845 is purchased from Colt.

REQUIRED

a. State the net relevant costs.

b. State the net relevant cost to purchase the part.

c. Write a memo to management with your recommendations for this decision.

(CPA adapted)

4-35   SEGMENT ANALYSIS Vernom Corporation, which produces and sells to wholesalers a line of summer lotions and insect repellents, has decided to diversify in order to stabilize sales over the year. A natural area for the company to consider is the production of winter lotions and creams to prevent dry and chapped skin.

CO 2

After considerable research, a winter products line has been developed. However, because of a cautious management, Vernom's president has decided to introduce only one of the new products for this coming winter. If it is a success, more winter products will be added in future years.

The product selected (called Chap-off) is a lip balm that will be sold in a lipstick-type tube. It will be sold to wholesalers in boxes of 24 tubes for $8 per box. Because of available capacity, no additional fixed charges will be incurred to produce the product. However, a $100,000 fixed charge will be absorbed by the new product to allocate a fair share of the company's present fixed costs to it.

Using the estimated sales and production of 100,000 boxes of Chap-off as the standard volume, the accounting department has developed the following costs per box:

Direct labor	$2.00
Direct material	$3.00
Total overhead	$1.50
Total cost	$6.50

Vernom has approached a cosmetics manufacturer to discuss the possibility of purchasing the tubes for Chap-off. The purchase price of the empty tubes from the cosmetics manufacturer would be $.90 per 24 tubes. If Vernom Corporation accepts the purchase proposal, it is estimated that direct labor and variable overhead costs would be reduced by 10% and direct material costs would be reduced by 20%.

REQUIRED

a. State the relevant costs per box of Chap-off.

b. State the costs per box of Chap-off saved by purchasing the tubes.

c. Calculate the maximum purchase price Vernom would be willing to pay for each box of 24 tubes.

d. Calculate the cost Vernom would incur by making 125,000 boxes, assuming that additional equipment, at an annual rental of $10,000, must be acquired to produce this volume.

e. Explain whether buying the 125,000 boxes would save money, and if so, how much.

4-36   CONTRIBUTION MARGIN INCOME STATEMENT Montana Company has four major product lines, M, N, O, and P. A summary income statement (in thousands) for a typical month follows:

CO 2

	M	N	O	P	Total
Sales	$64.0	$120	$72.0	$160.0	$416.0
Less: Cost of Goods Sold	44.8	64	52.8	102.4	264.0
Gross Profit	$19.2	$ 56	$19.2	$ 57.6	$152.0
Less: Operating Expenses	22.4	36	21.6	41.6	121.6
Net Income	$(3.2)	$ 20	$(2.4)	$ 16.0	$ 30.4

Additional analysis produces the following information:

	M	N	O	P
Units sold	2,000	2,500	3,000	4,000
Sales price per unit	$32.00	$48.00	$24.00	$40.00
Variable manufacturing costs per unit	$16.00	$19.20	$11.20	$19.20
Variable marketing costs per unit	$ 8.00	$ 9.60	$ 4.80	$ 6.40

All fixed costs are incurred at the firmwide level. Fixed manufacturing costs are allocated among the products on the basis of units produced and sold. Fixed marketing costs are allocated on the basis of each product line's sales revenue.

REQUIRED

a. Prepare a contribution margin income statement for the four lines.

b. Explain why the contribution income statement is superior to the traditional statement for management use.

c. Explain whether any of these products should be dropped.

4-37 SELL OR PROCESS FURTHER Fryer Company, produces Products X, Y, and Z from a joint process. Each product may be sold at the point of split-off or processed further. Additional processing requires no special facilities, and the production costs of further processing are entirely variable and traceable to the products involved. Last year all three products were processed beyond split-off. Joint production costs for the year were $72,000. Sales values and costs needed to evaluate Fryer's production policy are as follows:

CO 3

Product	Units Produced	Sales Value at Split-off	Sales Value	Additional Costs
			If Processed Further	
X	6,000	$30,000	$50,400	$10,800
Y	4,000	49,200	54,000	8,400
Z	2,000	28,800	38,400	9,600

Joint costs are allocated to the products in proportion to the relative physical volume of output.

REQUIRED

a. State the unit production costs most relevant to the sell-or-process-further decision.

b. Calculate which products Fryer should subject to additional processing in order to maximize profits.

c. Prepare a memo to management outlining your reasoning.

(CPA adapted)

4-38   **SELL OR PROCESS FURTHER** Ozone Corporation uses a joint process to produce three products, H, O, and C, all derived from one input. The company can sell these products at the point of split-off or process them further. The joint production costs during October were $780,000. Ozone allocates joint costs to the products in proportion to the relative physical volume of output. Other information follows:

CO 3

			If Processed Further	
Product	Units Produced	Sales Price at Split-off	Unit Sales Price	Unit Additional Costs
H	8,000	$32.00	$40.00	$6.00
O	16,000	18.00	32.00	9.60
C	12,000	24.00	30.00	7.20

REQUIRED

a. Determine the gross margin from the production process if all products were sold at the split-off point during October.

b. Assuming sufficient demand exists, Ozone could sell all the products at the prices above at either the split-off point or after further processing. State what Ozone should do in order to maximize its profits.

c. Prepare a memo to management outlining your recommendation.

(CPA adapted)

4-39   **MAKE OR BUY** Ready Light Company needs 100,000 units of a certain part to be used in its production cycle. If it buys the part from Ithaca Company instead of making it, Ready Light could not use the released facilities in another manufacturing activity. Sixty percent of the fixed overhead will continue regardless of what decision is made. The following information is available:

CO 4

Cost to Ready Light to make the part:	
Direct materials	$ 25.20
Direct labor	100.80
Variable overhead	50.40
Fixed overhead	63.00
	$239.40
Cost to buy the part from Ithaca Company	$222.60

REQUIRED

a. State Ready Light's total relevant costs to make the part.

b. What should Ready Light do?

c. Detail your analysis in a memo to management.

4-40 MAKE OR BUY The Blade Division of Brock Company produces carbon steel blades. One-third of the Blade Division's output is sold to Brock's Lawn Products Division; the remainder is sold to outside customers. The Blade Division's estimated sales and cost data for the year are as follows (amounts are in thousands):

CO 4

	Lawn Products	Outside Customers
Sales	$37,500	$100,000
Variable costs	(25,000)	(50,000)
Fixed costs	(7,500)	(15,000)
Gross margin	$ 5,000	$ 35,000
Unit sales	50,000	100,000

The Lawn Products Division has an opportunity to purchase 50,000,000 identical quality blades from an outside supplier at a cost of $.70 per unit on a continuing basis. Assume that the Blade Division cannot sell any additional products to outside customers.

REQUIRED

a. Determine whether Brock should allow its Lawn Products Division to purchase the blades from the outside supplier. State why or why not.

b. Assume that the Blade Division is now at capacity and sufficient demand exists to sell all production to outsiders at present prices. Calculate the incremental cost (benefit) of producing the blade internally.

(CPA adapted)

4-41 MAKE OR BUY Meadow Company manufactures Part Z for use in its production cycle. The costs per unit for 5,000 units of Part Z are as follows:

CO 4

Direct materials	$ 3.60
Direct labor	18.00
Variable overhead	7.20
Fixed overhead	9.60
Total cost per unit	$38.40

Lea Company has offered to sell Meadow 5,000 units of this part for $36 per unit. If Meadow accepts Lea's offer, the released facilities could be used to save $54,000 in relevant costs in the manufacture of Part Y. In addition, $6 per unit of the fixed overhead applied to Part Z would be eliminated.

REQUIRED

a. State the total relevant costs to manufacture Part Z.

b. State the total relevant costs to buy Part Z.

c. Calculate which alternative is more desirable and by what amount.

d. Write a memo to management describing your analysis.

(CPA adapted)

CO 5, 6

4-42   LIMITED CAPACITY Preston Company manufactures two models, standard and deluxe. Each product must be processed in the machining and polishing departments. The standard model requires two hours of machining and three hours of polishing. The deluxe model requires three hours of machining and four hours of polishing. The contribution margin is $13.50 for the standard model and $15 for the deluxe model. Preston has four grinding machines and five finishing machines, which run sixteen hours a day for six days a week.

REQUIRED

a. Explain how the restriction (constraint) for the departments would be expressed.

b. Explain how the objective function for Preston Company would be expressed.

c. Prepare a memo to management outlining the value of using linear programming given production constraints.

CO 6

4-43   LINEAR PROGRAMMING Forrest, Inc., plans to expand its sales force by opening several new branch offices. Forrest has $5,200,000 in capital available for new branch offices, and it considers opening only two types of branches: ten-employee branches (Type A) and five-employee branches (Type B). Expected initial cash outlays are $650,000 for a Type A branch and $335,000 for a Type B branch. Expected annual cash inflow, net of income taxes, is $46,000 for a Type A branch and $18,000 for a Type B branch. Forrest will hire no more than 100 employees for the new branch offices and will not open more than ten branch offices. Linear programming will be used to help decide how many branch offices should be opened.

REQUIRED

a. Identify the objective function.

b. Identify the constraints.

c. Explain to management the value of linear programming.

(CPA adapted)

CO 6

4-44   LINEAR PROGRAMMING Platinum Manufacturing, Inc., wants to maximize the profits on Products Q, R, and S. The contribution margin for each product follows:

Product	Contribution Margin
Q	$20
R	$50
S	$40

The production requirements and departmental capacities, by department, are as follows:

Department	Production Requirements by Product (Hours)		
	Q	R	S
Assembly	4	9	8
Painting	2	6	8
Finishing	4	9	2

Department	Department Capacity (Total Hours)
Assembly	50,000
Painting	58,000
Finishing	58,000

REQUIRED

a. State the profit-maximization formula for Platinum Manufacturing, Inc.

b. State the constraints.

Business Decision Case

CO 3

Herman's, a men's suit manufacturer, is planning to market a new suit for the coming season. Six yards of material are required to lay out the suit pattern. Some material remains after cutting that can be sold as remnants.

The leftover material could also be used to manufacture a matching vest and cap. However, if the leftover material is to be used for the vest and cap, more care will be required in the cutting, which will increase the cutting costs.

The company expects to sell 1,000 suits if no matching vest and cap are available. Market research reveals that suit sales will be 20% higher if a matching vest and cap are available. The research indicates that the vest and cap should not be sold individually but only as accessories with the suit. The various combinations of suits, vests, and caps that are expected to be sold by retailers are as follows:

	Percent of Total
Complete sets of suit, vest, and cap	75%
Suit and vest	6
Suit and cap	12
Suit only	7
Total	100%

The material used in the suit costs $17.50 a yard, or $105 for each suit. The cost of cutting the suit if the vest and cap are not manufactured is estimated at $30 a suit, and the resulting remnants can be sold for $15 for each suit cut out. If the vest and cap are to be manufactured, the cutting costs will be increased by $15 per suit. There will be no salable remnants if the vests and caps are manufactured in the quantities estimated.

The selling prices and the costs to complete the three items once they are cut are as follows:

	Selling Price per Unit	Unit Cost to Complete (Excludes Cost of Material and Cutting Operation)
Suit	$350	$100.00
Vest	30	24.50
Cap	15	12.50

REQUIRED

Present the calculations showing whether Herman's should sell suits only or should sell suit combinations.

(CMA adapted)

Chapter   5

Budgets

CHAPTER OBJECTIVES

After reading Chapter 5, you should be able to:

1. Explain the planning aspects of budgeting (pp. 143-44).

2. Explain the control aspects of budgeting (pp. 144-45).

3. Describe the interdependencies of the master budget and the subsidiary budgets (pp. 145-47).

4. Explain continuous budgeting and participative budgeting (pp. 147-48).

5. Discuss the steps in the preparation of the master budget for a merchandiser (pp. 148-57).

6. Prepare and analyze the inventory management budgets for a manufacturer (pp. 157-64).

7. Identify decision support systems for budgeting (pp. 164-68).

8. Discuss the behavioral aspects of budgeting (p. 165).

*M*anagers, investors, creditors, and taxpayers are interested in the formal quantitative plans of organizations with which they are associated. In this chapter we will examine the entire organizational plan, known as the *budget*. Although most of these business plans are sometimes referred to as "profit plans" or by other such terms, budgets should be prepared by profit-oriented and nonprofit entities alike. This chapter focuses on the master budget (that is, the overall plan), as well as the preparation of the subsidiary budgets, for merchandisers and manufacturers. The master budget is a key tool for managers because it helps managers to plan the operations of the firm, it helps them control operations, and it facilitates communication within the organization.

The master budget and the subsidiary budgets are highly interrelated. We will see that these interrelationships are reflected in an integrated set of budgets that permit interested parties to examine expected changes to the financial structure of the organization. As budgeting is primarily future oriented, it is an integral part of what management accounting is all about. In fact, without proper budgeting, it is impossible to exert any organizational control or provide incentives for the attainment of goals. Accordingly, this chapter focuses on budgeting for the operating structure of the organization, rather than on budgeting for capital projects budgets, which we will examine in Chapter 14.

BUDGETING AND MANAGEMENT FUNCTIONS

Planning

CHAPTER
OBJECTIVE 1
*Planning and
budgeting*

If you recall the discussion in Chapter 1 regarding the setting of strategic goals and other management tasks, you know that managers must quantify these goals and objectives into some form of a plan. A budget is a quantitative model of a plan as developed by management. It permits management to look ahead, coordinate, and control the organization to achieve its goals. The budget is future-oriented and expresses management's expectations in financial and other quantitative terms.

The master budget, also called the *profit plan* or *business plan*, expresses management's financial expectations for the organization as a whole. The master budget summarizes the entire set of subsidiary budgets and other schedules necessary to arrive at the total overview of the financial future of the organization. The master budget usually includes a budgeted income statement, a budgeted balance sheet, a budget of cash receipts and disbursements, and supporting budgets necessary to achieve these overall budgets. Some of these supporting budgets include, but are not limited to, the materials budget, the direct labor budget, the overhead budget, and the selling and general administrative expenses budget. By quantifying the goals of the organization, management is setting specific subgoals for the sales, production, marketing, and financing functions.

Planning Advantages to Budgets. Because budgets require estimates of the future, and therefore contains many uncertain elements, managers must make intuitive assumptions all the time. Budgeting forces management to quantify these assumptions. Budgeting, by definition, requires a commitment of resources (mostly time) from the organization. However, the advantages of budgeting usually outweigh the cost of the effort:

143

1. Budgeting formalizes the manager's concepts of the future and its relationship to the organizational goals.
2. Budgeting structures the manager's responsibilities for both planning and control.
3. Budgeting helps communicate to other managers and users what the objectives of the firm are and how each subunit fits into that overall scheme.

Successful budgeting involves not only planning and budgetary control but also communication. Therefore, top management's involvement and support of the budget system is necessary for the success of the organization as well as for the budget process. Top management's attitude toward budgeting and its usefulness in improving the organization sets the tone for the rest of the firm.

When management must quantify its expectations for the future, it must plan ahead. That is, management must think and anticipate what challenges and opportunities the future may bring and what that future impact may be on its segment of the organization or on the entire organization itself. The budgeting process elevates planning for the future into a definite management task.

Given the pressures of day-to-day operations, and impelled by events from one crisis to the next, many managers simply do not take the time or the effort to get beyond the nearest event horizon. Consequently, they simply eliminate planning entirely from the framework of their management tasks. The potent argument against crisis-to-crisis management is simply that the organizational goals can never be developed much less completed—and both management and organization are almost invariably doomed to failure of one form or another. That is, the firm may go out of business or may simply not earn the rate of return appropriate for an organization in that industry. In addition, control of such organizations is clearly at a minimum. Budgeting in the first place can help avoid many of the crises that *prevent* budgeting during such times.

Budgetary Control

CHAPTER
OBJECTIVE 2
Control and budgeting

Recall the discussion about *control* in Chapter 1, and that by control we mean management's ability to regulate and direct employees to work toward the organization's goals. If this can be achieved, we call this *goal congruence.*

Budgeting is a key tool of management to achieve control and strive for goal congruence. When the budget is used as a control mechanism, it is sometimes referred to as budgetary control. Evaluations of performance against a standard are very common in our society because they are more effective at changing future performance than are simply rewarding performance on its own current merits. The problem of the latter approach is that it typically overemphasizes the present at the expense of the future by encouraging current activity (which may be mediocre) as contributing to the work of the organization. Budgetary control tries to "stretch" people by motivating them toward excellence rather than mediocrity.

A manager must understand the phenomena behind the budget in order to achieve the control that is desired. That is, managers need to understand whether the budget is really motivating people to achieve their best or whether it is a subterfuge for maintaining mediocrity (an attempt to get rewarded while doing little work).

Parents, for example, might try to impose a grade point average budget for their child in high school or college. ("If you get a 3.5, I'll buy you a car.") Such an attempt at budgetary control might fail, however, since it does not look at the phenomena behind the numerical measurement. For example, you may have achieved a higher grade point average in the previous semester than in this one, but now you are learning more while taking more rigorous courses. If your parents try to impose a grade point average budget for higher and higher grades only, you might just substitute easier courses for harder courses. You might not learn as much, but you'll get the car. The parents, however, want you to learn something. If you avoid the harder courses, that goal might never be reached. The parents must look at the phenomena behind the numbers if they (and you) are going to achieve the educational goals they wish for you.

Managers face the same issues. They want to motivate employees to work toward the corporate goals, and to have a budget that impels people in that direction. But managers need to ask whether the budget is really doing its job. They must understand the business phenomena behind the budgeted and the actual numbers so that they can know how well the budget is controlling behavior. Management accountants are invaluable in providing help to managers in setting up an effective budget. They are also helpful in measuring performance against the budget and in interpreting the numbers.

The Budget as a Means of Communication

Motivating people in the organization requires some way of intertwining the operations and financial activities so that the goals of the individual segments and their managers mesh with the larger organizational goals. By using the budget to communicate its vision of the future, the organization tries to motivate people toward a common goal. What the marketing group is planning for sales volume, for example, directly affects the production department, which then affects purchasing. Both production and purchasing departments depend on the personnel group, which is mandated to find the employees to produce the product as well as to purchase raw materials that must all be brought together in a salable product. Clearly, the use of a budget mandates that management examine and communicate the interrelationships of the organization.

An Overview of the Master Budget

CHAPTER OBJECTIVE 3
The master budget and its subsidiary budgets

The master budget is actually made up of an interconnected group of component budgets, as depicted in Exhibit 5-1. The budgeted income statement indicates the future revenues, expenses, and income of the organization. The cash budget displays the cash expected to be received by the firm and the cash expected to be disbursed. The capital projects budget reveals cash outlays needed for investments in new projects. The budgeted balance sheet discloses the forecasted assets, liabilities, and stockholders' or owners' equity of the organization. The sales budget presents the estimated revenues of the company. The production budget (for manufacturers) indicates the number of units to produce and the expected cost of this production. It helps managers forecast future costs of goods sold and the cost of future inventory. The *responsibility center budgets* depict the general, administrative, and selling expenses of the organization. The *financing and investing budget* pinpoints when cash shortages will occur so that management knows how much cash must be raised and when, and it indicates when cash excesses are expected so that management can invest the funds to earn interest or dividends. The *product development budget* tries to determine the feasibility of developing and selling new products.

The *capital projects budget* shows the investment of cash in long-term projects. The *long-range sales forecast* helps in the development of the capital projects budget by highlighting future capital needs.

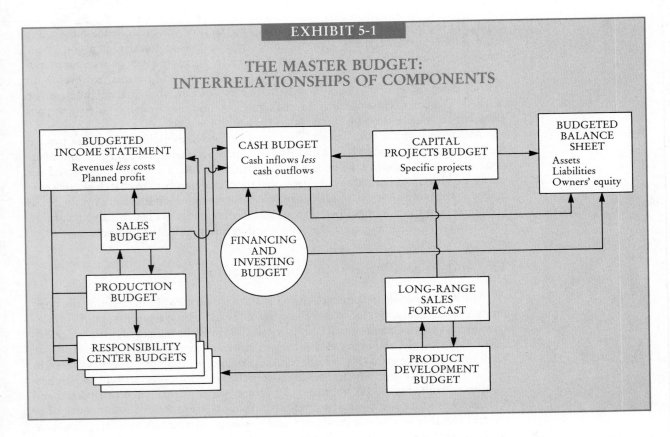

EXHIBIT 5-1

**THE MASTER BUDGET:
INTERRELATIONSHIPS OF COMPONENTS**

The interconnectedness among these budgets should be observed. The budgeted income statement shows the estimated revenues (from the sales budget) minus the estimated cost of goods sold (from the production budget) and other expenses (from the responsibility center budgets).

The cash budget outlines the estimated cash inflows. These inflows primarily come from cash sales and collections from credit sales (from the sales budget) and from financing and the sale of investments (shown on the financing and investing budget). The cash budget also forecasts cash outflows, which are usually for cost of sales (from the production budget), for cash expenditures (from the responsibility center budgets), for interest charges (from the financing and investing budget), and for investments for capital projects (from the capital projects budget).

The budgeted balance sheet is constructed from the data of last year's actual balance sheet and adjusted for changes in the assets, liabilities, and owners' equity. The adjustments are found in the budgeted income statement, the cash budget, the capital projects budget, and the financing and investing budget.

There are four prerequisites to using budgets as an effective control device:

1. The information system must be appropriate and must generate the data necessary for planning and control purposes.

2. The organization must actually isolate the costs and revenues by segment or other reasonable unit of activity delineations.

3. Management must have control over the costs and revenues under evaluation.

4. The firm can generate budgets reflecting each of the above prerequisites, which then can be used as the evaluative standard for management control.

Managerial Aspects of the Master Budget

CHAPTER OBJECTIVE 4
Continuous and participative budgeting

A **continuous budget** permits us to examine a period of one year or longer and add on periods in the future as the period just completed is eliminated. Continuous budgets force management to think continually of the period ahead in order to keep the focus on a rolling horizon in the future. If the continuous budget is done for a 12-month period, management is constantly thinking about results at the 12th month out from the beginning of the budget. If the continuous budget is for two or three years, management is constantly examining the second or third year out in the budget cycle. (Budget review consists of continual review and reiteration of the budget and evaluation process.)

Continuous budgets require that supervisors and subordinates alike must clearly and frequently communicate their expectations for budget estimates. Budgets that are summarily imposed from above often minimize job satisfaction and certainly alienate managers. It is better to have a mutually agreed-upon budget in which subordinates are given general guidelines and then return after preparing their own budgets. This is called **participative budgeting,** and it has clear advantages over budget "edicts":

1. Individuals on a variety of levels within the organization are perceived as part of the organization.

2. Employees become more committed to the budget and the achievement of the budgeted goals because they helped set these goals.

3. Employees closest to a project usually have a better idea of the true nature, time, and cost of the activity than do those removed from it by management layers, segments, or departments. Their view can increase the budget's accuracy.

4. An interactive budget process permits more congruent behavior because managers unable to meet budgeted goals usually will be more introspective about their lack of achievement. In other words, they will examine their own performance more closely to determine how they may have failed in meeting the budgeted goals, how they achieved those budgeted goals, and even whether the goals they helped formulate were unrealistic in the first place.

By permitting lower-level personnel to help prepare the budget and encouraging interaction between levels of management, participative budgeting promotes a system of checks and balances in the process. The management level most familiar with the day-to-day operating costs provides detailed budget analyses to middle and upper levels. Conversely, top management has a strategic perspective on the organization and can communicate this by way of the budget. Middle managers analyze the budget and facilitate the communication. Each management level contributes particular expertise to the budget process. Again, organizations have a behavior that forces management to examine their expectations, goals, objectives, cost structure, and evaluation system within the organization. The examination of all these factors increases communication to reach a budget that is acceptable at all levels.

The emphasis on communication in the budgeting process is essential because the budget affects almost every behavior in an organization. Therefore, the budget should be used as a positive influence rather than a means of finding fault or blame with particular employees for a particular problem. The successful integration of a rigorous, high-quality budget process requires communication ability on the part of top management and the other individuals concerned. Budgeting must be perceived as a positive support system for everyone in the organization.

An appropriate way to build in communications and coordination is to form a **budget committee.** This committee is a steering group for the organization's budget process. The budget committee is usually an advisory group to the chief management accountant or chief financial officer in charge of the entire budget process. Various subcommittees may be formed to examine elements of the budget if necessary. The budget committee receives periodic reports from all departments and subcommittees on the progress of the organization in achieving its goals. In addition, the budget committee can serve as an arbiter to disagreements among various organizational units. Finally, the budget committee is usually the final arbiter of the entire budget process and it signs off on that particular budget.

PREPARATION OF THE MASTER BUDGET FOR A MERCHANDISING FIRM

CHAPTER OBJECTIVE 5
Budgeting steps for merchandisers

In this section we will prepare a master budget for Malux Company, a merchandising firm, in order to demonstrate the integration of the subsidiary budgets into the master budget. (Manufacturing organizations have additional steps to follow, which are described in the next section.) The starting point for any master budget is the balance sheet, which reveals the assets and equities of the organization as of the close of the period. Malux Company prepares its annual budget on a quarterly basis for the upcoming year. It is December 19X1 and Malux is budgeting for 19X2. (We assume that managers have the data for 19X1 up to December and can estimate December's results accurately so that in effect it already has the 19X1 financial statements.) The following budgets and schedules are assembled in this order in the budget process:

1. Sales budget.
2. Cash collections from sales.
3. Purchases budget.
4. Cash disbursements for purchases.
5. Budgeted operating expenses.
6. Cash disbursements for budgeted operating expenses.
7. Budgeted statement of cash receipts and disbursements.
8. Budgeted income statement.
9. Budgeted balance sheet.

Data for the Malux Company Budget

Exhibit 5-2 is the closing balance sheet for Malux Company for 19X1, the fiscal year just ended. Sales in the fourth quarter of 19X1 were $120,000. Based on this and past years' growth, quarterly sales for 19X2 and the first quarter of 19X3 are forecast as follows:

EXHIBIT 5-2

Malux Company
Balance Sheet
December 31, 19X1

ASSETS

Current Assets

Cash	$ 30,000	
Accounts Receivable, net		
(.4 × sales of $120,000)	48,000	
Merchandise Inventory		
[$60,000 + .8(.7 × next		
quarter's sales of $150,000)]	144,000	
Unexpired Insurance	5,400	$227,400
Plant, Property, and Equipment		
Equipment, Fixtures, and Other	$111,000	
Less: Accumulated Depreciation	38,400	$ 72,600
Total Assets		$300,000

LIABILITIES AND EQUITIES

Current Liabilities

Accounts payable		
(.5 × purchases of $100,800)	$ 50,400	
Accrued wages and commissions payable		
($3,750 + $9,000)	12,750	$ 63,150
Owner's Equity		236,850
Total Liabilities and Owner's Equity		$300,000

Q1 19X2	Q2 19X2	Q3 19X2	Q4 19X2	Q1 19X3
$150,000	$240,000	$180,000	$150,000	$120,000

Sales consist of 60% cash and 40% credit. All credit accounts are collected in the quarter following the sales. The $48,000 of accounts receivable represents credit sales made in previous quarter (40% of $120,000). Uncollectible accounts are ignored as negligible.

At the end of any quarter, Malux wishes to maintain an inventory of $60,000 plus 80% of the cost of goods to be sold in the following quarter. The cost of goods sold averages 70% of sales. Therefore, the inventory on March 31, 19X2, the end of the first quarter, is expected to be $194,400 [$60,000 + .8(.7 × $240,000 second quarter sales)]. The purchase terms available to the company are net 30 days. A given quarter's purchases are paid as follows: 50% during that quarter and 50% during the next quarter.

Wages and commissions are paid half in the quarter earned and half in the quarter after they are earned. They are divided into two portions: (a) quarterly fixed wages of $7,500, and (b) commissions, which are 15% of sales that take place evenly throughout each month. Therefore, the balance of Accrued Wages and Commissions Payable in the first quarter of 19X2 consists of $12,750 $[(.5 \times \$7,500) + .5(.15 \times \$120,000)]$. This $12,750 will be paid on April 15. A used delivery truck will be purchased for $9,000 cash in the first quarter.

Other quarterly expenses are as follows:

Miscellaneous expenses	5% of sales, paid as incurred
Rent	$6,000, paid as incurred
Insurance	$600 expiration per quarter
Depreciation, including truck	$1,500

Management for Malux Company wishes to maintain a minimum cash balance of $30,000 at the end of each month. Money can be borrowed or repaid in multiples of $3,000, at an interest rate of 18% per annum. Management does not want to borrow any more cash than necessary and wants to repay it as promptly as possible. At the time the principal is repaid, interest is computed and paid only on the portion of principal that is repaid. For simplicity, assume that borrowing takes place at the beginning and repayment at the end of the quarters in question.

Steps in the Master Budget Process

The following six steps are taken to prepare the master budget for a merchandiser:

1. Determine projected sales and cash collections from these sales. Two schedules are prepared: the sales budget and the cash receipts from sales.
2. Estimate purchases of inventory and cash payments for these purchases. Two schedules are prepared: the purchases budget and the cash disbursements for purchases.
3. Forecast the operating expenses and the cash disbursements for these expenses.
4. Prepare the cash budget and estimate any necessary financing activities.
5. Prepare the budgeted income statement.
6. Prepare the budgeted balance sheet.

These six steps are discussed in detail for Malux Company next.

Step 1: The Sales Budget and Cash Collections from Sales.   The driving force of most, if not all, organizations is the sales forecast or *sales budget.* Such forecasts predict sales using various data and methods such as trend predictions, correlation analysis, and other operations research techniques. Organizations use the sales budget for production planning, control, estimation of cash receipts and disbursements (cash flows), forecasting of employment patterns, and many other functions. To arrive at the total estimated dollar sales for a period, the estimated number of units to be sold is multiplied by the estimated selling price per unit. In addition, management identifies the expected ratio of cash sales to credit sales. As mentioned earlier, for Malux Company this is 40% credit sales and 60% cash sales. We will need this assumption in order to calculate

EXHIBIT 5-3

SALES BUDGET

	Q4 19X1	Q1 19X2	Q2 19X2	Q3 19X2	Q4 19X2	19X2 Total
Credit sales, 40%	$ 48,000	$ 60,000	$ 96,000	$ 72,000	$ 60,000	$288,000
Cash sales, 60%	72,000	90,000	144,000	108,000	90,000	432,000
Total sales, 100%	$120,000	$150,000	$240,000	$180,000	$150,000	$720,000

Malux's cash receipts collections from sales. Even nonprofit organizations make some type of revenue estimation in order to determine their expected cash flows.

The sales budget for Malux Company is shown in Exhibit 5-3. Total sales for each quarter are taken from the original forecast data and divided into credit sales and cash sales. Credit sales equal 40% of total sales and cash sales equal 60% of total sales. Also shown are the fourth quarter sales for 19X1, since this data is needed when determining cash collections for the first quarter of 19X2.

Cash collections from sales, obtained from the sales budget in Exhibit 5-3, are calculated and the results described in a schedule, shown in Exhibit 5-4. Since credit sales are entirely collected in the following quarters, cash receipts in a quarter are equal to the cash sales made in that quarter plus the credit sales made in the previous quarter. For example, the cash expected to be received in the second quarter is equal to the cash sales in the second quarter ($144,000) plus the credit sales of the first quarter ($60,000). Thus, cash collection in the second quarter is anticipated to be $204,000.

Step 2: The Purchases Budget and Cash Disbursements for Purchases.
Recognizing that inventory must be managed is important for understanding the operations of an organization. Firms maintain inventories so that they can fill customers' orders quickly and therefore can be paid more readily. The opportunity cost of not holding inventories is frequently lost sales, since the customer could go to another dealer who could fill the order more quickly. Without planning, inventories can fluctuate according to essentially random variables or to the degree of competence of those in the

EXHIBIT 5-4

BUDGETED CASH COLLECTIONS

	Q1 19X2	Q2 19X2	Q3 19X2	Q4 19X2	19X2 Total
Cash sales this quarter	$ 90,000	$144,000	$108,000	$ 90,000	$432,000
Previous quarter's credit sales	48,000	60,000	96,000	72,000	276,000
	$138,000	$204,000	$204,000	$162,000	$708,000

EXHIBIT 5-5

PURCHASES BUDGET

	Q4 19X1	Q1 19X2	Q2 19X2	Q3 19X2	Q4 19X2	19X2 Total
Cost of goods sold	$ 84,000*	$105,000	$168,000	$126,000	$105,000	$504,000
Ending inventory	144,000	194,400	160,800	144,000	127,200	
Total needed	$228,000	$299,400	$328,800	$270,000	$232,200	
Beginning inventory	127,200†	144,000	194,400	160,800	144,000	
Purchases	$100,800	$155,400	$134,400	$109,200	$ 88,200	

*.7 × $120,000 fourth quarter, 19X1, sales
†$60,000 + .8(.7 × $120,000 fourth quarter, 19X1, sales)

organization that affect inventory levels. That is, crisis management would become the byword regarding inventory management. So the **purchases budget** is used to plan for inventory needs.

Beginning inventory plus purchases yields the cost of goods available for sale. These goods are either sold or still in inventory. This fact is often expressed as cost of goods available for sale minus ending inventory equals cost of goods sold:

$$\text{Beginning Inventory} + \text{Purchases} - \text{Ending Inventory} = \text{Cost of Goods Sold}$$

For planning purposes, this equation is often rearranged to solve for purchases:

$$\text{Purchases} = \text{Cost of Goods Sold} + \text{Ending Inventory} - \text{Beginning Inventory}$$

The purchases budget is an enactment of the above relationship.

The purchases budget for Malux Company is shown in Exhibit 5-5. Notice that purchases is computed by summing cost of goods sold and ending inventory and subtracting beginning inventory from the total. Recall the assumption that cost of goods sold averages 70% of sales; thus, the amounts for cost of goods sold in the purchases budget are 70% of the total sales shown in Exhibit 5-3. For example, the first quarter's cost of goods sold of $105,000 is equal to 70% of the first quarter's sales, $150,000.

As stated earlier, management wishes to maintain an inventory level of $60,000 plus 80% of the cost of goods sold in the following quarter. For example, the inventory on June 30 (the end of the second quarter) is $160,800. This value is obtained as follows: $60,000 + 80% of 70% of $180,000 (the sales in the third quarter). Note also that this $160,800 is both the ending inventory of the second quarter and the beginning inventory of the third quarter. For all quarters, the beginning inventory is the same as the ending inventory of the previous quarter.

Purchases can then be computed with the equation cited above. For example, for the second quarter, purchases are obtained by adding the projected cost of goods sold, $168,000, and the projected ending inventory, $160,800, and subtracting from the total

	EXHIBIT 5-6				
	CASH DISBURSEMENTS FOR PURCHASES				
	Q1 19X2	Q2 19X2	Q3 19X2	Q4 19X2	19X2 Total
50% of last quarter's purchases	$ 50,400	$ 77,700	$ 67,200	$54,600	$249,900
50% of this quarter's purchases	77,700	67,200	54,600	44,100	243,600
Cash disbursements	$128,100	$144,900	$121,800	$98,700	$493,500

the projected beginning inventory, $194,400. Projected purchases for the second quarter totals $134,400.

Exhibit 5-6 is the schedule for cash disbursements for purchases. Recall that management assumes that 50% of a given quarter's purchases are paid during that quarter and 50% are paid during the next quarter. The cash disbursements for a quarter are comprised of 50% of the purchases of the previous quarter and 50% of the purchases of the current quarter. In the second quarter of 19X2, this amount is $77,700 (50% of last quarter's purchases, $155,400) plus $67,200 (50% of the current quarter's purchases, $134,400), or $144,900.

Step 3: Budgeted Operating Expenses and Cash Disbursements for Operating Expenses.   The selling, general, and administrative expenses constitute the total budgeted operating expenses. Management requires that disbursements for budgeted operating expenses must be made based on a cash disbursements schedule. The budgeting process for purchases of long-term assets is included in Chapter 14, "Capital Budgeting."

The operating expense budget is depicted in Exhibit 5-7. The fixed component of wages is $7,500 per quarter. Commissions equal 15% of sales. For example, the projected sales for the second quarter are $240,000; therefore, the projected commissions will be 15% of the $240,000, or $36,000. Miscellaneous expenses (such as computer costs and legal fees) are assumed to be 5% of sales. For example, the miscellaneous expenses for the second quarter would be calculated as 5% of $240,000, or $12,000. Rent, insurance, and depreciation are all fixed costs. They are assumed to be $6,000, $600, and $1,500 per quarter, respectively. The total operating expenses are simply the sum of the above expenses.

The schedule of cash disbursements for budgeted operating expenses shown in Exhibit 5-8 is based on management's assumption that 50% of the wages and commissions will be paid in the quarter incurred and the rest paid in the following quarter. In other words, the quarterly cash disbursements for wages and commissions consist of 50% of the current quarter's wages and commissions plus 50% of the previous quarter's amount. For the second quarter, cash disbursements equal $15,000 (50% of the last quarter's $30,000 expense) plus $21,750 (50% of the second quarter's wages and commissions of $43,500). Rent and insurance are paid in the quarter they are expensed, so the numbers come unaltered from the operating expense budget in Exhibit 5-7.

EXHIBIT 5-7

OPERATING EXPENSE BUDGET

	Q4 19X1	Q1 19X2	Q2 19X2	Q3 19X2	Q4 19X2	19X2 Total
Wages, all fixed	$ 7,500	$ 7,500	$ 7,500	$ 7,500	$ 7,500	$ 30,000
Commission (15% of current quarter's sales)	18,000	22,500	36,000	27,000	22,500	108,000
Total wages and commissions	$25,500	$30,000	$43,500	$34,500	$30,000	$138,000
Miscellaneous expenses (5% of current quarter's sales)	$ 6,000	$ 7,500	$12,000	$ 9,000	$ 7,500	$36,000
Rent	6,000	6,000	6,000	6,000	6,000	24,000
Insurance	600	600	600	600	600	2,400
Depreciation	1,500	1,500	1,500	1,500	1,500	6,000
Subtotal	$14,100	$15,600	$20,100	$17,100	$15,600	$ 68,400
Total operating expenses	$39,600	$45,600	$63,600	$51,600	$45,600	$206,400

EXHIBIT 5-8

CASH DISBURSEMENTS FOR BUDGETED OPERATING EXPENSES

	Q1 19X2	Q2 19X2	Q3 19X2	Q4 19X2	19X2 Total
Wages and Commissions:					
50% of last quarter's expenses	$12,750	$15,000	$21,750	$17,250	$ 66,750
50% of this quarter's expenses	15,000	21,750	17,250	15,000	69,000
Total wages and commissions	$27,750	$36,750	$39,000	$32,250	$135,750
Miscellaneous expenses	7,500	12,000	9,000	7,500	36,000
Rent	6,000	6,000	6,000	6,000	24,000
Total disbursements	$41,250	$54,750	$54,000	$45,750	$195,750

Depreciation and expiration of prepaid insurance are expenses that have no cash flow. Accordingly, they never appear on a cash disbursements schedule.

Step 4: The Budgeted Statement of Cash Receipts and Disbursements.   The budgeted statement of cash receipts and disbursements, or *cash budget*, summarizes the data in the operating budget reflecting budgeted cash receipts and disbursements. The cash budget contains the following information, shown in Exhibit 5-9. A section on the beginning cash balance (equal to the previous ending balance) must be included along with the receipts in order to provide the total cash available prior to any financing

EXHIBIT 5-9

CASH BUDGET

	Q1 19X2	Q2 19X2	Q3 19X2	Q4 19X2	19X2 Total	Data Source
Beginning cash balance	$ 30,000	$ 31,650	$ 32,730	$ 30,285	$ 30,000	
Cash receipts:						
Collections from customers	138,000	204,000	204,000	162,000	708,000	Budgeted cash collections (Exh. 5-4)
W. Total cash available for needs, before financing	$168,000	$235,650	$236,730	$192,285	$738,000	
Cash disbursements:						
Merchandise	$128,100	$144,900	$121,800	$ 98,700	$493,500	Cash disbursements for purchases (Exh. 5-6)
Operating expenses	41,250	54,750	54,000	45,750	195,750	Cash disbursements for budgeted operating expenses (Exh. 5-8)
Truck purchase (given)	9,000	—	—	—	9,000	
X. Total disbursements	$178,350	$199,650	$175,800	$144,450	$698,250	
Minimum cash balance desired	30,000	30,000	30,000	30,000	30,000	
Total cash needed	$208,350	$229,650	$205,800	$174,450	$728,250	
Excess (deficiency) of total cash available over total cash needed before current financing	$(40,350)	$ 6,000	$ 30,930	$ 17,835	$ 9,750	
Financing:						
Borrowings (at beginning)	$ 42,000*				$ 42,000	
Repayments (at end)	—	$ (3,000)	$(27,000)	$(12,000)	(42,000)	
Interest (at 18% per year)†	—	(270)	(3,645)	(2,160)	(6,075)	
Y. Total effects of financing	$ 42,000	$ (3,270)	$(30,645)	$(14,160)	$ (6,075)	
Z. Ending cash balance (W + Y − X)	$ 31,650	$ 32,730	$ 30,285	$ 33,675	$ 33,675	

*Borrowings and repayments of principal are made in multiples of $3,000, at an interest rate of 18% per year.
†Interest computations: $.18 \times \$3,000 \times 6/12 = \$270$; $.18 \times \$27,000 \times 9/12 = \$3,645$; $.18 \times \$12,000 \times 12/12 = \$2160$.

EXHIBIT 5-10

BUDGETED INCOME STATEMENT

For the Year Ended December 31, 19X2

			Data Source
Sales		$720,000	Sales budget (Exhibit 5-3)
Cost of Goods Sold		504,000	Purchases budget (Exhibit 5-5)
Gross Margin		$216,000	
Operating Expenses:			
Wages and Commissions	$138,000		Operating expense budget (Exhibit 5-7)
Miscellaneous Expenses	36,000		Operating expense budget (Exhibit 5-7)
Rent	24,000		Operating expense budget (Exhibit 5-7)
Insurance	2,400		Operating expense budget (Exhibit 5-7)
Depreciation	6,000		
Total Operating Expenses		$206,400	
Income from Operations		$ 9,600	
Interest Expense		6,075	Cash budget (Exhibit 5-9)
Net Income		$ 3,525	

activities (here called line W). The cash receipts are extracted from the totals of the cash collections schedule in Exhibit 5-4. Next is a section on cash disbursements for merchandise purchases (from the schedule in Exhibit 5-6), operating expenses (from the schedule in Exhibit 5-8), and other capital items (in this example, a truck). This section provides the total disbursements for the period (here called line X). In addition, if the organization wishes to maintain a minimum cash balance (in this example, it is $30,000), this amount would be added to total disbursements to provide an estimate of the total cash needed.

The final portion of this section provides amounts for the excess or deficiency of budgeted cash available (or budgeted cash needed) prior to the "financing" arrangements. These financing arrangements consist of borrowing money or repaying previous debts (including interest). This excess or deficiency is equal to the total cash available for needs before financing minus the total cash disbursements and minus the minimum cash balance desired.

A financing section shows the borrowings that are assumed to occur at the beginning of the period and repayments that occur at the end of the period, at which time the interest has been paid. Note that the management accountants would first determine the payment terms in order to develop this cash budget. This statement shows management the total effects of financing, which includes either borrowings or repayments including interest (here called line Y). The financing section of the cash budget in Exhibit 5-9 may be better understood as follows. The first quarter of 19X2 reflects a projected deficit of $40,350. To overcome this deficit, the firm expects to borrow $42,000 (let's assume that it must borrow in multiples of $3,000). In the remaining quarters, the firm will use the excess cash to pay off part of the loan. The interest charge is the interest on the amount repaid; the remaining interest is paid later. For example, in the second quarter there will be excess cash of $6,000. Of this excess, $3,000 will be used to pay off part of the principal. The interest is computed as the principal times the annual rate times the amount of time as monthly fractions of a year. In the second quarter, this interest charge will amount to $270 ($3,000 × .18 × 6/12).

More will be said about the statement of cash receipts and disbursements in Chapter 6.

Step 5: The Budgeted Income Statement.   *A budgeted income statement* is simply a listing of the projected sales less cost of sales less operating expenses less interest. For the example, we obtain a total budgeted net income of $3,525, as shown in Exhibit 5-10. Each of the line items in this income statement has been computed in the totals columns of the schedules in previous exhibits.

Step 6: Budgeted Balance Sheet.   The final statement, the *budgeted balance sheet,* is revealed in Exhibit 5-11. The cash balance is taken from Exhibit 5-9. The balances of the following accounts are found in these exhibits: Accounts Receivable, Exhibit 5-3; Merchandise Inventory, Exhibit 5-5; Accounts Payable, Exhibit 5-5; and Accrued Wages and Commissions Payable, Exhibit 5-7. The remaining three asset balances (Unexpired Insurance; Equipment, Fixtures, and Other; and Accumulated Depreciation) are equal to the beginning balance plus or minus the appropriate adjustment. Finally, owner's equity equals the beginning balance plus net income.

THE MASTER BUDGET FOR A MANUFACTURING FIRM

CHAPTER OBJECTIVE 6
Budgeting steps for manufacturers

The discussion thus far has focused on the master budget and its subsidiary schedules for a merchandising firm. In this section we assume for simplicity that Malux Company is a manufacturer. Consequently, its master budget must be expanded to account for the costs of manufacturing.

Recall that there are three types of manufacturing costs. *Direct materials* are the costs of the raw materials from which the product is made. *Direct labor* is the cost of the labor to make the item. *Overhead* is all other manufacturing costs. The master budget must account for these manufacturing costs.

A merchandiser has one type of inventory, called *merchandise inventory,* consisting of items bought from others and held for resale to customers. In comparison, a manufacturer has three types of inventory. *Raw materials inventory* consists of the raw materials held for production. They have not yet been put into the production process. *Work in process inventory* is the manufacturing costs of items started in production but not yet completed. *Finished goods inventory* consists of the manufacturing costs of items that have completed the production process and are held for sale. It is important to note that the cost of work in process inventory and finished goods inventory—but not raw materials inventory—include the costs of direct materials, direct labor, and overhead.

Steps in the Master Budget Process

The following ten steps are taken to prepare the master budget for a manufacturer:

1. Determine projected sales and cash collections from these sales.
2. Prepare the *production budget,* which estimates how many units will be produced.

EXHIBIT 5-11

BUDGETED BALANCE SHEET

December 31, 19X2

ASSETS

			Data Source
Current Assets			
Cash	$ 33,675		Cash budget (Exhibit 5-9)
Accounts Receivable (.40 × $150,000 fourth quarter sales)	60,000		Sales budget (Exhibit 5-3)
Merchandise Inventory	127,200		Purchases budget (Exhibit 5-5)
Unexpired Insurance ($5,400 old balance − $2,400 expired)	3,000	$223,875	
Plant			
Equipment, Fixtures, and Other ($111,000 + $9,000 truck)	$120,000		Prior balance sheet (Exhibit 5-2)
Accumulated Depreciation ($38,400 + $6,000 depreciation)	44,400	$ 75,600	Income statement and prior balance sheet (Exhibits 5-2 and 5-10)
Total Assets		$299,475	

LIABILITIES AND EQUITIES

Current Liabilities			
Accounts Payable (.5 × $88,200 fourth quarter purchases)	$44,100		Purchases budget (Exhibit 5-5)
Accrued Wages and Commissions Payable (.5 × $30,000)	15,000	$ 59,100	Operating expense budget (Exhibit 5-7)
Owner's Equity			
($236,850 + $3,525 net income)		240,375	Income statement and prior balance sheet (Exhibits 5-2 and 5-10)
Total Liabilities and Owner's Equity		$299,475	

Note: Beginning balances were used as a start for the computations of unexpired insurance, plant, and owner's equity.

3. Project the cost of direct materials for the budgeted number of units.

4. Project the cost of direct labor to produce the budgeted number of units.

5. Project the cost of factory overhead (sometimes called manufacturing overhead) for the budgeted number of units.

6. Prepare the finished goods inventory budget. (We will assume that all units started in production are finished in the same period, thus ignoring work in process for now.)

7. Forecast the operating expenses and the cash disbursements for these expenses.

8. Prepare the cash budget and estimate any necessary financing activities.

EXHIBIT 5-12

PRODUCTION BUDGET

	Quarter				
	Q1	Q2	Q3	Q4	Year
Budgeted unit sales	3,000	4,500	6,000	4,500	18,000
Add: Desired ending inventory of finished goods	900	1,200	900	660	660
Total desired	3,900	5,700	6,900	5,160	18,660
Less: Beginning inventory of finished goods	600	900	1,200	900	600
Units to be produced	3,300	4,800	5,700	4,260	18,060

9. Prepare the budgeted income statement.

10. Prepare the budgeted balance sheet.

Note the similarity between the budgeting processes for merchandiser and manufacturer. Both have the same first step. Step 2 for the merchandiser is similar to step 3 of the manufacturer. Steps 3–6 of the merchandiser correspond to steps 7–10 for the manufacturer. New for the manufacturer are steps 2–6, which pertain only to the manufacturing process. In the example that follows we will concentrate on these new steps in the procedure.

Rather than repeating the entire analysis, especially since so many steps are redundant, we will only demonstrate the new steps and schedules. Also, work in process is ignored for the present.

Step 2: The Production Budget.   Assume that the manufacturing firm estimates its quarterly unit sales for 19X2 as follows:

Q1	Q2	Q3	Q4
3,000	4,500	6,000	4,500

The desired ending inventory of finished goods for each quarter is 20% of the next quarter's projected sales. The *production budget* using these assumptions is shown in Exhibit 5-12. Also assume that sales in first quarter 19X3 are 3,300 units.

The budgeted unit sales plus the desired ending finished goods inventory less the desired beginning finished goods inventory results in the number of units needed to be produced. From this number the manufacturing costs may be projected in Steps 3–6.

Step 3: Direct Materials Budget.   Assume that for each unit to be produced, 3 pounds of raw material is required. Each pound costs $3. Management desires to have on hand in raw materials inventory 25% of the next quarter's budget. With this data, the direct materials budget can be constructed, such as in Exhibit 5-13. Beginning raw materials inventory is 2,500 units.

EXHIBIT 5-13

DIRECT MATERIALS BUDGET

	Q1	Q2	Q3	Q4	Year	Data Source
			Quarter			
Units to be produced	3,300	4,800	5,700	4,260	18,060	Production budget (Exhibit 5-12)
Raw materials needs per unit (lbs.)	× 3	× 3	× 3	× 3	× 3	
Raw materials needed for production (lbs.)	9,900	14,400	17,100	12,780	54,180	
Budgeted ending raw materials inventory (lbs.)*	3,600	4,275	3,195	2,475	2,475	
Total raw materials needed (lbs.)	13,500	18,675	20,295	15,255	56,655	
Less: Beginning raw materials inventory (lbs.)	2,500	3,600	4,275	3,195	2,500	
Raw materials to be purchased (lbs.)	11,000	15,075	16,020	12,060	54,155	
Raw materials cost per lb.	× $3	× $3	× $3	× $3	× $3	
Cost of raw materials to be purchased	$33,000	$45,225	$48,060	$36,180	$162,465	

*25% of the next quarter's production budget. For example, the second quarter production budget is 14,400 lbs. Therefore, the budgeted ending inventory for the first quarter is 25% × 14,400 lbs. = 3,600 lbs.

Production needs (in pounds) are computed by multiplying the units to be produced by the amount of raw materials needed per unit to produce (here, 3 pounds). Ending raw materials inventory equals 25% of next quarter's products. For example, consider the second quarter in Exhibit 5-13. Production needs are 14,400 pounds; therefore, management wants to hold 25% of that amount, or 3,600 pounds, in inventory. Total raw materials needed equals the raw materials needed for production plus the desired ending raw materials inventory. We subtract the beginning inventory of raw materials (the previous quarter's ending inventory of raw materials) to obtain the raw materials to be purchased. By multiplying the cost per pound of the raw materials, we can calculate the total cost of raw materials to be purchased. (Notice the analogy with the purchases of merchandise inventory in Step 2 for a merchandiser. As explained in Chapter 2, the cost of raw materials used is calculated in a way quite similar to cost of goods sold for a merchandiser.) The balance sheet would show the raw materials ending inventory as $7,425 (2,475 pounds × $3).

EXHIBIT 5-14

DIRECT LABOR BUDGET

	Quarter					
	Q1	Q2	Q3	Q4	Year	Data Source
Units to be produced	3,300	4,800	5,700	4,260	18,060	Production
Direct labor time						budget
per unit (hours)	× 2	× 2	× 2	× 2	× 2	(Exh. 5-12)
Total hours of direct						
labor time needed	6,600	9,600	11,400	8,520	36,120	
Direct labor cost						
per hour	× $12	× $12	× $12	× $12	× $12	
Total direct labor cost	$79,200	$115,200	$136,800	$102,240	$433,440	

EXHIBIT 5-15

FACTORY OVERHEAD BUDGET

	Quarter					
	Q1	Q2	Q3	Q4	Year	Data Source
Budgeted direct labor	6,600	9,600	11,400	8,520	36,120	Direct labor
hours						budget
						(Exh. 5-14)
Variable overhead rate	× $1	× $1	× $1	× $1	× $1	
Budgeted variable overhead	$ 6,600	$ 9,600	$11,400	$ 8,520	$ 36,120	
Budgeted fixed overhead	50,000	50,000	50,000	50,000	200,000	
Total budgeted overhead	$56,600	$59,600	$61,400	$58,520	$236,120	

Step 4: The Direct Labor Budget.   Each unit produced requires two hours of direct labor and each hour of direct labor costs $12. From this data we can prepare the **direct labor budget,** shown in Exhibit 5-14.

The total hours of direct labor needed equals the number of units to be produced times the direct labor time per unit (in this case, two). By multiplying the total hours of direct labor time needed by the direct labor cost per hour (in this example, $12), the total direct labor cost is found.

Step 5: The Factory Overhead Budget.   The final manufacturing cost is factory overhead, and it is estimated on the **factory overhead budget,** as shown in Exhibit 5-15. From past experience it is known that the variable portion of the overhead is $1 per direct labor hour. (We will discuss how to compute this figure in Chapter 7.) The variable overhead is then determined by multiplying the budgeted direct labor hours from the direct labor budget in Exhibit 5-14 by the variable overhead rate. The fixed overhead is assumed to be $50,000 per quarter. The total budgeted overhead is found by simply adding together the variable and the fixed components.

Sometimes variable and fixed overhead are bundled together to obtain an overhead rate. To estimate total overhead costs, we would multiply the overhead rate by some value such as direct labor hours. In such cases, overhead is said to be applied at the overhead rate. We will discuss these points in greater detail in Chapters 7 and 8.

Step 6: The Finished Goods Inventory Budget.   These costs can now be accumulated and partitioned between cost of goods sold and the ending finished goods inventory. There are two ways this can be done: the **variable costing** method, displayed in Exhibit 5-16; and the **full costing** method, displayed in Exhibit 5-17. (These topics are fully described in Chapter 13.) The two methods differ in how they treat fixed overhead costs. This will be shown more fully as the example is developed.

The variable production cost per unit is $35, as shown in Exhibit 5-16. This cost per unit includes direct materials (from Exhibit 5-13), direct labor (from Exhibit 5-14), and variable overhead (from Exhibit 5-15).

The budgeted year-end number of units in ending inventory is 660 (see Exhibit 5-12). The cost of finished goods inventory is then 660 × $35, or $23,100. The budgeted number of units sold for the year is 18,000 (again see Exhibit 5-12). The cost of goods sold is comprised of the cost of beginning finished goods inventory plus the cost

---

EXHIBIT 5-16

FINISHED GOODS INVENTORY BUDGET
(VARIABLE COSTING)

			Data Source
Variable production cost per unit			
Direct materials	$	9	Direct materials budget (Exhibit 5-13)
Direct labor		24	Direct labor budget (Exhibit 5-14)
Variable overhead		2	Factory overhead budget (Exhibit 5-15)
Total	$	35	
Budgeted finished goods inventory			
Ending units of finished goods inventory		660	Production budget (Exhibit 5-12)
Variable production cost per unit	×	$35	
Ending finished goods inventory in dollars		$ 23,100	
Budgeted variable cost of goods sold			
Cost of beginning inventory (600 units)		$ 20,400	
Cost of units produced and sold			
(17,400 units × $35)		609,000	
Budgeted cost of goods sold		$629,400	

EXHIBIT 5-17

FINISHED GOODS INVENTORY BUDGET
(FULL COSTING)

Production costs		Data Source
Direct materials (18,060 × $9)	$162,540.00	
Direct labor	433,440.00	Direct labor budget (Exhibit 5-14)
Variable overhead	36,120.00	Factory overhead budget
Fixed overhead	200,000.00	(Exhibit 5-15)
Total production costs	$832,100.00	
Cost per unit ($832,100/18,060) rounded	$ 46.07	
Budgeted ending finished goods inventory		
Ending finished goods inventory, units	660	Production budget (Exhibit 5-12)
Production cost per unit	$ 46.07	
Budgeted ending finished goods inventory	$ 30,406.20	
Budgeted cost of goods sold		
Cost of beginning inventory	$ 27,000.00	
Cost of goods manufactured	832,100.00	
Cost of goods available for sale	$859,100.00	
Cost of ending inventory	30,406.20	
Budgeted cost of goods sold	$828,693.80	

---

of those units produced and sold in the current period. Note that this assumes the use of the first-in, first-out (FIFO) inventory method. Assume the cost of beginning inventory is 600 units times $34 per unit, $20,400. There are 17,400 units produced and sold in the current year and their variable cost is $35 per unit; thus, the total cost is $609,000. These components are added together to obtain $629,400 for the cost of goods sold.

When the budgeted balance sheet is prepared, the ending finished goods inventory is placed in the current assets section. When the budgeted income statement is prepared, the cost of goods sold is put in the variable expenses section and the fixed overhead costs are placed in the fixed expenses section.

The second method of allocating costs, called full costing, includes the fixed overhead costs in inventory and cost of goods sold. This method is reflected in the finished goods inventory budget in Exhibit 5-17.

In full costing, one determines the total production costs (including the variable costs, as before, plus the fixed overhead costs) and the production cost per unit. The budgeted ending finished goods inventory can then be calculated as the production cost per unit times the number of units in ending finished goods inventory.

Budgeted cost of goods sold equals the cost of beginning inventory plus the cost of units produced and sold this period. Assuming that the cost of beginning inventory is $27,000, the cost of the 17,400 units produced and sold ($801,693.80) is found by subtracting the cost of ending finished goods inventory ($30,406.20) from the total production costs ($832,100). The cost of goods sold is $27,000 + $801,693.80 = $828,693.80. Alternatively, as shown in Exhibit 5-17, cost of goods sold equals the cost of beginning inventory ($27,000) plus the cost of goods manufactured ($832,100) minus the loss of ending inventory ($30,406.20).

The budgeted ending finished goods inventory goes on the budgeted balance sheet. The budgeted cost of goods sold goes on the budgeted income statement. Note that there is no separate fixed overhead amount because it is passed on to ending inventory and to cost of goods sold.

The essential difference between variable costing (also called *direct costing*) and full costing (also called *absorption costing*) is the treatment of fixed overhead. Fixed overhead is kept as a separate item in variable costing; it is passed on to inventory and cost of goods sold in full costing.

Steps 7–10. This now completes the steps unique to manufacturers. One would continue to complete the master budget—that is, to prepare the operating expenses budget (step 7), the budgeted cash receipts and disbursements (step 8), the budgeted income statement (step 9), and the budgeted balance sheet (step 10). These steps, however, are essentially the same as the corresponding steps 3–6 for merchandisers.

DECISION SUPPORT SYSTEMS AND BUDGETING

CHAPTER OBJECTIVE 7
Decision support systems

As you can imagine, preparing a full budget for an organization is a substantial and complex task. In addition, the budget must rely on uncertain estimates of future activities. The *sales forecast* is clearly one example of the importance of being able to estimate what might happen in the future. Usually, the sales forecast is under the direction of someone other than the chief management accountant, such as a corporate economist who works closely with the chief management accountant. They must be able to understand the effects of general economic conditions, competition, the interrelationships of variables that affect the sales pattern, market research studies, and a variety of possible marketing plans. Developing sales estimates requires an eclectic viewpoint and the ability to work with subjective opinions and highly qualitative methods. None of these provides definitive answers for estimating future sales.

Finally, nonprofit organizations and government entities face severe difficulties in forecasting revenues. For example, a state may have forecast that oil prices would be at a certain level in order to estimate the gasoline tax revenue generated for its highway funds, only to find that current oil prices vary significantly from what was estimated due to a geopolitical event. Or a city may ordinarily rely on substantial tax revenues from tourists but discover that vacation travel patterns have changed since the previous year for a variety of reasons. Regardless of whether the budget is for a profit-making organization or a nonprofit organization, each of these examples shows that it is based on a set of assumptions that must be reviewed continually.

There are a number of **financial planning languages** that allow users to take a "model-building" approach (constructing equations to solve for financial variables) to the master budget. Many financial planning languages, and spreadsheet programs such as Lotus 1-2-3, use a nonprocedural English-like language in which the user may model the particular situation. Many financial planning languages also allow users to test the degree of change in net income or other significant variables by changing the assumptions through either sensitivity (what-if) analysis or through a simulation (attatching probability estimates to the numbers and determining the average expected results). Finally, some of the financial planning languages enable management accountants to develop a master budget with selected constraints and to optimize functions (linear programming) such as those discussed in Chapter 4 within that master budget.

BEHAVIORAL ASPECTS OF THE BUDGETING PROCESS

CHAPTER OBJECTIVE 8
Behavioral aspects

Budgeting is a dynamic process in which subordinates and supervisors alike must interact constructively and communicate wisely in order to achieve goal congruence. Budgeting is also a planning and control function, and managers' effectiveness and efficiency are measured against rising standards, with incentives and penalties assessed to match their performance. Clearly, therefore, the need for effective human relations skills in the budgeting process cannot be overstated.

Indeed, behavioral factors are becoming increasingly critical as budgets become more important as a planning tool. In their emerging role as the primary means of organizational planning, budgets also become the primary means of control—and thus affect organizational behavior to a greater extent than ever before.

It is easy to visualize a scenario in which the budget is manipulated as more and more pressure is brought to bear on managers to meet the budget or to create a budget that is acceptable to top management. Managers would respond by avoiding honest, objective analyses of budgets in preparation, preferring to engage in "budget games." For example, a subordinate might pad an expense account to allow for cost overruns or other inefficiencies (also referred to as budget slack).

Management needs good budget data because of the interlinking nature of the subbudgets. If an element or a segment of the organization perceives that it needs to manipulate the numbers through its data flows in order to be fairly represented in the final budget, the rest of the budget cycle will be affected by way of related budgets of many other departments. Effective use of budgets requires commitment and dedication on the part of management.

From time to time, a variety of budgeting methods arise into use, receive attention, and fall into disfavor. One of those in the recent past has been program, planning, budgeting systems (PPBS) in which the budget requests were classified by programs. Its primary use was for nonprofit organizations in which the budget preparer incorporated subjective and objective analysis of the benefits derived from a particular expenditure. In addition, PPBS was also used for some long-range planning goals, which depended on subjective analysis of expectations for validity. Variations of PPBS can be found today.

Another new approach is zero-based budgeting, in which management is required to estimate what resources it would need if the organization or department had to start over from nothing. Management must therefore justify every cost within the proposal. The assumption is that this process would provide checks and balances within the budget process for all items in order to minimize the amount of "deadwood" or slack within the budget. In concept, this seems a reasonable approach. Operationally, it meets with great difficulty because a great deal of effort is necessary to go back to zero and start over. The more appropriate response to zero-based budgeting requirements may be to analyze certain subsegments within a segment on a zero-based budgeting cycle of perhaps three to five years. In other words, each three to five years a particular element would be heavily scrutinized to the extent that its portion of the master budget would be zero based.

FINANCIAL PLANNING SYSTEM FOR A BANK

The following is an excerpt from an article, first published in 1981, discussing the successful implementation of a financial planning system at the then Louisiana National Bank, now part of Premier Bancorp. It is based on interviews with officers of the bank. Although you should focus on the system's budgeting features for this chapter, you may recognize aspects of our discussions from other chapters. Also briefly discussed in the article, but not included here for space reasons, are examples of how this system aided in the bank's asset/liability management and how it helped the bank's managers respond to changes in liquidity, overhead expenses, and banking regulation.

In the fall of 1973, the Louisiana National Bank in Baton Rouge was faced with decreasing profits and an increasing level of short-term borrowed funds. The situation was not responding to traditional management practices, and the underlying reasons were not obvious.

Since the early 1960s, the bank had made innovation its unofficial trademark. It was first in the city to offer credit cards and automatic teller machines (ATMs). It developed a sophisticated computerized financial accounting system and an advanced transaction cost accounting system.

While innovation was significant in marketing and operations, the bank held to traditional management policies in asset/liability management until 1973. Lending officers granted loans to credit worthy customers at the prevailing interest rates. Public deposits were actively sought. In short, the bank accepted all deposits offered and gave loans to anyone who met credit standards.

Against this background, in mid-1973 the bank found itself in trouble. Daily operations were characterized by excessive short-term borrowing to support the expanding loan portfolio and bank examiners were indicating displeasure with the bank's liquidity position. In the words of the chief financial officer, "We suddenly discovered that we were not making money. More seriously, we did not know why."

THE FINANCIAL PLANNING SYSTEM

To tackle the problem, the bank decided to implement a set of tools that would meet the challenge of the situation. The statement of management needs was straightforward: Something to help manage the bank at the top level, especially in the areas of profit planning and liquidity analysis. The need was not phrased in terms of technology or information required, but in terms of final results.

The specific task evolved as the development and implementation of a system that would provide reporting, analysis and forecasting. The resulting system extracts data from primary management information systems and presents it in summary reports; forecasts the coming 12 months and five years on a "constant horizon" basis; and analyzes the historical data and emphasizes key asset/liability management issues such as resource allocations, interest rates, liquidity, growth and capital. . . .

BENEFITS

The top management team is unanimous in its praise of the system; indeed the most important benefit is that it has helped make the bank more profitable. LNB's profit had fallen from $3.4 million in 1972 to $2.5 million in 1973 and $2.1 million in 1974. In 1975, LNB's profits rebounded to $3.9 million, an increase of 92% over the previous year. The chairman of the board attributed the profit turnaround to ". . . management's creative use of the Financial Planning System. The system enabled us to identify ways to restructure our asset and liability relationships and allowed us to test alternative action plans." . . .

HOW THE SYSTEM IS USED

The planning system (FPS) is used in three general ways: At the beginning of each month to report the previous month's activity; during the month to explore special issues or prepare strategic plans; and in the fall of each year to facilitate the budgeting process.

FPS produces the primary input to the planning committee meeting on the first Tuesday of each month. The committee is comprised of the chairman and CEO, the president, the chief financial officer, and the vice presidents in charge of each major market segment of the bank. The vice president of corporate planning uses FPS to prepare the reports and graphs and serves as the resource for questions about the information. The general purpose of this meeting is to review the previous month's performance, examine the newly prepared 12-month forecast and discuss anticipated changes or pending issues.

There are frequently questions and possibilities which need to be explored further with additional runs of FPS and considered at the next meeting. The committee currently meets twice a month, but in periods of rapid change or when a major set of strategies is under consideration, it meets weekly. The system is frequently used to prepare forecasts which test alternative strategies. Every officer has become interested in the bankwide impact of decisions because they all know their recommendations and actions will be examined in this context.

Special runs are also done to investigate the impact of pending changes in money market rates, banking regulations, market trends and internal policy changes.

Although completely separate, the financial planning system facilitates the budgeting process in the fall of the year. The budget is a detailed accounting budget, part of the automated financial control system which includes a cost accounting module, the general ledger and the budgeting system. A "grass roots" budget, as it is called, is composed of about 9,000 data items—one for each budget line item, for each of the cost centers, for each of the 12 months of the coming year.

The data are initially gathered from the cost center managers and entered into the budgeting sytem. Summaries are then extracted and entered into FPS in the same way that actual data are transferred after the end of each month. The tentative budget summary is then analyzed using FPS to assess the combined impact of the budget estimates, examine the reasonableness of the estimates compared to top management's judgment and search for any inconsistencies in interrelated areas. If necessary, adjustments are made through negotiation between top management and cost center managers, and the budget is approved by mid-December. The detailed budget is then carried in the automated accounting system, which produces monthly budget variance reports for each cost center during the year. The summary form of the budget is also stored in FPS for use in summary reports and comparative analyses.

It is important to note that the bank considered and rejected a combined budgeting/planning system. Management found that there are major differences in the purpose, procedure and format of budgeting versus planning. The budget mechanism is primarily a motivation and control device that requires fine levels of detail. Such detail tends to become "quicksand" for planning. Effective planning on concise data can reveal rather than obscure trends and underlying relationships. Plans must also be subject to change and extend across fiscal year reporting boundaries. For these reasons, FPS was designed to be separate from the budgeting segment of the automated accounting system.

A DECISION SUPPORT SYSTEM

The evolution of information technology has seen major developments, successes, failures and shifts in thinking. The concept of large-scale, all encompassing "management information systems" was recognized in the early 1970s. More recently, however, the concept of top management, modeling-based, summary-level "decision support systems," has become recognized as a logical approach for strategic analysis, planning and decision making. The financial planning system at Louisiana National Bank is a good illustration of a decision support system. The system is a summary model of the bank's automated financial control system; operates in an on-line computer environment which gives managerial access at any time rather than on a fixed processing schedule; permits experimental forecasting to test alternative assumptions and strategies; uses its own independent data base; and permits rapid redesign to accommodate changing circumstances.

(continued)

SYSTEM COMPONENTS

Data

At the end of each month, summary accounting data are extracted from the general ledger system. The process of reformatting and data entry requires about two hours of clerical effort. No adjustments or modifications are made to the data; that is, the summary statements produced by FPS will agree precisely with those produced by general ledger. As we shall see, this is a critical point.

Each month, the data are added to the historical data base which maintains up to three years of monthly figures and up to 7.5 years of quarterly figures. In addition, 12 periods of future data in the same format are maintained. These data are developed from the forecasting and simulation capability.

Reports and Analysis

Each month the system produces a full set of summary financial statements, including the balance sheet, income statement and standard operating ratio reports. The current monthly actual data are compared with the forecast, budget and actual for the previous year. The system also produces a series of special reports which analyze critical areas of the bank. Of particular importance is the interest rate-volume-mix analysis, and an analysis of product lines. The latter portrays the sources and uses of funds for three major segments of the bank—retail or consumer sector, public sector and commercial sector.

Forecasts

The reports outlined above are also available for each of the coming 12 months which are forecast by the system. Independent variables may be entered by management or generated by statistical techniques with management override capability. A built-in optimization model is available when needed. The forecast is a "rolling" or "constant horizon" forecast, always covering the next 12 periods, and is recast at the beginning of each new month. In addition, the bank may expand the horizons as far into the future as it desires on a monthly or quarterly basis.

CONTINUING BENEFITS

The continued growth and profitability of the bank is paralleled by a set of interacting benefits involving the planning system that facilitate management of the bank. Some of these contributing benefits include the following:

● Establishing a mechanism for managing the balance sheet over time. Two important parts of this mechanism are liquidity management and the capital analysis that monitors the bank's most critical constraints.

● Providing a framework and structured discipline around which to organize and coordinate the decision-making of the top management team. Such a system gets everyone focused on the same issues and working toward the same organizational goals.

● Providing a mechanism for statisfying the bank examiners' reporting requirements, and giving management a tool for communicating its analyses to the examiners.

● Enabling the top management team to anticipate and respond to changes in regulations, market opportunities and internal operations.

● Reducing the clerical cost, time and effort of preparing required periodic reports for management, regulators and others. . . .

A recent analysis revealed a growth in credit card loans beyond the ability of the retail sector to support them. A decision was made to sell off a large portion of credit card loans. With the bank's history as the regional lender in credit cards, this move would have been strongly opposed by several managers without the convincing analysis generated through the use of the FPS. . . .

SOURCE: Adapted from Ronald L. Olson and Ralph H. Sprague, "Financial Planning in Action," *The Magazine of Bank Administration* (February 1981), pp. 54–64. Copyright 1981 by Bank Administration Institute. Reprinted by permission.

Demonstration Problem

The following data relate to Garland Company:

a. Cash balance on October 31 was $74,400.

b. Sales for October were $492,000.

c. Expected sales for November are $630,000.

d. Purchases for October were $384,000.

e. Expected purchases for November are $336,000.

f. Expected cash selling expenses for November are $108,200.

g. Expected cash administrative expenses for November are $95,200.

h. In the month of sale 70% of sales are collected; the remaining 30% are collected in the following month. All purchases are made on credit and are paid for fully in the month following the purchase.

REQUIRED

Calculate the planned cash balance on November 30.

SOLUTION TO DEMONSTRATION PROBLEM

Garland Company
Cash Budget
For the Month of November

Cash receipts

Current sales (70% × $630,000)	$441,000
Accounts receivable (30% × $492,000)	147,600
	$588,600

Cash disbursements

Purchases—accounts payable	$384,000
Selling expenses	108,200
General and administrative expenses	95,200
	$587,400

Cash balance

Beginning cash balance	$ 74,400
Receipts	588,600
Disbursements	(587,400)
Ending cash balance	$ 75,600

Review of Chapter Objectives

1. Explain the planning aspects of budgeting (pp. 143-44).

   ■ Planning is a way of preparing for the future so that one can anticipate and capitalize on opportunities and be prepared for problems. A budget is a quantitative model of a plan developed by management. Budgeting does not encompass all of planning, for there are many qualitative variables to consider. Budgeting does help, however, since it expresses the financial expectations for the firm as a whole.

2. Explain the control aspects of budgeting (pp. 144–45).

- Control is the process of trying to match up actual performance with the planned objectives and goals. Did a manager perform as expected? If not, why not? Such questions are the essence of the control process.

- To achieve more effective control, managers must communicate effectively with one another. The master budget is one vehicle for increasing communication, since it articulates who is responsible for what and expresses what each segment of the firm is expected to accomplish. It makes visible the organization's expectations for its segments and provides guidelines that will be used to evaluate performance.

- Both planning aspects and control aspects can generally be improved by participative budgeting. This means that those affected by the budget should have something to say about it. In other words, it allows those to be controlled by the budget a chance to challenge the assumptions of the budget and the reasonableness of the expectations. Such an interactive communication often leads to more realistic budgets, enhances the planning process, and allows a fairer method for evaluating performance, improving the control process.

- For budgets to be effective control devices, several things are needed. A good information system is required, one must have the ability to partition the costs and revenues in a useful fashion, controllable items need to be distinguished from noncontrollable ones, and the budget must be generated sufficiently early and in enough detail so that managers can try to achieve the goals.

3. Describe the interdependencies of the master budget and the subsidiary budgets (pp. 145–47).

- This learning objective is met by studying and understanding Exhibit 5-1, which summarizes graphically the interrelationships among the various budgets.

- The sales budget often drives the rest of the schedules. Sales levels determine the production goals that need to be achieved and the various other expenses which are necessary to support sales. These also affect the cash budget, in which the actual receipts (inflows) and disbursements (outflows) of cash are estimated. These items in turn affect the budgeted income statement and the budgeted balance sheet.

4. Explain continuous budgeting and participative budgeting (pp. 147–48).

- A continuous budget is a budget prepared for a constant amount of time into the future. It helps managers focus on the future by planning within this fixed time horizon.

- In participative budgeting, the subordinates help to determine the budget. This motivates employees to commit themselves to the budget and to try to achieve the goals of the organization.

5. Discuss the steps in the preparation of the master budget for a merchandiser (pp. 148–57).

- There are six steps to preparing the master budget for a merchandiser. First, determine projected sales and cash collections from these sales. Second, estimate purchases of inventory and cash payments for these purchases. Third, forecast the operating expenses and the cash disbursements for these expenses. Fourth, prepare the cash budget, which is simply a listing of the projected cash receipts and disbursements and any necessary financing activities. Fifth, prepare the budgeted income statement. Sixth, prepare the budgeted balance sheet.

■ An extended illustration was given in the text to show the mechanics of the process. Do not get lost in the detail; keep a clear head about what is desired and the master budget becomes relatively clear. The cash budget is very important because it shows whether the firm will generate funds or whether top management should prepare to seek financing. To establish a cash budget, estimate the cash receipts from sales and the cash disbursements from purchases and other operating expenses.

■ Another product of the budgeting process is the budgeted income statement. This report helps managers assess the efficiency of operations. To prepare a budgeted income statement, one needs an estimate of sales, cost of goods sold, and operating expenses.

■ A third product from the budgeting process is the budgeted balance sheet. This helps managers determine whether its debt and equity proportions are desirable and see the growth in assets. To construct a balance sheet, the accountant needs the previous balance sheet and the changes in the accounts, such as Cash, Accounts Receivable, and Inventory.

6. Prepare and analyze inventory management budgets for a manufacturer (pp. 157–64).

■ This learning objective focuses on the steps in the preparation of the master budget for a manufacturer. We have stated it in these terms because the steps for a manufacturer are like those for a merchandiser, except for the inventory budgets.

■ As does the merchandiser, the manufacturer begins with the sales budget. The difference between the two types of organization arises at this point. After completing the sales budget, the manufacturer forecasts various aspects of manufacturing inventory: the production budget, followed by the forecasts of the cost of direct materials, cost of direct labor, cost of factory overhead, and cost of finished goods inventory.

7. Identify decision support systems for budgeting (pp. 164–68).

■ Performing what-if analyses on estimated sales is an important feature of real-world sales forecasts. Such forecasts are critical but difficult to estimate. Asking what-if questions can sensitize managers to the impact of various changes in the sales forecast.

■ Financial planning languages exist to carry out the analysis directly. The user can perform what-if analyses, goal-seeking, and analysis of the variables.

8. Discuss the behavioral aspects of budgeting (p. 165).

■ Perhaps the most interesting aspect of budgeting involves budget slack. Nearly everyone is averse to evaluation, especially if there exists the chance of negative evaluation and its possible negative consequences. So managers must watch for subordinates and colleagues creating slack in their budgets in an attempt to minimize the risk of not meeting the budget.

■ There are several innovations in the budgeting process that attempt to overcome the difficulties of budgeting. Program, planning, budgeting systems try to focus on program activity. Zero-based budgeting requires a complete justification for proposals and is an attempt to reduce budget slack.

Glossary

budget   Quantification of a plan.

budget committee   A steering committee to advise the chief management accountant or chief financial officer and coordinate the overall budget process.

budget slack   Padding in the budget, usually by lowering revenues or increasing expenses, to make budgeted levels easier to achieve.

budgetary control   The actions necessary to ensure that budget objectives, plans, policies, and standards are attained or revised.

budgeted balance sheet   Balance sheet prepared as a result of predicted operations linking the previous balance sheet to the budgeted income statement.

budgeted income statement   Income statement prepared as a result of predicted operations.

budgeting   The process of planning all flows of financial resources into, within, and from an entity during some specified future period. It includes providing for the detailed allocation of expected available future resources to projects, functions, responsibilities, and time periods.

cash budget   A period-by-period statement of cash on hand at the start of a budget period; expected cash receipts classified by source; expected cash disbursements classified by function, responsibility, and form; and the resulting cash balance at the end of the budget period.

continuous budget   A budget that adds a time period in the future as the time period just ended is dropped.

direct labor budget   A budget that estimates the cost of direct labor for the future production process.

direct materials budget   A budget that estimates the purchases of direct or raw materials.

factory overhead budget   A prediction of all production costs for a budget period, except direct material and direct labor costs, classified by responsibility, function, or form.

financial planning languages   Programming languages that permit modeling of the financial interactions and simulation of the results.

full costing   A method of costing which allocates the fixed overhead to ending inventory and cost of goods sold.

goals   An objective established to coordinate and direct a group in the pursuit of desired activities.

master budget   A set of interrelated budgets depicting the interrelationships of all the subsidiary budgets.

operating expense budget   A schedule of the various production, administration, and distribution expenses, classified by the nature of the expense, of an organizational unit or subunit required to attain unit objectives during a period.

participative budgeting   A budgeting approach in which subordinates and supervisors work together to establish the budget.

production budget   A prediction of the cost of producing the goods needed to meet the sales budget and maintain suitable inventories.

program, planning, budgeting systems   Budgets classified by programs. Used by some non-profit organizations.

purchases budget   A prediction, by types of material, of the cost and time needed to provide budgeted material requirements.

sales budget   A prediction, classified by responsibility, product, and area, of the net revenue from sales expected to be available to an organization in a period of time.

sales forecasting   A prediction of the sales for the budget period using various data and methods such as trend projections, correlation analysis, operations research techniques, and computer simulation, or less rigorous prediction procedures.

variable costing   A method of costing that does not allocate fixed overhead to ending inventory and cost of goods sold. Instead, fixed overhead is kept as a separate expense on the income statement.

zero-based budgeting   The process of developing a periodic budget on the assumption that the enterprise is initiating operations at the beginning of the budget period; thus a total budget must be developed anew for each successive period rather than relying on budgets based on incremental changes from period to period.

Review Questions

5-1   Define the terms *budget, master budget,* and *cash budget.*

5-2   What are the three main objectives of budgeting?

5-3   Why is budgeting so inextricably linked with planning and with control?

5-4   Provide an outline advocating budgeting to a management group that has not formally used budgeting as a management tool.

5-5   Do you agree or disagree that the basis for performance evaluation should be budgeted performance rather than past performance? Why?

5-6   Why is communications so important to the budget process?

5-7   What is participative budgeting? How is this process controlled?

5-8   What are the steps for preparing the master budget for a merchandising organization?

5-9   Why is the sales forecast or sales budget the driving force in the entire budget process?

5-10

5-11   Does the cash budget focus only on the ending balance of cash in the budgeted balance sheet? If not, why not?

5-12   List the contents of a cash budget.

5-13   Define the term "financing" in cash budgets. Describe two general types of financing.

5-14   What can a company do it if finds out that its projected asset level (a) exceeds the amount of financing available? (b) Is less than the amount of financing available?

5-15   Why do cash receipts and disbursements sometimes occur in different months or quarters than sales revenues, purchases, and expenses?

5-16   What are the steps for preparing the master budget for a manufacturing organization?

5-17   What is the difference between an "imposed" budget and a "participatory" budget?

5-18   What is zero-base budgeting? How can it differ from an incremental approach to budgeting in its effect on expense items?

Discussion Questions

5-19   The chapter listed the steps to follow in preparing a master budget when the organization is a merchandising firm or when it is a manufacturer. What would be the steps for a service organization?

5-20   Jack and Jill are twin teenagers whose parents have instituted a point system for doing chores around the house. When they get a certain number of points, they receive privileges, such as the use of a car. What games can they play with this budget system?

5-21   (a) Describe, in general terms, a computerized procedure a company could use in determining short-term cash needs. (b) Discuss the future of budgeting in relationship to the power of financial planning languages and computers. What do you perceive as the advantages of these computer models as well as the disadvantages of the same models?

5-22   Rouge Corporation is a medium-sized company in the steel fabrication industry with six divisions located in different areas of the United States. Considerable autonomy in operational management is permitted in the divisions, due in part to the distance between corporate head-quarters in St. Louis and five of the six divisions. Corporate management establishes divisional budgets using data for the prior year adjusted for industry and economic changes expected for the coming year. Budgets are prepared by year and by quarter, with top management attempting to recognize problems unique to each division in the divisional budget-setting process. Once the year's divisional budgets have been set by corporate management, they cannot be modified by division management.

The budget for calendar year 19X6 projects total corporate net income before taxes of $3,750,000 for the year, including $937,500 for the first quarter. Results of first-quarter opera-tions presented to corporate management in early April showed corporate net income of $865,000, which was $72,500 below the projected net income for the quarter. The St. Louis divi-sion operated at 4.5% above its projected divisional net income, whereas the other five divisions showed net incomes with variances ranging from 1.5% to 22% below budgeted net income.

Corporate management is concerned with the first-quarter results because it believes strongly that differences among divisions had been recognized. An entire day in late November of last year had been spent presenting and explaining the corporate and divisional budgets to the division managers and their division controllers. A mid-April meeting of corporate and division manage-ment generated unusual candor. All five out-of-state division managers cited reasons why the first-quarter results in their respective divisions represented effective management and were the best that could be expected. Corporate management remained unconvinced and informed divi-sion managers that "results will be brought into line with the budget by the end of the second quarter."

a.   Identify the major defects in the procedures used by Rouge Corporation's corporate manage-ment in preparing and implementing the divisional budgets.

b.   Discuss the behavioral problems that may arise by requiring Rouge Corporation's division managers to meet the quarterly budgeted net income figures as well as the annual budgeted net income.

5-23   Springfield, Inc., operates on a calendar-year basis. It begins the annual budgeting process in late August, when the president establishes targets for the total dollar sales and net income before taxes for the next year.

The sales target is given to the marketing department, where the marketing manager formu-lates a sales budget by product line in both units and dollars. From this budget, sales quotas by product line in units and dollars are established for each of the corporation's sales districts.

The marketing manager also estimates the cost of the marketing activities required to support the target sales volume and prepares a tentative marketing expense budget.

The executive vice president uses the sales and profit targets, the sales budget by product line, and the tentative marketing expense budget to determine the dollar amounts that can be devoted to manufacturing and corporate office expense. The executive vice president prepares the budget for corporate expenses, and then forwards to the production department the product-line sales budget in units and the total dollar amount that can be devoted to manufacturing.

The production manager meets with the factory managers to develop a manufacturing plan that will produce the required units when needed within the cost constraints set by the executive vice president. The budgeting process usually comes to a halt at this point because the production department does not consider the financial resources allocated to be adequate.

When this standstill occurs, the vice president of finance, the executive vice president, the marketing manager, and the production manager meet to determine the final budgets for each of the areas. This normally results in a modest increase in the total amount available for manufactur-ing costs, while the marketing expense and corporate office expense budgets are cut. The total sales and net income figures proposed by the president are seldom changed. Although the participants are seldom pleased with the compromise, these budgets are final. Each executive then develops a new detailed budget for the operations in his or her area.

None of the areas has achieved its budget in recent years. Sales often run below the target. When budgeted sales are not achieved, each area is expected to cut costs so that the president's profit target can still be met. However, the profit target is seldom met because costs are not cut enough. In fact, costs often run above the original budget in all functional areas. The president is disturbed that Springfield has not been able to meet the sales and profit targets. He hired a consultant with considerable experience with companies in Springfield's industry. The consultant reviewed the budgets for the past four years. He concluded that the product-line sales budgets were reasonable and that the cost and expense budgets were adequate for the budgeted sales and production levels.

a. Discuss how the budgeting process used by Springfield, Inc., contributes to the failure to achieve the president's sales and profit targets.

b. Suggest how Springfield's budgeting process could be revised to correct the problems.

c. Should the functional areas be expected to cut their costs when sales volume falls below budget? Explain your answer.

Exercises

CO 5 (Steps 1–2)

5-24 BUDGETED CASH RECEIPTS Kyle Corporation has a December 31, 19X0, Accounts Receivable balance of $138,000, of which $108,000 are from December's sales. Sales for January 19X1 are budgeted at $330,000. Sixty percent of sales are collected in the month of sale, 25% in the following month, and 15% in the second following month. Prepare an estimate of cash receipts for January, 19X1.

CO 5 (Steps 1–2)

5-25 BUDGETED CASH RECEIPTS Bradley Company has budgeted sales for the first three quarters of 19X1. The estimates are: first quarter, $150,000; second quarter, $120,000; third quarter, $180,000. Seventy percent of sales are collected in the quarter of sale, and 28% of sales are collected in the following quarter. The remaining 2% of sales are uncollectible. Calculate Bradley Company's estimated cash receipts for the third quarter of 19X1.

CO 5 (Steps 1–2)

5-26 BUDGETED CASH RECEIPTS The following data apply to the collection of accounts receivable for McCoy Company:

1. Current balance, March 31, $175,000 (of which $120,000 relates to March sales).

2. Planned sales for April, $800,000.

3. Seventy percent of sales is collected in the month of sale; 20% in the following month; and the remaining 10% in the second month after the sale.

Prepare a schedule of planned collections and ending balance for accounts receivable as of April 30, 19X1.

CO 5 (Step 3)

5-27 PURCHASES BUDGET Slipper Shoe Store has prepared the following sales budget for the first four months of 19X1:

January	February	March	April
$75,600	$54,000	$64,800	$72,000

Cost of goods sold is 60% of sales, and the company likes to have enough inventory on hand at the end of a month to cover 80% of the next month's sales. The ending inventory on December 31, 19X0, was $36,288. Prepare a purchases budget for each of the first three months of 19X1.

5-28   PURCHASES BUDGET Mediocre Company has prepared its sales budget for the first two quarters of 19X1. Budgeted sales in units are 240,000 in the first quarter and 420,000 in the second quarter. The company likes to maintain an inventory at the end of each quarter equal to 25% of the next quarter's budgeted sales. The company had 45,000 units in inventory on December 31, 19X0. How many units does the Mediocre Company need to purchase during the first quarter of 19X1?

CO 5 (Step 3)

5-29   BUDGETED CASH DISBURSEMENTS The following data from Watson, Inc., is gathered so that the cash budget can be prepared:

CO 5 (Step 4)

	Purchases	Sales
January	$12,600	$21,600
February	4,400	19,800
March	10,800	18,000
April	16,200	23,400

Collections from Watson's customers are normally 70% in the month of sale, and 20% and 9% respectively, in the two months following the sale. The balance is uncollectible. Watson takes full advantage of the 2% discount allowed on purchases paid for by the tenth of the following month. Purchases for May are budgeted at $18,000, and sales for May are forecast at $19,800. Cash disbursements for expenses are expected to be $4,320 for May. Watson's cash balance on May 1 was $6,600.

a. What are the expected cash collections during May?

b. What are the expected cash disbursements for May?

c. What is the expected cash balance on May 31?

5-30   BUDGETED CASH DISBURSEMENTS Aloe Company is preparing its cash budget for the next month. Projections for the month include the following:

CO 5 (Step 4)

Sales	$600,000
Gross profit (based on sales)	25%
Increase in merchandise inventory	$45,000
Decrease in trade accounts payable (purchases)	$18,000

What are the estimated cash disbursements for merchandise inventory?

5-31   BUDGETED CASH DISBURSEMENTS Heyne Company is preparing its cash budget for the month of October. The following information is available concerning its inventories:

Inventories at beginning of October	$ 22,500
Estimated purchases for October	110,000
Estimated cost of goods sold for October	112,500

Estimated payments in October for purchases in September	18,750
Estimated payments in October for purchases prior to September	5,000
Estimated payments in October for purchases in October	75%

What are the estimated total cash disbursements for inventories in October?

5-32 BUDGETED CASH DISBURSEMENTS Lampke Company has projected purchases for 19X1 to be $110,000 in the first quarter, $140,000 in the second quarter, $130,000 in the third quarter, and $180,000 in the fourth quarter. All purchases are made on credit. Eighty percent of purchases are paid for in the quarter purchased; 20% are paid for in the quarter following purchase. Other cash expenses paid each quarter are: taxes, $20,000; wages and salaries, $60,000; rent, $8,000; interest, $2,000; and miscellaneous, $1,500. Calculate the planned cash disbursements for the second, third, and fourth quarters.

CO 5 (Step 4)

5-33 BUDGETED CASH RECEIPTS AND DISBURSEMENTS Selected account balances of Farthing Company at December 31, 19X1, are:

CO 5 (Step 5)

Accounts Payable	$37,500
Accrued Wages Payable	3,500
Accounts Receivable	45,000
Prepaid Expenses	5,500
Accrued Taxes Payable	27,500

For the month of January 19X2, the following estimates have been compiled:

Net sales	$137,500
Purchases	100,000
Wages expense	37,500
Rent expense	2,750
Taxes expense	2,500

All sales are on a credit basis, with approximately 70% collected in the month of sale and the balance in the following month. Purchases are paid for one-half in the month of purchase and the balance in the following month. Wages are paid 90% in the month of incurrence and the balance in the following month. Rent expense results from the amortization of the prepaid rent (shown as prepaid expenses of $5,500). Property taxes are due in February.

Calculate the estimated cash receipts and disbursements for Farthing Company for January.

5-34 BUDGETED CASH RECEIPTS AND DISBURSEMENTS Bezel Company sells desk clocks at $35 each. Sales for next quarter (ending June 30) are estimated at 1,600 clocks. Sales for the preceding quarter (ending March 31) were 1,300 clocks. Eighty percent of sales are cash sales, and the remainder are credit sales. All credit sales are collected in the month following sale. Prepare a schedule of planned cash receipts for the quarter ending June 30. Will the company need to borrow any money next quarter if it desires to maintain a minimum cash balance of $8,000? If so, how much? (Assume planned cash disbursements total $62,400 and that the beginning cash balance is $13,500.)

CO 5 (Step 5)

CO 6 (Step 2)

5-35 PRODUCTION BUDGET Webster Company's sales officer estimated sales for the year as follows:

Quarter	Units
First	3,000
Second	4,000
Third	2,250
Fourth	2,750
Total	12,000

Inventory at the end of the prior year and at the end of this year was budgeted at 900 units. The quantity of finished goods inventory at the end of each quarter is equal to 30% of the next quarter's budgeted sales in units. Provide a production budget.

CO 6 (Steps 1–2)

5-36 SALES AND PRODUCTION BUDGETS Jordan Shoe Company has decided to produce 180,000 pairs of shoes at a uniform rate in 19X1. The sales department has estimated sales for 19X1 according to the following schedule:

	Sales in units
First quarter	49,500
Second quarter	42,750
Third quarter	40,500
Fourth quarter	63,000
Total for 19X1	195,750

The December 31, 19X0, inventory is estimated to be 20,250 pairs of shoes. Prepare a schedule of planned sales and production (in units) for each of the quarters of 19X1.

CO 6 (Step 2)

5-37 PRODUCTION BUDGET Inflexible Company manufactures and sells a single product. Each product requires three pounds of raw material that costs $3.30 per pound. The company wants to have enough raw materials inventory on hand at the end of each month to cover the next month's budgeted production. The company also wants to have enough units in finished goods inventory at the end of each month to cover 50% of the next month's sales forecast.

On June 30, 19X1, Inflexible had the following inventories:

Raw materials	399,000 pounds
Finished goods	49,000 units

Given the following monthly sales estimates, prepare monthly production budgets for July, August, and September of 19X1 and purchases budgets for July and August of 19X1.

Sales Estimates for 19X1 (in units)

July	August	September	October
105,000	126,000	140,000	147,000

5-38 PRODUCTION BUDGET Kim Company has estimated sales of 5,000 units of Product Q during the next month. Production of one unit of Product Q requires two units of Material E.

CO 6 (Step 2)

	Actual on Hand	Budgeted End of Month
Product Q	1,000	500
Material E	1,250	900

How many units of Material E is Kim Company planning to purchase during the month?

5-39 BUDGETED INVENTORY Sales for next quarter are budgeted at 120,000 units. Finished goods inventory at the end of this quarter is 24,000 units. Planned production for next quarter is 168,000 units. Calculate the budgeted finished goods inventory at the end of next quarter.

CO 6 (Step 6)

5-40 BUDGETED INVENTORY Olive Oil Company has forecast its sales for the coming year as follows:

CO 6 (Step 6)

First quarter	40,000 units
Second quarter	64,000
Third quarter	80,000
Fourth quarter	48,000

There are 16,000 units in inventory at the beginning of the year. The company plans to produce a total of 240,000 units evenly throughout the year. Prepare a schedule showing the planned finished goods inventory at the end of each quarter.

Problems

5-41 BUDGETED RECEIPTS AND DISBURSEMENTS Agnew Retailers seeks your expertise to develop cash and other budget information for July, August, and September. On June 30, the company had cash of $9,000, accounts receivable of $602,750, inventories of $580,125, and accounts payable of $307,223. The budget is to be based on the following assumptions:

CO 5 (Step 7)

SALES
Each month's sales are billed on the last day of the month.

Customers are allowed a 2% discount if payment is made within 10 days after the billing date. Receivables are booked gross.

Sixty percent of the billings are collected within the discount period, 25% are collected by the end of the month, 13% are collected by the end of the second month, and 2% prove uncollectible.

PURCHASES
54% of all purchases of material and selling, general, and administrative expenses are paid in the month purchased and the remainder in the following month.

Each month's ending inventory in units is equal to 130% of the next month's unit sales.

The cost of each unit of inventory is $30.

Selling, general, and administrative expenses, of which $3,000 is depreciation, are equal to 15% of the current month's sales.

Actual and projected sales are as follows:

	Dollars	Units
May	$590,000	14,750
June	605,000	15,125
July	595,000	14,875
August	570,000	14,250
September	600,000	15,000
October	610,000	15,250

REQUIRED

Determine the total cash receipts and the total cash disbursements in a cash budget for July, August, and September.

5-42 CASH BUDGET Leaf Company has applied at a local bank for a short-term commercial loan of $75,000 starting on October 1. The loan will be repaid with interest at 10% on December 31. The bank's loan officer has requested a cash budget from the company for the quarter ending December 31. The following budget information is needed to prepare the cash budget for the quarter ending December 31:

CO 5 (Step 7)

Sales	$480,000
Purchases	180,000
Salaries and wages to be paid	63,000
Rent payments	36,000
Supplies (payments for)	24,000
Insurance payments	9,000
Other cash payments	11,100

A cash balance of $12,000 is planned for October 1 but assumes the loan is approved. Accounts receivable are expected to be $24,000 on October 1. All of the accounts will be collected in the quarter ending December 31. In general, sales are collected as follows: 90% in the quarter of sale and 10% in the quarter after sale.

Accounts payable will be $240,000 on October 1 and will be paid during the quarter ending December 31. All purchases are paid for in the quarter after purchase.

REQUIRED

a. Prepare a cash budget for the quarter ending December 31. Assume that the $75,000 loan will be made on October 1 and will be repaid with interest at 10% on December 31.

b. Will the company be able to repay the loan on December 31? If the company desires a minimum cash balance of $20,000, will the company be able to repay the loan as planned?

5-43 CASH BUDGET Doberman Corporation is planning its cash flows for the second quarter of 19X1. The second quarter is the peak sales season, and the company wishes to know whether or not it will need to borrow money to finance its peak inventory level. The following information has been gathered:

CO 5 (Step 7)

	February	March	April	May	June
Sales	$112,000	$120,000	$150,000	$180,000	$200,000
Purchases	60,000	56,000	110,000	140,000	120,000
Salaries (paid monthly)	8,000	8,000	8,000	8,000	8,000
Wages (paid monthly)	10,000	10,000	10,000	10,000	10,000
Rent (paid monthly)	2,000	2,000	2,000	2,000	2,000
Insurance (paid monthly)	500	500	500	500	500
Other cash expenses (paid monthly)	1,000	1,000	1,000	1,000	1,000
Equipment purchases	—	20,000	—	30,000	—
Cash dividends	—	—	1,000	—	—
Advertising campaign	—	—	10,000	40,000	—

Forty percent of sales are for cash; 60% are credit sales. Credit sales are collected as follows: 50% in the month of sale, 40% in the month after sale, and 10% in the second month after sale.

All purchases are made on credit and are paid for 40% in the month of purchase and 60% in the month after purchase. Equipment purchases, dividends, and advertising payments will be made in the months indicated.

The cash balance on April 1 is $11,000. A minimum balance of $10,000 is required. The company can borrow money at 10% interest. Money is to be borrowed at the beginning of a month in which a cash shortage is expected. The money will be repaid whenever the cash balance exceeds $10,000 at the end of a month.

REQUIRED

Prepare a cash budget for each month of the second quarter (April, May, and June). Include planned cash receipts, planned disbursements, and borrowings and repayments with interest. Borrowings must be in multiples of $500 (the company can borrow $500, $1,000, $1,500, and so on).

5-44 CASH BUDGET Mary Hartman, president of Hopechest, Inc., has just approached the company's bank with a request for a $120,000, 90-day loan. The purpose of the loan is to build inventories in support of peak June sales. But the company has had some difficulty in paying off its loans in the past; thus, the loan officer has asked for a cash budget to help determine whether the loan should be made. The following data are available for May to July, during which the loan will be used:

CO 5 (Step 7)

1. On May 1, the start of the loan period, the cash balance will be $52,000. Accounts receivable on May 1 will total $303,000, of which $282,000 will be collected during May and $14,400 will be collected during June. The remainder will be uncollectible.

2. Past data show that 25% of a month's sales are collected in the month of sale, 70% in the month following sale, and 4% in the second month following sale. Budgeted sales and expenses for the period follow:

	May	June	July
Sales	$400,000	$600,000	$500,000
Merchandise purchases	240,000	360,000	300,000
Payroll	18,000	18,000	16,000
Lease payments	20,000	20,000	20,000
Advertising	140,000	160,000	120,000
Equipment purchases	80,000	—	—
Depreciation	20,000	20,000	20,000

3. Merchandise purchases are paid in full during the month following purchases. Accounts payable for merchandise purchases on May 31 will be paid during June and total $216,000.

4. In preparing the cash budget, assume that the loan will be made in June and repaid July 31. Interest on the loan will total $9,000.

REQUIRED

a. Prepare a schedule of budgeted cash receipts for May, June, and July and for the three months in total.

b. Prepare a cash budget, by month and in total, for the three-month period.

c. If the company needs a minimum cash balance of $40,000 to start each month, can the loan be repaid as planned? Explain.

5-45   BUDGETED INCOME STATEMENT Samson Company prepares budgets on a quarterly basis for its fiscal year ending June 30. Given below is its post-closing trial balance at December 31, 19X1:

CO 5
(Step 3, 7, 8, 9)

	Debits	Credits
Cash	$138,000	
Accounts receivable	360,000	
Allowance for doubtful accounts		$ 12,000
Merchandise inventory	156,000	
Prepaid expenses	12,000	
Furniture and equipment	180,000	
Allowance for depreciation		12,000
Accounts payable		120,000
Accrued liabilities		36,000
Notes payable, 10% (due 19X5)		480,000
Capital stock		300,000
Retained earnings (deficit)	114,000	
	$960,000	$960,000

All the stock of Samson Company was recently purchased by Samuel Moses after the corporation suffered losses for a number of years. After the purchase, Moses loaned large sums of money to the corporation, which still owes him $480,000 on a 10% note. Because of these past losses, there are no accrued federal income taxes payable, but future earnings will be subject to taxation.

Moses is quite anxious to withdraw $120,000 from the corporation (as a payment on the note payable to him) but will not do so if it reduces the corporation's cash balance below $120,000. Thus, he is quite interested in the budgets for the quarter ending March 31, 19X2.

ADDITIONAL DATA

1. Sales for the next quarter are forecasted at $1,200,000; for the following quarter at $1,500,000. The gross margin is 40%. Inventory on hand at the end of a quarter should equal 20% of the next quarter's sales. All sales are on account. Ninety-five percent of the December 31, 19X1, receivables plus 70% of the current quarter's sales will be collected during the quarter ending March 31, 19X2.

2. Selling expenses are budgeted at $48,000 fixed plus 5% of sales. Purchasing expenses are budgeted at $34,800 fixed plus 6% of purchases for the quarter.

3. Administrative expenses are budgeted at $42,000 plus 2% of sales.

4. Interest accrues at 10% on the note payable and is credited to accrued liabilities.

5. Federal income taxes are budgeted at 45% of net earnings before taxes.

REQUIRED

a. Prepare a purchases budget for the quarter ending March 31, 19X2.

b. Prepare a schedule of operating expenses and interest expense for the quarter ended March 31, 19X2.

c. Prepare a budgeted income statement for the quarter ended March 31, 19X2.

d. Prepare a schedule of planned accounts receivable collections and ending balance for the quarter ended March 31, 19X2.

e. Name the other information needed to assist Moses.

5-46 BUDGETED INCOME STATEMENT AND BALANCE SHEET The balance sheet of Poladak, Inc., as of March 31, 19X1, is as follows:

CO 5 (Steps 7, 8, 9)

Poladak, Inc.
Balance Sheet
March 31, 19X1

Assets

Cash	$ 4,000
Accounts Receivable	13,500
Inventory	23,000
Plant and Equipment, net of depreciation	100,000
Total Assets	$140,500

Liabilities and Equity

Accounts Payable	$ 20,000
Note Payable	4,000
Capital Stock	75,000
Retained Earnings	41,500
Total Liabilities and Equity	$140,500

Poladak, Inc., has never budgeted before, and for this reason it is limiting its master budget planning horizon to just one month—April 19X1. The company has assembled the following budgeted information relating to April:

1. Sales are budgeted at $75,000. Of these sales, $30,000 will be for cash; the remainder will be credit sales. Fifty percent of credit sales are collected in the month the sales are made, and the remainder is collected in the following month. All of the March 31 accounts receivable will be collected during April.

2. Purchases of inventory are expected to total $40,000 during the month, all on account. Forty percent of all purchases are paid for in the month of purchase; the remainder is paid in the following month. All of the March 31 accounts payable to suppliers will be paid during April.

3. The April 30 inventory balance is budgeted at $18,000.

4. Operating expenses for April are budgeted at $25,000, exclusive of depreciation. These expenses will all be paid in cash. Depreciation is budgeted at $1,250 for the month.

5. Equipment costing $7,500 will be acquired on April 30. The company will give a note payable to its bank in order to obtain funds to cover the equipment cost. The note will be due in one year.

6. The note payable at March 31 will be paid in April, with $125 interest. (All of the interest relates to the month of April.)

REQUIRED

a. Prepare a cash budget for Poladak, Inc., for April 19X1. Support your budget with schedules showing budgeted cash receipts and budgeted cash payments for inventory purchases.

b. Prepare a budgeted income statement for April 19X1. Use the traditional income statement format. Ignore income taxes.

c. Prepare a budgeted balance sheet as of April 30, 19X1.

5-47   **MASTER BUDGET** Southstar Corporation prepares its master budget on a quarterly basis. The following data have been assembled to assist in preparation of the master budget for the

CO 5 (Steps 1–9)   second quarter of 19X1:

1. As of March 31, 19X1 (the end of the prior quarter), the company's balance sheet showed the following account balances:

	Dr.	Cr.
Cash	$ 19,800	
Accounts Receivable	105,600	
Inventory	27,720	
Plant, Property, and Equipment	440,000	
Accounts Payable		$ 40,260
Capital Stock		396,000
Retained Earnings		156,860
	$593,120	$593,120

2. Actual sales for March and budgeted sales for April-July are as follows:

March (actual)	$132,000
April	154,000
May	187,000
June	198,000
July	110,000

3. Sales are 30% for cash and 70% on credit. All credit sale terms are net/30; therefore, accounts are collected in the month following sale. The accounts receivable at March 31 are a result of March credit sales.

4. The company's gross profit rate is 40% of sales.

5. Monthly expenses are budgeted as follows: salaries and wages, $16,500 per month; freight-out, 5% of sales; advertising, $13,200 per month; depreciation, $4,400 per month; other expense, 6% of sales.

6. At the end of each month, inventory is to be equal to 30% of the following month's sales needs, stated at cost.

7. Half of a month's inventory purchases are paid for in the month of purchase and half in the following month.

8. Equipment purchases during the quarter will be as follows: April, $35,300; May, $18,150.

9. Dividends totaling $8,800 will be declared and paid in June.

10. The company must maintain a minimum cash balance of $17,600. A line of credit is available at a bank with borrowing done at the beginning of a month, and all repayments are made at the end of a month. Borrowings and repayments of principal must be in multiples of $1,000. Loan repayments are on a first-in, first-out (FIFO) basis. Interest is paid only at the time of repayment of principal; however, any interest on unpaid loans should be properly accrued when statements are prepared. The interest rate is 12% per annum. (Compute interest on whole months, e.g., 6/12, 2/12.)

11. Ignore taxes.

REQUIRED

Using the data above, complete the following statements and schedules for the second quarter by replacing the question marks with the correct amounts.

a. Schedule of expected cash collections:

	April	May	June	Total
Cash sales (30% of current month)	$ 46,200	?	?	?
Credit sales (70% of previous month)	105,600	?	?	?
Total collections	$151,800	?	?	?

b. 1. Inventory purchases budget:

	April	May	June	Total
Budgeted cost of goods sold (60%)	$ 92,400*	$112,200	?	?
Add: Desired ending inventory	33,600†	?	?	?
Total needs	$126,060	?	?	?
Deduct: Opening inventory	27,720	?	?	?
Required purchases	$ 98,340	?	?	?

*60% × $154,000 April sales.
†At April 30: $112,200 × 30%.

2. Schedule of cash disbursements for purchases:

	April	May	June	Total
For March purchases	$ 40,260	?	?	$40,260
For April purchases	49,170	$49,170	?	98,340
For May purchases	?	?	?	?
For June purchases	?	?	?	?
Total cash disbursements	$ 89,430	?	?	?

c. Schedule of cash disbursements for expenses:

	April	May	June	Total
Salaries and wages	$ 16,500	?	?	?
Freight-out (5%)	7,700	?	?	?
Advertising	13,200	?	?	?
Other expenses (6%)	9,240	?	?	?
Total cash disbursements	$ 46,640	?	?	?

d. Cash budget:

	April	May	June	Total
Cash balance, beginning	$ 19,800	?	?	?
Add cash collections	151,800	?	?	?
Total cash available	$171,600	?	?	?
Less disbursements:				
For inventory purchases	$ 89,430	?	?	?
For operating expenses	46,640	?	?	?
For equipment purchases	35,300	?	?	?
For dividends	–0–	?	?	?
Total disbursements	$171,370	?	?	?
Excess (deficiency) of cash	$ 230	?	?	?
Financing:				
Borrowing	?	?	?	?
Repayments	?	?	?	?
Interest	?	?	?	?
Total effects	?	?	?	?
Cash balance, ending	?	?	?	?

e. Prepare an income statement for the quarter ending June 30.

f. Prepare a balance sheet as of June 30.

(CPA adapted)

5-48   MASTER BUDGET Nittany Company is preparing its master budget for the third quarter. The following sales information is available:

CO 5 (Steps 1–9)

June (actual)	$160,000
July	200,000
August	256,000
September	320,000
October	144,000

1. Sales are 40% cash and 60% on credit. All credit sale terms are net/30; therefore, accounts are collected in the month following sale. The accounts receivable at June 30 are a result of June credit sales.

2. The gross profit rate is 30% of sales.

3. Monthly expenses are as follows: salaries and wages, 15% of sales; rent, $8,800 per month; and other expenses (excluding depreciation), 5% of sales. Depreciation is $4,000 per month.

4. At the end of each month, inventory is to be on hand equal to 75 percent of the cost of the following month's sales needs.

5. All inventory purchases are on credit terms. Half of a month's purchases are paid for in the month of purchase and half in the following month.

6. Equipment costing $10,000 will be purchased in August.

7. The company must maintain a minimum cash balance of $20,000. An open line of credit is available at a local bank. All borrowing is done at the beginning of a month, and all repayments are made at the end of the month. Borrowings and repayments of principal must be in multiples of $1,000. Loan repayments are on a first-in, first-out (FIFO) basis. Interest is paid only at the time of repayment of principal; however, any interest on unpaid loans should be properly accrued when statements are prepared. The interest rate is 12% per annum.

8. Dividends of $6,000 will be declared and paid in September.

9. Balances in various balance sheet accounts at June 30 follow:

Cash	$ 24,000
Accounts Receivable	96,000
Inventory	105,000
Plant and Equipment (net)	600,000
Accounts Payable	66,500
Capital Stock	700,000
Retained Earnings	58,500

10. Ignore taxes.

REQUIRED

Using the data above, complete the following statements and schedules:

a. Schedule of expected cash collections:

	July	August	September	Total
Cash sales	$ 80,000	?	?	?
Credit sales	96,000	?	?	?
Total collections	$176,000	?	?	?

b. 1. Purchases budget:

	July	August	September	Total
Budgeted cost of goods sold	$140,000*	$179,200	?	?
Add: Desired ending inventory	134,400†	?	?	?
Total needs	$274,400	?	?	?
Deduct: Opening inventory	105,000	?	?	?
Required purchases	$169,400	?	?	?

*70% × $200,000 July sales.
†$179,200 × 75%.

2. Schedule of expected cash disbursements for purchases:

	July	August	September	Total
For June purchases	$ 66,500	?	?	$ 66,500
For July purchases	84,700	$84,700	?	$169,400
For August purchases	?	?	?	?
For September purchases	?	?	?	?
Total	$151,520	?	?	?

c. Schedule of expected cash disbursements for expenses:

	July	August	September	Total
Salaries and wages	$ 30,000	?	?	?
Rent	8,800	?	?	?
Other expenses	10,000	?	?	?
Total cash disbursements	$ 48,800	?	?	?

d. Cash budget:

	July	August	September	Total
Cash balance, beginning	$ 24,000	?	?	?
Add cash collections	176,000	?	?	?
Total cash available	$200,000	?	?	?

(continued)

	July	August	September	Total
Less disbursements:				
For inventory purchases	$151,200	?	?	?
For expenses	48,800	?	?	?
For equipment purchases	—	?	?	?
For dividends	—	?	?	?
Total disbursements	$200,000	?	?	?
Excess (deficiency) of cash	$ -0-	?	?	?
Financing:				
Borrowing	?	?	?	?
Repayments	?	?	?	?
Interest	?	?	?	?
Total effects	?	?	?	?
Cash balance, ending	?	?	?	?

e. Prepare an income statement for the quarter ending September 30.

f. Prepare a balance sheet as of September 30.   (CPA adapted)

5-49   BUDGETED COST OF GOODS MANUFACTURED AND SOLD Apaliski Company wants to prepare a schedule of planned cost of goods sold and ending inventory for the quarters ending June 30, 19X1, and September 30, 19X2. The following data relate to the expected activity for the two quarters:

CO 6 (Steps 2–6)

1. Expected sales for the next three quarters are $900,000 (June), $1,000,000 (September), and $800,000 (December).

2. Selling price is $25 per unit.

3. Because of demand, the company wishes to carry a beginning inventory equal to 40% of the following quarter's expected activity.

4. Inventory of finished goods, March 31, 19X1, is 20,000 units valued at $20 per unit.

5. Cost of production:

Materials	$5 per unit
Direct labor	$3 per unit
Variable overhead	$1 per unit
Fixed overhead	$200,000 per quarter

6. There is no work in process inventory at the beginning or end of either period.

7. The company computes inventory on a FIFO basis.

REQUIRED

Prepare a schedule of planned cost of goods manufactured and sold for the quarters ending June 30, 19X1, and September 30, 19X1. Use full costing. (Hint: Prepare the production budget first.)

5-50 PRODUCTION BUDGET Coleslaw Company manufactures and distributes a number of products to retailers. One product, Cabbageditch, requires five units of Material A in the manufacture of each unit. The company is now planning raw materials needs for the fourth quarter of 19X1 when peak sales occur. In order to keep production and shipments moving smoothly, the company has the following inventory requirements.

CO 6 (Step 2)

1. The finished goods inventory on hand at the end of each month must be equal to 10,000 units plus 20% of the next month's sales. The finished goods inventory on September 30 is budgeted to be 18,000 units.

2. The raw materials inventory on hand at the end of each month must be equal to one half of the following month's production needs for raw materials. The raw materials inventory on September 30 for material A is budgeted to be 105,000 units.

3. The company maintains no work in process inventories. A sales budget for Cabbageditch for the last six months of 19X1 is as follows:

	Budgeted Sales in Units
October	40,000
November	50,000
December	70,000
January	35,000
February	20,000
March	10,000

REQUIRED

a. Prepare a production budget for Cabbageditch for October to January.

b. Examine the production budget you have prepared. Discuss why the company will produce more units than it sells in October and November and fewer units than it sells in December and January.

c. Prepare a budget showing the quantity of material A to be purchased for October, November, and December 19X1 and for the quarter in total.

5-51 INVENTORY BUDGET A sales budget is given below for one of the products manufactured by Van Gauge, Inc.

CO 6 (Steps 1–2)

Month	Sales Budget in Units
July	72,000
August	80,000
September	96,000
October	104,000
November	76,000
December	64,000

The inventory of finished goods at the end of each month must be equal to 20,000 units plus 10% of the next month's sales. On June 30, the finished goods inventory totaled 27,200 units.

Each unit of product requires three ounces of a special solution. Sometimes the solution is in short supply; for this reason, the company has a policy of maintaining an inventory at the end of each month equal to half the next month's production needs. This requirement was met on July 1 of the current year.

REQUIRED

Prepare a budget showing the quantity of the solution to be purchased each month from July to September and for the three-month period in total.

5-52   BUDGETED INCOME STATEMENT Rumeer Products, Inc., produces and sells a very popular product called Blackball. The company is in the process of preparing budgeted data on Blackball for the second quarter of 19X1. The following data are available:

CO 6 (Steps 2–7, 9)

1. The company expects to sell 90,000 cartons of Blackball during the second quarter of 19X1. The selling price is $30 per carton.

2. Each carton of Blackball requires 10 pounds of a material called Innu and 30 pounds of a material called Endo.

3. Inventory levels are planned as follows:

	Beginning of Quarter	End of Quarter
Finished bags of Blackball	24,000	18,000
Innu (lbs.)	130,000	105,000
Endo (lbs.)	230,000	190,000
Empty carton	60,000	40,000

4. Innu costs $1.20 per pound; Endo costs $.20 per pound; and empty cartons cost $1.60 each.

5. It requires 12 minutes of direct labor time to process and fill one carton of Blackball. Labor cost is $15 per hour.

6. Variable manufacturing overhead costs are $.90 per carton. Fixed manufacturing overhead costs total $120,000 per quarter.

7. Variable selling and administrative expenses are 5% of sales. Fixed selling and administrative expenses total $70,000 per quarter.

REQUIRED

a. Prepare a production budget for Blackball for the second quarter.

b. Prepare a raw materials purchases budget for Innu and Endo, and empty cartons for the second quarter. Show the budgeted purchases in dollars as well as in pounds or cartons.

c. Compute the budgeted variable manufacturing cost to manufacture one carton of finished Blackball.

d. Prepare a budgeted income statement for Blackball for the second quarter. Use the contribution approach (so use variable costing for the inventory and cost of goods sold) and show both per-unit and total cost data.

5-53 MANUFACTURING BUDGET Anything Corporation manufactures and sells two products, Itemone and Itemtwo. In July 19X1, Anything's budget department gathered the following data to project sales and budget requirements for 19X2:

CO 6 (Steps 1–5)

19X2 Projected Sales

Product	Units	Price
Itemone	30,000	$35
Itemtwo	20,000	50

19X2 Inventories (In Units)

Product	Expected January 1, 19X2	Desired December 31, 19X2
Itemone	10,000	12,500
Itemtwo	4,000	4,500

To produce one unit of Itemone and Itemtwo, the following raw materials are used:

Raw Material	Unit	Itemone	Itemtwo
A	lbs.	8	10
B	lbs.	4	6
C	each	—	2

Projected data for 19X2 with respect to raw materials is as follows:

Raw Material	Anticipated Purchase Price	Expected Inventories Jan. 1, 19X2	Desired Inventories Dec. 31, 19X2
A	$1.00	64,000 lbs.	72,000 lbs.
B	.50	58,000 lbs.	64,000 lbs.
C	1.50	12,000 units	14,000 units

Projected direct labor requirements for 19X2 and rates are as follows:

Itemone: 1 hour per unit @ $6 per hour
Itemtwo: 2 hours per unit @ $8 per hour

Overhead is applied at the rate of $4 per direct labor hour.

REQUIRED
Prepare (a) a sales budget, (b) a production budget, (c) raw materials budget, (d) a direct labor budget, and (e) an overhead budget.

Business Decision Case

The following data are presented for the J. R. Ewing Company for use in preparing its 19X1 operating budget:

Plant capacity	900,000 units
Budgeted sales	700,000 units
Budgeted production	700,000 units
Forecasted sales price	$20 per unit
Manufacturing costs:	
Variable costs:	
Raw material	$2.50 per unit
Direct labor	$5 per unit
Overhead	$2 per unit
Fixed costs	$175,000
Selling and administrative expenses:	
Variable costs	$2 per unit
Fixed costs	$3,500,000

Assume no beginning inventory. Taxes are 50% of pretax earnings.

REQUIRED

Prepare a budgeted income statement for the year ended December 31, 19X1.

Chapter

6

Statement of Cash Flows

CHAPTER OBJECTIVES

After reading Chapter 6, you should be able to:

1. Explain the purpose of the statement of cash flows (pp. 195–98).

2. State the fundamental funds equations (pp. 198–99).

3. Derive the cash received from revenues (pp. 199–203).

4. Compute the cash paid for expenses (pp. 204–207).

5. Calculate cash flows from operating activities (p. 208).

6. Explain investing and financing activities (p. 209).

7. Prepare a statement of cash flows (pp. 209–12, 213–21).

*M*uch of accounting is focused on the income statement. One reason for this emphasis is that it provides information for managers, investors, and creditors about the profit-making activities of the firm. This information allows investors and creditors, as well as managers, to assess the profitability of the company, its lines of business, and its products. A second reason for the emphasis is that the income statement is a vehicle for control. Managers can control subordinates responsible for the results of certain segments of the firm or certain products. This control can be in the form of salaries or continued employment. Investors and creditors can exert control based on their earnings through adjustment of stock prices, interest rate charges, and contracts.

The income statement, however, does not completely disclose the financial health of an enterprise. Although it does indicate profitability, it may not show the firm's *solvency*—that is, its ability to pay its bills. This deficiency is brought about by its use of accruals and deferrals. In other words, accountants include in the earnings statement several items that do not reflect cash flow, such as depreciation and accrued salaries. The accruals and deferrals may enhance the ability of the income statement to reflect profitability, but it lessens its capacity to measure solvency. To overcome this problem, the accounting profession has created the statement of cash flows. This statement is also useful in the budgeting process.

Cash budgets are related to statements of cash flows. Cash budgets show the forecast cash flows of the organization. In essence, a cash budget is nothing more than a forecast statement of cash flows. The two reports are frequently organized differently, but the content is quite similar. Cash budgets are almost exclusively used for managerial purposes, whereas statements of cash flows are also a part of the report sent to stockholders. When used internally, statements of cash flows can be analyzed and made a part of decision support systems. Their role in decision support systems is the same as that of cash budgets, discussed in the previous chapter.

THE PURPOSE OF THE STATEMENT OF CASH FLOWS

CHAPTER OBJECTIVE 1
Purpose of the statement

In the past corporations prepared a statement of changes in financial position. The purpose of this statement was to show the sources (increases) and uses (decreases) of funds during a specified period. Firms were allowed by accounting's governing bodies to use a variety of alternatives in preparing the statement. Specifically, funds accounted for on this statement could be defined as cash, cash plus marketable securities (called *cash equivalents*), cash plus marketable securities plus accounts receivables, or working capital, among other possibilities. The most popular definition was *working capital*, where working capital equals current assets minus current liabilities. However, the use of working capital as a measure of cash flow has been criticized because, like income, it does not represent solvency very well. Working capital from operations is highly correlated with net income; once net income is known, working capital from operations can be approximated. For these reasons, the working capital method is no longer acceptable for financial reporting purposes. However, as stated in Chapter 1, management need not follow these rules for internal purposes. Internally, management can meet the rules of financial accounting standard-setting bodies and, if it is more relevant and useful, mandate different reporting formats and data for managerial purposes.

Statements of cash flows are now required for external disclosure by the Financial Accounting Standards Board (FASB). This chapter will focus only on the statement of changes in financial position prepared on a cash basis, now referred to as the *statement of cash flows*. We focus only on this statement because it relates to the master budgeting process described in the previous chapter and it helps managers observe and control balances, and because it is required for external reporting purposes.

The purpose of the statement of cash flows is to reflect the cash inflows and cash outflows of the firm. A helpful way to categorize these cash flows is by their activity. The FASB classifies these cash flows into three groups: cash flows from operating activities, cash flows from investing activities, and cash flows from financing activities. An example is given in Exhibit 6-1.

The *cash flows from operating activities* section shows the cash inflows and the cash outflows from selling the firm's goods and services. It includes such items as cash received from customers and cash disbursed to suppliers of the inventory, to employees for wages, to governments for taxes, and to rentors for the use of their property.

The *cash flows from investing activities* section displays the cash inflows from selling assets other than the goods to customers and from interest and dividends earned on investments and the cash outflows from purchasing such assets. In Exhibit 6-1 it includes the cash outflows for the purchase of land and the purchase of machinery.

The *cash flows from financing activities* section presents the cash inflows from issuing debt and stock and the cash outflows for payments to the creditors and to the stockholders and from retiring debt and stock. Examples of cash flows from financing activities include cash inflows from the issuance of preferred stock and from the issuance of long-term notes payable. Another example is the cash outflow for dividends paid to common and preferred stockholders.

The format used in Exhibit 6-1 to display the cash flows from operating activities is called the *direct method*. When the direct method is used, a reconciliation schedule is required by the FASB for external reporting purposes. This reconciliation is shown in Exhibit 6-1 and is simply a conversion from net income to the cash flow provided by operating activities. (The process for reconciling these items will be explained later.) Alternatively, the FASB allows the reconciliation schedule to be placed in the cash flows from operating activities section. When this is done, the format is called the *indirect method*. In general, we feel that the direct method is superior because it indicates specifically the nature of the cash flows.

For internal purposes, management can do whatever it wants with regard to this statement. As said in Chapter 1, governments generally do not set rules for the accounting procedures used within the organization. Managers can have no statement of cash flows, a statement of cash flows exactly as required by FASB, or some modification thereof. An example of a modified statement of cash flows is shown in Exhibit 6-2. The operating activities section looks like an income statement but prepared on a cash basis. Managers might want to do this since the gross margin number on a cash basis could provide useful information. Dividends are removed to a separate section. Managers might want to do this so that they can see how much cash is available to pay to stockholders.

Unless stated otherwise, we will adopt the FASB convention with two provisos. We will always use the direct method, since we feel that it is more informative. Also we will not prepare the reconciliation schedule, since it duplicates the information shown in the direct method.

EXHIBIT 6-1

STATEMENT OF CASH FLOWS

Perfect Manufacturing Company
Statement of Cash Flows
For the Year Ended June 30, 19X0

Cash Flows from Operating Activities

Cash Received from Customers	$2,090,500	
Cash Paid to Suppliers	(1,120,000)	
Cash Paid to Employees	(75,000)	
Income Taxes Paid	(200,000)	
Cash Paid for Renting	(100,000)	
Net Cash Provided by Operating Activities		$ 595,500

Cash Flows from Investing Activities

Purchase of Land	$ (405,500)	
Purchase of Machinery	(900,000)	
Net Cash Used in Investing Activities		(1,305,500)

Cash Flows from Financing Activities

Proceeds from Issuance of Preferred Stock	$ 500,000	
Proceeds from Issuance of Long-term Notes Payable	750,000	
Dividends Paid	(250,000)	
Net Cash Provided by Investing Activities		1,000,000
Net Increase in Cash		$ 290,000

Reconciliation of Net Income to Net Cash
Provided by Operating Activities

Net Income		$ 645,000
Adjustments to reconcile net income to net cash provided by operating activities:		
Depreciation	$ 80,000	
Increase in Accounts Receivable	(100,000)	
Increase in Inventory	(60,000)	
Increase in Wages Payable	10,000	
Increase in Taxes Payable	20,000	(50,000)
Net Cash Provided by Operating Activities		$ 595,000

EXHIBIT 6-2

STATEMENT OF CASH FLOWS (MODIFIED ACTIVITIES FORMAT)

Perfect Manufacturing Company
Statement of Cash Flows
For the Year Ended June 30, 19X0

Cash Flows from Operating Activities

Revenues		$ 2,090,500
Cost of Goods Sold		(1,120,000)
Gross Margin		$ 970,500
Deduct:		
Wages	$ (75,000)	
Taxes	(200,000)	
Rent	(100,000)	(375,000)
Net Cash Provided by Operating Activities		$ 595,500

Cash Flows from Investing Activities

Purchase of Land	$(405,500)	
Purchase of Machinery	(900,000)	
Net Cash Used by Investing Activities		(1,305,500)

Cash Flows from Financing Activities

Issuance of Preferred Stock	$ 500,000	
Issuance of Notes Payable	750,000	
Net Cash Provided by Financing Activities		1,250,000
Cash Dividend Paid Out		(250,000)
Net Increase in Cash		$ 290,000

FUNDAMENTAL FUNDS EQUATIONS

CHAPTER OBJECTIVE 2
Fundamental funds equation

The balance sheet is a representation of the fundamental accounting equation:

$$\text{Assets} = \text{Liabilities} + \text{Owner's Equity}$$

The income statement is a display of the fundamental income equation:

$$\text{Income} = \text{Revenues} - \text{Expenses}$$

In a similar manner, the statement of cash flows may be said to be a presentation of the **fundamental funds equation**:

$$\text{Beginning Cash} + \text{Cash Inflows} - \text{Cash Outflows} = \text{Ending Cash}$$

Some common **cash inflows** are cash generated from operations, collection of long-term notes receivable, issuance of common and preferred stock, issuance of bonds and notes payable, and proceeds from the sale of property, plant, and equipment. Common **cash outflows** include purchase of property, plant, and equipment, paying off bonds and notes payable, purchase of other firms' securities (long-term investments), purchase of the firm's own stock (treasury stock), and cash dividends.

As stated before, an activities format is a useful way to classify the cash flows. If followed, one would divide cash flows into operating activities, investing activities, and financing activities. One would then report cash from **operating activities,** which are the firm's activities related to the sale of goods and services, the purchase of raw materials and supplies, the conversion of these raw materials into finished goods inventory, and the administrative and selling tasks of the firm. **Financing activities** are activities related to obtaining capital, including borrowing debt and issuing preferred and common stock. They also include paying interest and dividends, paying off debt, and reacquiring company stock. **Investing activities** include the purchase and the sale of long-term assets such as stocks and bonds of other corporations, property, plant, and equipment. In this format, the fundamental funds equation is written as follows:

$$\begin{aligned}\text{Beginning Cash} &+ \text{Cash from Operating Activities} \\ &+ \text{Cash from Investing Activities} \\ &+ \text{Cash from Financing Activities} \\ &= \text{Ending Cash}\end{aligned}$$

Frequently corporations focus on the change in cash rather than the beginning and ending cash balances (since the balances are given in the balance sheets). If this is done, the equation can be rewritten:

$$\begin{aligned}\text{Increase (Decrease) in Cash} = &\ \text{Cash from Operating Activities} \\ &+ \text{Cash from Investing Activities} \\ &+ \text{Cash from Financing Activities}\end{aligned}$$

DERIVATION OF CASH FROM OPERATING ACTIVITIES

CHAPTER OBJECTIVE 3
Derive cash received from revenues

The first, and most important, step in the preparation of the statement of cash flows is the derivation of cash from operating activities. Think of this measure as earnings on a cash basis. Cash from operations, therefore, is equal to revenues on a cash basis minus expenses on a cash basis. Since the revenues and the expenses are on the accrual basis of accounting, it is necessary for the accountant to adjust the revenues and the expenses to a cash basis. The procedure can adjust for five situations in which cash accounting and accrual accounting are different:

1. Cash is received before it is earned.
2. Cash is received after it is earned.

3. Cash is paid before it is expensed.

4. Cash is paid after it is expensed.

5. No cash is paid even though there is an expense.

The rest of this section examines each of these cases, with a detailed look at sales and cost of goods sold. The section ends with a formula that links all of these items together to obtain cash from operating activities.

Cash Received before Earned

When cash is received before it is earned, the cash is recognized as revenue on the cash basis of accounting in the period before it is recognized as a revenue on the accrual basis of accounting. For example, suppose a corporation receives $5,000 on December 31, 19X0, for renting office space to another company for 19X1 and then receives $6,000 on December 31, 19X1, for renting office space for 19X2. The revenue is recognized as follows:

Year	Cash Accounting	Accrual Accounting
19X0	$5,000	$ –0–
19X1	6,000	5,000
19X2	–0–	6,000

In practice, the accounts are maintained on an accrual basis of accounting. (Firms can keep the accounts any way they wish. It is permissible to maintain the accounts on a cash basis, and some small firms and some nonprofit entities do that. In that case, there are no adjustments to obtain cash from operations because the accounts will already reveal that when properly combined.) Thus, the data would be stored as follows:

Year	Balance Sheet (December 31): Unearned Rent Revenue	Income Statement: Rent Revenue
19X0	$5,000	$ –0–
19X1	6,000	5,000
19X2	–0–	6,000

The accountant must convert these data to obtain the cash flow (in this case, the rent revenue on a cash basis of accounting). The cash from rent revenue is calculated by increasing or decreasing the accrual Rent Revenue account by the amount of change in the Unearned Revenue account. Assuming this account began in 19X0, the entire amount in Unearned Rent Revenue ($5,000) is added to the Rent Revenue account. For 19X0, cash from renting equals:

$ –0– Rent Revenue account

+ 5,000 Increase in Unearned Rent Revenue account

$5,000 Cash from rent revenue

The $5,000 in the Unearned Rent Revenue account implies that additional cash has been received but not earned as an accrual revenue. Therefore, the increase is added to Rent Revenue to obtain the cash from rent revenue amount.

For 19X1, cash from renting equals:

$5,000 Rent Revenue account
+ 1,000 Increase in Unearned Rent Revenue account
$6,000 Cash from rent revenue

Notice that Rent Revenue is increased by the difference between the amounts in the Unearned Rent Revenue account from 19X0 to 19X1.

For 19X2, cash from renting equals:

$6,000 Rent Revenue account
− 6,000 Decrease in Unearned Rent Revenue account
$ −0− Cash from rent revenue

The decrease to Unearned Rent Revenue from 19X1 to 19X2 implies that the firm is recognizing the rent as revenue in that period, but that the cash was received in an earlier period. Therefore, Rent Revenue is decreased by the amount of unearned rent revenue to obtain the amount for cash from rent revenue.

These principles may be summarized in the following formula:

$$\text{Cash from Rent Revenue} = \text{Rent Revenue} \begin{cases} + \text{Increase in Unearned Rent Revenue} \\ or \\ - \text{Decrease in Unearned Rent Revenue} \end{cases}$$

Cash Received after Earned

When cash is received after it is earned, the cash is recognized as a revenue on the cash basis of accounting in the year after it is recognized as revenue on the accrual basis of accounting. For example, suppose that an enterprise earns interest of $20,000 in 19X0 but does not receive the cash until 19X1 and that it earns interest of $24,000 in 19X1 but does not receive the cash until 19X2. The revenue is recognized as follows:

Year	Cash Accounting	Accrual Accounting
19X0	$ −0−	$20,000
19X1	20,000	24,000
19X2	24,000	−0−

In practice, the accounts are maintained on an accrual basis of accounting. Thus, the data are stored as follows:

Year	Balance Sheet (December 31): Interest Receivable	Income Statement: Interest Revenue
19X0	$20,000	$20,000
19X1	24,000	24,000
19X2	–0–	–0–

The accountant needs to convert these data to obtain the cash flow (in this case, the interest revenue on a cash basis of accounting). The amount of cash received from interest revenue is calculated by increasing or decreasing the accrual Interest Revenue account by the change in the Interest Receivable account. Assuming this account began in 19X0, the entire amount in Interest Receivable ($20,000) is subtracted from the Interest Revenue account. For 19X0, cash from interest would equal:

$20,000 Interest Revenue account
– 20,000 Increase in Interest Receivable account
$ –0– Cash from interest revenue

The interest receivable of $20,000 implies that the revenue was recognized even though the cash had not been received. Therefore, the increase is subtracted from the Interest Revenue to obtain cash from interest.

For 19X1, cash from interest equals:

$24,000 Interest Revenue account
– 4,000 Increase in Interest Receivable account
$20,000 Cash from interest revenue

For this conversion, the interest revenue decreases by the difference between the amounts in the Interest Receivable account from 19X0 to 19X1.

For 19X2, cash from interest equals:

$ –0– Interest Revenue account
+ 24,000 Decrease in Interest Receivable account
$24,000 Cash from interest revenue

The decrease in Interest Receivable from 19X1 to 19X2 implies that cash was received for interest but that the revenue was recorded in an earlier period. Therefore, the Interest Revenue account is increased by the change in the Interest Receivable account to obtain cash from interest.

These principles may be summarized in the following formula:

$$\text{Cash from Interest Revenue} = \text{Interest Revenue} \begin{cases} + \text{Decrease in Interest Receivable} \\ or \\ - \text{Increase in Interest Receivable} \end{cases}$$

Sales. A very important example of the situation in which cash is received after the income is recognized involves sales. When sales are made on account, the cash is received after it is earned. Sales can be made for cash directly, too. Fortunately, this does not change the formula for obtaining cash generated from operations.

Suppose a firm has cash sales of $20,000 and credit sales of $280,000 in 19X0. Cash sales are $25,000 in 19X1 with credit sales amounting to $325,000. Collections of receivables are $190,000 and $330,000 in 19X0 and 19X1, respectively. What is the cash generated from sales in those two years? Revenue recognition is as follows:

Year	Cash Accounting	Accrual Accounting
19X0	$210,000	$300,000
19X1	355,000	350,000

Given that the accounts are kept on an accrual basis, we have the following balances:

Year	Balance Sheet (December 31): Accounts Receivable	Income Statement: Sales
19X0	$90,000	$300,000
19X1	85,000	350,000

The formula for adjustment is as follows:

$$\text{Cash from Sales} = \text{Accrual Sales} \begin{cases} +\text{Decrease in Accounts Receivable} \\ or \\ -\text{Increase in Accounts Receivable} \end{cases}$$

This formula is similar to the previous adjustment for interest revenue. The amount of cash sales does not affect this calculation, since cash from sales are already embedded in the Sales account and they need no adjustment.

With these facts, we can compute the cash generated from sales. In 19X0, it is:

$300,000 Sales
− 90,000 Increase in Accounts Receivable
$210,000 Cash collections from sales

The $90,000 represents sales for which cash has not yet been received. In 19X1, the amount is:

$350,000 Sales
+ 5,000 Decrease in Accounts Receivable
$355,000 Cash collections from sales

Hence, the $5,000 measures the net amount of cash received for which the sales were recorded in a previous period.

Cash Paid out before Expensed

When cash is paid out before it is expensed, the cash is reported as an expense on the cash basis of accounting in the period before it is recorded as an expense on the accrual basis of accounting. For example, assume a business pays out $15,000 on December 31, 19X0, for a one-year insurance policy (to be effective during 19X1). Also assume that the company pays out $18,000 on December 31, 19X1, for insurance coverage in 19X2. The expense is reported as follows:

Year	Cash Accounting	Accrual Accounting
19X0	$15,000	$ –0–
19X1	18,000	15,000
19X2	–0–	18,000

In practice, the accounts are maintained on an accrual basis of accounting. Thus, the data is stored as follows:

Year	Balance Sheet (December 31): Prepaid Insurance Expense	Income Statement: Insurance Expense
19X0	$15,000	$ –0–
19X1	18,000	15,000
19X2	–0–	18,000

The accountant must convert these data to obtain the cash flow (in this case, the insurance expense on a cash basis of accounting). The cash for insurance expense is calculated by increasing or decreasing the accrual Insurance Expense account by the amount of change in the Prepaid Insurance Expense account. Assuming this account began in 19X0, the entire amount in Prepaid Insurance Expense ($15,000) is added to the Insurance Expense account. For 19X0, cash for insurance equals:

$$
\begin{array}{rl}
\$ \ –0– & \text{Insurance Expense account} \\
+ \ \underline{15,000} & \text{Increase in Prepaid Insurance Expense account} \\
\underline{\$15,000} & \text{Cash for insurance expenditure}
\end{array}
$$

The Prepaid Insurance Expense account of $15,000 implies that cash has been paid out even though the expense has not yet been reported.

For 19X1, cash for insurance equals:

$$
\begin{array}{rl}
\$15,000 & \text{Insurance Expense account} \\
+ \ \underline{3,000} & \text{Increase in Prepaid Insurance Expense account} \\
\underline{\$18,000} & \text{Cash for insurance expenditure}
\end{array}
$$

The Insurance Expense account is increased by the difference between the amounts in the Prepaid Insurance Expense account from 19X0 to 19X1. For 19X2, cash for insurance equals:

$18,000   Insurance Expense account
− 18,000   Decrease in Prepaid Insurance Expense account
$ −0−   Cash for insurance expenditure

The decrease in Prepaid Insurance Expense from 19X1 to 19X2 implies that the firm has recognized that decrease as an expense but that the cash was dispensed in an earlier period. These principles may be summarized in the following formula:

$$\text{Cash for Insurance Expense} = \text{Insurance Expense} \begin{cases} + \text{Increase in Prepaid} \\ \quad \text{Insurance} \\ or \\ - \text{Decrease in Prepaid} \\ \quad \text{Insurance} \end{cases}$$

Cash Paid out after Expensed

When cash is paid out after it is expensed, the cash is recognized as an expense on the cash basis of accounting in the year after it is recognized as an expense on the accrual basis of accounting. For example, suppose that a firm pays $250,000 in wages in 19X0 that were earned by the employees in 19X0 and that it still owes $5,000 wages to its employees in 19X0 that would not be paid until 19X1. Also suppose that the entity owes $6,000 in wages to its employees in 19X1 but that the amount is not paid until 19X2. The corporation also paid $270,000 in wages in 19X1 that were earned in 19X1 and paid $300,000 in wages in 19X2 that were earned in 19X2. The wages expense is recognized as follows. (The reader should verify these numbers. For example, 19X1 cash wages were $270,000 of 19X1 wages paid in 19X1 plus $5,000 of 19X0 wages paid in 19X1.)

Year	Cash Accounting	Accrual Accounting
19X0	$250,000	$255,000
19X1	275,000	276,000
19X2	306,000	300,000

In practice, the accounts are maintained on an accrual basis of accounting. Thus, the data is stored as follows:

Year	Balance Sheet (December 31): Wages Payable	Income Statement: Wages Expense
19X0	$5,000	$255,000
19X1	6,000	276,000
19X2	−0−	300,000

The accountant must convert these data to obtain the cash flow (in this case, the wages expense on a cash basis of accounting). The cash paid for wages expense is calculated by increasing or decreasing the accrual Wages Expense account by the amount of change in the Wages Payable account. Assuming this particular account began in 19X0, the entire amount in Wages Payable ($5,000) is subtracted from the Wages Expense account. For 19X0, cash for wages equals:

$255,000 Wages Expense account
−   5,000 Increase in Wages Payable account
$250,000 Cash for wages expenditure

The use of Wages Payable implies that the expense was recorded even though the cash has not yet been paid out. Therefore, the increase is subtracted from Wages Expense to obtain cash paid for wages expense.

For 19X1, cash for wages equals:

$276,000 Wages Expense
−   1,000 Increase in Wages Payable
$275,000 Cash for wages expenditure

Notice that Wages Expense is decreased by the difference between the amounts in the Wages Payable account from 19X0 to 19X1.

For 19X2, cash for wages equals:

$300,000 Wages Expense account
+   6,000 Decrease in Wages Payable account
$306,000 Cash for wages expenditure

The decrease in Wages Payable from 19X1 to 19X2 implies that cash was paid for those wages but that the expense was recorded in an earlier period.

These principles may be summarized in the following formula:

$$\text{Cash for Wages Expense} = \text{Wages Expense} \begin{cases} +\text{Decrease in Wages Payable} \\ or \\ -\text{Increase in Wages Payable} \end{cases}$$

Cost of Goods Sold.   Computing cash cost of goods sold is a bit more complicated since it depends on the interactions of two accounts: Inventory and Accounts Payable. Inventory is adjusted in a manner similar to the example dealing with cash being paid out prior to the expense recognition, but accounts payable is adjusted similar to the example in which cash was paid out after the expense was recognized. The algorithm is:

$$\begin{matrix} \text{Cash for} \\ \text{Cost of} \\ \text{Goods Sold} \end{matrix} = \begin{matrix} \text{Cost of} \\ \text{Goods} \\ \text{Sold} \end{matrix} \begin{cases} +\text{Increase in} \\ \text{Inventory} \\ or \\ -\text{Decrease in} \\ \text{Inventory} \end{cases} and \begin{cases} +\text{Decrease in} \\ \text{Accounts Payable} \\ or \\ -\text{Increase in} \\ \text{Accounts Payable} \end{cases}$$

The rationale for the above formula is the following. If inventory is acquired and paid for, but is still on hand at the end of the year, then cash was paid out but the item not entered into cost of goods sold. Thus, the increase in Inventory is added in the above formula to determine the amount disbursed. Likewise, if Inventory decreases, it was acquired in an earlier period but expensed currently. It must be subtracted out in the above formula to get the cash amount. If Accounts Payable rises, then the amount needs to be subtracted out from cost of goods sold. This shows that the increase in Accounts Payable reflects no cash outflow. Likewise, if Accounts Payable declines, cash was disbursed to pay off the debt. This amount needs to be added to cost of goods sold to determine the cash outlay.

Things get complicated when one realizes that inventory can be acquired on account. An increase in Inventory can be off-set by an increase in Accounts Payable, and the result is no cash outflow. Myriad possibilities exist of how to link inventory and accounts payable. Fortunately, the formula stays the same.

For example, suppose there is a firm which acquires $50,000 inventory with cash and $250,000 of inventory on credit in 19X0. Beginning inventory is $30,000 and $260,000 of inventory was sold during the year. $200,000 of the accounts payable was paid in 19X0. How much is the cash paid out for cost of goods sold?

Notice cost of goods sold is $260,000 and that cash paid out is $250,000 ($50,000 cash purchase + $200,000 payment on accounts payable). How does one calculate this with the accounts? As follows:

$$
\begin{array}{rl}
\$260,000 & \text{Cost of Goods Sold} \\
+\quad 40,000 & \text{Increase in Inventory} \\
-\quad 50,000 & \text{Increase in Accounts Payable} \\
\hline
\$250,000 & \text{Cash cost of goods sold}
\end{array}
$$

Ending inventory is $70,000 which is the beginning inventory $30,000 plus purchases $300,000 minus cost of goods sold $260,000. There is an increase of $40,000 over the beginning inventory of $30,000. Assuming Accounts Payable has a zero beginning balance, the account increases by the $250,000 credit purchases and decreases by the $200,000 worth of payments. There is a net increase in Accounts Payable of $50,000.

No Cash Flow with Expense

Some expenses and revenues generate no cash flow. An example is depreciation. Other examples include depletion, amortization of intangibles, amortization of premiums and discounts on bonds payable, and amortization of premiums and discounts on bond investments.

The entry for depreciation is debit Depreciation Expense and credit Accumulated Depreciation. This entry is made regardless of the method used to calculate depreciation. The method simply determines the amount. The rationale for depreciation is that it better matches revenues and costs. Depreciation, however, has no cash flow attached to it; depreciation is ignored when preparing figures for cash from operations. If one begins with earnings, depreciation may be added back to obtain cash flow. This add-back simply reverses the depreciation deduction.

THERE'S CASH FLOW, AND THERE'S CASH FLOW

On Sundays, Mormon Bishop Donald Yacktman tends to his 400-strong congregation in suburban Chicago, chairing meetings and overseeing his church's main weekly religious service. Says he, "It's usually the longest day of the week."

On Monday mornings Yacktman, 48, returns to the world of mammon, trading stocks for the $350 million Selected American Shares. There Yacktman seems to be on the side of the angels, with a fund that joined the *Forbes* honor roll this year. He has returned 19% a year since taking over the fund six years ago, versus 15.5% for the S&P 500.

Yacktman uses a common enough stock picking method, looking for companies that are cheap in relation to disposable cash flow. But he concedes that this method is flawed. "Ultimately, what you would like to look at is operating cash flow, which would be what an LBO [leveraged buyout] person would look at," he says. "You'd look at cash flow before depreciation, amortization, interest and taxes. Then you need to take away from that maintenance capital expenditures. That's the tough part. Unless you're inside the company, it's virtually impossible to know what that number is." How is an outsider to know whether a firm has bolstered cash flow by skimping on maintenance, for example? How is he to decide how much of capital spending is merely for upkeep and how much actually enhances the value of the company?

Yacktman does his own arithmetic. Says he, "You end up using shortcut methods, like looking at cash flows of businesses that are similar, or looking at price/earnings ratios."

Valuing companies at a multiple of free cash flow is a popular tool of analysis these days but one often misapplied. In one version applauded recently in another business journal, you subtract dividends as well as capital replacement costs to get free cash flow. Such a deduction makes the preposterous assumption that a company generating $1 a share in excess cash per year would become worthless if it declared a $1 dividend. . . .

In addition to cash flow, Yacktman also tries to assess whether a company's chief executive has a good strategy for using retained earnings. "The reason the chief executive is so critical is because each year he's making a new layer of investment," argues Yacktman. "The cash that is generated by a business ends up in one of four places. Either it's used for expanding the existing business, for making acquisitions, for paying dividends or for shrinking the capitalization by buying back stock." . . .

SOURCE: Jonathan Clements, "There's Cash Flow, and There's Cash Flow, *Forbes* (September 18, 1989), pp. 138, 141. Excerpted by permission of *Forbes* magazine. © Forbes Inc., 1989.

Summary

CHAPTER OBJECTIVE 5
Cash from operating activities

As stated at the beginning of this section, cash from operations is equal to revenues on a cash basis minus expenses on a cash basis. Each of the subsections has indicated how to adjust a revenue or an expense from the accrual basis to the cash basis. Once these adjustments are completed, cash from operations is computed as follows:

$$
\begin{aligned}
\text{Cash from Operations} = &\ \text{Sales (cash)} \\
&- \text{Cost of goods sold (cash)} \\
&- \text{Other expenses (cash)} \\
&+ \text{Other revenues (cash)}
\end{aligned}
$$

Depreciation is omitted from this formula. Operating activities involve the sale of the normal product or service in the ordinary course of business.

INVESTING AND FINANCING ACTIVITIES

CHAPTER OBJECTIVE 6
Investing and financing activities

Investing activities encompass the acquisition of property, plant, and equipment and other assets used over several years. The sale of such assets is also classified as investing activities. Investing activities are distinguished from operations in that they also are not associated with the buying and selling of goods and services for a single period.

As previously mentioned, financing activities bring in cash by taking on more debt or issuing more stock. They also represent disbursements of cash for retirement of debt or stock. Financing activities are distinguished from operations in that they are not associated with the selling of goods and services or with the production of those goods and services.

It is not always easy to distinguish operations from these other two activities. Suppose a firm sells a long-term asset that has a historical cost of $30 and an accumulated depreciation of $25 (thus a book value of $5) for $7. There is a gain on the sale of $2. The question is: How should the cash inflow of $7 be treated? One viewpoint is to consider the transaction as a disinvestment and place the entire $7 in the investing section. The rationale is that the event is incidental to the major line of business engaged in by the corporation. The opposite viewpoint takes a broader perspective on what operations involve. According to this thought, the firm *must* engage in some transactions such as this. Although they are infrequent and perhaps incidental, they are still part of doing business. Therefore, the entire $7 would be considered a part of cash generated from operations. In practice, the usual treatment is a compromise between these two views. The book value portion of the cash flow ($5) is treated as investments; the rest ($2) is treated as part of operations.

It is also possible for a business to conduct combined financing and investing activities. Suppose an entity acquires a piece of property valued at $50,000 by issuing common stock of the corporation. Although the transaction does not generate any cash flows, it is advisable to think of it as a two-part transaction. The first part is a financing transaction. Namely, think of it as if the $50,000 cash were obtained by the issuance of stock. The second part is an investment. It is as if there were disbursements of $50,000 for the purpose of buying the property. The reason for interpreting the event this way is that the acquisition did have a cost to the firm: common stock. Also, the firm obtained something of value from the issuance of the stock: the property. The managers may not always be able to link the two together. So that managers and other users may understand the transaction better, the two-part interpretation is used because it does not show the activities linked together. Technically, the FASB does not require this interpretation (though an earlier pronouncement did); nonetheless, we adopt this convention since it gives greater insights into the activities of the enterprise.

Cash dividends are a return to stockholders; cash is paid out as dividends to preferred and common shareholders. Declaration of dividends alone do not involve a cash flow and so are excluded. Also excluded are stock dividends and stock splits since these transactions do not involve cash flows.

Demonstration Problem

CHAPTER OBJECTIVE 6
Prepare a statement of cash flows

Ben's Bakery is a new corporation. In its first year of operations, which ended December 31, 19X0, the following transactions occurred:

1. Obtained $100,000 upon issuance of common stock.

2. Bought property costing $30,000.

3. Acquired a building for $50,000.

4. Obtained $60,000 of inventory on account.

5. Made $10,000 worth of cash sales.

6. Made credit sales of $90,000.

7. Cost of goods sold was $40,000.

8. Collected $75,000 of the accounts receivable.

9. Paid $55,000 of the accounts payable.

10. The building was depreciated at $5,000.

11. The firm incurred first-year's taxes of $20,000.

12. Paid $17,500 of the taxes.

13. Declared and paid cash dividends of $12,000.

REQUIRED

Prepare the statement of cash flows for Ben's Bakery for its first year of operations.

SOLUTION TO DEMONSTRATION PROBLEM

Although not required, it is helpful to draw up the income statement and the balance sheet, as we have done. We compute each of the components of the statement of cash flows and then bring them together. An alternative approach to preparing the statement of cash flows is the *T-account approach*, which is described in Appendix B.

Ben's Bakery
Income Statement
(accrual basis)
For the Year Ended December 31, 19X0

Sales	$100,000
Cost of Goods Sold	40,000
Gross Margin	$ 60,000
Depreciation Expense	5,000
Earnings before Taxes	$ 55,000
Tax Expense	20,000
Net Income	$ 35,000

Ben's Bakery
Balance Sheet
December 31, 19X0

ASSETS

Current Assets	
Cash	$ 20,500
Accounts Receivable	15,000
Inventory	20,000
Current Assets	$ 55,500

(continued)

Long-term Assets

Property		$ 30,000
Building	$50,000	
Less: Accumulated Depreciation	5,000	45,000
Long-term Assets		$ 75,000
Total Assets		$130,500

EQUITIES

Accounts Payable		$ 5,000
Taxes Payable		2,500
Current Liabilities		$ 7,500
Common Stock		$100,000
Retained Earnings		23,000
Stockholders' Equity		$123,000
Total Equities		$130,500

Cash collections from sales equal cash sales of $10,000 plus $75,000 cash collected from credit sales. Cash collections are thus $85,000.

Cost of goods sold is $40,000. Inventory increased from $0 (since this is a new firm) to $20,000 ($60,000 bought minus $40,000 sold). The increase in accounts payable is $5,000 ($60,000 for the inventory minus the $55,000 paid). Thus the cash outlay for the cost of goods sold is $55,000 ($40,000 + $20,000 − $5,000).

The cash flow from gross margin is $85,000 cash collections from sales minus $55,000 cash paid out for cost of goods sold, or $30,000.

The only other cash expenditure for operations involves taxes. This is $17,500. Cash from operations is therefore $12,500 ($30,000 − $17,500).

Ben's had two investing activities, for it purchased property for $30,000 cash and it purchased a building for $50,000 cash.

Ben's had two financing transactions. Ben's issued common stock and received $100,000 cash. Finally, the entity paid out $12,000 as a cash dividend.

Compiling these items, we construct the following statement of cash flows. The statement tells the reader that Ben's Bakery increased its cash by $20,500.

Cash Flows from Operating Activities

Sales		$ 85,000
Cost of Goods Sold		(55,000)
Gross Margin		$ 30,000
Deduct: Taxes		(17,500)
Net Cash Provided by Operating Activities		$ 12,500

Cash Flows from Investing Activities

Purchase of Property	$ (30,000)	
Purchase of Building	(50,000)	
Net Cash Used by Operating Activities		

Cash Flows from Financing Activities

Issuance of Common Stock	$100,000	
Cash Dividend Paid Out	(12,000)	
Net Cash Provided by		
Financing Activities		88,000
Net Increase in Cash		$ 20,500

Review of Chapter Objectives

1. Explain the purpose of the statement of cash flows (pp. 195–98).

   ■ The statement of cash flows explains why the cash balance has changed during the period (usually one year). The statement is organized in an activities format. In this format, cash flows are categorized as operating, investing, and financing activities. Operating activities refer to the profit-making activities of the organization, activities related to the sale of goods and services of the firm; investing activities refer to the purchase and sale of investments including property, plant, and equipment; financing activities refer to the obtaining and repayment of debt and stock.

2. State the fundamental funds equation (pp. 198–99).

   ■ The fundamental funds equation explains the change in the cash balance and so is the essence of the statement of cash flows. The equation is:

   Beginning Cash + Cash from Operating Activities
   + Cash from Investing Activities
   + Cash from Financing Activities
   = Ending Cash

3. Derive the cash received from revenues (pp. 199–203).

   ■ There are two formulas for obtaining the cash received from revenues, depending on whether the associated account is a liability or an asset. An example of the former is Rent Revenue and Unearned Rent Revenue. An example of the latter is Interest Revenue and Interest Receivable.

   ■ When the associated account is a liability, the adjustment is as follows: Cash generated from the revenue is equal to the revenue measured on an accrual basis plus the increase (or minus the decrease) in the liability.

   ■ When the associated account is an asset, the adjustment is made as follows: Cash generated from the revenue is equal to the revenue measured on an accrual basis plus the decrease (or minus the increase) in the asset.

Compute the cash paid for expenses (pp. 204–207).

   Similar to the previous situation, there are two formulas for obtaining the cash paid for expenses, depending on whether the associated account is an asset or a liability. An example of the former is Insurance Expense and Prepaid Insurance Expense. An illustration of the latter is Wages Expense and Wages Payable.

   When the associated account is an asset, the following formula is used: The cash paid for the expense is equal to the expense measured on an accrual basis plus the increase (or minus the decrease) in the asset.

(80,000) (continued)

- When the associated account is a liability, then the following adjustment is made: The cash paid for the expense is equal to the expense measured on an accrual basis plus the decrease (or minus the increase) in the liability.
- Keep in mind that some accrual expenses have no cash flow. The classic example of this is depreciation. In computation of cash flows from operations, depreciation is simply ignored because of the lack of any associated cash expenditure.

5. Calculate cash flows from operating activities (p. 208).

- Cash from operations equals cash from sales minus cash disbursed for expenses. Again notice that depreciation and other noncash items are omitted from this formula.

6. Explain investing and financing activities (p. 209).

- Cash flows from investing activities consist of the cash inflows from selling assets (not inventory) and from interest and dividends earned on investments, and of the cash outflows from buying assets such as property, plant, and equipment. Determine the cash inflow or outflow and report it on the statement of cash flows.
- Cash flows from financing activities consist of the cash inflow from borrowing money or selling stock and the cash outflow from paying off debts or buying back stock or paying cash dividends on the stock. Determine the cash inflow or outflow and report it on the statement of cash flows.

7. Prepare a statement of cash flows (pp. 209–12, 213–21).

- A statement of cash flows depicts the cash flows from operating activities, investing activities, and financing activities. These have been extensively summarized in the previous four points. The statement of cash flows simply collects these different items and reports them so that the net increase or decrease in cash is shown. In other words, the statement of cash flows is an elaboration of the fundamental funds equation.

APPENDIX B

T-Account Approach

The T-account approach consists of several steps, the result of which is a set of T accounts that contain the values needed to prepare the statement of cash flows. These T accounts are worksheet accounts only. The entries made to these accounts are worksheet entries and are not posted to the actual accounts. The steps are the following:

CHAPTER OBJECTIVE 7
Prepare a statement of cash flows

1. Set up a T account for Cash, Cash Sales, Cash Cost of Goods Sold, and one for each additional revenue and expense account for which there is a cash flow. In addition, set up a T account for every other balance sheet account.
2. Specify in the T account the change in each balance sheet account that occurred in the period.
3. Prepare a trial balance of T-account balances to catch any errors up to this point.
4. Prepare entries that explain the changes that occurred in the balance sheet accounts over the period.
5. Close out the cash revenue and cash expense accounts to Cash.
6. Verify that the additions and subtractions to Cash net to the increase or decrease in that account.

Once these six steps are completed, the statement of cash flows itself is prepared. Cash from operations is contained in the cash revenue and the cash expense accounts (not accounts in the ledger). The amount closed to Cash is equal to the cash generated from operations. Other sources and uses of cash are contained in the Cash account. Cash inflows are shown on the debit side; cash outflows on are shown on the credit side. To use the activities format, one needs to know whether the transactions are operating, investing, or financing activities.

We now illustrate the T-account approach using the example in the Demonstration Problem on pages 209–12. Suppose that a new corporation entitled Ben's Bakery is started. During 19X0, its first year of operation, Ben's Bakery had the following transactions. The journal entries are also shown.

1. Obtained $100,000 upon issuance of common stock.

Cash	100,000	
Common Stock		100,000

2. Bought property costing $30,000.

Property	30,000	
Cash		30,000

3. Acquired a building for $50,000.

Building	50,000	
Cash		50,000

4. Obtained $60,000 of inventory on account.

Inventory	60,000	
Accounts Payable		60,000

5. Made $10,000 worth of cash sales.

Cash	10,000	
Sales		10,000

6. Made credit sales of $90,000.

Accounts Receivable	90,000	
Sales		90,000

7. Cost of goods sold was $40,000.

Cost of Goods Sold	40,000	
Inventory		40,000

8. Collected $75,000 of the accounts receivable.

Cash	75,000	
Accounts Receivable		75,000

9. Paid $55,000 of the accounts payable.

Accounts Payable	55,000	
Cash		55,000

10. The building has a 10-year life and no salvage value. Straight-line depreciation is used. Thus, the building is depreciated at $5,000.

Depreciation Expense	5,000	
Accumulated Depreciation		5,000

11. The firm incurred first-year's taxes of $20,000.

Tax Expense	20,000	
Taxes Payable		20,000

12. Paid $17,500 of the taxes.

Taxes Payable	17,500	
Cash		17,500

13. Declared and paid cash dividends of $12,000.

Retained Earnings	12,000	
Cash		12,000

Step 1 is to set up the various T accounts for all accounts. From the balance sheet and the income statement we see that a T-account is needed for Cash, Cash Sales, Cash Cost of Goods Sold, Cash Taxes, Accounts Receivable, Inventory, Property, Building, Accumulated Depreciation, Accounts Payable, Taxes Payable, Common Stock, and Retained Earnings.

Step 2 is to write down the changes in the balance sheet account (see the balance sheet on pages 210–11). For example, beginning Inventory is $0 and ending Inventory is $20,000. The increase in Inventory is $20,000. The increase is put on the debit side, following the usual rules for debits and credits.

The results of the first two steps is shown in Exhibit B-1. A line is drawn under the changes to differentiate the change from the entries that follow.

Step 3 is to prepare a trial balance. The debits are Cash, $20,500; Accounts Receivable, $15,000; Inventory, $20,000; Property, $30,000; and Building, $50,000. Total debits are $135,500. Credits are Accumulated Depreciation, $5,000; Accounts Payable, $5,000; Taxes Payable, $2,500; Common Stock, $100,000; Retained Earnings, $23,000. Total credits are $135,500. Debits equal credits, so we may proceed.

Step 4 is to prepare entries that explain the changes in the balance sheet accounts as a result of the flows of cash during the period. This includes the income transactions since they affect retained earnings. The entries are shown in Exhibit B-2. The numbers in parentheses are cross-references to transaction numbers, to make the T account entries easier to follow.

Entries 1–13 given earlier are entered in the T accounts. Expenses are debited and revenues are credited to Retained Earnings. Cash transactions related to the operations

EXHIBIT B-1

T-ACCOUNT APPROACH (STEPS 1 AND 2)

Cash		Cash Sales	
20,500			

Cash Cost of Goods Sold		Cash Taxes	

Accounts Receivable		Inventory	
15,000		20,000	

Property		Building	
30,000		50,000	

Accumulated Depreciation		Accounts Payable	
	5,000		5,000

(continued)

EXHIBIT B-1   T-ACCOUNT APPROACH (STEPS 1 AND 2) *(CONTINUED)*

Taxes Payable		Common Stock	
	2,500		100,000

Retained Earnings	
	23,000

of the enterprise are entered into one of the cash revenue or cash expense T accounts. In this example, cash sales and collections of accounts receivable are entered in Cash Sales. Payments of accounts payable are entered in Cash Cost of Goods Sold. Payment of taxes payable is placed in Cash Taxes.

Cash transactions not related to operations are entered in the Cash account. Included in this illustration are cash from sale of common stock, cash paid for the property and for the building, and cash dividends.

Step 4 is completed when all of the balance sheet accounts, except Cash, are explained. For example, look at the Retained Earnings account in Exhibit B-2. That account has debits of $77,000 from entries 7, 10, 11, and 13, and credits of $100,000 from entries 5 and 6. Credits exceed debits by $23,000. This amount is the same as the change in the account noted in Step 2. Thus, the preparer is finished with the Retained Earnings account. All balance sheet accounts, except Cash, should be explained at this point.

Note the treatment of depreciation, entry 10. Retained Earnings is debited $5,000 and Accumulated Depreciation is credited $5,000. Of course, there is no entry to a cash expense account, since depreciation has no cash flow.

Step 5 is to close out the cash revenue and cash expense accounts to Cash. Entry 14 is as follows:

Cash	12,500	
Cash Cost of Goods Sold	55,000	
Cash Taxes	17,500	
Cash Sales		85,000

Note that the $12,500 debited to Cash represents the cash from operating activities. Also note that these are *worksheet* entries and not made in the accounting journal or ledger.

Step 6 is to verify the entries to the Cash account. Entries 1 and 14 are debits totaling $112,500. Entries 2, 3, and 13 are credits totaling $92,000. The net increase is $20,500, the same as it was in the Demonstration Problem.

EXHIBIT B-2

T-ACCOUNT APPROACH (STEPS 3–6)

Cash			Cash Sales		
20,500			(5) 10,000		
			(8) 75,000	(14) 85,000	
(1) 100,000	(2) 30,000				
(14) 12,500	(3) 50,000				
	(13) 12,000				

Cash Cost of Goods Sold		Cash Taxes	
(14) 55,000	(9) 55,000	(14) 17,500	(12) 17,500

Accounts Receivable		Inventory	
15,000		20,000	
(6) 90,000	(8) 75,000	(4) 60,000	(7) 40,000

Property		Building	
30,000		50,000	
(2) 30,000		(3) 50,000	

Accumulated Depreciation		Accounts Payable	
	5,000		5,000
	(10) 5,000	(9) 55,000	(4) 60,000

(continued)

EXHIBIT B-2   T-ACCOUNT APPROACH (STEPS 3–6) *(CONTINUED)*

Taxes Payable			Common Stock	
	2,500			100,000
(12) 17,500	(11) 20,000			(1) 100,000

Retained Earnings	
	23,000
(7) 40,000	(5) 10,000
(10) 5,000	(6) 90,000
(11) 20,000	
(13) 12,000	

The T-account approach is now completed. The statement of cash flows can be prepared now from the data gathered from the T-account approach and reflected in Exhibit B-2. The resulting statement is the same as that shown in the Demonstration Problem, pages 211–12. Net cash flows from operating activities equals $12,500. The components are taken from the Cash Revenue and the Cash Expense T accounts. The other cash inflows and outflows are obtained from the Cash account in Exhibit B-2. Entry 1 reflects the issuance of common stock, which is a financing transaction. Entries 2 and 3 reflect the purchase of property and building, which are investing transactions. Finally, entry 13 shows the cash dividends paid to common stockholders.

Alternative T-account Approach

The data requirements for doing the T-account approach as presented in Exhibit B-2 are more stringent than really needed. The T-account approach can still be done if we do not know the cash sales and the credit sales, for example. All that is needed are the sales figures and the *change* in Accounts Receivable over the period. This follows from the discussion earlier in the chapter that cash from sales equals Sales (on an accrual basis) plus the decrease (or minus the increase) in Accounts Receivable. Similar statements can be made about the other cash revenues and cash expenses.

If performed on the changes, the T-account approach would produce the results shown in Exhibit B-3. (The entry numbers do not match those in Exhibit B-2 or in the listing of the transaction because we aggregate certain items.) Entry 4 in Exhibit B-3 explains the change in accrual sales of $100,000 over the period (from $0 at startup to $100,000 at the end of the first year), which is taken from the income statement in the Demonstration Problem on page 210. Entry 5 is an adjustment for the change in accounts receivable, thus giving the $85,000 cash sales (part of entry 12). Entry 6 explains the change in accrual cost of goods sold of $40,000 (again, from $0 at startup to $40,000 at the end of the year), again taken from the income statement on page 210. Entry 7 adjusts for the change in inventory, and entry 8 adjusts for the change in accounts

EXHIBIT B-3

ALTERNATIVE T-ACCOUNT APPROACH

Cash

20,500	

(1) 100,000	(2) 30,000
(13) 12,500	(3) 50,000
	(12) 12,000

Cash Sales

(4) 100,000	(5) 15,000
	(13) 85,000

Cash Cost of Goods Sold

(8) 5,000	(6) 40,000
(13) 55,000	(7) 20,000

Cash Taxes

(11) 2,500	(10) 20,000
(13) 17,500	

Accounts Receivable

15,000	
(5) 15,000	

Inventory

20,000	
(7) 20,000	

Property

30,000	
(2) 30,000	

Building

50,000	
(3) 50,000	

Accumulated Depreciation

	5,000
	(9) 5,000

Accounts Payable

	5,000
	(8) 5,000

(continued)

EXHIBIT B-3 ALTERNATIVE T-ACCOUNT APPROACH (CONTINUED)

Taxes Payable		Common Stock	
	2,500		100,000
	(11) 2,500		(1) 100,000

Retained Earnings	
	23,000
(6) 40,000	(4) 100,000
(9) 5,000	
(10) 20,000	
(12) 12,000	

payable over the period. Entry 9 is the entry for depreciation. Entry 10 reflects the income tax expense, while entry 11 indicates that $2,500 of the tax expense was not paid this year. Entry 12 reflects the cash dividend. Entry 13 closes out the cash revenue and cash expense accounts. The statement of cash flows prepared using Exhibit B-3 is the same as that prepared in the Demonstration Problem on pages 211–12.

Glossary of Key Terms

cash inflow   An activity that increases cash.

cash outflow   An activity that decreases cash.

financing activities   Activities relating to obtaining capital. They include borrowing funds and issuing preferred and common stock. They also include repayment of debt and reacquisition of stock.

fundamental funds equation   The equation that states that the net increase in cash is equal to cash inflows minus cash outflows.

investing activities   Activities relating to obtaining long-term assets. They include the purchase and the sale of long-term assets such as stocks and bonds of other corporations, property, plant, and equipment.

operating activities   Activities relating to the profit-making aspects of the firm. They include the sale of goods and services, the purchase of raw materials and supplies, the conversion of these raw materials into finished goods inventory, and the administrative and selling tasks of the firm.

solvency   A firm's ability to pay its debts.

statement of cash flows   A financial statement that shows the cash inflows and outflows of the entity.

T-account approach (Appendix B)   A method that helps one to prepare statements of cash flows. It consists of a series of account entries such that the debit side of the cash accounts indicates a cash inflow and the credit side shows cash outflows.

Review Questions

6-1　What is a statement of cash flows? What is its purpose?

6-2　How does the statement of cash flows complement the income statement?

6-3　What is meant by *solvency*?

6-4　What is a cash inflow? What is a cash outflow?

6-5　Name the three major activities of a firm. Define each of the activities.

6-6　What is the fundamental funds equation?

6-7　Name some common cash inflows.

6-8　Name some common cash outflows.

6-9　How is cash from operating activities measured?

6-10　What is the formula for measuring cash revenues in terms of accrual revenues when cash is received before it is earned?

6-11　What is the formula for measuring cash revenues in terms of accrual revenues when cash is received after it is earned?

6-12　What is the formula for measuring cash expenses in terms of accrual expenses when cash is paid before it is expensed?

6-13　What is the formula for measuring cash expenses in terms of accrual expenses when cash is paid after it is expensed?

6-14　What is the formula for measuring cash cost of goods sold in terms of accrual cost of goods sold?

6-15　What is the formula for measuring cash depreciation in terms of accrual depreciation.

6-16　A company sells an asset having a book value of $100 for $80. How is this transaction shown on the statement of cash flows?

6-17　A building is constructed for $100,000. It required a down payment of $20,000; the rest was mortgaged. How should this event be depicted on the statement of cash flows using the two-transaction interpretation?

6-18　What steps comprise the T-account approach?

Discussion Questions

6-19　Cash from operating activities can be calculated by:

$$\text{Cash from Operating Activities} = \text{Income}$$
$$+ \text{Depreciation}$$
$$- \text{Increase in Current Assets (except cash)}$$
$$+ \text{Increase in Current Liabilities}$$

Decreases would change the signs. Explain why this formula works. *Hint:* Put cash from operations in terms of cash revenues and cash expenses and then adjust them from the cash basis to the accrual basis.

6-20　How can a firm go bankrupt and have good earnings?

6-21　Ben's Bakery issues the following statement of operations, which combines an income statement and a statement of cash flows. Critique it.

Ben's Bakery
Statement of Operations
For the Year Ended December 31, 19X0

	Accrual	Cash
Sales	$100,000	$85,000
Cost of Goods Sold	40,000	55,000
Gross Margin	$ 60,000	$30,000
Depreciation	5,000	
Earnings before Tax	$ 55,000	$30,000
Taxes	20,000	17,500
Net Income	$ 35,000	$12,500

Exercises

6-22 INFLOWS AND OUTFLOWS For each of the following transactions, indicate whether it is a inflow or outflow of cash, neither, or both. Also list in which section the item would be placed on the statement of cash flows using the activities format.

CO 1

a. Cash sales.

b. Issuance of bonds payable.

c. Credit sales.

d. Purchase of machinery.

e. Purchase of inventory for cash.

f. Issuance of preferred stock.

g. Purchase of property with a mortgage.

h. Collection of accounts receivable.

i. Issuance of a stock dividend.

j. Retirement of part of the bonds payable.

6-23 CASH FLOW AND ACCOUNTS A corporation receives $10,000 cash on July 1, 19X0, in advance for the one-year rental of office space it owns. The rental is from July 1, 19X0, to June 30, 19X1. It receives $12,000 cash on July 1, 19X1, in advance for the one-year rental from July 1, 19X1 to June 30, 19X0 of that office space.

CO 3

a. Show how much rent revenue there is each year on the cash basis and the accrual basis. The fiscal year ends on December 31.

b. Show the account balances on December 31, 19X0, 19X1, and 19X2.

c. Show how cash rent revenue is computed from accrual rent revenue.

6-24 CASH FLOW AND ACCRUALS An enterprise earns interest of $25,000 in 19X0 but does not receive the cash until 19X1. Also, in 19X1 the company earns interest of $30,000, for which it receives $25,000 in 19X1 and the rest in 19X2. The fiscal year ends on December 31.

CO 3

a. Show how much interest revenue there is for each year on the cash basis and the accrual basis.

b. Show the account balances on December 31, 19X0, 19X1, and 19X2.

c. Show how cash interest revenue is computed from accrual interest revenue.

6-25 CASH FLOW AND ACCRUALS A corporation pays out $12,000 on July 1, 19X0 for a one-year insurance policy from July 1, 19X0, to June 30, 19X1. The firm also pays out $14,000 on July 1, 19X1 for another one-year policy running from July 1, 19X1, to June 30, 19X2. The fiscal year ends December 31.

CO 4

a. Show how much insurance expense there is for each year on the cash basis and the accrual basis.

b. Show the account balances on December 31, 19X0, 19X1, and 19X2.

c. Show how cash insurance expense is computed from accrual insurance expense.

6-26 CASH FLOW AND ACCRUALS A company owes $6,000 in wages to its employees in 19X0 that is not paid until 19X1. It owes $100,000 for wages incurred in 19X1, of which $90,000 is paid in 19X1 and $10,000 paid in 19X2.

CO 4

a. Show how much wages expense there is for each year on the cash basis and the accrual basis.

b. Show the account balances on December 31, 19X0, 19X1, and 19X2.

c. Show how cash Wages Expense is computed from accrual Wages Expense.

6-27 CASH FROM SALES For the following independent cases a–f, replace the question marks with the correct amounts.

CO 3

	Beginning Accounts Receivable	Ending Accounts Receivable	Increase in Accounts Receivable	Credit Sales	Cash Sales during Period	Total Accrual Sales	Collection on Credit Sales	Sales on Cash Basis
a.	$ 10,000	$30,000	$?	$80,000	$20,000	$?	$?	$?
b.	10,000	?	20,000	90,000	10,000	?	?	?
c.	?	30,000	20,000	95,000	?	100,000	?	?
d.	20,000	40,000	?	80,000	20,000	?	?	?
e.	30,000	50,000	?	?	5,000	?	?	80,000
f.	110,000	?	20,000	?	10,000	?	70,000	?

6-28 CASH FOR INVENTORY Fill in the blanks in the two tables below and on page 225. The lines for a, b, c, and so on in both tables refer to the same company.

CO 4

	Beginning Inventory	Cash Purchases	Credit Purchases	Total Purchases	Ending Inventory	Increase in Inventory
a.	$ 10,000	$ –0–	$?	$?	$ 35,000	$?
b.	?	10,000	?	?	50,000	25,000
c.	40,000	?	100,000	?	?	25,000
d.	100,000	15,000	?	?	125,000	?
e.	?	?	?	125,000	25,000	25,000
f.	60,000	12,000	?	?	?	25,000

	Beginning Accounts Payable	Ending Accounts Payable	Increase in Accounts Payable	Cash Payment for Accounts Payable	Accrual Cost of Goods Sold	Cash Cost of Goods Sold
a.	$ 20,000	$ 30,000	$?	$?	$100,000	$?
b.	?	60,000	10,000	?	100,000	?
c.	–0–	?	10,000	?	100,000	?
d.	100,000	110,000	?	?	?	115,000
e.	45,000	55,000	?	95,000	?	?
f.	?	22,000	10,000	?	100,000	?

6-29 CASH FLOW AND ACCRUALS The information below is taken from the books of Snoozer Company:

CO 3, 4, 5

	End of Year	Beginning of Year
Accounts Receivable	$ 30,100	$15,100
Inventory	33,000	49,000
Prepaid Rent	2,800	1,700
Accounts Payable	35,000	24,000
Wages Payable	600	800
Sales	250,000	–0–
Cost of Goods Sold	110,000	–0–
Expenses (Rent, Wages, and $15,000 depreciation)	70,000	–0–

Compute (a) cash sales; (b) cash cost of goods sold; (c) cash expenses; (d) cash from operating activities.

6-30 STATEMENT OF CASH FLOWS The following cash accounts of Bluejay Restaurant are on a cash basis and are in alphabetical order. Prepare a statement of cash flows using the activities format for the year ended December 31, 19X0, its first year of operation.

CO 5, 6, 7

Cost of Goods Sold	$ 45,000
Dividends Paid Out	5,000
Issuance of Notes Payable	22,000
Purchase of Equipment	50,000
Retirement of Bonds Payable	30,000
Sale of Machinery	10,000
Sales	100,000
Taxes	12,000

Problems

6-31 STATEMENT OF CASH FLOWS Leininger Sports Co. began operations in 19X0. Its summary transactions follow.

CO 7

1. Leininger put $50,000 of his money into the business.
2. Bought $10,000 property and $50,000 building for $6,000 cash and $54,000 mortgage payable.

3. Bought $20,000 inventory on account.

4. Made $25,000 cash sales.

5. Made $55,000 credit sales.

6. Collected $40,000 receivables.

7. Paid $18,000 accounts payable.

8. Paid $5,000 taxes in cash.

9. Depreciated building $2,500.

10. Leininger withdrew $1,000 for personal use.

11. Ending inventory is $2,000.

REQUIRED

Prepare the income statement, balance sheet, and statement of cash flows for Leininger Sports Co.

6-32 STATEMENT OF CASH FLOWS Holly's Consulting, Inc., was initiated in 19X9. The summary transactions for its first-year operations follow.

CO 7

1. Issued 20,000 shares of common stock, par value $10, for $15.

2. Rented office space for $20,000. The payment covers a two-year period.

3. Bought a car for $15,000 cash.

4. Consulting fees totaled $100,000.

5. Collected $80,000 of the consulting fees.

6. Wages incurred amounted to $40,000.

7. Paid $36,000 of the wages.

8. Incurred taxes payable of $10,000.

9. Paid $7,000 of the taxes.

10. Depreciation on car was $3,000.

REQUIRED

Prepare the income statement, balance sheet, and statement of cash flows for 19X9, for Holly's Consulting, Inc.

6-33 STATEMENT OF CASH FLOWS Following is the income statement, and the comparative balance sheet for Gillespie Gizmos, Inc.:

CO 7

Gillespie Gizmos, Inc.
Income Statement
For the Year Ended December 31, 19X0

Sales	$400,000	
Cost of Goods Sold	220,000	
Gross Margin		$180,000
Wages Expense	$ 50,000	
Rent Expense	60,000	
Depreciation Expense	4,000	114,000
Earnings before Taxes		66,000
Taxes Expense		24,000
Net Income		$ 42,000

Gillespie Gizmos, Inc.
Balance Sheet
December 31, 19X9 and 19X0

	19X9	19X0
Assets		
Cash	$ 20,000	$ 60,000
Accounts Receivable	25,000	30,000
Inventory	11,000	10,000
Prepaid Rent	10,000	5,000
Land	40,000	40,000
Equipment	300,000	350,000
Accumulated Depreciation	(126,000)	(130,000)
Total Assets	$280,000	$365,000
Equities		
Accounts Payable	$ 15,000	$ 35,000
Wages Payable	3,000	3,000
Taxes Payable	2,000	5,000
Bonds Payable	60,000	60,000
Common Stock	100,000	120,000
Retained Earnings	100,000	142,000
Total Equities	$280,000	$365,000

REQUIRED

Prepare a statement of cash flows from these documents for the year ended December 31, 19X0.

6-34 **STATEMENT OF CASH FLOWS** Following is the income statement and the comparative balance sheet for Charity's Horse Stables:

CO 7

Charity's Horse Stables
Income Statement
For the Year Ended June 30, 19X1

Boarding Revenues	$120,000	
Teaching Revenues	45,000	
Total Revenues		$165,000
Wages Expense	$ 60,000	
Supplies Expense	40,000	
Insurance Expense	10,000	
Taxes Expense	15,000	
Total Expenses		$125,000
Net Income		$ 40,000

Charity's Horse Stables
Balance Sheet
June 30, 19X0 and 19X1

	19X0	19X1
Cash	$20,000	$ 25,000
Accounts Receivable	10,000	5,000
Supplies	5,000	10,000
Prepaid Insurance	1,000	2,000
Barn	50,000	50,000
Accumulated Depreciation	(50,000)	(50,000)
Horses	60,000	80,000
Total Assets	$96,000	$122,000
Wages Payable	$ 1,000	$ 2,000
Taxes Payable	1,000	3,000
Charity, Capital	94,000	117,000
Total Equities	$96,000	$122,000

REQUIRED

Prepare a statement of cash flows from these documents for the year ended June 30, 19X1.

6-35   Following is an adjusted trial balance of Joey Z's for December 31, 19X1 and 19X2.

CO 7

	December 31, 19X1		December 31, 19X2	
	Dr.	Cr.	Dr.	Cr.
Cash	$ 35		$ 50	
Marketable Securities	–0–		110	
Accounts Receivable	94		80	
Inventory	260		200	
Prepaid Insurance Expense	4		3	
Land	80		80	
Equipment	320		400	
Patents	40		30	
Cost of Goods Sold	250		300	
Insurance Expense	25		25	
Taxes	50		60	
Depreciation Expense	20		20	
Patent Amortization	10		10	
Dividends	40		40	
Accum. Depr.—Equipment		$ 130		$ 150
Accounts Payable		100		55
Common Stock		400		400
Retained Earnings (beginning)		98		203
Sales		500		600
	$1,228	$1,228	$1,408	$1,408

REQUIRED

Prepare a statement of cash flows for Joey Z's for the year ended December 31, 19X2.

6-36 **STATEMENT OF CASH FLOWS** Following is an adjusted trial balance of Seago's Seascape for December 31, 19X0 and 19X1.

CO 7

	December 31	
	19X0	19X1
Debits		
Cash	$ 50	$ 25
Marketable Securities	50	0
Accounts Receivable	90	120
Inventory	300	350
Land	100	0
Equipment	500	500
Cost of Goods Sold	500	700
Depreciation Expense	25	25
Wages Expense	200	200
Bond Interest Expense	50	50
Taxes Expense	100	80
Dividends	10	10
Total Debits	$1,975	$2,060
Credits		
Accumulated Depreciation	$ 100	$ 125
Accounts Payable	200	60
Wages Payable	10	10
Bonds Payable	500	500
Premium on Bonds Payable	150	125
Common Stock	100	100
Retained Earnings (beginning)	115	30
Sales	800	1100
Gain on Sale of Marketable Securities	–0–	10
	$1,975	$2,060

REQUIRED

Prepare a statement of cash flows for Seago's Seascape for the year ended December 31, 19X1.

 6-37 **STATEMENT OF CASH FLOWS** Following is the income statement and the comparative balance sheet for Teichman's Tie Company.

CO 7

Teichman's Tie Company
Income Statement
For the Year Ended June 30, 19X2

Sales	$600,000
Cost of Goods Sold	350,000
Gross Margin	$250,000
Wages Expense	$120,000
Depreciation Expense	30,000
Supplies Expense	30,000
Patent Amortization	5,000
Operating Expenses	$185,000
	$ 65,000
Gain on Sale of Marketable	
Securities	15,000
Earnings before Taxes	$ 80,000
Tax Expense	20,000
Net Income	$ 60,000

Teichman's Tie Company
Balance Sheet
June 30, 19X1 and 19X2

	19X1	19X2
Assets		
Cash	$ 50,000	$ 70,000
Marketable Securities	250,000	50,000
Accounts Receivable	40,000	60,000
Inventory	60,000	70,000
Supplies Inventory	5,000	10,000
Current Assets	$405,000	$260,000
Land	$100,000	$120,000
Equipment	450,000	600,000
Less: Accumulated Depreciation	(130,000)	(160,000)
Patents	50,000	45,000
Long-term Assets	$470,000	$605,000
Total Assets	$875,000	$865,000

(continued)

Liabilities

Accounts Payable	$ 90,000	$ 25,000
Wages Payable	10,000	5,000
Taxes Payable	25,000	5,000
Current Debts	$125,000	$ 35,000
Notes Payable	$300,000	$350,000
Total Debts	$425,000	$385,000
Common Stock	$200,000	$200,000
Retained Earnings	250,000	280,000
Total Stockholders' Equity	$450,000	$480,000
Total Equities	$875,000	$865,000

Note: Additional equipment partly financed with Notes Payable.

REQUIRED

Prepare a statement of cash flows for Teichman's Tie Company for the year ended June 30, 19X2.

6-38 STATEMENT OF CASH FLOWS AND INCOME STATEMENT Following is the income statement and comparative balance sheet for Sartore's Safari Equipment.

CO 7

Sartore's Safari Equipment
Income Statement
For the Year Ended October 31, 19X1

Sales	$500,000
Cost of Goods Sold	200,000
Gross Margin	$300,000
Wages Expense	$100,000
Depreciation Expense	25,000
Interest Expense	50,000
Rent Expense	50,000
Operating Expenses	$225,000
Subtotal	$ 75,000
Gain on Sale of Equipment	25,000
Earnings before Taxes	$100,000
Tax Expense	30,000
Net Income	$ 70,000

Sartore's Safari Equipment
Balance Sheet
October 31, 19X0 and 19X1

	19X0	19X1
Cash	$ 60,000	$ 90,000
Accounts Receivable	40,000	45,000
Inventory	200,000	220,000
Prepaid Rent	100,000	90,000
Current Assets	$400,000	$445,000
Land*	$120,000	$220,000
Equipment†	500,000	400,000
Less: Accumulated Depreciation	(350,000)	(325,000)
Long-term Assets	$270,000	$295,000
Total Assets	$670,000	$740,000
Accounts Payable	$ 50,000	$ 60,000
Wages Payable	5,000	8,000
Taxes Payable	5,000	12,000
Current Debts	$ 60,000	$ 80,000
Bonds Payable	$100,000	$100,000
Discount on Bonds Payable	(15,000)	(10,000)
Long-term Debts	$ 85,000	$ 90,000
Common Stock	$200,000	$220,000
Retained Earnings	325,000	350,000
Stockholders' Equity	$525,000	$570,000
Total Equities	$670,000	$740,000

*The additional land was obtained by issuing $20,000 common stock and paying $80,000 cash.
†Treat the sale of equipment as a disinvestment.

REQUIRED
Prepare the statement of cash flows for Sartore's Safari Equipment from these documents for the year ended October 31, 19X1.

6-39   Following are the comparative balance sheets and statement of cash flows for Backwards Bananas, Inc.

CO 2, 3, 4

Backwards Bananas, Inc.
Balance Sheets
December 31, 19X0 and 19X1

	19X0	19X1
Cash	$ 10	$ 25
Accounts Receivable	100	120
Inventory	200	175
Prepaid Insurance	10	15
Interest Receivable	15	5
Current Assets	$335	$340
Land	$100	$120
Equipment	500	600
Less: Accumulated Depreciation	(125)	(175)
Long-term Assets	$475	$545
Total Assets	$810	$885
Accounts Payable	$150	$200
Wages Payable	30	45
Taxes Payable	20	40
Current Debts	$200	$285
Notes Payable	$300	$200
Total Debts	$500	$485
Common Stock	$200	$270
Retained Earnings	110	130
Stockholders' Equity	$310	$400
Total Equities	$810	$885

Backwards Bananas, Inc.
Statement of Cash Flows
For the Year Ended December 31, 19X1

Cash Flows from Operating Activities

Sales		$600
Cost of Goods Sold		(225)
Gross Margin		$375
Deduct:		
Insurance	$ (25)	
Wages	(85)	
Taxes	(55)	(165)
Interest Revenue		45
Net Cash Provided by Operating Activities		$255

Cash Flows from Investing Activities

Purchase of Land	$ (20)	
Purchase of Equipment	(100)	
Net Cash Used by Investing Activities		$(120)

Cash Flows from Financing Activities

Issuance of Common Stock	$ 70	
Retirement of Notes Payable	(100)	
Cash Dividends Paid Out	(90)	
Net Cash Provided by Financing Activities		$(120)
Net Increase in Cash		$ 15

REQUIRED

Prepare the income statement for Backwards Bananas, Inc., for 19X1 from these documents.

6-40 **CASH AND NEAR CASH** Refer to Problem 6-37 for Teichman's Tie Company.

CO 7   *REQUIRED*

Revise the statement of cash flows prepared for Teichman's Tie Company in Problem 6-37 to treat marketable securities as near cash. (*Hint:* Combine the two accounts into one.)

6-41 **CASH BUDGET AND STATEMENT OF CASH FLOWS** Recall the discussion of Malux Company in Chapter 5. Specifically, recall Exhibit 5-9 that presented the cash budget of CO 1, 7 Malux Company. It is reproduced here in abbreviated form for the year 19X2.

Cash balance, beginning			$ 30,000
Cash collections from customers			708,000
W. Total cash available			$738,000
Cash disbursements:			
Merchandise		$ 493,500	
Operating expenses		195,750	
Truck purchase		9,000	
X. Total disbursements		$ 698,250	
Minimum cash balance desired		30,000	
Total cash needed			$728,250
Excess of total cash available			
over total cash needed			$ 9,750
Financing:			
Borrowings		$ 42,000	
Repayments		(42,000)	
Interest		(6,075)	
Y. Total effects of financing			(6,075)
Z. Cash balance, ending (W + Y − X)			$ 33,675

REQUIRED

a. Restate this data in the form of a statement of cash flows.

b. Discuss the relative merits of the cash budget and the statement of cash flows.

Business Decision Case

Darryl Semlow is looking at his financial statements and has asked his consultant Hana Breen for help. The comparative balance sheets and income statements are as follows:

Semlow Industries
Balance Sheets
December 31, 19X1 and 19X2
(000,000 omitted)

	19X1	19X2
Assets		
Cash	$ 100	$ 50
Accounts Receivable	200	300
Merchandise Inventory	300	550
Building and Equipment	1,000	1,000
Accumulated Depreciation	(100)	(200)
Total Assets	$1,500	$1,700
Liabilities and Owners' Equity		
Accounts Payable	$ 300	$ 300
Common Stock	500	500
Retained Earnings	700	900
Total Liabilities and Owners' Equity	$1,500	$1,700

Semlow Industries
Income Statement
For the Year Ended December 31, 19X2
(000,000 omitted)

Sales		$1,000
Cost of Goods Sold		400
Gross Margin		$ 600
Operating Expenses (cash)	$200	
Depreciation Expense	100	300
Net Income		$ 300

Darryl Semlow asks Hana Breen, "What is going on? My income is $300,000,000 and I pay out dividends of $100,000,000. Why has my cash balance decreased by $50,000,000. I don't understand it. I thought I was making money."

REQUIRED

Prepare Hana's response to Darryl.

PRODUCT COSTING: PLANNING AND CONTROL

Standard Costs: Materials, Direct Labor, and Variable Overhead

CHAPTER OBJECTIVES

After reading Chapter 7, you should be able to:

1. State the purposes served by standard costs (pp. 239–41).

2. Calculate the material price variance and the material quantity variance (pp. 241–46).

3. Compute the labor rate variance and the labor efficiency variance (pp. 246–48).

4. Define *predetermined variable manufacturing overhead rate* (pp. 248–50).

5. Calculate the variable manufacturing overhead spending variance and variable manufacturing overhead efficiency variance (pp. 250–55).

6. Describe the general variance model based on input and output standards (pp. 256–60).

The control of business operations depends on management planning the amount of output considered reasonable given the amount of resources available to the operation. *Standard costs* are the result of a study of quantities and of costs necessary to make the product. These standard costs play an important role in controlling operations. Journal entries can be used to record standard costs and variances. Discussion of journal entries is delayed until Chapter 10, where we discuss standard costing in relation to product costing.

STANDARD COSTS

CHAPTER OBJECTIVE 1
Purposes of standard costs

Effectiveness refers to how well a plan is met or a purpose is served. *Efficiency* refers to the productivity of some work; informally, it is the useful output per input. Standard costs are used to assess efficiency, not effectiveness.

In order to evaluate properly the efficiency of business operations, it is important to have a well-founded notion of the relationship that should exist between the resources (direct material, direct labor, and factory or manufacturing overhead) and the output (the product). A *standard cost* is a predetermined cost of the product. It is a goal managers set under projected conditions. The standard costs and the variances (defined later) are determined with a standard cost system. The standard cost system relies heavily on a study of the product from a product design viewpoint. The purpose of the study is to estimate the quantities of each type of material necessary to complete the product and the quantity of direct labor necessary to fabricate and assemble the direct materials.

Consider the following example. Buchanan Company manufactures a stereo cabinet that it sells to a major retailer. (We will also use this company in Chapter 8.) Buchanan sells the cabinet at a set price agreed to by both parties—Buchanan Company and the retailer. Thus, Buchanan's cost inefficiencies may not be passed on in the form of higher prices but instead would have to be absorbed by Buchanan in the form of lower margin. Therefore, Buchanan's accounting system must provide information for its management to make appropriate cost decisions. A study of the cabinet specifications reveals that the following materials are necessary to complete one cabinet:

> 38 sq. ft. of birch panels for top, three sides, and shelf
> 20 sq. ft. of hardboard panels for bottom and rear
> 50 linear ft. of spruce for structural support

The specifications also reveal the required number of cuts with a saw, the extent to which the edges of the birch panel for the top will require beveling, and the extent to which the front birch panel will require special cutting to accommodate the speakers. A person familiar with these labor operations will be capable of estimating the amount of time required to complete each of the operations necessary to fabricate the components and assemble the cabinet. Assume that such a person studying the specifications estimates that the following direct labor will be required for each cabinet:

Fabrication Department: 3 direct labor hours
Assembly Department: 2 direct labor hours

The Fabrication Department cuts the wood, bevels the edges of the top, and cuts the holes for the speakers. Reference to the labor contract (if unionized) or expected pay rates would permit an estimate of the expected labor costs. At Buchanan workers earn $8 an hour in the Fabrication Department and $6 per hour in the Assembly Department.

The purchasing manager is capable of providing an estimate of the cost of materials necessary to manufacture the cabinet. Let's assume that the purchasing manager provided the following estimates:

Birch panels: $1 per sq. ft. in 4 ft. × 8 ft. panels
Hardboard panels: $.18 per sq. ft. in 4 ft. × 8 ft. panels
Spruce structural members: $.20 per linear ft. in 1 in. × 2 in. dimensions

Screws, glue, and other parts are considered indirect materials and are discussed in conjunction with variable overhead later in this chapter. Some companies choose to consider these items as direct materials and include them in this analysis.

Summarizing all of this quantity and cost information, we arrive at the ideal standard cost for one stereo cabinet (see Exhibit 7-1). *Prime costs* (first mentioned in Chapter 2) consist of the cost of direct materials plus the cost of direct labor.

This standard cost of $87.60 per cabinet is the ideal cost. However, the ideal standard cost is based on quantities that may not be easily attained in actual production. Because the birch and hardboard panels arrive in standard 4 ft. × 8 ft. panels, it is likely that cutting those panels into the required smaller panels will result in some waste.

Likewise, the estimates of labor hours required have made no allowance for random machine malfunctions, delays from lack of materials, and other workplace factors that may tend to slow down the manufacturing process.

Practical standard costs may be developed by manufacturing the stereo cabinet on a pilot basis for a short period of time to determine the quantity estimates that are capable of being attained. Assume that a two-week pilot run revealed the following quantity usage per stereo cabinet.

Birch panels: 42 sq. ft.
Hardboard panels: 24 sq. ft.
Spruce structural members: 52 linear ft.
Fabrication Department direct labor: 3.5 hrs.
Assembly Department direct labor: 2.25 hrs.

These more reasonable quantity estimates may be used to arrive at the standard prime cost of a stereo cabinet based on practical standards. The practical standard prime cost is $98.22, as depicted in Exhibit 7-2 (page 242).

We have now developed two standards for producing the stereo cabinet. The ideal standard indicates a prime cost for $87.60 per cabinet and the practical standard indicates a prime cost of $98.22 per cabinet. Clearly, it is the practical standard of $98.22

EXHIBIT 7-1

IDEAL STANDARD PRIME COST PER UNIT OF PRODUCT

Direct Materials:

Birch panels, 38 sq. ft. @ $1 per sq. ft.	$38.00
Hardboard panels, 20 sq. ft. @ $.18 per sq. ft.	3.60
Spruce structural members, 50 linear ft. @ $.20 per linear ft.	10.00
Total Direct Materials	$51.60

Direct Labor:

Fabrication Department, 3 direct labor hours @ $8 per hr.	$24.00
Assembly Department, 2 direct labor hours @ $6 per hr.	12.00
Total Direct Labor	36.00
Total Prime Costs (ideal standard)	$87.60

that is most useful in planning, control, and decision making. Recall that pricing decision must be accurate, as prices cannot rise to absorb higher costs. The ideal standard is of little use once the practical standard has been determined through a pilot study.

USE OF STANDARD COSTS IN CONTROLLING DIRECT MATERIALS

CHAPTER OBJECTIVE 2
Materials variances

The profitability of any company is closely related to the control of direct material and direct labor costs. Once the selling price of the stereo cabinet is established in the marketplace, adverse changes in direct materials, direct labor, or manufacturing overhead (manufacturing overhead will be discussed later in this chapter and in Chapter 8) will have an adverse effect on profits. Thus, the company must have a formal system to monitor these costs.

Before we examine the methods used to monitor material costs, we should review the process by which materials are requisitioned, purchased, and issued to the Fabrication Department. As an order of stereo cabinets is received, the Fabrication Department supervisor checks the birch panels, hardboard panels, and spruce structural members on hand in the raw materials storeroom (or warehouse) to determine whether additional materials should be ordered. If additional quantities are required, a requisition is prepared and sent to the purchasing manager. The purchasing manager requests quotations from several potential suppliers and selects the supplier that offers the requisite quality wood at the lowest cost.

When the materials are received from the supplier, they are placed in the raw materials storeroom, where they are held until the supervisor of the Fabrication Department requests that they be delivered to his or her department for production. In some

---

EXHIBIT 7-2

PRACTICAL STANDARD PRIME COST
PER UNIT OF PRODUCT

Direct Materials:		
Birch panels, 42 sq. ft. @ $1 per sq. ft.	$42.00	
Hardboard panels, 24 sq. ft. @ $.18		
per sq. ft.	4.32	
Spruce structural members, 52 linear ft. @		
$.20 per linear ft.	10.40	
Total Direct Materials		$56.72
Direct Labor:		
Fabrication Department, 3.5 direct labor hours		
@ $8 per hr.	$28.00	
Assembly Department, 2.25 direct labor hours		
@ $6 per hr.	13.50	
Total Direct Labor		41.50
Total Prime Costs (practical standard)		$98.22

---

companies, the materials for a specific job are identified and held in the warehouse until the job is started.

In monitoring the cost of direct materials, we focus on the performance of two separate managers who are responsible for the costs incurred. The *purchasing manager* is responsible for the price paid for the materials, and the *manufacturing manager* is responsible for the quantities used in manufacturing the product.

A variance is the difference between the actual cost and the practical standard cost. (As is customary, we will simply use *standard* in the rest of the textbook.) A variance is favorable when the actual result is better than the standard and it is unfavorable when the actual result is not as good as the standard. Variances are important because they act as signals (unless there are extenuating circumstances) that aid in the evaluation of the manager and in the investigation of the cause of the variance.

Material Price Variance

The material price variance is the responsibility of the purchasing manager and it is determined at the time of purchase for all direct materials purchased. This material price variance is calculated by comparing the total cost of direct materials purchased with the cost that would have been incurred had the items been purchased at the standard cost per unit.

At the beginning of June, the purchasing manager purchased the following direct materials that were expected to be used by the Fabrication Department in June and July:

Birch panels, 16,800 sq. ft. × $1.25	$21,000
Hardboard panels, 9,600 sq. ft. × $.17	1,632
Spruce structural members, 20,800 linear ft. × $.21	4,368
Total Actual Cost of Items Purchased	$27,000

The standard cost for the items purchased was as follows:

Birch panels, 16,800 sq. ft. × $1	$16,800
Hardboard panels, 9,600 sq. ft. × $.18	1,728
Spruce structural members, 20,800 linear ft. × $.20	4,160
Total Standard Cost of Items Purchased	$22,688

From this information, the controller could prepare a report designed to help improve the performance of the purchasing manager. Such a report for June 19X1 is presented in Exhibit 7-3. This performance report will be sent to the purchasing manager and his or her supervisor. It shows that there is a significant cost control problem with the birch panels. This report should prompt a discussion between the purchasing manager and the supervisor. The discussion should seek to identify courses of action to counter the unfavorable cost increase for the birch panels.

There are three ways of indicating whether a variance is favorable or unfavorable in a report. A favorable variance is denoted by the word *favorable*, the letter *F*, or by showing the number as a positive number. Correspondingly, an unfavorable variance is shown by the word *unfavorable*, the letter *U*, or by showing the number as a negative number (often by enclosing it within parentheses).

The price variance shown in this report is calculated using the following formula. (Here, of course, the parentheses only indicate aggregation.)

$$\begin{array}{c}\text{Material}\\\text{Price}\\\text{Variance}\end{array} = \left(\begin{array}{c}\text{Actual}\\\text{Quantity}\\\text{Purchased}\end{array} \times \begin{array}{c}\text{Actual}\\\text{Cost per}\\\text{Unit}\end{array}\right) - \left(\begin{array}{c}\text{Actual}\\\text{Quantity}\\\text{Purchased}\end{array} \times \begin{array}{c}\text{Standard}\\\text{Cost per}\\\text{Unit}\end{array}\right)$$

or alternatively:

$$\begin{array}{c}\text{Material}\\\text{Price}\\\text{Variance}\end{array} = \begin{array}{c}\text{Actual}\\\text{Quantity}\\\text{Purchased}\end{array} \times \left(\begin{array}{c}\text{Actual}\\\text{Cost per}\\\text{Unit}\end{array} - \begin{array}{c}\text{Standard}\\\text{Cost per}\\\text{Unit}\end{array}\right)$$

Using the birch panel amounts with each of these formulas, we get:

(16,800 sq. ft. × $1.25) − (16,800 sq. ft. × $1) = $4,200 Unfavorable

or:

16,800 sq. ft. × ($1.25 − $1) = $4,200 Unfavorable

The variance is unfavorable because the company paid more for the materials than the standard cost.

	EXHIBIT 7-3		

Purchasing Manager's Performance Report
For June 19X1

Item Purchased	Actual Cost	Standard Cost	Price Variance
Birch panels	$21,000	$16,800	$4,200 Unfavorable
Hardboard panels	1,632	1,728	96 Favorable
Spruce structural members	4,368	4,160	208 Unfavorable
Total Cost	$27,000	$22,688	$4,312 Unfavorable

Material Quantity Variance

The manufacturing manager is responsible for the quantities of materials used. He or she is in a position to enforce material usage standards and monitor the cutting methods used in manufacturing the stereo cabinets. In monitoring the manufacturing manager's performance, the focus is on materials issued from the raw materials storeroom rather than materials purchased. The controller must rely on a system that documents the quantity of materials issued from the storeroom to the production line and a system that documents the quantity of finished stereo cabinets completed and transferred to finished goods inventory.

In June, the following materials were issued from the raw materials storeroom to the production line for use in manufacturing stereo cabinets.

Birch panels: 10,000 sq. ft.
Hardboard panels: 6,000 sq. ft.
Spruce structural members: 10,250 linear ft.

During this month, 200 stereo cabinets were completed or partially completed (185 were sold, 5 were in finished goods inventory, and 10 had just left the Fabrication Department and were about to be assembled). Thus, the following quantities should have been used:

Birch panels: 200 stereo cabinets × 42 sq. ft. = 8,400 sq. ft.
Hardboard panels: 200 stereo cabinets × 24 sq. ft. = 4,800 sq. ft.
Spruce structural members: 200 stereo cabinets × 52 linear ft. = 10,400 linear ft.

This information concerning quantities coupled with the standard cost information permits a calculation of **material quantity variance** that is meaningful in evaluating the performance of the manufacturing manager.

EXHIBIT 7-4

Manufacturing Manager's Performance Report
(Materials Portion Only)
June 19X1

	Input Standard Cost	Output Standard Cost	Material Quantity Variance	
Direct Material				
Birch Panels	$10,000	$ 8,400	$1,600	Unfavorable
Hardboard Panels	1,080	864	216	Unfavorable
Spruce Structural				
Members	2,050	2,080	30	Favorable
Total Cost	$13,130	$11,344	$1,786	Unfavorable

$$\begin{matrix}\text{Material}\\\text{Quantity}\\\text{Variance}\end{matrix} = \left(\begin{matrix}\text{Actual}\\\text{Quantity}\\\text{Issued}\end{matrix} \times \begin{matrix}\text{Standard}\\\text{Cost per}\\\text{Unit}\end{matrix}\right) - \left(\begin{matrix}\text{Standard}\\\text{Quantity}\\\text{Based on}\\\text{Output}\end{matrix} \times \begin{matrix}\text{Standard}\\\text{Cost per}\\\text{Unit}\end{matrix}\right)$$

or alternatively:

$$\begin{matrix}\text{Material}\\\text{Quantity}\\\text{Variance}\end{matrix} = \begin{matrix}\text{Standard}\\\text{Cost per}\\\text{Unit}\end{matrix} \times \left(\begin{matrix}\text{Actual}\\\text{Quantity}\\\text{Issued}\end{matrix} - \begin{matrix}\text{Standard}\\\text{Quantity}\\\text{Based on}\\\text{Output}\end{matrix}\right)$$

Using the birch amounts with the first of these formulations, we get:

Input Standard Cost   **Output Standard Cost**
(10,000 sq. ft. × $1/sq. ft.) − (8,400 sq. ft. × $1/sq. ft.) = $1,600 Unfavorable

The left-hand portion of the preceding formula is called input standard cost because it represents the standard costs that are associated with the direct materials placed in production (input). The right-hand portion of the formula is called output standard cost because it represents the standard costs that are associated with the items manufactured (output) during the period based on the quantities of materials that should have been used in manufacturing the items. The variance is unfavorable because more materials were used in production than should have been, based on practical standards.

From the foregoing information, the controller could prepare the report in Exhibit 7-4, which is designed to monitor the performance of the manufacturing manager. The report would be sent to the manufacturing manager and his or her supervisor in order to permit the supervisor to determine whether discussion with the manufacturing manager is necessary.

The June 19X1 report should invite a discussion of the unfavorable material quantity variances associated with birch panels and hardboard panels. Inquiries may reveal that the saw blades are not being changed when the power saw operators switch from the more easily cut hardboard panels to the birch panels, which are more difficult to cut. Such a revelation might prompt a change in processing to eliminate scrapping birch panels that are ruined in the cutting operation.

The unfavorable material quantity variances associated with the hardboard panels may be the result of a cause that is not under the control of the manufacturing manager even though it appears on that manager's performance report. When we calculated the materials price variance in May 19X1, we found that the purchasing manager had a favorable material price variance for hardboard panels. The purchasing manager purchased the hardboard at $.17 per panel. That cost was $.01 per panel below the standard cost of a hardboard panel. It is possible that the purchasing manager bought a lower-quality panel in order to realize a favorable material price variance. That action appears to have had an adverse effect on the quantity of hardboard panels used, as the lower-quality panels are more easily chipped, rendering them unusable during the cutting operation.

Thus, even though this system of monitoring materials costs attempts to attribute responsibility for cost variances to the manager responsible for creating the variance, the system is not perfect. The proper use of cost standards for control of operations must rely on managerial judgment in order to be effective.

USE OF STANDARD COSTS IN CONTROLLING DIRECT LABOR

CHAPTER OBJECTIVE 3
Labor variances

Direct labor costs may also be analyzed from the viewpoint of price and quantity variances. However, the price variance for direct labor is called the *labor rate variance* and the quantity variance is called the *labor efficiency variance*. The manufacturing manager is often the one person in the position to control both the labor rate variance and the labor efficiency variance. As we will see in this section, the manufacturing manager's performance report would include the labor rate variance and the labor efficiency variance, as well as the material quantity variance discussed earlier.

Labor Rate Variance

The labor rate variance is the result of the difference between the average pay rate for each department and the wage rate that was used in arriving at the product's standard cost. One might wonder why the manufacturing manager should be held responsible for the labor rate when that rate is often determined by labor negotiations between the labor union and the personnel department or the human resources department. However, the manufacturing manager does influence the average labor rate in a significant way: The manager exercises control over the assignment of personnel to tasks. Because there are various labor rates within the department (based on seniority, productivity, and function, for example), the manager influences the average labor rate by assigning tasks to personnel.

Buchanan Company experienced the following actual labor costs in June 19XX:

Fabrication Department, 750 direct labor hours @ $7.76 $5,820
Assembly Department, 550 direct labor hours @ $6.30   3,465
Total Direct Labor Costs $9,285

The labor rate variance is calculated by comparing the actual labor costs with the input standard costs as follows:

$$\text{Labor Rate Variance} = \text{Actual Cost} - \left(\begin{array}{c} \text{Actual} \\ \text{Direct Labor} \\ \text{Hours} \end{array} \times \begin{array}{c} \text{Standard} \\ \text{Wage} \\ \text{Rate} \end{array} \right)$$

or alternatively, since actual cost equals actual direct labor hours times the actual wage rate:

$$\text{Labor Rate Variance} = \begin{array}{c} \text{Actual} \\ \text{Direct Labor} \\ \text{Hours} \end{array} \times \left(\begin{array}{c} \text{Actual} \\ \text{Wage} \\ \text{Rate} \end{array} - \begin{array}{c} \text{Standard} \\ \text{Wage} \\ \text{Rate} \end{array} \right)$$

Thus, the labor rate variance for the Fabrication Department is calculated as follows:

$$\$5,820 - (750 \times \$8) = \$180 \text{ Favorable}$$

or:

$$750 \times (\$7.76 - \$8) = \$180 \text{ Favorable}$$

The variance is considered to be favorable because the actual average wage rate was $.24 per hour less than the standard rate of $8 per hour.

Labor Efficiency Variance

At the end of June, ten of the 200 cabinets that were worked on by the Fabrication Department are still in work in process inventory, as the Assembly Department will assemble them in July. Thus the Assembly Department completed 190 cabinets in June. Based on the production of 200 stereo cabinets by the Fabrication Department and 190 cabinets by the Assembly Department, the following costs should have been incurred in June 19XX:

Fabrication Department

200 cabinets × (3.5 standard direct labor hours × $8 per hr.) $5,600

Assembly Department

190 cabinets × (2.25 standard direct labor hours × $6 per hr.)   2,565
Total standard cost (output standard) $8,165

The labor efficiency variance is calculated by comparing the input standard cost used in calculating the labor rate variance with the output standard costs shown above. The formula is as follows:

$$\begin{matrix} \text{Labor} \\ \text{Efficiency} \\ \text{Variance} \end{matrix} = \left(\begin{matrix} \text{Actual} \\ \text{Direct Labor} \\ \text{Hours} \end{matrix} \times \begin{matrix} \text{Standard} \\ \text{Wage} \\ \text{Rate} \end{matrix} \right) - \left(\begin{matrix} \text{Standard Direct} \\ \text{Labor Hours for} \\ \text{Units Produced} \end{matrix} \times \begin{matrix} \text{Standard} \\ \text{Wage} \\ \text{Rate} \end{matrix} \right)$$

or alternatively:

$$\begin{matrix} \text{Labor} \\ \text{Efficiency} \\ \text{Variance} \end{matrix} = \begin{matrix} \text{Standard} \\ \text{Wage} \\ \text{Rate} \end{matrix} \times \left(\begin{matrix} \text{Actual} \\ \text{Direct Labor} \\ \text{Hours} \end{matrix} - \begin{matrix} \text{Standard Direct Labor} \\ \text{Hours for Units} \\ \text{Produced} \end{matrix} \right)$$

Using the alternate formula shown above, the labor efficiency variance for the assembly department is calculated as follows:

$6 per hour × (550 actual direct labor hours − 427.5 standard direct labor hours for the 190 cabinets produced) = $735 Unfavorable

The labor efficiency variance is unfavorable because it took more direct labor hours to produce the 190 cabinets than it should have taken based on practical standards.

The labor rate variances and labor efficiency variances would likely be summarized in the same manufacturing manager's performance report that was used to report the materials quantity variances. The labor portion of that report is shown in Exhibit 7-5.

Firms in an automated environment might not be too interested in these labor variances. If labor costs are an insignificant part of manufacturing costs, management might prefer to look at *machine efficiency* instead of labor efficiency. This would be analyzed in a manner analogous to labor efficiency. For example:

$$\begin{matrix} \text{Machine} \\ \text{Efficiency} \\ \text{Variance} \end{matrix} = \left(\begin{matrix} \text{Actual} \\ \text{Machine} \\ \text{Hours} \end{matrix} \times \begin{matrix} \text{Standard} \\ \text{Machine} \\ \text{Rate} \end{matrix} \right) - \left(\begin{matrix} \text{Standard} \\ \text{Machine} \\ \text{Hours} \end{matrix} \times \begin{matrix} \text{Standard} \\ \text{Machine} \\ \text{Rate} \end{matrix} \right)$$

THE NATURE OF OVERHEAD COSTS

CHAPTER OBJECTIVE 4
Variable overhead rate

Factory overhead costs are manufacturing costs that are incurred in support of the overall manufacturing effort without becoming directly linked to any one unit of product. Examples of manufacturing overhead costs include the depreciation of the factory building, the costs of heat and light, and the cost of manufacturing supervision.

The distinction between variable manufacturing overhead and fixed manufacturing overhead is based on the behavior of manufacturing costs in response to changes in the level of production. Recall the definitions of variable and fixed costs from Chapters 2 and 3. *Variable manufacturing overhead costs* are nondirect manufacturing costs that change in direct response to changes in the level of production. An example of variable manufacturing costs would include the cost of electricity. Electricity is used to provide power to the machines, to provide light for the entire plant, and, in some instances, to

EXHIBIT 7-5

Manufacturing Manager's Performance Report
(Labor Portion Only)
June 19X1

	Actual Cost	Input Standard Cost	Output Standard Cost	Labor Rate Variance	Labor Efficiency Variance
Fabrication Department	$5,820	$6,000*	$5,600	$180F	$ 400U
Assembly Department	3,465	3,300*	2,565	165U	735U
	$9,285	$9,300	$8,165	$ 15F	$1,135U

*The calculations for input standard cost are:
  Fabrication Department = 750 actual hours × $8 standard cost per direct labor hour
           = $6,000
   Assembly Department = 550 actual hours × $6 standard cost per direct labor hour
           = $3,300
F   Favorable.
U   Unfavorable.

provide heat for the plant. Because electricity usage is not specifically identified with each item of machinery (except for certain heavy-use machines), the cost of electricity should not be regarded as a direct cost. Instead, we must regard it as an indirect cost and make a distinction between the variable and fixed components of the cost. In the case of electricity, a study of the rate agreement with the electric utility or the utility bill would likely reveal the variable cost per kilowatt-hour used.

Another type of variable overhead cost is one that would appear to be a direct material cost, such as the cost of glue used to attach the various components of a cabinet. Because glue is a relatively inexpensive component of the cabinet, the material cost procedures typically associated with direct materials are not cost effective. Consequently, materials of relatively low value are often regarded as indirect costs and thus a component of variable overhead. As such, the costs of those items are controlled and applied to units of product using the variable manufacturing overhead standard costing techniques described in the following sections.

Fixed overhead is the portion of manufacturing overhead that does not change in response to changes (within the relevant range) in levels of production. The cost associated with depreciation of plant and equipment is regarded as a fixed manufacturing overhead cost. Given a factory with the capacity to produce 100,000 units of product per year, the level of production could vary between 80,000 and 100,000 units per year (its *relevant range*) without the cost of depreciation changing. If production went beyond 100,000 units per year, additional equipment would have to be purchased and the depreciation cost would increase; thus the concept of relevant range is important in discussions of fixed costs.

Under the *full costing* (or *absorption costing*) method of product costing required for financial and tax accounting purposes (first introduced in Chapter 5), overhead costs must be applied (attached) to units of product. The method by which the overhead costs are identified with units of product is very different from the method used to identify direct material and direct labor costs with units of product.

In the case of direct materials, a *materials issue slip* links the materials with a particular product or production run. In the case of direct labor, a *time card* links the labor with a particular product or production run. However, in the case of overhead costs, there *is* no routinely prepared document that links the cost to the product. Instead, overhead costs are applied to the product through the use of **overhead rates** that are tied to a resource (sometimes called a **cost driver** or *production divisor*) that has a direct relationship to the product. Typically, the resource having a direct relationship to the product is direct labor hours. Direct labor hours are documented on the time card.

Before the start of each new fiscal year, manufacturing companies establish a **predetermined variable manufacturing overhead rate.** This is the rate at which variable manufacturing overhead is applied to production (explained later in this chapter and in greater detail in Chapters 10 and 11). This rate can be estimated by an analysis of all of the variable budgeted overhead items (such as electricity and glue). The total of these variable overhead costs is related to a resource (cost driver, as mentioned earlier), such as direct labor hours, that has a measured and direct relationship to a unit of product. For example, during preparation of the Buchanan Company budget, the variable manufacturing overhead for the Fabrication Department is estimated at $160,000. The direct labor hours is estimated to be 80,000. Then the overhead rate is derived as $160,000/ 80,000 hours, or $2 per direct labor hour. Thus the following predetermined variable manufacturing overhead rates apply to Buchanan's cabinet manufacturing operation (the Assembly Department's variable manufacturing overhead would be computed in a similar manner):

Fabrication	$2 per direct labor hour
Assembly	$4 per direct labor hour

Based on the standard direct labor hours per unit, we are able to establish the following standards for variable manufacturing overhead:

$$\text{Fabrication Overhead Rate} = 3.5 \text{ standard hours per unit } [\textit{from Exhibit 7-2}] \times \$2 \text{ per direct labor hour} = \$7 \text{ per unit of product}$$

$$\text{Assembly Overhead Rate} = 2.25 \text{ standard hours per unit } [\textit{from Exhibit 7-2}] \times \$4 \text{ per direct labor hour} = \$9 \text{ per unit of product}$$

The total predetermined variable manufacturing overhead rate is $16 per unit of product ($7 + $9).

VARIABLE OVERHEAD AND PERFORMANCE EVALUATION

CHAPTER OBJECTIVE 5
Variable overhead variances

The primary use of standard costs is to aid in the evaluation of managers of organizational units (responsibility centers, as explained in Chapter 1). We have seen how standard costs enable us to evaluate the purchasing manager based on the material price variance and the manufacturing manager based on the material quantity variance, the labor rate variance, and the labor efficiency variance. We will now examine the variable overhead cost variances and explore how they might be used for managerial performance evaluation.

Variable Overhead Spending Variance

The total variable overhead variance may be fragmented into two separate variances that will give us additional insight into the department manager's performance in the area of cost control.

The method used to fragment this variance is the same one that was discussed in the previous sections on materials and labor. We use it here to calculate the variable manufacturing overhead spending variance and the variable manufacturing overhead efficiency variance. The formula for **variable manufacturing overhead spending variance** is as follows:

$$\begin{matrix} \text{Variable Manufacturing} \\ \text{Overhead Spending} \\ \text{Variance} \end{matrix} = \begin{matrix} \text{Actual} \\ \text{Cost} \end{matrix} - \left(\begin{matrix} \text{Actual} \\ \text{Direct Labor} \\ \text{Hours} \end{matrix} \times \begin{matrix} \text{Standard Variable} \\ \text{Overhead Rate per} \\ \text{Direct Labor Hour} \end{matrix} \right)$$

(Rather than direct labor hours, some other input could be used, such as machine hours.)

The general ledger at the end of June revealed that the Fabrication Department incurred variable manufacturing overhead costs of $1,700. The Assembly Department incurred variable manufacturing overhead costs of $1,500. These actual costs may be compared with the input standard costs to determine the variable manufacturing overhead spending variance for each department. That calculation is shown below.

Fabrication Department: $1,700 - (750 \times \$2) = \$200$ Unfavorable
Assembly Department: $1,500 - (550 \times \$4) = \underline{\quad 700}$ Favorable
Variable Manufacturing Overhead Spending Variance = $\underline{\underline{\$500}}$ Favorable

This variance expresses the extent to which the actual price of the variable overhead components differed from the standard price and the extent to which actual quantities used differed from the standard quantities used. The separate effects of price and quantity cannot be isolated because there was no standard quantity established for each of the resources included in the variable overhead category.

For example, this variance could be favorable because Buchanan paid a lower price for glue than the price considered when the variable overhead rate per direct labor hour was estimated. Or this variance could be favorable because we used less glue than the quantity considered when the variable overhead rate per direct labor hour was estimated. Or the variance could be favorable because of various combinations of causes related to price and quantity. Further, one of the components of variable overhead, such as electricity, could have had an unfavorable variance and another component, such as glue, could have had a favorable variance.

A problem in using this variance to evaluate the performance of managers is that the responsibility for the variance is shared between the purchasing manager and the manufacturing manager. The purchasing manager is responsible for the portion of the variance related to price and the manufacturing manager is responsible for the portion of the variance related to quantity usage. Because we are unable to separate these shared responsibilities into distinct variances, we include the manufacturing overhead spending variance on the performance report of the manufacturing manager and use caution in interpreting the meaning of the variance. An alternative approach would be to establish

TELEPHONE INDUSTRY DEVELOPS NEW COST STANDARDS

The AT&T divestiture, deregulation, and increased competition have had a considerable impact on the telephone industry—and telephone users. These changes were well publicized, but less well known is the significant impact on telephone industry accounting.

Accounting for telephone companies had been frozen in a form dating from 1934. In that year, as part of its regulatory function, the Federal Communications Commission (FCC) prescribed a Uniform System of Accounts (USOA) for telephone companies. This chart of accounts has never incorporated the generally accepted accounting principles issued by the Accounting Principles Board or the Financial Accounting Standards Board.

In 1978, the FCC began working on the design and implementation of a new financial accounting process. It appointed an industry advisory committee to update the Uniform System of Accounts. Six years later, the advisory committee made its recommendations. After subsequent hearings and revisions, the FCC ordered a new Uniform System of Accounts to be implemented by all telephone companies on January 1, 1988.

This method of designing an accounting process was a new approach for the government. When Congress became concerned about cost accounting in the defense industry, it created a Cost Accounting Standards Board (CASB), which issued 21 statements on cost accounting. The statements were produced on a centralized basis; an appointed board hired researchers, who made proposals, which were reviewed and reacted to by the industry. Although the CASB statements were requirements for defense contractors, they had an impact on the cost accounting process in general.

In regard to the telephone industry, Congress and regulators decided to try a different approach. Instead of having proposals made by a centralized board, the FCC issued an order that outlined accounting safeguard requirements for a telephone company to enter the nonregulated marketplace.

The FCC had previously allowed telephone companies to enter deregulated services only through fully separated subsidiary operations. This corporate structure required separate books of account, and it provided assurance to ratepayers that regulated revenues would not be used to subsidize nonregulated business activities. It also provided assurance that the telephone companies could not enter into unfair competition (e.g., predatory pricing). The separate subsidiary was prohibited from using any employees from the regulated company. As a result of these safeguards, many services were priced beyond the customer's willingness to pay.

This outcome gave the regulators some concern. Their goal was eventual deregulation, but this deregulation could be accomplished more readily if prices for existing regulated services were declining. If the telephone industry were allowed to enter lucrative new lines of business—with adequate safeguards against subsidization—the burden on regulated services would decrease, and the cost of telephone services would go down.

As a safeguard against subsidization, under the new order, the FCC required telephone companies with more than $100 million in annual revenues to file a cost manual for review and approval.

The FCC "experiment" took the dedication of a vast amount of resources to produce and publish cost accounting information. For two years, management accountants in the telephone industry worked to develop procedures to implement the new accounting requirement in their companies. The United States Telephone Association (USTA) hired Price Waterhouse to develop a prototype manual for the telephone industry and during 1987 sponsored seminars nationally for telephone accountants to acquaint them with the ramifications of the new requirements. Pacific Bell participated in the USTA forums and used the prototype for the format of its cost manual.

The FCC has reviewed these cost manuals and has requested more detail regarding the proposed methods of regulated/nonregulated allocation. FCC approval is necessary prior to a telephone company's entry into nonregulated businesses. The jury is still out on whether or not existing restrictions will be modified to allow telephone companies to compete in the most lucrative nonregulated markets. . . .

a standard price and standard usage rates per unit of product for each of the resources included in this category. Such an approach would permit a distinction between the two causes of variance; however, there are a large number of individual cost categories included in variable overhead and such precision would not be cost effective.

Variable Overhead Efficiency Variance

The formula for variable manufacturing overhead efficiency is the following:

$$
\begin{array}{l}
\text{Variable Manufacturing} \\
\text{Overhead Efficiency} \\
\text{Variance}
\end{array} =
\left(
\begin{array}{l}
\text{Actual} \\
\text{Direct Labor} \times \\
\text{Hours}
\end{array}
\begin{array}{l}
\text{Standard Variable} \\
\text{Overhead Rate per} \\
\text{Direct Labor Hour}
\end{array}
\right) -
\left(
\begin{array}{l}
\text{Standard Direct Labor} \\
\text{Hours for Units} \\
\text{Produced}
\end{array}
\times
\begin{array}{l}
\text{Standard Variable} \\
\text{Overhead Rate per} \\
\text{Direct Labor Hour}
\end{array}
\right)
$$

Alternatively:

$$
\begin{array}{l}
\text{Variable Manufacturing} \\
\text{Overhead Efficiency} \\
\text{Variance}
\end{array} =
\begin{array}{l}
\text{Standard Variable} \\
\text{Overhead Rate per} \\
\text{Direct Labor Hour}
\end{array}
\times
\left(
\begin{array}{l}
\text{Actual} \\
\text{Direct Labor} - \\
\text{Hours}
\end{array}
\begin{array}{l}
\text{Standard Direct Labor} \\
\text{Hours for Units} \\
\text{Produced}
\end{array}
\right)
$$

(Machine hours or some other logical input could be used instead of direct labor hours.)
The variable overhead efficiency variance for each of the two departments for June is as follows:

Fabrication:
(750 × $2) − (200 units × 3.50 hours × $2) = $100 Unfavorable
Assembly:
(550 × $4) − (190 units × 2.25 hours × $4) =   490 Unfavorable
Variable Manufacturing Overhead Efficiency
    Variance $590 Unfavorable

This variance adds nothing to our understanding of the reasons why actual variable overhead cost exceeded standard variable overhead cost. In fact, the only two possible causes of actual costs exceeding standard costs are captured in the variable overhead spending variance explained above—that is, paying a price different from the standard price and using quantities different from standard quantities.

This variable overhead efficiency variance is influenced by the measured resource or base used to apply this cost to the product. That measured resource is usually direct labor hours or machine hours. If direct labor hours are used to apply variable manufacturing overhead to the product, as it is in the Buchanan cabinet manufacturing example, then the variable manufacturing overhead efficiency variance will be related to the labor efficiency variance. The same factors that cause an unfavorable labor efficiency variance (discussed earlier in this chapter) will also cause an unfavorable variable manufacturing overhead efficiency variance. Thus, if production of 200 units used more direct labor hours than are allowed by the labor standards, there will be an unfavorable direct labor efficiency variance and an unfavorable variable overhead efficiency variance.

In fact, the two efficiency variances (direct labor and variable overhead) will be related to each other in such a way that if you know the dollar amount of the direct labor efficiency variance you can determine the dollar amount of the variable overhead efficiency variance by considering the relationship that exists between the standard wage rate and the standard variable overhead rate (as long as direct labor hours is the cost driver).

This can be demonstrated using Buchanan's Fabrication Department as an example. The standard direct labor wage rate for the Fabrication Department is $8 per direct labor hour and the standard variable overhead rate for that department is $2 per direct labor hour. Because the ratio of the hourly rates is 4:1, the efficiency variances will also have a ratio of 4:1. Earlier in this chapter we determined that the Fabrication Department had a $400 unfavorable direct labor efficiency variance. We could have concluded, based on that calculation, that the variable overhead efficiency variance would be one-fourth of that amount, or $100. The detailed calculation in this chapter shows that the Fabrication Department variable manufacturing overhead efficiency variance is, in fact, $100 unfavorable.

Although this variable overhead efficiency variance tells us nothing new about the cause of the variance, it does put the impact of direct labor inefficiency in a different perspective. For example, the dollar impact of the inefficient use of direct labor in the Fabrication Department is not just the $400 direct labor efficiency variance; it is $500, the sum of the direct labor efficiency variance and the variable overhead efficiency variance.

Manufacturing Manager's Performance Report

Now that we have examined the methods used in calculating the variable cost variances that are under the control of the manufacturing manager, we are able to prepare a performance report for the manufacturing manager, as in Exhibit 7-6.

The formal report permits an evaluation of the manager's use of material, labor, and variable overhead resources that were employed in assembling 190 stereo cabinets and fabricating 200 stereo cabinets. On the surface it appears that the manufacturing manager had a very poor performance during June. However, keep in mind that that manager's material quantity variance for hardboard panels was negatively affected by the purchase of inferior-quality materials.

EXHIBIT 7-6

Manufacturing Manager's Performance Report
June 19X1

Direct Materials	Actual Cost	Input Standard Cost	Output Standard Cost	Material Quantity Variance
Birch panels	N.A.	$10,000	$ 8,400	$1,600U
Hardboard panels	N.A.	1,080	864	216U
Spruce	N.A.	2,050	2,080	30F
Total Direct Material		$13,130	$11,344	$1,786U

Direct Labor	Actual Cost	Input Standard Cost	Output Standard Cost	Labor Rate Variance	Labor Efficiency Variance
Fabrication Department	$5,820	$6,000	$5,600	$180F	$ 400U
Assembly Department	3,465	3,300	2,565	165U	735U
Total Direct Labor	$9,285	$9,300	$8,165	$ 15F	$1,135U

Variable Overhead	Actual Cost	Input Standard Cost	Output Standard Cost	Labor Rate Variance	Labor Efficiency Variance
				VOSV	VOEV
Fabrication Department	$1,700	$1,500	$1,400	$200U	$100U
Assembly Department	1,500	2,200	1,710	700F	490U
Total Variable Overhead	$3,200	$3,700	$3,110	$500F	$590U

F   Favorable
U   Unfavorable

Those low-quality materials might also have caused much of the $400 unfavorable Fabrication Department labor efficiency variance. Consider the labor hours that are wasted as saw operators cut the hardboard panels and find that the panel is not usable only after a portion of the cutting has been completed. As the panel is discarded, the labor cost expended in partially cutting the panel—and disposing of the extraordinary waste—provides no benefits to the department.

Certainly, the $735 unfavorable labor efficiency variance in the Assembly Department would not have been caused by the low-quality hardboard panels because only usable panels would have made it to the Assembly Department. This report would prompt the manager to investigate the cause of such a large unfavorable variance. The investigation may necessitate a change in assembly methods in order to attain the standards that were developed during the pilot manufacturing operation.

It is important to note that the actual direct material cost and the material price variance are not shown on the manufacturing manager's performance report. Those amounts were excluded because the purchasing manager, rather than the manufacturing manager, is responsible for the material price variance.

THE GENERAL MODEL OF MATERIAL, LABOR, AND VARIABLE OVERHEAD VARIANCES

CHAPTER OBJECTIVE 6
General variance model

The same methods were used in calculating the price and the quantity variances for direct material, the labor rate and the efficiency variances for labor, and the spending and efficiency variances for variable manufacturing overhead. Those methods are illustrated in the general variance model presented in Exhibit 7-7.

There are two important features of the general variance model that require further clarification. Column 3 is based on the standard quantity expected for the actual output. That quantity is determined by first counting the actual output for the period and multiplying that output by the standard resource quantity allowed for each unit of output. The standard resource quantity allowed for each unit of output is determined by reference to the standard quantities established for that product. The price variance is the actual cost less the input standard. The quantity variance is the input standard minus the output standard.

The other feature requiring clarification is related to the calculation of material variances. The actual quantity used for materials in columns 1 and 2 is not likely to be the same quantity for both the material price variance and the material quantity variance. This is true because the material price variance is the responsibility of the purchasing manager and it should be based on the quantity actually purchased. On the other hand, the material quantity variance is the responsibility of the manufacturing manager and it should be based in the quantity actually used in production.

EXHIBIT 7-7

GENERAL VARIANCE MODEL FOR VARIABLE COSTS VARIANCE ANALYSIS

1 **Actual Cost** Actual quantity of inputs times actual price per unit $(AQ \times AP)$	2 **Input Standard Cost** Actual quantity of inputs times standard price per unit $(AQ \times SP)$	3 **Output Standard Cost** Standard quantity expected for actual output times standard price per unit $(SQ \times SP)$
Price Variance *(Column 1 less Column 2)* Use for: 1. Material price variance. 2. Labor rate variance. 3. Variable manufacturing spending variance.		**Quantity Variance** *(Column 2 less Column 3)* Use for: 1. Material quantity variance. 2. Labor efficiency variance. 3. Variable manufacturing efficiency variance.
Total Variance		

(Some firms compute the material price variance based on the quantity used in production. The advantage of this alternative is that it fits the general variance method. The advantage of using the quantity purchased is that it better measures the performance of the purchasing manager.)

To illustrate the general model to variance analysis shown in Exhibit 7-7, consider the following example. Nelson Company established the following standards for the single product that it manufactures:

Direct materials	5 lbs. at $2 per pound
Direct labor	2 hrs. at $6 per hour
Variable overhead	$3 per direct labor hour

Standard Cost per Unit:

Direct material	5 lbs. × $2/lb. =	$10.00
Direct labor	2 hrs. × $6/hr. =	12.00
Variable overhead	2 hrs. × $3/hr. =	6.00
Total standard Variable Costs per Unit		$28.00

During August 19XX, Nelson experienced the following production, resource use, and costs:

Direct materials purchased	50,000 lbs.
Direct materials purchase price	$2.10 per lb.
Direct materials used in production	34,000 lbs.
Direct labor hours used in production	12,360 hrs.
Direct labor wage rate	$6.05 per hr.
Actual production	6,500 units
Actual variable overhead	$40,000

Based on the above data, the variances for direct material, direct labor, and variable overhead are shown in Exhibits 7-8, 7-9, and 7-10 (pages 258 and 259).

DECISION SUPPORT SYSTEMS AND BEHAVIORAL ASPECTS OF STANDARD COSTING

Decision support systems are designed to help managers make better decisions. To do this they need accurate and relevant data. The concept of standard costing is helpful because it requires managers to enunciate benchmarks that delineate between good and poor performance. Setting the standards requires careful planning. Once set, these standards help managers to interpret and analyze how well the organization is doing.

Standard costing helps organizations communicate expectations to its managers. Communication occurs when the standard costs are set (Are they proper? Are they fair?). Communication also takes place when the actual results are measured and analyzed against the benchmarks. Finally, since the variances are not perfect, communication must take place in debates about the interpretation of the variances.

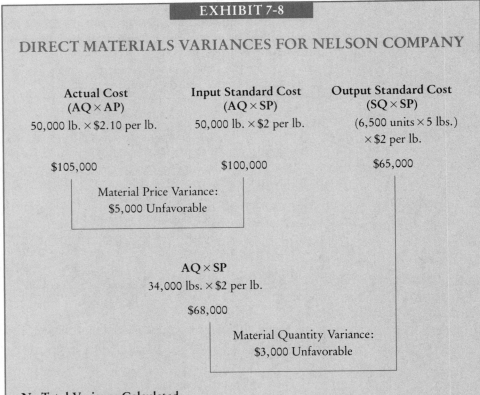

EXHIBIT 7-8

DIRECT MATERIALS VARIANCES FOR NELSON COMPANY

Actual Cost (AQ × AP)	Input Standard Cost (AQ × SP)	Output Standard Cost (SQ × SP)
50,000 lb. × $2.10 per lb.	50,000 lb. × $2 per lb.	(6,500 units × 5 lbs.) × $2 per lb.
$105,000	$100,000	$65,000

Material Price Variance:
$5,000 Unfavorable

AQ × SP
34,000 lbs. × $2 per lb.

$68,000

Material Quantity Variance:
$3,000 Unfavorable

No Total Variance Calculated

It is not appropriate to calculate the total direct materials variance by adding the two material variances together, because each variance is based on a different actual quantity (50,000 lbs. in the case of the material price variance and 34,000 lbs. in the case of the material quantity variance).

The model for calculating material variances does not agree precisely with the general model presented earlier. The reason for this is that the material price variance is based on the actual quantity of 50,000 lbs. purchased, whereas the material quantity variance is based on the 34,000 lbs. that were used.

The variances also help top management pinpoint possible problems. Under a system called *exception reporting,* top managers are sent a special report only when problems exist. For example, when a large unfavorable variance occurs, a report is sent to top managers to alert them of the situation. Exception reporting is a way for a manager to avoid information overload (discussed in Chapter 4). It calls for his or her attention only when needed.

One problem with standard costs is that they may become a driving force of the entity. They may be viewed as an end rather than a means to an end. In other words, managers might behave in a manner to achieve favorable variances (or at least avoid unfavorable variances) and not keep in mind the strategic objectives of the corporation. Given that setting standards is not perfect, a manager should not put complete reliance on the variances. For example, unforeseen changes in the business environment might

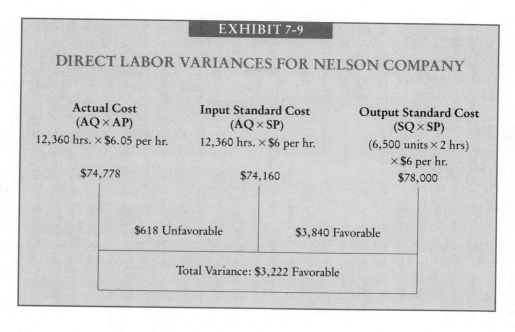

EXHIBIT 7-9

DIRECT LABOR VARIANCES FOR NELSON COMPANY

Actual Cost (AQ × AP)	Input Standard Cost (AQ × SP)	Output Standard Cost (SQ × SP)
12,360 hrs. × $6.05 per hr.	12,360 hrs. × $6 per hr.	(6,500 units × 2 hrs) × $6 per hr.
$74,778	$74,160	$78,000
	$618 Unfavorable	$3,840 Favorable
	Total Variance: $3,222 Favorable	

render standards obsolete. As a more specific example, unforeseen changes in the Soviet Union might make cost standards obsolete for a defense contractor.

Another behavioral problem is that variance analysis invites "gaming" on the part of those controlled. Employees will wish to obtain favorable variances, but ones that are not too large. If the favorable variances are viewed by top management as being very large, it might conclude that the standard was too low in the first place and thus raise it. Employees generally will try to avoid having the standards tightened. In other words,

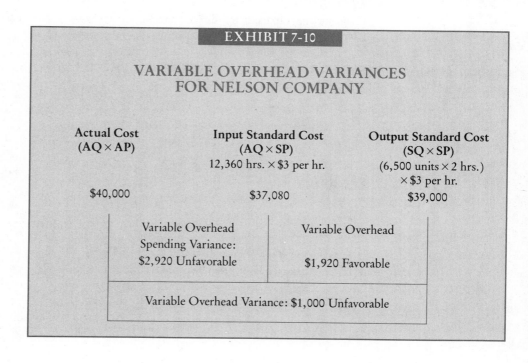

EXHIBIT 7-10

VARIABLE OVERHEAD VARIANCES FOR NELSON COMPANY

Actual Cost (AQ × AP)	Input Standard Cost (AQ × SP)	Output Standard Cost (SQ × SP)
	12,360 hrs. × $3 per hr.	(6,500 units × 2 hrs.) × $3 per hr.
$40,000	$37,080	$39,000
	Variable Overhead Spending Variance: $2,920 Unfavorable	Variable Overhead $1,920 Favorable
	Variable Overhead Variance: $1,000 Unfavorable	

employees want to obtain favorable variances so they can avoid punishment (such as embarrassment or, in the extreme, being fired) and be rewarded (such as praise or the receipt of a bonus). But employees do not want to exceed the budget by a large amount else the standard will be raised. If the standard is raised, there is a higher chance of being punished and a lower chance of being rewarded. This is an example of goal incongruence, defined in Chapter 4.

Demonstration Problem

Boden Company established the following standard costs for one of its products.

Direct material: 10 lbs. @ $4 per lb.
Direct labor: 1/10 hrs. @ $12 per hr.
Variable overhead: $2 per lb. of direct material used

During March, Boden Company experienced the following results:

Direct materials purchased	82,000 lbs.
Direct materials purchase price	$3.90 per lb.
Direct materials used in production	105,000 lbs.
Direct labor hours used in production	980 hrs.
Direct labor wage rate	$12 per hr.
Actual production	10,000 units
Actual variable overhead	$190,000

REQUIRED
Calculate the variances for direct material, direct labor, and variable overhead for Boden Company.

SOLUTION TO DEMONSTRATION PROBLEM
The standard cost per unit produced is:

Direct material: 10 lbs. @ $4 per lb.	$40.00
Direct labor: 1/10 hr. @ $12 per hr.	1.20
Variable overhead: 10 lbs. @ $2 per lb.	20.00
Total Standard Cost per Unit Produced	$61.20

The variances are as follows:

Material price variance = 82,000 × ($4 − $3.90)	= $ 8,200F
Material quantity variance = $4 × (100,000 − 105,000)	= $20,000U
Labor rate variance = 980 × ($12 − $12)	= $ -0-
Labor efficiency variance = $12 × (1,000 − 980)	= $ 240F
Variable overhead spending variance = (105,000 × $2) − $190,000	= $20,000F
Variable overhead efficiency variance = $2 × (100,000 − 105,000)	= $10,000U

Review of
Chapter
Objectives

1. State the purposes served by standard costs (pp. 239–41).

   ■ To evaluate efficiency, an organization needs a good standard cost system. This system tries to assess how well managers did (actual) compared to what they could have done (standard). This purpose is put into operation when standards are set.

   ■ Standard costs should not be considered ideal costs because then the standards are very hard or even impossible to meet. Further, unrealistically tight standards lose their ability to provide incentives. Practical standards help to focus expectations and yet keep them reasonable.

2. Calculate the material price variance and the material quantity variance (pp. 241–46).

   ■ The material price variance is equal to the actual quantity purchased times the difference between the actual cost per unit and the standard cost per unit. The material price variance is the responsibility of the purchasing manager. The variance is favorable when the actual cost per unit is less than the standard cost per unit. It is unfavorable when the actual cost per unit is greater than the standard cost per unit.

   ■ The material quantity variance is equal to the standard cost per unit times the difference between the actual quantity issued and used and the standard quantity to use based on output. The manufacturing manager is responsible for the quantities of materials used. The variance is favorable when the actual quantity used is less than the standard quantity. It is unfavorable when the actual quantity is greater than the standard quantity.

   ■ The management accountant must keep in mind how these two variances can interact. The purchasing manager can buy inferior raw materials at a cheap price, thereby getting a favorable price variance. However, the material quantity variance may become unfavorable since during manufacture these inferior materials may generate more waste and scrap per unit of materials put in production than standard-grade material.

3. Compute the labor rate variance and the labor efficiency variance (pp. 246–48).

   ■ The labor rate variance is equal to the actual direct labor hours multiplied by the difference between the actual cost per hour and the standard wage rate per hour. The labor rate variance is favorable when the actual cost per hour is less than the standard wage rate per hour. The labor rate variance is unfavorable when the actual cost per hour is more than the standard wage rate per hour.

   ■ The labor efficiency variance is the standard wage rate times the difference between the actual direct labor hours and the standard direct labor hours for units produced. The variance is favorable when the actual direct labor hours is less than the standard direct labor hours. The variance is unfavorable when the actual direct labor hours is greater than the standard direct labor hours.

   ■ The manufacturing manager is responsible for both of these variances.

4. Define *predetermined variable manufacturing overhead rate* (pp. 248–50).

   ■ Any manufacturing cost not a direct materials cost or a direct labor cost is lumped together as overhead. In this chapter we described the relationship between product costing and variable manufacturing overhead costs. In the next chapter fixed manufacturing overhead costs are examined.

- The predetermined variable manufacturing overhead rate is the rate at which variable manufacturing overhead is applied to production. It is based on the ratio of total budgeted variable overhead costs for a period of time to the expected total of some measure of activity. Common measures of activity (cost drivers) are machine hours and direct labor hours.

5. Calculate the variable manufacturing overhead spending variance and the variable manufacturing overhead efficiency variance (pp. 250–55).

- The variable manufacturing overhead spending variance is measured as the actual variable overhead costs minus the product of the actual direct labor hours times the standard variable overhead rate per direct labor hour. This variance is favorable when the actual variable overhead costs is less than the product of the actual direct labor hours and the standard variable overhead rate per direct labor hour. It is unfavorable when the actual variable overhead costs are greater. Responsibility for this variance is shared by the purchasing manager and the manufacturing manager.

- The variable overhead manufacturing efficiency variance is computed as the standard variable manufacturing overhead rate per direct labor hour times the difference between the actual direct labor hours and the standard direct labor hours. The variable overhead efficiency variance is favorable if the actual direct labor hours is less than the standard direct labor hours. It is unfavorable if the number of actual direct labor hours is greater than the number of standard direct labor hours. The manufacturing manager is usually responsible for this variance.

6. Describe the general variance model based on input and output standards (pp. 256–60).

- A generalized approach to variance analysis is as follows. The actual cost is the actual quantity times the actual price per unit. The input standard cost is the actual quantity of inputs times the standard price. The output standard cost is the standard quantity expected times the standard price.

- These standards can then be used to obtain the variances. The price variance is the actual costs minus the input standard. The quantity variance is the input standard minus the output standard.

Glossary of Key Terms

cost driver   The divisor used in calculating the predetermined variable manufacturing overhead rate. This divisor is the estimate of the expected level of production. It is often expressed in terms of machine hours or direct labor hours.

general variance model   A model that characterizes all variances to be equal to a price variance (which is actual cost minus input standard cost) plus a quantity variance (which is input standard cost minus output standard cost).

ideal standard cost   The minimum cost that would result if all productive inputs were combined under ideal conditions to achieve a given output level. Due to its premise, such cost is meaningful only in a relative and not in a practical sense.

input standard cost   A general term that refers to the actual quantity of input multiplied by the standard price.

labor efficiency variance   The difference between the actual direct labor cost at the standard wage rate and the standard direct labor hours times the standard wage rate.

labor rate variance   The difference between actual wage rate and standard wage rate multiplied by the actual hours of direct labor used.

material price variance   The difference between actual cost per unit and standard cost per unit multiplied by the actual quantity of material purchased.

material quantity variance   The difference between the actual unit usage of materials and the established standard unit usage, multiplied by the standard unit price for the material.

output standard cost   A general term that refers to the standard quantity of inputs for the actual output multiplied by the standard price.

overhead rate   The ratio of overhead costs for a period of time to the amount of some measurable associated causal factor in the same period of time. For example, the expected or standard overhead costs divided by the expected or standard productive output.

practical standard cost   A realistic expectation of the cost that would result under typical operating conditions, in which there is unavoidable material waste and normal nonproductive labor hours.

predetermined variable manufacturing overhead rate   The rate at which variable manufacturing overhead is applied to production, based on the ratio of total budgeted variable overhead costs for a period of time to the expected total of some measure of activity (cost driver) for the same period, such as machine hours or direct labor hours.

price variance   A general term used to refer to the difference between actual input costs and their standard costs. The more specific terms are *material price variance, labor rate variance, and variable overhead spending variance.*

quantity variance   A general term used to refer to the difference between input standard cost and output standard cost. The more specific terms are *material quantity variance, labor efficiency variance, and variable overhead efficiency variance.*

standard cost   A predetermined cost of the product that management sets as the goal to be attained under projected conditions.

standard cost system   An accounting technique whereby costs are recorded on the basis of predetermined standards while deviations (variances) from such standards are identified separately for analysis and control.

standard quantity expected   The standard quantity of inputs that is allowed given the actual quantity produced.

variable manufacturing overhead efficiency variance   The difference between actual direct labor hours incurred and the standard direct labor hours of actual production, multiplied by the standard variable overhead rate per direct labor hour, where direct labor hours is the basis for applying overhead (other appropriate bases could be used).

variable manufacturing overhead spending variance   The difference between actual variable overhead costs incurred and the actual number of units of input (direct labor hours or machine hours) multiplied by the actual variable overhead rate per unit of input.

variance   The difference between actual cost and standard cost.

Review Questions

7-1   Why are standard costs used in business?

7-2   How does one distinguish between a standard cost per unit and a standard quantity?

7-3   How does one distinguish between ideal standards and practical standards?

7-4   What role do standard costs play in establishing a selling price for a product?

7-5   What role do standard costs play in controlling the cost of manufacturing the product?

7-6   Why are actual material *purchases* used to calculate the material price variance, when actual material issues *from the storeroom* are used to calculate the material quantity variance?

7-7   In analyzing the variance between actual costs and standard costs for materials, why is it necessary to make a distinction between the material price variance and the material quantity variance?

7-8   How does one distinguish between the input standard cost and the output standard cost?

7-9   Under what circumstances might a labor rate variance be unfavorable?

7-10   In what way might the material quantity variance be related to the material price variance?

7-11   In what way might the labor rate variance be related to the labor efficiency variance?

7-12   Why are variable overhead costs regarded as indirect costs?

7-13   What method is used to "attach" variable overhead costs to the product?

7-14   Why might a manufacturing manager feel powerless in controlling the variable overhead spending variance?

7-15   If direct labor hours are used to apply variable manufacturing overhead to the product, what is the relationship between the labor efficiency variance and the variable manufacturing overhead efficiency variance?

7-16   Who is responsible for the labor efficiency variance? The material quantity variance? The material price variance?

7-17   How do you calculate the input standard cost?

7-18   How is the output standard cost calculated?

Discussion Questions

7-19   Suppose a firm automates its manufacturing process so that there is little direct labor involved. What are the likely changes in the variance analysis?

7-20   Management is not happy with the traditional variable overhead category. The management team feels that it is important to lump energy costs together and analyze them separately from the other overhead costs. They ask for your assistance. Assuming that energy costs are variable, what do you recommend?

Exercises

7-21   **MATERIAL AND LABOR VARIANCES** EMF Company uses a standard cost system. The standard cost of the company's only product is as follows:

CO 2, 3

Materials		
Labor	4 hours @ $3 per hour	12
Total standard cost per unit of product		$18

In a recent period, 1,000 units of finished product were completed using 4,200 direct labor hours. Direct labor costs averaged $3.30 per hour and 2,900 units of material were used. Materials purchased during the period were 2,500 units at a cost of $5,250.

a. Calculate the material price variance and the material quantity variance.

b. Calculate the labor rate variance and the labor efficiency variance.

7-22 MATERIAL AND LABOR VARIANCES Hal-McGuire Company uses a standard cost system in controlling the costs of manufacturing a toy aircraft carrier. The standard cost system is designed to isolate the variances as soon as possible. The standards and partial actual information is presented below:

	Standard	Actual
Materials used	10 lbs. per toy	?
Materials purchased	$5 per lb.	?
Direct labor wage rate	$4 per hour	?
Direct labor usage	20 hours per toy	13,000 hrs.

CO 2, 3

a. If 600 toy aircraft carriers were produced and the material quantity variance was $2,000 favorable, what was the cost of the material used in making the 600 toys?

b. If 600 toy aircraft carriers were produced and the total labor variance was $3,350 unfavorable, what was the actual labor cost per hour?

7-23 LABOR AND VARIABLE OVERHEAD VARIANCES Wilkins Company manufactures a single product called Nu-Time that has the following standard costs:

CO 3, 5

Direct material	2 lbs. @ $5 per pound	$10
Direct labor	4 hours at $3 per hour	12
Variable overhead	$2 per direct labor hour	8
Total standard cost per unit of product		$30

During a recent month 10,000 units of Nu-Time were produced and the following costs were incurred:

Materials purchased and used: 21,000 lbs. @ $4.50 each	$ 94,500
Direct labor: 45,000 hours @ $3.50 per hour	157,500
Variable overhead costs	112,500
Total actual costs for the month	$364,500

a. What direct labor cost should have been incurred during the month? 120,000

b. What effect did the efficiency or inefficiency of labor have on the variable manufacturing overhead efficiency variance during the month?

7-24 DIRECT LABOR AND VARIABLE MANUFACTURING OVERHEAD VARIANCES Coppage Spoon Company manufactures spoons. The operating employees are expected to produce 40 spoons per hour and the standard wage rate is $5 per direct labor hour. During a period in which 50,000 spoons were produced, 1,200 direct labor hours were used. The standard variable manufacturing overhead rate is $2.50 per direct labor hour.

CO 3, 5

a. What is the amount of the direct labor efficiency variance?

b. What is the amount of the variable manufacturing overhead efficiency variance?

7-25 INTERACTION OF MATERIAL PRICE AND MATERIAL QUANTITY VARIANCE Marbone Corporation manufactures small wooden bookcases. In order for its power saws to operate efficiently, wood of a particular quality must be used in manufacturing the

CO 2

bookcases. The standards as they apply to wood are as follows: Each bookcase requires 65 square feet of wood at a cost of $2.50 per square foot.

During June the purchasing manager bought 35,000 square feet of wood at a cost of $2 per square foot. During the same period the manufacturing manager used 38,000 square feet of wood to manufacture 550 bookcases.

a. Calculate the material price variance and the material quantity variance for June.

b. If the manufacturing manager were asked by the division manager to explain the material quantity variance, what explanation would you expect to be given?

7-26   DIRECT LABOR AND VARIABLE OVERHEAD VARIANCES Sturm, Inc., prints textbooks. A study has shown that the variable overhead has traditionally been $4 per direct labor hour. The average wage rate is $8 per direct labor hour. In establishing the variable overhead rate for the next year, they chose to use a rate 50% that of the direct labor rate. In August print production was such that 5,000 direct labor hours should have been used. The actual direct labor hours used were 5,300 and the actual average wage rate was $7.90. The variable manufacturing overhead during the month was $23,000.

CO 3, 5

a. Calculate the labor rate variance and the labor efficiency variance.

b. Calculate the variable overhead spending variance and the variable overhead efficiency variance.

c. Comment on the relationship between the labor efficiency variance and the variable manufacturing overhead variance.

7-27   MATERIAL QUANTITY VARIANCE AND LABOR EFFICIENCY VARI-ANCE Attaway Corporation manufactures tables. The tables are made from a type of wood that must be free of knotholes. In September the company purchased some wood containing flaws that were not obvious until the wood had been partially sawed. The standards for the table were as follows:

CO 2, 3

Direct materials:	40 square feet @ $6 per square foot	=	$240.00
Direct labor:	5 hours per table @ $10 per hour	=	50.00
Variable overhead:	75% of the direct labor standard cost	=	37.50
	Total standard variable cost of table		$327.50

The actual costs during September, when 100 tables were produced, were as follows:

Direct materials used = 4,500 feet @ $6 per square foot = $27,000
Direct labor = 535 hours @ $10 per hour = $5,350
Variable manufacturing overhead = $4,200

a. Calculate the material quantity variance.

b. Calculate the labor efficiency variance.

c. Comment on the way the material quantity variance and the labor efficiency variance are related.

7-28   VARIABLE OVERHEAD SPENDING AND EFFICIENCY VARIANCES Brown Corporation manufactures bicycles. In an attempt to control the cost of variable manufacturing overhead, Brown has installed a standard cost system. The variable manufacturing overhead includes small items such as valve stems and decals that are included with the bicycle. In

CO 5

establishing the standard variable manufacturing overhead rate, the cost accountant studied the cost of those items in relation to the standard direct labor hours allowed to manufacture the units produced in the past two years.

That study indicated that the standard cost of the variable manufacturing overhead items was $1.50 per direct labor hour. The standard direct labor hours per bicycle were 5 direct labor hours. During a month in which 200 bicycles were produced, the variable manufacturing overhead costs were $1,700 and the direct labor hours were 950 direct labor hours.

a. Calculate the variable manufacturing overhead spending variance.

b. Calculate the variable manufacturing overhead efficiency variance.

c. Comment on the cause of the variable manufacturing overhead spending variance.

Problems

7-29   INPUT STANDARDS VS. OUTPUT STANDARDS Glycerin, which is a flavoring used by toothpaste companies, is manufactured by Preston Company. In preparing the budget Preston's managers use direct labor hours to develop manufacturing costs. After receiving his monthly report, the production manager tells you he needs your help to interpret it. The information contained in the report is as follows:

CO 2, 3, 5

	Actual Cost at 15,000 Direct Labor Hours	Budgeted Cost for 15,000 Hours
Materials used at standard prices	$ 30,000	$ 28,500
Direct labor	105,000	108,750
Indirect labor	51,000	49,500
Other variable overhead	45,000	44,550
Total variable costs	$231,000	$231,300

140,000 gallons were produced during the period, which at standard performance would have required 14,000 direct labor hours.

REQUIRED

Determine all variances for the components of cost.

7-30   UNIT COSTS The new cost accountant at Zebart Corporation prepared the following performance report and sent it to the foreman of the machining department:

CO 2, 3, 5

	Cost per Unit		
	Budget	**Actual**	**Variance**
Materials	$ 3.20	$ 3.10	$0.10
Direct labor (1.25 hours per unit at standard)	5.00	5.082	(0.082)
Variable overhead			
Indirect labor	2.15	2.20	(0.05)
Power	0.85	0.87	(0.02)
Fixed overhead	3.50	4.50	(1.00)
Totals	$14.70	$15.752	$(1.052)

Actual cost per unit for fixed overhead is actual cost incurred divided by actual production units.

Budgeted production was 12,500 units, and actual production was 10,000 units. Budgeted fixed overhead per unit is based on budgeted production. Actual material cost in this report is based on standard prices, and all other actual cost figures are based on actual prices and quantities.

Actual cost of direct labor was $3.85 per unit. The foreman is not responsible for these rates, nor is she responsible for variable overhead spending variances. She is responsible for fixed overhead budget variances.

REQUIRED

Prepare a new report showing only those items for which the foreman is responsible. (You may want to present your report differently than the one shown.)

7-31   **STANDARDS AND VARIANCES FOR TWO PRODUCTS** York Company manufactures two items, I and II. The prime costs (direct material and labor) are recorded for the items as a whole. The company does not maintain records of the quantity of material and the labor used in manufacturing each item. Standard cost data are as follows:

CO 2, 3, 4, 5

	Item I	Item II
Direct Materials:		
4 lbs. @ $7 per lb.	$ 28	
7 lbs. @ $7 per lb.		$ 49
Direct Labor:		
5 hrs. @ $12 per hr.	60	
9 hrs. @ $12 per hr.		108
Variable Overhead:		
$10 per direct labor hr.	$ 50	$ 90
Total Standard Variable Costs	$138	$247

Both items are made up of the same material. Assembly workers earn $12 per hour and the variable overhead rate is $10 per direct labor hour.

During October, the company had the following outcome:

Direct materials purchased	8,000 lbs.
Direct materials purchase price	$6.50 per lb.
Direct materials used in production	7,700 lbs.
Direct labor hours used in production	9,800 hrs.
Direct labor wage rate	$11.85 per hr.
Actual production	
Item I	1,000
Item II	500
Actual variable overhead	$90,000

REQUIRED

a. Compute all variable cost variances for production.

b. State why you cannot compute variances for each item. State why you might want to isolate variances to individual items.

7-32 INVESTIGATION OF VARIANCES The plant manager of Clarkson, Inc., practices a style of management that concentrates on areas that deserve attention and disregards areas that are running smoothly. Performance reports are generally used for analysis, although further observations may be needed if a variance is greater than 15% of total standard cost. The plant manager does not take responsibility for price variances, although he is interested in efficiency variances.

CO 2, 3, 5

During May, 1,375 units were produced using 7,000 direct labor hours and 6,300 gallons. One unit of product requires 4 gallons of material at $5 per gallon, while direct labor per unit requires 5 hours at $7 per hour. Variable overhead consists of $9 per direct labor hour, therefore total standard variable cost per unit is $100 per unit.

REQUIRED

a. Compute only the variances for which the plant manager is to be held responsible.

b. Determine which variances the plant manager should be concerned with based on the guidelines he set.

7-33 COST OF LABOR INEFFICIENCY Just Doors Company produces three types of aluminum storm doors for residences. The company sells these doors to retail stores. There is not a steady demand for storm doors, thus the company endures months in which production is low and months in which the production supply cannot meet the demand of the retail stores. In months that production demand exceeds the supply, sales are lost to competitors. The construction process constrains the amount of direct labor hours available, and the company can obtain a maximum of 20,000 direct labor hours per month. The typical product mix results in the following standards:

CO 3

Direct labor hours	3 hours per unit
Standard labor rate	$ 7 per hour
Standard variable overhead	$ 4 per direct labor hour
Standard material costs	$ 77 per unit
Selling price	$145 per unit

Production results for February and August appear below. Orders for August exceeded production.

	February	August
Actual units	5,200	6,300
Actual hours	16,000	20,000

Assume that during those months material costs and the actual labor rate equaled the standard costs. Variable overhead equaled $4 times the actual direct labor hours in both months.

REQUIRED

a. Compute the labor efficiency variance and variable overhead efficiency variance for each month.

b. Decide whether the variances for both months reflect the true cost to the firm of labor inefficiency. Explain your answer.

7-34 STANDARD COSTS: MACHINE-HOUR BASIS Since Kinderman Company uses machines for cutting and preparing its product, it has chosen machine hours as the basis for

CO 2, 3, 5

setting the standard variable costs per unit of product. The standard variable overhead rate is $10 per machine hour. Also, the labor required to operate this machine is so minimal that all the labor is counted as indirect labor and is accounted for in the variable overhead. It takes two hours for the machines to complete one unit of output. Four inches of raw material are required for each unit of output. The cost of the raw material is $63 per yard.

During June, 6,500 yards of material were purchased for $415,350 and 5,625 yards were issued from the raw materials storeroom to the factory for the month. There were 50,000 units finished during the month. There were 99,850 machine hours used. Variable overhead costs charged to the manufacturing overhead control account were $997,000.

REQUIRED

a. Compute the standard variable cost of a unit of product.

b. Compute all of the relevant variances for June.

7-35   STANDARD COSTS: JOINT PRODUCTS

CO 2, 3, 5

Aliseen, Inc., takes a single substance and converts it into two interim products, helmit and tole. Helmit and tole are additionally processed into final products. There are no additional materials needed.

From current data gathered, it takes 8 laborers 2 hours to convert one ton of raw material, at a material cost of $200, into 1,100 pounds of helmit and 800 pounds of tole. The remaining 100 pounds is waste that has no selling value. One supervisor oversees this process. It takes 3 laborers 6 hours to finish processing the 1,100 pounds of helmit, and 2 laborers 5 hours to process the 800 pounds of tole. A supervisor is separately assigned to each process. All workers have a wage rate of $8 per hour. The variable overhead cost has been calculated to be $5 per direct labor hour. After all processing is completed, helmit and tole final products sell for $.73 and $.94 respectively.

REQUIRED

a. Compute the standard costs necessary for control and performance evaluation.

b. Compute the standard costs necessary for product costing purposes. For this requirement the joint costs should be allocated between the joint products based on relative contribution margin. Hint: Allocation based on relative contribution margin is like allocation based on relative sales value (p. 117), except that contribution margin is used instead of sales value.

7-36   DEVELOPING STANDARD COSTS

CO 1, 4

You have been engaged by Furrina, Inc., to change its present cost system to incorporate standard variable costing for its product, Pur-r-rfect cat food. The controller wishes the standard to be based on current production capabilities. The following data is the actual cost for 19X7:

Materials used (4,000,000 lbs. @ $.10 per lb.)		$ 400,000
Direct labor (55,000 hrs. @ $7.45 per hr.)		409,750
Variable overhead:		
Indirect labor	$105,000	
Maintenance and repair	68,750	
Packaging materials	140,000	
Other variable overhead	137,500	451,250
Total variable production costs		$1,261,000

Pur-r-rfect, is distributed to retailers in cases of 48 cans, 6 ounces each. During 19X7, 200,000 cases were produced. Data shows that 10% of the material is lost in production. The suppliers have notified Furrina of an increase in material costs of $0.025 per pound for 19X8.

Since 19X7 was the first year of operation, the workers were inexperienced. The controller feels direct labor hours will be decreased by 20% during 19X8, once the workers settle into their tasks. The labor contract provides for a wage rate of $7.50 for 19X8.

Indirect labor will receive a wage increase of 5%. Since packaging is related only to the number of cases produced the labor hours are not expected to decrease.

REQUIRED

Calculate the standard variable cost for Furrina, Inc., per case of Pur-r-rfect cat food.

7-37 STANDARD COSTS, VARIANCES, AND EVALUATION Valdez Corp. makes and sells only one product. The standard variable costs per unit are as follows:

CO 2, 3, 5

Direct materials (2 ft. @ $5 per foot)	$10
Direct labor (45 mins. @ $8 per hour)	6
Variable overhead	3
Total standard variable cost	$19

Variable costs are related to production through units produced rather than direct labor hours, because overhead incurred was seen to be caused by the units produced. The budgeted variable overhead components are based on a production volume of 75,000 units per year and are as follows:

Indirect labor (15,500 hrs. @ $8 per hour)	$124,000
Screws, bolts, and nuts (125,000 @ $.30 each)	37,500
Variable maintenance (7,500 hrs. @ $2.50 per unit)	18,750
Total budgeted variable overhead	$180,250

Budgeted fixed overhead components, also based on a production volume of 75,000 units yearly, are as follows:

Supervisors' salaries	$ 42,000
Depreciation	38,000
Miscellaneous fixed overhead	22,000
Total budgeted fixed overhead	$102,000

In May, 6,500 units were produced. Actual costs in May 19X0 were as follows:

Materials issued (13,200 ft. @ $4.50 per foot)	$ 59,400
Direct labor (4,500 @ $7.50 per hour)	33,750
Indirect labor (1,200 @ $7.50 per hour)	9,000
Screws, bolts, and nuts (10,000 @ $.30 each)	3,000
Variable maintenance costs (625 hrs. @ $3 per unit)	1,875
Supervisors' salaries	2,500
Depreciation	3,100
Miscellaneous fixed overhead	1,800
Total	$114,425

Material purchases were 14,000 ft. @ $4.50 per foot. The firm has allocated responsibilities of material usage, labor usage, and overhead variances to the production manager. The material price variance is the responsibility of the purchasing manager.

REQUIRED
a. Calculate the following:
  1. Material price variance.
  2. Material quantity variance.
  3. Labor rate variance.
  4. Labor efficiency variance.
  5. Variable manufacturing overhead spending variance.
  6. Variable manufacturing overhead efficiency variance.

b. Prepare performance reports for the production manager and the purchasing manager.

7-38   INPUT STANDARDS VERSUS OUTPUT STANDARDS Shane Company manufactures a wood glue for use in the construction industry. The company's budgeted manufacturing costs are based on direct labor hours. The production manager has just received a report for June 19X2 containing the data in the following list and does not know how to interpret it. He asks you for your help.

CO 2, 3, 4, 5

	Actual Cost at 20,000 Direct Labor Hours	Budgeted Cost for 20,000 Direct Labor Hours
Direct materials used (at standard prices)	$ 32,000	$ 30,000
Direct labor	97,500	98,000
Indirect labor	37,450	36,500
Other variable overhead	37,400	37,300
Total variable costs	$204,350	$201,800

68,000 gallons were produced during the period. At standard performance, this would require 18,600 direct labor hours.

REQUIRED
Determine the variance due to efficiency (or inefficiency), and the variance due to price or spending, for each component of cost. Prepare a more explanatory report for the production manager using this information.

Business Decision Case

Farley Chemical Company manufactures a stain remover called Ridstain that is sold in 32-ounce (1/4 gallon) plastic bottles. The stain remover can be made using either one of two basic raw materials—greasocide or mudocide. Their respective costs are $5 and $3 per pound. The product is bottled and packed into cartons of 12 bottles each.

The basic batch size is made with 750 gallons of water costing $.25 per 100 gallons. The chemical agents other than the raw materials mentioned above cost $75 per batch. If greasocide is used, 50 pounds of it are mixed with water and chemical agents. If mudocide is used, 60 pounds are needed. The mixing process takes two hours and requires the services of two laborers (a total of four hours per batch).

The mixture is then cooked—for 60 minutes if greasocide is used or for 45 minutes if mudocide is used. One worker is needed for this process. Using either raw material, the output of the cooking process is 660 gallons due to evaporation. Bottling and packing requires one laborer working for three hours.

All laborers are paid $10 per hour. Variable overhead is based on time required in each process because the high degree of mechanization makes direct labor a poor measure of volume for variable overhead. The overhead per hour for the mixing process is $10, $100 for the cooking process, and $50 for the bottling and packing process. Bottles are $.05 each, and the cartons cost $.40 each.

REQUIRED

a. Compute the standard cost of a carton of Ridstain assuming (1) greasocide is used and (2) mudocide is used.

b. Suppose that each carton sells for $15 and that cooking time available each month is 1,000 hours. Which material should be used?

8

Standard Costs: Fixed Overhead

CHAPTER OBJECTIVES

After reading Chapter 8, you should be able to:

1. Define *predetermined fixed manufacturing overhead rate* and *cost driver* (production divisor) and indicate their importance in planning and evaluating fixed overhead costs (pp. 275–77).

2. Calculate the variance used to control fixed manufacturing costs (pp. 277–79).

3. Explain how standard costs are used in product costing for determining income and valuing inventory (pp. 279–85).

4. Describe the manufacturing manager's performance report (pp. 285–88).

5. Describe the general variance model based on input and output standards as applied to fixed overhead (pp. 288–89).

6. Explain the purposes of activity-based costing and how it is applied (pp. 289–94).

7. Interpret the variance analysis from a decision support systems viewpoint (pp. 294–95).

*D*irect material, direct labor, and variable overhead are not the only manufacturing costs for which standards are developed and used for product costing and cost control. The fixed overhead costs must also be applied to the product for product costing purposes. These indirect manufacturing costs should also be subjected to managerial control through the comparison of actual overhead costs with standard overhead costs.

The conventional division of costs into fixed and variable, implicit in the textbook up to this point, is becoming less useful for many companies as they discover that *how* they apply resources for making their products (some activity basis) can have more effect on costs than *how much* of the product they produce and sell (the conventional volume basis of costing). Consequently, *activity-based costing* is emerging as a proper costing method for many manufacturing processes.

THE PREDETERMINED FIXED MANUFACTURING OVERHEAD RATE

CHAPTER OBJECTIVE 1
Overhead rate and cost drivers

In Chapter 7 we examined standard costs for direct materials, direct labor, and variable manufacturing overhead. We pointed out that direct materials and direct labor have material issue slips and time cards to identify the quantity of direct material and direct labor used in manufacturing products. Variable overhead has no such document; therefore, some other measured indicator, such as direct labor hours or machine hours, is used in determining the amount of variable overhead allowed for a certain level of production.

As will soon be demonstrated, fixed manufacturing overhead is accounted for in nearly the same way as with variable manufacturing overhead. A **predetermined fixed manufacturing overhead rate** is estimated and then that rate is used to determine the amount of fixed overhead that should be applied to, assigned to, or charged to the product.

The discussion of fixed overhead costs continues to use Buchanan Company, the subject of the ongoing example in Chapter 7. The continued use of Buchanan Company permits us to demonstrate how standard costs are used for both income determination and performance evaluation. The Buchanan Company example will be continued in Chapter 10 in order to demonstrate how job costing is integrated with income determination and performance evaluation.

Prior to the start of the new fiscal year, the sales manager, the production manager, and the controller hold a planning meeting as part of their master budget preparation. The sales manager contributes an estimate of unit sales so the production manager can estimate unit production. The production manager would use the unit sales estimate, consider existing versus desired level of inventory, and arrive at a planned unit production level for the next year. The controller would take the planned unit production and arrive at next year's planned labor hours based on standard labor hours per unit.

The production manager estimates production to be 210 units per month for each of the 12 months of the next year. Recall from Chapter 7 that the Fabrication Department takes 3.5 hours to work on the product and the Assembly Department takes 2.25 hours. So it takes 5.75 direct labor hours to make the product. The planned labor hours can be calculated as follows:

[handwritten margin note: Overhead = Deprec. Expense = fixed cost]

$$\frac{\text{Required Labor Hours}}{\text{for Next Year}} = \frac{\text{210 Units per Month}}{\times 5.75 \text{ direct labor hours per unit} \times 12 \text{ months}}$$
$$= 14,490 \text{ direct labor hours}$$

The controller would then estimate the fixed overhead costs for the next year. This estimate would be based on fixed overhead costs incurred in the current year adjusted for expected price changes, planned capital expenditures, and any other factors expected to influence the fixed manufacturing overhead costs for the next year. Let us assume that the controller's estimate of fixed manufacturing overhead was $173,880 for the next year.

The fixed manufacturing overhead rate is now calculated by dividing the estimated fixed manufacturing overhead costs ($173,880) by the estimated direct labor hours (14,490 direct labor hours). The estimated direct labor hours is called the *production divisor* or the cost driver. The value of this variable is sometimes called the denominator activity level.

$$\frac{\text{Predetermined}}{\text{Fixed Manufacturing}} = \frac{\$173,880}{14,490 \text{ Direct Labor Hours}}$$
$$\text{Overhead Rate}$$
$$= \$12 \text{ per direct labor hour}$$

Some manufacturers calculate a predetermined fixed manufacturing overhead rate for each department. The controller could have calculated one rate for fabrication and one rate for assembly. However, such precision would have required the controller to estimate the annual fixed manufacturing overhead costs for each department rather than for the entire factory.

It is important to note that this overhead rate is called the predetermined fixed manufacturing overhead rate because it is determined prior to the year in which it will be used for product costing. This rate is based on three estimates—estimated unit production, estimated direct labor hours per unit, and estimated fixed manufacturing overhead cost per year. (Sometimes we will add the predetermined fixed manufacturing overhead rate to the predetermined variable manufacturing overhead rate. We should refer to the sum as the predetermined manufacturing overhead rate.)

Once the controller has arrived at the predetermined fixed manufacturing overhead rate, that rate is used to calculate the standard fixed manufacturing overhead per unit of product.

$$\frac{\text{Standard Fixed}}{\text{Manufacturing Overhead}} = \frac{5.75 \text{ direct labor hours}}{\text{per unit of product}}$$
$$\text{per Unit of Product} \quad \times \$12 \text{ per direct labor hour}$$
$$= \$69 \text{ per unit of product}$$

When the variable overhead and fixed overhead costs are combined, we arrive at the total overhead per unit of product as follows:

Standard variable manufacturing overhead per unit of product (from Chapter 7)	$16
Standard fixed manufacturing overhead per unit of product	69
Standard manufacturing overhead per unit of product	$85

Recall from Chapter 7 that the standard direct labor cost was $41.50 per unit of product. Thus, the standard overhead is 205% of the standard direct labor ($85 vs. $41.50). It is not unusual to have the overhead expressed as a percentage of the direct labor component. As manufacturers become more automated, there is a trend toward a larger overhead component in relation to the direct labor component and thus a larger percentage.

In highly automated factories, or departments within factories, there may be only a small amount of direct labor expended in producing the product. In such situations, direct labor is not considered an appropriate base on which to allocate overhead to the product. Instead, machine hours, which are measured by timing devices on the machines, are often used as the cost driver in calculating the predetermined overhead rates. The standard number of machine hours and the predetermined overhead rate are used to calculate the standard overhead costs. In highly automated factories, the control of overhead costs, especially fixed costs, is very important.

FIXED OVERHEAD VARIANCES

CHAPTER OBJECTIVE 2
Fixed overhead variances

The fixed overhead variance can be fragmented into two component parts, the fixed manufacturing overhead budget variance and the fixed manufacturing overhead volume variance. The first of these is useful in evaluating the cost control efforts of a manager, and the second is not useful (and even counterproductive) in that evaluation.

If the actual overhead costs exceed the overhead charged to the products using predetermined rates (the absorbed overhead), the overhead is said to be underabsorbed or *underapplied*. If the actual overhead costs is less than the absorbed overhead, the overhead is said to be overabsorbed or *overapplied*.

The method used to fragment this variance makes use of the estimate of total fixed manufacturing overhead for the year. Recall that in calculating the predetermined fixed manufacturing overhead rate, the controller used a budget of $173,880. That annual amount may be divided by 12 months to obtain the budget of $14,490 per month.

When this budget of $14,490 per month is used, it enables us to break the fixed manufacturing overhead variance into two separate variances—the fixed manufacturing overhead *budget variance* and the fixed manufacturing overhead *volume variance*, discussed next.

Fixed Manufacturing Overhead Budget Variance

The formula for the fixed manufacturing overhead budget variance is as follows:

$$
\begin{matrix}
\text{Fixed Manufacturing} \\
\text{Overhead Budget} \\
\text{Variance}
\end{matrix}
=
\begin{matrix}
\text{Actual Fixed} \\
\text{Manufacturing} \\
\text{Overhead Costs}
\end{matrix}
-
\begin{matrix}
\text{Budgeted Fixed} \\
\text{Manufacturing} \\
\text{Overhead Costs}
\end{matrix}
$$

Suppose that the actual fixed manufacturing overhead costs are $12,450 in June. Thus, the fixed manufacturing overhead budget variance for June is $2,040 favorable ($12,450 − $14,490).

This variance provides insight into the extent to which managers have exercised control over fixed manufacturing overhead. The variance is usually not calculated for each department within the factory because departmental managers typically do not have the authority to control the types of costs that are included in fixed manufacturing overhead. Instead, the fixed manufacturing overhead budget variance is calculated for the entire manufacturing operation and is used as an indicator of the extent to which the plant manager has been effective in controlling fixed manufacturing overhead costs.

In June, which had a favorable $2,040 variance, the plant manager may have saved fixed manufacturing overhead by not filling an open fork-lift operator position that was included in the budget or by deferring maintenance. The plant manager may have found a means of more effectively using the other fork-lift operator and thus eliminated the need for the planned hiring of the second operator. Deferring maintenance, however, may lead to problems. For example, in the long run, machinery could wear out more quickly than necessary.

Fixed Manufacturing Overhead Volume Variance

The formula for calculating the fixed manufacturing overhead volume variance is shown below:

$$
\begin{matrix}
\text{Fixed Manufacturing} \\
\text{Overhead Volume} \\
\text{Variance}
\end{matrix}
=
\begin{matrix}
\text{Budgeted Fixed} \\
\text{Manufacturing} \\
\text{Overhead Costs}
\end{matrix}
-
\left(
\begin{matrix}
\text{Standard Direct Labor} \\
\text{Hours for Units} \\
\text{Produced}
\end{matrix}
\times
\begin{matrix}
\text{Predetermined Fixed} \\
\text{Manufacturing Overhead} \\
\text{Rate per Hour}
\end{matrix}
\right)
$$

The fixed manufacturing overhead volume variance for June is as follows:

No good →

$$
\begin{aligned}
\begin{matrix}\text{Fixed Manufacturing}\\ \text{Overhead Volume}\\ \text{Variance}\end{matrix}
&= \$14{,}490 - \{[(200 \text{ units} \times 3.50 \text{ hours}) + (190 \text{ units} \times 2.25 \text{ hours})] \\
&\quad \times \$12\} \\
&= \$14{,}490 - \$13{,}530 \\
&= \$960 \text{ Unfavorable}
\end{aligned}
$$

This variance, although it can be calculated, is not useful for cost control purposes. In fact, its use for cost control purposes could result in dysfunctional action on the part of the plant manager.

In Buchanan's cabinet manufacturing operation, examined in Chapter 7, the Fabrication Department produced 200 cabinets and the Assembly Department produced 190 cabinets in June. Recall that the standard direct labor hours associated with that production was as follows:

Fabrication	200 units × 3.5 hrs. per unit	=	700.0 hrs.
Assembly	190 units × 2.25 hrs. per unit	=	427.5 hrs.
Total standard hours			1,127.5 hrs.

The number of direct labor hours that should have been used based on estimates prior to the start of the year were as follows:

Budgeted Monthly Production		**Direct Labor Hours per Unit**		
210 units	×	(3.5 hrs. + 2.25 hrs.)	=	1,207.5 hrs.

Thus, the company planned on using 1,207.5 direct labor hours when it established the predetermined overhead rate of $12 per direct labor hour. However, we used only 1,127.5 direct labor hours because fabrication produced only 200 units and assembly produced only 190 units in June. Thus, the actual level was lower than the planned production level. Consequently, the standard hours associated with actual production were 80 hours less than planned. That 80 direct labor hours when multiplied by the predetermined fixed manufacturing overhead rate of $12 yields $960. This $960 amount is the $960 unfavorable fixed manufacturing overhead volume variance that was calculated earlier using the formula.

The fixed manufacturing overhead volume variance is considered to be unfavorable because Buchanan produced fewer units than were expected based on its plan for 210 units per month. However, consider that the production of fewer units than planned could have been the result of fewer unit sales than expected. In that case, it would be unreasonable to hold the plant manager responsible for a $960 unfavorable overhead volume variance when he or she merely cut back on production because of the failure of the sales department to sell all of the units that had been planned.

There is another reason why we should not hold the plant manager responsible for this variance. If the fixed overhead volume variance were regarded as the responsibility of the plant manager, the manager could cause it to be a favorable variance by producing more units than were planned or needed. In June, the plant manager could have had a $690 favorable variance (10 units difference × 5.75 hours per unit × $12 per hour) if he or she had produced 220 units, or 10 units more than the 210 units planned. However, given sales of only 185 units, finished goods inventory would have increased to the point that there would be no more storage space for that inventory. Thus, holding the plant manager responsible for this variance is not in the best interest of the company because a cost control system should not stand in the way of the plant manager developing a production schedule that is coordinated with the sales department's product sales.

There may be some justification for holding the sales manager responsible for this variance because the sales manager is in a position to influence the variance positively by increasing sales effort. Increased sales will allow increased production, and production in excess of 210 units per month will generate a favorable fixed manufacturing overhead volume variance.

Why should an organization have a fixed manufacturing overhead volume variance if it is not useful for cost control? The comparison of actual fixed overhead costs with standard overhead cost simply yields a variance that includes two variances, each with different causes. One of the variances, the fixed manufacturing overhead budget variance, is useful for cost control purposes. Breaking out the fixed overhead budget variance from the overall fixed overhead variance generates a variance (the fixed overhead volume variance) that is just a natural fall-out from the calculation of the fixed overhead budget variance and arises from the selection of the production divisor.

PRODUCT COSTING AND INCOME DETERMINATION

CHAPTER OBJECTIVE 3
Standard costs in product costing

The calculation of cost of goods sold relies on the standard cost per unit of product. In Buchanan's cabinet manufacturing operation that was examined beginning in Chapter 7, the standard costs were determined to be as follows:

Direct material	$ 56.72
Direct labor	41.50
Variable manufacturing overhead	16.00
Fixed manufacturing overhead	69.00
Total cost	$183.22

The standard cost of $183.22 per unit will be used to determine the cost of the finished goods inventory at the end of the accounting period and also the cost of goods sold during the accounting period.

If the physical inventory reveals five completed cabinets in the finished goods warehouse, the cost of the finished goods inventory would be as follows:

$$5 \times \$183.22 = \$916.10$$

The work in process inventory (product on which work has been started but not yet finished at the end of the accounting period) will be counted based on the department in which it is located and the labor operation last performed.

If, on the last day of the fiscal year, a physical inventory reveals that work in process includes ten cabinets that have just left the Fabrication Department and are about to enter the Assembly Department, the standard cost of those cabinets would be $1,337.20, as shown in Exhibit 8-1. Notice that this figure includes all the production costs up to this point in time. It includes all the direct materials, the direct labor for the Fabrication Department, and the overhead related to the Fabrication Department.

The standard cost of the raw materials in the raw materials storeroom would be the product of the number of units per the physical inventory times the standard direct material cost per item of raw material.

If the physical inventory revealed the following raw materials in the storeroom at the end of the accounting period, the standard cost of the raw material inventory would be as follows:

Raw Material Item in Inventory	Quantity in Raw Material Inventory	Standard Cost per Unit	Total Cost
Birch panels	6,800 sq. ft.	$1.00	$6,800
Hardboard panels	3,600 sq. ft.	.18	648
Spruce structural members	10,550 linear ft.	.20	2,110
Total standard cost of ending raw materials inventory			$9,558

The standard cost of the inventory reported on the balance sheet at the end of the accounting period is given in Exhibit 8-2. Each of the three inventories is placed on the balance sheet in the current assets section.

If 185 cabinets were sold during June, the standard cost of goods sold as shown on the income statement would be as follows:

$$185 \text{ units} \times \$183.22 \text{ per unit} = \$33,895.70$$

EXHIBIT 8-1

STANDARD COST OF ITEMS IN WORK IN PROCESS INVENTORY

	Standard Cost per Unit in Work in Process
Direct material [all of the material would have already been cut and ready for assembly]	$ 56.72
Direct labor (for Fabrication Department only— 3.5 direct labor hours × $8 per hour)	28.00
Variable manufacturing overhead (3.5 direct labor hours × $2 per direct labor hour)	7.00
Fixed manufacturing overhead (3.5 direct labor hours × $12 per direct labor hour)	42.00
Total cost per fabricated (but not assembled) cabinet	$ 133.72
	× 10 cabinets
Standard cost of work in process inventory at end of accounting period	$1,337.20

EXHIBIT 8-2

PARTIAL BALANCE SHEET SHOWING INVENTORIES AT STANDARD COST

Buchanan Company
Balance Sheet
As of June 30, 19X1
(Current Assets Portion Only)

ASSETS

Current Assets		
Cash		$XXXXXX.XX
Inventory		
Finished Goods	$ 916.10	
Work in Process	1,337.20	
Raw Materials	9,558.00	
Total Inventories		$ 11,811.30
Other Current Assets		XXXXXX.XX
Total Current Assets		$XXXXXX.XX

Based on a sales price per unit of $250, the gross profit portion of the income statement is shown below. As usual, sales less cost of goods sold equals gross profit.

Buchanan Company
Income Statement
Month of June 19X1
(Gross Profit Portion Only)

Sales (185 units × $250 per unit)	$46,250.00
Less: Standard Cost of Goods Sold	33,895.70
Standard Gross Profit	$12,354.30

However, this partial income statement ignores the fact that actual costs were different from standard costs. In Chapter 7 we revealed that actual direct material costs were $6,098 greater than standard direct material costs (a $4,312 unfavorable materials price variance and $1,786 unfavorable materials quantity variance), actual direct labor costs were $1,120 greater than standard direct labor costs (a $15 favorable wage rate variance and $1,135 unfavorable labor efficiency variance), and actual variable overhead costs were $90 greater than standard variable overhead costs ($500 favorable spending variance and $590 unfavorable efficiency variance). Unless those variances are considered when calculating the actual gross profit for the month of June, net income will be incorrect.

We must also consider that the overhead amounts in Exhibit 8-3 have been applied to the units of product that have been produced or partially produced (in work in process inventory).

It is not likely that the actual overhead costs for any month will exactly equal the standard overhead amounts. In fact, suppose Buchanan's general ledger revealed the actual June overhead costs to be as follows:

Actual variable overhead	$ 3,200.00*
Actual fixed overhead	12,450.00
Actual total overhead	$15,650.00

*$1,700 for the Fabrication Department and $1,500 for the Assembly Department.

Thus, the overhead cost variances from standard for June are as depicted in Exhibit 8-4.

There is another way in which we might calculate the total unfavorable variance of $6,228. This can be done by contrasting the actual costs incurred during the month of June with the sum of the standard cost of goods sold as shown on the income statement and the standard cost of the ending inventory as shown on the balance sheet. By comparing the two exhibits, we may see that there are two ways of finding the total variance. We could accumulate the individual variances, as done in Exhibit 8-4, or we could obtain the difference between total actual manufacturing costs and total standard manufacturing costs, as shown in Exhibit 8-5.

It is unlikely that the unfavorable and favorable variances would be revealed in a set of financial statements released to persons outside of the company (creditors, investors, or potential investors). Instead, the income statement would probably be stated as follows on page 284:

EXHIBIT 8-3

ANALYSIS OF STANDARD OVERHEAD COSTS APPLIED TO PRODUCT

	Cost of Goods Sold	Finished Goods Inventory	Work in Process Inventory	Overhead Applied to Product
Variable overhead	$ 2,960	$ 80	$ 70	$ 3,110
	(185 × $16)	(5 × $16)	(10 × $7)	
Fixed overhead	$12,765	$345	$420	13,530
	(185 × $69)	(5 × $69)	(10 × 3.5 × $12)	
Total				$16,640

EXHIBIT 8-4

PARTIAL STATEMENT OF INCOME WITH VARIANCES SHOWN

Buchanan Company
Income Statement
Month of June 19XX
(Gross Profit Portion Only)

Sales	$46,250.00	
Less: Standard Cost of Goods Sold	33,895.70	
Standard Gross Profit	$12,354.30	
Less: Unfavorable Variances from Standard:		
Unfavorable Material Price Variance	(4,312.00)	
Unfavorable Material Quantity Variance	(1,786.00)	
Unfavorable Labor Efficiency Variance	(1,135.00)	
Unfavorable Variable Overhead Variance	(90.00)	Total Variance:
Unfavorable Volume Variance	(960.00)	$6,228
Add: Favorable Variances from Standard:		Unfavorable
Favorable Labor Rate Variance	15.00	
Favorable Budget Variance	2,040.00	
Actual Gross Profit	$ 6,126.30	

EXHIBIT 8-5

DETAILED COMPARISON OF ACTUAL COSTS AND STANDARD COSTS

Actual Manufacturing Costs Incurred in June

Birch panels	$21,000	
Hardboard panels	1,632	
Spruce structural members	4,368	
Fabrication department labor	5,820	
Assembly department labor	3,465	
Fabrication department variable overhead	1,700	
Assembly department variable overhead	1,500	
Fixed manufacturing overhead	12,450	
Total actual manufacturing costs incurred		$51,935.00

Standard Manufacturing Costs Accounted for in June

Costs of goods sold	$33,895.70	
Finished goods inventory	916.10	
Work in process inventory	1,337.20	
Raw materials inventory	9,558.00	
Total standard costs applied to product		45,707.00
Extent to which actual costs exceeded standard costs		$6,228.00

Buchanan
Income Statement
Month of June 19XX
(Gross Profit Portion Only)

Sales	$46,250.00
Less: cost of goods sold	40,123.70
Gross profit	$ 6,126.30

The $40,123.70 cost of goods sold is the sum of the standard cost of goods sold, $33,895.70, and the unfavorable variances from standard, or $6,228, from Exhibits 8-4 and 8-5. Of course, the inventory amounts would be reported on the balance sheet at the standard cost amounts as shown earlier.

Purpose of Variance Analysis Reexamined

A common question at this point is, "Why did we go to the trouble of calculating the variances from standard if we are not going to reveal those variances in the financial statements?" First, as demonstrated in Chapter 7, the variances are reported on managerial performance reports that are prepared for use within the company. Second, even though the variances from standard are not reported on the financial statements released outside of the company, the standards themselves serve a useful purpose for management. Finally, firms do not wish to release information not desired by investors and creditors but that could help competitors.

The standard cost is useful in establishing a selling price when there is no competitively established market price. Even when there is such a price established, the standard cost determined before production starts aids management in deciding whether or not the profit margin will be enough to justify production.

The establishment of cost standards also aids in planning. Knowing how many hours are necessary to produce a unit of product or how many units of raw materials are required per unit of product aids in personnel and materials planning.

The use of standards also aids in inventory costing. When standard costs are used, there is no need to determine the actual cost of each item in inventory. The inventory is costed at standard costs and any variances between actual and standard cost are used to adjust the standard cost of goods sold to the actual cost of goods sold.

This practice of permitting all variances to be regarded as an adjustment to the standard cost of goods sold sometimes seems counter to the interest of accounting precision. The cabinet-making operation in Buchanan Company provides an example.

The $6,228 unfavorable variance was used to adjust the standard cost of goods sold to the actual cost of goods sold. A major portion of that $6,228 variance was related to the material price variance. In the previous chapter we calculated an unfavorable materials price variance of $4,312 based on the purchase of materials for approximately two months' production. Much of that $4,312 unfavorable variance is related to raw materials that remained in raw materials inventory at the end of June. Those materials will be used in July, yet its portion of the $4,312 unfavorable material price variance was used to reduce the gross profit in June.

Even though that accounting treatment may seem to ignore the matching principle of accounting, it is expected that when looked at from the perspective of a year rather than just a month, the impact will be immaterial.

If, on the other hand, the variance is material when viewed from the annual perspective, there may be justification for prorating some portion of the variance to the inventories. For example, if there is a variance for 60 units of a product of which 50 are sold and 10 are in finished goods inventory, 5/6 of the variance is assigned to cost of goods sold and 1/6 is assigned to finished goods inventory. More realistically, the total variance would be prorated among cost of goods sold, raw materials inventory, work in process inventory, and finished goods inventory.

A large variance from standard at the end of the year should also suggest that the standards need to be reevaluated. Companies typically revise standards periodically to reflect changes in the cost of resources and in production methods.

MANUFACTURING MANAGER'S PERFORMANCE REPORT

CHAPTER OBJECTIVE 4
Performance report

In Chapter 7, we presented a formal report, the manufacturing manager's performance report, that could be used to evaluate the performance of the manufacturing manager (see page 255). That report may now be completed with the inclusion of fixed overhead costs, as in Exhibit 8-6 on page 287. This report merely combines many of the exhibits presented in Chapter 7 and earlier in this chapter.

HOW COST ACCOUNTING DISTORTS PRODUCT COSTS

The authors of the following article visited and documented the management accounting practices at 20 firms, among them the three firms mentioned at the beginning of this excerpt.

One message comes through overwhelmingly in our experiences with the three firms, and with the many others we talked and worked with. Almost all product-related decisions—introduction, pricing, and discontinuance—are long-term. Management accounting thinking (and teaching) during the past half-century has concentrated on information for making short-run incremental decisions based on variable, incremental, or relevant costs. It has missed the most important aspect of product decisions. Invariably, the time period for measuring "variable," "incremental," or "relevant" costs has been about a month (the time period corresponding to the cycle of the firm's internal financial reporting system). While academics admonish that notions of fixed and variable are meaningful only with respect to a particular time period, they immediately discard this warning and teach from the perspective of one-month decision horizons.

This short-term focus for product costing has led all the companies we visited to view a large and growing proportion of their total manufacturing costs as "fixed." In fact, however, what they call "fixed" costs have been the most variable and rapidly increasing costs. This paradox has seemingly eluded most accounting practitioners and scholars. Two fundamental changes in our thinking about cost behavior must be introduced.

First, the allocation of costs from the cost pools to the products should be achieved using bases that reflect cost drivers. Because many overhead costs are driven by the complexity of production, not the volume of production, non-volume-related bases are required. Second, many of these overhead costs are somewhat discretionary. While they vary with changes in the complexity of the production process, these changes are intermittent. A traditional cost system that defines variable costs as varying in the short term with production volume will misclassify these costs as fixed.

The misclassification also arises from an inadequate understanding of the actual cost drivers for most overhead costs. Many overhead costs vary with transactions: transactions to order, schedule, receive, inspect, and pay for shipments; to move, track, and count inventory; to schedule production work; to set up machines; to perform quality assurance; to implement engineering change orders; and to expedite and ship orders. The cost of these transactions is largely independent of the size of the order being handled; the cost does not vary with the amount of inputs or outputs. It does vary, however, with the need for the transaction itself. If the firm introduces more products, if it needs to expedite more orders, or if it needs to inspect more components, then it will need larger overhead departments to perform these additional transactions.

SOURCE: Reprinted by permission of Harvard Business School Press, Boston. Excerpts from Robin Cooper and Robert S. Kaplan, "How Cost Accounting Systematically Distorts Product Costs" in William J. Bruns, Jr., and Robert S. Kaplan, eds., *Accounting and Management: Field Study Perspectives*, pp. 224–26. Copyright © 1987 by the President and Fellows of Harvard College. As published in *Management Accounting* (April 1988), pp. 20–27.

According to this performance report, the manufacturing manager is responsible for a net of $956 in unfavorable variances for the month of June 19XX. This report reveals the subdepartment managers who contributed to that variance and it also reveals the resource (direct material, direct labor, variable overhead, and fixed overhead) that contributed to the variance. Additionally, the report categorizes the variances according to cause (for example, spending and rate variances are isolated from efficiency variances).

The manufacturing manager's total variance of $956 unfavorable, when added to the purchasing department manager's variance of $4,312 unfavorable (as calculated in

EXHIBIT 8-6

MANUFACTURING MANAGER'S PERFORMANCE REPORT
JUNE 19XX

	Actual Cost	Input Standard Cost	Output Standard Cost	Labor Rate and Variable Overhead Spending Variances	Material Quantity, Labor Efficiency, and Variable Overhead Variances	Total Variance
Direct Material						
Birch panels	N.A.	$10,000	$ 8,400	N.A.	$1,600U	$1,600U
Hardboard panels	N.A.	1,080	864	N.A.	216U	216U
Spruce structural members	N.A.	2,050	2,080	N.A.	30F	30F
Total direct material		$13,130	$11,344		$1,786U	$1,786U
Direct Labor						
Fabrication dept.	$5,820	$ 6,000	$ 5,600	$180F	$ 400U	$ 220U
Assembly dept.	3,465	3,300	2,565	165U	735U	900U
Total direct labor	$9,285	$ 9,300	$ 8,165	$ 15F	$1,135U	$1,120U
Variable Overhead						
Fabrication dept.	$1,700	$ 1,500	$ 1,400	$200U	$ 100U	$ 300U
Assembly dept.	1,500	2,200	1,710	700F	490U	210F
Total variable overhead	$3,200	$ 3,700	$ 3,110	$500F	$ 590U	$ 90U

	Actual Cost	Fixed Cost Budget	Fixed Overhead Budget Variance	Fixed Overhead Volume Variance	Total Variance
Fixed Overhead					
All departments	$12,450	$14,490	$2,040F	N.A.	$2,040F

			Spending Variances	Efficiency Variances	Total Variances
Grand Total					
Variance			$2,555F	$3,511U	$ 956U

F   Favorable
U   Unfavorable

the previous chapter) and added to the $960 unfavorable fixed manufacturing overhead volume variance (for which no manager is held responsible), yields a total variance of $6,228 unfavorable. That $6,228 is the same amount used to adjust the standard gross profit to the actual gross profit on page 283 of this chapter.

GENERAL MODEL FOR FIXED OVERHEAD VARIANCES

CHAPTER OBJECTIVE 5
General variance model

In Chapter 7 we illustrated the general model used in calculating the variances related to the variables costs. The *general variance model*, defined in Chapter 7, is applied to fixed overhead variances and is presented in Exhibit 8-7.

The following comprehensive example illustrates the use of the general model given in Exhibit 8-7. The management accountant at Nelson Company compiled the following information to aid in the establishment of predetermined overhead rates to be used for the next fiscal year, which starts on August 1.

Budgeted annual fixed overhead costs	$1,382,400
Planned annual unit sales	77,400 units
Planned annual unit production	76,800 units
Current year's variable manufacturing overhead rate	$2.73 per direct labor hour
Expected price increase on variable overhead cost components	10%
Direct labor hours per unit of product	2 direct labor hours

Using this information, the management accountant calculates the predetermined overhead rates as follows. First, the variable manufacturing overhead rate is computed:

$$\text{Variable Manufacturing Overhead Rate} = \$2.73 \text{ per direct labor hour} + (.10 \times \$2.73)$$
$$= \$3 \text{ per direct labor hour}$$

The rate for the current year was increased by 10% because it was expected that items included in variable overhead would increase 10% in price. Second, the predetermined fixed manufacturing overhead rate is computed:

$$\text{Fixed Manufacturing Overhead Rate} = \$1,382,400/(76,800 \text{ units} \times 2 \text{ direct labor hours per unit})$$
$$= \$1,382,400/153,600 \text{ direct labor hours}$$
$$= \$9 \text{ per direct labor hour}$$

Notice that the planned units produced, and not the planned unit sales, were multiplied by the standard direct labor hours to arrive at planned direct labor hours. The planned direct labor hours is divided into the budgeted fixed manufacturing overhead to arrive at the predetermined fixed manufacturing overhead rate of $9 per direct labor hour.

During August 19XX, Nelson Company experienced the following actual overhead costs, direct labor hours and units of production:

Actual variable manufacturing overhead costs	$ 40,000
Actual fixed manufacturing overhead costs	$116,500
Actual direct labor hours	12,360 direct labor hours
Actual production	6,500 units

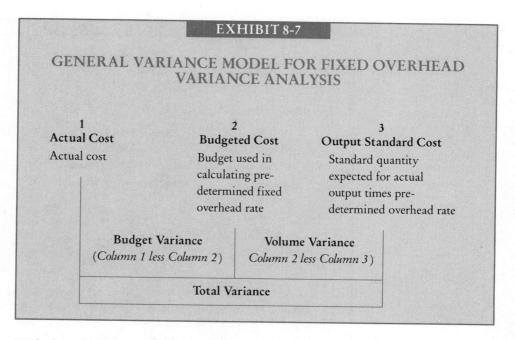

With these data, the overhead variances are calculations in Exhibit 8-8 on page 290.

The overhead variances computed in Exhibit 8-8 follow the general model presented in Exhibit 8-7. First, we examine the variable manufacturing overhead variances. The actual variable overhead cost is $40,000. The input standard is $37,080 which is the actual direct labor hours (12,360) times the variable overhead rate ($3). The output standard is $39,000 which is the actual production (6,500 units) times the standard number of direct labor hours per unit of product (2) times the variable overhead rate ($3). The spending variance is the actual cost ($40,000) less the input standard ($37,080) for $2,920 unfavorable. The efficiency variance is the difference between the input standard ($37,080) and the output standard ($39,000) which equals $1,920 favorable.

Now, we measure the fixed manufacturing overhead variances, again using the general model in Exhibit 8-7. The actual fixed overhead is $116,500. The input standard or budgeted figure is $1,382,400/12 months, or $115,200. The output standard is the actual production (6,500 units) times the standard number of direct labor units per unit of product (2) times the fixed overhead rate ($9). The output standard is thus $117,000. The budget variance is the difference between the actual cost ($116,500) and the input standard ($115,200), which is $1,300 unfavorable. The volume variance is $1,800 favorable and is the difference between the input standard ($115,200) and the output standard ($117,000).

ACTIVITY-BASED COSTING

CHAPTER OBJECTIVE 6
The purpose and application of activity-based costing

Up to this point in the textbook, we have assumed that costs can be divided into two types, variable and fixed. In addition, we have implicitly assumed that the only factor that causes costs to vary is the volume of activity. In Chapter 2, for example, we defined a variable cost as a cost that varies in proportion with changes in activity level and we defined a fixed cost as a cost that does not vary as the activity level changes. In Chapter 3, we described cost–volume–profit analysis using this distinction. Contribution margin analysis, also in Chapter 3, depends on the concepts of fixed and variable costs.

EXHIBIT 8-8

OVERHEAD VARIANCE CALCULATIONS

Variable Overhead Variances

Actual Cost (AQ × AP)	Input Standard Cost (AQ × SP)	Output Standard Cost (SQ × SP)
(Unable to express in terms of quantity times price.)	12,360 direct labor hours × $3	6,500 units × 2 direct labor hours × $3
$40,000	$37,080	$39,000

Variable Manufacturing Spending Variance: $2,920 Unfavorable	Variable Manufacturing Efficiency Variance: $1,920 Favorable

Total Variance: $1,000 Unfavorable

Fixed Overhead Variances

Actual Cost	Budgeted Cost	Output Standard Cost
		6,500 units × 2 direct labor hours × $9
$116,500	$115,200*	$117,000

Fixed Manufacturing Overhead Budget Variance: $1,300 Unfavorable	Fixed Manufacturing Overhead Volume Variance: $1,800 Favorable

Total Variance: $500 Favorable

*Monthly basis ($1,382,400 annual budget/12 months = $115,200).

Historically, the classification of costs as either variable or fixed, depending on their relationship with the activity level, has worked well in most companies. More recently, however, this cost scheme has faltered. Because of these problems, *activity-based costing* has been developed.

Limitations of Conventional Costing

In recent years some corporations have discovered that the so-called fixed costs are the ones that varied the most! In addition, some firms have found that their product costs are not reasonable estimates of the resources expended on the product. A third problem is that high-volume products seem to be costed excessively, whereas low-volume products are not costed enough. Given these anomalies, management accountants have probed for reasons to explain such phenomena. Several things have been learned, especially in how manufacturing overhead should be analyzed.

Management accountants have found that volume is not the only factor that causes costs to change. Other factors can also affect the level of cost that a firm incurs, such as the number of setups, the number of quality inspections, the number of production runs, the number and extent of repairs, and the level of maintenance. As these factors have increased in proportion to the total cost, it has become clearer that the conventional way of costing products can be inaccurate.

As a simple example of this distortion, consider a company that sells two products, 800 units of A and 200 units of B. The manufacturing overhead is $1,000. A traditional management accounting costing scheme would allocate to Product A 80% (800 units/ 1,000 total units) of the overhead cost, or $800 (80% of $1,000). The allocation to Product B would be $200 (20% of $1,000). But suppose that on further analysis the management accountant discovers that the overhead costs are due entirely to the number of setups and that Product B requires substantially more setups, and more expensive ones, than does Product A. In particular, she finds that Product A's setups cost $100 whereas Product B's setups cost $900. Thus the conventional costing system is misleading, since the volume-related allocations lead to product costs that are in contrast to the real economic factor causing the overhead costs: the number of setups.

Conventional versus Activity-based Costing

Activity-based costing traces costs to activities and then traces costs to the product. In the above example, the accountant would trace overhead costs to the number of setups and then trace these setup costs to products A and B. In a more realistic setting, the accountant would follow these steps:

1. Determine the factors that require resources of the firm.
2. Group activities whose costs are determined by one factor and collect the costs of these activities (called a cost pool).
3. Determine and use cost drivers that can estimate the cost of these causal factors and assign them to the cost pools.
4. Cost the product by using the cost drivers determined above.

Steps 1, 2, and 3 are often referred to as the *first stage* of activity-based costing, in which costs are traced to activities. Step 4 is the *second stage*, in which costs are traced from activities to products. In other words, the first stage sets up the cost pools and the pool rate, which is the cost per unit of the cost driver. In the second stage the overhead is applied to products by using the pool rate.

EXHIBIT 8-9

COMPARISON OF CONVENTIONAL AND ACTIVITY-BASED COSTING

Attribute	Conventional Costing	Activity-based Costing
1. Factors that cause resources to be used	Only volume	Several factors such as the number of setups or the number of production runs
2. Number of cost pools	One	Multiple, one for each factor that causes use of resources
3. Number of cost drivers	One	Multiple, one for each cost pool
4. How products are costed	Use the volume cost driver	Use each of the cost drivers

tween conventional costing and activity-based costing. (These contrasts are summarized in Exhibit 8-9.) Conventional costing assumes that the only factor that causes resources to be used is volume (that is, the more units that are produced, the greater the production costs). Activity-based costing says that there are multiple causes of resource use, one of which is probably volume. Accordingly, conventional costing has only one cost pool for overhead, whereas activity-based costing has multiple cost pools. Conventional costing uses only one cost driver and it is volume related. Common cost drivers under conventional costing are number of units produced, direct labor hours, and machine hours. Activity-based costing uses several cost drivers, one for each cost pool. Finally, conventional costing costs the product by using the one and only cost driver. Activity-based costing costs the product by using the different cost drivers for the various cost pools.

Illustration of Activity-based Costing

Suppose that Umpity Toy Corporation makes two products, Grump and Trump. The production process of each good is that it goes through the Machining Department and then through the Assembly Department. After investigating the production process, Umpity Corporation decides that there are four causes or components of overhead cost (for this example, we will not be concerned with direct materials or direct labor): indirect labor, indirect materials, power, and setup costs. As shown in Exhibit 8-10, the major costs are power and setup costs.

The management accountant creates two cost pools: the Machining Department and the Assembly Department. Cost pools do not need to be created this way, but if they can, this provides a practical basis for accumulating costs. The key point is that the

EXHIBIT 8-10

FIRST STAGE OF ACTIVITY-BASED COSTING

Overhead Item	Machining Department	Assembly Department
Indirect labor	$ 10,000	$ 10,000
Indirect materials	15,000	5,000
Power	170,000	25,000
Setup costs	5,000	60,000
Total	$200,000	$100,000
Number of machine hours	2,000	
Number of production runs		500
Cost per machine hour	$100	
Cost per production run		$200

costs in each pool should be as homogeneous as possible. As depicted in Exhibit 8-10, the Machining Department consists mostly of power costs, whereas the Assembly Department primarily involves setup costs.

The next step is to select a cost driver for each cost pool. Since most of the cost in the Machining Department is for power to run the machinery, the cost driver there is machine hours. The largest cost in the Assembly Department is for setups, so a logical cost driver for that cost pool is number of production runs.

The budget for Umpity Corporation yields the data in Exhibit 8-10. From these projections, the management accountant can estimate the pool rate, the cost per unit of the cost driver. For the Machinery Department, the total estimated costs are $200,000 and the estimated number of machine hours is 2,000; thus the pool rate equals $100 per machine hour. In the Assembly Department, the total estimated costs are $100,000. The estimated number of production runs is 500. These data indicate a pool rate of $200 per production run.

The overhead is applied when the goods are actually produced. Here there are two overhead rates—not just one, as in conventional product costing. In April Umpity Corporation makes 15,000 units of Grump and 6,000 units of Trump. While making Grump, the firm incurs 150 machine hours and makes 10 production runs. The total cost of Grump, as shown in Exhibit 8-11, is $17,000 [(150 × $100) + (10 × $200)]. Grump's cost per unit is $1.13 ($17,000/15,000 units).

Similarly, we can calculate the cost of producing Trump. Trump requires 30 machine hours and 30 production runs. Trump's cost in the Machinery Department is 30 × $100, or $3,000. Trump's cost in the Assembly Department is 30 × $200, or $6,000. The total cost in April of producing 6,000 units of Trump is $3,000 + $6,000, or $9,000. Trump's cost per unit is $1.50 ($9,000/6,000 units).

The superiority of activity-based costing can be seen by comparing this analysis with a more conventional costing analysis. Suppose the costs are aggregated into one pool. Total overhead costs are estimated at $300,000 ($200,000 + $100,000). Assume that machine hours is the cost driver. The overhead rate becomes $300,000/2,000

EXHIBIT 8-11		
SECOND STAGE OF ACTIVITY-BASED COSTING		
	Grump	**Trump**
Units produced	15,000	6,000
Machine hours	150	30
Production runs	10	30
Cost of machine hours		
($100 per hour)	$15,000	$3,000
Cost of production runs		
($200 per run)	$ 2,000	$6,000
Total cost	$17,000	$9,000
Cost per unit	$1.13	$1.50

machine hours, or $150 per machine hour. Grump is then costed at 150 machine hours × $150, or $22,500. On a per-unit basis, Grump costs $1.50 ($22,500/15,000 units). Trump is costed at 30 machine hours × $150, or $4,500. Trump costs $.75 per unit ($4,500/6,000 units). The distortion in the costs comes about because conventional costing ignores the setup costs, especially in the assembly of the products. In particular, the product consuming more of the cost driver (Grump uses more machine hours) is charged more costs and thus *looks less profitable than it really is.* The product consuming less of the cost driver (in this example, it is Trump) is absorbing less of the production costs and so *looks more profitable than it really is.*

Activity-based costing is always proper and correct, since it allocates the actual use of resources to those products that consume them. Conventional costing is proper only when it provides cost figures approximately the same as activity-based costing. This may happen if there is only one cost pool or only one product, or in the manufacture of products that use resources in the same proportion as their individual volume to total volume.

DECISION SUPPORT SYSTEMS AND BEHAVIORAL ASPECTS OF VARIANCE ANALYSIS

CHAPTER OBJECTIVE 7
Variance analysis and decision support

Standard costs are a tool used to implement a management control system and to focus management attention on exceptional situations. The variances generated by the management control system should be regarded as springboards for further inquiry.

As we have discussed, the variances for some resources are difficult to interpret without further investigation. In judging whether or not a variance warrants further review, it is important to consider the extent to which the resource is under control of the manager, the persistence of the variance, and the materiality of the item.

Even though a variance appears on the performance report of a manager, it does not mean that the manager has complete control of the variance. An example is fixed manufacturing overhead. The manager might control a portion of that cost—for example, the cost of material handling—but he or she may have no control over the depreciation expense portion of fixed overhead. If the company president is the only person authorized to acquire new equipment, it is the president who controls the depreciation portion of fixed manufacturing overhead.

A variance should be included on the manufacturing manager's performance report only if he or she is capable of influencing some portion of the costs. However, the noncontrollable portion is not easily extracted from the analysis because it must be included in fixed manufacturing overhead for product costing purposes.

Accounting systems, physical inventories, and the accountants who compile the reports are not completely accurate. Given the inaccurate environment of management accounting and managerial performance evaluations, the management accountants should not overreact when the performance report indicates a variance. What is more important is the *trend* associated with the variance.

If the variance is the result of an inventory count error, the error will likely correct itself at the end of the next accounting period. An overstatement in one period generally becomes an understatement in the next period, and vice versa. If the error is in compiling the report, the same error will probably not recur consistently. One way to isolate the random errors from problems that require management's attention is to plot the variances on a graph and assess the trend of the variance. Statistical techniques could be applied to the variances that appear to stand out consistently from the rest. If we assume that random errors will have a normal distribution, then any observation that is outside of the range of the mean plus or minus three standard deviations should receive special attention.

Demonstration Problem

Capablanca Company budgeted the following activities with respect to its fixed overhead.

Planned annual fixed overhead cost	$8,100,000
Planned annual unit sales	1,200,000
Planned annual unit production	1,000,000
Planned machine hours per unit of product	2 hours

Capablanca Company uses planned machine hours instead of direct labor hours for the allocation of fixed manufacturing overhead costs.

During July Capablanca Company experienced the following actual overhead costs and production:

Actual fixed manufacturing overhead costs	$650,000
Actual production	80,000

REQUIRED
Compute the fixed overhead variances in July for Capablanca Company.

SOLUTION TO DEMONSTRATION PROBLEM
The first thing to do is to compute the predetermined fixed manufacturing overhead rate. It is the budgeted annual fixed overhead costs divided by the planned machine hours to produce the planned annual production:

$$\$8,100,000/(1,000,000 \times 2) = \$4.05 \text{ per machine hour}$$

Also note that the planned monthly fixed overhead cost is 1/12 of $8,100,000, or $675,000. The fixed overhead variances can now be computed for Capablanca Company:

$$\text{Fixed Overhead Budget Variance} = \$675,000 - \$650,000$$
$$= \$25,000\text{F}$$
$$\text{Fixed Overhead Volume Variance} = (80,000 \times 2 \times \$4.05) - \$675,000$$
$$= \$27,000\text{U}$$

Review of Chapter Objectives

1. Define *predetermined fixed manufacturing overhead rate* and *cost driver* (production divisor) and indicate their importance in planning and evaluating fixed overhead costs (pp. 275–77).

   ▪ A predetermined fixed manufacturing overhead rate is an estimate of the fixed overhead costs per some unit of activity. This activity is called the cost driver or production divisor. It is the estimate of the expected level of production and is often expressed in direct labor hours or machine hours.

   ▪ During the budgeting process, managers estimate unit production, direct labor hours per unit (or machine hours per unit), and fixed manufacturing overhead costs. Thus, the predetermined fixed manufacturing overhead rate and the cost driver are established during the planning process. They are used to plan for the future manufacturing activities of the organization.

   ▪ The predetermined fixed manufacturing overhead rate is also used in determining the overhead rate of a product. The standard fixed manufacturing overhead per unit of product is equal to direct labor hours per unit of product times the predetermined overhead rate per direct labor hour. If a different cost driver is used, then the formula is changed appropriately.

   ▪ Variances are calculated during the evaluation stage. Among the variances computed are the fixed overhead variances. These variances are calculated using the predetermined overhead rate.

2. Calculate the variance used to control fixed manufacturing costs (pp. 277–79).

   ▪ There are two fixed manufacturing overhead variances. The first is the budget variance. It is equal to the actual fixed manufacturing overhead costs less the budgeted fixed manufacturing overhead cost. The second variance is called the volume variance. This variance is equal to the budgeted fixed manufacturing overhead costs minus the product of the standard direct labor hours for units produced times the predetermined fixed manufacturing overhead rate. Although the budget variance is useful when evaluating the performance of a plant manager, the volume variance is not.

   ▪ As firms become more automated, their fixed costs become relatively larger while the variable costs become relatively small. For these companies fixed overhead costs deserve attention. The overhead variances should help these managers control fixed costs.

3. Explain how standard costs are used in product costing for determining income and valuing inventory (pp. 279–85).

   ▪ Work in process inventory can be accounted for at standard cost, which includes standard direct materials cost, standard direct labor costs, standard variable manufacturing overhead cost, and standard fixed manufacturing overhead cost.

When the product is completed, it is transferred into finished goods inventory, which can be accounted for at standard cost as well.

- When the item is sold to a customer, it is transferred from finished goods inventory to cost of goods sold. If the finished goods inventory is kept at standard costs, then the cost of goods sold will be also. Thus, the standard cost of the product is expensed when the product is sold.

- This process must be altered when the actual costs differ from the standard. The issue is how to account for the difference between the standard and the actual costs. What is to be done with the variances? In practice, the variances are generally charged against cost of goods sold. Theoretically, the variances are also the result of items still in direct materials inventory and in work in process inventory. However, unless the amounts are substantial, most firms simply charge all of the variances against cost of goods sold as a practical solution to the problem.

4. Describe the manufacturing manager's performance report (pp. 285–88).

- Combining the variances defined in Chapter 7 with the two in this chapter, one can prepare a report by which the manager of manufacturing operations can be evaluated. The manufacturing manager's performance report details the standard and actual costs of direct materials, direct labor, variable overhead, and fixed overhead. It also pinpoints favorable and unfavorable variances.

5. Describe the general variance model based on input and output standards as applied to fixed overhead (pp. 288–89).

- The general variance model also applies to the computation of the two fixed overhead variances. This is done, analogous to the way presented in Chapter 7, by comparing the actual cost and the input standard and the output standard. The budget variance is equal to the actual cost less the input standard. The volume variance is equal to the input standard minus the output standard. The input standard is the budgeted fixed overhead cost (and comes from the master budget).

6. Explain the purpose of activity-based costing and how it is applied (pp. 289–94).

- Conventional costing fails when the underlying factors that explain the use of resources in manufacturing are not volume related. Activity-based costing overcomes these problems by tracing costs to activities and then tracing costs to products. In the first stage, the management accountant determines activities that explain costs and then collects these costs (in what are called cost pools) for each of these activities. For each cost pool, a cost driver is determined that measures how much of the resource is used. In the second stage, the costs are applied to the products by adding the costs from each cost pool. The cost from a cost pool is obtained by multiplying the pool rate by the amount of the cost driver used in making the product.

7. Interpret the variance analysis from a decision support systems viewpoint (pp. 294–95).

- Variances are not measured without error; managers should examine the cost models based under different measurements. More importantly, variances provide mixed signals because they can be caused by a multitude of factors, both within and outside the control of managers whose performance is under review. Decision support systems should help managers to interpret the variances. One way of doing this is by looking for trends. Variances that recur from month to month need to be examined closely. Organizations should be structured to highlight effective and ineffective performance.

Glossary of Key Terms

absorbed overhead The portion of factory indirect cost that has been allocated to a specific product. The allocation process is usually carried out by the application of an appropriate overhead rate to specific units of production.

activity-based costing A cost system that traces costs to activities and then traces costs to products.

budget variance The difference between budgeted fixed manufacturing overhead and the standard direct labor hours for units produced times the predetermined fixed manufacturing overhead rate.

cost driver The divisor used in calculating the predetermined overhead rate. This divisor is the estimate of the expected level of production. It is often expressed in terms of direct labor hours or machine hours.

cost pool A group of factors, as nearly homogeneous as possible, that cause resources to be used in making a product. Cost pools are used in activity-based costing.

denominator activity level The value of the cost driver. It is the denominator of the fraction comprising the predetermined fixed manufacturing overhead rate.

overabsorbed overhead The excess of manufacturing overhead applied to production over the actual expenses incurred. Synonymous with *overapplied overhead*.

pool rate The cost per unit of the cost driver for a given cost pool. It is equal to the estimated costs of the cost pool divided by the estimated measure of the cost driver.

predetermined fixed manufacturing overhead rate The rate at which fixed manufacturing overhead is applied to production, based on the ratio of total budgeted fixed overhead costs for a period of time to the expected total of some measure of activity (cost driver) for the same period, such as machine hours or direct labor hours.

predetermined manufacturing overhead rate The predetermined variable manufacturing overhead rate plus the predetermined fixed overhead rate.

underabsorbed overhead The excess of actual manufacturing expenses incurred over the amount of manufacturing overhead applied to production. Synonymous with *underapplied overhead*.

volume variance The difference between fixed cost assigned to products in a specified time period and budgeted fixed manufacturing overhead.

Review Questions

8-1 Discuss the role of the production manager, the sales manager, and the controller in determining the predetermined fixed manufacturing overhead rate.

8-2 Once the expected production for the next year is estimated, what role does the standard labor hours per unit of product play in determining the predetermined fixed manufacturing overhead rate?

8-3 Some companies establish a separate predetermined fixed manufacturing overhead rate for each production department. Why would a company choose to establish separate rates for each department?

8-4 Direct materials, direct labor, variable manufacturing overhead, and fixed manufacturing overhead are considered product costs. It is easier to understand why the variable-cost items are regarded as product costs than it is to understand why fixed manufacturing cost is regarded as a product cost. Why is fixed manufacturing overhead considered a product cost?

8-5 What are the two variances into which the overall fixed manufacturing overhead may be decomposed?

8-6 What does the fixed manufacturing overhead budget variance tell us about the control of costs in the manufacturing facility?

8-7 How should the fixed manufacturing overhead volume variance be interpreted?

8-8 Why should the fixed manufacturing overhead volume variance not be used in the evaluation of the performance of the production manager?

8-9 How does one determine whether the fixed manufacturing overhead volume variance is favorable or unfavorable?

8-10 What does the term *applied overhead* mean?

8-11 How is the total amount of the overapplied or underapplied overhead related to the total overhead cost variance?

8-12 How should a management accountant react to variances that appear on the production manager's performance report?

8-13 What is the preferred method of disposing of the variances between actual costs and standard costs at the end of the accounting period?

8-14 Why might a company decide to use machine hours rather than direct labor hours as a basis for determining the predetermined fixed manufacturing overhead rate?

8-15 What role does the predetermined fixed manufacturing overhead rate play in valuing finished goods inventory?

8-16 What role does the predetermined fixed manufacturing overhead rate play in valuing work in process inventory?

8-17 What role does the predetermined fixed manufacturing overhead rate play in valuing raw materials inventory?

8-18 What is activity-based costing?

8-19 When is it proper to use activity-based costing?

8-20 Compare and contrast conventional and activity-based costing.

8-21 What is a cost pool? How does an accountant establish a cost pool?

8-22 What is a pool rate and how is it used?

Discussion Questions

8-23 How can a manager use standard variable cost per unit in decision making? Standard variable plus standard fixed cost per unit? Are the data relevant to the sales manager, the purchasing manager, or the manufacturing manager?

8-24 Explain how applying fixed costs to product costing is treating fixed costs as if they were variable costs. How does this fact affect the interpretation of the fixed overhead variances?

8-25 Conventional costing may be viewed as a special case of activity-based costing. Explain.

Exercises

8-26 **PREDETERMINED FIXED MANUFACTURING OVERHEAD RATE** Based on the following information, calculate the predetermined fixed manufacturing overhead rate for

CO 1 each of the two production departments within the factory.

	Machining Department	Assembly Department
Units of production	50,000	52,000
Machine hours per unit	3	–0–
Direct labor hours per unit	–0–	4
Estimated fixed manufacturing overhead for the year	$75,000	$316,000

8-27   FIXED MANUFACTURING OVERHEAD VARIANCES Adams Company calculated a predetermined fixed manufacturing overhead rate of $2 per direct labor hour based on the

CO 2   following information:

Estimated fixed manufacturing overhead	$1,000,000
Estimated direct labor hours	500,000 hours
Predetermined Fixed Manufacturing Overhead	$1,000,000/500,000 direct labor hours, or $2 per direct labor hour

The actual fixed manufacturing overhead for the year was $1,050,000 and the actual direct labor hours used were 510,000 hours.

a. Calculate the amount of the fixed manufacturing overhead budget variance and indicate if the variance is favorable or unfavorable.

b. Calculate the amount of the fixed manufacturing overhead volume variance and indicate if the variance is favorable or unfavorable.

8-28   DISPOSITION OF FIXED OVERHEAD VOLUME VARIANCE Frost Company had an unfavorable fixed manufacturing budget variance of $3,000, a favorable fixed manufacturing volume variance of $1,200, and a standard cost of goods sold of $130,000. The finished goods

CO 3   inventory at the end of the accounting period was $30,000 and the work in process at the end of the accounting period was $10,000. Calculate the actual cost of goods sold for the accounting period.

8-29   UNDERAPPLIED OR OVERAPPLIED FIXED MANUFACTURING OVERHEAD Scott Company used a predetermined fixed manufacturing overhead rate of $4 per ma-

CO 2   chine hour during the entire year. It was a year in which the company used 80,000 machine hours. Actual fixed manufacturing overhead was $330,000. Determine the amount of underapplied or overapplied fixed manufacturing overhead.

8-30   FIXED MANUFACTURING OVERHEAD VOLUME VARIANCE Famous Frog Legs Co. produced 200,000 units in a year in which it expected to produce 180,000 units. The

CO 2   predetermined fixed manufacturing overhead rate used during the year was $.25. What is the amount of favorable or unfavorable fixed manufacturing overhead volume variance?

8-31   FIXED MANUFACTURING OVERHEAD BUDGET VARIANCE When Brakett Company closed its accounting records at the end of the period, the fixed manufacturing over-

CO 2   head account was underapplied by $5,000. The company determined that the number of units

produced was 20,000 fewer than were expected to be produced. The fixed manufacturing overhead rate used during the year was $1 per unit produced. Determine the amount of the fixed manufacturing overhead budget variance and indicate if the variance is favorable or unfavorable.

8-32 FIXED MANUFACTURING OVERHEAD VOLUME VARIANCE Rimstidt Manufacturing Company established the fixed manufacturing overhead rate based on expected fixed manufacturing costs of $5,000,000 per year and estimated production of 1,000,000 units of product. Each unit of product requires 2 direct labor hours.

At the end of the year, it was determined that 2,400,000 direct labor hours were used and the actual fixed manufacturing overhead was $4,900,000.

Calculate the fixed manufacturing overhead volume variance and indicate if the variance is favorable or unfavorable.

8-33 FIXED MANUFACTURING OVERHEAD BUDGET VARIANCE Kindelsperger Products estimated that it would produce 2,000,000 units of product during the next year and that level of production would require 7,000,000 machine hours. The estimated fixed manufacturing overhead costs during the year was $3,000,000.

At the end of the year it was determined that the actual machine hours used was 7,500,000. The actual fixed manufacturing overhead cost were $3,400,000.

Calculate the fixed manufacturing overhead budget variance and indicate if the variance is favorable or unfavorable.

8-34 TOTAL FIXED MANUFACTURING OVERHEAD VARIANCE Pimlot Manufacturing Company estimates that total production during the year will be 2,000,000 units and the estimated fixed manufacturing overhead costs will be $5,000,000 during the year.

At the end of the year it was determined that the actual production was 2,400,000 units and the actual fixed manufacturing overhead costs were $4,800,000.

Calculate the total fixed manufacturing overhead variance (the combination of fixed manufacturing overhead budget variance and fixed manufacturing overhead volume variance) and indicate if the variance is favorable or unfavorable.

8-35 ACTIVITY-BASED COSTING Ryerson Company produces only two products, Wright and Wrong. After analyzing the cost factors, Ryerson concludes that it has only one cost pool and its cost driver is machine hours. Total estimates overhead costs are $600,000. Ryerson plans to produce 1,000 units each of Wright and Wrong. One unit of Wright requires one hour of direct labor and two machine hours. To make a unit of Wrong takes two hours of direct labor and three machine hours. During July, Ryerson manufactures 100 units of Wright and 80 units of Wrong.

a. Use conventional costing with direct labor hours as the cost driver. What is the overhead rate? What are the product costs in July?

b. Use conventional costing and use machine hours as the cost driver. What is the overhead rate? What are the product costs in July?

c. Use activity-based costing and use machine hours as the cost driver. What is the pool rate? What are the product costs in July?

d. What can you conclude about conventional versus activity-based costing?

8-36 ACTIVITY-BASED COSTING Godfrey Manufacturing makes KEB, which involves two stages, machining and drying. Accordingly, the accountants at Godfrey set up two cost pools. The cost driver of the machining cost pool is machine hours. The cost driver of the drying cost pool is kilowatt hours.

Yearly estimated costs of the machining cost pool and the drying cost pool, respectively, are $500,000 and $200,000. Godfrey anticipates that it will make 100,000 units of KEB. Each unit of KEB requires two direct labor hours, one machine hour in the machining stage, and one kilowatt hour in the drying stage.

During September 19X1, Godfrey makes 15,000 units of KEB.

a. Use conventional costing with direct labor hours as the cost driver. What is the overhead rate? What is the cost of goods manufactured in September?

b. Use activity-based costing. What are the pool rates? What is the cost of goods manufactured in September?

c. What can you conclude about conventional versus activity-based costing?

CO 6

8-37   **ACTIVITY-BASED COSTING** Pushkin makes and sells TIC and TAC. Both goods go through Cutting and then through Polishing. The cost drivers for these departments are production runs and machine hours.

When the budget was prepared, the firm estimated that it would produce 10,000 units of TIC and 15,000 units of TAC. The Cutting Department will have $800,000 of costs while the Polishing Department will incur $600,000 of costs. Furthermore, the firm estimated that the total number of production runs would be 500 and that the total number of machine hours would be 10,000.

During May, Pushkin makes 1,000 units of TIC and 1,000 units of TAC. Building TIC requires 20 production runs and 500 machine hours. TAC, on the other hand, takes 15 production runs and 400 machine hours.

a. What are the total costs and the cost per unit of TIC?

b. What are the total costs and the cost per unit of TAC?

Problems

CO 2

8-38   **OVERHEAD VARIANCE ANALYSIS** Westlake Company, a major producer of stereos, is capable of producing 130,000 stereo headsets per month. The cost accounting department has determined that 5 hours and 45 minutes of variable overhead at $.85 per hour and 5 hours of fixed overhead at $2 per hour are required to complete one headset.

During May, Westlake produced 137,000 headsets, incurring variable factory overhead of $735,000 and fixed overhead of $1,119,000. Actual hours of input were 852,000.

REQUIRED

Prepare an analysis of all variable overhead and fixed overhead variances.

8-39   **SELECTING A COST DRIVER** The controller of Rogers-Stanley Manufacturing Company developed the following estimates of total factory overhead costs.

CO 1

	Volume	
	88,000 Direct Labor Hours	110,000 Direct Labor Hours
Variable overhead @ $5.25 per unit	$ 462,000	$ 577,500
Fixed overhead	770,000	993,300
Total factory overhead costs	$1,232,000	$1,570,800

Fixed overhead is higher at the practical capacity of 110,000 direct labor hours due to increased requirements for maintenance and supervisory personnel. The controller expected actual volume to be 90,000 direct labor hours, but considered using practical capacity as the basis for applying overhead for the tax advantage it affords. She realized doing so could cause problems in using the variances for control purposes.

REQUIRED

a. Calculate the fixed overhead application rate using the cost and volume at practical capacity.

b. Assuming that actual direct labor hours are 94,000 and that actual fixed overhead is $860,000, calculate the fixed overhead budget variance and volume variance using the practical capacity overhead rate.

c. Explain why or why not these variances appear to be useful controls.

CO 2

8-40 OVERHEAD VARIANCE ANALYSIS Fix-It-All Repair and Supply Outlet has had trouble controlling its accounts receivable. Bills for repair work and housing contractors have on occasion been inaccurate and late. This has caused an increase in bad debts as well as intolerable levels of receivables.

You were a consultant to Fix-It-All on this matter. After carefully studying the billing operation, you developed some currently attainable standards that were implemented with a budget four weeks ago. You had divided costs into fixed and variable categories. The bill is regarded as the product, the unit of output.

You have reasonable confidence that the underlying source documents for compiling the results have been accurately tallied. However, the bookkeeper has had some trouble summarizing the data and has provided the following:

Standard variable costs, allowed per hour	$ 8
Fixed overhead budget variance, favorable	180
Combined budgeted costs for the bills produced	21,000
Production volume variance, favorable	1,200
Variable-cost spending variance, unfavorable	2,300
Variable-cost efficiency variance, favorable	2,500
Standard hours allowed for the bills produced	1,600 hours

REQUIRED

Compute the following:

a. Actual hours of input

b. Fixed-overhead budget

c. Standard fixed overhead applied

d. Amount of direct labor hours (according to the master budget)

8-41   OVERHEAD VARIANCE ANALYSIS Winner Widgets uses a standard cost system to determine rates and variances for the next year. By using a denominator activity level of 53,000 units per month for a base, management determined that standard costs included 7 hours per widget of variable overhead at $1 per hour, and 7 hours per widget per fixed overhead at $1.55 per hour. In January, Winner actually produced 55,000 widgets. As a result actual variable factory overhead was $375,000, actual hours of input were 400,000, and actual fixed overhead was $550,000.

CO 1, 2

REQUIRED

Prepare an analysis of all variable overhead and fixed overhead variances.

8-42   OVERHEAD VARIANCE ANALYSIS Overhead is budgeted based on departmental rates for Marcy, Inc. The bases for these rates are as follows:

CO 2

Fabrication Department

Annual fixed overhead	$6,000,000
Variable overhead	$20 per direct labor hour

Assembly Department

Annual fixed overhead	$7,800,000
Variable overhead	$30 per direct labor hour

Overhead application is based on 600,000 labor hours per year for each department.

REQUIRED

Answer each of the following independent questions.

a. What would the total standard overhead per unit for a product be if that product has a standard of 4 hours in the Fabrication Department and 3 hours in the Assembly Department?

b. During January the following occurred:

	Actual Hours	Standard Hours Given the Output
Fabrication Department	65,000	64,000
Assembly	55,000	57,000

Actual overhead for January was as follows:

	Variable Overhead	Fixed Overhead
Fabrication Department	$1,300,000.00	$650,000.00
Assembly	1,543,255.81	681,744.19

Calculate the spending, efficiency, and budget variances.

8-43   DEPARTMENTAL AND PLANTWIDE OVERHEAD   Galaxy Comic Company has introduced a new product line based on its comic characters. The new line is composed of different sets of silver figurines. Departmental rates for overhead costs and a plantwide rate for common costs are based on the following information:

CO 2

Smelting

Annual fixed overhead	$12,600,000
Variable overhead	$18 per direct labor hour

Molding and Design

Annual fixed overhead	$6,600,000
Variable overhead	$12 per direct labor hour

Common Costs

Annual fixed overhead	$2,400,000

Overhead applied is based on 600,000 labor hours per year for each of the two departments.

REQUIRED
Solve the following independently:

a. If a set of figurines has a standard of 6 hours in the Smelting Department and 4 hours in the Molding and Design Department, find the total standard fixed overhead per set of figurines.

b. For July, the budgeted fixed overhead is $1,050,000 for the Smelting Department and $550,000 for the Molding and Design Department. Also, $200,000 is budgeted for common manufacturing overhead. The following occurred during July:

	Actual Hours	Standard Hours Given the Output
Smelting Department	76,000	80,000
Molding and Design Department	58,000	60,000

Additionally, overhead in July occurred as follows:

Smelting Department	$2,375,000
Molding and Design Department	1,062,500
Common manufacturing overhead	165,000

With this information, calculate the combined variable overhead spending variance and fixed overhead budget variance. Also compute the variable overhead efficiency variance.

8-44   BASIC MANUFACTURING OVERHEAD VARIANCES The Bat Factory is a manufacturer of wood baseball bats. The following report is a comparison of budgeted and actual overhead costs:

CO 2, 4

	Budget	Actual	Favorable or (Unfavorable) Variance
Bats (quantity produced)	30,000	32,000	
Variable factory overhead:			
Budgeted (15,000 machine hours @ $4 per hour)	$ 60,000		$(2,700)
Actual (16,500 machine hours)		$ 62,700	
Fixed factory overhead:			
Budgeted	$240,000		$ 5,000
Actual		$235,000	
Total Overhead Costs	$300,000	$297,700	$ 2,300

There is no beginning or ending inventory. The factory fixed overhead rate is $8 per bat.

REQUIRED

a. Compute all possible variances for the month.

b. State which variances should not be shown on the manufacturing manager's performance report and why.

8-45 OVERHEAD COSTS IN A SERVICE BUSINESS Turfscape Company provides landscaping services in a large metropolitan area. The controller of the company developed a fixed overhead rate based on the expected fixed overhead costs of $50,000 for the year. The production divisor of 100,000 square feet of landscaping was used to arrive at a fixed overhead rate of $.50 per square foot of landscaping.

Actual fixed overhead costs for the year were $52,000, and 105,000 square feet of landscaping services were provided to customers during the year.

REQUIRED

a. Calculate the fixed overhead budget variance.

b. Calculate the fixed overhead volume variance.

8-46 BASIC MANUFACTURING VARIANCES: REVIEW PROBLEM FOR CHAPTERS 7 AND 8 The results of Stuart Company's June production as well as the standard costs are given below.

CO 2, 4, 7

	Direct Materials	Direct Labor	Variable Factory Overhead	Fixed Factory Overhead
Standard quantity	6 units	3 hours	3 direct labor hours	3 direct labor hours
Standard price or rate	$ 5	$10	$13	$15
Total	$30	$30	$39	$45

Budgeted fixed costs per period	$180,000
Units manufactured	3,900

Purchases of raw materials:

Units	24,000
Cost per unit	$4.95
Total	$118,800
Use of raw materials in units	23,700

Direct labor:

Actual hours	11,500
Actual rate	$10.25
Total	$117,875

Actual factory overhead:

Variable	$151,000
Fixed	$175,000

REQUIRED

Prepare the performance report for the month of June showing the eight possible variances.

8-47   BASIC MANUFACTURING VARIANCES: REVIEW PROBLEM FOR CHAPTERS 7 AND 8 Stanton Company manufactures standard-sized pillow cases. Stanton uses standard costs with separate standards established for each product. Pillow case coverings for throw pillows are manufactured in the Specialty Department. Production volume is measured by direct labor hours in this department and a flexible budget system is used to plan and control department overhead.

CO 2, 4, 7

Standard costs for these special pillow cases are determined annually in October for the coming year. The standard cost of a specialty pillow case for 19XX was $55, as follows:

Direct Materials:		
Fabric	5 yds @ $6 =	$30
Dye	1 gal. @ $5 =	5
Direct Labor	2 hrs. @ $6 =	12
Var. Overhead	2 hrs. @ $3 =	6
Fixed Overhead	2 hrs. @ $1 =	2
Total		$55

Overhead rates were based on normal and expected monthly capacity for 19XX, both of which were 3,000 direct labor hours. Practical capacity for this department is 3,500 direct labor hours per month. Variable costs are expected to vary with the number of direct labor hours actually used.

During September, 1,000 specialty pillow cases were produced. This was below what was expected because a labor dispute disrupted production. Once the dispute was settled, the department scheduled overtime in order to catch up to expected production levels. Actual costs incurred in September were as follows:

Direct Materials:	Purchased	Issued
Fabric	5,500 @ $6.05	5,400
Dye	2,500 @ 5.01	1,400

Direct labor:

Regular time	1,500 @ $6.25
	1,000 @ 6.50
Variable overhead	$11,200
Fixed overhead	7,650

REQUIRED

Prepare a complete analysis of all variances and provide performance reports associated with the particular variances.

Business Decision Case

Cascade Products has established standards for its Gelid X-2000 ice cooler. They are as follows:

Material:
Polyethylene, 8.5 lbs. @ $2.80 per lb.
Metal handles, 2 @ $.10 each
Labor:
15 minutes per cooler
Labor rate:
$12 per hour
Overhead:
Variable, $10 per hour
Fixed, $13 per hour

For fixed cost per unit, a budgeted 130,000 coolers were used.

In May actual production was 14,400 coolers using 3,575 hours at a labor cost of $43,750. In this month, 121,000 pounds of polyethylene were used, while 200,000 pounds were purchased for $566,000. There were no beginning inventories for the polyethylene. A total of 28,800 metal handles were used, and 10,000 were purchased at $.15 each. Variable overhead amounted to $35,800 and fixed overhead was $36,100.

REQUIRED

a. Determine how many standard hours of labor are required to produce 14,400 coolers.

b. How many standard pounds of polyethylene are required to produce 14,400 coolers?

c. What is the expected cost of overhead per cooler?

d. Compute the following variances:

   1. (a) Material price variance, (b) material quantity variance

   2. (a) Labor rate variance, (b) labor efficiency variance

    3. (a) Variable overhead spending variance, (b) variable overhead efficiency variance

    4. (a) Budget variance, (b) volume variance

e. Explain the overhead variances.

f. Explain possible causes of the material and labor variances.

Chapter 9

Flexible Budgets

CHAPTER OBJECTIVES

After reading Chapter 9, you should be able to:

1. Describe the advantages of flexible budgeting compared to static budgeting (pp. 311–12).

2. Prepare a flexible budget (pp. 312–15).

3. Define *master budget variance, activity variance, flexible budget variance,* and *sales variance* (pp. 314–15).

4. Explain the variety of activity levels and the importance of selecting the appropriate budgeted activity level (pp. 315–16).

5. Describe the relationship between standards and flexible budgets (pp. 316–18).

6. Interpret cost variances in terms of the flexible budget (pp. 318–28).

Chapter 5 stressed the planning, control, and communication aspects of the budgeting process, as well as the mechanics of preparing the master budget and the supporting budgets or schedules. It demonstrated that budgets may be prepared on an organization-wide basis to encompass all activities from overall sales to the smallest activity. Yet each of these budgets and schedules was static, or inflexible. Each was an estimate of expected achievements if all activities in the firm matched the fixed assumptions used to draw up the budget. In other words, these budgets gave no latitude for changes in the activity level and the effects of these changes throughout the master budget. This inflexibility in the master budget indicates that another type of budget is needed, the *flexible budget*, which can compare budgeted and actual performance for a variety of activity levels.

Chapter 5 also examined the contingency approach that management must take in planning, organizing, staffing, directing, and controlling the organization. The uncertainty and the dynamic nature of the business environment requires management to be able to adjust performance evaluations for a manager's performance whatever the actual activity level the segment achieves. When used alone, the static budget is unable to do this. For example, an activity level may be budgeted at 10,000 units under the assumptions of a static budget, but for a variety of reasons outside the responsible manager's control, the firm's activity level was actually 9,000 units (or 11,000 units, or any other deviation from the original). It would be inappropriate to use the static budget at the 10,000-unit level to evaluate the manager's performance at the 9,000-unit level. Flexible budgets allow evaluation of actual results as if the actual activity level were known before it occurred.

STATIC BUDGETS VERSUS FLEXIBLE BUDGETS

CHAPTER
OBJECTIVE 1
Advantages of flexible budgets

A static budget is an estimate or goal based on assumptions for one level of activity. Budgets such as these are useful planning and communication tools because they communicate the overall goals and objectives of the firm that the organization and each of its segments are expected to achieve. The master budget in Chapter 5 attempted to express the relationships of the segments and the variables that comprise the master budget in such a way that the managers of the segments could accept their supporting budgets as statements of the approach needed to achieve the firm's overall goal. Thus many of the communication and planning goals are achieved through the master budget. In addition, the master budget process requires management to create the interrelationships and formulas that link the activities and segments into a whole.

However, the static budget suffers from a deficiency: it represents an estimate based on a particular point—one activity level, hence one revenue and cost level to be achieved for each budgeted item. When comparing that budgeted estimate to the actual results, it would be most unusual—if not impossible—for the actual activity level achieved to match exactly the activity level estimated in the budget. Thus performance goals, management controls, and evaluations of managers' performance cannot be met through static budgets alone. They must be achieved through an understanding of the relationships established between activities and segments in the master budget tempered by the results adjusted for actual levels in the flexible budget.

In short, master budgets, including the supporting budgets and schedules for sales, production, cash flow, raw materials, inventory, and other activities, share the two characteristics common to all static budgets: (1) they are based on one planned activity level and (2) they are inflexible in the face of actual levels of activity. These characteristics indicate that a performance evaluation comparing actual results against a static budget cannot distinguish between results due to managerial skill and results due to changes in the actual activity level that are outside the manager's control.

However, the relationships established in the static budget process provide an opportunity for each of the budgets to be adjusted to any particular activity level within the relevant range. These adjustments permit management to generate a variety of flexible budgets for planning as well as create a flexible budget for evaluation and control purposes after the fact. Management can analyze the flexible budget that would have been prepared if the resulted activity level had been known. (This is not to say that flexible budgets could not go outside the relevant range, but that the budgeted relationships might not remain the same.)

In short, the important characteristics of flexible budgeting are that: (1) it is oriented toward *all* activity levels within the relevant range; (2) it is *contingent* in nature rather than static; and (3) it can be developed for any activity level within the relevant range *even after the time period is over.* Budgets at different activity levels direct the manager to compare the actual activity level achieved to the appropriate flexible budget level that contains the costs and revenues that should have been incurred at that activity level.

Overview of Flexible Budgets

Essentially, the flexible budget uses the concepts discussed in Chapter 3. Recall that costs are assumed to be either fixed or variable or a mixture of the two over some relevant range. Fixed costs do not vary in relation to the activity level. Variable costs vary in relation to the activity level in a linear fashion. In other words, total variable costs equal variable cost per unit times the number of units produced. (Activity levels can be stated in other terms, but number of units produced is common.) A mixed cost is equal to the fixed component plus the variable component.

Revenues are considered to be variable. That is, revenues vary in relation to the activity level in a linear fashion. Specifically, revenues equal selling price per unit multiplied by the number of units sold.

Often we will also assume that the number of units sold is equal to the number of units produced. This is not a crucial assumption, however, and may be changed. We typically invoke this assumption, as in cost–volume–profit analysis, because we wish to eliminate any effect that an inventory costing method would have on the analysis.

In short, the assumptions of flexible budgets are the same as in cost–volume–profit analysis. (You may wish to review Exhibit 3-1 before proceeding.) Flexible budgeting makes the additional assumption that revenues are variable and linear with respect to number of units sold.

Example of Flexible Budgeting

CHAPTER
OBJECTIVE 2
Prepare a flexible budget

Hallinan Company had prepared a static budget that assumed a production and sales level of 7,500 units for the period. This was the best estimate that management could make prior to the period in which the actual activity took place. During the actual production run, the output level was 6,000 units, a shortfall of 1,500 units

EXHIBIT 9-1

Hallinan Company
Department A
Budgeted Income Statement
7,500 Units

Sales		$135,000
Cost of goods sold		
Direct materials	$30,000	
Direct labor	22,500	
Variable overhead	15,000	
Fixed overhead	7,500	
Total cost		75,000
Net income		$ 60,000

EXHIBIT 9-2

STATIC BUDGET VERSUS ACTUAL COSTS

Hallinan Company
Department A

	Master Budget (7,500 Units)	Actual (6,000 Units)	Variance
Sales	$135,000	$102,000	$(33,000)
Direct materials	$ 30,000	$ 25,000	$ 5,000
Direct labor	22,500	17,500	5,000
Variable overhead	15,000	12,500	2,500
Fixed overhead	7,500	8,000	(500)
Total costs	$ 75,000	$ 63,000	$ 12,000
Net income	$ 60,000	$ 39,000	$(21,000)

produced and sold. The static budget in Exhibit 9-1 indicates that for 7,500 units of output, the expected cost was $75,000. Expected sales are $135,000 and so expected income is $60,000. Overhead is separated into variable and fixed components, as is also necessary in all flexible budgeting activities.

The actual results are displayed in Exhibit 9-2. These actual results are also contrasted with the budget from Exhibit 9-1. The difference between the budgeted income and the actual income is ($21,000). The line item differences or variances are also noted in the right column in Exhibit 9-2; however, these variances do not indicate whether they are due to poor managerial performance or to the change in the number of units produced and sold. Flexible budgets can modify the master budget for the latter effect so that any remaining variances may be attributed to managerial performance.

There are a number of ways of calculating the flexible budget. One approach involves calculating cost per unit of all variable items and then multiplying the cost per unit by the actual number of units produced and sold. For example, to find direct materials, 7,500 is divided into $30,000 to reveal a $4 per unit direct materials cost. Thus, direct materials for 6,000 units should cost $24,000; for 5,000 units, $20,000; for 8,000 units, $32,000; and so on. A second approach is as follows. Since we budgeted 7,500 units and actually produced 6,000 units, all variable items should have been at 80% (6,000/7,500) of the static budget. For example, direct materials cost of $30,000 in a 7,500-unit budget would be $30,000 × 80% for 6,000 units, or $24,000. Either of these methods would have permitted us to develop a flexible budget at the activity level actually achieved. Fixed costs, of course, do not change.

Exhibit 9-3 demonstrates this. Note that the direct materials cost budgeted at 6,000 units would be $24,000 and the actual still stands at $25,000, indicating that we actually overspent by $1,000, given actual production and sales of 6,000 units. Direct labor and variable overhead are computed similarly, whereas fixed overhead remains fixed in total within the flexible budget as compared against the actual fixed overhead for a $500 unfavorable variance.

The difference between the master budget income of $60,000 and the actual income of $39,000 is $21,000 and is an unfavorable variance. This difference is not particularly helpful for an evaluation of management. It is disaggregated further, as follows, in order to provide a more useful way of assessing the management team.

CHAPTER
OBJECTIVE 3
Define variances

This master budget variance can be broken into two parts by using the flexible budget in Exhibit 9-3. The master budget indicates that income should be $60,000, whereas the flexible budget shows that it is expected to be $46,500. The difference is $13,500, and it is unfavorable. This difference is sometimes called the activity variance. It can be caused by macroeconomic factors such as growth in gross national product, interest rates, and trade deficits; it might also be due to management's marketing strategy or product competition. Since these factors are for the most part external to the organization, no manager should be held responsible for the activity variance.

The difference between the flexible budget income and the actual income is called the flexible budget variance (sometimes called the *price/cost variance*). For this example it is the difference between $46,500 and $39,000 or $7,500 unfavorable. Note that the activity variance $13,500U, plus the flexible budget variance $7,500U equals the master budget variance of $21,000U. The flexible budget variance is useful because it does reflect management's ability to generate a profit for the corporation. Usually it is broken down into several other parts. This process is carried out for each line item in Exhibit 9-3.

For example, the sales variance is the difference in the flexible budget sales revenues and the actual sales revenues. In this case, it is the difference between $108,000 and $102,000, respectively. Thus, the sales variance is $6,000 unfavorable. This variance reflects the ability of the organization to determine the selling price per unit. It was set at $18 ($108,000/6,000 units), but the actual selling price was $17 per unit ($102,000/6,000 units).

Variances can be found for each of the production costs: direct materials, direct labor, variable overhead, and fixed overhead. For each of them, the variance is computed by comparing the flexible budget amount against the actual amount. As shown in Exhibit 9-3, the *direct materials variance* is $1,000 unfavorable; the *direct labor variance* is $500 favorable; the *variable overhead variance* is $500 unfavorable; and the *fixed*

EXHIBIT 9-3

FLEXIBLE BUDGET VERSUS ACTUAL COSTS

Hallinan Company
Department A

	Flexible Budget (6,000 Units)	Actual (6,000 Units)	Flexible Budget Variance
Sales	$108,000	$102,000	$(6,000)
Direct materials	$ 24,000	$ 25,000	$(1,000)
Direct labor	18,000	17,500	500
Variable overhead	12,000	12,500	(500)
Fixed overhead	7,500	8,000	(500)
Total costs	$ 61,500	$ 63,000	$(1,500)
Net income	$ 46,500	$ 39,000	$(7,500)

overhead variance is $500 unfavorable. Management can be evaluated on each of these variances just as in the discussion in Chapters 7 and 8.

More complex flexible budgets may be created simply by examining the relationships that develop each flexible budget item. By recognizing these relationships, each budget line item and sub-line item can be calculated based on the relationships of costs and revenues that have been established. Using the methods just described, management at Hallinan Company could request a flexible budget for Department A for any activity level within the relevant range and it could be provided.

CHOICE OF ACTIVITY LEVEL

CHAPTER OBJECTIVE 4
Choosing an activity level

There are many different activity levels within any relevant range. Further, there are any number of activities that could be chosen as the one around which the budget is built. Therefore, there is no one best way of determining the relationship between a variable and its activity level, because this varies from organization to organization. Three common factors that determine the choice of activity level are: (1) attempt to identify the relationship that appears to have a cause and effect between the activity and the budget variable; (2) do not use dollars in the activity level relationship established if at all possible; (3) keep the activity measure simple. Let us briefly discuss each of these.

1. **Identify the cause-and-effect standard.** The causal relationship between the activity and the budget variable is based on the manager's knowledge of the organization and is critical to flexible budgeting. Given the increasing prevalence of technology and capital investment in society, many activity bases or rates are no longer tied to direct labor but are instead a result of technological measurements, machine outputs, and data processing. Regardless of what happens, the concept is that a cause–effect relationship should establish the activity base for the budget variable.

For example, consider a manufacturer of electronic products. The costs are probably related to the amount of machine hours; therefore, machine hours is an acceptable choice for the activity level. That is, a greater (or lesser) number of machine hours probably implies greater (or lesser) cost. There appears to be a cause-and-effect relationship between the two, and this lends confidence that the relationship will hold in the future. On the other hand, there might be an accidental relationship, perhaps assessed by linear regression, between costs and baseball scores. Since there does not appear to be a cause-and-effect relationship between costs and baseball scores, one should infer that any relationship between them is spurious. In other words, since there does not appear to be a cause-and-effect relationship between them, we do not have confidence that the relationship will hold under future conditions.

2. **Avoid the use of dollars.** In determining the relationship between a variable and its activity level, it is much better to use units rather than dollars because of the possible change in certain variables due to wage contracts, new technology, purchase orders, etc., the types of things affecting the dollar price for a particular item. One can partially overcome this deficiency by using standard dollar cost rather than actual dollar cost.

Suppose that one does try to relate activity to some dollar measure such as sales. Further, let us assume that there is a cause-and-effect relationship between them. The relationship is acceptable—but only to the extent that it is stable. The problem is that in the real world the relationship has a small chance of staying constant. New technology will affect the selling price, and the relationship between variable costs and sales must change. Or changes in the political climate of one of the corporation's markets might affect the ability to sell there, causing sales to change and along with it the relationship between sales and variable costs. Avoid the use of dollars because the relationship is usually unstable.

3. **Keep the activity measure simple.** The budget variables and relationships chosen should be simple and understandable to management. A complex relationship not understood by management will not gain their commitment for planning and control purposes and thus defeats the purpose of flexible budgeting.

STANDARDS VERSUS BUDGETING

CHAPTER
OBJECTIVE 5
Standards and budgets

A *standard* is a cost or revenue that is usually perceived to be currently obtainable under present operating conditions. In essence, a standard is a budgeted cost or price for one unit within the organization. For example, in Hallinan Company, the direct material standard cost was $4 per unit and the budgeted amount for 6,000 units was $24,000. However, many organizations use budget and standard interchangeably in examining the performance of a subunit.

Operationally, direct materials and direct labor lend themselves well to standard costs, whereas other costs may require different consideration. We can determine direct labor and direct materials individually as long as they are oriented toward relatively large amounts and thus important for planning and control purposes.

There are a variety of ways of establishing standard costs: past experience, currently obtainable standards, engineering standards, and the ideal standard. The role of *past experience* is a usual starting point for examining a standard cost, but we should not rely solely on this for standard costs nor for our budgeting purposes, for past experience

MEASURING PRODUCT PROFITABILITY IN TODAY'S MANUFACTURING ENVIRONMENT

The competitive environment in the manufacturing industry has created an emphasis on the following: product quality, customer service, automation, and employee involvement. This shift in emphasis can lead to changes in companies' manufacturing processes and cost structures. Examples of these changes follow.

Change in the relative size of product cost components. A nonautomated manufacturer might expect a product's cost to consist of equal parts of direct material, direct labor, and overhead. As productivity improves or automation increases, the product cost makeup shifts toward a mix of 50% direct material, 40% overhead, and 10% direct labor.

The nature of manufacturing costs is also affected. In a nonautomated environment, the only components of product costs that are conventionally classified as direct are direct material and direct labor. Such manufacturing costs as supplies, maintenance, energy, and depreciation are classified as indirect, largely because these costs must be allocated to products. In an automated environment, especially one that uses manufacturing cells, it may not be necessary to allocate all depreciation, maintenance, and other indirect costs to products; they may be defined as direct costs.

Change in direct labor. As automation and productivity increase, the relative amount of direct labor falls, labor becomes more fixed, and the skills required can change significantly. Factory workers become technicians rather than laborers. Parts are made by machines with the help of an operator instead of by an operator with the help of a machine.

Change in the composition of factory overhead. As manufacturers improve their operations, the makeup and size of the overhead cost component undergo the following changes:

- Purchases of computers and other equipment increase depreciation expenses.
- CAD/CAE reduces design, engineering, drafting, and clerical efforts.
- Quality control and purchasing staffs have different and more vital roles.
- Training and employee relations are emphasized.
- More attention is given to maintenance (especially preventive maintenance) of sophisticated machinery.

As cost systems are revised to reflect these changes, manufacturing companies should focus on their ability to adequately measure the profitability of their products. Although a company's income statement provides an overall measure of performance, to survive in today's highly competitive economy, a firm should know not only its total profit but also the profitability of each of its products so that it can:

- Assess its competitive position.
- Compare the relative profitability of its products with the firm's overall profitability.
- Decide which products should be added or discontinued.
- Price and market its products intelligently.
- Develop strategic plans.
- Identify the best capital investment opportunities.

often has some inefficiencies. In management accounting we are constantly looking to the future; therefore, the role of past experience in leading us toward estimating the future should be our primary concern. If the past helps predict the future, then we should use it. After all, management wishes to estimate future costs for budget purposes, not past costs.

The *currently attainable standard* is usually considered the standard that is achievable under fairly rigorous conditions and efficient operations. These expectations are usually agreed to by both upper or middle management and the subunit manager in order to challenge employees somewhat without being unreasonable. Currently attainable standards are not as strict as ideal standards, which are based on perfection. Currently attainable standards recognize that unachievable goals do not motivate people toward that expectation but rather decrease motivation and increase animosity toward the system.

To compute standards, both inputs and outputs must be analyzed in order to be realistic and to facilitate the variance analysis that comes later. Note that the flexible budget is the actual outputs achieved multiplied by appropriate resources or input allowed for that particular unit. In essence, the total standard amount of cost is computed that would be allowed for that activity level. Performance is evaluated by examining the total standard allowed versus the actual achieved and determining to what extent pricing or costing factors (price variances) versus efficiency or usage factors (quantity variances) have contributed to the total variance.

VARIANCE ANALYSIS AND FLEXIBLE BUDGETING

CHAPTER OBJECTIVE 6
Variances and the flexible budget

Given the mechanics of flexible budgeting, we can now reanalyze the variances discussed in Chapters 7 and 8. As we will see, these variances are very much dependent on the flexible budget.

Each of the product costs has a product cost variance: direct materials variance, direct labor variance, variable overhead variance, and fixed overhead variance. Each of these variances is computed as the actual cost minus the standard cost. The cost itself is equal to the quantity times the price per unit.

Let AQ represent the actual quantity, AP the actual price, SQ the standard quantity, and SP the standard price. The variance is

$$(AQ \times AP) - (SP \times SQ)$$

In Chapters 7 and 8, each variance was partitioned into two parts: a price variance and a quantity variance. These variances are listed in Exhibit 9-4 with the names we used in the previous chapters. The goal is to partition the cost variance into a price variance and a quantity difference. The method management accountants use is to compare the actual cost ($AQ \times AP$) or standard cost ($SQ \times SP$) to the actual quantity at the standard price, or $AQ \times SP$. Thus:

$$
\begin{aligned}
\text{Cost Variance} &= (AQ \times AP) - (SQ \times SP) \\
&= (AQ \times AP) + [-(AQ \times SP) + (AQ \times SP)] - (SQ \times SP) \\
&= [(AQ \times AP) - (AQ \times SP)] + [(AQ \times SP) - (SQ \times SP)] \\
&= [\text{actual cost} - (AQ \times SP)] + [(AQ \times SP) - \text{standard cost}] \\
&= \underbrace{AQ(AP - SP)} + \underbrace{(AQ - SQ)SP}
\end{aligned}
$$

$$= \text{Price Variance} + \text{Quantity Variance}$$

Therefore, each cost variance is divided into a price variance and a quantity variance. This partitioning is exactly what was done in Chapters 7 and 8 (review Exhibits 7-8, 7-9, 7-10, and 8-8 if necessary).

EXHIBIT 9-4

CLASSIFICATION OF VARIANCES

Product Cost	Quantity Variance $(AQ - SQ) \times SP$	Price Variance $(AP - SP) \times AQ$
Direct materials	Material quantity variance	Material price variance
Direct labor	Labor efficiency variance	Labor rate variance
Variable overhead	Variable overhead efficiency variance	Variable overhead spending variance
Fixed overhead	Volume variance	Budget variance

What is the significance of $AQ \times SP$? Very simply, it is the budgeted cost amount from the flexible budget at the activity level of AQ. Thus, the price variance is the difference between the actual costs and the flexible budget amount. The quantity variance is the difference between the flexible budget amount and the standard amount. The standard amount, $SP \times SQ$, is the flexible budget amount at the activity level of SQ.

The following example not only reinforces the concepts contained in Chapters 7 and 8, but it also illustrates how this general characterization of variance analysis is related to the flexible budget. There are two exceptions to the general model. First, the direct material price variance is based on the purchased amount of direct materials. If the amount of purchased direct materials equals the amount of direct materials placed into production, then the general model will still hold. Second, the formula works for fixed overhead, but only because firms treat fixed overhead in a variable fashion. That is, they determine a fixed overhead rate by dividing estimated fixed overhead costs by the presumed activity level for the year. Then they apply this rate to determine the cost of jobs or processes (discussed in greater detail in the next two chapters). Only in this manner is a standard fixed overhead cost created, which is the applied fixed overhead.

Example of Variance Analysis

The data in Exhibit 9-5 comprises the product costs for Classen Company. From it we will compute the eight variances previously described. Revenues are ignored since they do not affect the product cost variances.

The data in Exhibit 9-5 can be used to prepare a flexible budget for Classen, shown in Exhibit 9-6. The flexible budget is constructed for 2,000, 2,200, 2,400, 2,600, 2,800, and 3,000 units of output. These levels correspond to 1,000, 1,100, 1,200, 1,300, 1,400, and 1,500 direct labor hours, since the standard is to produce two units of output per direct labor hour.

Direct materials cost is equal to the number of units times $8 per unit. Direct labor cost equals the number of direct labor hours times $16 per direct labor hour. Factory supplies is the number of direct labor hours times $1. Power and heat equals $500 plus the number of direct labor hours times $2. For example, at 1,300 hours, power and heat is projected to be $500 + (1,300 \times $2)$, or $3,100. Repairs are $500 plus the number of

EXHIBIT 9-5

DATA FOR FLEXIBLE BUDGET AND VARIANCES EXAMPLE

Classen Company

Raw materials	$8 per unit produced (2 feet at $4 per foot)
Direct labor	$16 per direct labor hour
Factory supplies	$1 per direct labor hour
Power and heat	$500 per month plus $2 per direct labor hour
Repairs	$500 per month plus $1 per direct labor hour
Depreciation	$2,000 per month
Rent	$2,000 per month
Supervision	$3,000 per month

EXHIBIT 9-6

FLEXIBLE BUDGET

Classen Company
Typical Month
1,000 to 1,500 Direct Labor Hours
(2 Units of Output per Direct Labor Hour)

Direct labor hours	1,000	1,100	1,200	1,300	1,400	1,500
Units of output	2,000	2,200	2,400	2,600	2,800	3,000
Product costs:						
Direct materials	$16,000	$17,600	$19,200	$20,800	$22,400	$24,000
Direct labor	16,000	17,600	19,200	20,800	22,400	24,000
Factory supplies	1,000	1,100	1,200	1,300	1,400	1,500
Power and heat	2,500	2,700	2,900	3,100	3,300	3,500
Repairs	1,500	1,600	1,700	1,800	1,900	2,000
Depreciation	2,000	2,000	2,000	2,000	2,000	2,000
Rent	2,000	2,000	2,000	2,000	2,000	2,000
Supervision	3,000	3,000	3,000	3,000	3,000	3,000
Total costs	$44,000	$47,600	$51,200	$54,800	$58,400	$62,000

direct labor hours multiplied by $1. Depreciation is always $2,000. Rent is $2,000 at all activity levels. Finally, supervision is fixed at $3,000.

The actual results are provided in Exhibit 9-7. From Exhibits 9-5, 9-6, and 9-7, we will compute the product cost variances. First, the overhead items are grouped into

EXHIBIT 9-7

ACTUAL RESULTS FOR FLEXIBLE BUDGET AND VARIANCES EXAMPLE

Classen Company

Actual production	2,600 units
Direct labor worked	1,250 hours
Direct materials purchased and used	
(5,400 ft. @ $3.90 per foot)	$21,060
Actual direct labor ($17 per hour)	21,250
Factory supplies	1,280
Power and heat*	3,000
Repairs*	1,600
Depreciation _budget?_	2,000
Rent	2,000
Supervision	3,200

*Fixed component expended as expected.

fixed and variable categories, yielding the flexible budget presented in Exhibit 9-8. This budget is reclassified from Exhibit 9-6. Specifically, variable overhead is computed as follows:

Factory supplies	$1 per direct labor hour
Power and heat	2 per direct labor hour
Repairs	1 per direct labor hour
Total	$4 per direct labor hour

Thus, in Exhibit 9-8 the variable overhead costs are computed as the number of direct labor hours multiplied by $4. The fixed overhead is calculated as follows:

Power and heat	$ 500
Repairs	500
Depreciation	2,000
Rent	2,000
Supervision	3,000
Total	$8,000

Therefore, in Exhibit 9-8 the fixed overhead costs are $8,000 at each activity level.

EXHIBIT 9-8

RECLASSIFIED FLEXIBLE BUDGET

Classen Company
Typical Month
1,000 to 1,500 Direct Labor Hours
(2 Units of Output per Direct Labor Hour)

Direct labor hours	1,000	1,100	1,200	1,300	1,400	1,500
Units of output	2,000	2,200	2,400	2,600	2,800	3,000
Direct materials	$16,000	$17,600	$19,200	$20,800	$22,400	$24,000
Direct labor	16,000	17,600	19,200	20,800	22,400	24,000
Variable overhead	4,000	4,400	4,800	5,200	5,600	6,000
Fixed overhead	8,000	8,000	8,000	8,000	8,000	8,000
Total costs	$44,000	$47,600	$51,200	$54,800	$58,400	$62,000

EXHIBIT 9-9

FLEXIBLE VERSUS ACTUAL COSTS

Classen Company
Production at 2,600 Units

Product Cost	Budgeted Amount	Actual Amount	Variance
Direct materials	$20,800	$21,060	$260U
Direct labor	20,800	21,250	450U
Variable overhead	5,200	4,880	320F
Fixed overhead	8,000	8,200	200U

Price and Quantity Variances for Each Product Cost

The four product cost variances are shown in Exhibit 9-9 as the difference between the flexible budget allowed amount and the actual cost. The flexible budget amounts are extracted from Exhibit 9-8 at the activity level of 2,600 production units. The actual costs may be found in Exhibit 9-7.

The variances for direct materials, direct labor, and variable overhead are the overall cost variances and they must be partitioned into price and quantity effects. The fixed overhead variance is actually the budget variance; more will be said about this later. Notice in the following calculations that the standard costs and the actual costs are both compared with the flexible budget amount at the actual quantity.

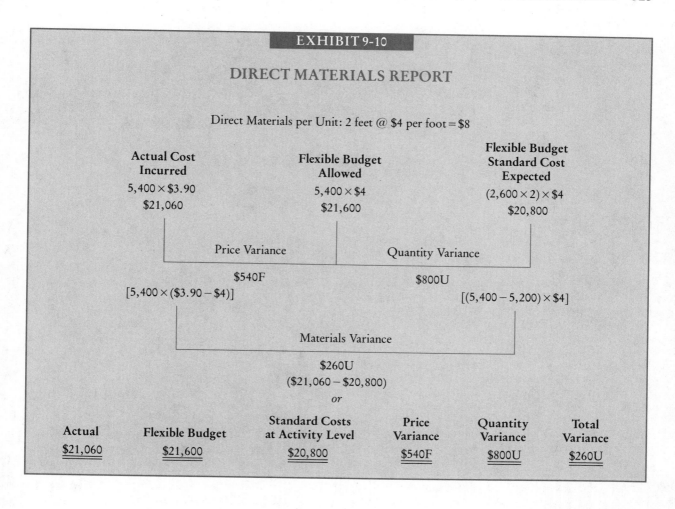

EXHIBIT 9-10

DIRECT MATERIALS REPORT

Direct Materials per Unit: 2 feet @ $4 per foot = $8

Actual Cost Incurred	Flexible Budget Allowed	Flexible Budget Standard Cost Expected
5,400 × $3.90	5,400 × $4	(2,600 × 2) × $4
$21,060	$21,600	$20,800

Price Variance

$540F

[5,400 × ($3.90 − $4)]

Quantity Variance

$800U

[(5,400 − 5,200) × $4]

Materials Variance

$260U

($21,060 − $20,800)

or

Actual	Flexible Budget	Standard Costs at Activity Level	Price Variance	Quantity Variance	Total Variance
$21,060	$21,600	$20,800	$540F	$800U	$260U

The direct materials report for Classen Company is displayed in Exhibit 9-10. The flexible budget allowed is the 5,400 actual quantity times the $4 standard cost. The direct materials variance can then be divided into a price variance of $540 favorable and a quantity variance of $800 unfavorable. The two variances add up to $260 unfavorable direct materials variance, which agrees with the figure in Exhibit 9-9. The direct materials exception to the general model, mentioned on page 319, is not found here because the raw materials purchased equal the raw materials placed into production.

Exhibit 9-11 performs the analogous operations on direct labor cost. The flexible budget allowed is 1,250 direct labor hours multiplied by $16 per hour, or $20,000. The direct labor cost variance of $450 unfavorable may be divided into a direct labor rate variance of $1,250 unfavorable and a direct labor efficiency variance of $800 favorable.

Similarly, the partitioning of the variable overhead variance is demonstrated in Exhibit 9-12 on page 325. The flexible budget allowed is 1,250 direct labor hours times the $4 per hour variable overhead rate. This amount is $5,000, and it allows partitioning the variable overhead variance. Thus, the variable overhead variance of $320 favorable equals the spending variance of $120 favorable plus the variable overhead efficiency variance of $200 favorable.

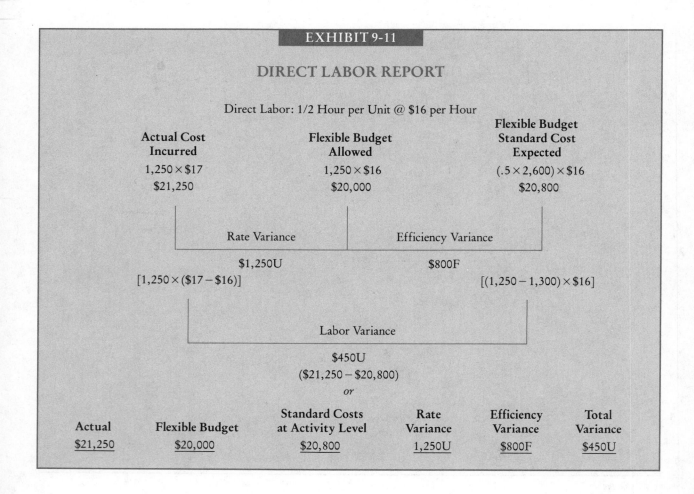

These calculations are equivalent to those found in Chapter 7. The point in this chapter is that each of the product cost variances can be divided into a price variance and a quantity variance. This partitioning is done by comparing the actual or the standard costs to the flexible budget amount at the activity level of the actual quantity.

The last item is fixed overhead cost. The reclassified flexible budget in Exhibit 9-8 indicates that this amount should be $8,000 at all activity levels. By comparing the actual with the budgeted amount, as in Exhibit 9-13 on page 326, we obtain a variance of $200 unfavorable. This is actually the budget variance.

To allow the fixed costs variance to be divided into a price variance and a quantity variance, as the previous three costs were, one needs to view the fixed overhead as it is applied to jobs. In particular, this depends on the master budget and how much is expected to be produced and sold. Suppose it is 3,200 units. The predetermined fixed overhead rate becomes $8,000 fixed costs divided by 1,600 direct labor hours (the amount needed to produce 3,200 units), or $5. If only 2,600 units are made and sold, only 1,300 hours are costed out. In other words, applied fixed overhead is $6,500 (1,300 × $5). The volume variance is the difference between the flexible budget of $8,000 and the applied overhead of $6,500, or $1,500 unfavorable. Underapplied fixed overhead is unfavorable because it indicates that the number of units specified in the

EXHIBIT 9-12

VARIABLE OVERHEAD COSTS

Factory supplies = $1 per direct labor hour
Power and heat = $2 per direct labor hour ($500 fixed portion was spent)
Repairs   = $1 per direct labor hour ($500 fixed portion was spent)
                  $4 per direct labor hour

Variable Overhead Costs	Actual Total	Less Fixed	Variable Overhead
Factory supplies	$1,280	$ –0–	$1,280
Power and heat	3,000	500	2,500
Maintenance	1,600	500	1,100
	$5,880	$1,000	$4,880

Actual Cost Incurred	Flexible Budget Allowed	Flexible Budget Standard Variable Overhead Costs Expected
	1,250 × $4	1,300 × $4
$4,880 (per above)	$5,000	$5,200

Spending Variance | Efficiency Variance

$120F | $200F

Variable Overhead Variance

$320F
($4,800 – $5,200)
or

Actual	Flexible Budget	Standard Costs Expected (Applied)	Spending Variance	Efficiency Variance	Total Variable Overhead Variance
$4,880	$5,000	$5,200	$120F	$200F	$320F

master budget has not been achieved. (Overapplied fixed overhead would be favorable since the firm would have sold more units than were budgeted.)

In this sense, then, the fixed overhead variance is $1,700 unfavorable, as shown in Exhibit 9-14. This amount is equal to the budget variance of $200 unfavorable plus the volume variance of $1,500 unfavorable.

	EXHIBIT 9-13	

FIXED OVERHEAD BUDGET VARIANCE

	Actual Costs Incurred	Flexible Budget	Budget Variance
Power and heat	$ 500	$ 500	$–0–
Repairs	500	500	–0–
Depreciation	2,000	2,000	–0–
Rent	2,000	2,000	–0–
Supervision	3,200	3,000	200U
	$8,200	$8,000	$200U

	EXHIBIT 9-14	

FIXED OVERHEAD COSTS

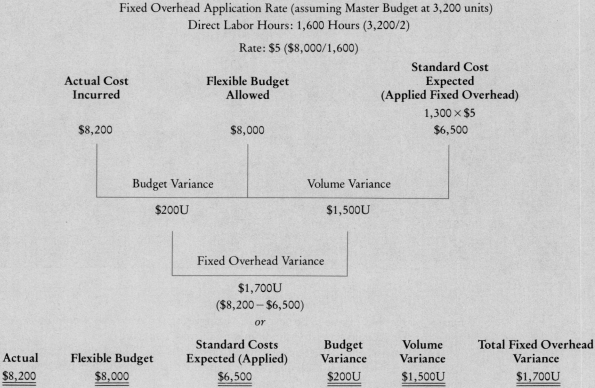

Fixed Overhead Application Rate (assuming Master Budget at 3,200 units)
Direct Labor Hours: 1,600 Hours (3,200/2)

Rate: $5 ($8,000/1,600)

Actual Cost Incurred	Flexible Budget Allowed	Standard Cost Expected (Applied Fixed Overhead)
		$1,300 \times \$5$
$8,200	$8,000	$6,500

	Budget Variance	Volume Variance
	$200U	$1,500U

Fixed Overhead Variance

$1,700U
($8,200 − $6,500)

or

Actual	Flexible Budget	Standard Costs Expected (Applied)	Budget Variance	Volume Variance	Total Fixed Overhead Variance
$8,200	$8,000	$6,500	$200U	$1,500U	$1,700U

Demonstration Problem

Product costs for Botvinnik, Inc., are given below. The manufacturing process is virtually 100% robotic; therefore, there is no direct labor.

Raw materials	$4 per unit produced ($4 per lb.)
Factory supplies	$1 per machine hour
Power and heat	$1,000 per month plus $3 per machine hour
Depreciation	$5,000 per month
Rent	$3,000 per month
Supervision	$3,000 per month

It is estimated that it takes 1/2 machine hours to produce one unit of output. The actual results for Botvinnik during 19X1 are as follows:

Actual production	2,500 units
Machine hours worked	1,300 hours
Raw materials purchased and used	
(2,600 lbs. @ $4.10 per lb.)	$10,660
Factory supplies	1,200
Power and heat (fixed)	1,000
Power and heat (variable)	3,800
Depreciation	5,000
Rent	3,000
Supervision	3,000

The master budget called for the manufacture of 3,000 units.

REQUIRED

a. Prepare the flexible budget for Botvinnik, Inc., for 1,500, 2,000, 2,500, and 3,000 units of output.

b. Calculate the materials variances, the variable overhead variances, and the fixed overhead variances. (You will also need to compute the predetermined fixed overhead rate.)

SOLUTION TO DEMONSTRATION PROBLEM

a. The flexible budget is prepared as follows:

Botvinnik, Inc.
Flexible Budget
For the Year Ended December 31, 19X1

Units of output	1,500	2,000	2,500	3,000
Machine hours	750	1,000	1,250	1,500
Direct materials	$ 6,000	$ 8,000	$10,000	$12,000
Variable overhead	3,000	4,000	5,000	6,000
($4 per machine hour)				
Fixed overhead	12,000	12,000	12,000	12,000
Total costs	$21,000	$24,000	$27,000	$30,000

b.

Material price variance	$2,600 \times (\$4 - \$4.10)$	$= \$260U$
Material quantity variance	$\$4 \times (2,500 - 2,600)$	$= \$400U$
Variable overhead spending variance	$(1,300 \times \$4) - 5,000$	$= \$200F$
Variable overhead efficiency variance	$\$4 \times (1,250 - 1,300)$	$= \$200U$
Fixed overhead budget variance	$\$12,000 - \$12,000$	$= \$0$

To obtain the fixed overhead volume variance, one needs to know the predetermined fixed overhead rate. This rate is $12,000 fixed costs divided by 1,500 machine hours (3,000 master budget units × 1/2), or $8 per machine hour.

Given this predetermined fixed overhead rate, the applied fixed overhead is $10,000 (1,250 × $8). We can now compute the last variance:

$$\text{Fixed overhead volume variance} = \$10,000 - \$12,000$$
$$= \$2,000U$$

Review of Chapter Objectives

1. Describe the advantages of flexible budgeting when compared to static budgeting (pp. 311–12).

   ■ Static budgets are not adjusted for changes in the activity level. This fact makes it hard to interpret actual results because any differences between the budget and the actual result may be attributed to managerial performance or to change in the activity level. Flexible budgets help overcome this problem. Differences between the flexible budget and the actual result are due to managerial performance.

   ■ Flexible budgets are created by recomputing the revenues and the variable costs. Once the activity level is determined, the revenues are recalculated as the selling price per unit times the number of units. The variable costs are recalculated as the variable cost per unit multiplied by the number of units produced and sold. Fixed costs stay the same.

   ■ Therefore, the advantage of using flexible budgets is that it helps in planning when the activity level is uncertain and it helps in evaluating the performance of managers by factoring out differences due only to changes in the activity level.

2. Prepare a flexible budget (pp. 312–15).

   ■ One way of preparing the flexible budget is to calculate the unit cost of all variable items and multiply this unit cost by the actual number of units produced and sold. A second way is to assess the actual activity level as a percentage of the activity level in the static budget (number of units divided by the number of budgeted units). Then multiply this percentage by the budgeted amount for all variable items in the static budget. Nothing needs to be done to fixed costs, since by definition they do not change.

3. Define *master budget variance*, *activity variance*, *flexible budget variance*, and *sales variance* (pp. 314–15).

   ■ Developing a flexible budget allows several new variances. The master budget variance is the difference between the income projected by the master budget and the actual income. The master budget variance can be broken into two parts. The master budget variance is equal to the activity variance plus the flexible budget variance.

- The activity variance is the difference between the income projected by the master budget and the income projected by the flexible budget. It is favorable when the flexible budget income is greater than the master budget income. It is unfavorable when the flexible budget income is less than the master budget income. In other words, the activity variance is favorable when the actual activity level exceeds the activity level budgeted in the master budget. It is unfavorable when the actual activity level is less than the master budget activity level.

- The flexible budget variance is the difference between income predicted by the flexible budget and the actual income. It is favorable when the actual income is greater than the flexible budget income and is unfavorable when the actual income is less than the flexible budget income.

- The sales variance is the difference between the sales predicted by the flexible budget and the actual sales. It is favorable if the actual sales are greater than the flexible budget sales. It is unfavorable if the actual sales are less than the flexible budget sales.

4. Explain the variety of activity levels and the importance of selecting the appropriate budgeted activity level (pp. 315–16).

- A number of measures of the activity level are possible. They include, but are not limited to, number of units produced, number of sales orders, direct labor hours, and machine hours. Three principles should be considered when choosing an activity level. (1) Attempt to identify the relationship that appears to have a cause and effect between the activity and the budget variable. (2) Do not use dollars in the activity level. (3) Keep the activity measure simple.

5. Describe the relationship between standards and flexible budgets (pp. 316–18).

- Standard costs, such as that discussed in the previous two chapters, can be thought of as the budget formulas used in flexible budgeting. To obtain an amount of some cost in a flexible budget, multiply the activity level by the cost per unit of activity. The cost per unit of activity is the standard cost when a standard costing system is used.

6. Interpret cost variances in terms of the flexible budget (pp. 318–28).

- The cost variance is the actual cost minus the standard cost. Further, the cost variance is equal to the price variance plus the quantity variance. The price variance is equal to the actual quantity times the difference between the actual cost and the standard cost. The quantity variance is equal to the standard cost times the difference between the actual quantity and the standard quantity.

- The budgeted amount from the flexible budget is the actual quantity multiplied by the standard cost per unit. Thus, the price variance is the difference between the actual costs and the flexible budget amount. The quantity variance is the difference between the flexible budget amount and the standard cost.

- This characterization is true also for fixed overhead when it is treated in a variable fashion. This occurs when firms take the master budget amount of fixed overhead and divide it by the activity level to determine a fixed overhead rate. This rate is used when costing products and is referred to as applied overhead.

Glossary of Key Terms

activity variance   The difference between the income projected by the master budget and the income projected by the flexible budget.

flexible budget   A budget structure in which the budget amounts may be adjusted to any activity level.

flexible budget variance   The difference between the income predicted by the flexible budget and the actual income.

master budget variance   The difference between the income predicted by the master budget and the actual income.

sales variance   The differences between the sales revenues predicted by the flexible budget and the actual sales revenues.

static budget   Master budget made for only one activity level.

Review Questions

9-1   What is a static budget? What major assumption does a static budget entail?

9-2   What is a flexible budget?

9-3   Why is a flexible budget often more useful than a static budget?

9-4   How is flexible budgeting like cost–volume–profit analysis?

9-5   A static budget can be compared with actual costs. What does this comparison show? What does the comparison *not* show?

9-6   How can a flexible budget be calculated?

9-7   What is the master budget variance? Is it controllable by managers?

9-8   What is the activity variance? What causes it?

9-9   What is the flexible budget variance? What does it reflect?

9-10   How are the master budget variance, the activity variance, and the flexible budget variance related?

9-11   What is the sales variance?

9-12   What factors determine the choice of activity measure?

9-13   How are standards and flexible budgeting similar?

9-14   A cost variance can be dichotomized into what two components? Give the formulas for these variables.

9-15   One variable in variance analysis is the actual quantity times the standard price. What is its significance?

9-16   Another variable in variance analysis is the standard price times the standard quantity. What is its significance?

9-17   Cost variances can be determined either with the flexible budget or with the appropriate price and quantity variances. Explain.

9-18   In terms of the flexible budget, how is a price variance computed?

9-19   In terms of the flexible budget, how is a quantity variance computed?

9-20   Partitioning direct materials variance into price and quantity variances may not always work. Why not? How can it be made always to work?

9-21   Fixed overhead cost variance can also be partitioned into price and quantity variances. How is this accomplished?

Discussion Questions

9-22 The technique of flexible budgeting can be applied to service organizations as well as to manufacturers. What might be used to measure activity in a hospital? Prepare an illustration that applies flexible budgeting to a hospital with the activity measure.

9-23 In this chapter the examples have assumed that only one department is involved. Suppose there are two departments. What changes? Prepare an illustration that applies flexible budgeting to a two-department organization.

Exercises

9-24 **FLEXIBLE BUDGET** Ayres Company has developed the following budget formulas:

CO 2

Cost	Formula
Direct materials	$10 per unit
Direct labor	$2 per unit
Variable overhead	$4 per unit
Fixed overhead	$700,000 per year

Prepare a flexible budget of production costs for 19X1 for 100,000 units to 200,000 units with increment of 20,000 units.

9-25 **FLEXIBLE BUDGET** Wolfson, Inc., has derived the following budget formulas:

CO 2

Cost	Formula
Direct materials	$5 per machine hour
Direct labor	$20 per machine hour
Factory overhead	$10 per machine hour plus $5,000 per year

Prepare a flexible budget of production costs for 19X2 for 200,000 machine hours to 400,000 machine hours with increment of 50,000 machine hours.

9-26 **FLEXIBLE BUDGET** Jackson Company has prepared the following budget:

CO 2

Sales (80,000 units × $100 per unit)	$8,000,000
Less: Variable costs:	
Direct materials	$1,600,000
Direct labor	400,000
Variable overhead	400,000
Selling expenses	160,000
Total variable costs	$2,560,000
Contribution margin	$5,440,000
Less: Fixed costs:	
Fixed overhead	$2,000,000
Administrative expenses	1,100,000
Total fixed costs	$3,100,000
Net income	$2,340,000

Prepare the budget if the number of units produced and sold is 70,000 or 90,000.

9-27   FLEXIBLE BUDGET Outslay, Inc., has the following master budget and actual results.

CO 1, 2

	Master Budget (10,000 units)	Actual (12,000 units)	Variance
Sales	$200,000	$240,000	$ 40,000
Direct materials	$ 60,000	$ 70,000	$(10,000)
Direct labor	10,000	12,000	(2,000)
Variable overhead	30,000	33,000	(3,000)
Fixed overhead	50,000	55,000	(5,000)
Total costs	$150,000	$170,000	$(20,000)
Net income	$ 50,000	$ 70,000	$ 20,000

The president attributes the good fortune of making an extra $20,000 to sales. He declares, "If we did a better job of controlling costs, we would have done even better. If we could have held them to budget we would have made yet another $20,000." Respond.

9-28   FLEXIBLE BUDGET AND VARIANCE Hite Company has the following master budget and actual results.

CO 3

	Master Budget (10,000 units)	Actual (9,000 units)	Variance
Sales	$500,000	$450,000	$(50,000)
Direct materials	$100,000	$ 95,000	$ 5,000
Direct labor	50,000	47,000	3,000
Variable overhead	150,000	140,000	10,000
Fixed overhead	100,000	100,000	–0–
Total costs	$400,000	$382,000	$ 18,000
Net income	$100,000	$ 68,000	$(32,000)

Compute the master budget variance, the activity variance, the flexible budget variance, and the sales variance.

9-29   FLEXIBLE BUDGET Thornton, Inc., has the following partially completed flexible budget. Complete the statement.

CO 2

Sales	$300,000	$?	$540,000
Direct materials	$ 50,000	$?	$?
Direct labor	10,000	14,000	?
Variable overhead	?	126,000	?
Fixed overhead	?	100,000	?
Total costs	$250,000	$?	$?
Net income	$?	$?	$?

CO 2, 6

9-30 DIRECT MATERIALS VARIANCES Rhea, Inc., purchases 1,000,000 pounds of gloxin at $5 per pound. The standard set by the firm calls for 10 pounds of gloxin to be used to make one unit at a standard cost of $49 per unit. The company actually makes 90,000 units and uses 920,000 pounds of gloxin.

a. Compute the price and quantity variances for direct materials. Use the flexible budget in computing these variances.

b. Show that the sum of these variances does not work if the price variance is based on the pounds purchased.

CO 6

9-31 DIRECT LABOR VARIANCES Wolk Company has determined that it takes two direct labor hours to manufacture one gidget. The pay should be $30 per direct labor hour. During the year Wolk makes 1,000 gidgets and uses 1,960 hours of direct labor at a cost of $60,760. Compute the price and quantity variances for direct labor. Use the flexible budget in computing these variances.

CO 6

9-32 VARIABLE OVERHEAD VARIANCES In manufacturing gadgets Martin Company ascertains that it takes one-half machine hour to make one gadget. Variable overhead is applied at $40 per machine hour. Martin makes 20,000 gadgets with 11,000 machine hours. The actual variable overhead costs is $410,000. Compute the price and quantity variances for variable overhead. Use the flexible budget in computing these variances.

CO 6

9-33 FIXED OVERHEAD VARIANCES Burns Manufacturing Company assessed in its master budget that it would produce 8,000 red wagons. It also estimated that fixed manufacturing overhead would amount to $640,000. A red wagon requires one-half hour of direct labor time. For the year Burns actually produced only 7,000 red wagons at a fixed manufacturing overhead of $630,000. Compute the budget variance and the volume variances for fixed overhead. Use the flexible budget in computing these variances.

CO 1, 6

9-34 VARIABLE OVERHEAD VARIANCES Hicks Distributors prepared the following for the variable overhead portion of its flexible budget.

Overhead Item	Direct Labor Hours		
	25,000	30,000	35,000
Indirect materials	$25,000	$ 30,000	$ 35,000
Indirect labor	50,000	60,000	70,000
Electricity	12,500	15,000	17,500
Maintenance	2,500	3,000	3,500
Total variable overhead	$90,000	$108,000	$126,000

During the period the company expected to use 32,000 direct labor hours for the number of units it produced. It actually incurred 33,000 direct labor hours. The actual costs were:

Indirect materials	$30,000
Indirect labor	69,000
Electricity	17,000
Maintenance	2,900

REQUIRED

a. Provide the cost formula for each of the variable overhead cost items.

b. Compute price and quantity variances for each of the individual items and for the total variable overhead.

Problems

9-35   FLEXIBLE BUDGET FOR SERVICE ORGANIZATION Doolittle, Inc., is a hair stylist. Doolittle is preparing a flexible budget for the upcoming period 19X1 and has developed the following data:

CO 2

Cost	Formula
Depreciation—Building	$25,000 per year
Electricity	$10,000 per year plus $.50 per hair styling
Insurance	$5,000 per year
Labor	$164,000 per year
Supplies	$4 per hair styling
Telephone	$3,000 per year

The price of a hair styling is $10.

REQUIRED

Prepare a flexible budget for Doolittle, Inc., for the year ended December 31, 19X1, at 100,000, 150,000, 200,000, and 250,000 hair stylings.

9-36   FLEXIBLE BUDGET FOR A MERCHANDISER Steve Morgan owns Morgan's Stereo Company. The stereo will be priced at $500 per unit during the upcoming period 19X1. He has asked you to help him in his planning for next year's activities. Expected costs are as follows:

CO 2

Cost	Formula
Advertising	$20,000 per year
Direct materials (stereos)	$200 per unit
Heat and light	$25,000 per year
Insurance	$10,000 per year
Labor	$80,000 per year plus a bonus of $75 per unit sold
Rent	$60,000 per year
Telephone	$5,000 per year
Transportation in	$25 per unit

REQUIRED

a. Compute the breakeven point for Morgan's Stereo Company.

b. Prepare the flexible budget for the year ending December 31, 19X1, for the breakeven point, for 200 units less than the breakeven point, and for 200 units greater than the breakeven point.

CO 2

9-37 FLEXIBLE BUDGETING FOR A MANUFACTURER Bear Thomas Corporation makes glow-in-the-dark calculators and sells them for $25 each. Costs for Bear Thomas are as follows:

Cost	Formula
Depreciation on building	$150,000 per year
Depreciation on machinery	$75,000 per year
Direct labor	$8 per calculator
Direct materials	$4 per calculator
Indirect labor	$1 per calculator
Indirect materials	$1 per calculator
Marketing	$100,000 per year
Office expenses	$275,000 per year
Real estate taxes	$300,000 per year
Utilities	$600,000 per year plus $1 per calculator

REQUIRED

a. Determine the breakeven point.

b. Prepare a flexible budget for the year ending December 31, 19X1, for the breakeven point, for 10,000 units less than the breakeven point, and for 10,000 units more than the breakeven point.

CO 2

9-38 FLEXIBLE BUDGETING FOR A MANUFACTURER Joel Goff has invented a new electronic security device for the home. Because of its looks, it is referred to as a goff ball. Joel Goff, Inc., plans to sell it for $1,000 each. The factory is totally automated, so there is no direct labor. The activity level is measured in robotic hours. Costs can be determined by the following relationships.

Cost	Formula
Administrative expenses	$400,000 per year
Depreciation for robots	$60 per robot hour
Direct materials	$300 per unit
Maintenance	$300,000 per year plus $40 per robot hour
Indirect labor	$800,000 per year
Selling expenses	$200,000 per year
Utilities	$700,000 per year plus $100 per robot hour

Each unit of output requires two robot hours.

REQUIRED

a. Compute the breakeven point in terms of robot hours.

b. Prepare the flexible budget for the year ending December 31, 19X1, for 20,000 and 24,000 robot hours.

9-39   FLEXIBLE BUDGET VS. TRADITIONAL BUDGETED INCOME STATE-MENT Klauss Manufacturing has generated the following flexible budget.

CO 1, 2

	10,000 Units	12,000 Units	14,000 Units
Sales	$1,000,000	$1,200,000	$1,400,000
Variable costs			
Direct materials	$ 200,000	$ 240,000	$ 280,000
Direct labor	20,000	24,000	28,000
Variable overhead	100,000	120,000	140,000
Administrative	40,000	48,000	56,000
Selling	10,000	12,000	14,000
Total variable costs	$ 370,000	$ 444,000	$ 518,000
Fixed costs			
Fixed overhead	$ 200,000	$ 200,000	$ 200,000
Administrative	120,000	120,000	120,000
Selling	70,000	70,000	70,000
Total fixed costs	$ 390,000	$ 390,000	$ 390,000
Total costs	$ 760,000	$ 834,000	$ 908,000
Net income	$ 240,000	$ 366,000	$ 492,000

a. Prepare a traditional budgeted income statement for the year ending December 31, 19X1, assuming that 12,000 units will be produced and sold.

b. Explain what the flexible budget indicates that the budgeted income statement does not.

9-40   MASTER BUDGET VS. FLEXIBLE BUDGET North Company prepared a master budget for 19X0. At the end of the year the management team contrasts the master budget with the actual results:

CO 1, 2, 3, 6

	Master Budget 8,000 Units	Actual 10,000 Units	Variance
Sales	$80,000	$96,000	$ 16,000
Direct materials	$32,000	$41,000	$ (9,000)
Direct labor	8,000	9,000	(1,000)
Variable overhead	16,000	25,000	(9,000)
Fixed overhead	8,000	10,000	(2,000)
Total cost	$64,000	$85,000	$(21,000)
Net income	$16,000	$11,000	$ (5,000)

REQUIRED

a. Prepare a flexible budget for North Company at 10,000 units.

b. Contrast the flexible budget at 10,000 units against the actual results and show the variances.

c. Compute the master budget variance, the activity variance, the flexible budget variance, and the sales variance.

9-41   **EFFECTS OF DIFFERENT ACTIVITY MEASURES**   Moore and McGuffey, Inc., manufacture filing cabinets. Making one filing cabinet requires three hours of machine time and two hours of direct labor. The corporation's master budget for the period 19X1 and its actual results are as follows:

CO 4, 5, 6

	Master Budget 10,000 Cabinets	Actual 12,000 Cabinets
Sales	$100,000	$120,000
Direct materials	$ 30,000	$ 35,000
Direct labor	10,000	10,000
Variable overhead	15,000	20,000
Fixed overhead	30,000	31,000
Total costs	$ 85,000	$ 96,000
Net income	$ 15,000	$ 24,000

Moore and McGuffey incurred 42,000 machine hours during 19X1 and 22,000 direct labor hours.

REQUIRED

a. Use the number of cabinets sold as the activity measure for determining costs. Prepare the flexible budget for the year ending December 31, 19X1, and contrast it with the actual results.

b. Use machine hours as the activity measure for determining costs. Prepare the flexible budget and contrast it with the actual results.

c. Use direct labor hours as the activity measure for determining costs. Prepare the flexible budget and contrast it with the actual results.

9-42   **CHOOSING ACTIVITY MEASURE USING REGRESSION ANALYSIS** Management often has many possible measures of activity to choose from. One way of deciding which to use is regression analysis (discussed in the Appendix A following Chapter 3). Suppose the following data are available to management:

CO 4

Cost ($000s)	Direct Labor Hours (000s)	Machine Hours (000s)
$1,000	200	100
2,200	300	200
3,000	600	300
4,200	1,200	400
5,500	900	500

REQUIRED

a. Regress direct labor hours against cost.

b. Regress machine hours against cost.

c. Determine which is better according to the criterion of R^2.

9-43   **ANALYSIS OF ELEMENTS OF VARIABLE OVERHEAD** Hodges, Inc., shows the following details of its variable overhead in its flexible budget.

CO 5, 6

Items in Variable Overhead	Machine Hours		
	8,000	10,000	12,000
Electricity	$4,000	$5,000	$ 6,000
Indirect labor	800	1,000	1,200
Lubricants	80	100	120
Maintenance	2,400	3,000	3,600
Supplies	400	500	600
Total variable overhead	$7,680	$9,600	$11,520

Actual work during the period involved 11,000 machine hours. Actual costs are:

Electricity	$5,400
Indirect labor	1,200
Lubricants	150
Maintenance	3,400
Supplies	520

REQUIRED

a. Prepare the projected costs for these items at 11,000 machine hours. Contrast these amounts from the flexible budget with the actual costs and calculate the variances.

b. Explain whether it is more helpful in general for a manager to focus on the total variable overhead or on the line-by-line elements of variable overhead.

9-44   **ANALYSIS OF ELEMENTS OF FIXED OVERHEAD** Benston, Inc., shows the following details of its fixed overhead in its flexible budget:

CO 5, 6

Items in Fixed Overhead	Machine Hours
	10,000
Depreciation of equipment	$ 2,000
Depreciation of factory	5,000
Insurance	2,500
Property taxes	3,500
Supervisory salaries	8,000
Utilities	10,000
Total	$31,000

Actual work during the period involved 11,000 machine hours. Actual costs are:

Depreciation of equipment	$2,100
Depreciation of factory	5,000
Insurance	3,000
Property taxes	3,500
Supervisory salaries	10,000
Utilities	9,000

REQUIRED

a. Prepare the projected cost for these items at 11,000 machine hours. Contrast these amounts from the flexible budget with the actual costs and calculate the variances.

b. Explain whether it is more helpful for a manager to focus on the total fixed overhead or on the line-by-line elements of fixed overhead.

c. State why fixed costs might not be projected perfectly.

Business Decision Case

Cox Company manufactures widgets with the following standard costs:

Raw materials (5 lb. per unit)	$30 per lb.
Direct labor (2 hours per unit)	$20 per hour
Depreciation on equipment	$10,000 per year
Electricity (1/2 machine hour per unit)	$60 per machine hour
Rent	$90,000 per year
Supervisory wages	$120,000 per year

Cox estimated that it would produce and sell 1,000 widgets (selling at $600 each) during the period. With this prediction, Cox prepares the following master budget for 19X0:

Sales	$600,000
Direct materials	$150,000
Direct labor	40,000
Variable overhead	30,000
Fixed overhead	220,000
Total costs	$440,000
Net income	$160,000

Actual results for 19X0 are as follows:

Actual production and sale	900 units
Raw materials purchased and used ($4,600 lbs. @ $29 per lb.)	$133,400
Direct labor ($1,900 hours $21 per hour)	$ 39,900
Depreciation on equipment	$ 10,000
Electricity (430 machine hours @ $62 per machine hours)	$ 26,660
Rent	$ 95,000
Supervisory wages	$120,000

REQUIRED

a. Make a flexible budget for Cox for the year ending December 31, 19X0 for 800, 900, 1,100, and 1,200 units.

b. Compute the master budget variance, the activity variance, the flexible budget variance, and the sales variance.

c. Determine the predetermined fixed overhead rate using number of units as the activity level.

d. Calculate the materials variances, labor variances, variable overhead variances, and fixed overhead variances.

e. If the activity level is number of machine hours, determine the predetermined fixed overhead rate. Recompute the fixed overhead variances.

Product Costing Using Job Costing

CHAPTER OBJECTIVES

After reading Chapter 10, you should be able to:

1. Identify the elements of product costs (pp. 341–42).

2. Identify situations appropriate for job costing (pp. 342–43).

3. Visualize the use of database management software in job costing (p. 343).

4. Identify the documents used in job costing (pp. 344–45).

5. Prepare a job cost report (pp. 346–48).

6. Calculate the standard cost variances related to a job (pp. 347–48).

7. Prepare journal entries that reflect the flow of costs (pp. 348–57).

8. Prepare journal entries that reflect the standard cost variances by job (pp. 348–57).

9. Discuss the decision support systems and behavioral aspects of job costing (p. 357).

Product costing is important because it helps managers assess the financial viability of the product. It is also useful because it facilitates the preparation of financial statements in accordance with generally accepted accounting principles. In particular, it facilitates the allocation of manufacturing costs among work in process inventory, finished goods inventory, and cost of goods sold. This allocation process allows firms to match their costs with their revenues. (You may wish to review the cost flows in organizations shown in Exhibits 2-3 [page 32] and 2-6 [page 35] and especially in Exhibit 2-11 [page 40].)

Product costing generally is carried out in either of two ways. *Job costing* (or job order costing) accumulates costs for a particular manufacturing job. *Process costing* accumulates costs for a particular department. Job costing is the subject of this chapter, and process costing is the subject of Chapter 11.

Product costing can be implemented with actual costs or with standard costs, which was discussed in Chapters 8 and 9. If standard costs are applied, variance analysis can then be used with either type of costing. The application of overhead is another aspect of our coverage of both job costing and process costing.

PRODUCT COSTING

CHAPTER
OBJECTIVE 1
*Elements of product
costing*

Chapters 7 and 8 on standard costs introduced the idea of product costing even though those chapters focused on the performance evaluation of managers. Product costing is also necessary in order to permit the allocation of total manufacturing costs between cost of goods sold and inventory.

This allocation process actually involves identifying the direct costs (direct materials and direct labor) with each unit of product and allocating variable and fixed manufacturing overhead to the product. This allocation is necessary to keep the firm in accordance with the full costing (absorption costing) rules of generally accepted accounting principles.

The identification and allocation of costs to products is also important for decisions concerning the price of the product. In negotiated contracts with the government, manufacturing cost is often a very important element in pricing the product. The variable cost elements of the product cost are also important considerations in decisions concerning make-or-buy and capital expenditures.

The manufacturing environment dictates the type of product costing system to be used. If there are multiple products, multiple customers, and the customers are known when the manufacturing process begins, then the job costing system would be used because the items being produced are being made to customer specifications. An example would be a printing shop.

On the other hand, if the customer is not known—such as in the production of inventory from which a customer will select—then the process costing system would likely be used. An example would be an oil refinery.

Job costing is used in situations in which the lot of product being produced can be uniquely identified with a customer or with the customer's specifications. Process costing is used in situations in which there is no way to distinguish one lot from another. This chapter is devoted to job costing; the next chapter is devoted to process costing.

COMPETITOR COST ANALYSIS AT CATERPILLAR

At Caterpillar we are spending hundreds of millions of dollars on factory modernization. Our continuing objective is to be the lowest-cost, highest-value producer in our industry on a sustained basis. Before we developed our modernization plans, we analyzed the competitive situation. This was done from perspectives of price, cost, industry capacity, and competitor strategies. This effort resulted in the establishment of a total company-wide structural cost reduction target and individual product-by-product targets.

These targets provided the impetus for strategies for modernizing manufacturing operations and reducing costs, and provide the benchmarks against which the unfolding improvements are monitored.

There is a key aspect of competitor analysis that must be understood: there is a point at which a competitor's cost advantage is large enough that it cannot be eliminated through evolutionary or "business as usual" cost reduction efforts. When a manufacturer's cost problems are beyond that point, revolutionary change is required. The competitor analysis should provide the information for making that determination. It is too much to ask of a management team that it plan strategy for future competitiveness while "in the dark" as to the nature and extent of any cost disadvantages it may have. How can a major manufacturer successfully plan to achieve optimal competitiveness without knowledge of the strategies and costs of its key competitors?

The managerial accountant must play the major role in seeing that his company has this knowledge. *This responsibility can't be abdicated.* Admittedly, for many, competitor analyses will be a venture into "uncharted waters." They will require thought, understanding, and planning.

Probably the simplest form of analysis would be simply to divide a competitor's costs from the published financial statements by the units produced and determine an average product cost. But this would not yield very useful information for trying to analyze the cost of complex, multiproduct manufacturers.

At the other end of the spectrum would be the ideal: the development of very specific product cost estimates based on detailed information about the competitor's cost structure, products, and the product's costs in the production process. When an organization does mobilize itself to do competitor analysis it is important that it approaches the effort with the "ideal" as a frame of reference. Of course, this information is, understandably, not available. So available published information is used as the basis for analyses.

Obtaining reliable internal product costs is a prerequisite for competitor cost analysis. If a company's own product cost system can't meet this test then competitor evaluations will be of little value. But for the company with a good product specific costing system, competitor analysis is a powerful tool for maintaining or gaining competitive advantage. . . .

SOURCE: Adapted from Lou Jones, "Competitor Cost Analysis at Caterpillar," *Management Accounting* (October 1988), pp. 32–38. Adapted by permission.

JOB COSTING

CHAPTER OBJECTIVE 2
When to use job costing

Job costing, or *job order costing*, relies on documentation that relates the expending of resources (direct material and direct labor) directly to a lot or a batch of production. Usually this is accomplished by assigning each customer order a job order number. The job order number is then used when direct materials are issued from the raw materials storeroom to the production floor and it is used by the machine operators or assemblers when they begin work on that customer's order.

In order to get an overview of the job costing procedure, we will focus on Buchanan Company, which builds furniture. Buchanan was introduced in Chapters 7 and 8.

Managers of Buchanan need a cost accounting system that will inform them of the costs of the furniture that is manufactured. If the firm makes a stereo cabinet, costs should be accumulated for that cabinet so that managers can assess how efficiently the firm is making it. They need this information in order to make intelligent pricing decisions, for example. The identification of product costs with each customer order is also necessary because the manufacturing costs associated with the stereo cabinet will be classified as work in process inventory (when still being worked on at the end of the accounting period), finished goods inventory (when the cabinet is produced but is not yet sold), or as cost of goods sold (when the product is sold). This proper identification of manufacturing costs with the specific customer order is necessary if the income for the accounting period is to be calculated in accordance with generally accepted accounting principles. This cost system would, of course, be applied not only to stereo cabinets, but also to dining room tables, china cabinets, bookcases, and all of the other products Buchanan Company makes.

Job costing is the appropriate system to use in situations such as the one just described. A job costing system in use at Buchanan would require a carpenter to record, probably on a daily basis, the number of hours worked on each of the projects he or she worked on. Likewise, any materials issued from the central materials warehouse would have to be documented so that the accountant could determine which materials went to which furniture-building project. The documents used to provide this information to the accountant are the worker's *time card* used for direct labor and the *materials issue slip* used for direct materials. These documents are described and discussed more completely later in this chapter.

The direct material and labor costs are usually identified rather precisely with their related furniture-building projects. Direct materials and direct labor costs, however, are only part of the total manufacturing costs that are accounted for. The other cost is manufacturing overhead.

The application of variable overhead was described in Chapter 7 and the application of fixed overhead in Chapter 8. The same ideas are used in the job costing system. Manufacturing overhead costs are typically allocated to each of the projects based on direct labor hours or machine hours (or whatever is the cost driver) identified as being associated with each project. If direct labor hours are used, the data would be obtained from the workers' time cards. If machine hours are used as the cost driver, a meter would measure the amount of time the machine was deployed on the project and the data entered on machine time cards.

The direct materials, direct labor, and manufacturing overhead costs are thus identified with or allocated to the projects in order to determine the total manufacturing costs of each project. It is this process that permits the cost of goods sold to be deducted from the revenues recorded from the sale of the furniture to arrive at gross profit for the year. This system also yields the proper cost of ending inventory to be placed on the balance sheet.

Database Management Software and Job Costing

CHAPTER OBJECTIVE 3
Computerizing job costing

Database management software is very useful in computerizing job costing systems. Database management software is software that permits the user to store data and establish relationships among the stored data.

For example, the database management software is capable of calculating the cost of materials issued to each job, the actual cost of direct labor used on each job, and the overhead charged to each job.

```
┌─────────────────────────────────────────────────────────────┐
│                      EXHIBIT 10-1                            │
│                                                              │
│              DIRECT MATERIALS ISSUE SLIP                    │
│                                                              │
│   Date June 19, 19X1                    Issue Slip No. 15378│
│   Department Fabrication         Job No. to Be Charged 157  │
│                                                              │
│   Direct Material Description    Part Number    Quantity    │
│   Birch panels                      W523        384 sq. ft. │
│   Hardboard panels                  W412        224 sq. ft. │
│   Spruce structural members         W751        470 lin. ft.│
│   _____  │
│                                                              │
│   Receipt of Items Acknowledged by: _____ │
└─────────────────────────────────────────────────────────────┘
```

Direct Materials Issue Slip

CHAPTER
OBJECTIVE 4
*Documents for
job costing*

When materials are needed on the production line, the department supervisor completes a *direct materials issue slip* and presents it to the attendant in the direct materials storeroom. The attendant gives the material to the supervisor and the supervisor signs the issue slip acknowledging receipt of the quantities issued. The signed receipt for one day's estimated material requirements is shown in Exhibit 10-1.

The data from the direct materials issue slip would be entered into the computerized database. Each direct material part number and related description and standard cost per unit would have previously been entered into the computer. When the issue slip part numbers and related quantities are entered into the computer from the issue slip, the computer can make the following calculation:

Materials Issue Slip Number	Part Description	Part Number	Quantity Issued	Standard Unit Cost	Total Cost
15378	Birch panels	W523	384 sq. ft.	$1.00	$384.00
15378	Hardboard panels	W412	224 sq. ft.	.18	40.32
15378	Spruce structural members	W751	470 linear ft.	.20	94.00
	Total				$518.32

The total direct material cost of $518.32 will be retained in the database and related to job 157. When the costs for job 157 are later summarized, the $518.32 amount will appear on the report as the standard cost of direct material issued in job 157.

Direct Labor Time Card

Those employees who comprise the direct labor force are required to complete a *time card* indicating the number of hours they worked on each job order. This time card is the basis for calculating the employee's pay and also for determining the direct labor cost that will be charged to each job order.

In a job order manufacturing environment there are procedures established to ensure that each employee knows the job order number of the job on which he or she is working. When the employee changes from one job order to another, the time of that change is noted on the time card.

That time card is sent to the accounting department at the end of each week, and it calculates the number of hours associated with each job order. A summary of one week's time card data might appear as in Exhibit 10-2. The employee number, total hours worked, and hours worked on each job are entered into the database, where the employee's department and actual wage rate are already associated with the employee. The database management software then calculates the employee's net pay and also the dollar amount of the direct labor charge to each job order.

Information in the summary of charges section at the bottom of Exhibit 10-2 will be retained in the database for use in preparing the job cost report, discussed next, for each of the two job orders that were worked on during the week ending June 23, 19X1.

EXHIBIT 10-2

Direct Labor Charges to Job Orders
Week Ending June 23, 19X1

Employee Number	Department	Job Order	Direct Labor Hours	Actual Labor Rate	Direct Labor Charged to Job
243	Fabrication	157	12.0	$7.50	$ 90.00
243	Fabrication	158	28.0	$7.50	210.00
127	Fabrication	157	8.0	$7.95	63.60
127	Fabrication	158	32.0	$7.95	254.40
089	Fabrication	157	6.0	$7.75	46.50
089	Fabrication	158	34.0	$7.75	263.50
132	Fabrication	157	8.0	$8.05	64.40
132	Fabrication	158	32.0	$8.05	257.60
102	Assembly	157	4.0	$6.35	25.40
102	Assembly	158	36.0	$6.35	228.60
212	Assembly	157	7.0	$6.25	43.75
212	Assembly	158	33.0	$6.25	206.25
183	Assembly	157	8.0	$6.30	50.40
183	Assembly	158	32.0	$6.30	201.60
	Total		280.0		$2,006.00

Summary of Charges:

Amount charged to Fabrication—Job 157	34 hours	$264.50
Amount charged to Assembly—Job 157	19 hours	119.55
Total for Job 157		$ 384.05
Amount charged to Fabrication—Job 158	126 hours	985.50
Amount charged to Assembly—Job 158	101 hours	636.45
Total for Job 158		1,621.95
Total Charges	280 hours	$2,006.00

Job Cost Report

The job cost report is a summary report of all the actual charges to a particular job order. This report also includes descriptive information about the job order and the record of the standard cost and variances associated with the project. Exhibit 10-3 illustrates a job cost report prepared by database management software.

The job cost report shows the summary information concerning direct material cost and direct labor cost. References, such as the issue slip number and the date associated with an individual's time card, are also indicated to permit an examination of the details from which the summary information is derived.

EXHIBIT 10-3

JOB COST REPORT
(PREPARED BY DATABASE MANAGEMENT SOFTWARE)

Job Cost Report
For Job Order 157

Date Started 6-19-19X1
Number of Units Ordered 9
Number of Units Completed 9
Production Identification Stereo Cabinet B26389

Promised Delivery Date 6-26-19X1
Date Completed 6-23-19X1
Customer Music City

MATERIALS		DIRECT LABOR						
Issue Slip Number	Actual Cost	Week Ending	Employee Number	Department	Actual Hours	Actual Labor Rate	Actual Amount
15378	$518.32	6-23-19X1	243	Fabrication	12.0	$7.50	$ 90.00
15384	28.68	6-23-19X1	127	Fabrication	8.0	$7.95	63.60
		6-23-19X1	089	Fabrication	6.0	$7.75	46.50
		6-23-19X1	132	Fabrication	8.0	$8.05	64.40
		6-23-19X1	102	Assembly	4.0	$6.35	25.40
		6-23-19X1	212	Assembly	7.0	$6.25	43.75
		6-23-19X1	183	Assembly	8.0	$6.30	50.40
	$547.00				53.0 hours		$384.05

(continued)

EXHIBIT 10-3 *continued*

Variance Analysis

	Actual	Input Standard	Output Standard		Material Quantity Variance
Direct Materials	$547.00	$547.00	$510.48[a]		$36.52U

Direct Labor:

	Actual	Input Standard	Output Standard	Labor Rate Variance	Labor Efficiency Variance
Fabrication	$264.50	$272.00[b]	$252.00[c]	$7.50F	$20.00U
Assembly	119.55	114.00[d]	121.50[e]	5.55U	7.50F
Total direct labor	$384.05	$386.00	$373.50	$1.95F	$12.50U

Overhead Charges:
Variable

Fabrication	9 units × 3.50 hours × $2	$ 63.00
Assembly	9 units × 2.25 hours × $4	81.00
	(Standard cost per Chapter 7)	$ 144.00

Fixed

Both departments	9 units × 5.75 hours × $12 *(Standard cost per Chapter 8)*	621.00
Overhead charges		$ 765.00

Standard Cost of Job Order:

Direct materials	$ 510.48
Direct labor	373.50
Overhead	765.00
Standard cost of job order	$1,648.98

[a]9 units × $56.72 per unit standard cost (from Exh. 7-2, p. 242).
[b]34 hours × $8 per hour standard rate (from Exh. 7-2).
[c]9 units × 3.5 hours × $8 per hour standard rate (from Exh. 7-2).
[d]19 hours × $6 per hour standard rate (from Exh. 7-2).
[e]9 units × 2.25 hours × $6 per hour standard rate (from Exh. 7-2).

CHAPTER OBJECTIVE 6
Cost variances for a job

The actual direct material and direct labor costs are compared with the input standard costs and the output standard costs to permit the calculation of variances that are helpful in assessing the extent to which the direct costs were within the limits established by the standards. The input standard costs and output standard costs are calculated by the database management software because the database contains the standards associated with the product which was manufactured—Stereo Cabinet B26389 for this job order.

The job cost record also shows the amount of overhead that was charged to the job order. No attempt is made to determine the overhead variances associated with a particular job order because there is no reasonable means of assigning actual variable and fixed overhead costs to a job order. The standard overhead costs are determined and added to the other standard costs (direct materials and direct labor) to provide a record of the amount that is charged to finished goods inventory when the job order is completed.

This method of using database management software to store standard costs and actual costs results in a job cost report that is useful for evaluating the control of direct cost associated with the job order. On this job, which involved the manufacture of nine stereo cabinets, there was a $36.52 unfavorable material quantity variance and only a slightly unfavorable labor efficiency variance. The labor rate variance was marginally favorable.

JOB COSTING AND THE FLOW OF COSTS

CHAPTER OBJECTIVE 7
Cost flows

With the help of documents such as vendors' invoices, receiving reports, direct materials issue slips, and time cards, the accounting department uses computerized accounting systems (such as the database management software) to prepare job cost reports and to account for the cost in the general ledger accounting system. Exhibit 10-4 describes the flow of documents through the accounting system.

Direct Material Cost Flow

CHAPTER OBJECTIVE 8
Variances

Chapter 7 discussed the purchase of raw materials estimated to meet production needs for two months, June and July 19X1 (refer to pages 241–44 and Exhibit 7-3). Those raw materials would have been paid for upon receipt of an invoice from the supplier (vendor) and a receiving report from the raw materials storeroom attendant.

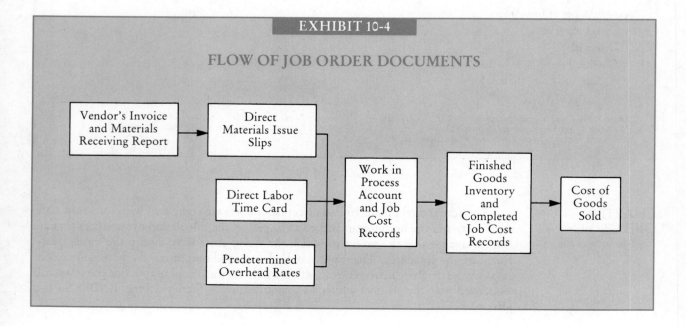

EXHIBIT 10-4

FLOW OF JOB ORDER DOCUMENTS

The journal entry to record the receipt of those raw materials would be as follows:

1.	Raw Materials Inventory	22,688	
	Direct Material Price Variance	4,312	
	Accounts Payable		27,000

The invoice and the receiving report, along with the standard cost for each category of raw material as stored in the database, are used to create this entry, which values the materials in the Raw Materials Inventory account at the standard cost and recognizes the material price variance at the time of purchase.

The direct materials issue slips are processed through the accounting department and the information on those slips is entered into the database. The database management software then calculates the standard cost of material issued as shown in Exhibit 10-3.

The journal entry prepared from this calculation of the input standard cost of materials issued is as follows:

2.	Work in Process—Job 157	547	
	Raw Materials Inventory		547

In addition to being posted to the appropriate general ledger accounts, the $547 would be summarized on the job cost record for job order 157.

Note that the material price variance is recognized and recorded in the accounting records at the date of purchase. Further, the raw materials are put into and removed from the Raw Materials Inventory account at the standard cost. This practice results in the Raw Materials Inventory account having a balance that appropriately reflects the standard cost of the materials. Additionally, the material price variance is revealed on management reports in the month in which the variance occurs.

Direct Labor Cost Flow

Soon after the payroll is calculated using the time cards, a journal entry is prepared to record the gross payroll, withholdings, and accrued wages payable. Using the payroll report shown in Exhibit 10-2, the following entry (shown in summary form) would be prepared:

3.	Gross Payroll Control	2,006	
	Accrued Wages Payable (and other liability accounts for tax withholdings)		2,006

The debits to the Gross Payroll Control account would then be distributed to the various work in process accounts as follows (based on the database management software calculations illustrated in Exhibit 10-2):

4.	Work in Process—Job 157	384.05	
	Work in Process—Job 156	1,621.95	
	Gross Payroll Control		2,006.00

This entry has the effect of distributing the payroll to the various job orders that were worked on during that week.

Variable Manufacturing Overhead Cost Flow

As mentioned in Chapter 7, variable manufacturing overhead includes items of low unit value that are used in manufacturing, such as glue, nails, and so on. Because of the low unit value of these items, no standards are developed for them. Thus, when these items are purchased, they are not accounted for as if they were a part of raw materials inventory. Even though they will likely be placed in the raw materials storeroom for safekeeping, they are not included in the raw materials inventory, which is maintained at standard cost. Additionally, when these items are needed in manufacturing, they are issued from the raw materials store without the need for a materials issue slip. The low unit value is the justification for this relaxed approach to dealing with the items included in variable manufacturing overhead. When variable overhead items are purchased, the following journal entry is prepared to record the purchase:

5.	Variable Manufacturing Overhead Control—		
	Fabrication Department	1,700	
	Variable Manufacturing Overhead Control—		
	Assembly Department	1,500	
	Accounts Payable		3,200

Because there are no documents to trace the flow of these variable overhead items into work in process, their flow is facilitated by the use of the predetermined variable overhead rate and the count of units completed.

When job order 157 is completed on June 23, the actual number of units produced during the month, nine units, is used to determine the amount of variable overhead that should be charged to work in process. That calculation would also be accomplished by the database management software through the multiplication of the nine units times the standard direct labor hours per unit times the predetermined variable manufacturing overhead rate per direct labor hour. The calculation for the completed job order 157 is as follows:

Fabrication Department: 9 units × 3.5 hours × $2 per hour = $63
Assembly Department: 9 units × 2.25 hours × $4 per hour = $81

The journal entry to record the application of variable overhead is as follows:

6.	Work in Process—Job 157	144	
	Variable Manufacturing Overhead		
	Applied—Fabrication Department		63
	Variable Manufacturing Overhead		
	Applied—Assembly Department		81

If the job order is not complete at the end of a month, the number of units that were completed during the month is determined and the variable overhead applied to that job is calculated using that number of units completed.

Fixed Manufacturing Overhead Cost Flow

Fixed manufacturing overhead includes items such as factory supervision, insurance, and depreciation. The incurrence of those costs is recorded as shown in the following journal entry:

7.	Supervisory Payroll	6,000	
	Factory Depreciation	4,450	
	Insurance Expense	2,000	
	Accrued Salaries Payable		6,000
	Accumulated Depreciation		4,450
	Accounts Payable		2,000

The various debits, because they are all components of fixed manufacturing overhead, are distributed to the fixed manufacturing overhead control account with the following journal entry:

8.	Fixed Manufacturing Overhead Control	12,450	
	Supervisory Payroll		6,000
	Factory Depreciation		4,450
	Insurance Expense		2,000

The flow of fixed manufacturing overhead from the control account to work in process is accomplished just as it is for variable manufacturing overhead. Once the number of units completed has been determined, that number of units is multiplied by the standard direct labor hours per unit times the predetermined fixed manufacturing overhead rate per direct labor hour. The calculation for completed job order 157 is as follows:

$$9 \text{ units completed} \times 5.75 \text{ hours} \times \$12 \text{ per hour} = \$621$$

The journal entry to record the application of fixed overhead is as follows:

9.	Work in Process—Job 157	621	
	Fixed Manufacturing Overhead Applied		621

Closing the Fixed and Variable Overhead Accounts

We now assume that other jobs on which work was performed in June 19XX had applied overhead that resulted in the following journal entry (in summary form).

10. Work in Process—Various Jobs 15,875
　　　Variable Manufacturing Overhead
　　　　Applied—Fabrication Department 1,337
　　　Variable Manufacturing Overhead
　　　　Applied—Assembly Department 1,629
　　　Fixed Manufacturing Overhead Applied 12,909

After posting previous journal entries in the Overhead Applied and the Overhead Control accounts, totals for those accounts are shown in T-account form in Exhibit 10-5. These overhead accounts are usually closed at the end of each year. However, in this situation they are being closed at the end of the month of June in order to demonstrate the method used in closing the accounts. The journal entries used to close the accounts are shown on page 353:

EXHIBIT 10-5

STATUS OF GENERAL LEDGER OVERHEAD ACCOUNTS AT END OF JUNE

Prior to Closing Entry

Variable Manufacturing Overhead Control—Fabrication Department

(5) $1,700	
Bal. $1,700	

Variable Manufacturing Overhead Applied—Fabrication Department

	(6) $ 63
	(10) 1,337
	Bal. $1,400

Variable Manufacturing Overhead Control—Assembly Department

(5) $1,500	
Bal. $1,500	

Variable Manufacturing Overhead Applied—Assembly Department

	(6) $ 81
	(10) 1,629
	Bal. $1,710

Fixed Manufacturing Overhead Control

(8) $12,450	
Bal. $12,450	

Fixed Manufacturing Overhead Applied

	(9) $ 621
	(10) 12,909
	Bal. $13,530

11. Variable Manufacturing Overhead
      Applied—Fabrication Department   1,400
    Variable Manufacturing Overhead
        Variance—Fabrication Department   300
        Variable Manufacturing Overhead
            Control—Fabrication Department   1,700

12. Variable Manufacturing Overhead
      Applied—Assembly Department   1,710
        Variable Manufacturing Overhead
            Variance—Assembly Department   210
        Variable Manufacturing Overhead
            Control—Assembly Department   1,080

13. Fixed Manufacturing Overhead Applied   13,530
        Fixed Manufacturing Overhead Control   12,450
        Fixed Manufacturing Overhead Variance   1,080

After these journal entries are made, the general ledger accounts for the overhead control and the overhead applied accounts have a zero balance and the overhead variance accounts are established with debit (unfavorable, as an expense) and credit (favorable, as a revenue) balances reflecting the underapplied (unfavorable) and overapplied (favorable) condition of the overhead accounts.

Recall from Chapter 8, page 280 that 185 units were sold in June at a selling price of $250 per unit, 5 completed units were still in finished goods inventory at the end of the month, and 10 partially completed units were in work process inventory at the end of the month.

The journal entry to move the standard cost of the 190 units (185 units sold and 5 units in finished goods inventory) from work in process inventory to finished goods inventory is based on the following calculation:

$$190 \text{ units} \times \$183.22 \text{ standard cost per unit} = \$34,811.80$$

The journal entry that results from that calculation is as follows:

14. Finished Goods Inventory   34,811.80
        Work in Process Inventory   34,811.80

The cost of goods sold at standard cost is calculated as follows:

$$185 \text{ units} \times \$183.22 \text{ standard cost per unit} = \$33,895.70$$

The journal entry to record the sales is as follows:

15. Accounts Receivable   42,250.00
     Cost of Goods Sold   33,895.70
        Sales   42,250.00
        Finished Goods Inventory   33,895.70

EXHIBIT 10-6

STATUS OF SELECTED GENERAL LEDGER ACCOUNTS
AT END OF JUNE

After Closing of Overhead Accounts

Raw Materials Inventory

(1) $22,688	(2) $547
	(16) 12,583
Bal. $ 9,558	

Work in Process Inventory

(2) $ 547.00	(14) $ 34,811.80
(4) 384.05	(19) 1,786.00
(4) 1,621.95	(21) 1,135.00
(6) 144.00	
(9) 621.00	
(10) 15,875.00	
(16) 12,583.00	
(18) 7,279.00	
(20) 15.00	
Bal. $ 1,337.20	

Finished Goods Inventory

(14) $34,811.80	(15) $ 33,895.70
Bal. $ 916.10	

Cost of Goods Sold

(15) $33,895.70	

Material Quantity Variance

(19) $1,786	

Labor Efficiency Variance

(21) $1,135	

Direct Materials Price Variance

(1) $4,312	

**Variable Overhead Variance
—Fabricating Department**

(11) $300	

**Variable Overhead Variance
—Assembly Department**

	(12) $210

Fixed Overhead Variance

	(13) $1,080

Labor Rate Variance

	(20) $15

Before we post the journal entries to the general ledger accounts we must show the journal entries for direct materials and direct labor used on other jobs. The following journal entries will record these items. These entries, in summary form, are for work started but uncompleted at the end of the period.

16.	Work in Process—All Other Jobs	12,583	
	Raw Materials Inventory		12,583
17.	Gross Payroll Control	7,279	
	Accrued Wages Payable		7,279
18.	Work in Process—All Other Jobs	7,279	
	Gross Payroll Control		7,279

Summing the material quantity variances, labor rate variances, and labor efficiency variances from the individual job cost reports for all jobs completed or in process will permit the following journal entries:

19.	Material Quantity Variance	1,786	
	Work in Process		1,786
20.	Work in Process	15	
	Labor Rate Variance		15
21.	Labor Efficiency Variance	1,135	
	Work in Process		1,135

The amounts used in these last three journal entries agree with the variances shown on the manufacturing manager's performance report for June in Chapter 7 (Exhibit 7-6). Thus, in a job costing system these variances can be analyzed by job. As we saw in Exhibit 10-3, Job 157 contributed $36.52 toward the unfavorable material quantity variance, $1.95 toward the favorable wage rate variance, and $12.50 toward the unfavorable labor efficiency variance. Other jobs completed or in process at the end of June accounted for the remainder of the variances.

After those journal entries have been made, selected general ledger accounts will show their activity and balances as in Exhibit 10-6. From the balances in the general ledger accounts, the following financial statements may be prepared. The partial balance sheet is displayed in Exhibit 10-7, and the partial income statement is in Exhibit 10-8. These statements are identical with the statements shown earlier in Chapter 8 as Exhibits 8-2 (page 281) and 8-4 (page 283).

Job Costing and Activity-based Costing

Activity-based costing, discussed in Chapter 8, can be used with job costing. Recall that in the first stage of activity-based costing the management accountant groups activities whose costs are determined by some economic factor and collects the costs of these activities in what is termed a *cost pool*. A cost driver is selected for this cost pool and a *pool rate* is determined.

EXHIBIT 10-7

PARTIAL BALANCE SHEET SHOWING INVENTORIES AT STANDARD COST

Buchanan Company
Balance Sheet
As of June 30, 19X1
(Current Asset Portion Only)

ASSETS

Current Assets

Cash		$XXXXXX.XX
Inventory		
Finished Goods	$ 916.10	
Work in Process	1,337.20	
Raw Materials	9,558.00	
Total Inventories		11,811.30
Other Current Assets		XXXXXX.XX
Total Current Assets		$XXXXXX.XX

EXHIBIT 10-8

PARTIAL INCOME STATEMENT WITH VARIANCES SHOWN

Buchanan Company
Income Statement
Month of June 19X1
(Gross Profit Portion Only)

Sales	$46,250.00	
Less: Standard Cost of Goods Sold	33,895.70	
Standard Gross Profit	$12,354.30	
Less: Unfavorable Variances from Standard:		
Unfavorable Material Price Variance	(4,312.00)	
Unfavorable Material Quantity Variance	(1,786.00)	
Unfavorable Labor Efficiency Variance	(1,135.00)	Total Variance:
Unfavorable Variable Overhead Variance	(90.00)	$6,228
Unfavorable Volume Variance	(960.00)	Unfavorable
Add: Favorable Variances from Standard:		
Favorable Labor Rate Variance	15.00	
Favorable Budget Variance	2,040.00	
Actual Gross Profit	$ 6,126.30	

In this chapter we have implicitly assumed that there is only one cost pool with direct labor hours as the cost driver. The logic of job costing is essentially the same if there are several cost pools. Consider a job that makes 100 widgets. It uses two gallons of goo at $4 per gallon, one-half hour of direct labor at $10 per hour, two machine hours at $15 per hour, and one setup at $45 per setup. The job costs $88, or $.88 per widget, and is calculated as follows:

Direct materials (2 × $4)	$ 8
Direct labor (1/2 × $10)	5
Machine hours (2 × $15)	30
Setups (1 × $45)	45
Total	$88

Thus, job costing can be easily modified to handle activity-based costing.

DECISION SUPPORT SYSTEMS AND BEHAVIORAL ASPECTS OF JOB COSTING

CHAPTER OBJECTIVE 9
DSS and behavioral impact

This chapter discussed the use of database management software to support the accumulation of costs by specific job. It is only in recent years that accountants have had the advantage of software to support the job costing task. The advent of such software has made job costing systems available to small businesses. Prior to the availability of such software for use with the personal computer, these small businesses typically had no formal system of costing products.

The increased use of job costing by small businesses (both manufacturing and service-oriented businesses) has provided valuable information to the managers of those businesses. Managers now have the information necessary to develop pricing strategies that tend to ensure that the price will exceed the cost and yield the desired profit. Additionally, the manager may use the standard costing system with the job costing system to evaluate those who are responsible for the job. The variances from standard costs are helpful to the manager as he or she seeks to evaluate the extent to which the costs of the job were under control. Knowing that the manager has this capability, those responsible for job performance are more likely to be vigilant in controlling costs.

Demonstration Problem

Pressler and Company had the following activity related to jobs 101 and 102.

	Job 101	Job 102
Units produced (started and finished)	1,000	5,000
Machining Department		
Direct materials cost	$9,600	$3,500
Machine hours worked	20	10
Fabrication Department		
Direct materials cost	$1,000	$900
Machine hours worked	5	5

Because the factory is so automated, direct labor is considered insignificant and is included in factory overhead. The overhead rates are $124 per machine hour in the Machining Department and $72 per machine hour in the Fabrication Department.

REQUIRED

Assume that Pressler uses a job order cost system. Compute the cost of job 101 and the cost of job 102.

SOLUTION TO DEMONSTRATION PROBLEM

Job 101

Machining Department:		
Direct materials cost	$9,600	
Overhead—machining (20 hours @ $124 per hour)	2,480	$12,080
Fabrication Department:		
Direct materials cost	$1,000	
Overhead—fabricating (5 hours @ $72 per hour)	360	1,360
Total cost		$13,440
Cost per unit		$13.44

Job 102

Machining Department:		
Direct materials cost	$3,500	
Overhead—machining (10 hours @ $124 per hour)	1,240	$ 4,740
Fabrication Department:		
Direct materials cost	$ 900	
Overhead—fabricating (5 hours @ $72 per hour)	360	1,260
Total cost		$6,000
Cost per unit		$1.20

Review of Chapter Objectives

1. Identify the elements of product costs (pp. 341–42).

   ■ The elements of product cost are direct materials, direct labor, variable manufacturing overhead, and fixed manufacturing overhead. The overhead costs are allocated to the product rather than being directly identified with each product.

2. Identify situations appropriate for job costing (pp. 342–43).

   ■ The manufacturing environment dictates the type of product costing system that will be used. If the manufacturing environment is such that there are multiple customers, and the customers are known when the manufacturing process begins, then job costing would be used because the items are being produced to customer specifications.

3. Visualize the use of database management software in job costing (p. 343).

   ■ Database management software is useful in recording the information from the direct materials issue slip and the direct labor time card and classifying it in such a way that it is identified with the appropriate job. This database management system may be used to multiply items of direct material and hours of direct labor times the unit costs stored in the database to arrive at costs charged to each job.

4. Identify the documents used in job costing (pp. 344–45).

   ■ The documents used in job costing include the direct materials issue slip and the direct labor time card.

5. Prepare a job cost report (pp. 346–48).

   ■ The job cost report is the report on which all of the cost charges to a job are summarized. The information is recorded in such a way that the source of the information may be readily determined. The job cost report includes a calculation of the total direct material costs, the total direct labor costs, and the overhead charged to a job.

6. Calculate the standard cost variances related to a job (pp. 347–48).

   ■ If standard costs are used, it is possible to couple standard costing with job costing. In such a situation, it is possible to determine what the job should have cost and then contrast that expected cost with the actual cost. The difference between the two is the cost variance. The total cost variance can be fragmented into various causes such as the material quantity variance, the labor rate variance, and the labor efficiency variance.

7. Prepare journal entries that reflect the flow of costs (pp. 348–57).

   ■ As costs move from raw materials inventory and gross payroll into the manufacturing facility, a journal entry is prepared transferring those costs to work in process inventory. When the job is completed, the work in process costs are transferred to finished goods inventory through the use of a journal entry. When the job is delivered to the customer, a journal entry is used to transfer the cost from finished goods inventory to cost of goods sold.

8. Prepare journal entries that reflect the standard cost variances by job (pp. 348–57).

   ■ If standard costs are used and variances from standard costs are identified with specific jobs, those variances may be entered into the accounting records through journal entries. These entries permit the internal financial statements used by management to reveal the cost variances by job. In such a situation, the gross profit based on standard costs is reported and then that amount is adjusted through the use of revealed cost variances to arrive at actual gross profit.

   ■ Activity-based costing can be easily incorporated into job costing. This is done by costing a job for its use of direct materials, direct labor, and the various activities that make up overhead (such as machine hours, setups, and quality inspections).

9. Discuss the decision support systems and behavioral aspects of job costing (p. 357).

   ■ Throughout this chapter, we have shown how the management accountant can use computer software packages to support job costing. The use of such database management software simplifies the accountant's task and can lead to more accurate product costing. This computerization also facilitates variance analysis, which can be used to reward and punish managers for their good and bad performance.

Glossary of Key Terms

job cost report   The detailed record for the accumulation of job costs (that is, the material, labor, and overhead cost incurred on a job or specific production).

job costing   A method of cost accounting in which costs for material, labor, and overhead (either actual or standard) are charged to a specific job or lot. The job or lot may consist of either a single unit or like units and pertains to either goods or services.

product costing   The use of a system of accounting to determine the cost of a unit of product or service. There are two basic systems of product costing: job costing (q.v.) and process costing (discussed in Chapter 11).

Review Questions

10-1   Why is it necessary to determine the cost of each product that is produced by a business enterprise?

10-2   In what business situation would a job costing system be most appropriate?

10-3   In what business situation would a process costing system be most appropriate?

10-4   What documents are necessary to trace the cost of raw materials to the jobs or departments to which the cost is charged?

10-5   What documents are necessary to trace the cost of direct labor to the jobs or departments to which the cost is charged?

10-6   What is a job cost report and how is it used?

10-7   How might database management software be used to generate the direct materials portion of a job cost report?

10-8   How might database management software be used to generate the direct labor portion of a job cost report?

10-9   Why does the job costing system focus on jobs whereas the process costing system focuses on departments?

10-10   How does a well-maintained job costing system contribute to a determination of cost of goods sold?

10-11   What advantage is there to using standard costs with a job costing system?

10-12   Why are the variances from standard costs reported on the income statement that is used within the company?

10-13   Why is it not possible to associate manufacturing overhead variances with particular jobs?

10-14   When a job spans two years, should the current-year job cost report include the costs for both years or just the costs for the current year?

10-15   Why is it necessary that the signature of the person receiving the goods issued from the raw materials storeroom be affixed to the materials issue slip?

10-16   How does a job costing system used in a manufacturing company differ from a job costing system used in a company that sells a service rather than a product?

10-17   If a worker works 40 hours in a week but only shows 30 of those hours as related to particular jobs, how is the cost associated with the other 10 hours treated?

10-18   If the manufacturing overhead is underapplied during a year, what can we conclude about the cost of the jobs that were worked on during that year?

Discussion Questions

10-19   Job costing may be used by merchandisers as well as by manufacturers. Discuss how a merchandising organization might use job costing when evaluating the profitability of a particular product. (Recall that merchandisers have only one inventory, merchandise inventory.) Can merchandisers incorporate standard costs with a job costing system?

10-20   Job costing may also be used by service organizations. Consider a financial consultant who is considering whether to bid on a government contract and asks for help in redesigning her budgeting system. How might job costing be used by the financial consultant? (Note that the service organization does not have inventories; we ignore supplies inventory and treat it as an item of overhead.) Can service organizations incorporate standard costs with a job order cost system?

Exercises

10-21   **PREPARATION OF JOB COST REPORT** Longdon Manufacturing Company manufactures specialized machinery according to customer specifications. During a recent month, the following material requisitions and labor charges were recorded by the accounting department:

CO 1, 4, 5

	Material Requisitions			Labor Charges	
Date	Job Number	Amount		Job Number	Amount
Sept. 1	1253	$2,000		1240	$3,000
Sept. 5	1250	1,500		1245	2,000
Sept. 10	1245	1,250		1253	2,500
Sept. 13	1245	3,250		1245	1,500
Sept. 18	1251	800		1250	1,700
Sept. 22	1250	1,400		1251	700
Sept. 28	1245	1,100			

Manufacturing overhead is applied at the rate of 200% of direct labor cost. Job 1245 was started and completed during the month, consisting of one specialized machine manufactured for Spiller Company.

Prepare a job cost report for Job 1245. Indicate on the report the amount of manufacturing overhead charged to this job.

10-22   **MULTIPLE-DEPARTMENT JOB COST REPORT** Following is the data collected for two jobs. The manufacturing overhead rate is $10 per direct labor hour.

CO 1, 5

	Job 432	Job 433
Units produced	1,000	1,500
Cutting Department:		
Direct labor hours	500	300
Direct labor cost	$4,000	$2,400
Direct materials	$8,000	$5,000
Molding Department:		
Direct labor hours	300	100
Direct labor cost	$2,700	$ 900
Assembly Department:		
Direct labor hours	100	40
Direct labor cost	$ 700	$ 280
Direct material	$ 100	$ 50

Prepare a job cost report for Job 432 that shows the department in which the direct costs originated. Also include on the job cost report the calculation of the manufacturing overhead cost charged to Job 432.

10-23   JOB COSTING: JOURNAL ENTRIES AND COST PER UNIT The Mount Company manufactures wire winding equipment to customer specifications. During January, the company devoted its entire production effort to manufacturing 10 winding machines for Reliable Electric Company. No other jobs were in process during this period. At the end of January, the 10 completed units were placed in the finished goods warehouse to await delivery to Reliable.

CO 1, 7

The costs for January were as follows:

1. Direct labor hours: 5,000 hours @ $10 per hour

2. Direct materials: $100,000

3. Predetermined overhead rate: $30 per direct labor hour

a. Prepare the journal entries to record these costs.

b. Calculate the cost per unit.

10-24   JOB COSTING: JOURNAL ENTRIES AND WORK IN PROCESS BALANCE Shelley Company uses a job costing system to accumulate the costs of producing valves to customer specifications. The following information relates to the current month:

CO 1, 7

1. Direct materials issued from the raw materials storeroom, $100,000.

2. Direct labor costs incurred, $75,000.

3. The company applies manufacturing overhead to production at the rate of $2.50 per direct labor hour. During the month there were 75,000 direct labor hours used.

4. Actual manufacturing overhead costs totaled $190,000 during the month.

5. Orders costing $300,000 were completed and shipped to customers during the month. The sales price associated with these shipped orders was $400,000.

a. Prepare the journal entries to record the transactions and information provided above.

b. Calculate the balance in the Work in Process account at the end of the month.

10-25   ANALYSIS OF WORK IN PROCESS ACCOUNT At the end of the first month of operations, Hanover Company's Work in Process account appeared in T-account form as follows:

CO 1, 5, 7

Work in Process

Direct Materials $20,000	$130,000 To Finished Goods Inventory
Labor 45,000	
Manufacturing Overhead 90,000	

Hanover Company manufactures to customer specifications and applies overhead to the product at 200% of the direct labor cost. At the end of the month, the company had one job that remained in work in process inventory, job 325. That job had been charged with $6,000 of direct labor.

Complete the job cost report for the partially completed Job 325 as of the end of the first month.

10-26 STANDARD COST VARIANCE ANALYSIS Kindelsperger Company uses a standard cost job costing system to account for costs associated with each of their lawn care jobs. The accounting department, by working with the operations department, has established a labor standard of 2 direct labor hours for each 1,000 square yards of lawn cared for. The standard direct labor wage rate is established at $7.50 per hour.

CO 5, 6

In a recent week, the company cared for two large estates. The Belmore estate had 50,000 square yards of lawn; and the Crane estate had 70,000 square yards of lawn. The lawn care of both estates was started at the beginning of the week and finished by the end of the week. Care of the Belmore estate required 110 actual direct labor hours during the week, and the Crane estate required 120 actual direct labor hours. Because of overtime pay, the average actual wage rate was $8.25 per hour.

Standards had not yet been established for direct materials used in caring for lawns. Instead, the actual issues to each job were documented on material issue slips prepared when the materials were taken from the central storage area. The direct material issue slips prepared during the week were as follows:

Issue Slip Number	Items of Material	Job	Cost
43679	Chemicals	Belmore	$150
43680	Chemicals	Crane	200
43681	Seed	Belmore	50
43682	Seed	Crane	80

a. Prepare a job cost report for each of the two jobs for the week from June 1, 19X0 to June 6, 19X0. This schedule should show only the prime costs (direct materials and direct labor), because the problem does not reveal the overhead rates the company uses.

b. At the bottom of each of the job cost reports show the variance analysis as it applies to direct labor used on each job.

10-27 STANDARD COST VARIANCES AND JOURNAL ENTRIES Cupp Company is a telemarketing company that makes telephone calls to raise funds for various charities. In order to control the costs of the callers who place the calls and solicit the funds, Cupp establishes standards for each of the charities with which the company enters into a contract.

CO 7, 8

During a recent month, Cupp Company solicited funds for two charities (the Wild Bear Fund and the Save the Darter Fund). It was determined that callers for the Wild Bear Fund should complete 12 telephone calls per hour and the callers for the Save the Darter Fund should complete 6 telephone calls per hour (the latter callers must take more time to explain what a "Darter" is and why it should be saved).

The variance analysis section of the job cost report for each of the two jobs are summarized as follows:

Variance Analysis

Labor	Actual Cost	Input Standard Cost	Output Standard Cost	Labor Rate Variance	Labor Efficiency Variance
Wild Bear	$ 6,000	$5,800	$6,200	$(200)	$400
Darter	4,000	3,700	3,500	(300)	(200)
Total	$10,000	$9,500	$9,700	$(500)	$200

Prepare the journal entries to record the labor costs and to record the labor rate and labor efficiency variances.

10-28   DATABASE MANAGEMENT SYSTEM: DIRECT LABOR The cost accountant at Stillhamer Corporation has been given the responsibility for converting the company's manually prepared job costing system to a database management system for use on a computer.

CO 3

Focusing only on the information related to direct labor, do the following:

a. Identify the information that must be obtained from the direct laborer's weekly time card.

b. Identify the information that must be obtained when the direct laborer is hired or when his or her status changes.

10-29   DESIGN OF DATABASE MANAGEMENT SYSTEM: DIRECT MATERIAL Coppage Corporation is in the process of converting its manually prepared job costing system to a database management system. Coppage intends to start the conversion by designing the direct material portion of the database management system first.

CO 3

Focusing only on the information related to direct material, do the following:

a. Identify the information that must be obtained from the direct material issue slip.

b. Identify the information that must be obtained from the purchasing department when the various items of direct materials are initially identified as being required for a job.

10-30   STANDARD COST VARIANCES FOR OVERHEAD: JOURNAL ENTRIES The variance analysis section of the Job Cost Reports for the jobs that Costa Corporation worked on during a recent year are summarized as follows:

CO 7

Variance Analysis

Labor	Actual Cost	Input Standard Cost	Output Standard Cost	Labor Rate Variance	Labor Efficiency Variance
Job 245	$ 89,000	$ 92,000	$ 86,000	$3,000	$(6,000)
Job 246	74,000	72,000	72,000	(2,000)	–0–
Total	$163,000	$164,000	$158,000	$1,000	$(6,000)

The company has established predetermined manufacturing overhead rates as follows:

Variable manufacturing overhead: 50% of standard direct labor cost
Fixed manufacturing overhead: 200% of standard direct labor cost

The actual cost for overhead was as follows:

Variable manufacturing overhead	$82,000
Fixed manufacturing overhead	$320,000

Prepare the journal entries to record the actual and the applied overhead costs for variable overhead and for fixed overhead.

Problems

10-31   INCOME DETERMINATION DePauw Company maintains a job costing account-ing system. At the beginning of the most recent fiscal year, the balance sheet indicated the follow-ing inventory account balances:

CO 1, 7

Raw Materials	$10,000
Work in Process	50,000
Finished Goods	70,000

During the year the following transactions took place:

1. Raw materials purchased on account, $500,000.
2. Direct labor, $700,000.
3. Factory heat and light, $30,000.
4. Manufacturing depreciation, $50,000.
5. Selling and administrative expense incurred, $300,000.
6. Other manufacturing overhead expense, $280,000.
7. Raw materials removed from the storeroom and used in production, $490,000.
8. The company applies manufacturing overhead to the product at the rate of 50% of direct labor costs.
9. Finished goods with a manufacturing cost of $1,500,000 were moved to the finished goods warehouse during the year.
10. Finished goods with a cost of $1,550,000 were sold to customers for $2,000,000.

REQUIRED

a. Prepare journal entries to record the information given above.

b. Prepare T accounts for the inventory accounts and the Manufacturing Overhead Control ac-count and determine the ending balance for each account.

c. Prepare the journal entry to close the Manufacturing Overhead Control account to the Cost of Goods Sold account.

d. Prepare the income statement for the year to show the pretax income.

CO 1, 4

10-32 INCOMPLETE AND COMPLETED JOBS Franklin Company, which uses a job costing system, had two jobs in process at the beginning of the year. The jobs and the costs associated with those jobs per the beginning work in process inventory were as follows:

	Job RS-10	Job KT-34
Direct material	$ 8,000	$12,000
Direct labor	6,000	20,000
Manufacturing overhead	6,000	20,000
Total	$20,000	$52,000

The beginning work in process inventory was the total of those two incomplete jobs, or $72,000.

The following costs were incurred during the year on the jobs indicated:

	Job RS-10	Job GT-33	Job HY-20	Job KT-34	Total
Direct material	$12,000	$ 50,000	$35,000	$100,000	$197,000
Direct labor	50,000	200,000	75,000	350,000	675,000

Overhead was applied at the rate of 100% of direct labor cost. Jobs RS-10, KT-34, and GT-33 were completed and sold during the year; and Job HY-20 was still in process at the end of the year. The amount invoiced to customers for the three completed jobs was as follows:

	Invoice Amount
Job RS-10	$ 200,000
Job KT-34	1,500,000
Job GT-33	800,000

Selling and administrative costs for the year were $300,000.

REQUIRED

a. Compute the cost of completed jobs.

b. Compute the value of ending work in process inventory.

c. Compute the pretax income for the year.

CO 1, 4

10-33 JOURNAL ENTRIES IN JOB COSTING SYSTEM Smart Company compiled the following data for 19X1, a year in which there were only two jobs worked on. Of the current costs of production, 60% of the costs were incurred for Job WT-10 and the remaining 40% was incurred for Job RL-23.

Payroll costs	
(75% is direct labor)	$ 300,000
Direct materials purchased	250,000
Direct materials used	210,000
Factory equipment depreciation	30,000
Factory building depreciation	150,000
Indirect factory supplies used	20,000
Miscellaneous factory overhead	30,000
Sales	1,000,000

Manufacturing overhead is applied to the jobs at the rate of 100% of direct labor. There is no beginning or ending work in process inventory. Both jobs were completed and sent to the finished goods warehouse. The customer for Job WT-10 picked up the entire job before the end of the year. The customer for Job RL-23 had picked up all but 10% of the product. That remaining 10% will have to be classified as ending finished goods inventory on the balance sheet of Smart Company.

REQUIRED

Prepare journal entries to reflect the information shown above.

10-34 WORK IN PROCESS ENDING INVENTORY Manchester Company uses a job costing accounting system and manufacturing overhead is applied to jobs at the rate of 150% of direct labor cost. Work in process at the beginning of the period was as follows:

CO 1, 3

	R-3	R-4	R-5	R-6
Direct materials	$2,000	$3,000	$ 4,000	$ 5,000
Direct labor	1,500	2,000	2,500	3,000
Applied overhead	2,250	3,000	3,750	4,500
Total	$5,750	$8,000	$10,250	$12,500

The total work in process inventory at the beginning of the period was the total of the jobs shown above: $36,500.

The following materials and labor costs were incurred during the period:

	Direct Materials	Direct Labor
R-3	$ 1,000	$ 500
R-4	2,000	1,000
R-5	1,500	800
R-6	500	300
R-7	2,700	900
R-8	3,200	2,000
R-9	2,400	1,100
Total	$13,300	$6,600

Actual factory overhead costs were $10,000 for the period. Jobs R-8 and R-9 were still in process at the end of the period. All other jobs had been delivered to the customers.

REQUIRED

a. Compute the work in process inventory at the end of the period.

b. Calculate the cost of goods sold.

10-35 JOURNAL ENTRIES Earlham Company uses a job cost system. Transactions completed during one month were as follows. There were no beginning inventories.

CO 1, 7

1. Purchased raw materials and supplies at a cost of $25,000.

2. Raw materials and supplies were issued from the storeroom during the month as follows:

Direct materials:

Job MS-10	$4,000	
Job MS-11	8,000	
Job MS-12	7,000	
Total direct materials		$19,000
Add: Factory supplies		3,000
Total materials used		$22,000

3. The factory payroll was as follows:

Direct labor:

Job MS-10	$ 8,000	
Job MS-11	12,000	
Job MS-12	11,000	
Total direct labor		$31,000
Add: Indirect labor		9,000
Total labor		$40,000

4. Other factory overhead costs were $6,000 for the month.

5. Manufacturing overhead was applied to product at the rate of 60% of direct labor cost.

6. Jobs MS-10 and MS-11 were completed and transferred to finished goods inventory.

7. Job MS-10 was delivered to the customer prior to the end of the month and the customer was charged $22,000.

REQUIRED

Prepare the journal entries to record the transactions shown above. Include the journal entry that closes out the manufacturing overhead control account for the overapplied or underapplied manufacturing overhead.

10-36   **JOB COST REPORT, STANDARD COSTS, VARIANCE ANALYSIS** Sewanee Corporation builds redwood patios to customers' specifications. In a recent month, Sewanee CO 1, 5, 6   Corporation built patios for two different customers. The following information was assembled by the accounting department:

	Job 244	Job 245
Standard cost of materials for the job	$1,000	$1,800
Actual cost of materials used	$1,100	$1,950
Standard hours of direct labor	100	160
Standard cost of labor for the job	$800	$1,280
Actual hours of direct labor	130	150
Actual cost of labor for the job	$1,105	$1,275

The variable overhead rate is $4 per standard direct labor hour. The fixed manufacturing overhead rate is $6 per standard direct labor hour.

REQUIRED

a. Prepare a job cost report for each job to show the actual materials and direct labor costs and the applied variable and fixed manufacturing overhead. Prepare a variance analysis section at the bottom of the report to show the variances associated with direct materials and direct labor.

10-37 **JOB COST REPORT, JOURNAL ENTRIES, INVENTORY ACCOUNTS**
Ireland Company's accounting records indicate the following information related to June 19X1.

CO 4, 5, 7   1. The raw materials inventory at the end of May was as follows:

Material XX	$30,000
Material YY	20,000
Total	$50,000

2. Receipt of raw materials during June:

Material XX	$10,000
Material YY	5,000

3. Issue of direct materials from the raw materials inventory storeroom per issue slips dated in June:

Material XX for Job 632	$8,000
Material XX for Job 633	3,000
Material YY for Job 632	4,000
Material YY for Job 633	1,000

4. The beginning work in process inventory includes the following:

Job 632	$70,000
Job 633	50,000

The job cost reports for jobs 632 and 633 at the end of May showed the following details:

	Job 632	Job 633
Direct materials	$26,000	$28,000
Direct labor	20,000	10,000
Variable manufacturing overhead applied	4,000	2,000
Fixed manufacturing overhead applied	20,000	10,000
Total	$70,000	$50,000

5. The beginning finished goods inventory consisted of the following:

Job 630	$120,000
Job 631	80,000

6. Direct labor payroll for June was as follows:

Job 632	$30,000
Job 633	10,000

7. Variable manufacturing overhead is applied to jobs based on 20% of direct labor costs, and fixed manufacturing overhead is applied to jobs based on 100% of direct labor costs.

8. Job 632 was completed in June and sent to finished goods inventory to await shipment to the customer in July.

9. Job 630 and Job 631 were shipped to the customers in early June. The customer for Job 630 was billed $150,000 and the customer for Job 631 was billed $110,000.

REQUIRED

a. Prepare the journal entries to record the relevant information shown above.

b. Prepare the job cost reports for Jobs 632 and 633.

c. Prepare the T accounts for the raw materials inventory, the work in process inventory, and the finished goods inventory to determine the balance in each of those accounts at the end of June.

10-38 JOB COST REPORT, JOURNAL ENTRIES, INVENTORY ACCOUNTS

CO 4, 5, 7

Halgarth Company uses a job costing system to account for the costs of various jobs that are undertaken for clients. Information pertaining to November is as follows:

1. The beginning work in process inventory on November 1 had a balance of $150,000. The job cost reports for the two jobs that were in process at the end of October showed the following:

	Job 813	Job 814	Total
Direct material	$30,000	$ 40,000	$ 70,000
Direct labor	10,000	30,000	40,000
Manufacturing overhead applied			
(variable and fixed)	10,000	30,000	40,000
Total	$50,000	$100,000	$150,000

2. During November, the following direct costs were incurred:

	Job 813	Job 814	Job 815
Direct materials issued	$10,000	$15,000	$25,000
Direct labor costs	15,000	12,000	20,000

3. The company has established a predetermined manufacturing overhead rate that is as follows:

Variable manufacturing overhead	30% of direct labor costs
Fixed manufacturing overhead	70% of direct labor costs

4. The beginning inventory for raw materials inventory at November 1 was $80,000. During November, direct materials with a cost of $13,000 were purchased and received into the raw materials inventory storeroom.

5. Beginning finished goods inventory is zero. During November, Job 813 was completed, moved to finished goods, and then delivered to the customer. The customer was billed $100,000 for the job.

REQUIRED

a. Prepare the journal entries suggested by the relevant transactions listed above.

b. Prepare a summary that shows the costs accumulated on each job at the end of November.

c. Using T accounts, calculate the balance in all of the inventory accounts at the end of November.

10-39 INCOME STATEMENT AND PROFITABILITY ANALYSIS FOR A SERVICE ORGANIZATION Aviel and Associates is an architectural firm that has a job costing system to account for the costs incurred on the various jobs undertaken by the firm. A summary of the job cost reports for the year ended December 31, 19X2, is as follows:

CO 4, 5, 7

Job Cost Report
Aviel & Associates
19X2

	Resort Job	Hotel Job	Stadium Job	Total
Work in process at beginning of year:				
Direct labor	$120,000	$180,000	$220,000	$ 520,000
Supplies	8,000	10,000	25,000	43,000
Application of overhead	60,000	90,000	110,000	260,000
Total	$188,000	$280,000	$355,000	$ 823,000
Cost in current year:				
Direct labor	$200,000	$ 50,000	$300,000	$ 550,000
Supplies	10,000	20,000	15,000	45,000
Application of overhead	100,000	25,000	150,000	275,000
Total for job	$498,000	$375,000	$820,000	$1,693,000

As indicated by the preceding summary, the rate used for application of overhead was 50% of direct labor. The actual overhead costs during the current year were $285,000.

As in all service organizations, there are no inventories. The costs are treated as expenses in the year in which they are incurred, and the client is typically billed periodically throughout the year. In this year, billings to clients totaled $1,030,000. This amount was associated with the three jobs as follows:

	19X2 Revenues
Resort job	$ 400,000
Hotel job	80,000
Stadium job	550,000
Total	$1,030,000

Billings on the three jobs in the prior year (or years) were as follows:

	Prior-year Revenues
Resort job	$200,000
Hotel job	290,000
Stadium job	450,000
Total	$940,000

The marketing expenses during this year were $80,000. These expenses are not included in the calculation of the overhead rate.

REQUIRED

a. Based on the information shown above, prepare the income statement for the year 19X2. Show the underapplied overhead separately.

b. Prepare a schedule that shows the profitability of each of the three jobs.

c. The hotel job was complete as of December 31, 19X2, and the final billing has been submitted to the client. The resort job was 50% complete as of December 31 of that year, and 50% of the agreed-upon fee of $1,200,000 has been billed the client. The stadium job was 90% complete as of the end of 19X2, and the final billing of $50,000 is expected to be sent to the client on January 15, 19X3.

All of these jobs were awarded to Aviel Associates based on a bidding process. The amount of each bid and the expected profit for each job at the time of the bid is shown below:

	Amount of Bid	Expected Profit
Resort job	$1,200,000	$200,000
Hotel job	370,000	50,000
Stadium job	1,050,000	400,000

Based on your answers given in requirements a and b, comment on the extent to which each job is likely to achieve its expected profit.

Business Decision Case

La Jolla Corporation manufactures specialized machinery based on customer specifications. During the first month of operations, the company undertook two major jobs. One of the jobs, Job 573, was completed during the month and delivered to the customer before the end of the month. The other job, Job 574, was still in process at the end of the first month. The process engineer estimated that 80% of the work (as budgeted) had been completed on Job 574 and that all of the materials that were going to be used on Job 574 had already been issued to the job.

The accounting department has summarized the materials issue slips and time cards as follows:

	Job 573	Job 574
Materials used (standard cost)	$12,000	$18,000
Actual labor hours	1,250	1,700
Actual labor cost	$20,000	$25,500

The engineering department had made the following estimates based on standard costs when the bids were prepared for these two jobs:

	Job 573	Job 574
Materials expected to be used at standard costs	$12,500	$18,900
Labor hours expected to be used	1,200	2,100
Standard labor rate per hour	$15.50	$15.50
Variable manufacturing overhead rate per standard (expected) labor hour	$5	$5
Fixed manufacturing overhead rate per standard (expected) labor hour	$12	$12

Additional information is as follows:

Actual variable manufacturing overhead	$17,000
Actual fixed manufacturing overhead	39,000
Actual general and administrative costs	15,000

The engineering department bid $75,000 for Job 573 and $100,000 for Job 574; those bids were accepted by the customers.

REQUIRED

a. Prepare a job cost report for each of the two jobs. At the bottom of the report, show the variance analysis and the total standard cost of each job.

b. Prepare the journal entries necessary to permit the preparation of the financial statements at the end of the month.

c. Prepare the inventory section of the balance sheet at the end of the first month and prepare the income statement showing favorable and unfavorable variances for the first month.

d. Analyze the income statement and advise La Jolla's vice president for manufacturing about areas of concern.

11

Product Costing Using Process Costing

CHAPTER OBJECTIVES

After reading Chapter 11 you should be able to:

1. Calculate equivalent production units for various resource uses in manufacturing products in a particular department for a particular accounting period (pp. 378–80).

2. Prepare the cost of production report for a department that has no beginning inventory (pp. 380–83).

3. Prepare the cost of production report for a department where manufacturing begins that has beginning work in process inventory and uses the weighted average cost flow assumption (pp. 384–87).

4. Prepare the cost of production report for a department where

manufacturing begins that has beginning work in process inventory and uses the first in, first out (FIFO) cost flow assumption (pp. 387–91).

5. Prepare the cost of production report for a department that receives work in process from another department, has beginning inventory, and uses the first-in, first-out (FIFO) cost flow assumption (pp. 391–94).

6. Discuss the decision support systems and behavioral aspects of process costing (p. 394).

C hapter 10 introduced product costing and focused on job costing. This chapter concentrates on process costing, the other means of product costing. As Chapter 10 mentioned briefly, the manufacturing environment dictates whether process costing or job costing should be used. Process costing is indicated when (1) the customer is not known, as in the production of goods from which customers will select, and (2) there is no way to distinguish one lot of product from another.

PROCESS COSTING

While the job costing system is centered around a job order, the process costing system is centered around the department. Instead of being issued to identifiable jobs, materials are issued to departments. Instead of charging time to jobs, employees charge their time to the department in which they work.

The focus of process costing systems is on the accumulation of costs by department within the factory. Because the lots of product are not uniquely identified, issues from the raw materials storeroom and direct labor recorded on the time card are charged to the departments to which the material was issued and the department in which the employee worked.

The cost per unit for direct materials and direct labor is determined by dividing the number of units produced during a time period into the cost of the resource used during that period. The overhead costs are allocated to the units of product based on an overhead rate that is related to direct labor hours or some other indicator of overhead usage.

The following discussion of process costing pertains to a company that manufactures a product in two producing departments, machining and assembly. The period of time that will be covered is two monthly accounting periods, October and November. Actual costs rather than standard costs will be used, even though standard costs with variances could be used in a process cost system. First, the *weighted average* cost flow assumption will be demonstrated and discussed; then the *first in, first out (FIFO)* cost flow assumption will be demonstrated and discussed.

Cost of Production Report: An Overview

Process costing involves the creation of a *cost of production report* instead of job tickets. This report is designed to show which costs move from one department to another and to finished goods during the month and which costs remain in work in process inventory. Because we will be allocating total manufacturing costs among cost of goods sold, finished goods inventory, and assembly department work in process inventory, the necessity of a cost flow assumption (weighted average or FIFO) should be clear.

Cost Flow Assumptions

As a refresher of cost flow assumptions, consider the following. Suppose a firm has 100 units of beginning inventory at $1 each. It purchases 100 units at $2 each and later purchases another 100 units at $3 each. During the period, the entity sells 250 units, so

50 units are left as ending inventory. Notice that the cost of goods available for sale is $600 [(100 × $1) + (100 × $2) + (100 × $3)]. How much is the cost of goods sold and how much is the ending inventory? To determine these amounts, one must invoke a cost flow assumption. We will focus on only two possibilities, weighted average and FIFO.

To use the weighted average method, calculate the weighted average cost per unit. Then multiply this number by the units sold to get cost of goods sold; multiply it by the units left in inventory to obtain the cost of ending inventory. The weighted average cost per unit is the cost of goods available for sale divided by the number of units available for sale. In this example, the weighted average cost per unit is $600/300 units, or $2. Thus, the cost of goods sold is $2 × 250 units, or $500. The cost of ending inventory is $2 × 50 units, or $100. Of course, the cost of goods sold plus the cost of ending inventory equals the cost of goods available for sale.

FIFO assumes that the goods are sold in the order they were acquired. In this example, the first 100 units sold are out of beginning inventory, the second 100 units sold are out of the first purchase lot, and the last 50 units sold are out of the second purchase lot. Then, the cost of goods sold is $450 [($1 × 100) + ($2 × 100) + ($3 × 50)]. The cost of the ending inventory is $150 ($3 × 50). Again, cost of goods sold plus the cost of ending inventory equals the cost of goods available for sale.

Example of Cost of Production Report

The cost of production report contains two basic sections. The first section concerns units of production and the second section concerns cost. The units section contains a statement about which department the units came from and which department the units go to next. In a properly prepared report the units to be accounted for equal the units accounted for. In the cost section, the same balance of units in process exists. The costs placed into production must equal the costs transferred out plus those remaining in work in process.

In order to prepare the cost of production reports for October, the first month of operation (thus there is no beginning inventory), we will assume the following information. Note: The distinction between the weighted average and the FIFO cost flow assumptions is not important when there is no beginning inventory.

1. All of the materials are issued to the Machining Department.

2. The Machining Department has the materials in hand when it begins work on the product.

3. Labor is expended on a pro rata basis throughout both departments. If the partially completed product has moved to the mid-point of either department, we can assume that one-half of the labor of that department has been expended on the product.

4. The product is inspected by quality control personnel before it leaves the Machining Department and also before it leaves the Assembly Department and moves to finished goods inventory. An inspection report is sent to the accounting department.

5. When there are beginning work in process inventories (as there will be at the beginning of November), the weighted average cost flow assumption will be used.

HOW MILLIKEN STAYS ON TOP

Milliken & Co., a leading textile manufacturer, recently changed its cost accounting system by simplifying its standard cost system and implementing nonfinancial measures of performance such as reductions in lead time, set-up time, and down time. These changes have improved operations and reduced cost, according to the article from which this excerpt is drawn.

OVERVIEW OF COST SYSTEM

Milliken uses a "process cost" system, which means manufacturing costs are accumulated at each process, or cost center. Because the costs of raw materials, such as cotton, fluctuate widely over short periods of time, and because these costs represent a large portion of total costs, raw materials are costed at "actual." Other manufacturing costs are accumulated at "standard costs" established by plant managers and industrial engineers for such variables as labor, supplies, indirect materials and waste. Overhead is applied on machine hours, except for such labor-related overhead as payroll taxes and fringe benefits, which is applied on labor hours.

RECOMMENDED CHANGES

. . . Milliken developed three broad recommendations designed to improve and upgrade the old cost accounting system.

1. *Emphasize actual costs for process and cost control and deemphasize standard costs.* By focusing on actual costs, managers would know their impact on company profits and could concentrate on reducing them—and increasing margins—rather than on meeting standards. . . .

2. *Continue using plant standards for product costing but update them quarterly rather than annually.* Thus, the standards would reflect more current conditions, and realistic costs would lead to better decisions—including those on product pricing.

3. *Include nonfinancial measures for process and cost control.* Developing nonfinancial measures for process and cost control would result in more timely, relevant feedback, enabling production personnel and plant managers to make immediate adjustments to improve operations. . . .

THE BOTTOM LINE

While management accounting experts have long recommended the adoption of nonfinancial measures to enhance productivity, Milliken's experience proves these measures can result in concomitant improvements in cost control and reduction. . . .

SOURCE: Adapted from James Don Edwards, Cynthia D. Heagy, and Harold W. Rakes, "How Milliken Stays on Top," *Journal of Accountancy* (April 1989), pp. 63–74. Adapted by permission.

The following activities occurred in October:

1. The Machining Department started 9,000 units into production.
2. Quality control inspected 8,500 units during the month. All of these units were sent on to the Assembly Department.
3. Five hundred partially completed units remained in the machining department at the end of October.
4. Direct materials with a cost of $18,000 were charged to the Machining Department in October.

5. Direct labor and manufacturing overhead (*conversion costs*) of $8,875 were charged to the Machining Department in October. This charge was based on time cards and the predetermined overhead rate that was applied using actual direct labor hours.

6. The 500 units in work in process inventory were approximately 75% complete as of the end of October. Thus, because of the pro rata application of labor assumption, we assume that three-fourths of the total labor in the Machining Department has been expended on these units.

The cost of production report is prepared for the Machining Department for the month of October to determine the portion of the costs charged to the department that moved on to the Assembly Department in October.

The Machining Department's cost of production report is contained in Exhibit 11-1. Started in production are 9,000 units; of these, 8,500 are completed and transferred to the next department, the rest are incomplete and stay in machining.

CHAPTER OBJECTIVE 1
Calculate equivalent units

Equivalent units are the number of units that could have been completed if the entire effort were spent only on making whole units. To clarify, consider in this example that 8,500 units were started and completed in this month. Five hundred additional units were started but not completed. But these 500 units are 100% complete with respect to materials. So the equivalent units with respect to materials is $8,500 + 500 = 9,000$ units. These same 500 units, however, are only 75% complete with respect to conversion (labor and overhead). So the equivalent units with respect to conversion is 75% of 500 or 375. The total number of equivalent units with respect to conversion is 8,875 (8,500 + 375).

As stated before and as shown in Exhibit 11-1, the organization expended $18,000 for materials (for a cost per equivalent unit of $2 [$18,000/9,000]) and $8,875 for **conversion costs** (for a cost per equivalent unit of $1 [$8,875/8,875]). Armed with this data, we can now cost the units transferred to the Assembly Department and those units still in the Machining Department. The cost of units transferred to assembly is as follows:

$$8,500 \times (\$2 + \$1) = \$25,500$$

The cost of units still in machining is

$$500 \times \$2 = \$1,000$$
$$375 \times \$1 = \underline{\quad 375}$$
$$\underline{\underline{\$1,375}}$$

The cost of production report for October reflects the fact that the following journal entry had been made during the month to charge the Machining Department's Work in Process account for the resources used:

1.	Work in Process—Machining Department	26,875	
	Direct Materials		18,000
	Conversion Costs		8,875

EXHIBIT 11-1

MACHINING DEPARTMENT OCTOBER COST OF PRODUCTION REPORT

Cost of Production Report
Machining Department
October 19XX

Units to Be Accounted For:

Units Started	9,000 units

Units Accounted For:

Transferred to Assembly Department	8,500
In ending work in process inventory (100% materials, 75% conversion)	500
Total units accounted for	9,000 units

Costs to Be Accounted For:

Resource	Cost	Equivalent Production	Cost per Unit
Materials	$18,000	9,000 units	$2
Conversion	8,875	8,875 units	1
Total costs to be accounted for	$26,875		$3

Costs Accounted For:

Cost of units transferred to Assembly Department (8,500 × $3)		$25,500
Ending work in process inventory in Machining Department:		
Materials portion (500 × $2)	$1,000	
Conversion portion (500 × .75 × $1)	375	
Total ending work in process inventory		1,375
Total costs accounted for		$26,875

The cost of production report is the basis on which the following journal entry is made to transfer some of the cost to the Assembly Department.

2.	Work in Process—Assembly Department	25,500	
	Work in Process—Machining Department		25,500

After the last entry is made, the balance in the Work in Process—Machining account will be $1,375 ($26,875 − $25,500), the amount shown on the cost of production report as the work in process ending inventory amount.

Process Costing and Activity-based Costing

Activity-based costing was described in Chapter 8. In Chapter 10 it was pointed out that activity-based costing can be used with job costing. In a similar way, activity-based costing can be linked with process costing.

In the first stage of activity-based costing, the management accountant groups activities whose costs are determined by the same economic factor. He or she collects the costs of these activities in what is termed a *cost pool*. A cost driver is selected for this cost pool and a pool rate is determined. This pool rate is then used to cost that particular resource.

In this chapter we have implicitly assumed that there is only one cost pool per department. But process costing can still be applied if there are multiple cost pools per department. We simply determine how much of the cost driver is used for a cost pool and charge the process for that amount times the pool rate. We do this for each cost pool. These costs, along with direct materials and direct labor, will give the costs for the processing department for that time period.

As a practical matter, however, firms might set up the cost pools as departments. Then each department will charge one and only one pool rate. The product, however, is charged several pool rates as it goes through the various departments. In the previous example, the Machining Department might charge one pool rate while the Assembly Department charges another rate. In other words, if the departments are established as cost pools, traditional process costing actually uses activity-based costing.

PREPARING THE COST OF PRODUCTION REPORT: NO BEGINNING INVENTORY

The purpose of the cost of production report is to permit the accounting department to make the journal entry just shown. That journal entry will be accurate only to the extent that the departmental cost per unit is accurate.

The accuracy of the departmental cost per unit depends on several elements:

1. *Proper accounting for the units.* You must know how many units were transferred to the next department and how many units remain in ending work in process inventory. Further, you must know the percentage of completion of the units in ending work in process inventory.

2. *Proper accounting for the costs.* The costs charged to the department are determined by reference to the appropriate general ledger accounts. However, a major challenge is determining the cost per unit. It is this cost per unit that is necessary to determine the amount of cost that was attached to the units that were moved to the next department.

3. *Correct calculation of the equivalent units.* The calculation of equivalent units is an attempt to relate the cost of each resource (materials and conversion) to a number of units that will yield an appropriate cost per unit. In doing this we ask the question, "How much production did that cost incurred buy?" In the case of

materials costs, it is the $18,000 paid for the materials in all of the units transferred to assembly (8,500 units) and in all of the units in work in process inventory (500 units). Thus, the equivalent production for the materials resource is 9,000 units. This is true because we are certain that each unit in work in process inventory has its required materials.

For the conversion resource, the equivalent production equals the 8,500 units transferred to assembly plus three-fourths of the units in work in process inventory, or 375 units. Thus, the equivalent production associated with the conversion resource is 8,875 units.

The use of 375 units to represent the number of equivalent production units in work in process inventory deserves more explanation. Ending work in process inventory in the Machining Department is considered to be three-fourths complete. That probably means that no work in process unit is completely finished but that each unit is partially complete. Although contrary to fact, we reason as if 375 of the 500 work in process units were completely finished and thus apply all of the conversion resource to them. This is a convenient assumption to arrive at a cost per unit.

4. *Proper costing of the units transferred.* Once the cost per unit is determined using the correct equivalent production, the units transferred to the next department may be costed and the costs move to the next department along with the units.

5. *The equality of units to be accounted for and units accounted for and the equality of costs to be accounted for and costs accounted for.* In the Machining Department for October, 9,000 units are accounted for and all of the $26,875 in costs is accounted for.

The cost of production report for the Assembly Department for October is shown in Exhibit 11-2. You will notice that units and costs transferred from the Machining Department in October appear as units and costs *transferred into* this department in the same month.

Prior to the preparation of the cost of production report for October, the following journal entry would have been prepared to charge the Assembly Department for conversion costs it incurred during the month:

3.	Work in Process—Assembly Department	11,250	
	Conversion Costs		11,250

From the information on the cost of production report for October for the Assembly Department, the following journal entry will be prepared:

4.	Finished Goods Inventory	31,500	
	Work in Process—Assembly Department		31,500

Assuming that 6,000 of the 7,000 units transferred to finished goods inventory were sold during October at a price of $6 per unit, the following journal entry would

EXHIBIT 11-2

ASSEMBLY DEPARTMENT OCTOBER COST OF PRODUCTION REPORT

Cost of Production Report
Assembly Department
October 19XX

Units to Be Accounted For:

Transferred in from Machining Department	8,500 units

Units Accounted For:

Transferred to finished goods inventory	7,000
In ending work in process inventory (1/3 conversion)	1,500
Total units accounted for	8,500 units

Costs to Be Accounted For:

Resource	Cost	Equivalent Production	Cost per Unit
Units and cost from preceding department	$25,500	8,500 units	$3.00
Materials	–0–	–0–	–0–
Conversion	11,250	7,500 units	1.50
Total costs to be accounted for	$36,750		$4.50

Costs Accounted For:

Transferred to finished goods inventory (7,000 × $4.50)		$31,500
Ending work in process inventory in Assembly Department:		
Costs from preceding department (1,500 × $3)	$4,500	
Conversion portion (1,500 × .333 × $1.50)	750	
Total ending work in process inventory		5,250
Total costs accounted for		$36,750

be made to record the sale and remove 6/7 of the cost from finished goods inventory. (The "6/7" refers to the fact that 6,000 of the 7,000 units transferred to finished goods were sold.)

5.	Accounts Receivable	36,000	
	Sales		36,000
6.	Cost of Goods Sold	27,000	
	Finished Goods Inventory		27,000

EXHIBIT 11-3

SELECTED GENERAL LEDGER ACCOUNTS
AT END OF OCTOBER

Work in Process—
Machining Department

(1) $26,875	(2) $25,500
Bal. $ 1,375	

Work in Process—
Assembly Department

(2) $25,500	(4) $31,500
(3) $11,250	
Bal. $ 5,250	

Finished Goods Inventory

(4) $31,500	(6) $27,000
Bal. $ 4,500	

Cost of Goods Sold

(6) $27,000	
Bal. $27,000	

After these journal entries are posted, selected general ledger accounts would appear at the end of October as shown in Exhibit 11-3.

A balance sheet prepared on October 31 would include the following inventory accounts balances:

Work in Process—Machining Department	$1,375	
Work in Process—Assembly Department	5,250	
Total Work in Process Inventory		$6,625
Finished Goods Inventory		$4,500

Notice that the Machining Department's work in process inventory of $1,375 and the Assembly Department's work in process inventory of $5,250 agree with the amounts shown in ending work in process inventory of the cost of production reports for each of the departments.

PREPARING THE COST OF PRODUCTION REPORT: BEGINNING INVENTORY, WEIGHTED AVERAGE ASSUMPTION

CHAPTER
OBJECTIVE 3
*Cost of production
report—beginning
inventory, weighted
average*

The ending work in process balances for October will appear on the cost of production reports for November as beginning inventory balances. It is the presence of a beginning work in process inventory for the second month that forces a choice concerning the cost flow assumption to be used in preparing the cost of production report. First, we demonstrate and discuss the *weighted average* cost flow assumption. The demonstration and discussion of the FIFO cost flow assumption follows this section.

The November cost of production report using the weighted average assumption is shown in Exhibit 11-4. There are several elements of this report that require additional discussion.

1. Among the units to be accounted for are the 500 units in the Machining Department's ending work in process inventory at the end of October. That quantity is regarded as beginning inventory in November.

2. The "costs to be accounted for" section contains a separate identification of the costs included in the prior month's ending inventory. Refer to the Machining Department's October cost of production report (Exhibit 11-1). The ending inventory contained $1,000 of materials costs and $375 of conversion costs. Those costs are added to the costs incurred in the current period (November) to arrive at the cost of each resource that must be accounted for.

3. The equivalent production associated with the cost included in the beginning work in process inventory is determined by reference to the prior month's cost of production report for this department. Thus, the number of units associated with the material cost of $1,000 was 500 units; and the number of units associated with the $375 was 375 units (75% of 500).

4. The equivalent production associated with the current period costs is determined as follows (equivalent production for conversion is used as an example):

Units transferred out	8,500 units
Less: Beginning work in process inventory	
(in equivalent units)	375 units
	8,125 units
Add: Ending work in process inventory	
(in equivalent units)	1,000 units
Total equivalent production	9,125 units

5. The equivalent production for beginning inventory is added to the equivalent production for the current period to arrive at a total called the *production divisor*. For material costs, the production divisor of 10,500 units is divided into the total material costs of $21,525 to arrive at material cost per unit of $2.05 (see Exhibit 11-4).

6. Several lines in the cost per unit column contain "N.A." for "not applicable." This is because the cost per unit is the quotient of cost divided by the production divisor, not the sum of the cost per unit for beginning inventory and the cost per unit for the current period.

EXHIBIT 11-4

MACHINING DEPARTMENT NOVEMBER COST OF PRODUCTION REPORT (WEIGHTED AVERAGE COST FLOW ASSUMPTION)

Cost of Production Report
Machining Department
November 19XX

Units to Be Accounted For:

Beginning work in process inventory (100% materials, 75% conversion)	500 units
Units started	10,000 units
Total units to be accounted for	10,500 units

Units Accounted For:

Transferred to Assembly Department	8,500 units
In ending work in process inventory (100% materials, 50% conversion)	2,000 units
Total units accounted for	10,500 units

Costs to Be Accounted For:

Resource	Cost	Equivalent Production	Cost per Unit
Materials:			
Beginning inventory	$ 1,000	500 units	N.A.
Current period	20,525	10,000 units	N.A.
	$21,525	10,500 units	$2.05
Conversion:			
Beginning inventory	$ 375	375 units	N.A.
Current period	10,075	9,125 units	N.A.
	$10,450	9,500 units	$1.10
Total costs to be accounted for	$31,975		$3.15

Costs Accounted For:

Cost of units transferred to Assembly Department (8,500 × $3.15)		$26,775
Ending work in process inventory in Machining Department:		
Materials portion (2,000 × $2.05)	$4,100	
Conversion portion (2,000 × .50 × $1.10)	1,100	
Total ending work in process inventory		5,200
Total costs accounted for		$31,975

EXHIBIT 11-5

ASSEMBLY DEPARTMENT
NOVEMBER COST OF PRODUCTION REPORT
(WEIGHTED AVERAGE COST FLOW ASSUMPTION)

Cost of Production Report
Assembly Department
November 19XX

Units to Be Accounted For:

Beginning work in process inventory	
(100% preceding department, 1/3 conversion)	1,500 units
Transferred in from Machining Department	8,500 units
Total units to be accounted for	10,000 units

Units Accounted For:

Transferred to finished goods inventory	8,000 units
In ending work in process inventory	
(20% conversion)	2,000 units
Total units accounted for	10,000 units

Costs to Be Accounted For:

Resource	Cost	Equivalent Production	Cost per Unit
Cost transferred from preceding department:			
Beginning inventory	$ 4,500	1,500 units	N.A.
Current period	26,775	8,500 units	N.A.
	$31,275	10,000 units	$3.1275
Conversion:			
Beginning inventory	$ 750	500 units	N.A.
Current period	12,690	7,900 units	N.A.
	$13,440	8,400 units	$1.60
Total costs to be accounted for	$44,715		$4.7275

Costs Accounted For:

Cost of units transferred to finished goods inventory		
(8,000 units × $4.7275)		$37,820
Ending work in process inventory in Assembly Department:		
Costs from preceding department (2,000 units × $3.1275)	$6,255	
Conversion portion (2,000 units × .20 × $1.60)	640	
Total ending work in process inventory		6,895
Total costs accounted for		$44,715

The cost of production report for the Assembly Department in November reflects costs from three separate sources: (1) costs incurred in the Assembly Department in November, (2) costs incurred in the Machining Department during November and transferred to the Assembly Department during that period, and (3) costs incurred in a prior month (October) and held in the Assembly Department's ending work in process inventory at October 31.

The Assembly Department's cost of production report for November is shown in Exhibit 11-5.

There are some additional elements of the November cost of production report for the Assembly Department that require clarification:

1. The beginning inventory cost associated with the units transferred from the Machining Department ($4,500) plus the beginning inventory cost associated with conversion ($750) yield a total of $5,250. That amount, and the details supporting it, were reported as the ending inventory cost for the Assembly Department in October. This $5,250 moves into the cost to be accounted for by the Assembly Department in November.

2. The equivalent production associated with the beginning inventory costs come from the October cost of production report for the Assembly Department. The 1,500 units were multiplied by $3 on that report to arrive at the cost of $4,500. Likewise, the 500 units (1,500 × 1/3) for conversion were multiplied by $1.50 to arrive at the cost of $750.

3. The equivalent production associated with the current period costs was determined as follows:

	Transferred from Preceding Department	Conversion
Units transferred out	8,000 units	8,000 units
Less: Beginning work in process inventory (in equivalent units)	1,500 units	500 units
	6,500	7,500
Add: Ending work in process inventory (in equivalent units)	2,000 units	400 units
Total equivalent units	8,500 units	7,900 units

PREPARING THE COST OF PRODUCTION REPORT: BEGINNING INVENTORY, FIFO

CHAPTER OBJECTIVE 4
Cost of production report—beginning inventory, FIFO

As mentioned earlier, the presence of ending work in process inventory at the end of October forces a choice concerning the cost flow assumptions to be used in preparing the cost of production report for November. In the previous section we prepared the cost of production report based on the weighted average cost flow assumption. In this section we discuss and demonstrate the *first-in, first-out (FIFO)* cost flow assumption.

The November cost of production report for the Machining Department is shown in Exhibit 11-6. There are several elements of the November cost of production based on the FIFO assumption that require additional discussion.

1. The units portion of the cost of production report is identical to that in the cost of production report prepared using the weighted average cost flow assumption. There are no differences between the weighted average method and the FIFO method in accounting for units.

2. One of the differences between the two cost flow assumptions lies in the "costs to be accounted for" section of the cost of production report. This section is organized differently when using the weighted average method than when using the FIFO method. In the FIFO cost of production report, the costs of resources are organized with a primary focus on whether the costs are from beginning inventory or from the current period. In contrast, the weighted average cost of production report organizes the costs of resources with a primary focus on the type of resource (Materials or Conversion). The "costs to be accounted for" section for the two different cost flow assumptions is contrasted below:

Weighted Average	**FIFO**
Materials:	Beginning Inventory:
Beginning Inventory	Materials
Current Period	Conversion
Conversion:	Current Period:
Beginning Inventory	Materials
Current Period	Conversion

3. The different organization of the "costs to be accounted for" section occasions a different use of the equivalent production column to calculate the cost per unit column. The theory of the FIFO method is to regard the costs associated with the beginning inventory to be the first costs moved from the machining department to the assembly department as the month begins. The costs incurred during the current month are used to cost all other units completed and moved to the next department. Thus, we see the application of the first in, first out (FIFO) concept.

The calculation of equivalent production is the same for both methods; however, the manner in which the equivalent production is used is different in the FIFO method than in the weighted average method. Examination of the "costs to be accounted for" section of Exhibit 11-6 shows that the cost per unit is calculated for every resource item included in the resource column. In Exhibit 11-6, the cost per unit of the beginning inventory is $3; whereas the current-period cost is $3.1566 per unit. This indicates that the machining department's cost per unit has increased from October to November.

In contrast, the cost of production report in Exhibit 11-4, which uses the weighted average method, makes no distinction between costs incurred in October and costs incurred in November. Under the weighted average method, there was no need to make such a distinction because the purpose was to average the October costs with the November costs to arrive at a weighted average of the costs of materials and a weighted average of the costs of conversion.

4. The "costs accounted for" section of the FIFO cost of production report differs significantly from the same section in the weighted average cost of production report. The FIFO cost of production report requires an explanatory note in which a subcalculation is made.

That note, as shown below the "costs accounted for" section, is designed to calculate the equivalent units both finished and transferred to the next department in the current period. The equivalent units must be determined because they are the units transferred that must be costed using the unit costs experienced in the current period. The note, at the bottom of the "costs accounted for" section in Exhibit 11-6, reveals that of the 8,500 units transferred from Machining to Assembly in November, 500 equivalent units (for materials) are known to have come from beginning inventory. The remainder of the units transferred must have come from equivalent units completed during the current period.

EXHIBIT 11-6

MACHINING DEPARTMENT
NOVEMBER COST OF PRODUCTION REPORT
(FIFO COST FLOW ASSUMPTION)

Cost of Production Report
Machining Department
November 19XX

Units to Be Accounted For:

Beginning work in process inventory (100% materials, 75% conversion)	500 units
Units started	10,000 units
Total units to be accounted for	10,500 units

Units Accounted For:

Transferred to Assembly Department	8,500 units
In ending work in process inventory (100% materials, 50% conversion)	2,000 units
Total units accounted for	10,500 units

Costs to Be Accounted For:

Resource	Cost	Equivalent Production	Cost per Unit
Beginning inventory:			
Materials	$ 1,000	500 units	$2
Conversion	375	375 units	1
	$ 1,375		$3
Current period:			
Materials	$20,525	10,000 units	$2.0525
Conversion	10,075	9,125 units	1.1041
	$30,600		
Total costs to be accounted for	$31,975		$3.1566

EXHIBIT 11-6 *(continued)*

Costs Accounted For:

Cost of units transferred to Assembly Department:		
Materials (beginning inventory) (500 units × $2)	$ 1,000	
Conversion (beginning inventory) (375 units × $1)	375	
Costs from beginning inventory		$ 1,375
Materials (current period) (8,000 units × $2.0525)*	$16,420	
Conversion (current period) (8,125 units × $1.1041)*	8,971	
Costs related to current period		25,391
Total cost of units transferred to Assembly Department		$26,766
Ending work in process inventory in Machining Department:		
Materials (current period) (2,000 units × $2.0525)	$ 4,105	
Conversion (current period) (1,000 units × $1.1041)	1,104	
Total ending work in process inventory		5,209
Total costs accounted for		$31,975

*NOTE: The units transferred to the next department that are costed at the current period cost are determined as follows:

	Materials	Conversion
Units transferred	8,500	8,500
Less: Equivalent units from beginning inventory	500	375
Equivalent units finished and transferred in current period	8,000	8,125

It is important to remember that to the extent that units in beginning inventory are not complete, they must be completed in the current period. When they are completed in the current period, they incur current-period costs. This is illustrated by reference to the conversion column of the note beneath the "costs accounted for" section in Exhibit 11-6.

In the Machining Department for November, there were 500 units in beginning work in process inventory. However, those 500 units were only 75% complete with regard to conversion. Thus, only 375 of the 500 units were regarded as completed. The remaining 125 units had to be completed in November. This is documented in the calculation in the note, which shows that of the 8,500 units transferred, 375 units came from beginning inventory and the remaining 8,125 units (8,500 − 375) were completed and transferred in November.

5. The cost of units transferred to the Assembly Department (the next department) includes the cost attached to the equivalent units in inventory ($1,375 in Exhibit 11-6) plus the cost of the equivalent units finished and transferred in the current period. These finished and transferred equivalent units are obtained from the calculations in the note at the bottom of Exhibit 11-6, and they are costed using the current-period per-unit costs calculated for each resource in the "costs to be accounted for" section. The total cost of the units transferred is the sum of the

costs in beginning inventory plus the cost of the units completed and transferred in the current period. As Exhibit 11-6 shows, the total cost transferred is $26,766.

In accounting for the total costs, it is necessary to determine the cost of the units that are found in inventory at the *end* of the month. First the number of units in ending inventory are determined; then those units are converted to equivalent units based on the percentage of completion of each resource. The ending inventory in the machining department for November was 2,000 units that were 100% complete with regard to materials and 50% complete with regard to conversion. Thus, the ending inventory equivalent units for materials are 2,000 units; and the ending inventory equivalent units for conversion are 1,000 units (2,000 units × 50%).

In determining the cost associated with ending inventory, the equivalent units associated with each resource is costed using the per-unit cost calculated for each resource for the current period. As shown in Exhibit 11-6, this costing process results in an ending inventory cost of $5,209. When the cost of units transferred ($26,766) is added to the cost of ending inventory ($5,209), the sum ($31,975) is the same amount as the total of the costs to be accounted on the cost of production report.

CHAPTER OBJECTIVE 5
Cost of production report—receives work in process, beginning inventory, FIFO

As a result of the application of the preceding elements, the units transferred to the next department have costs that were incurred in the prior month and costs that were incurred in the current period. The units that remain in the ending inventory have only costs that were incurred in the current month. This result is consistent with the first in, first out cost flow assumption.

The Assembly Department's cost of production report for November is shown in Exhibit 11-7. Unlike Exhibit 11-5, which was prepared for the Assembly Department

---

EXHIBIT 11-7

ASSEMBLY DEPARTMENT
NOVEMBER COST OF PRODUCTION REPORT
(FIFO COST FLOW ASSUMPTION)

Cost of Production Report
Assembly Department
November 19XX

Units to Be Accounted For:

Beginning work in process inventory	
(100% preceding department, 1/3 conversion)	1,500 units
Transferred in from Machining Department	8,500 units
Total units to be accounted for	10,000 units

Units Accounted For:

Transferred to finished goods inventory	8,000 units
In ending work in process inventory	
(20% conversion)	2,000 units
Total units accounted for	10,000 units

EXHIBIT 11-7 *(continued)*

Costs to Be Accounted For:

Resource	Cost	Equivalent Production	Cost per Unit
Beginning inventory:			
Preceding department	$ 4,500	1,500 units	$3.00
Conversion	750	500 units	1.50
	$5,250		$4.50
Current period:			
Preceding department	$26,766	8,500 units	$3.1489
Conversion	12,690	7,900 units	1.6063
	$39,456		$4.7552
Total costs to be accounted for	$44,706		

Costs Accounted For:

Cost of units transferred to Assembly Department:		
Preceding department (beginning inventory)		
(1,500 units × $3)	$ 4,500	
Conversion (beginning inventory) (500 units × $1.50)	750	
Costs from beginning inventory		$ 5,250
Preceding department (current period) (6,500 units ×		
$3.1489)*	$20,468	
Conversion (current period) (7,500 units × $1.6063)*	12,047	
Costs related to current period		32,515
Total cost of units transferred to Assembly Department		$37,765
Ending work in process inventory in Machining Department:		
Preceding department (current period) (2,000 units ×		
$3.1489)	$ 6,298	
Conversion (current period) (400 units × $1.6063)	643	
Total ending work in process inventory		6,941
Total costs accounted for		$44,706

*NOTE: The units transferred to the next department that are costed at the current period cost are determined as follows:

	Preceding Department	Conversion
Units transferred	8,000	8,000
Less: Equivalent units from		
beginning inventory	1,500	500
Equivalent units finished		
and transferred in		
current period	6,500	7,500

for November using the weighted average cost flow assumption, Exhibit 11-7 was prepared using the FIFO cost flow assumption. All of the comments about Exhibit 11-6 apply to Exhibit 11-7 because both exhibits were prepared using the FIFO cost flow assumption. However, Exhibit 11-7 requires additional discussion because, unlike the Machining Department, the Assembly Department receives work in process from another department. The Machining Department, on the other hand, started the manufacturing process; thus, it did not receive work in process from another department.

The Assembly Department receives work in process from the Machining Department and merely assembles the product without adding any more direct material. Therefore, the resources that are itemized to specify the costs to be accounted for are labeled "preceding department" and "conversion." The resource "materials" is not specified because there are no materials added in the Assembly Department.

The resource called "preceding department" should be thought of as the partially completed product in the in-process state when in leaves the Machining Department and is transferred to the Assembly Department. This resource has had direct materials and conversion costs devoted to it in a prior department.

The resource called "preceding department" in the beginning inventory section of the "costs to be accounted for" section of the production report is the partially completed product that was transferred from the Machining Department to the Assembly Department in October. This is the resource that was in the Assembly Department's work in process inventory at the beginning of November. Exhibit 11-7 shows that 1,500 units of equivalent production of preceding department was in beginning inventory for the Assembly Department on November 1. These 1,500 units had a per-unit cost of $3 and they were 100% complete with regard to the preceding department.

As one would expect, the cost of $4,500 and the per-unit cost of $3 are obtained from the "costs accounted for" section of the October cost of production report for the Assembly Department (Exhibit 11-2). Those amounts are shown in the ending work in process inventory element of that section. It is important to note that the $3 per unit amount is derived from the machining department's cost of production report for October (Exhibit 11-1) in the "costs to be accounted for" section. Thus, the $3 per unit is calculated on the October cost of production report for the Machining Department; it is used in calculating the ending inventory of work in process items in the Assembly Department at the end of October; and under the FIFO cost flow assumption it is among the first costs to move out of the Assembly Department into the finished goods inventory in November.

If the items received from the preceding department have some limited assembly work performed on them between the date they are received and the end of the month, then the Assembly Department's beginning work in process inventory will have two resources applied to them (preceding department and conversion). That was the case in the Assembly Department at the end of October. As indicated in the "units to be accounted for" section of Exhibit 11-7, the 1,500 units in beginning work in process inventory were 100% complete with regard to the preceding department and one-third complete with regard to conversion. This means that between the time the Assembly Department received the last partially completed batch of 1,500 items from the Machining Department and the end of October, the Assembly Department worked on the batch and completed one-third of the work necessary to complete the units and move them to finished goods inventory.

That explains why the conversion portion of the beginning inventory in Exhibit 11-7 shows equivalent production of 500 units (1/3 × 1,500 units). The $750 cost associated with those 500 equivalent production units is determined by reference to the cost of production report for the Assembly Department for October (Exhibit 11-2) in the ending inventory element of the "costs accounted for" section. That is the same section from which we obtained the costs associated with the preceding department. In fact, it should now be clear that the beginning inventory information in Exhibit 11-7 is obtained from the ending inventory section of Exhibit 11-2.

If 8,000 units were completed by the Assembly Department and transferred to finished goods inventory in November, and if 1,500 of those units were 100% complete with regard to the preceding department's operations at the end of the prior month, then 6,500 equivalent units (8,000 − 1,500) were transferred to Assembly and then on to finished goods inventory in November (see the note at the bottom of Exhibit 11-7). These 6,500 units have a cost of $3.1489 per unit based on the current-period costs that are transferred from the Machining Department to the Assembly Department in November. That $3.1489 is determined by dividing the $26,766 in cost transferred from the Machining Department in November by the number of equivalent units (8,500) associated with the preceding department.

DECISION SUPPORT SYSTEMS AND BEHAVIORAL ASPECTS OF PROCESS COSTING

CHAPTER OBJECTIVE 6
DSS and behavioral aspects

The cost of production report is prepared to determine the dollar amount that will appear in the journal entry that credits work in process for one department and debits work in process for the next department in the sequence of departments. That certainly seems like a lot of work to get just one number—the cost of units transferred. As you might expect, the cost of production report can be prepared using the computer and database management software or electronic spreadsheet software.

In the preparation of the cost of production report for one department for one month, information is obtained from the cost of production report from a preceding department and from the cost of production report from the prior month. If these referenced reports are accessible by the computer, the information calculated in one cost of production report may be simultaneously used in the calculations in another cost of production report.

Just as standard costs were used in the job cost report in Chapter 10, standard costs can be used in conjunction with the cost of production reports, which can be used to evaluate the performance of the manager of each department. Such an evaluation would encourage cost control in the various departments.

Demonstration Problem

This demonstration problem uses the same case situation that was used in the demonstration problem in Chapter 10, page 357. By using the same case for both the job costing chapter and the process costing chapter, we are able to highlight the weaknesses associated with process costing when its use is not appropriate.

Pressler and Company had the following activity for each department in a particular month:

Units started and completed during month	6,000 units	
Machining Department		
Direct materials costs	$13,100	
Overhead—machining (30 hours × $124)	3,720	
Total Machining Department	$16,820	
Machining Department cost per unit		$2.80
Fabrication Department		
Direct materials costs	$ 1,900	
Overhead—fabrication (10 hours × $72)	720	
Total Fabricating Department	$ 2,620	
Fabricating Department cost per unit		.44
Total cost per unit		$3.24

The costs shown above are the same costs (on an aggregated basis) that were used in the demonstration problem in Chapter 10. As in that problem, 6,000 units were started and completed during the month.

REQUIRED

a. Calculate the cost of each of the two jobs discussed in the demonstration problem in the prior chapter based on 1,000 units for job 101 and 5,000 units for job 102. Use the cost per unit derived from the process costing system cited above.

b. Compare the cost of each job under the job costing system and under the process costing system and comment on the appropriateness of the process costing system when each job is unique and significantly different from all other jobs.

SOLUTION TO DEMONSTRATION PROBLEM

a. Job 101   1,000 units @ $3.24 = $3,240
   Job 102   5,000 units @ $3.24 = $16,200

b.

	Job 101
Cost per process costing system	$ 3,240
Cost per job costing system	13,440
Difference	$10,200

	Job 102
Cost per process costing system	$16,200
Cost per job costing system	6,000
Difference	$10,200

As in the problem for Chapter 10, job 101 is a product that is substantially different from job 102. The job costing system, which traces materials directly to the job where they are used, showed that the cost per unit of job 101 was $13.44 and of job 102 was only $1.20. That difference in cost strongly suggests that the two jobs involve very different products. In spite of that difference, the process costing system regards each of the 6,000 units produced during the month as having a unit cost of $3.24.

The differences in the costs per unit between the two costing systems indicates that the process costing system is appropriate only when there is a homogeneity among the products manufactured by the departments. If the products that are processed through the departments are diverse, serious thought should be given to implementing a job cost system to capture the cost differences between and among the diverse products. One of the major problems associated with small manufacturing businesses is that they do not have accounting systems that are adequate to properly determine the cost of the various products. Many of these small businesses manufacture a diverse group of products but use a process costing system when they should be using job costing systems.

A recent development in product costing involves the reorganization of the production facility so the departments do, in fact, manufacture a closely related group of products. Grouping operations in this manner does permit the use of process costing systems rather than job costing systems.

Review of Chapter Objectives

1. Calculate equivalent production units for various resource uses in manufacturing products in a particular department for a particular accounting period (pp. 378–80).

   ■ The equivalent production units must be calculated for each resource (materials, conversion, and prior department work in process) for each department's monthly production report. That calculation is based on the following example:

Units transferred out	8,500 units
Less: Beginning work in process inventory	
(actual count in equivalent units)	375 units
	8,125 units
Add: Ending work in process inventory	
(actual count in equivalent units)	1,000 units
Total equivalent production	9,125 units

   ■ Activity-based costing can be easily incorporated into process costing. This can be done by costing a batch of goods through a department for its use of direct materials, direct labor, and for various activities that make up overhead in that department (e.g., machine hours, setups, and quality inspections). If departments are created as single cost pools, process costing is automatically using activity-based costing.

2. Prepare the cost of production report for a department that has no beginning inventory (pp. 380–83).

   ■ When there is no beginning inventory, there is no need to deal with the "cost flow assumption" issue. That is true because all costs associated with production are costs that were incurred in the current month. This is the simplest of all the cost of production reports because we do not have to make any assumptions about which costs flow first into the next department.

3. Prepare the cost of production report for a department where manufacturing begins that has beginning work in process inventory and uses the weighted average cost flow assumption (pp. 384–87).

   ■ This type of cost of production report requires an assumption about the flow of costs. It uses the weighted average cost flow assumption and thus averages the costs in the beginning inventory with the costs incurred in the current period to arrive at the costs per unit to use in costing the units transferred to the next department.

4. Prepare the cost of production report for a department where manufacturing begins that has beginning work in process inventory and uses the first-in, first-out (FIFO) cost flow assumption (pp. 387–91).

■ This type of cost of production report requires an assumption about the flow of costs. It uses the first-in, first-out (FIFO) cost flow assumption and thus assumes that the beginning inventory costs move with the work in process transferred to the next department prior to the attachment of the current costs to the work in process transferred. Using this assumption, the ending work in process inventory is costed using the current-period costs.

5. Prepare the cost of production report for a department that receives work in process from another department, has beginning inventory, and uses the first-in, first-out (FIFO) cost flow assumption (pp. 391–94).

■ When work in process is received from another department, we regard that work in process as a resource on a par with the resources of materials and conversion. This treatment of work in process received from a previous department is difficult for beginning students to grasp because the work in process is a combination of direct materials and conversion that were combined in a previous department and, to a certain extent, in a previous month. However, it is necessary to regard this work in process as a resource just as direct materials and conversion are resources.

6. Discuss the decision support systems and behavioral aspects of process costing (p. 394).

■ Product costing under a process costing system is summarized in the cost of production report. This report is often computerized so that the data manipulation of process costing can be minimized. The data calculated in a cost of production report for one department can be saved. Later the data can be retrieved when the next department prepares its cost of production report. Thus, the data can be comingled in a company database.

Glossary of Key Terms

equivalent units The number of units that could have been completed if the entire effort were spent only on making whole units.

process costing A method of cost accounting wherein costs (either actual or standard) are charged to processes, operations, or departments. This method of costing is used where there is continuous mass production of like units that usually pass in consecutive order through a series of production steps called operations or processes. Costs are accumulated by those operations or processes for a specified period of time; an average cost per unit of output is developed for costing purposes.

Review Questions

11-1 What is a cost of production report and how is it used?

11-2 Why is a cost of production report prepared monthly for each department in the factory?

11-3 What are equivalent units and what role do they play in the completion of the cost of production report?

11-4   Why is it necessary to make a cost flow assumption (average cost, FIFO, or LIFO) in regard to the process costing system when it is not an important consideration with a job costing system?

11-5   Why are direct labor and overhead costs combined and regarded as "conversion costs" in a process costing system?

11-6   What role do journal entries play in a product costing system (either job cost or process cost)?

11-7   What use could be made of the ending work in process inventory information on the cost of production report?

11-8   Discuss the difference between the unit cost calculation section of the cost of production report using the weighted average method and the FIFO method.

11-9   The equivalent units calculation is an important calculation in a process costing system. Should the equivalent units be in terms of units of input material (such as barrels of crude oil) or should the equivalent units be in terms of units of output material (such as gallons of gasoline)?

11-10   What is the formula for calculating equivalent units?

11-11   Why is the percentage of completion for materials most often different from the percentage of completion for conversion?

11-12   Under what condition would the percentage of completion for conversion and materials be the same?

11-13   Are there any conditions under which any percentage other than "100% complete" would be used in conjunction with the units and related cost of units transferred from the preceding department?

11-14   When were the beginning inventory costs incurred?

Discussion Questions

11-15   Suppose that goods are manufactured in such a way that inventories are kept to low levels—so low that beginning work in process inventory and ending work in process inventory are essentially zero. (This can happen, for example, in a "just-in-time" environment, to be discussed in Chapter 17.) How does this condition simplify process costing?

11-16   The manufacture of an aircraft carrier is usually accounted for with job costing while the manufacture of automobiles is usually accounted for with process costing. What accounts for the different accounting treatments?

Exercises

11-17   NO BEGINNING INVENTORY; COST OF PRODUCTION REPORT Horn, Inc., instituted a new chemical process in October. During October, 9,000 gallons of the chemical called Drezon were started in the Heating Department. Of the gallons started, 7,000 were transferred to the Stirring Department and 2,000 remained in work in process in the Heating Department on October 31. The work in process in the Heating Department on October 31 was 100% complete with regard to material costs and 50% complete with regard to conversion costs.

CO 1, 2

Material costs of $27,000 and conversion costs of $40,000 were charged to the Heating Department during October. What were the total costs transferred to the Stirring Department in October?

11-18   BEGINNING INVENTORY; WEIGHTED AVERAGE COST FLOW ASSUMPTION; CONVERSION COST ONLY Russell Corp. has a process costing system to account for the transfer of product costs from one department to another department. The company

CO 1, 3

produces a cake mix and it mixes the ingredients in the Mixing Department. The following information relates to the Mixing Department for April:

	Units in Process	Conversion Percentage Completed	Conversion Cost
Beginning inventory	10,000	40%	$18,000
Ending inventory	8,000	75%	?

During April, $73,450 in conversion cost was incurred in the Mixing Department and 25,000 units were completed and transferred to the Packaging Department. What unit cost would be used to cost the units in ending inventory for the Mixing Department for conversion costs? The company uses the weighted average cost flow assumption.

11-19 NO BEGINNING INVENTORY; CALCULATION OF UNITS TRANS-FERRED Big Red Paint Company manufactures paint and sells it by the gallon. During the first month of production, the following production information was collected by the accounting department:

CO 1, 2

Gallons started into production	10,000 gallons
Cost of raw materials introduced at the beginning of the process	$37,500
Direct labor costs incurred	$28,750
Manufacturing overhead	$42,500

Ending work in process was 1,000 gallons that were 50% complete with regard to conversion. Prepare a cost of production report for the first month of operations.

11-20 CALCULATION OF EQUIVALENT PRODUCTION Information for four independent process costing situations, A–D is presented below. Use this information to calculate the equivalent production units (for both material and conversion) for each situation.

CO 1

	A	B	C	D
Beginning inventory (units)	1,000	5,000	3,000	–0–
Materials—percent completed	50%	100%	40%	0%
Conversion—percent completed	40%	60%	50%	0%
Units started	10,000	20,000	30,000	40,000
Ending inventory (units)	2,000	3,000	2,000	5,000
Materials—percent completed	75%	100%	60%	100%
Conversion—percent completed	60%	80%	30%	70%

CO 2 11-21 JOURNAL ENTRIES; NO BEGINNING INVENTORY The cost portion of the April cost of production report for the Painting Department is shown below:

Costs to Be Accounted For:

Resource	Cost	Equivalent Units	Cost per Unit
Direct material	$40,000	100,000	$.40
Conversion	$20,000	80,000	.25
Total costs to be accounted for	$60,000		$.65

(continued)

Costs Accounted For:

Costs transferred to next department (60,000 units × $.65)		$39,000
Costs in ending inventory:		
Materials (40,000 units × $.40)	$16,000	
Conversion (40,000 units × 50% × $.25)	5,000	
Total work in process ending inventory		21,000
Total costs accounted for		$60,000

a. Prepare the journal entry that would have charged the costs to the department during the month of April.

b. Prepare the journal entry that would be prepared to remove the cost from the Painting Department and move those costs to the Drying Department.

11-22   NO BEGINNING INVENTORY; PRIOR DEPARTMENT COSTS Koussa Company produced a chemical in three production departments. Those departments in the sequence in which they worked on the product were Heating, Mixing, and Packaging. During June, the Mixing Department received partially completed chemicals with a cost of $50,000 from the Heating Department.

CO 1, 2

The Mixing Department had no beginning inventory at the start of June. There were 25,000 gallons of the partially completed chemical transferred from the Heating Department to the Mixing Department during the month of June. No new materials are added to the chemical in the Mixing Department.

At the end of June, there were 5,000 gallons of the chemical remaining in the Mixing Department. That 5,000 gallons was 50% complete with regard to the mixing in the Mixing Department.

Prepare a cost of production report for the Mixing Department for June.

11-23   BEGINNING INVENTORY; FIFO COST FLOW ASSUMPTION; CONVERSION COST ONLY Pimlott Company uses a process costing system to account for the transfer of products from one department to another. The company mixes chemicals in one department and then transfers the mixed chemicals to the Heating Department, where it is heated prior to being packaged. The following information relates to the Mixing Department for the month of January:

CO 1, 4

	Units in Process	Conversion Percentage Completed	Conversion Cost
Beginning inventory	20,000	40%	$36,000
Ending inventory	16,000	75%	?

During January, $248,400 in conversion cost was incurred in the Mixing Department and 50,000 units were completed and transferred to the Heating Department. What is the cost associated with the conversion cost portion of the ending work in process inventory in the Mixing Department? (The company uses the FIFO cost flow assumption.)

11-24   BEGINNING INVENTORY; FIFO COST FLOW ASSUMPTION; COST OF ENDING INVENTORY; COST OF PRODUCT TRANSFERRED Taib Company uses the FIFO cost flow assumption in its process costing system. The company manufactures a food

CO 4

product that is processed through three departments. The Grain Crushing Department is the first of these three departments. The following information pertains to the Grain Crushing Department during a recent month:

Beginning inventory (100% materials, 60% conversion)	20,000 units
Units started in the Grain Crushing Department during month	80,000 units
Ending inventory (100% materials, 30% conversion)	10,000 units

The costs associated with the components of the beginning inventory were as follows:

Materials	$10,000
Conversion	2,400
Beginning inventory cost	$12,400

The cost per equivalent unit for the units started during the month were as follows:

Materials cost	$.55
Conversion cost	.22
Total	$.77

a. Determine the number of units transferred to the next department during the month.

b. Determine the cost of the units transferred to the next department.

c. Determine the cost of the ending inventory.

11-25 BEGINNING INVENTORY; FIFO COST FLOW ASSUMPTION; CALCU-LATE UNIT COSTS Bloom Company manufactures a product that is produced in two departments. All of the materials are added in the first department; and thus, the only resources to account for in the second department are conversion and preceding-department resources. The following information relates to the operation of the second of those departments during the month of March:

CO 4

Units to Be Accounted For:

Beginning work in process (60% complete)	4,000 units
Units transferred from first department in March	20,000 units
Total units to be accounted for	24,000 units

Units Accounted For:

Ending work in process (30% complete)	? units
Units transferred to finished goods inventory	22,000 units
Total units accounted for	?

The beginning work in process inventory includes the following costs:

Preceding department	$40,000
Conversion	36,000
Cost of beginning inventory	$76,000

The costs incurred in the month of March by the second department were as follows:

Preceding department (20,000 units)	$220,000
Conversion	313,100
Total costs in current month	$533,100

Prepare a schedule showing the cost per unit, assuming that the company uses the FIFO cost flow assumption.

11-26   BEGINNING INVENTORY; WEIGHTED AVERAGE COST FLOW ASSUMP-TION; CALCULATE UNIT COSTS Refer to the information presented in Exercise 11-25. Prepare a schedule showing the cost per unit, assuming that the company uses the weighted average cost flow assumption.

CO 3

Problems

11-27   NO BEGINNING INVENTORIES; EQUIVALENT PRODUCTION CALCU-LATIONS Chatham Company uses a process costing system to account for its product, which moves through three departments during the manufacturing process: the Fabrication Department, the Machining Department, and the Assembly Department. When the units leave the Assembly Department, they are sent to the finished goods warehouse to await shipment to the customer. None of the departments had beginning inventory.

CO 1, 2

The following information was summarized at the end of the first year of operations:

1. *Fabrication Department*: 1,000 units, 100% complete with regard to direct materials, 50% complete with regard to conversion costs, in ending work in process inventory. During the year, 25,000 units were transferred to the Machining Department.

2. *Machining Department:* 1,500 units, 100% complete with regard to direct materials, 25% complete with regard to conversion costs, in ending work in process inventory. During the year, 23,500 units were transferred to the Assembly Department.

3. *Assembly Department:* 2,000 units, 75% complete with regard to direct materials, 75% complete with regard to conversion costs, in ending work in process inventory. During the year, 21,500 units were transferred to Finished Goods Inventory.

REQUIRED

a. Determine the equivalent units for all resources for the Fabrication Department.

b. Determine the equivalent units for all resources for the Machining Department.

c. Determine the equivalent units for all resources for the Assembly Department.

11-28   EQUIVALENT PRODUCTION CALCULATIONS; BEGINNING INVENTO-RIES; WEIGHTED AVERAGE COST FLOW ASSUMPTION Chatham Company, the company introduced in Problem 11-27 summarized its operations for the second year of operations as follows:

CO 1, 3

1. *Fabrication Department:* The beginning work in process inventory was 1,000 units, as indicated in Problem 11-27. This 1,000 unit beginning inventory was 100% complete with regard to direct materials and 50% complete with regard to conversion. During this second year, 30,000 units were transferred to the Machining Department. At the end of the

second year this department had 2,000 units remaining in work in process ending inventory. That 2,000 units was 100% complete with regard to direct materials and 30% complete with regard to conversion.

2. *Machining Department:* The beginning work in process inventory was 1,500 units, as indicated in Problem 11-27. This 1,500 unit beginning inventory was 100% complete with regard to direct materials and 25% complete with regard to conversion. During this second year, 28,500 units were transferred to the Assembly Department. At the end of the second year, this department had 3,000 units remaining in work in process inventory. That 3,000 units was 100% complete with regard to direct materials and 60% complete with regard to conversion.

3. *Assembly Department:* The beginning work in process inventory was 2,000 units, as indicated in Problem 11-27. This 2,000 unit beginning inventory was 75% complete with regard to direct materials and 75% complete with regard to conversion. During this second year, 28,000 units were transferred to the finished goods inventory. At the end of the year this department had 2,500 units remaining in work in process inventory. That 2,500 units was 80% complete with regard to direct materials and 70% complete with regard to conversion.

REQUIRED

Determine the following based on the weighted average cost flow assumption:

a. The equivalent units for all resources for the Fabrication Department.

b. The equivalent units for all resources for the Machining Department.

c. The equivalent units for all resources for the Assembly Department.

11-29 COST OF PRODUCTION REPORT; BEGINNING INVENTORY; WEIGHTED AVERAGE COST FLOW ASSUMPTION Miami Company uses a process costing system and the weighted average cost flow assumption. There is only one department in the factory. The following information is available for the year just completed:

CO 1, 3

	Units
Beginning work in process inventory (100% complete with regard to materials and 70% complete with regard to conversion)	20,000
Units started in process during the year	300,000
Units transferred to finished goods	290,000
Units completed and on hand in finished goods inventory	5,000
Ending work in process inventory (100% complete with regard to materials and 25% complete with regard to conversion costs)	30,000

	Costs	
Opening Work in Process:		
Direct materials	$ 5,000	
Direct labor	7,000	
Manufacturing overhead	3,500	$ 15,500
Costs Incurred during the Year:		
Direct materials	$ 78,200	
Direct labor	139,800	
Manufacturing overhead	69,850	287,850
		$303,350

REQUIRED

Prepare a cost of production report for the year ended using the weighted average cost flow assumption.

11-30 BEGINNING INVENTORY; FIFO COST FLOW ASSUMPTION; FOCUS ON SECOND DEPARTMENT; COST OF PRODUCTION REPORT The Abpst Company manufactures a product that requires processing through two departments. The Cutting Department cuts the metal into the proper shape, and then the metal is transferred to the Assembly Department, where the metal pieces are attached to each other to complete the product. There are no materials used in the Assembly Department. The relatively inexpensive items used to attach the metal pieces are regarded as variable manufacturing overhead and classified as conversion costs. The company uses the FIFO cost flow assumption in conjunction with a process costing system.

CO 1, 5

The following information is provided concerning the Assembly Department during November:

1. During November, the Cutting Department transferred the metal parts necessary for making 2,000 units of product to the Assembly Department. The cost transferred with these 2,000 units was $10,000. Additionally, the Assembly Department incurred conversion costs of $50,000.

2. The beginning inventory in the Assembly Department at the beginning of the month of November was 1,500 units. These 1,500 units were 100% complete with regard to prior department and 1/3 complete with regard to conversion. The costs in the beginning inventory were as follows:

Prior department	$ 8,250
Conversion	10,500
Cost of beginning inventory	$18,750

3. The ending work in process inventory in the Assembly Department at the end of the month of November was 1,000 units, which were 100% complete with regard to prior department and 50% complete with regard to conversion.

REQUIRED

Prepare the cost of production report for the Assembly Department for the month of November.

11-31 BEGINNING INVENTORY; FIFO COST FLOW ASSUMPTION; FOCUS ON FIRST DEPARTMENT; COST OF PRODUCTION REPORT Madison Manufacturing Company processes wheat into flour. The first department in the process grinds the grain to a certain fineness before it is transferred to the next department, which grinds the product into a finer consistency. This problem concentrates on the first department in this process.

CO 1, 4

The accounting department collected the following information for the first department during July:

Beginning work in process inventory	
(100% materials; 75% conversion)	20,000 units
Transferred in from the grain	
storage bins during July	150,000 units
Ending work in process inventory	
(100% materials; 40% conversion)	30,000 units

The costs associated with the beginning inventory were as follows:

Materials	$100,000
Conversion	10,000
Cost of beginning inventory	$110,000

The costs incurred in the first department during July were as follows:

Materials	$ 960,000
Conversion	959,000
Costs incurred in July	$1,919,000

REQUIRED

Prepare the cost of production report for the first department for July. Assume that the company uses the FIFO cost flow assumption.

11-32   BEGINNING INVENTORY; WEIGHTED AVERAGE COST FLOW ASSUMPTION; FOCUS ON FIRST DEPARTMENT; COST OF PRODUCTION REPORT Refer to the information presented in Problem 11-31.

CO 1, 3

REQUIRED

Prepare the cost of production report for the first department for July. Assume that the company uses the weighted average cost flow assumption.

11-33   BEGINNING INVENTORY; WEIGHTED AVERAGE COST FLOW ASSUMPTION; FOCUS ON FIRST DEPARTMENT; COST OF PRODUCTION REPORT Wile Company is a chemical company that combines basic chemicals in such a way to create solvents. The Mixing Department is the first department in the process, and it is the department in which the basic chemicals are combined and mixed. After the chemicals are mixed, they are transferred to the Heating Department, where they are heated prior to being placed in containers.

CO 1, 3

The following information is available for the Heating Department for October:

		Cost
Beginning inventory	4,000 units	
Materials (100% complete)		$120,000
Conversion (25% complete)		15,000
Beginning inventory		$135,000
Ending inventory	6,000 units	
Materials (100% complete)		?
Conversion (80% complete)		?
Ending inventory cost		?
Materials transferred to the Heating Department in October	100,000 units	
Cost of materials transferred to the Heating Department in October		$3,200,000
Conversion costs incurred in the Heating Department in October		$1,628,000

REQUIRED

Assume that the company uses the weighted average cost flow assumption. Prepare the cost of production report for the Heating Department for October.

11-34 BEGINNING INVENTORY; FIFO COST FLOW ASSUMPTION; FOCUS ON FIRST DEPARTMENT; COST OF PRODUCTION REPORT Refer to the information in Problem 11-33.

CO 1, 4

REQUIRED

Prepare the cost of production report for the Heating Department for October. Assume that the company uses the FIFO cost flow assumption.

11-35 BEGINNING INVENTORY; FIFO COST FLOW ASSUMPTION; FOCUS ON FIRST AND SECOND DEPARTMENTS; COST OF PRODUCTION REPORTS The Evergreen Manufacturing Company manufactures a product in two departments. The materials are introduced into the Fabrication Department, and then the partially completed product is sent to the Assembly Department for final assembly. No materials are added in the Assembly Department. The company has a process costing system and it uses the FIFO cost flow assumption. The following information pertains to both departments in the month of September:

CO 1, 4, 5

	Fabrication Department		Assembly Department	
	Units	Cost	Units	Cost
Beginning inventory	3,000			
Materials (100%)		$ 30,000		
Conversion (75%)		$ 15,750		
Beginning inventory			4,000	
Preceding department (100%)				$ 68,400
Conversion (50%)				$ 24,000
Current Month:				
Materials started	10,000	$100,000		
Conversion costs		$ 61,755		$148,840
Units transferred in				
from preceding department			?	?
Ending inventory	2,000			
Materials (100%)		?		
Conversion (10%)		?		
Ending inventory			4,000	
Preceding department (100%)				?
Conversion (80%)				?

REQUIRED

Prepare a cost of production report for each of the two departments, finding the unknown amounts. (*Hint:* Prepare the report for the Fabrication Department first in order to determine the number of units transferred to the Assembly Department in September).

Business Decision Case

Kenyon Company produces a special chemical in three departments. The raw material is introduced in the Mixing Department. After the product is properly mixed it goes to the Heating Department. When the heating process is completed, the product is sent to the Cooling Department. When the product is properly cooled, it is sent to the finished goods warehouse. In all of the departments the conversion costs are incurred evenly throughout the department.

The following incomplete Work in Process T account is for June for the Mixing Department:

Work in Process—Mixing Department

June 1 inventory (10,000 gallons 75% complete)	$ 5,000	Completed and transferred to Heating Department (? gallons)	?
June cost added:			
Raw materials (60,000 gallons)	12,000		
Labor	10,550		
Overhead	10,550		
June 30 inventory (13,000 gallons, 25 complete)	?		

The materials cost portion of the $5,000 opening inventory cost is $2,000. The company uses the weighted average cost flow assumption.

REQUIRED

a. Determine how many gallons of mixed materials were transferred to the Heating Department in June.

b. Determine the average cost of conversion and the average cost of materials to be used for June.

c. Determine the cost of the units transferred to the Heating Department during June.

d. Determine the cost of the ending work in process inventory at June 30.

4

PERFORMANCE
EVALUATION

Chapter

12

Responsibility Centers and Performance Evaluation

CHAPTER OBJECTIVES

After reading Chapter 12, you should be able to:

1. Explain how decentralization affects managerial span of control (pp. 411–14).

2. Describe the three basic types of responsibility centers (pp. 414–16).

3. Discuss how to measure investment center performance (pp. 416–19).

4. Show how residual income is superior to return on investment when

linked with incentive compensation plans (pp. 419–20).

5. Explain why automated manufacturing environments are changing the concept of direct labor cost control (pp. 421–22).

6. Explain how transfer prices are determined for products or services transferred between responsibility centers (pp. 422–26).

This chapter concerns the performance evaluation of the managers of organizational units. These organizational units are called *responsibility centers.* The span of control, the number of subordinates directly answering to one manager, determines the specific type of responsibility center and the appropriate means of performance evaluation.

RESPONSIBILITY ACCOUNTING: A REPRISE

Responsibility accounting, as discussed in Chapter 1, refers to the accumulation of data and the reporting of information necessary to evaluate managers of organizational units. The controller of the organization is charged with tailoring a responsibility accounting system to the information needs of the managers at varying levels. Those informational needs are dictated to a great extent by the structure of the organization.

In an organization with highly centralized authority, one person, the owner of the business, may make all of the decisions. On the other hand, in a highly decentralized organization, the authority for decision making is given to persons at various levels within the organization. (Recall the discussion in Chapter 1 about centralization and decentralization.) The organization with centralized authority may only have limited need for a responsibility accounting system; however, the decentralized organization needs a rather extensive system. The responsibility accounting system permits a periodic (monthly, quarterly, and annual) evaluation of the decisions made by managers within the organization. Through this means of evaluation, the owner of the business or the director of the organization is informed about the effect of managers' decisions and is in a position to plan and organize for better decisions. The owner or director can use these evaluations to control decisions that do not result in a contribution to the organizational unit's goals. In addition, the owner or director is in a position to structure incentive compensation plans to motivate the managers.

RESPONSIBILITY ACCOUNTING IN A DECENTRALIZED ORGANIZATION

CHAPTER OBJECTIVE 1
Decentralization and span of control

Because decentralized organizations make more extensive use of the responsibility accounting system, we will use data related to the highly decentralized McCallum Company to illustrate a responsibility accounting system. McCallum is a diversified manufacturer of wood products. McCallum Company has three product groups, each headed by a group vice-president. We will focus on the Furniture Group, which includes three divisions: the Eastern Division, the Midwestern Division, and the Western Division. Each division general manager is responsible for selling furniture within a specified geographic area and for manufacturing the furniture at plants located in the same area. We will concentrate on the Midwestern Division, which has four manufacturing facilities and a marketing department. The organization chart for McCallum Company is shown in Exhibit 12-1.

In order to simplify the organizational chart, the details of the organization beneath the vice-presidents of the Fiberboard Group and the Timber Group have not been

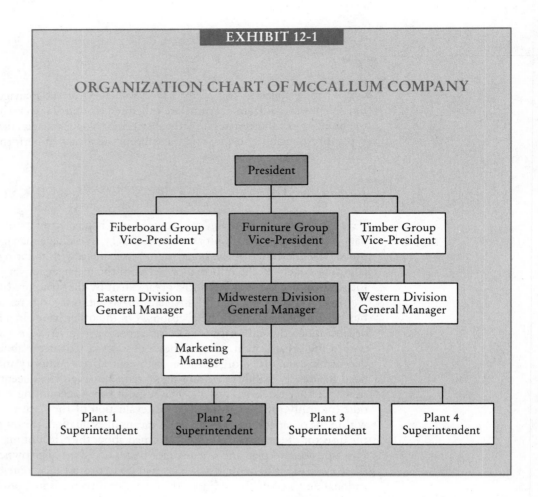

EXHIBIT 12-1

ORGANIZATION CHART OF McCALLUM COMPANY

shown. Those suborganizations have a structure similar to that shown for the Furniture Group's vice-president. The organizational units of primary focus are indicated by shading.

A sound responsibility accounting system must take into consideration the managerial responsibility associated with each organizational level. Within McCallum Company the managerial responsibility of each of the managers is defined as follows:

- *Plant superintendent:* This manager is responsible for producing a product of a specified quality at the lowest possible cost.

- *Marketing manager:* This manager is responsible for marketing furniture within the specified geographical territory. The manager makes decisions concerning the compensation of salespersons, the expenditures for advertising and promotion, and the selling price of the product. The manager sells only furniture manufactured by plants within the specified geographical territory.

- *Division general manager:* This manager coordinates the efforts of the marketing manager and the plant superintendents of the plants located in the territory. The purpose of this coordination is to ensure that only products that are profitable are being produced and sold and that the products that are being demanded are the products that are being produced.

EXHIBIT 12-2

McCallum Company
Responsibility Accounting Reports
For the Year Ended December 31, 19XX

Furniture Group Vice-President

The president of the company evaluates the group vice-president's performance based on controllable profits and controllable investment.

	Actual	Flexible Budget	Variance
Controllable Profit			
Eastern Division	XX	XX	XX
Midwestern Division	$ 35,000	$ 34,000	$ 1,000F
Western Division	XX	XX	XX
Less Group Administrative Expenses	XX	XX	XX
Controllable Profit	$175,000	$165,000	$10,000F
Controllable Investment			
Group Assets	$800,000	$840,000	
Less Group Liabilities	100,000	110,000	
Controllable Investment	$700,000	$730,000	$30,000F

Midwestern Division General Manager

The group vice-president evaluates the division manager's performance based on this report.

	Actual	Flexible Budget	Variance
Controllable Profit			
Controllable Revenue	XXX	XXX	X
Less Controllable Expenses:			
Plant 1	XX	XX	X
Plant 2	$ 10,000	$ 9,500	$ 500U
Plant 3	XX	XX	X
Plant 4	XX	XX	X
Controllable Gross Profit	XX	XX	X
Less Controllable Marketing and Administrative Expenses	X	X	X
Controllable Profit	$ 35,000	$ 34,000	$ 1,000F

Plant 2 Superintendent

The plant superintendent's performance would be evaluated based on this report. In its more complete form it would include all of the controllable variances.

	Actual	Flexible Budget	Variance
Controllable Expenses			
Direct Materials	XX	XX	X
Direct Labor	XX	XX	X
Manufacturing Overhead	XX	XX	X
Total	$ 10,000	$ 9,500	$ 500U

● *Group vice-president:* This manager is responsible for making decisions concerning the amount of capital that should be invested in the group operations and particularly in each division within the group. This person has the authority to decide to close a plant and sell off the assets if such a decision were considered appropriate. This manager also has the authority to make relatively large commitments of capital for the expansion or modernization of plant facilities. Additionally, he or she is responsible for establishing inventory control policies, credit policies, and providing financing for the operations of the divisions within the group. The group vice-president in this decentralized company is closely comparable to the owner of his or her own business.

● *President:* The president of the company is responsible for identifying new investment opportunities and reviewing the performance of the group vice-presidents.

RESPONSIBILITY REPORTING AND RESPONSIBILITY CENTERS

**CHAPTER
OBJECTIVE 2**
*Types of responsibility
centers*

A basic tenet of management theory is that a manager should be held accountable for only the variables that that manager can control. In structuring a responsibility reporting system, this tenet is a guiding principle.

A responsibility report system for McCallum Company is illustrated in Exhibit 12-2 (see page 413). Note that the performance reports for the lower organizational levels become, in summary form, a part of the performance reports for higher organizational levels. Although not shown in Exhibit 12-2, there is a report that the shareholders use to evaluate the performance of the president: the quarterly or annual report released to the shareholders, the annual report usually audited by independent accountants. That report would include, as a minimum, the income statement, the balance sheet, and the statement of cash flows for the company. Note that the responsibility report focuses on the controllable items of the manager. The key concept is controllability at a specific level of authority.

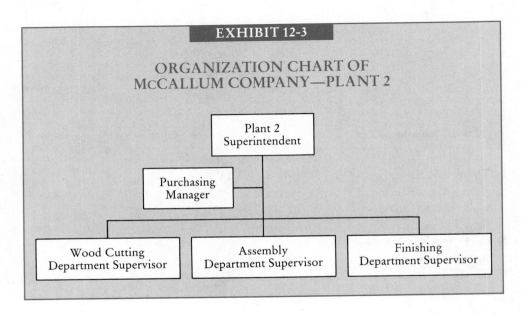

EXHIBIT 12-3

**ORGANIZATION CHART OF
McCALLUM COMPANY—PLANT 2**

Plant 2
Superintendent

Purchasing
Manager

Wood Cutting
Department Supervisor

Assembly
Department Supervisor

Finishing
Department Supervisor

EXHIBIT 12-4

Supervisor's Performance Report
McCallum Company
Wood Cutting Department
For the Year Ended December 31, 19XX

Material quantity variance	$XXXF
Labor efficiency variance	XXXU
Labor rate variance	XXXU
Variable overhead spending variance	XXXF
Variable overhead efficiency variance	XXXU
Fixed overhead budget variance	XXXF
Total variances	$XXXF

Cost Centers

A responsibility center is a cost center (organizational unit) when the manager exercises control over cost incurrence. (You may wish to review the discussion about controllable costs in Chapter 2.) These managers have no control, or only limited control, over revenues and the amount of capital investment in their operations. In McCallum Company, the plant superintendents are cost center managers. They control costs of manufacturing the product; but they cannot establish the product selling price, make decisions concerning advertising or promotion, or decide, for example, to replace an obsolete wood-cutting lathe with a more modern lathe. Given the limited authority of the superintendent, the responsibility accounting system should generate a report that focuses only on the costs that the superintendent controls.

Managers who are subordinate to the plant superintendent are also cost center managers. Various manufacturing functions are performed by different departments in Plant 2 of McCallum Company, as shown in Exhibit 12-3.

In evaluating these departmental supervisors, the plant superintendent would rely on the responsibility accounting system to generate reports that focus on the costs controlled by each supervisor. An illustrative performance report for the Wood Cutting Department supervisor is presented in Exhibit 12-4. These variances are the same performance indicators that were discussed in Chapters 7 and 8.

Profit Centers

Profit centers are responsibility centers that are headed by managers who exercise control over both costs and revenues. However, profit center managers do not have control over capital investment. In McCallum Company, the division general managers are profit center managers. They exercise control over both the plant superintendents, who control only costs, and the marketing manager, who is in a position to influence revenues. Because they control both revenues and costs, a performance report that focuses on controllable profits (controllable revenues less *controllable costs*) is an appropriate gauge of the performance of division managers. The center section of Exhibit 12-2 illustrates a profit center–oriented performance report for the Midwestern Division's general manager.

Incentive systems are often structured with a focus on controllable profit. The incentive system could be a profit-sharing arrangement based on predetermined expectations or it could be a bonus system based on the group vice-president's judgment of the division general manager's performance. In either case, a properly developed responsibility accounting system is essential.

Investment Centers

Investment centers are responsibility centers that are headed by managers who exercise control over costs, revenues, and the amount of capital invested. In McCallum Company there are investment center managers at two different organizational levels of the company. The group vice-presidents are investment center managers at one level and the president is an investment center manager at another level. Both the group vice-presidents and the president control costs, revenues, and the amount of investment; however, the president controls those elements more comprehensively than do the group vice-presidents.

MEASURING INVESTMENT CENTER PERFORMANCE

CHAPTER OBJECTIVE 3
Investment center performance

Because the investment center manager controls all three elements essential to the economic viability of the organization—costs, revenues, and capital investments—the performance evaluation is more useful for investment center managers than for profit center managers or for cost center managers. This power will be revealed as we explore the two different ways by which investment center managerial performance may be measured. Those two ways are *return on investment* and *residual income*.

Return on Investment

Controllable return on investment (ROI) is calculated as follows:

$$\text{Controllable Return on Investment} = \frac{\text{Controllable Profit}}{\text{Controllable Investment}}$$

The necessary information for calculating the controllable return on investment for the vice-president of the Furniture Group is shown in Exhibit 12-2. Actual controllable profit is $175,000 and actual controllable investment is $700,000. Using the equation presented above, the controllable return on investment for 19XX is as follows:

$$\frac{\$175,000}{\$700,000} = 25\%$$

Using the same equation, the budgeted controllable return on investment is calculated as follows:

$$\frac{\$165,000}{\$730,000} = 22.6\%$$

EXHIBIT 12-5	
CONTROLLABLE INVESTMENT DATA	
	Actual January 31, 19XX
Controllable Group Assets	
Accounts receivable	$ 75,000
Inventory	125,000
Property, plant, and equipment	600,000
Total controllable assets	$800,000
Controllable Group Liabilities	
Accounts payable	$ 25,000
Notes payable	75,000
Total controllable liabilities	$100,000
Net Controllable Investment	$700,000

The details of Exhibit 12-2 present sufficient information to permit an assessment of the items that are included in controllable profit. However, the controllable investment is presented only in summary form. In determining which items should be considered in arriving at the controllable investment, we must consider which balance sheet items are controlled by the investment center manager. As previously mentioned, the group vice-presidents have the authority to make capital investment decisions, establish inventory policies, establish credit policies, and provide financing for operations within the group.

Given this authority, the controllable investment should include the items shown in Exhibit 12-5. The controllable balance sheet items are accounts receivable; inventory; property, plant, and equipment; accounts payable; and notes payable. Cash is notably absent from the assets because the company treasurer controls the level of cash throughout the company. When the treasurer observes that excess cash is available in one group, that cash will be taken to be used in other groups or invested in other activities.

The inclusion of accounts receivable, inventory, and accounts payable among the items used to determine controllable investment may cause some difficulty to some readers. Admittedly, those items are not under the direct control of the group vice-president, because the level of activity at the division level has an influence on the dollar amount of these items. However, because the group vice-president has authority to establish policies regarding these items, he or she has more comprehensive control over the items than does the manager of any organizational sub-unit.

Return on investment is regarded as a powerful measure of performance because its use encourages the manager to seek the optimal level of investment given the profit potential of the business enterprise. Its use, coupled with an incentive compensation system that rewards the manager for improvement in ROI, spurs the manager continually to evaluate and consider expansion opportunities that would enhance ROI, capital improvements that would increase ROI, and even the divestiture of unprofitable products that have had a negative effect on ROI. Performance evaluation of cost centers and profit centers are not as conducive to the development of such comprehensive incentive compensation systems.

ARE YOUR PERFORMANCE MEASURES OBSOLETE?

The authors of the following article address the manager's constant question, "How will I be measured?" as they explore the principles on which they believe valid performance measures must be based.

BASIC BELIEFS REGARDING PERFORMANCE MEASURES

Performance measures derive from strategy. Every corporation and every major business unit of the corporation has either an explicit or implicit business mission—specific management targets, generally measured as share of the market, specified earning goals, or desired return on investment. Guided by insight into customer needs, management selects strategies to meet these objectives and to achieve competitive advantage.

Performance measures are hierarchical as well as integrated across business functions. Performance measures are interrelated throughout an organization. But consider for a moment the impact that a performance measure such as return on investment will have at the lowest level of the organization. How does an accounts payable clerk, for example, maximize the company's return on investment? How does a lathe operator contribute to long-term shareholder wealth? Performance measures as they extend down through the organization must become increasingly specific. They must encompass shorter planning horizons, and some must emphasize cost performance. Internally consistent performance measures are difficult to formulate, much less express—they take some thought. When in doubt, the company needs to ask itself whether a particular performance measure supports or inhibits overall strategy. For many companies, the problem is that *there are too many performance measures*—too many that are obsolete and too many that are not consistent.

Performance measures must support the company's multidimensional environment. Every organization tends to have an internal bias. It spends a great deal of time on its internal performance measurements, often at the expense of external comparisons.

Performance measures must be based on a thorough understanding of cost relationships and cost behavior. Having stated that performance measures do not necessarily have to be expressed as cost, we understand, nonetheless, that cost is a most important basis for performance measurement. And in American industry, notions of cost are being challenged with increasing regularity. No one who seriously studies the cost management systems of manufacturing companies finds them adequate. They are based on the ghosts-of-management-past.

WHERE SHOULD WE START?

Look to strategy. For many companies, the central problem is not that they lack performance measures, but that they have too many—and too many irrelevant ones. Start with strategy. What are the strategic objectives of the company? How do these strategic objectives translate into divisional goals and individual management action? How do you populate the performance measurement matrix and select a small number that will cause strategy to happen? How do you translate overall performance measures into ones that are meaningful at a low level in the organization?

Look to budgeting. Next, turn your attention to the process of instilling performance measures into management thinking. There is a well-developed vehicle for doing this in most organizations—the budget. Unfortunately, we think of budgets in financial terms. Budgets can be even more useful if they are considered the annual performance-measurement-setting exercise. Average product shipments per day can be budgeted. Percent "first pass" quality inspections can be budgeted. Number of customer complaints (carefully defined) can be budgeted. Even the number of invoices processed (per dollar of sales) can be budgeted. The budgets do not have to be linear. They can incorporate concepts of continual improvement by targeting advancements each quarter.

EXORCISING THE GHOSTS

We have taken a long trip through the world of performance measurement, seeking to exorcise the ghosts-of-management-past. Consider the principles again. First, performance measures *do* guide management action, for good or not so good; therefore, they should derive from strategy. If strategy has not been set, performance measurement discussion will be a frustrating exercise. Second, performance measures are hierarchical as well as integrated across business functions. The integration measurements are the most difficult to identify and articulate. Third, performance measures must support a company's multidimensional environment. And last, performance measures must be based on a thorough understanding of cost. In this regard, your present cost accounting system may not be adequate.

SOURCE: Adapted from Daniel P. Keegan, Robert G. Eiler, and Charles R. Jones, "Are Your Performance Measures Obsolete?" *Management Accounting* (June 1989), pp. 45-50. Adapted by permission.

Residual Income

Residual income (RI), the other means of evaluating investment center managers, uses the same controllable profit and investment used in the ROI calculation. However, residual income relies on another item of information: the minimum required rate of return.

The **minimum required rate of return** is the rate of return that reflects the company's estimated cost of capital and growth expectations. (Cost of capital is described at greater length in Chapter 14.) Certainly, to establish a minimum required rate of return below the cost of capital would not be prudent. To do so would encourage managers to invest in projects that would yield a return less than the cost of the capital devoted to the project. A minimum required rate of return equal to the cost of capital might encourage managers to undertake projects that merely break even (return equals capital cost). On the other hand, a minimum required rate of return greater than the estimated cost of capital will tend to result in profit growth as investment center managers identify projects with a return that exceeds the cost of capital.

Residual income is calculated by subtracting a capital charge from the controllable profits. The **capital charge** is determined by multiplying the minimum required rate of return times the controllable investment. If we assume that the minimum required rate of return for McCallum Company is 15%, then the actual residual income for 19XX is as follows:

Controllable profit	$175,000
Less: Capital charge	
(15% × $700,000 controllable investment)	105,000
Residual income	$ 70,000

The residual income of $70,000 implies that the investment center manager was successful in using the assets under his or her control in a manner that yielded a profit greater than the minimum profit required to foster profit growth.

The same considerations for determining the items included in controllable investment also apply to residual income. Moreover, as powerful as ROI is in evaluating investment center performance, residual income is even more powerful, as the next section makes clear.

BEHAVIORAL ASPECTS OF INVESTMENT CENTERS

CHAPTER OBJECTIVE 4
Residual income versus return on investment

The structure of the performance evaluation system has a significant effect on the behavior of the center managers. The performance evaluation system and the related incentive compensation system should be designed so that the managers are persuaded to make decisions that are in the best interests of the company. (Recall from Chapter 4 that this is referred to as *goal congruency*.) As we will see in this section, the use of the residual income method of investment center managerial evaluation demands greater goal congruence from the manager, and is thus a more powerful means of evaluation than is return on investment.

The actual results for 19XX for the Furniture Group reveal that return on investment was 25%, versus a budgeted return on investment of 22.6% ($165,000/$730,000). If return on investment were the basis for rewarding the Furniture Group vice-president, it is easy to imagine that he or she might be expecting a sizable bonus and words of congratulations from the company president at year-end.

Suppose that soon after the 19XX performance evaluation report was released, the group vice-president received a formal request from the general manager of the Midwestern Division for $150,000 to replace a nearly obsolete lathe. The request indicates that the annual savings in lathe operating costs were expected to be $30,000, yielding a return on investment of 20% ($30,000/$150,000).

The group vice-president would likely deny the request for funds to acquire the lathe. Acquiring the lathe and increasing the investment would have the effect of diluting the Furniture Group's return on investment to an amount less than the current 25%. Denying the request would be contrary to the best interests of the company, however, because the president had declared that the minimum required rate of return is 15%. The lathe replacement would actually raise company profits because the annual return on the lathe replacement would be in excess of the company's estimated cost of providing the funds to acquire the lathe.

An incentive compensation system that uses return on investment as the basis of investment center managerial performance evaluation invites the kind of dysfunctional decision making described above. Although generally a powerful indicator, return on investment is weak when the manager is faced with an investment decision in which the proposed investment has an expected return on investment greater than the company's minimum required rate of return but less than the manager's existing return on investment.

An incentive compensation system that relies on residual income as the managerial performance indicator would overcome that disadvantage. A top-level manager chooses a minimum required rate of return for all divisions. Income over the capital charge is the division's residual income. In McCallum Company's situation, the Furniture Group vice-president, when faced with the lathe replacement decision, concluded that the lathe replacement would increase the group's residual income, as shown in Exhibit 12-6. Thus, the group vice-president would be inclined to acquire the new lathe, just as the company president would hope. The use of residual income to support an incentive compensation plan is more likely to cause investment center managers to make decisions that are in the best interests of the center and the company alike.

There is one disadvantage associated with using residual income as a basis of performance. Because it is an absolute, rather than a relative, indicator of performance, residual income is not appropriate to use in comparing the performance of managers of investment centers of different sizes. The manager of a large investment center is likely to have a larger residual income than the manager of a small investment center. The difference between residual incomes is more a function of the size of the entity than of the comparative effectiveness of the managers. Return on investment and the resulting percentages allow comparisons among different-size units.

EXHIBIT 12-6	
CALCULATION OF RESIDUAL INCOME RELATED TO THE PROPOSED LATHE REPLACEMENT	
Annual operating cost savings (an increase in controllable profit)	$30,000
Less: Capital charge of 15% (minimum required rate of return) times the $150,000 cost of the new lathe	22,500
Increase in Furniture Group's residual income	$ 7,500

MANAGEMENT ACCOUNTING IN AN AUTOMATED MANUFACTURING ENVIRONMENT

CHAPTER OBJECTIVE 5
Automated manufacturing and direct labor cost

Managerial performance evaluation at the cost center level was emphasized in Chapters 7–11 and in this chapter. Up to now, we have thought of the cost center manager as responsible for the prudent use of direct material, direct labor, and overhead items. However, recent innovations in manufacturing technology have caused management accountants to begin to reevaluate the extent to which the traditional standard costing approaches to cost control are effective in this new manufacturing environment.

Automated manufacturing processes are becoming more prevalent in industry. Manufacturers are converting entire plants from labor-intensive operations to highly automated operations through the use of robotics. New plants are being constructed in which the use of direct labor in the manufacturing process is minimal.

Direct material, although still an important element in the manufacture of products, has become subjected to intense quality scrutiny under the currently popular *just-in-time manufacturing process* (discussed in Chapter 17). *Just-in-time* refers to an approach to production management that attempts to minimize inventories by having the raw materials, work in process, and finished goods arrive just as they are needed. The raw materials arrive just as they are needed in the department where they are introduced in the production system. The work in process inventory arrives just as it is needed at the next machine or the next process, and the finished goods are completed just as the truck is ready to leave for delivery to the customer.

In order for a just-in-time process to function properly, the raw materials being received must pass rigid quality control tests. This is necessary, because the just-in-time system is often supported by a highly automated manufacturing process that does not tolerate raw materials that fail to meet quality and dimensional specifications.

Given the decline in direct labor involved in manufacturing and the greater reliance on quality control personnel for control of direct material costs, management accountants have begun to reconsider the appropriateness of the continued emphasis on direct material and direct labor cost control when evaluating the performance of manufacturing cost center managers.

Management accountants have begun to realize that indirect costs such as equipment maintenance, depreciation, insurance, equipment operating expenses, and indirect labor are fast replacing direct labor and direct material as the costs that the cost center manager must control. Therefore, management accountants are attempting to develop cost control concepts that are appropriate for the control of indirect costs in an automated manufacturing environment. For example, indirect costs (electricity, robots, computers, and so on) are greater than labor costs in the auto industry.

Some have argued that management accountants should begin to focus on the element of overhead costs that relates to equipment. They contend that in automated manufacturing processes equipment costs are so large that it is no longer sufficient to control them using the traditional overhead cost control techniques. They suggest that equipment related costs should be removed from the overhead category and monitored separately using budgets for the expected costs and output for each major item of equipment or each major group of equipment items.

Other authors have suggested the establishment of standards for cost categories currently regarded as part of overhead but directly related to equipment use, such as an indirect laborer who maintains a group of related items of equipment. The establishment of maintenance performance standards based on machine use would aid in the assessment of maintenance efficiency.

This emerging area of automation in manufacturing represents a definite challenge to management accountants to develop innovative approaches to controlling costs through responsibility accounting systems at the cost center level of the company.

TRANSFER PRICING

CHAPTER OBJECTIVE 6
Transferring goods between responsibility centers

The performance evaluation of profit center and investment center managers becomes more difficult when one organizational unit (segment) sells products or services to another within the company. The difficulty arises concerning the **transfer price** that should be charged for the product or service that is transferred from one segment to another segment of the same company. As you would expect, the buying segment wants the lowest possible price, whereas the selling segment wants the highest possible price in order to obtain the best performance evaluations.

In a normal business environment with two separate companies, the market forces would result in a price that favors neither the buyer nor the seller. If the buyer thinks the price is too high, he or she can seek other sellers who might be willing to sell at a lower price. Likewise, if the seller thinks the price is too low, he or she can seek other buyers who might be willing to buy at a higher price.

Intracompany transfers do not take place under the normal circumstances just described. Sellers are often compelled to sell and buyers are often compelled to buy from segments within the company in order to make use of what would otherwise be idle capacity. Thus, a transaction that is not in the best interest of either manager may be in the best interest of the company as a whole.

An Example of Transfer Pricing

Wile Company is a company that manufactures various glass and ceramic products. Additionally, the company has an aeronautics division that develops and manufactures space satellites. The Aeronautics Division buys ceramic parts from the Ceramics Division for use as critical heat-resistant components in the satellites. To illustrate how the overall company interests might be different from the interests of the two

EXHIBIT 12-7

CERAMICS DIVISION FINANCIAL AND OPERATING DATA

Monthly productive capacity	160,000 lbs.
Expected average monthly production for next six months	80,000 lbs.
Expected capacity utilization	50%
Market price per pound of ceramic product	$9.00
Variable costs per pound of ceramic product:	
Direct material	$3.00
Direct labor	1.40
Variable manufacturing overhead	2.10
Total variable cost per pound of ceramic product	$6.50
Fixed costs per month:	
Fixed manufacturing overhead	$200,000
Marketing expenses	30,000
Administrative expenses	45,000
Total fixed costs per month	$275,000

division managers, we will look at the financial and operating data of the Ceramics Division, shown in Exhibit 12-7, and evaluate the consequences of alternative transfer prices.

The Ceramics Division sells to ceramics users both inside and outside Wile Company and is currently operating at 50% of capacity as a result of an economic downturn that has affected the entire ceramics industry. The market price charged by all producers for the kinds of ceramics made by the Ceramics Division has been $9 per pound. However, there have been reports that some ceramics producers have begun to offer special discounts in order to more fully utilize their production capacity.

In response to a large satellite order, the Aeronautics Division has requested that the Ceramics Division provide 60,000 pounds of ceramics per month for each of the next six months. The day after the large satellite order was announced in *The Wall Street Journal,* a competitor of the Ceramics Division contacted the manager of the Aeronautics Division to offer the necessary ceramics at $8 per pound. The Aeronautics Division manager called the manager of the Ceramics Division to report the $8-per-pound offer and to request that the intracompany transfer be made at that price. The Ceramics Division manager refused to sell at such a large discount.

The financial consequences of the Ceramics Division manager's refusal to sell 60,000 pound of ceramics at $8 per pound are displayed in Exhibit 12-8.

The difference in income to the Ceramics Division with and without the internal sale is $90,000—income is $(75,000) without the internal sale and $15,000 with it. This difference is due to the incremental revenues of $480,000 less the incremental costs of $390,000.

EXHIBIT 12-8		
CERAMICS DIVISION INCOME STATEMENTS: FINANCIAL CONSEQUENCES OF REFUSAL TO SELL INTERNALLY		
	With No Internal Sale	With Internal Sale
Expected sales (80,000 lbs. @ $9 per lb.)	$720,000	$ 720,000
Additional sales to Aeronautics		
Division (60,000 lbs. @ $8 per lb.)	–0–	480,000
Total sales	$720,000	$1,200,000
Less: Variable costs:		
Related to normal external sales		
(80,000 lbs. @ $6.50 per lb.)	520,000	520,000
Related to additional internal		
sales to Aeronautics Division		
(60,000 lbs. @ $6.50 per lb.)	–0–	390,000
Contribution margin	$200,000	$ 290,000
Less: Fixed costs	275,000	275,000
Net income or (loss)	$(75,000)	$ 15,000

Clearly, it is advantageous to Wile Company and to the Ceramics Division for the additional ceramics products to be produced internally. The production of the additional 60,000 pounds of ceramics will result in an increase of $90,000 per month in company profits and an improvement of $90,000 per month in the controllable profits of the Ceramics Division. Because this additional production will require no additional capital investment by the Ceramics Division, the additional order will significantly enhance its manager's controllable return on investment and controllable residual income. The Aeronautics Division manager is indifferent about whether the ceramics are purchased internally or externally if they could be purchased from either source at $8 per pound, because her performance evaluation will be the same (given the price of $8) whether the order is purchased internally or externally.

Market Price as Transfer Price

The use of the product's market price as the transfer price is considered the best solution to solving the problems associated with internal transfers of products or services. The use of the market price means that each manager's performance evaluation is equally affected by the supply-and-demand forces that influence that market price. Thus, the performance evaluation would not be influenced by any bargaining advantage that the internal buyer had over the internal seller, or vice versa.

The problem, of course, is determining the true market price. The Aeronautics Division manager regarded $8 per pound as the market price and the Ceramics Division manager regarded $9 per pound as the market price. However, given the assumed economic condition of the ceramics industry, $8 per pound may be close to the "true" market price because the Aeronautics Division manager has a firm quote of $8 per pound from a viable supplier. If out of stubbornness or misinformation the manager of the Ceramics Division remains unwilling to transfer the ceramics at $8 per pound, there should be some mechanism whereby Wile Company's president could offer advice about making the transfer—relying heavily on the data developed as in Exhibit 12-8.

The situation changes drastically if the Ceramics Division is operating at capacity when the order for an additional 60,000 pounds of ceramics is placed with the Ceramics Division. If all of the production were currently being sold to outside users for $9 per pound, there would be no compelling reason to displace 60,000 pounds per month and sell it to the Aeronautics Division at $8 per pound (a quote provided by a ceramics supplier that had idle capacity). The displacement of 60,000 pounds of $9-per-pound ceramics by 60,000 pounds of $8-per-pound ceramics would result in a decline in profits of $60,000 per month and an impaired performance evaluation for the Ceramics Division. Moreover, there would be no offsetting profit advantage to the Aeronautics Division because it can obtain the $8 per pound price from an outside supplier. When the selling division is operating at full capacity, both the total company and the selling division gain by refusing to divert product to an internal division at a selling price that is less than the price at which it can be sold to outside users. The buying division also gains because it is able to benefit from the price concessions made by a producer with idle capacity.

Cost as a Transfer Price

Often the product or service transferred from one division to another has no market price. In such instances, the transfer pricing principles discussed earlier are not particularly useful.

Assume that the Aeronautics Division receives a government order for satellites that require ceramic components having unique heat-transfer properties. The Aeronautics Division manager's discussions with the Ceramics Division manager revealed that ceramic components with those properties were not available from any ceramic producer. However, the Ceramics Division could produce the components with the acquisition of a special heat-treating oven.

In the absence of an established market price, it is tempting to rely on product cost as the transfer price. In fact, many contracts negotiated with the U.S. government contain a provision that unique components transferred from one division to another must be done so at cost when no market value for them is ascertainable.

Behavioral Aspects of Product Cost as Transfer Cost.   There are at least three behavioral problems associated with the use of product cost as the transfer price. The first is the dysfunctional decisions that such a transfer price invites. The cost-based transfer price, unlike the market-based transfer price, provides no mechanism for revealing to the manager whether or not the company would benefit by the transfer.

The second problem is that any profit associated with the production of the unique components appears in the performance report of the division manager who sells the end product to an outside customer. Realizing this, the manager of the supplying division has no real incentive to produce the components because they merely displace profitable business with outside customers.

The third problem is that the use of cost-based transfer prices fails to foster an attitude of cost control among the personnel in the producing division. Because all costs associated with production of the item are transferred to the using division, the producing division has limited incentive to control those costs in order to maximize profit. This problem can be partially overcome by the use of *standard costs* rather than actual costs as the basis for the transfer price. The use of standard costs has the advantage of not passing on inefficiencies from one division to another. Unfavorable variances charged to the first division (as the responsibility of that division's manager) would then not be passed on to the second division, as would occur under an actual cost-based system.

As mentioned, cost-based transfer prices are often found in companies that contract with the U.S. government. Such a practice is probably the result of negotiated contracts that specify cost-based transfer prices for unique components. When government contracts specify cost-based transfer prices, the performance evaluation system often used cost-based transfer prices in spite of all the behavioral problems associated with cost-based transfer prices. The accountants who designed the performance evaluation systems failed to realize that in this era of nearly universal computerized processing of data, cost-based transfer prices could be used for contract costing and market-based transfer prices could be used for performance evaluations by coding the transfer document with both the cost and the market price when it is ascertainable.

Divisional Autonomy versus Intervention by Higher-level Management

In the discussion of Wile Company, it was mentioned that Wile's president might find it necessary to counsel the Ceramics Division manager to sell internally for the sake of the company as a whole despite apparent divisional disincentives to do so. The philosophy of decentralized operations is based on willingness to let responsibility center managers make decisions concerning their own operations without undue interference from higher-level managers. Certainly, the performance evaluation system and the incentive compensation system work best in such an environment.

However, that philosophy also has associated risks. Higher authority must take the risk that responsibility center managers will not always make decisions that are in the best interest of the company or even in the best interest of their own responsibility center.

Wile Company's president is faced with a dilemma: Should he support the philosophy of divisional autonomy, or intervene to avoid the suboptimal (not optimal from firm's point of view) use of company resources? There is no easy answer. Proponents of divisional autonomy would argue that persistent stubbornness on the part of the division manager will be revealed by the performance evaluation system and the manager will be forced to deal with it or lose his or her job. Others might argue that such stubbornness should be dealt with where it surfaces in order to enhance the profits of the company. Regardless of your philosophical position on this point, you must remember that, as a manager, you will also be subject to performance evaluations based on your performance in managing those who report to you. Often the profit pressures on you will be so great that they will tend to overcome even the strongest philosophical position.

Demonstration Problem

Omega Company has two divisions. Alpha Division has controllable profits of $250,000 and controllable investments of $1,000,000. Beta Division has controllable profits of $400,000 and controllable investments of $2,000,000. Additional corporate expenses are $50,000 interest (after-tax) charges that are not allocated to the divisions. Capital charges can be assessed at 15%.

A customer has come to Beta Division and offers to buy 100,000 units of a new gadget at $10 each. Beta would need to invest an additional $1,000,000 of plant and equipment. Beta can obtain the parts it needs from an outsider or it can buy them from Alpha Division. If Beta buys from an outsider, the cost per unit will be $6. If it buys from Alpha, the cost per unit will be $4.

If Alpha Division makes the parts, it will cost the division $2 per unit. It can then sell them to Beta for $4 per unit. If it agrees to this transaction, Alpha Division will incur an additional $500,000 of investments.

Assume a tax rate of 50%.

REQUIRED

a. Determine the current ROI and RI for each division and for the company overall.

b. Determine the ROI and RI for Beta Division and the company overall if the new deal is accepted and Beta buys the parts from an outsider.

c. Explain why Alpha Division might reject making the part.

d. Determine the ROI and RI for each division and for the company overall if the new deal is accepted and Alpha makes the parts.

SOLUTION TO DEMONSTRATION PROBLEM

a. The current ROI and RI:

	Alpha	Beta	Omega
Controllable profit	$ 250,000	$ 400,000	$ 600,000
Controllable investment	1,000,000	2,000,000	3,000,000
Return on investment (ROI)	25%	20%	20%
Controllable profit	$ 250,000	$ 400,000	$ 600,000
Capital charge (15%)	150,000	300,000	450,000
Residual income (RI)	$ 100,000	$ 100,000	$ 150,000

b. The incremental profit to Beta (and to Omega) if the deal is accepted and the parts are bought from an outsider:

Sales (100,000 units @ $10 per unit)	$1,000,000
Cost of sales (100,000 units @ $6 per unit)	600,000
Profit before tax	$ 400,000
Tax	200,000
Profit	$ 200,000

The incremental investment to Beta (and to Omega) is $1,000,000. With this data the new ROI and RI can be obtained:

	Alpha	Beta	Omega
Controllable profit	$ 250,000	$ 600,000	$ 800,000
Controllable investment	1,000,000	3,000,000	4,000,000
Return on investment (ROI)	25%	20%	20%
Controllable profit	$ 250,000	$ 600,000	$ 800,000
Capital charge (15%)	150,000	450,000	600,000
Residual income (RI)	$ 100,000	$ 150,000	$ 200,000

Beta and Omega show no change in ROI. On the other hand, they both show $50,000 more of residual income. This result occurs because the new project earns the previous level of ROI, which is above the minimum required rate of return.

c. The incremental investment to Alpha Division, if it makes the parts, is $500,000. Next we determine the incremental profit to Alpha:

Sales (100,000 units @ $4 per unit)	$400,000
Cost of sales (100,000 units @ $2 per unit)	200,000
Profit before tax	$200,000
Tax	100,000
Profit	$100,000

The new ROI for Alpha would be 23.3%. Alpha Division might reject the offer because its ROI declines.

d. If Beta buys the parts from Alpha at $4, its profit would be:

Sales (100,000 units @ 10 per unit)	$1,000,000
Cost of sales (100,000 units @ $4 per unit)	400,000
Profit before tax	$ 600,000
Tax	300,000
Profit	$ 300,000

If Beta buys the parts from Alpha, the ROIs and the RIs would be:

	Alpha	Beta	Omega
Controllable profit	$ 350,000	$ 700,000	$1,000,000
Controllable investment	1,500,000	3,000,000	4,500,000
ROI	23%	23%	22%
Controllable profit	$ 350,000	$ 700,000	$1,000,000
Capital charge (15%)	225,000	450,000	675,000
Residual income	$ 125,000	$ 250,000	$ 325,000

Review of Chapter Objectives

1. Explain how decentralization affects managerial span of control (pp. 411–14).

   ■ *Span of control* refers to the number of subordinates directly answering to one manager. In a decentralized organization, the authority for decision making is given to persons at various levels within the organization. Control of the firm's finances may become more difficult because there are more people with authority and because authority is spread throughout the organization in uneven ways. Some may be responsible for product costs, such as plant superintendents;

some may assume responsibility for sales, such as marketing managers; and so on. The key point is to evaluate the managers on the basis of what they are responsible for.

■ Responsibility accounting focuses on the performance evaluation of managers of responsibility centers. This performance evaluation is often coupled with an incentive compensation system designed to reward managers for their performance. Basic to the performance evaluation system is the upward communication of actual results versus expected results through a set of hierarchical reports.

2. Describe the three basic types of responsibility centers (pp. 414–16).

■ Responsibility centers are distinguished by what is considered controllable by the manager or management team being evaluated. There are three types of responsibility centers: cost centers, profit centers, and investment centers. Each focuses on controllable items, whether they are costs, profits, or investments.

■ The responsibility centers in which costs are the only element over which the manager exercises control are called cost centers. Responsibility centers in which the manager has control over both costs and revenues are called profit centers. Responsibility centers in which the manager controls costs, revenues, and the capital investment are called investment centers.

■ The cost center manager is evaluated by contrasting actual controllable costs and budgeted controllable costs. The management accountant determines variances of the controllable costs under control of the cost center manager. The evaluation of profit center managers is accomplished by focusing on controllable profit. This is done by examining actual controllable profit against budgeted controllable profit. Finally, the evaluation of investment centers is carried out by observing the actual performance of the investment center against the budgeted amount.

3. Discuss how to measure investment center performance (pp. 416–19).

■ Return on investment is a popular means of evaluating investment center managers. Controllable return on investment is equal to controllable profit divided by controllable investment. A second way to measure performance is called residual income. Residual income is equal to controllable profit minus a capital charge. The capital charge is determined by multiplying the minimum required rate of return times the controllable investment.

4. Show how residual income is superior to return on investment when linked with incentive compensation plans (pp. 419–20).

■ Residual income is superior to the return on investment measure in one important way. The use of return on investment coupled with an incentive compensation system could result in managers ignoring investment opportunities that would tend to lower his or her unit's controllable return on investment even though the investment opportunity might be attractive from the viewpoint of the overall company. The residual income method of performance evaluation overcomes this weakness through the use of a minimum required rate of return, which is established at a high level within the organization for use by all investment center managers within the organization.

5. Explain why automated manufacturing environments are changing the concept of direct labor cost control (pp. 421–22).

■ Automation and the just-in-time manufacturing process are greatly changing the manufacturing situation. Indirect costs such as equipment maintenance, depreciation, insurance, equipment operating expenses, and indirect labor are becoming greater (in some firms much greater) than direct materials and direct labor. Managers who want to control costs should then refocus their attention from direct materials and direct labor to these various indirect costs.

6. Explain how transfer prices are determined for products or services transferred between responsibility centers (pp. 422–26).

■ Intracompany transfers pose particular difficulties as companies increasingly strive to establish an equitable means of evaluating managers. The use of an established market price as the transfer price tends to cause the managers to act in the best interest of the company as they seek to maximize their own performance. However, disagreement over the established market price represents a potential for suboptimal decisions or disagreements among responsibility center managers.

Glossary of Key Terms

capital charge   Controllable investment times the minimum required rate of return. Used in calculating residual income.

controllable investment   The net of assets and liabilities that can be significantly influenced by the decisions of the responsibility center managers.

controllable revenues   Revenues that can be significantly influenced by the decisions of the responsibility center manager.

cost center   A group of operating activities having some common characteristics for the measurement of performance and the assignment of responsibility for the incurrence of costs.

investment center   A unit headed by a manager responsible for costs, revenues, and long-term outlays.

minimum required rate of return   Used in computing residual income, it is the rate of return that reflects the company's estimated cost of capital and growth expectations.

profit center   A segment of a business for which revenues and costs are directly traceable to a segment manager and are accumulated in the accounts. Such data are then used to evaluate managerial performance and accountability.

residual income (controllable)   The net income that the investment center manager is able to earn above the capital charge. The capital charge is based on the controllable investment.

responsibility accounting   A reporting system in which costs and revenues are assigned to the level of the organization having responsibility for them.

return on investment (controllable)   The ratio of controllable profit to controllable investment.

span of control   The number of subordinates directly answering to one manager.

transfer price   The price charged on a good transferred between divisions of the same company.

Review Questions

12-1 What is a responsibility center?

12-2 What is a responsibility accounting system?

12-3 Why is it necessary to understand the responsibility of the managers of each organizational level when developing a responsibility accounting system.

12-4 What is a cost center?

12-5 What is a profit center?

12-6 What is an investment center?

12-7 What is the significance of the word *controllable* in the term *controllable return of investment?*

12-8 Explain the concept of residual income.

12-9 How does residual income differ from return on investment?

12-10 Why is residual income more powerful as an indicator of managerial performance than is return on investment?

12-11 What does the term *just-in-time* refer to?

12-12 Why has the just-in-time approach to production management resulted in reduced focus on direct material and direct labor cost control?

12-13 Why has the just-in-time approach to production management resulted in increased focus on manufacturing overhead control?

12-14 What are transfer prices?

12-15 Why is the market price the most appropriate transfer price when there is idle capacity at the factory of the producer of the item or service being transferred?

12-16 Why is the cost of the item being transferred not an appropriate transfer price?

12-17 Under what conditions is the cost of the item the appropriate transfer price?

12-18 What transfer pricing policy would be most appropriate when the producer of the item is operating at full capacity?

Discussion Questions

12-19 One criticism of using return on investment as a measure of management performance arises when the investment center has old plant and equipment. The manager has an incentive not to invest in new plant and equipment, but instead continues to use the old. Explain this phenomenon. What might be done to overcome this problem?

12-20 What advantages are there to using standard cost as the transfer price?

Exercises

CO 2, 3   12-21 **EVALUATING PROFIT CENTER MANAGERS** Wabash Company has three operating divisions for which it reported the following information:

Division	Sales	Cost of Goods Sold	Marketing Expenses	Controllable Assets
Alpha	$ 50,000	$ 30,000	$ 5,000	$ 75,000
Beta	100,000	65,000	12,000	110,000
Delta	75,000	45,000	15,000	50,000

a. Calculate the controllable return on investment for each division.

b. Calculate the controllable residual income for each division assuming that the corporation's minimum required rate of return is 20%.

12-22   RETURN ON INVESTMENT VERSUS RESIDUAL INCOME The Purdue Division of Big Ten Corporation achieved a profit of $2,000,000 on a controllable investment of $8,000,000 for the year just ended. Now the Purdue Division manager is evaluating an investment proposal that has been submitted by the supervisor of the Milling Department. This proposal would require the investment of $200,000 immediately. The investment would result in annual operating expense savings of $40,000. The president of Big Ten Corporation has stated that acquisition proposals that earn in excess of 15% annually should get favorable consideration.

CO 3

a. Calculate the return on investment for the year just ended.

b. Calculate the residual income for the year just ended. Use 15% as the minimum required rate of return.

c. If the manager of the Purdue Division is evaluated based on return on investment, what is that manager likely to decide with regard to the proposed investment? Why?

d. If the manager of the Purdue Division is evaluated based on residual income, what is that manager likely to decide with regard to the proposed investment? Why?

12-23   CONTROLLABLE RETURN ON INVESTMENT Monmouth Company has three operating divisions. One of the divisions, Gamma Division, had the following divisional financial statements for the year just ended:

CO 3

Partial Income Statement

Revenue	$3,000,000
Less: Cost of Goods Sold	2,000,000
Gross Profit	$1,000,000
Less: Operating Expenses:	
Incurred by the Division	300,000
Allocated Corporate Expenses	100,000
Net Income	$ 600,000

Partial Balance Sheet

ASSETS

Current Assets

Cash	$ 100,000	
Accounts Receivable	400,000	
Inventory	1,000,000	
Total Current Assets		$1,500,000

(continued)

Fixed Assets

Assets used in the Division (net of depreciation)	2,000,000	
Corporate Assets Allocated to the Division	500,000	2,500,000
Total Assets		$4,000,000

LIABILITIES

Current Liabilities

Accounts Payable	$ 500,000	
Other	100,000	
Total Current Liabilities		$ 600,000

Long-term Liabilities

Long-term Debt	1,000,000	
Division Equity	2,400,000	3,400,000
Total Liabilities and Equity		$4,000,000

The manager of Gamma Division has no responsibility for the long-term debt or the other current liabilities on the balance sheet.

Prepare a schedule that shows the calculation of the controllable return on investment.

12-24 RESIDUAL INCOME AND RETURN ON INVESTMENT Supply the missing data in the following table:

CO 3

	Division		
	Sigma	**Iota**	**Rho**
Sales	$100,000	$150,000	$200,000
Controllable income	?	$ 45,000	$ 65,000
Controllable assets	$200,000	?	$500,000
Controllable return on investment	12.5%	15%	13%
Minimum required rate of return	15%	10%	?
Residual income	$ (5,000)	$ 15,000	$(35,000)

12-25 INVESTMENT DECISIONS USING RESIDUAL INCOME Selected financial information for the three operating divisions of Knox Company is presented in the following table. The manager of each of these divisions is an investment center manager who is evaluated based on residual income.

CO 3, 4

	Division A	Division B	Division C
Controllable income	$ 100,000	$150,000	$ 200,000
Controllable investment	$1,000,000	$750,000	$1,500,000
Minimum required rate of return	15%	15%	15%

a. Compute the residual income for the manager of each division.

b. Assume that each division manager is presented with an investment opportunity that will involve an investment of $500,000 and will yield operating expense savings of $85,000 per year.

Which division managers will be likely to make the investment of $500,000? If you were the president of the company, would you agree with the decision of each division manager?

12-26 COST CENTER VS. PROFIT CENTER Albion Company is organized into divisions with a vice-president in charge of each division. The division vice-president is in charge of manufacturing and selling the product through a director of marketing who reports to the division vice-president. The director of manufacturing also reports to the division vice-president.

CO 2

The division vice-president is not permitted to make major investment decisions without the approval of the president of the company. The division vice-president also does not have the authority to borrow money to use within his or her division.

a. What level of responsibility accounting should be used to evaluate the performance of the division vice-president?

b. What responsibility accounting method should be used to evaluate the performance of the director of manufacturing?

12-27 PROFIT CENTER VS. INVESTMENT CENTER Hillsdale Company is organized into product groups with each group including several operating divisions. The operating divisions are headed by division directors who are responsible for manufacturing and marketing the products produced by the division. The vice-president in charge of each product group is responsible for the divisions reporting to him or her. Additionally, the group vice-president is responsible for making investment decisions for all of the divisions within the group.

CO 2, 3

a. What responsibility accounting method should be used to evaluate the performance of the group vice-president?

b. What responsibility accounting method should be used to evaluate the performance of the division directors?

12-28 TRANSFER PRICE UNDER IDLE CAPACITY The vice president of administration for Wooster Company has established an intracompany price of $40 per hour for computer programming services performed by the Systems Department. That department has sufficient personnel to perform 20,000 more hours of computer programming services per year than it currently performs.

CO 6

The Central Division, a profit center, needs approximately 3,000 hours of computer programming during the next year; but the division vice-president objects to paying the intracompany charge of $40 per hour when she has found a qualified computer programmer outside the company who will perform the services at $35 per hour.

In discussing the situation with the vice president of administration, the Central Division vice president has threatened to use the outside programmer unless the intracompany price is lowered to $35.

How should the vice president of administration react to the threat when you consider that the president of the corporation desires the implementation of systems that encourage cooperation among divisions for the sake of the company's larger goals?

12-29 TRANSFER PRICING UNDER PURE COMPETITION Coe Company is a division of Grinnell Corporation, which produces a product that is sold in a market characterized by pure competition. The product sells for $30 per unit. The total manufacturing cost is $20 per unit; and $15 of that amount is variable manufacturing cost. Coe's productive capacity is 3,000 units per year. Another division of Grinnell, Beloit Company, has requested 4,000 units of the product for the next year.

CO 6

a. At what price should the transfer be made between Coe Company and Beloit Company?

b. What is the difference in total profits to Grinnell Corporation if Coe Company sells the 3,000 units to an outside company at $30 each and Beloit Company buys the 3,000 units from an outside company at $30 each? Explain.

12-30   TRANSFER PRICE RANGE Center Company is a decentralized company having several divisions that are evaluated on residual income. Whitenburg Division has capacity to make 10,000 units of its product. The variable costs of the product are $50 per unit. Oxford Division can use the Whitenburg Division product in the manufacture of its product. Oxford requires $20 of variable cost to convert the Whitenburg product to a product that sells for $130.

CO 6

Answer the following questions, which are independent of each other.

a. Whitenburg Division can sell all that it produces at a price of $80 per unit. Oxford Division needs 1,000 units. What is the proper transfer price?

b. Whitenburg Division can sell 8,000 units at $80 per unit. There is no market for the other 2,000 units of capacity except for Oxford Division, which needs 1,000 units. What is the bargaining range for transfer pricing purposes?

12-31   TRANSFER PRICING Georgetown Company has two operating divisions, Bluffton Division and Earlham Division. Components of Bluffton Division's product are purchased from outside suppliers at a cost of $80 per unit. However, the components are also available from Earlham Division. Earlham Division has unused capacity and is able to produce the components needed by Bluffton Division at a variable cost of $55 per unit.

CO 6

If a transfer price of $75 per unit is established and 4,000 units are transferred to Earlham Division with no reduction in Bluffton Division's current sales:

a. How much would Georgetown Company's total profits increase?

b. How much would Bluffton Division's profits increase?

c. How much would Earlham Division's profits increase?

Problems

12-32   PERFORMANCE EVALUATION The most recent income statement of the Lawrence Division of Ripon Company is represented below:

CO 3

Sales	$5,000,000
Less: Cost of Goods Sold	3,000,000
Gross Profit	2,000,000
Less: Operating Expense	1,300,000
Controllable Income	$ 700,000
Controllable Investment	$4,000,000

The president of Ripon Company has stated that he expects the vice-president in charge of the Lawrence Division to earn a controllable return on investment of 20% by the end of next year if he is to remain with the company. The Lawrence Division manager is pondering the following alternatives:

Proposal A: Discontinue a product line. This line has a controllable profit of $100,000 per year and $400,000 of controllable investment associated with it.

Proposal B: Purchase new equipment for $200,000 to replace $30,000 of direct labor annually as it automates a particular production process.

Proposal C: Eliminate the contract transportation that is used to deliver the products. Instead, lease three trucks to provide the transportation. Contract transportation costs of $120,000 would be eliminated; and the costs of leasing, driving, and operating the three leased trucks would be only $100,000 per year. The lease would be regarded as an operating lease and not a capital lease.

REQUIRED

Analyze the three proposals and determine which ones should be implemented in order to achieve the objective of a 20% controllable return on investment for the division.

12-33 RESIDUAL INCOME VS. RETURN ON INVESTMENT Carleton Company has four operating divisions. The managers of these divisions are evaluated and rewarded based on the controllable return on investment for the division. The financial results for the Educational Division for the year just ended were as follows:

Sales	$9,000,000
Less: Variable expense	6,000,000
Contribution margin	$3,000,000
Less: Fixed expense	1,700,000
Controllable income	$1,300,000
Controllable investment	$6,500,000

Carleton Company had a return on investment of 15% on a consolidated basis (the entire company). The Educational Division which has an opportunity to add a computer training course to its line, would require an additional investment of $1,000,000. It is estimated that the new computer training course would have the following annual data:

Sales	$3,000,000
Less: Variable expenses	2,000,000
Contribution margin	$1,000,000
Less: Fixed expenses	820,000
Controllable income	$ 180,000

REQUIRED

a. Assuming you are the head of the Education Division, decide whether you would be inclined to implement the proposed new computer training course. Explain and support your explanations with calculations.

b. Assuming you are the president of Carleton Company, decide whether you would urge the head of the Education Division to implement the new computer training course. Explain and support your explanations with calculations.

c. Assume that the president of the company considers the minimum acceptable rate of return to be 16% and the division managers are evaluated using the controllable residual income rather than the controllable return on investment. Explain whether the head of the Education Division would choose to implement the new computer training offering. Explain and support your explanation with calculations.

12-34 ANALYSIS USING RESIDUAL INCOME St. Olaf Company uses the residual income to evaluate the performance of division managers. The president of the company has determined that the minimum required rate of return used in determining the residual income should be 20%. One of the division managers is considering three investment proposals that have been suggested by operating personnel. Information on those three proposals is given as follows:

	Investment 1	Investment 2	Investment 3
Expected annual income	$2,000	$150,000	$200,000
Expected investment	$8,000	$900,000	$950,000

REQUIRED

a. Explain which investment opportunity you would consider the most promising if you were the division manager.

b. State whether you would select more than just one of the investment alternatives and why.

12-35 PROFIT CENTER AND COST CENTER PERFORMANCE REPORTS
Budgeted and actual results for the Westminster Division of Rose Corporation are as follows as of December 31, 19X1.

CO 2, 3

Division Profit
($000s)

	Actual	Budget	Variance
Revenues	$800.0	$850.0	$(50.0)
Less: Cost of goods sold:			
Direct materials	225.0	245.0	20.0
Direct labor	150.0	120.0	(30.0)
Manufacturing overhead	175.0	160.0	(15.0)
Gross profit	$250.0	$325.0	$(75.0)
Less: Operating expenses:			
Marketing expense	90.0	100.0	10.0
Administrative expense	60.0	80.0	20.0
Net income	$100.0	$145.0	$(45.0)

REQUIRED

Restructure the information on the performance report in order to prepare one report that is appropriate to evaluate the performance of the manufacturing manager and another report that is appropriate to evaluate the performance of the marketing manager.

12-36 CONTROL OF COSTS IN AUTOMATED MANUFACTURING Williams Company has operated a manufacturing facility that was recently converted from a labor-intensive manufacturing operation to one that is operated using the just-in-time philosophy and is highly automated with robots. The cost center performance report for the manufacturing manager for the last year of labor-intensive operations is as follows:

CO 5

Manufacturing Manager's Performance Report
Williams Company
For the Year Ended December 31, 19X0
($000s)

	Actual	Budget	Variance
Direct materials	$1,200	$1,250	$ 50
Direct labor	4,000	3,700	(300)
Manufacturing overhead	2,000	2,100	100
Total manufacturing costs	$7,200	$7,050	$(150)

The actual cost information collected by the accounting department during the first year of operations in an automated just-in-time environment is shown below:

Actual Manufacturing Costs
($000s)
For 19X1

Direct material	$1,300
Direct labor	400
Depreciation	2,000
Maintenance	1,000
Scheduling	1,500
Indirect labor	500

The budgeted cost information for the first year of just-in-time operations is shown below:

Budgeted Manufacturing Costs
($000s)
For 19X1

Direct material	$1,200
Direct labor	450
Depreciation	2,000
Maintenance	900
Scheduling	1,700
Indirect labor	600

REQUIRED

a. Prepare a performance evaluation report for the manager of the manufacturing cost center for the year 19X1, the first year of just-in-time operations.

b. Compare the performance report prepared before the conversion to just-in-time operation with the performance report prepared in response to requirement a. Comment on the differences between the two reports and relate those differences to the essential characteristics of an automated just-in-time manufacturing process.

CO 6   12-37 **TRANSFER PRICING** The Hamline Division of Macalester Company has the following budget for next year:

Revenues (300,000 units @ $5 per unit)	$1,500,000
Less: Variable expenses ($3 per unit)	900,000
Contribution margin	$ 600,000
Fixed expenses	400,000
Pretax profits	$ 200,000

The Alverno Division of Macalester Company wants to acquire 25,000 units of the Hamline Division's product in the first year. The Alverno Division would take the component from the Hamline Division and modify it at an additional variable cost of $1 per unit and then sell the final product for $9 per unit.

Hamline has a productive capacity of 330,000 units per year.

REQUIRED

a. Calculate what would happen to the profit of Macalester Company if the transaction took place at a transfer price of $4 per unit.

b. Calculate what would happen to the contribution margin of each division if the transaction took place at a transfer price of $4 per unit.

c. State the minimum transfer price per unit that the Hamline Division should accept for the additional production of 25,000 units. Decide whether that is the minimum transfer price that the president of Macalester Company would agree to.

12-38 TRANSFER PRICING Wheaton Company recently acquired a ball bearing producer in order to provide a source of ball bearings for its other operating division, which manufactures conveyer equipment. The Ball Bearing Division has a productive capacity of 2,000,000 bearing sets per year and it has been selling them for $3.50 per set. The Conveyer Division has been buying the same type of ball bearing sets for $3.45 per set.

CO 6

An analysis of the costs for the newly acquired ball bearing division reveals the following information:

	Costs per Ball Bearing Set
Direct material	$1.10
Direct labor	.50
Variable manufacturing overhead	.40
Fixed manufacturing overhead ($2,000,000 per year)	1.00
Total cost per set	$3.00

The Ball Bearing Division has sales to outsiders of 1,600,000 bearing sets per year. The Conveyer Division needs 400,000 sets per year.

REQUIRED

a. Show whether the manager of the Ball Bearing Division should sell the ball bearing sets to the Conveyer Division for $3.45. Find the lowest transfer price that manager could agree to without decreasing the division's profit below what it would be without the order from the Conveyer Division.

b. Suppose that the Ball Bearing Division agrees to transfer the 400,000 ball bearing sets at $3.50 per set, rather than the $3.45 price in requirement a. Explain how each of the three entities' profits would be affected by the choice of the $3.50 transfer price.

c. If the Ball Bearing Division had orders for 2,000,000 sets per year (the entire production capacity) to outsiders, and the president of Wheaton Company decides that 400,000 sets should be diverted to the Conveyer Division at $3.45 per unit, explain the effect on profits for Wheaton Company. Assume that the sets could be sold to outsiders at $3.50 per unit and the sets could be purchased from others by the Conveyer Division at $3.45 per set.

12-39 **COST CENTER VS. PROFIT CENTER IN TRANSFER PRICING CON-TEXT** Grace Company's Grain Division provides the grain necessary for the production of breakfast cereal in the Breakfast Food Division. The Grain Division sells all of its output to the Breakfast Food Division. The grain is produced at the costs indicated below:

CO 2, 3, 6

	Cost per Unit of Grain
Direct material	$5.00
Direct labor	2.00
Variable manufacturing overhead	1.00
Fixed manufacturing overhead	1.50
Total	$9.50

Both of the division managers are evaluated based on the controllable profits of their divisions. The Grain Division has been transferring grain to the Breakfast Food Division at $12 per unit; however, the manager of the Breakfast Food Division recently received a bid of $11 per unit from an outside competitor of the Grain Division.

When the Breakfast Food Division manager approached the Grain Division manager about reducing the transfer price to $11, the manager of the Grain Division refused to consider the reduction in transfer price.

Before placing the order with the outside supplier, the manager of the Breakfast Food Division contacts you, the corporate controller, to advise you of the action he was about to take in order to enhance his division's controllable profit. You have had prior experience with the Grain Division manager and you know that he is unlikely to change his mind about reducing the transfer price. Explain your actions in this situation.

Business Decision Case

Adolphus Company has three operating divisions. Division X and Division Y each make a component that is sent to Division Z for assembly into the final product. One unit of Division X's component and one unit of Division Y's component are required to make one unit of the Division Z final product. Information on the final product is as follows:

Selling price	$150
Variable expenses:	
Division X	$ 40
Division Y	30
Division Z	20
Total variable expenses	$ 90

The capacity of all divisions is 20,000 units and all operate at full capacity.

The transfer price for Division X's component is $50 and the transfer price for Division Y's component is $38. However, Division Z has been offered the opportunity to buy Division X's component from an outside supplier for $47, $3 per unit below the transfer price.

REQUIRED

a. Determine whether the offer from the outside supplier should be accepted. In making this determination, consider that Division X will lower the transfer price to $47 if requested.

b. Assume that Division X is able to sell its entire output of 20,000 units if it does additional work on the component to ready it for a slightly different market. This additional work would enable Division X to sell the modified component for $60, and the additional variable costs per unit to make the modification would be only $4 per unit. No additional fixed costs would have to be incurred in order to make the modification. Determine whether Division X should meet the $47 price of the outside supplier or modify the component for sale to outsiders at the $60 price. Use calculations to support your answer.

Chapter

13

Segment Reporting

CHAPTER OBJECTIVES

After reading Chapter 13, you should be able to:

1. Indicate the difference between separable and common fixed costs (p. 443).

2. Explain the difference between segment margin and contribution margin (pp. 443–47).

3. Describe a business segment report (pp. 443–49).

4. Discuss the way in which direct costing differs from absorption costing and the implication for performance evaluation (pp. 449–59).

5. Describe the behavioral aspects of absorption costing (pp. 457–58).

6. Explain how to price products (pp. 459–63).

7. Discuss the overhead allocation of service departments (Appendix C) (pp. 465–71).

*I*n this chapter we shift the focus of performance evaluation from the manager of an organizational unit, which was discussed in the previous chapter, to the organizational unit itself. The evaluation of organizational units is important if management is to make informed decisions about the economic viability of these units.

Organizational units are called *segments,* and a segment is any organizational entity that can be separately described. Examples of business segments would include a product line, an operating division, a department, or a marketing territory.

THE SEGMENT REPORT

Separable vs. Common Costs

CHAPTER
OBJECTIVE 1
*Separable vs. common
fixed costs*

Just as responsibility accounting relies on a distinction between controllable and noncontrollable costs, segment reporting relies upon a distinction between separable and common costs. Separable costs (sometimes called *traceable costs*) are costs that are so directly associated with the segment that they would be eliminated if the segment were eliminated. Examples might include the salary of the manager of the segment, the supplies used by the segment, or the direct materials used in the product manufactured by the segment.

Common costs, as defined in Chapter 4, are costs that are not directly associated with one segment. These include costs that would tend to recur even if the segment were eliminated. In a multidivision company, the salary of the president of the company would be a common cost when viewed from the perspective of one of the company's divisions. The president's salary is regarded as a common cost because the services provided by that person are shared by all divisions. The elimination of one of the divisions is not likely to result in the elimination of the president.

An Example of a Segment Report

CHAPTER
OBJECTIVE 2
*Segment margin versus
contribution margin*

Ruble Company is a manufacturer of leather and metal specialty items. The company's organization chart is described in Exhibit 13-1.

Although the metal products are manufactured in plants that are separate from the leather product manufacturing facilities, the marketing effort is organized around geographical territories with the salespersons in each of the two territories selling both leather and metal products.

The distinction between separable and common costs, and the proper structuring of the accounting information based on that distinction, will permit an evaluation of the economic viability of the various identifiable segments within the company. As we will see, it is virtually impossible to evaluate segments without properly structuring the accounting information.

CHAPTER
OBJECTIVE 3
*Business segment
report*

Exhibit 13-2 shows a skeletal form of the calculation of segment margin. Sales made by the segment less the variable costs of the segment yields the segment's contribution margin. The contribution margin of the segment less the separable fixed costs of the segment gives the segment margin. As will be shown, this segment margin is used to evaluate the economic effectiveness of the segment.

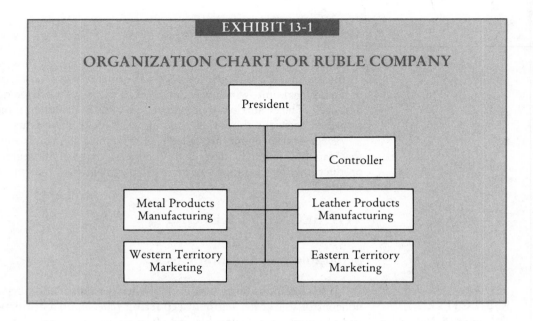

EXHIBIT 13-1

ORGANIZATION CHART FOR RUBLE COMPANY

President

Controller

Metal Products Manufacturing

Leather Products Manufacturing

Western Territory Marketing

Eastern Territory Marketing

EXHIBIT 13-2

CALCULATION OF SEGMENT MARGIN

Segment sales	$XXX
Less: Segment variable costs	XXX
Segment contribution margin	$XXX
Less: Segment separable fixed costs	XXX
Segment margin	$XXX

The upper portion of Exhibit 13-3 focuses on the segments regarded as the two product lines that Ruble Company manufactures. The report shows that during the month of July the leather products line had sales exceeding the separable expenses by $40,000. On the other hand, the metal products line had separable expenses that were greater than the sales of those products. The difference between sales and separable expenses is called the *segment margin* when used in a general context. Once the segment has been identified, as it has been in this situation (where the segment is the product), we may more specifically identify the difference between sales and separable expenses as the product margin.

The product margin of $(15,000) for the metal products line indicates that the financial results for July would have been enhanced if there had been no metal products. In fact, if the company management expects the prospects for metal products to continue at the same level, the line should be discontinued. Discontinuance would result in loss of the sales, but it would also result in the elimination of a greater amount of separable expenses that are identified with those products.

EXHIBIT 13-3

Ruble Company Segment Report
July 19XX

Segments

	Metal Products	Leather Products	Total Company
Sales	$150,000	$225,000	$375,000
Less: Separable variable expenses:			
Direct material, direct labor, overhead	60,000	85,000	145,000
Administrative and marketing	15,000	20,000	35,000
Contribution margin	$ 75,000	$120,000	$195,000
Less: Separable fixed expenses:			
Overhead	85,000	70,000	$155,000
Administrative and marketing	5,000	10,000	15,000
Segment (product) margin	$(15,000)	$ 40,000	$ 25,000
Less: Common fixed expenses			10,000
Net income			$ 15,000

Metal Products

	Western Territory	Eastern Territory	Total Metal Products
Sales	$50,000	$100,000	$150,000
Less: Separable variable expenses:			
Direct material, direct labor, overhead	20,000	40,000	60,000
Administrative and marketing	5,000	10,000	15,000
Contribution margin	$25,000	$ 50,000	$ 75,000
Less: Separable fixed expenses:			
Administrative and marketing	1,000	1,000	2,000
Segment (territory) margin	$24,000	$ 49,000	$ 73,000
Less: Common fixed expenses:			
Overhead			85,000
Administrative and marketing			3,000
Segment (product) margin			$(15,000)

Leather Products

	Western Territory	Eastern Territory	Total Leather Products
Sales	$200,000	$25,000	$225,000
Less: Separable variable expenses:			
Direct material, direct labor, overhead	65,000	20,000	85,000
Administrative and marketing	15,000	5,000	20,000
Contribution margin	$120,000	$ –0–	$120,000
Less: Separable fixed expenses:			
Administrative and marketing	2,000	2,000	4,000
Segment (territory) margin	$118,000	$(2,000)	$116,000
Less: Common fixed expenses:			
Overhead			70,000
Administrative and marketing			6,000
Segment (product) margin			$ 40,000

In Exhibit 13-3, a subtotal entitled "contribution margin" precedes the segment margin. Such a subtotal is useful for short-term decisions. In addition, it is convenient because the distinction between separable and common costs is facilitated by the fixed-versus-variable distinction that is important in arriving at the contribution margin. Variable costs may always be regarded as separable costs, because if the segment were eliminated the segment's variable costs, by their very nature, will also be eliminated. Thus, after identifying costs as variable and fixed, the further identification of separable costs requires a focus on only the fixed costs.

The separable fixed expenses associated with the metal products line include $85,000 of fixed manufacturing overhead and $5,000 of administrative and marketing expenses. The recommendation to discontinue the metal products line was based on the assumption that if the line were eliminated the manufacturing overhead would be eliminated through the disposal of the manufacturing facilities.

The $10,000 of common fixed expenses, shown in the total company column of the upper portion of Exhibit 13-3, includes the fixed costs associated with the president and the controller of the company. These expenses are not directly associated with either segment; they are expenses incurred in support of both lines. The elimination of either of the lines will not eliminate the need for the president's or the controller's services. However, if it were expected that the cost of the controller's activity could be trimmed if a line were eliminated, then some part of the expense associated with the controller could appropriately be classified as separable.

In the lower part of Exhibit 13-3, the $(15,000) product margin for the metal products line and the $40,000 product margin for the leather products line are further detailed in terms of the territories in which they were marketed. The report shows that the metal products were more profitable in the eastern market than in the western market and that the opposite was true of the leather products.

The $75,000 of contribution margin for the metal products line is detailed to show that $25,000 was generated by the western territory and $50,000 was generated by the eastern territory. At the contribution margin level, the sum of the territory contribution margins $(25,000 + $50,000) is equal to the product contribution margin of $75,000.

The same is not true at the segment margin level. The territory margins of $24,000 and $49,000 do not sum to the product margin of $(15,000). The reason for this difference between the contribution margin level and the segment margin level is that variable expenses used in arriving at contribution margin are separable under all circumstances, whereas the fixed costs subtracted from contribution margin are *not* separable under all circumstances. The $85,000 of fixed manufacturing overhead for metal products is related to the manufacturing facility and may only be eliminated by eliminating the entire product.

The elimination of one of the marketing territories would not permit the elimination of any of those manufacturing overhead expenses because the facility would still be necessary to manufacture the product for sale in the territory that remained. Manufacturing overhead related to metal products is a common cost when viewed from the perspective of the marketing territories.

The same phenomenon occurs with the administrative and marketing expense. When viewed from the perspective of the metal products segment, the separable amount of administrative and marketing expense is $5,000. When viewed from the perspective of the marketing territories, the total separable amount is only $2,000 ($1,000 for each territory). The difference of $3,000 is considered a cost that is common to both territories when viewed from a territory perspective. This difference may be explained by describing the $5,000 as the metal products segments' separable fixed administrative and marketing expense. Of the $5,000 amount, $2,000 relates to advertising in regional publications. One-half of the latter amount was spent in each of the two marketing territories. The remaining $3,000 relates to administrative and marketing expenses that are common to both territories and thus relate uniquely to neither of the territories.

Necessity of Multiple Perspectives

It is possible that the segment report could have been prepared with only a marketing territory perspective. Such a report would have revealed a segment profit for the metal products line in both the western territory and the eastern territory and led the company management to believe that the line was making a contribution to covering the common fixed costs of the company. However, it must be remembered that the separable fixed costs on the marketing territory report do not include the manufacturing overhead. Those costs are included in the report's common fixed costs. The preparation of a report from the product line perspective permits an appropriate assessment of the economic viability of each product line. Thus, it is important to note that there is an important decision regarding the appropriate type of segment report.

If the accounting system were designed to identify sales and costs of the product items associated with each product line, it would be possible to prepare a segment report that would show the product item margin for each of the products included in the product line. Such a report might reveal that only one type of metal product is causing the unfavorable performance of the metal products line because of unusually high variable costs or because of extraordinarily high fixed overhead costs uniquely related to the product. Such a report would indicate that only one product, rather then the entire product line, should be eliminated.

Reference to Exhibit 13-3 will also reveal another reason why multiple-perspective segment reports are helpful in management decision making. The territory margin for the leather products line in the eastern territory has a loss of $(2,000). If such performance were expected to persist, it would be prudent to discontinue offering the leather products line in the eastern market. This might permit an increased marketing effort in the western territory or, at minimum, a reallocation of effort and resources.

The negative metal product line margin and the negative eastern territory margin for the leather products line could persuade company management to eliminate all segments except the leather products line sold in the western territory. However, the company could try another course of action. It could use the segment reports to guide its efforts to bolster company profits by developing strategies for improving the prospects for the weaker segments. Regardless of the action of management, the appropriate view of costs as separable or common and the proper structuring of the accounting information toward this distinction is a tremendous aid to management control by alerting management to the need for corrective action. Some corrective action is required for the unprofitable segments.

ALLOCATION OF COMMON COSTS

Often in practice, common costs are allocated to segments in the interest of determining the "full cost" associated with the segment. This allocation is rationalized on the assumption that common costs are support costs that would have had to be incurred by

---

EXHIBIT 13-4

SEGMENT INCOME STATEMENT (NOT "FULL COST" APPROACH)

Spiller Company
Segment Income Statement
August 19XX

	Product 1	Product 2	Product 3	Total Company
Sales	$30,000	$50,000	$20,000	$100,000
Less: Separable variable expenses:				
Direct material, direct labor, overhead	18,000	25,000	14,000	57,000
Contribution margin	$12,000	$25,000	$ 6,000	$ 43,000
Less: Separable fixed expenses:				
Advertising expense	6,000	10,000	4,000	20,000
Product margin	$ 6,000	$15,000	$ 2,000	$ 23,000
Common fixed expenses:				
Marketing expense				$ 12,000
Administrative expense				8,000
Net income				$ 3,000

---

the segment if the segment were completely autonomous. This arbitrary "full costs" approach is often applied to products in an attempt to determine the total costs of the product.

Spiller Company manufactures three related products and markets them through a group of salaried salespersons. From a segment reporting viewpoint, the August 19XX product report revealed the segment performances described in Exhibit 13-4. Using the "full cost" approach, a profit-oriented evaluation showing each product would indicate the report shown in Exhibit 13-5. Exhibit 13-5 is based on an allocation of common fixed costs using relative sales as the basis of allocation (for a review, see p. 117).

The dangers of preparing "full cost" profit-oriented segment reports are clear when the two reports are compared. The use of the "full cost" approach reveals that the net income of product 1 is zero and product 3 has a loss of $2,000. Yet the segment report in which common costs were not allocated indicated that all three products were profitable at the product margin level.

Clearly, the report that does *not* allocate common fixed costs is the report that is appropriate for evaluating the economic viability of the products. The "full cost" profit-oriented product report is not useful for control or decision-making purposes because it is based on a misconception regarding costs. *The misconception is that the marketing costs of $12,000 and administrative costs of $8,000 are expenses that are in some way related to the level of sales.* By relating those costs to sales we are, in effect, regarding them as variable costs; in fact, they are fixed costs that are not likely to be influenced by the level of sales.

EXHIBIT 13-5

SEGMENT INCOME STATEMENT ("FULL COST" APPROACH)

Spiller Company
Segment Income Statement
August 19XX

	Product 1	Product 2	Product 3	Total Company
Sales	$30,000	$50,000	$20,000	$100,000
Less: Variable expenses:				
Direct material	$12,000	$18,000	$10,000	$ 40,000
Direct labor	3,000	3,000	2,000	8,000
Overhead	3,000	4,000	2,000	9,000
Total variable expense	$18,000	$25,000	$14,000	$ 57,000
Contribution margin	$12,000	$25,000	$ 6,000	$ 43,000
Less: Fixed expenses:				
Advertising expense	$ 6,000	$10,000	$ 4,000	$ 20,000
Allocated marketing expense*	3,600	6,000	2,400	12,000
Allocated administrative expense*	2,400	4,000	1,600	8,000
Total fixed expenses	$12,000	$20,000	$ 8,000	$ 40,000
Net income	$ –0–	$ 5,000	$(2,000)	$ 3,000

*Product 1 had 30% of the total company sales for the month ($30,000/$100,000), thus Product 1 is allocated 30% of the total marketing expense (.3 × $12,000 = $3,600) and 30% of the total administrative expense (.3 × $8,000 = $2,400).

A related issue is the overhead allocation of service departments. This is covered in Appendix C, pages 465–71, at the end of this chapter.

ABSORPTION COSTING VS. DIRECT COSTING

CHAPTER OBJECTIVE 4
How direct costing differs from absorption costing

In Chapter 5, and briefly in Chapter 7, we discussed the *absorption* method of costing also known as "full costing." That method of costing inventories is the proper method from a financial accounting viewpoint. Financial statements released to the public must be based on the absorption method of costing inventories. For a manufacturing company, the absorption method of costing results in inventory costs that include both variable costs and fixed manufacturing costs. The variable costs are the direct material, direct labor, and variable manufacturing overhead. The fixed costs include the fixed manufacturing overhead items such as depreciation, maintenance expenses, and supervisory salaries.

As we will demonstrate in this section, the use of absorption costing for performance evaluation purpose may result in dysfunctional actions by managers, who are concerned about their own evaluations or about the evaluation of the segmental unit with which they are associated. In particular, by producing more goods a manager can increase income under absorption costing, even if they are not sold. A manager might be tempted to produce more goods than the corporation desires in order to increase the net income. (An example of this is shown later, in Exhibit 13-12.)

Direct costing (or variable costing) is an inventory costing method that includes only the variable manufacturing costs in inventory costs. This method differs from absorption costing only in the treatment of fixed manufacturing overhead. Absorption costing includes a portion of fixed manufacturing overhead in inventories, whereas direct costing does not. Instead, the direct costing method regards fixed manufacturing overhead as a period cost just as marketing and administrative costs are regarded as period costs. This difference between the two inventory costing systems has significant implications from a control viewpoint.

Unit Costs under Both Methods

CHAPTER OBJECTIVE 4
Direct costing vs. absorption costing

Bullock Manufacturing Company produces one product. The costs associated with that product are given in Exhibit 13-6. The unit costs under both the absorption and direct costing methods are derived in Exhibits 13-7 and 13-8.

Costs per unit for direct materials, direct labor, and variable manufacturing overhead, as given in Exhibit 13-6, is relevant to both absorption costing and direct costing. These numbers are included in both computations, as can be seen by comparing

---

EXHIBIT 13-6

INFORMATION USED IN CALCULATING PRODUCT COSTS

Variable costs per unit:	
Direct materials	$5
Direct labor	$4
Variable manufacturing overhead	$2
Variable marketing expense	$1
Fixed costs per year:	
Fixed manufacturing overhead	$24,000
Fixed marketing expense	$ 5,000
Fixed administrative expense	$10,000
Annual production	8,000 units

EXHIBIT 13-7

PRODUCT COSTS PER UNIT (ABSORPTION COSTING)

Direct materials	$ 5
Direct labor	4
Variable manufacturing overhead	2
Total variable manufacturing costs	$11
Fixed manufacturing overhead	
($24,000/8,000 units)	3
Total absorption cost per unit	$14

EXHIBIT 13-8

PRODUCT COSTS PER UNIT (DIRECT COSTING)

Direct materials	$ 5
Direct labor	4
Variable manufacturing overhead	2
Total direct cost per unit	$11

Exhibits 13-7 and 13-8. Direct costing includes only these three items. So the direct cost per unit of inventory is $11 ($5 + $4 + $2).

Absorption costing also includes the fixed manufacturing overhead, which totals $24,000 (see Exhibit 13-6). The cost per unit for fixed manufacturing overhead is $3 ($24,000/8,000 units). Thus the absorption cost per unit is $14 ($5 + $4 + $2 + $3). Note that the variable marketing expense, the fixed marketing expense, and the fixed administrative expense are irrelevant to either product costing scheme. These costs are not product costs.

Under the absorption costing method, every unit that Bullock Manufacturing Company sells will result in $14 being added to cost of goods sold. Likewise, every unit added to inventory will add $14 to inventory. Under the direct costing method, the sale of one unit would increase cost of goods sold by only $11. The addition of one unit to inventory would increase inventories by only $11. The fixed manufacturing overhead that was included in the absorption costing method at $3 per unit is not included under the direct costing method. Of course, that $3 amount must be included somewhere when the direct costing method is used. The $3 amount, in its total dollar form of $24,000 ($3 × 8,000 units), is deducted from sales as a period cost just as are marketing and administrative expenses.

Absorption Costing and Direct Costing Compared: An Example

By making additional assumptions concerning inventory and sales at Bullock Manufacturing Company, we may demonstrate the differences in net income under absorption and direct costing. The income differences in Exhibits 13-9 and 13-10 result from the different methods of accounting for overhead. We assume the following about Bullock:

Sales price per unit	$20
Units sold in 19X1	6,000 units
Units produced in 19X1	8,000 units

(The marketing and administrative expense is the $15,000 fixed portion plus the $6,000 variable portion [6,000 units × $1 per unit].) A comparison of the net incomes shown in Exhibit 13-9 ($15,000) and Exhibit 13-10 ($9,000) reveals that there is a $6,000 difference between the two, with the absorption cost income statement having higher net income than the direct cost income statement. A comparison of the partial balance sheets reveals that the inventory cost on the absorption cost balance sheet is $6,000 greater than the inventory cost on the direct cost balance sheet.

EXHIBIT 13-9

BULLOCK MANUFACTURING COMPANY
FINANCIAL STATEMENTS (ABSORPTION COSTING)

Income Statement for the Year Ended December 31, 19X1

Sales (6,000 units × $20 per unit)		$120,000
Less: Cost of Goods Sold:		
Beginning Inventory	$ –0–	
Cost of Goods Manufactured (8,000 units × $14 per unit)	112,000	
Goods Available for Sale	$112,000	
Less: Ending Inventory (2,000 units × $14 per unit)	28,000	
Cost of Goods Sold		84,000
Gross Profit		$ 36,000
Less: Marketing and Administrative Expense		21,000
Net Income		$ 15,000

Partial Balance Sheet as of December 31, 19X1

Assets	
Cash	$ XXX
Accounts Receivable	XXX
Inventory (2,000 units × $14 per unit)	28,000
Total Current Assets	$ XXX
Plant and Equipment	XXX
Total Assets	$ XXX

EXHIBIT 13-10

BULLOCK MANUFACTURING COMPANY
FINANCIAL STATEMENTS (DIRECT COSTING)

Income Statement for the Year Ended December 31, 19X1

Sales (6,000 units @ $20 per unit)		$120,000
Less: Cost of Goods Sold (direct costing basis):		
Beginning Inventory	$ –0–	
Variable Manufacturing Costs (8,000 units × $11 per unit)	88,000	
Goods Available for Sale	$88,000	
Less: Ending Inventory (2,000 units × $11 per unit)	22,000	
Cost of Goods Sold		66,000
Gross Profit (direct costing)		$ 54,000
Less:		
Fixed Manufacturing Overhead	$24,000	
Marketing and Administration Expense	21,000	
Total Fixed Income		45,000
Net Income		$ 9,000

Partial Balance Sheet as of December 31, 19X1

Assets	
Cash	$ XXX
Accounts Receivable	XXX
Inventory (2,000 units × $11 per unit)	22,000
Total Current Assets	$ XXX
Plant and Equipment	XXX
Total Assets	$ XXX

The $6,000 difference on both comparisons is a direct result of the $3-per-unit difference between the product cost associated with the absorption costing method ($14) and the product cost associated with the direct costing method ($11). That $3 difference between the two methods multiplied by the 2,000 units in ending inventory explains the $6,000 difference in inventory cost and thus the $6,000 difference in net income.

Under both systems, the total cost for the year is $133,000. The costs to be accounted for are the same:

Direct material (8,000 × $5)	$ 40,000
Direct labor (8,000 × $4)	32,000
Variable overhead (8,000 × $2)	16,000
Fixed overhead (8,000 × $3)	24,000
Marketing and administration	21,000
Total cost	$133,000

But these costs are accounted for in different ways. Absorption costing accounts for the costs in this manner:

Ending inventory (2,000 × $14)		$ 28,000
Expenses:		
Cost of sales (6,000 × $14)	$84,000	
Marketing and administration	21,000	105,000
Total cost		$133,000

On the other hand, direct costing partitions the total cost in the following way:

Ending inventory (2,000 × $11)		$ 22,000
Expenses:		
Cost of sales (6,000 × $11)	$66,000	
Marketing and administration	21,000	
Fixed overhead	24,000	111,000
Total cost		$133,000

Under both costing methods the total cost for the year was $133,000. Manufacturing costs must be classified as either an expense or an asset (inventory) when the financial statements are prepared. These two costing methods differ in how each takes the total cost and splits it between expenses and an asset (inventory). The reconciliation between absorption costing and direct costing (variable costing) is always attributable to the difference between the amount of fixed manufacturing overhead in beginning and ending inventories.

Absorption Costing vs. Direct Costing in Multiple Years

Now that we have examined the differences between the absorption and direct costing methods, we will focus on the implications of those differences by showing a series of consecutive years in which the unit sales per year remain unchanged but production changes from one year to another. Such a situation results in inventories changing from one year-end to another year-end.

Miller Manufacturing Company started operations in 19X1. Operating and cost data for the single product Miller manufactures is presented below for years 19X1, 19X2, and 19X3. With this data, the manufacturing cost per unit can be computed. The results are shown in Exhibit 13-11. As usual, the direct cost per unit equals the direct materials cost per unit plus the direct labor cost per unit plus the variable manufacturing overhead cost per unit. The absorption cost per unit equals these costs plus the fixed manufacturing overhead cost per unit. Following is the inventory data for Miller Manufacturing over the three years:

> ### EXHIBIT 13-11
>
> ## MILLER MANUFACTURING COMPANY
> ## COST PER UNIT
>
> | | 19X1 | 19X2 | 19X3 |
> |---|---|---|---|
> | Direct material | $ 6 | $ 6 | $ 6 |
> | Direct labor | 4 | 4 | 4 |
> | Variable manufacturing overhead | 3 | 3 | 3 |
> | Total variable manufacturing costs | $13 | $13 | $13 |
> | Fixed manufacturing overhead* | 8 | 6 | 12 |
> | Total manufacturing costs | $21 | $19 | $25 |
>
> *Fixed manufacturing overhead of $48,000 allocated to units based on production in each year:
> 19X1: $48,000/6,000 units produced = $8 per unit
> 19X2: $48,000/8,000 units produced = $6 per unit
> 19X3: $48,000/4,000 units produced = $12 per unit

	19X1	19X2	19X3	Total for Three Years
Beginning inventory (units)	–0–	–0–	2,000	N.A.
Units produced	6,000	8,000	4,000	18,000
Units sold	6,000	6,000	6,000	18,000
Ending inventory (units)	–0–	2,000	–0–	N.A.

Exhibit 13-12 indicates that in 19X1, when production is 6,000 units and sales are 6,000 units, the ending inventory remains at zero and the net income is the same for both costing methods ($26,000).

In 19X2, when production was 8,000 units and sales were 6,000 units, inventories increased by 2,000 units. Under the absorption costing method, each unit of inventory has $6 of fixed manufacturing overhead attached to it (2,000 × $6 = $12,000); whereas, under the direct costing method, no fixed manufacturing overhead attaches to inventory (2,000 × $0 = $0). That $12,000 difference in inventories results in absorption costing net income ($38,000) that is $12,000 greater than direct costing net income ($26,000). Thus, *when inventories increase, absorption costing results in greater net income than the net income reported under direct costing.*

In 19X3, sales were 6,000 units and production was 4,000 units. Thus, the 2,000 units in inventory at the end of 19X2 were sold in 19X3. The sale of those 2,000 units released $38,000 into 19X3 cost of goods sold under the absorption costing method. Under the direct costing method, $26,000 was released from inventory into cost of goods sold. That $12,000 difference in costs released from inventory into cost of goods sold under absorption costing resulted in direct costing net income that was $12,000 greater than the net income under absorption costing. Thus, *when inventories decline, direct costing results in greater net income than the net income reported under absorption costing.*

EXHIBIT 13-12

MILLER MANUFACTURING COMPANY
COMPARISON
ABSORPTION AND DIRECT COSTING
FINANCIAL STATEMENTS

Absorption Costing

	19X1	19X2	19X3	Total for Three Years
Sales (6,000 units × $27)	$162,000	$162,000	$162,000	$486,000
Less: Cost of Goods Sold:				
Beginning Inventory	$ –0–	$ –0–	$ 38,000	Total not applicable
Cost of Goods Manufactured:				
Variable Manufacturing Costs*	78,000	104,000	52,000	234,000
Fixed Manufacturing Costs†	48,000	48,000	48,000	144,000
Goods Available for Sale	126,000	152,000	138,000	378,000
Less: Ending Inventory‡	–0–	38,000	–0–	Total not applicable
Cost of Goods Sold	126,000	114,000	138,000	378,000
Gross Margin	36,000	48,000	24,000	108,000
Less Marketing and Administrative Expenses	10,000	10,000	10,000	30,000
Net Income	$ 26,000	$ 38,000	$ 14,000	$ 78,000

Direct Costing

	19X1	19X2	19X3	Total for Three Years
Sales	$162,000	$162,000	$162,000	$486,000
Less: Variable Cost of Goods Sold:				
Beginning Inventory	$ –0–	$ –0–	$ 26,000	Total not applicable
Cost of Goods Manufactured:				
Variable manufacturing costs*	78,000	104,000	52,000	234,000
Goods available for sale	78,000	104,000	78,000	234,000
Less: Ending Inventory‡	–0–	26,000	–0–	Total not applicable
Variable Cost of Goods Sold	78,000	78,000	78,000	234,000
Gross Margin (direct-cost basis)	84,000	84,000	84,000	252,000
Less:				
Fixed Manufacturing Expense†	48,000	48,000	48,000	144,000
Marketing and Administrative Expense	10,000	10,000	10,000	30,000
Net Income	$ 26,000	$ 26,000	$ 26,000	$ 78,000

EXHIBIT 13-12 (*continued*)

*Variable manufacturing costs	†Fixed manufacturing costs
19X1: 6,000 units × $13 = $ 78,000	19X1: 6,000 units × $ 8 = $48,000
19X2: 8,000 units × $13 = $104,000	19X2: 8,000 units × $ 6 = $48,000
19X3: 4,000 units × $13 = $ 52,000	19X3: 4,000 units × $12 = $48,000

‡Ending inventories on balance sheet

	Absorption Costing	Direct Costing	Difference
19X1	–0–	–0–	–0–
19X2	2,000 × $19 = $38,000	2,000 × $13 = $26,000	$12,000

Notice that sales were 6,000 units for each of the three years but the net income using absorption costing varies from a high of $38,000 to a low of $14,000. The fluctuations in units produced caused the variability in net income. Net income using the direct costing method remains at $26,000 for each of the three years. Net income for the total three years is the same for each costing method ($78,000). The example presented in Exhibit 13-12 illustrates an earlier point that under the absorption costing method managers have the opportunity to manipulate earnings by producing quantities different from quantities sold. Because of the possibilities of manipulation, managers must recognize the inherent deficiencies in using absorption costing financial statements for evaluative purposes. Direct costing does not offer that same opportunity to manipulate earnings because fixed manufacturing overhead is treated as a period cost rather than a product cost.

Behavioral Aspects of the Absorption Method

CHAPTER OBJECTIVE 5
Behavioral aspects of absorption costing

When inventories increased from zero to 2,000 units for Miller Manufacturing Company in the preceding section, the absorption method resulted in net income of $38,000, whereas the direct cost method yielded net income of $26,000. The absorption costing method will always result in a net income greater than the direct costing net income when inventories increase. This is because the absorption costing method treats fixed manufacturing overhead as if it were a variable cost. Under the absorption costing system, every unit of inventory has some amount of fixed manufacturing overhead attached to it. Under the direct costing system, the inventory has no fixed manufacturing overhead included in its costs. Costs not included in inventory must be treated as period expenses and deducted from sales to arrive at net income.

In a performance evaluation in which the manager or the business segment is being evaluated using a profit center approach, the manager is often under tremendous pressure to meet profit goals. The use of the absorption costing method for performance evaluation purposes invites the manager to increase net income by increasing inventories. An increase in inventories results in the classification of current-period fixed cost as assets rather than expenses. Classification as an asset defers the item from being deducted from revenue on the income statement. Thus, short-run profits are increased.

Absorption costing is required for external reporting and for income tax purposes. In spite of the fact that absorption costing is deeply ingrained in our accounting systems, there is a compelling reason why that method is not appropriate for performance reporting. In fact, when you consider that computer-based accounting systems are quite prevalent in the industrial sector of business, it is reasonable to expect that a well-designed accounting system could generate absorption costing financial statements for external reporting and tax purposes and direct costing financial statements for performance reporting purposes.

Direct Costing and Contribution Reporting

CHAPTER OBJECTIVE 4
Direct costing vs. absorption costing

Aside from its behavioral advantage mentioned earlier, direct costing is advantageous in another way. Because direct costing regards fixed manufacturing overhead as a period cost, the accounting system that supports direct costing must distinguish between fixed and variable manufacturing overhead. Such a distinction is also essential to the use of the contribution approach used in cost–volume–profit analysis, discussed in Chapter 3.

In the example presented in Exhibit 13-13, marketing expenses have been separated into variable ($40,000) and fixed ($15,000) components. The variable component is subtracted from the gross profit calculated on a direct costing basis to arrive at contribution margin. All of the fixed expenses, including fixed manufacturing overhead, are subtracted from contribution margin to arrive at net income.

A reporting system that combines the direct costing and the contribution approaches contributes to an appropriate evaluation of managerial or segment performance. At the same time, it provides information for use in cost–volume–profit studies such as breakeven or target-profit analysis (see Chapter 3).

Theoretical Considerations Favoring Direct Costing for Performance Evaluations

CHAPTER OBJECTIVE 4
Direct costing vs. absorption costing

At this point you are probably asking yourself, "If there are so many advantages to direct costing, why do we even bother with the absorption costing method?" The direct-costing-versus-absorption-costing controversy has been debated for many years.

The advocates of absorption costing believe that fixed manufacturing overhead cost incurrence is so closely associated with the production process that the accountant's *matching principle* supports the treatment of that overhead as a product cost. They reason that the fixed manufacturing overhead cost category includes costs such as depreciation on plant, equipment, and factory supervision, and that those costs must be incurred if the product is to be manufactured.

Advocates of absorption costing view the cost of depreciation on plant and equipment very differently from the rental cost of a computer used in the accounting department or the costs associated with the legal department. The depreciation on plant and equipment is inextricably linked to the production of the product, whereas the accounting and legal departmental expenses are only remotely associated with the production process. Thus, advocates of absorption costing feel justified in treating fixed manufacturing overhead as a product cost and accounting and legal departmental costs as period costs.

Advocates of direct costing argue that fixed manufacturing overhead may be closely associated with the production process, but that this is no justification for deferring them as product costs. To do so requires an allocation of some portion of the cost to an asset account (Inventory); and they have difficulty considering such allocated costs as an asset.

EXHIBIT 13-13

DIRECT COSTING AND CONTRIBUTION REPORTING COMBINED

Sales		$200,000
Less: Variable Cost of Goods Sold:		
Direct Materials	$40,000	
Direct Labor	15,000	
Variable Manufacturing Overhead	15,000	70,000
Gross Margin (direct costing basis)		$130,000
Less: Variable Marketing Expense		40,000
Contribution Margin		$ 90,000
Less: Fixed Expenses:		
Fixed Manufacturing Overhead	$25,000	
Fixed Marketing Overhead	15,000	
Fixed Administrative Expenses	30,000	70,000
Net Income		$ 20,000

Another objection that advocates of direct costing have is that absorption costing is often used in preparing the responsibility accounting reports for the evaluation of managerial performance. In Chapter 8, when we were discussing the treatment of fixed manufacturing overhead in the manufacturing manager's performance report, we stated that the fixed manufacturing overhead volume variance on the report would encourage the manufacturing manager to produce quantities in excess of those that can be sold. Inventories would grow, fixed overhead would be allocated to those inventories and away from the cost of goods sold, and net income would increase.

That dreaded manufacturing overhead volume variance is a direct result of the use of absorption costing. Because this variance is naturally generated by the use of absorption costing with standard cost systems, companies tend to place it on the performance report along with all of the other variances generated by the absorption cost-based standard costing system. If the absorption costing system were not mandatory for financial accounting purposes, companies would have no such inclination to let the variances generated by it be used inappropriately.

In this textbook the authors hold that absorption costing may be appropriate for external reporting to stockholders, lenders, and the Internal Revenue Service, but it is rarely appropriate for management accounting purposes. The control aspect of management accounting is better served by direct costing.

PRICING WITH PRODUCT COSTS

CHAPTER OBJECTIVE 6
How to price products

A common business decision is how to price a product. Many firms use a *cost-plus* formula for pricing decisions. In other words, they add a profit margin to the cost of the product to obtain the price. This approach can be adopted by managers using absorption costing as well as direct costing.

In both cases, the approach is to take the breakeven formula with a targeted net income and solve it for the selling price. Then the unit cost is deducted to obtain the "profit" per unit sold. By dividing this difference by the unit cost one gets the markup percentage.

Recall the breakeven formula from Chapter 3. Consider the case when management has a profit goal. The formula is:

$$Q = \frac{FC + TNI}{SP - VC}$$

where   Q = the units produced and sold (called the *breakeven point* in Chapter 3)
     FC = fixed costs
   TNI = target net income
     SP = selling price per unit
     VC = variable cost per unit

In Chapter 3 we assumed that FC, TNI, SP, and VC were known and solved for the quantity Q. In this presentation we assume that Q, FC, TNI, and VC are known or are estimated and solve for the selling price:

$$Q = \frac{FC + TNI}{SP - VC}$$

$$Q \times (SP - VC) = FC + TNI$$

$$(Q \times SP) - (Q \times VC) = FC + TNI$$

$$Q \times SP = FC + TNI + (Q \times VC)$$

$$SP = \frac{FC + TNI + (Q \times VC)}{Q}$$

If one knows the value of the various terms, it is a simple matter to compute the selling price per unit. In practice, however, it is conventional to extract the product cost and work toward the markup on the product cost. Since the cost can be either absorption cost or direct cost, we need a formula for each case.

Before proceeding, note that the direct cost per unit is VC. The contribution margin per unit is $SP - VC$. The markup is therefore $(SP - VC)/VC$. Absorption costing is a bit more complicated. Whereas VC is already in unit terms, fixed costs are not. We unitize them so that the fixed costs per unit is FC/Q. The absorption cost per unit is $VC + FC/Q$. The profit per unit is $SP - VC - FC/Q$. Thus, the markup is $(SP - VC - FC/Q)/(VC + FC/Q)$.

Finally, note that the answer one arrives at will be the same regardless of the product costing system. Both ways of solving the problem consider all of the incremental revenues and all of the incremental costs so that the targeted net income is achieved. This will be illustrated later by an example.

First, assume that direct costing is used. We will transfer the last equation discussed into a formula for the markup on direct costs.

$$SP = \frac{FC + TNI + (Q \times VC)}{Q}$$

$$SP - VC = \frac{FC + TNI}{Q}$$

$$\frac{SP - VC}{VC} = \frac{FC + TNI}{Q \times VC}$$

The markup percentage (direct cost) equals the fixed costs plus the target net income all divided by the product of the volume in units times the variable costs per unit.

Second, consider the absorption costing case. Again, begin with the formula for the selling price per unit.

$$SP = \frac{FC + TNI + (Q \times VC)}{Q}$$

$$SP - VC - \frac{FC}{Q} = \frac{TNI}{Q}$$

$$\frac{SP - VC - \dfrac{FC}{Q}}{VC + \dfrac{FC}{Q}} = \frac{\dfrac{TNI}{Q}}{VC + \dfrac{FC}{Q}}$$

$$= \frac{\dfrac{TNI}{Q}}{\dfrac{(VC \times Q) + FC}{Q}}$$

$$= \frac{TNI}{(VC \times Q) + FC}$$

$$= \frac{TNI}{Q \times \left(VC + \dfrac{FC}{Q} \right)}$$

The markup percentage (absorption cost) equals the target net income divided by the volume in units times the absorption cost per unit.

Both formulas become more complicated if we admit into the analysis nonmanufacturing fixed and variable costs such as administrative and selling expenses. Let FC_1 denote manufacturing fixed costs and FC_2 denote other fixed costs. Total fixed costs $FC = FC_1 + FC_2$. Similarly, let VC_1 denote manufacturing variable costs per unit and VC_2 denote other variable costs per unit. Total variable costs per unit $VC = VC_1 + VC_2$. Then the selling price per unit is:

$$SP = \frac{FC + TNI + (Q \times VC)}{Q}$$

$$= \frac{FC_1 + FC_2 + TNI + (Q \times VC_1) + (Q \times VC_2)}{Q}$$

PRICING STRATEGY IN THE AUTOMOTIVE GLASS INDUSTRY

As customers change their purchasing practices, automotive window glass manufacturers are faced with two questions:

● What is the proper product mix of windows given productive/distribution constraints;

● What prices should be set on individual windows to enhance profitability?

Their cost accounting systems generally are not capable of telling management what it really costs to make each window size. Current cost systems are geared to developing product costs for periodic inventory valuation and financial reporting. Thus current product costs are determined by allocating costs using traditional cost allocation bases.

A "true" product cost should reflect the value of production and distribution resources consumed in creating, packaging, and transporting the product to the customer. Cost assignment to a product should reflect direct or cause-and-effect relationships between small changes in product volume and resulting changes in the consumption of productive resources.

Aside from the direct costs of acquiring and moving raw materials, parts, and products through the plant, all other costs are related only indirectly to products and should be classified as overhead. The challenge to management accountants in the auto glass industry is to find the most meaningful approach to assigning overhead costs.

Historically, overhead costs have been allocated using bases such as square feet of glass or direct labor hours. In reality, production costs are not incurred in proportion to the square footage contained in a window, and direct labor has become too small and misleading a basis for linking costs to products.

COST ACCOUNTING AS A COMPETITIVE TOOL

The cost accounting system can be an effective competitive tool if the information it generates can help managers make better decisions. To do so, the system must bridge the gap between production and marketing. If production and marketing do not work together, marketing may be pursuing a mix of product orders that severely hampers the profitability of the firm. Coordinating what the firm is capable of selling with what it can produce begins with identifying the major bottlenecks, whether in production, distribution, or customer demand. Company employees must work together to identify and then push the most profitable volume through that bottleneck(s).

The allocation of costs to products is needed to determine whether current selling prices are adequate. The knowledge of which products are winners and losers and how best to use scarce resources should not be lost in the process of cost allocation. Throughput value is an important strategic method of determining product profitability.

SOURCE: Adapted from Robert J. Campbell, "Pricing Strategy in the Automotive Glass Industry," *Management Accounting* (July 1989), pp. 26–34. Adapted by permission.

It can be shown that the markup on direct costs is given by the formula:

$$Markup = \frac{FC_1 + FC_2 + TNI + (Q \times VC_2)}{Q \times VC_1}$$

And the markup on absorption cost is given by:

$$Markup = \frac{FC_2 + TNI + (Q \times VC_2)}{Q \times \left(VC_1 + \frac{FC_1}{Q}\right)}$$

Their derivations are left as an exercise to the reader.

Consider the following example. We use the data from Exhibit 13-6 and assume that the target net income is $25,000. What should the markup be? What should the sales price be?

We solve the problem for variable costing first. The unit product cost is $11 as discussed earlier in this chapter and shown in Exhibit 13-8. The markup to achieve a $25,000 profit will be:

$$\text{Markup} = \frac{\$39,000 + \$25,000 + (8,000 \times \$1)}{8,000 \times \$11}$$

$$= 81.81\% \text{ (rounded)}$$

Thus the markup is $9 (81.81% × $11). The selling price should be $20 ($11 product cost + $9 markup). Note that the $39,000 is the total fixed costs and that the $8,000 is the variable marketing expense.

Next we solve it with an absorption costing system. The product cost is calculated in Exhibit 13-7 to be $14 per unit. The markup is computed with the appropriate formula:

$$\text{Markup} = \frac{\$15,000 + \$25,000 + (8,000 \times \$1)}{8,000 \times \$14}$$

$$= 42.857\% \text{ (rounded)}$$

The $15,000 is the fixed marketing and administrative expenses. The $8,000 again is the variable marketing expense. The markup in dollars is $6 (42.857% × $14). The selling price should be $20 ($14 product cost + $6 markup).

The costing system did not affect the decision. Both cost methods yielded an answer of $20 per unit.

Note that the net incomes in Exhibit 13-9 and in Exhibit 13-10 are not $25,000. The reason for this is that previously we assumed that of the 8,000 units produced only 6,000 are sold. The formula assumes that all 8,000 are sold and does not concern itself with what happens when they are sold over more than one year. The income statements in Exhibits 13-9 and 13-10 should be revised assuming that all 8,000 units are sold. The correct answer is, of course, a net income of $25,000.

Demonstration Problem

A new product has the following financial characteristics.

Variable costs per unit:	
Direct materials	$20
Variable manufacturing overhead	
(includes the direct labor)	$10
Variable marketing expenses	$1
Fixed costs per year:	
Fixed manufacturing overhead	$100,000
Fixed marketing and administrative costs	$25,000
Annual production	10,000 units

REQUIRED

a. Determine the product cost under absorption costing and direct costing.

b. Estimate the selling price if the targeted net income is $65,000. Also determine the markups under absorption costing and direct costing.

c. Prepare the income statement under absorption costing and direct costing if 8,000 units are sold.

SOLUTION TO DEMONSTRATION PROBLEM

a. The product cost under absorption costing consists of the variable and fixed manufacturing costs, as follows:

Direct materials	$20
Variable manufacturing overhead	10
Fixed manufacturing overhead	10
Cost per unit	$40

The product cost under direct costing consists of the variable manufacturing costs, as follows:

Direct materials	$20
Variable manufacturing overhead	10
Cost per unit	$30

b. The selling price is computed by the following formula:

$$SP = \frac{FC + TNI + (Q \times VC)}{Q}$$

$$= \frac{\$125,000 + \$65,000 + (10,000 \times \$31)}{10,000}$$

$$= \$50$$

We next give the markups under the two costing methods:

$$\text{Markup (direct costing)} = \frac{\$100,000 + \$25,000 + \$65,000 + (10,000 \times \$1)}{10,000 \times \$30}$$

$$= 66.7\%$$

which is correct given the selling price [($50 − $30)/$30 = 66.7%].

$$\text{Markup (absorption costing)} = \frac{\$25,000 + \$65,000 + (10,000 \times \$1)}{10,000 \times \$40}$$

$$= 25\%$$

which is also correct [($50 − $40)/$40 = 25%].

c. The income statement under absorption costing is as follows.

Sales (8,000 × $50)	$400,000
Cost of Sales (8,000 × $40)	320,000
Gross Profit	$ 80,000
Less: Marketing and Administration Expenses (fixed, $25,000; variable, $8,000)	33,000
Net Income	$ 47,000

The income statement under direct costing will complete this discussion problem.

Sales		$400,000
Cost of Sales (8,000 × $30)		240,000
Gross Profit		$160,000
Less: Marketing and Administration		
Expenses	$ 33,000	
Fixed manufacturing costs	100,000	133,000
Net Income		$ 27,000

The difference in income lies in the treatment of fixed manufacturing costs. Under absorption costing, this item is unitized as $100,000/10,000 units = $10 per unit. There are 2,000 unsold units. Put as an asset—that is, included in ending inventory—it is 2,000 × $10, or $20,000 under absorption costing.

APPENDIX C

Overhead Allocation for Service and Producing Departments

OBJECTIVE 7
Overhead allocation for service departments

Within the factory there are two basic types of departments: service departments and producing departments. The product being manufactured does not typically flow through a service department but it must flow through a department that is regarded as a producing (or operating) department.

Service departments are manufacturing-oriented departments (usually located in the factory) that provide services to the producing departments. Examples of service departments include the maintenance department, the cafeteria, and the utilities department. Service departments do not include marketing departments or general administration departments, because their costs are not incurred in manufacturing a product. Marketing and general administration costs are considered period costs and should not be regarded as product costs.

Overhead Allocation

The distinction between service departments and producing departments is an important one because of the implications for developing the predetermined variable and fixed overhead rates. It is also important because producing departments are often held responsible not only for their own costs but also those of the service departments.

Because products do not move through the service departments, there is no direct basis for determining how much of the service department's cost attaches to each unit of product. Such is not the case with producing departments, where there are standards for the number of direct labor hours or machine hours required for each unit of product. Those standard hours permit us to appropriately attach the cost of the producing departments to each unit of product.

Allocation Using the Step Method

Because absorption costing requires that *all* manufacturing costs (service department and producing department) be attached to the product, a method of attaching service department costs to the product is needed. Exhibit C-1 illustrates how this is accomplished.

This exhibit is an oversimplification because it fails to recognize the interdependencies between and among the service departments. The cafeteria serves meals to those who work in the maintenance department, maintenance does work in the cafeteria, and the utilities provide service to both maintenance and the cafeteria. The actual relationships are more appropriately described in Exhibit C-2.

Properly accounting for these interrelationships among service departments is possible using the rather complex *reciprocal method* of cost allocation discussed in more advanced textbooks. In this textbook we discuss the more common, and less complex, step method of dealing with these interrelationships among service departments. Exhibit C-3 illustrates how the step method simplifies the interdependencies among service departments.

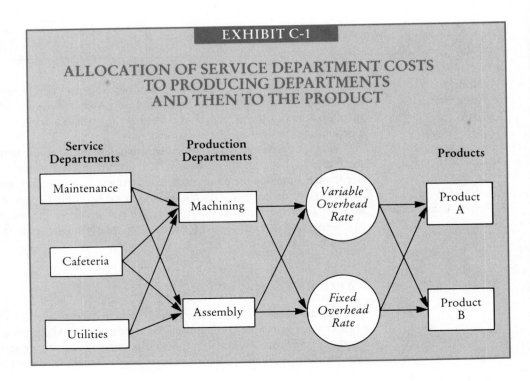

EXHIBIT C-1

ALLOCATION OF SERVICE DEPARTMENT COSTS TO PRODUCING DEPARTMENTS AND THEN TO THE PRODUCT

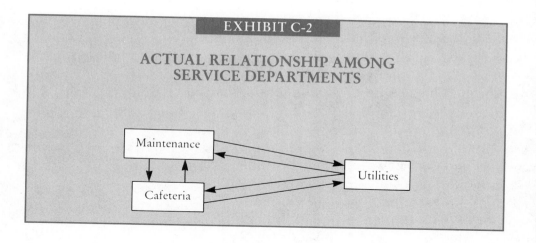

EXHIBIT C-2

ACTUAL RELATIONSHIP AMONG
SERVICE DEPARTMENTS

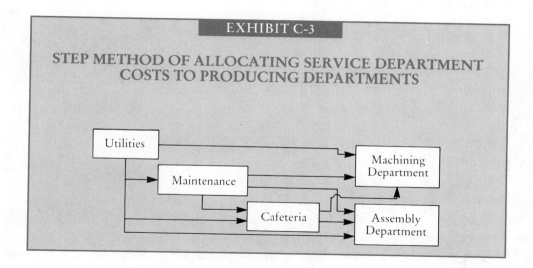

EXHIBIT C-3

STEP METHOD OF ALLOCATING SERVICE DEPARTMENT
COSTS TO PRODUCING DEPARTMENTS

The basis for allocating the service department cost to other service and producing departments is the unit of measure that best indicates the effort expended by the service department. Remember that this allocation process is done in order to establish predetermined overhead rates (variable and fixed). Therefore, the units of measure selected for allocation purposes will be the budgeted or expected amounts and not the actual amounts. Assume the budgeted costs of Exhibit C-4.

In order to perform the step method of cost allocation to determine the predetermined overhead rates for each producing department, it is also necessary to have a budget of how heavily the resources are to be used. The expectations for the next year are expressed in Exhibit C-5.

As indicated in Exhibit C-3, the service department's budgeted costs are allocated sequentially starting with the utilities department and then moving to the maintenance department and then to the cafeteria. The reason the utilities department is chosen as the department to start the allocation is that it has the largest variable overhead budget ($180,000) of the service departments. The maintenance department is the second

EXHIBIT C-4

BASIS OF ALLOCATION AND APPLICATION AND BUDGETED COST FOR SERVICE DEPARTMENTS AND PRODUCING DEPARTMENTS

Service Departments	Basis of Allocation	Budgeted Costs* Variable Portion	Fixed Portion
Utilities	Killowatt hour (KWH)	$180,000	$900,000
Maintenance	Maintenance worker hours	$120,000	$600,000
Cafeteria	Number of employees	$ 66,000	$ 15,000

Producing Departments	Basis of Application of Overhead	Budgeted Overhead Costs* Variable Portion	Fixed Portion
Machining	Machine hours	$ 48,000	$729,000
Assembly	Direct labor hours	$ 96,000	$240,000

*These budgeted nondirect material and labor cost amounts are based on the expected level of production of the producing departments for the next year.

EXHIBIT C-5

BUDGETED SERVICE USE, MACHINE HOURS, AND DIRECT LABOR HOURS

Service	Utilities Department	Maintenance Department	Cafeteria	Machining	Assembly	Total
Utilities	200,000 kwh	100,000 kwh	20,000 kwh	1,180,000 kwh	500,000 kwh	2,000,000 kwh
Maintenance	300 hrs.	600 hrs.	100 hrs.	4,000 hrs.	2,400 hrs.	7,400 hrs.
Cafeteria	4 emp.	3 emp.	5 emp.	20 emp.	50 emp.	82 emp.
Machining	N.A.	N.A.	N.A.	133,000 hrs.	N.A.	133,000 hrs.
Assembly	N.A.	N.A.	N.A.	N.A.	100,000 direct labor hours	100,000 direct labor hours

department in the sequence of departments allocated because it has the second highest budgeted cost ($120,000). The reasoning is that the service department that provides the most service should start the step allocation process. Often, the budgets of the service departments are used as indicators of the amount of service they provide.

The allocation of the variable overhead is demonstrated in Exhibit C-6. Utilities of $180,000 is allocated first and it is allocated on the basis of kilowatt-hours (kwh).

EXHIBIT C-6

CALCULATION OF PREDETERMINED VARIABLE OVERHEAD RATES FOR MACHINING AND ASSEMBLY DEPARTMENTS

	Service Departments			Producing Departments		
Utilities	Maintenance	Cafeteria		Machining	Assembly	Total
$180,000	$120,000	$66,000		$ 48,000	$ 96,000	$510,000
(180,000) Ⓐ	10,000	2,000		118,000	50,000	–0–
$ –0–	$130,000					
	(130,000) Ⓑ	2,000		80,000	48,000	–0–
	$ –0–	$70,000				
		(70,000) Ⓒ		20,000	50,000	–0–
		$ –0–		$266,000*	$244,000†	$510,000

ⒶThe departments to which utilities will be allocated are expected to use a total of 1,800,000 kwh. The variable cost budget is $180,000, or $.10 per kwh. Thus maintenance is allocated $10,000 (100,000 kwh × $.10).

ⒷThe $130,000 budgeted cost associated with the maintenance department is allocated to the departments to the right of the maintenance department on this schedule. Those three departments are expected to need 6,500 maintenance hours (100 for cafeteria, 4,000 for machining, and 2,400 for assembly). Thus the rate is $20 per hour ($130,000/6500 hours). The $2,000 charged to the cafeteria is that department's expected maintenance hours times $20 per hour. There is no allocation backward to utilities or to maintenance itself.

ⒸThis $70,000 will be allocated to the remaining two departments to the right (*never allocate to the left, or backward*). The $70,000 will be allocated over 70 employees at $1,000 per employee.

*Predetermined variable manufacturing overhead rate for the machining department is $2 per machine hour ($266,000/133,000 machine hours).
†Predetermined variable manufacturing overhead rate for the assembly department is $2.44 per direct labor hour ($244,000/100,000 direct labor hours).

Maintenance is allocated $10,000, which is equal to 100,000 kwh (from Exhibit C-5) divided by 1,800,000 kwh (the kwh in the remaining four departments) times the $180,000. The cafeteria is allocated $2,000 [(20,000/1,800,000) × $180,000]. Similarly, machining is allocated $118,000 and assembly $50,000. Notice that the four departments are allocated exactly the cost of the utilities ($10,000 + $2,000 + $118,000 + $50,000 = $180,000).

Next, we allocate the cost of the maintenance department, $130,000, to the remaining three departments. The basis is the number of maintenance hours. The number of hours in the remaining three departments is 100 + 4,000 + 2,400 = 6,500 (from Exhibit C-5). Therefore, the cafeteria is allocated $2,000 [(100/6,500) × $130,000]. Machining receives $80,000 [(4,000/6,500) × $130,000]. Assembly is allocated $48,000 [(2,400/6,500) × $130,000].

Finally we allocate the costs of the cafeteria to machining and assembly. From Exhibit C-6 note that the cafeteria cost is now $70,000. From Exhibit C-5, the basis is the number of employees and that machining and assembly have 20 and 50 employees, respectively. Thus, machining receives $20,000 [(20/70) × $70,000] and assembly receives $50,000 [(50/70) × $70,000].

EXHIBIT C-7

CALCULATION OF PREDETERMINED FIXED OVERHEAD RATES FOR MACHINING AND ASSEMBLY DEPARTMENTS

Service Departments			Producing Departments		
Utilities	Maintenance	Cafeteria	Machining	Assembly	Total
$900,000.00	$600,000	$15,000	$ 729,000	$240,000	$2,484,000
(900,000.00) ⓐ⇨	50,000	10,000	590,000	250,000	–0–
$ –0–	$650,000				
	(650,000) ⓑ⇨	10,000	400,000	240,000	–0–
	$ –0–	$35,000			
		(35,000) ⓒ⇨	10,000	25,000	–0–
		$ –0–	$1,729,000*	$755,000†	$2,484,000

ⓐ The departments to which utilities will be allocated are expected to use a total of 1,800,000 kwh. The fixed cost budget is $900,000, or $.50 per kwh. Thus maintenance is allocated $50,000 (100,000 kwh × $.50).

ⓑ The $650,000 ($600,000 original maintenance budget plus $50,000 of utilities cost allocated to maintenance) budget for maintenance fixed costs is allocated to those departments that are to the right of the maintenance department on this schedule. Those three departments are expecting to need 6,500 maintenance hours. Thus the rate is $100 per maintenance hour.

ⓒ This $35,000 will be allocated to the remaining two departments to the right of the cafeteria on this schedule. The $35,000 will be allocated over 70 employees at $500 per employee.

*Predetermined fixed manufacturing overhead rate for the machining department is $13 per machine hour ($1,729,000/133,000 machine hours).
†Predetermined fixed manufacturing overhead rate for the assembly department is $7.55 per direct labor hour ($755,000/100,000 direct labor hours).

The fixed overhead is allocated in similar fashion, using the details in Exhibit C-4 and C-5 to obtain the allocated costs. The calculation is shown in Exhibit C-7.

The predetermined fixed overhead rates of $13 per machine hour for the machining department and $7.55 per direct labor hour for the assembly department will be used with the variable overhead rates and the required machine hours and direct labor hours per unit of product to arrive at product costs.

Exhibit C-8 illustrates how those predetermined overhead rates are used to arrive at the standard overhead cost per unit of product.

The Inappropriateness of Allocation for Management Accounting

The allocation of service department costs to producing departments is necessary for complete adherence to absorption costing. However, such allocation is not appropriate or desirable for the performance evaluation aspects of management accounting.

EXHIBIT C-8

CALCULATION OF OVERHEAD COST PER UNIT OF PRODUCT

Standard machine hours per unit of product
in the machining department · · · · · · · · · · · · · · 3.75 machine hours

Standard direct labor hours per unit of product
in the assembly department · · · · · · · · · · · · · · 2.25 direct labor hours

Variable overhead cost:

Machining department (3.75 machine hours × $2) · · · · · · $ 7.50

Assembly department (2.25 direct labor hours × $2.44) · · · · 5.49

Standard variable overhead per unit of product · · · · · · · · · $12.99

Fixed overhead cost:

Machining department: (3.75 machine hours × $13) · · · · · · $48.75

Assembly department: (2.25 direct labor hours × $7.55) · · · · 16.99

Standard fixed overhead cost per unit of product · · · · · · · · $65.74

Total standard overhead cost per unit of product · · · · · · · · $78.73

The control system should strive to hold department managers responsible only for costs over which they are capable of exercising meaningful control. In accordance with that principle, the manager of the machining department should not be held responsible for the lack of cost control in service departments that are headed by other managers.

Designing an accounting system that meets the absorption costing needs of external reporting and the control needs of management accounting represents a challenge to accountants. Fortunately, the use of computers and accounting databases has made it possible to accomplish both purposes simultaneously.

Review of Chapter Objectives

1. Indicate the difference between separable and common fixed costs (p. 443).

   ■ Segment reporting requires a distinction between separable and common costs. Separable costs are costs that are so directly associated with a segment that they would be eliminated if the segment were eliminated. Common costs, on the other hand, are costs that are not directly associated with one segment. They are items that span two or more segments of the organization.

2. Explain the difference between segment margin and contribution margin (pp. 443–47).

   ■ Segment contribution margin is equal to segment sales minus segment variable costs. This is like our definition of contribution margin made in Chapter 3, except that it is computed only for the segment. Segment margin is equal to segment contribution margin less segment separable fixed costs. Thus the difference between segment margin and contribution margin is the separable fixed costs of the segment.

3. Describe a business segment report (pp. 443–49).

■ Segment reporting is the process of presenting financial and other information for components of a business organization. Recall that a segment is an identifiable collection of related resources and activities. Operationally it is a significant strategic or organizational component of an enterprise. It may be a subsidiary, a division, a department, or some other meaningful breakdown of the organization. The segment is a group having distinctive resources and activities that can be treated as a unit for planning or control purposes.

■ A business segment report shows the segment margin for each of the segments. It also shows the common costs, but it subtracts this item from the total segment margin to yield net income.

■ Segment performance reports are often hierarchical in nature with one segment being subdivided into even smaller segments. As the segments become smaller, the proportion of costs that are classified as common becomes greater, because the smaller the segment is, the greater the amount of services that are shared with other segments.

■ Segment reports are essential in evaluating the economic viability. Such an evaluation depends on the careful selection of the segment. An accounting system that permits the evaluation of segments at multiple levels within the organization contributes to more precise identification of situations that require corrective action.

■ In practice, common costs are often allocated in an attempt to determine the full cost associated with the segment. Such an allocation may be useful if the segment is a product and the allocation of common cost is an attempt to gain an understanding of the total cost associated with the product. However, the allocation of common costs to a segment is never appropriate for performance evaluation.

4. Discuss the way in which direct costing differs from absorption costing and the implication for performance evaluation (pp. 449–59).

■ Direct costing includes only the variable manufacturing costs in inventory costs. Absorption costing includes not only the variable manufacturing costs but also a portion of the fixed manufacturing overhead. The difference between the two methods of inventory costing lies in the treatment of fixed manufacturing overhead. More specifically, a reconciliation between absorption costing and direct costing is always due to the difference between the amount of fixed manufacturing overhead in beginning and ending inventories.

5. Describe the behavioral aspects of absorption costing (pp. 457–58).

■ A major problem with absorption costing is that it provides incentive for managers to overproduce. The mechanics of absorption costing imply that if inventories increase, profits increase. This is because absorption costing treats fixed manufacturing costs as if they were variable. By increasing production, some of these fixed costs are placed into inventory costs and less goes into costs of goods sold. By decreasing cost of goods sold, a manager can increase net income. Thus, the plant manager has an incentive to produce goods—even when they cannot be sold.

6. Explain how to price products (pp. 459–63).

- Formulas were devised in this chapter for choosing a price for a product. The basic formula is that the selling price equals the sum of the fixed costs plus the target net income plus the quantity times the variable cost per unit, all divided by the quantity. Formulas were also derived for the markup. Two formulas were obtained, one under absorption costing and one for direct costing.

- It should be kept in mind that the answer the formula yields must be assessed for its realism. The manager must compare the solution to the market forces to see whether the item can be sold for the suggested amount.

7. Discuss the overhead allocation of service departments (Appendix C) (pp. 465–71).

- Service departments provide services to the producing departments. The accounting question is how to allocate the costs of the service departments to the producing departments (assuming that such allocation needs to be done).

- The step method is one way for allocating the costs of service departments. (Other ways are discussed in more advanced texts.) This calls for determining a sequence for the allocation procedure. One picks which service department to allocate first, then second, and so on, until they are all allocated to the producing departments. When the allocation is carried out, the costs are allocated upon some reasonable basis of activity. Examples are kilowatt hours for a utilities department and number of employees for a cafeteria.

- This allocation scheme is necessary for the use of absorption costing, but it inherits the usual problems with absorption costing. Accordingly, this allocation is not appropriate for performance evaluation.

Glossary of Key Terms

product margin   The segment margin when the segment is a product.

segment margin   The contribution margin for each segment of a business less all separable fixed costs.

segment reporting   The process of presenting financial and other information for components of a business entity.

separable cost   The cost or resource uniquely associated with an organizational unit.

service department   Departments that do not produce goods but provide services to producing departments.

step method   A method for allocating costs of service departments.

Review Questions

13-1   What is a business segment? Is a segment different from a responsibility center that was discussed in the previous chapter?

13-2   How do we distinguish between separable fixed costs and common fixed costs? What does it mean to say that the distinction between separable and common fixed costs depends on the perspective?

13-3 Why is it possible to always consider variable costs as separable costs?

13-4 How does the contribution margin differ from the segment margin?

13-5 Why is is misleading to allocate common fixed costs to segments to arrive at a profit associated with each segment?

13-6 If direct costing is so much more advantageous than absorption costing, why is absorption costing more commonly used?

13-7 What is the essential difference between direct costing and absorption costing?

13-8 In what way is absorption costing advantageous from the viewpoint of the manager who is being evaluated using profit determined based upon absorption costing?

13-9 If the ending inventory increases from one year end to another, which method of income determination would you expect to report the higher profit? Why?

13-10 Why is it advantageous to combine contribution reporting with direct costing?

13-11 Distinguish between a producing department and a service department.

13-12 Why is it necessary to allocate the service department costs to the producing departments when developing the predetermined overhead rate?

13-13 If it is so important to avoid the allocation of common fixed costs in preparing segment reports, why is it necessary to allocate fixed overhead costs associated with service departments in arriving at the predetermined manufacturing overhead rate?

13-14 Why is the step method of service department allocation used rather than the reciprocal method?

13-15 What rule is used in arranging the service departments prior to the start of the step allocation process?

13-16 If the profit difference between the direct costing method and the absorption costing method is $12,000, with the direct costing method having the higher profit, what will be the difference in the ending inventory value between the two methods if the beginning inventory were the same under both methods?

13-17 Is it possible to have business segments within business segments?

13-18 Is it possible to have business segments that have, within each segment, elements of other segments?

Discussion Questions

13-19 Can segment reporting be applied to the firm as a whole?

13-20 Can the pricing formulas developed in this chapter be used by service companies? Consider, for example, a hair stylist. Can the price of a haircut and style be computed using these formulas?

13-21 Sometimes the costs of a centralized computer system are allocated to the producing departments. This allocation, however, might provide incentives for a producing department to buy its own personal computers or minicomputer. Why might this happen? Why would top management likely not allow this scenario to happen? What might be done to satisfy the divisional managers?

Exercises

CO 1, 2, 3

13-22 **SEGMENT REPORTING** The vice president of finance of Mills Company has heard about business segment reporting and has asked you to prepare a segment report based on product lines given the following information for a recent month:

Revenues	$200,000
Less: variable expenses	120,000
Contribution margin	$ 80,000
Less: Fixed expenses	50,000
Profit	$ 30,000

Mills Company produces two products. Each of the products has the following information for the same month as presented above:

	Product A	Product B
Sales	$80,000	$120,000
Variable costs as a percent of sales	45%	70%
Separable fixed costs	$10,000	$ 20,000

a. Prepare a segment report for Mills Company. The report should be structured to show the product margin for each product and the profit for the entire company for the month.

b. Mills Company has an opportunity to increase the sales of product B by 30%. In order to take advantage of this opportunity, the Mills Company would have to increase separable fixed costs for Product B by $15,000. Should the Mills Company increase the sales of Product B under these conditions? Explain.

13-23 SEGMENT REPORTING AND DECISION MAKING Reed Company's Brescia Division produces two products and the controller of the Brescia Division prepares segment reports in order to aid in decision making in regard to products. The segment report for the most recent period is as follows:

CO 1, 2, 3

	Brescia Division		
	Product 1	Product 2	Total Division
Revenues	$100,000	$150,000	$250,000
Less: Variable expenses	60,000	100,000	160,000
Contribution margin	$ 40,000	$ 50,000	$ 90,000
Less: Separable fixed expenses	30,000	40,000	70,000
Segment Margin	$ 10,000	$ 10,000	$ 20,000
Less: Common fixed expenses			5,000
Profit			$ 15,000

Reed Company is considering the expenditure of $5,000 for advertising for the Brescia Division. If the $5,000 of advertising expense is devoted to Product 1, the sales of Product 1 in units will increase by 10%. If the $5,000 is devoted to Product 2, the sales of Product 2 in units will increase by 8%.

Alternatively, Reed Company could be persuaded to devote the $5,000 of advertising to the total division. If the $5,000 were spent to advertise the entire division, Reed expects that the unit sales of Product 1 would increase by 7% and the unit sales of Product 2 would increase by 7% also.

a. What are the financial consequences of spending the advertising fund of $5,000 on Product 1?

b. What are the financial consequences of spending the advertising fund of $5,000 on Product 2?

c. What are the financial consequences of spending the advertising fund of $5,000 on the total division?

13-24   ANALYSIS OF PROFITABILITY USING SEGMENT REPORTING Data from Oberlin Company's most recent income statement is presented below:

CO 1, 2, 3

Revenues	$800,000
Less: Variable expenses	520,000
Contribution margin	$280,000
Less: fixed expenses	250,000
Net income	$ 30,000

The management team of Oberlin Company is not pleased with the very low profits for its company and they have asked you to analyze the situation and advise them on actions they might take to improve profitability.

By asking questions of the controller, you have learned the following additional information:

1. Oberlin has an Eastern Sales Territory and a Western Sales Territory. Of the total $800,000 sales, $600,000 are generated by the Eastern Sales Territory. The contribution margin associated with the two sales territories is identical.

2. The fixed expenses of $250,000 includes $100,000 of fixed expenses associated with the Eastern Sales Territory and $80,000 of fixed expenses associated with the Western Sales Division.

a. Prepare a segment report that reveals the segment margin associated with each sales territory and the total company profit.

b. Does the segment report prepared in requirement a suggest an action that would improve the profitability of the company? Explain.

13-25   ELIMINATION OF A SEGMENT Drake Company has two operating divisions. The financial results for the two divisions for the year just ended are presented below:

CO 3

	North Division	South Division
Revenues	$1,200,000	$800,000
Less: Variable expenses	900,000	480,000
Contribution margin	$ 300,000	$320,000
Less: Separable fixed expenses	200,000	180,000
Segment margin	$ 100,000	$140,000
Allocated corporate expenses	120,000	80,000
Net income	$ (20,000)	$ 60,000

The $20,000 loss associated with the North Division is of great concern to the management of the Drake Company. In the opinion of the management, it was not likely that the North Division's prospects can be improved.

Would you advise the management of the Drake Company to eliminate the North Division? Explain.

13-26 DIRECT COSTING VERSUS ABSORPTION COSTING Denison Company has just completed its first year of operations, and the results of operations on an absorption costing basis are presented in the following income statement:

CO 4

Revenues (20,000 units @ $100 per unit)		$2,000,000
Less: Cost of Goods Sold:		
Beginning Inventory	$ –0–	
Cost of Goods Produced		
(22,000 units @ $70 per unit)	1,540,000	
Goods Available for Sale	$1,540,000	
Less: Ending Inventory		
(2,000 units @ $70 per unit)	140,000	
Cost of Goods Sold		1,400,000
Gross Profit		$ 600,000
Less: Selling and Administrative Expense		400,000
Net Income		$ 200,000

The absorption cost per unit has the following components:

Direct material	$30
Direct labor	10
Variable overhead	15
Fixed overhead	15 ($330,000/22,000 units produced)
Total absorption cost per unit	$70

a. Prepare a revised income statement using the direct costing approach to income determination.

b. Explain any difference between the net income using the absorption costing approach and the net income using the direct costing approach. Use calculations to support your explanation of the difference.

13-27 ABSORPTION COSTING VS. DIRECT COSTING Ithaca Company's product has the following cost components:

CO 4

	Cost per Unit	Cost per Year	Annual Production
Direct materials	$7		
Direct labor	3		
Variable manufacturing overhead	2		
Fixed manufacturing overhead		$400,000	
Annual production in units			100,000

The selling price per unit is $25 and the selling and administrative expenses are $500,000, all fixed expenses.

a. Calculate the direct cost per unit.

b. Calculate the absorption cost per unit.

c. If 90,000 units are sold during a year in which 100,000 units were produced, what is the dollar amount difference between net income under the absorption costing approach and the direct costing approach? Which of the two approaches will have the highest net income?

13-28   ENDING INVENTORY UNDER DIRECT COSTING AND ABSORPTION COSTING Hampshire Company manufactures a single product whose cost characteristics are

CO 4   revealed below:

	Cost per Unit	Cost per Year	Annual Production
Direct materials	$12		
Direct labor	7		
Variable manufacturing overhead	3		
Fixed manufacturing overhead		$800,000	
Annual production in units			200,000

During the first year of operations the Hampshire Company produced 200,000 units but sold only 180,000 units.

a. What is the value of the ending inventory under the direct costing approach to income determination?

b. What is the value of the ending inventory under the absorption costing approach to income determination?

c. Based on your answers to parts a and b, above, what conclusions are you able to draw concerning the net income differences between the two approaches to income determination?

13-29   ABSORPTION VERSUS DIRECT COSTING: MULTIPLE YEARS Bucknell Company's absorption costing income statements for the past three years are presented below:

CO 4	19X1	19X2	19X3
Revenues	$400,000	$340,000	$460,000
Less: Cost of Goods Sold	280,000	238,000	322,000
Gross Margin	$120,000	$102,000	$138,000
Less: Selling and Administrative Expense	100,000	100,000	100,000
Net Income	$ 20,000	$ 2,000	$ 38,000
Unit Sales	20,000	17,000	23,000
Unit Production	20,000	20,000	20,000
Change in inventory units	–0–	3,000	(3,000)

The cost of goods sold includes $2 per unit for fixed manufacturing overhead.

a. Prepare direct costing income statements for each of the three years.

b. Compare the net incomes for each year for each of the income determination approaches (absorption and direct costing) and explain the differences.

13-30 **PRICING OF PRODUCTS** Data for three independent situations are given in the following table.

CO 6

	Products		
	A	B	C
Fixed costs	$50,000	$10,000	$5,000
Quantity of goods sold	26,000	2,000	10,000
Target net income	$80,000	$12,000	$35,000
Variable cost per unit	$2	$29	$16

Determine the price of each product. Also verify that the price is correct by preparing an income statement and verifying that the price yields the target net income.

13-31 **PRICING WITH ABSORPTION COSTING AND DIRECT COSTING MARKUPS** Data for two independent situations are given in the following table.

CO 6

	Products	
	A	B
Fixed costs	$20,000	$600,000
Quantity produced	10,000	30,000
Target net income	$40,000	$750,000
Variable cost per unit	$2	$5

Determine the cost, the markup percentage, and the selling price of each product under absorption costing and under direct costing.

13-32 **PRICING WITH ABSORPTION COSTING AND DIRECT COSTING MARKUPS** Derive the two formulas on p. 462 that determine the markup percentages under absorption costing and direct costing when nonmanufacturing fixed and variable costs are included in the analysis.

CO 6

13-33 **PREDETERMINED OVERHEAD RATE CALCULATION: SERVICE DE-PARTMENT (APPENDIX)** Hobart Company, in establishing its predetermined manufacturing overhead rate for the upcoming year, estimated that the Machining Department would use 20,000 machine hours during the year. The variable cost per machine hour is estimated to be $10 and the fixed cost per year for the Machining Department is estimated to be $800,000.

CO 7

The Maintenance Department, which devotes 60% of its maintenance time to the Machining Department, has estimated that it will work 5,000 maintenance hours in the upcoming year. The budgeted variable cost per maintenance hour in the Maintenance Department is $5. The fixed cost for operating the Maintenance Department for the next year is estimated to be $100,000.

a. Calculate the predetermined variable manufacturing overhead rate for the Machining Department. Include in the calculation the appropriate amount to reflect the support provided by the Maintenance Department.

b. Calculate the predetermined fixed manufacturing overhead rate for the Machining Department. Include in the calculation the appropriate amount to reflect the support provided by the Maintenance Department.

13-34 ALLOCATION OF SERVICE DEPARTMENT COSTS (APPENDIX) Furman Company has three service departments that provide manufacturing services to the only producing department in the factory. The budgets for the upcoming year for each of the three departments are as follows:

CO 7

	Service Department A	Service Department B	Service Department C
Variable expenses	$100,000	$150,000	$200,000
Fixed expenses	700,000	400,000	300,000
Total expenses	$800,000	$550,000	$500,000

The measurement of services provided by one service department to each other and to the producing department is presented below:

Measurement for the Department Below	Service Departments			Producing Department
	A	B	C	
Department A (kwh)	–0–	20,000	40,000	140,000
Department B (sq. ft.)	4,000	16,000	2,000	30,000
Department C (hours)	1,000	2,000	5,000	40,000

a. Prepare a schedule that can be used to calculate the amounts of service department variable costs that will be allocated to the producing department.

b. Prepare a schedule which can be used to calculate the amounts of service department fixed costs that will be allocated to the producing department.

13-35 ALLOCATION OF SERVICE DEPARTMENTS TO PRODUCING DEPARTMENTS (APPENDIX) Clemson Company has two service departments that provide manufacturing services to two producing departments. Information for the fixed manufacturing overhead for those departments is presented below:

CO 7

	Service Departments		Producing Departments	
	A	B	C	D
Fixed manufacturing overhead	$100,000	$50,000	$400,000	$600,000
Allocation base:				
Service Department A (hours)	1,000	4,000	20,000	26,000
Service Department B (persons)	5	15	45	55

Prepare a schedule that shows how the fixed manufacturing overhead of the Service Departments should be allocated to the Producing Departments.

Problems

13-36 SEGMENT REPORTING Lafayette Company produces and sells hats and ties. The income statement for the year 19X0 just ended is as follows:

CO 1, 2, 3

Lafayette Company
Income Statement
December 31, 19X0
($000s)

	Tie Segment	Hat Segment	Total
Revenues	$800	$900	$1,700
Less: Variable Expenses	600	600	1,200
Contribution Margin	$200	$300	$ 500
Less: Separable Fixed Expenses	100	150	250
Segment Margin	$100	$150	$ 250
Less: Common Fixed Expenses			150
Net Income			$ 100

The ties and hats are sold through both the retail outlet and a catalog department. Information on those two additional segments is presented below:

	Retail Segment	Catalog Segment
Tie revenues	$600	$200
Hat revenues	600	300

The common fixed expenses of $150 when viewed from the perspective of the retail and catalog revealed the following breakdown of the $150:

Retail segment separable fixed expenses	$ 60
Catalog segment separable fixed expenses	70
Common fixed expenses	20
Total common fixed expenses	$150

The separable fixed expenses of $100 for ties and $150 for hats, when viewed from the perspective of the retail and catalog segments, revealed the following breakdown of the $100 and $150.

	Tie Segment	Hat Segment
Retail segment separable fixed expense	$ 30	$ 50
Catalog segment separable fixed expense	45	70
Common fixed expenses	25	30
Total separable fixed expenses	$100	$150

REQUIRED

Prepare a segment report of net income for the company that shows the retail and the catalog segments rather than the tie and hat segments.

CO 1, 2, 3

13-37   SEGMENT REPORTING Baylor Corporation is a service-oriented business for the performing arts. It sells its services to vocalists and instrumentalists. These services are marketed through two channels: telemarketing and direct mail. Information for the year just ended for each of these segments is as follows:

	Vocalists	Instrumentalists
Revenues	$200,000	$300,000
Variable expenses as a percent of revenues	60%	60%
Separable fixed expenses	$ 50,000	$ 70,000
Common fixed expenses (allocated based on relative revenues)	$ 20,000	$ 30,000

	Telemarketing	Direct Mail
Percentage of revenues from vocalists	50%	50%
Percentage of revenues from instrumentalists	50%	50%
Separable fixed expenses	$110,000	$ 30,000
Common fixed expenses (allocated based on relative revenues)	$ 15,000	$ 15,000

REQUIRED

a. Prepare a segment report that shows the Vocalists and Instrumentalists segment incomes and the net income for the total company.

b. Prepare a segment report that shows the Telemarketing and the Direct Mail segment incomes and the net income for the total company.

c. What conclusions can you draw concerning the effectiveness of each marketing channel with regard to each client segment?

13-38   SEGMENT REPORTING: EVALUATING ALTERNATIVES Whitman Company sells two lines of products, Mugs and Bowls. The company's controller prepared the income statement for the most recent years using the segment reporting format. This is the first time that the controller has examined the segment margin of each of the products. The segment reports that she prepared are presented below:

	Mug Line	Bowl Line	Total
Revenues	$800,000	$600,000	$1,400,000
Less: Variable expenses	400,000	300,000	700,000
Contribution margin	$400,000	300,000	$ 700,000
Less: Separable fixed expense	200,000	350,000	550,000
Segment margin	$200,000	$(50,000)	$ 150,000
Less: common fixed expenses			80,000
Net income			$ 70,000

REQUIRED

a. Calculate by how much the total company net income would have increased if the Bowl product line had not existed during the year.

b. When the Bowl product manager saw the preceding segment report, she asked for additional information on the items included in the separable fixed costs associated with her segment. That additional information is as follows:

Bowl advertising	$150,000
Salaried Bowl salespersons	100,000
Bowl promotions	50,000
Salary of the Bowl product manager	50,000
Total separable Bowl fixed expenses	$350,000

Explain whether the Bowl product manager will object to any of the fixed costs that the controller attributed to her product.

c. After analyzing the segment report, the product manager examined some alternatives and concluded that she could convert her salespersons from salaried to commissioned employees. To do this, she would have to pay them 15% of their revenues from Bowl sales. She expects that if she converts them to commissioned salespersons they will increase revenues by 20%. Of course, this change would eliminate the separable fixed expenses of $100,000 for salespersons' salaries.

Prepare a schedule showing the Bowl segment income for one year based on the change in the method of compensating the salespersons.

13-39 ABSORPTION COSTING VS. DIRECT COSTING Adelphi Company is a manufacturer of metal mailboxes. The costs and other information related to a recent month are as follows:

CO 4

Beginning Inventory	–0–
Units sold	480
Units produced	500
Sales price per unit	$20
Manufacturing costs:	
Direct materials per unit	$3
Direct labor per unit	$1
Variable manufacturing overhead per unit	$1
Fixed manufacturing overhead per unit	
($60,000 divided by 6,000 units per year)	$10
Selling and administrative expense	$2,000

REQUIRED

a. Find the net income of the company for the recently ended month using the absorption costing approach.

b. Find the net income of the company for the recently ended month using the direct costing approach.

c. Explain the difference in net income between the two income determination approaches.

13-40 DIRECT COSTING INCOME STATEMENT Hollins Company's controller prepared the following absorption costing income statement for the year just ended:

CO 4

Revenues (2,000 units at $500 per unit)		$1,000,000
Less: Cost of Goods Sold:		
Beginning Inventory	$ –0–	
Cost of Goods Produced		
(2,500 units × $350 per unit)	875,000	
Cost of Goods Available for Sale	$875,000	
Less: Ending Inventory		
(500 units at $350 per unit)	175,000	
Cost of Goods Sold		700,000
Gross Profit		$ 300,000
Less: Selling and Administrative Expenses		100,000
Net Income		$ 200,000

The fixed manufacturing overhead costs were estimated at $500,000 per year when the predetermined overhead rate was calculated at the beginning of the year using an estimated production divisor of 2,500 units.

The company's variable manufacturing costs as a percentage of sales is 30%. The selling and administrative expenses are all fixed expenses.

REQUIRED

Prepare an income statement from the information provided on a direct costing basis.

13-41   ABSORPTION COSTING VS. DIRECT COSTING The president of Lehigh Company, reviewing the performance of her company for the past two years, read the following income statement information:

CO 4

	19X1		19X2	
Revenues		$2,400,000		$2,800,000
Less: Cost of Goods Sold:				
Beginning Inventory	$ –0–		$ 310,000	
Cost of Goods				
Manufactured	2,170,000		1,920,000	
Goods Available				
for Sale	$2,170,000		$2,230,000	
Less: Ending Inventory	310,000		–0–	
Cost of Goods Sold		1,860,000		2,230,000
Gross Profit		$ 540,000		$ 570,000
Less: Selling and Administrative				
Expenses		300,000		300,000
Net Income		$ 240,000		$ 270,000

Other information related to the last two years is presented below:

	19X1	19X2
Sales in units	60,000	70,000
Production in units	70,000	60,000
Fixed manufacturing overhead	$420,000	$420,000

(continued)

Fixed manufacturing overhead rate per unit	$6	$7
Variable manufacturing expense per unit	$25	$25
Selling price per unit	$40	$40

After reviewing the information, the president commented to the controller that she was confused by the information in the financial statements. Sales increased by 16.7% but net income increased by only 12.5%. These results were reported in spite of the fact that the variable manufacturing costs per unit, the fixed manufacturing overhead, the selling and administrative expense, and the sales price per unit remained unchanged from one year to the next.

When the president considered that the contribution margin per unit is $15 and the fixed costs remained unchanged, the 10,000 unit increase in sales should have increased net income by $150,000 ($15 × 10,000 units).

REQUIRED

a. Explain why the net income for 19X2 is different from the president's expectations.

b. Prepare revised income statements for 19X1 and 19X2 in order to properly reflect the kind of relationships that the president expected to find when she reviewed both income statements.

13-42 PRODUCT PRICING UNDER ABSORPTION AND DIRECT COSTING
CO 6   Linda Roan Associates has developed a new electronic green stamp tabulator. Its financial characteristics are as follows:

Variable costs per unit:	
Direct materials	$ 2.00
Direct labor	.50
Variable manufacturing overhead	10.00
Variable administrative and marketing	1.50
	$14.00

Fixed costs:	
Fixed manufacturing overhead	$125,000
Fixed administrative and marketing	75,000
	$200,000
Production	10,000 units

REQUIRED

a. Suppose the target net income is $10,000. Determine the product cost under absorption costing and direct costing. Also compute the selling price.

b. Suppose the target net income is $40,000. Determine the product cost under absorption costing and direct costing. Also compute the selling price.

13-43 SERVICE DEPARTMENT COST ALLOCATIONS: PREDETERMINED OVER-HEAD RATES (APPENDIX) Emory Company is a manufacturer of three-ring binders. The
CO 7   manufacturing facility has two producing departments: Cutting and Assembly. There are two service departments that support the producing departments: the Maintenance Department and the First Aid Department.

The predetermined manufacturing overhead rate is based on machine hours in the Cutting Department and based on direct labor hours in the Assembly Department. These bases reflect the fact that the Cutting Department is capital-intensive and the Assembly Department is labor-intensive.

Estimates for the upcoming year are presented below:

	Maintenance Department	First Aid Department	Cutting Department	Assembly Department
Variable manufacturing overhead	$ 20,000	$ 5,000	$ 40,000	$ 60,000
Fixed manufacturing overhead	80,000	20,000	200,000	80,000
Total manufacturing overhead	$100,000	$25,000	$240,000	$140,000
Maintenance hours	160	–0–	3,000	1,000
Number of employees	2	1	4	16
Machine hours			100,000	
Direct labor hours				40,000

REQUIRED

a. Using the step method, prepare a schedule that can be used to calculate the variable manufacturing overhead rate for the Cutting Department and the Assembly Department.

b. Using the step method, prepare a schedule that can be used to calculate the fixed manufacturing overhead rate for the Cutting Department and the Assembly Department.

c. Comment on the effect on the overhead rates if the First Aid Department were allocated first rather than the Maintenance Department. (The choice to allocate the Maintenance Department first is the appropriate choice. The purpose of this question is to challenge you to consider the impact of that choice.)

13-44   ALLOCATION OF SERVICE DEPARTMENT COSTS: COMBINED OVER-HEAD RATE (APPENDIX) Tulane Company has two producing departments and two service departments. The company controller is in the process of developing a manufacturing overhead rate for the factory. The manufacturing overhead rate will be used for inventory costing and income determination purposes in the following year, which will start in three months.

CO 7

Producing Department A is a highly capital-intensive department that has only a few direct laborers. On the other hand, producing Department B is a labor-intensive department that has many direct laborers.

In the past, the controller has established one manufacturing overhead rate for the entire factory. This one rate combined both the variable and fixed manufacturing overhead costs, and it was used in product costing as if there were not two producing departments in the factory. The rate was based on direct labor hours.

REQUIRED

Advise the controller concerning the appropriateness of a single overhead rate for the entire factory.

13-45   SERVICE DEPARTMENT ALLOCATION: DEPARTMENTAL VS. PLANT-WIDE—PRODUCT PRICE (APPENDIX) Drew Company has two producing and two service departments. In establishing manufacturing overhead rates, the company intends to use the following estimates for the upcoming year:

CO 7

	Service Departments		Producing Departments	
	A	B	1	2
Variable manufacturing overhead	$ 40,000	$ 30,000	$ 400,000	$ 600,000
Fixed manufacturing overhead	120,000	80,000	800,000	900,000
Total manufacturing overhead	$160,000	$110,000	$1,200,000	$1,500,000
Service Department A				
(maintenance hours)	–0–	400	1,600	2,000
Service Department B				
(sq. ft.)	1,000	3,000	10,000	10,000
Producing departments				
(direct labor hours)			40,000	20,000
Machine hours				100,000

The direct production costs for the single product manufactured by this company are as follows:

	Direct Costs per Unit
Direct material	$500
Producing Department 1	
Direct labor (4 hrs. @ $10 per hr.)	40
Producing Department 2	
Direct labor (2 hrs. @ $8 per hr.)	16
Total direct cost per unit of product	$556

Management has established a policy of pricing the product at 150% of total cost per unit. Total cost per unit is equal to the sum of the $556 per unit direct cost plus the fixed and variable manufacturing overhead per unit.

REQUIRED

a. Calculate the price that would be established for the product if the manufacturing overhead rate were based on direct labor hours for the entire factory as if there were not two separate producing departments within the factory.

b. Calculate the price that would be established for the product if there were a separate manufacturing overhead rate established for each of the two producing departments. Assume that Producing Department 1 uses direct labor hours and Producing Department 2 uses machine hours to establish an overhead rate for each producing department. Also assume that 10 machine hours are required in Producing Department 2 for each unit of product.

c. Compare the product price calculated in requirement a with the product price in requirement b. Explain why they are the same or different.

Business Decision Case

The now retired Judge Moore is running his own business and has developed a new product called Xorque. He is thinking about how to price it, but is uncertain of how much of it he can sell. Specifically, it is estimated that the fixed costs of this venture would be $2,624,000 and the variable costs $100 per unit. Unfortunately, he does not know how many he can sell but thinks it is between 6,000 and 10,000 units. Sally Nimmo, his marketing vice-president, has performed some market surveys and concludes that for the following prices the maximum quantity that can be sold is given accordingly.

Selling Price	Maximum Quantity that can be sold
$400	12,000
450	10,000
500	8,000
550	6,000
600	4,000

REQUIRED

Perform a what-if analysis using the quantity of goods produced and sold as 6,000 to 10,000 in increments of 1,000 units. For each of these levels determine the selling price. Then use Nimmo's marketing analysis to assess the feasibility of the price and quantity combination. Explain what Judge Moore should do if his target net income is $400,000.

Part

5

ADVANCED TOPICS IN
PLANNING AND
CONTROL

Chapter

14

Capital Budgeting

CHAPTER OBJECTIVES

After reading Chapter 14, you should be able to:

1. Describe the process of capital budgeting (pp. 491–95).

2. Define *time value of money* and distinguish between simple and compound interest (pp. 495–97).

3. Explain and compute future value and present value for single sums and annuities (pp. 497–500).

4. Calculate and explain the advantages and disadvantages of the methods used to evaluate proposed capital projects (payback, accounting rate of return, net present value,

discounted payback, and internal rate of return) (pp. 500–505).

5. Determine the impact of changes in the cost of capital on the various methods of capital budgeting (pp. 506–507).

6. Indicate the role of taxes in capital budgeting (pp. 507–512).

7. Explain how decision support systems help managers perform capital budgeting (pp. 512–14).

8. State how behavioral issues impact capital budgeting (p. 514).

*F*ixed or long-term assets tend to be expensive. Since these decisions involve large sums of money, such outlays require greater scrutiny than do smaller purchases. Special methods are required by which managers can evaluate investment in a particular long-term asset. These techniques are generally referred to as capital budgeting.

Capital, in the sense used in this chapter, refers to long-term assets used by the firm. A budget is simply a financial plan. It generally indicates the cash inflows and outflows of a particular project or asset. Thus, **capital budgeting** refers to a financial plan that examines the cash flows of proposed long-term assets. It encompasses the processes of creating, evaluating, and auditing these financial plans as well as the methods for aggregating and summarizing the cash inflows and outflows of an asset.

THE PROCESS OF CAPITAL BUDGETING

CHAPTER OBJECTIVE 1
The capital budgeting process

The first step in the process of capital budgeting is the development of the ideas. A manager or engineer or some other employee conceives of the long-term asset and how it might fit into the enterprise. The next step is to classify the project by its type. This helps upper management understand the nature of the proposed project and its fit within the organization. A formal project request is the third step. This request explains what is proposed and why. The fourth step is the estimation of the cash flows. In practice this step may be combined with and included in the formal request. These cash flows include both cash coming into the firm and cash that must be expended. Fifth, upper management evaluates the project and makes a decision about it. Two evaluation tools are the *payback method* and the *net present value* method. (These are often referred to as capital budgeting techniques.) The sixth and last step is to provide an audit of the project. Accepted projects need to be reexamined to see whether they were really good projects. This step involves, for example, a comparison between predicted cash flows and actual cash flows. These six steps are summarized in Exhibit 14-1.

The Generation of Ideas

The first step is the generation of ideas. Since capital projects are created by the organization, the firm needs some ways to generate ideas for capital projects. Ideas can come from a research and development staff whose job is to research, analyze, and search for new products and for new uses of existing projects. Ideas may come from engineers or employees in production. They may come from the sales staff who listen to customer's requests for new products. They may come from the legal staff who are aware of certain legal requirements such as the need for anti-pollution equipment. Indeed, ideas can arise from almost any employee in the firm. The generation of ideas for capital projects is a creative process. It is an art, not a science. Firms must master this step, in part by nurturing a culture within the firm conducive to producing ideas for capital projects.

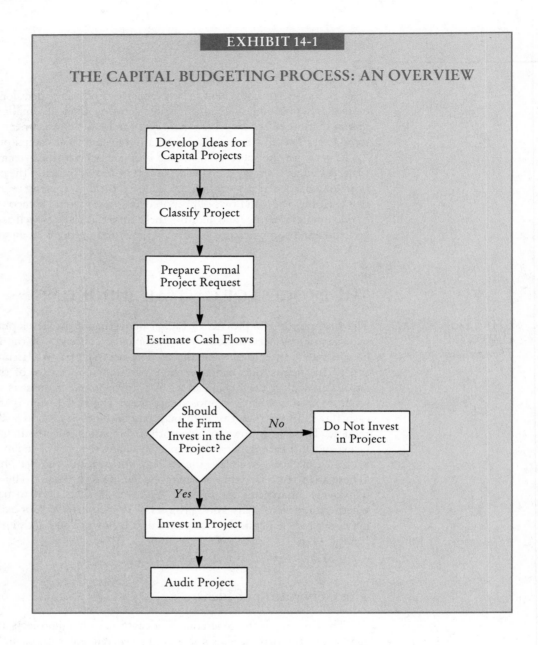

EXHIBIT 14-1

THE CAPITAL BUDGETING PROCESS: AN OVERVIEW

Develop Ideas for Capital Projects

Classify Project

Prepare Formal Project Request

Estimate Cash Flows

Should the Firm Invest in the Project? — *No* → Do Not Invest in Project

Yes

Invest in Project

Audit Project

The Classification of the Project

Next the proposed project is classified to help managers analyze it. There are many classification schemes in practice. The following classification scheme is typical:

1. **New product**   These expenditures are made to develop new products or new uses of existing products. (Some firms use two categories, differentiating between new products and new uses of existing products.)

2. **Replacement**   These expenditures are justified by a need to replace defective or worn-out assets.

3. **Cost reduction**   These capital expenditures are paid out because the project reduces the cost of existing manufacturing or production.

4. **Safety/environmental**   These funds are justified because they address safety concerns for employees or because of legal requirements to provide for safety or environmental quality on the job.

5. **Other**   Anything else, from parking lots to information systems.

Such a classification scheme helps managers understand the nature of the project and assess quickly how it fits into the plans of the organization. For example, a manager may be unwilling to approve a proposal to take on an unprofitable new product but would be willing to accept an unprofitable safety/environmental project in order to comply with the law.

The Formal Request

The third step of the capital budgeting process is to prepare a formal request. This step may be combined with several others (for example, steps two and four). In the request, the proposer states the nature of the project and explains its benefits. Frequently, the request also mentions the locale for the project, the timing of the project, and the funds necessary to carry it out. If combined with later steps, as is often done in practice, the request will enumerate the projected cash inflows and outflows and show the project evaluation in terms of, for example, the payback period and the net present value. There is usually space provided on the request for the necessary signatures of managers who approve (or disapprove) the project.

A sample corporate request is shown in Exhibit 14-2. Notice that this capital budgeting request states the corporate division initiating the proposal, the date of the request, the title of the project, the location of the project, and the amount of funds needed for the project. It also contains the project classification, the project description, a brief listing of project benefits, and the starting and ending dates (if approved). Cash flow estimates are listed as well as the payback period and the net present value. Space is provided for noting the approval or rejection of the project and additional notes explaining the reason for the decision.

Estimation of Cash Flows

The fourth step in capital budgeting is to estimate the cash flows. The manager who proposes the project provides a realistic and comprehensive assessment of these flows. All (and only) incremental costs are to be included. As stated in previous chapters, sunk costs should be ignored. Engineering estimates are often used in obtaining these estimates of cash flows.

Since the numbers are estimated, the evaluation techniques will be affected by the quality of the estimates. Sometimes firms use three sets of numbers: one for an optimistic case, one for a pessimistic scenario, and one for the most likely outcome. Some firms estimate the average and the standard deviation of the calculated flows. Other companies use simulation to try various cash flows and to investigate the impact of each on the financial viability of the project. These issues will be discussed further in the decision support systems section.

EXHIBIT 14-2

EXAMPLE OF A CAPITAL BUDGETING REQUEST

Division: Winding Gulf   *Date:* July 19X2
Title of Project: New conveyor belts
Location of Project: Black Gulf
Amount Requested: $2,000,000
Classification of Project: Replacement

Description of Request: A new conveyor belt will be installed in mines #2, 4, and 5 at Black Gulf.

Benefits of Project: The current conveyor belts are 12 years old. They are damaged in spots. Coal falls off the belts in many places, requiring special maintenance. Cash inflows are from cost reduction.

Starting Date: January 19X3
Completion Date: March 19X3

Predicted Cash Flows

	19X3	19X4	19X5	19X6	19X7
Cash inflow	$ 400,000	$400,000	$400,000	$400,000	$400,000
Cash outflow	2,000,000	—	—	—	—
Net cash flow	$(1,600,000)	$400,000	$400,000	$400,000	$400,000

	19X8	19X9	19Y0	19Y1	19Y2
Cash inflow	$ 400,000	$400,000	$400,000	$400,000	$400,000
Cash outflow	—	—	—	—	—
Net cash flow	$ 400,000	$400,000	$400,000	$400,000	$400,000

Payback Period: 5.0 years
Net Present Value: $7,520

Approved ☐   Rejected ☐   _____
                                                                            Division Manager

Evaluation of the Proposed Project

In the process of capital budgeting, the fifth step is the evaluation of the proposed project. Five common methods used in the evaluation phase are (1) the payback period, (2) the accounting rate of return, (3) the net present value, (4) the discounted payback method, and (5) the internal rate of return. These methods are explored in greater depth in a later section of the chapter. All of the methods aggregate the cash flows into a single number. Then the index is compared with some benchmark. If the comparison is favorable, then the project should be accepted. If the comparison is unfavorable, then it should be rejected. At times the five methods will conflict, in which case management must prioritize them based on the organization's strategy.

Many capital projects might be accepted even if the numbers are not acceptable. Safety/environmental projects, for example, are often accepted to comply with the law or with union contracts rather than because of their profitability. Corporations may accept projects on the basis of market share, penetration into new geographic areas, improved employee relations, or for research and development reasons. These considerations cannot be directly translated into money, so the economics of the project alone does not decide the issue.

In a similar manner, capital projects might be rejected even if the numbers *are* acceptable. Management might consider the risk of the project to be too high. The project might not fit in with the strategic goals of the organization. Alternatively, managers might have a limited amount of funds and desire to rank the projects. An otherwise acceptable project might be ranked behind other projects deemed economically more acceptable.

The Project Audit

The sixth and last step is to provide an audit of the completed project. In particular, the projected cash flows should be compared with the actual cash flows. If the budgeted and actual amounts differ significantly, the project should be investigated to determine why. The purpose of this project audit is to improve forecasts and to motivate behavior. If a manager knows that the forecast will be monitored and evaluated, then he or she has an incentive not to send forward low-quality forecasts. It is also hoped that a learning process is taking place. Managers should learn about what went right and what went wrong with previous projects and apply the knowledge to future proposals.

These steps should not be thought of as static and necessarily sequential. In practice, the process is dynamic and interactive. Steps two through five may be combined or reordered in several ways. These six steps are generally present in U.S. corporations in one form or another.

TIME VALUE OF MONEY

CHAPTER OBJECTIVE 2
Time value of money, simple vs. compound interest

Three of the five methods for evaluating capital projects are built on the concept of the time value of money. Very simply, the concept refers to the fact that $1 today is worth more than $1 received in the future, because the $1 received today may be put into a bank account to draw interest. The amount of the interest is the difference between the value of $1 received today and $1 received in the future.

Interest is the amount paid or received for the borrowing or lending of money. **Simple interest** determines the amount of interest as a function of the principal. Specifically, the formula for simple interest is:

$$I = P \times R \times T$$

where

> I = the amount of the interest
> P = the principal, the amount borrowed or lent
> R = the interest rate
> T = the amount of the time elapsed

The rate and the time must be in comparable units. Both are measured annually, semi-annually, quarterly, monthly, daily, or by some other unit of time.

If Paula has put $1,000 into a savings account at 8% annual interest, how much will she have at the end of six months? The interest is $40 computed as:

$$\$1,000 \times 8\% \times 6/12$$

The total at the end of six months is $1,040. Note that the interest rate and the time are on a yearly basis.

Compound interest is computed not only on the principal but also on any interest earned but yet not paid or received. The rationale is that once interest is earned it belongs to the creditor. If the interest is not paid out at that time, the creditor then earns new interest on the total amount loaned to the borrower, which is the principal plus the unpaid interest. If partial repayments of the loan are made, the principal is reduced. If Paula has a savings account that compounds interest semiannually, how much would she have at the end of one year? We know she has $1,040 after six months. To obtain the answer, calculate the interest for the next six months, keeping in mind that the principal this time is $1,040. The interest is $1,040 × 8% × 6/12, or $41.60. Thus, at the end of 12 months, Paula would have $1,081.60 in her savings account.

Compound interest plays an important part in the financial economy. The crucial point here is that compound interest is a fundamental aspect behind several of the capital budgeting techniques. Four situations arise in which compound interest is relevant. They are the future value of a single sum, the future value of an annuity, the present value of a single sum, and the present value of an annuity. These are explained in turn. The first two items deal with future value and the last two deal with present value.

Future value is the amount a cash flow made today will grow to at some future date. Present value is the worth today of a cash flow made in the future. Paula's problem is a future value problem because we know she has $1,000 today and we want to know how much she will have in the future.

If Paula asked us for the future value of that sum after 15 years, we could resolve the problem as before but use the simple interest formula 30 times, once for each six-month period. Each time, the interest would be added to the old principal to yield the new principal. The process is tedious and cumbersome. Fortunately, there is an easier way.

Appendix D, at the end of this chapter (page 528), contains four tables, D-1 to D-4, to handle the future and present values of single sums and annuities. (More elaborate tables are available that cover more periods and more interest rates.) We will use these tables throughout the chapter, as they will make calculating present and future values much easier. The tables correspond to the four circumstances with compound interest. Each table gives the period or number of periods down the first column. All of the numbers along the given row are for that particular period or number of periods. For example, the fifth row refers to factors for the fifth period. At the tops of the columns are the interest rates. All of the numbers down the given column are factors for that interest rate. For example, the numbers in the 6% column are for situations with 6% interest. To find the relevant interest factor to use in solving a problem, look at the intersection of a column showing the interest rate and a row depicting the period or number of periods.

The interest rate and the period or number of periods must correspond to the compounding time frame. If the compounding is annually, then the interest rate and the period should both be yearly numbers; if the compounding is semiannual, then both should be semiannual numbers; and so on. Note that for simple interest, it is enough for the interest rate and the period to be compatible, that is, measured in the same units of time. For compound interest, not only must they be compatible, they must also conform to the compounding time unit.

Future Value of a Single Sum

We are now ready to solve Paula's question. Recall that she begins with $1,000 and puts the money in a bank paying 8% interest compounded semiannually. How much will she have at the end of 15 years? By convention, interest rates are stated as annual rates. So we must convert it to a semiannual rate by dividing by two. The interest rate to use in solving the problem is 4%. Also convert the number of years to the number of semiannual periods. That gives 30 (15 × 2) semiannual periods. Look up the future value interest factor for 4% and 30 periods in Table D-1, pages 528–29. That number is 3.2434. The future value is $1,000 × 3.2434, yielding an answer of $3,243. Isn't that easier than using the simple interest formula 30 times?

Suppose the interest rate were 12%. The factor for this rate is found at the intersection of the "6%" column and the "30 period" row. The factor is 5.7435. Paula would have $1,000 × 5.7435, or $5,743 after 15 years. In general, other things equal, higher interest rates imply higher future values.

Finally, notice how the numbers in each column of Table D-1 are related. The first number in each column is one plus the interest rate. Each succeeding interest factor is equal to the interest factor for the prior period at the same rate of interest multiplied by one plus the interest rate. In other words, the column is constructed by successively multiplying the prior year's factor by one plus the interest rate.

Future Value of an Annuity

The above situation dealt with only one cash flow, called single sums. If there are several cash flows, we could treat each cash flow separately, computing the future value of each cash flow *individually* and then add up the future values. There is a short-cut method if the cash flows are equal in amount and occur uniformly. An annuity is a set of equal cash flows (commonly called *rents*) paid or received in equal time intervals. There are two types of annuities. In an ordinary annuity, the cash flows occur at the end of each period. In an *annuity due*, the cash flows occur at the beginning of each period. This chapter focuses only on ordinary annuities.

Suppose that Ted puts $2,000 into his pension fund each year at the end of the year for five years. How much will Ted have at the end of the fifth year if the pension fund earns 10% interest compounded annually? The problem involves the future value of an ordinary annuity and the interest factors are tabulated in Table D-2, pages 530–31. For five periods and an interest rate of 10%, the interest factor is 6.1051. Therefore, the amount of money Ted will have is $2,000 × 6.1051, or $12,210. Ted contributed a total of $10,000 so the total interest he earned is $2,210.

As just mentioned, we could have used Table D-1 to solve the problem, figuring the future amount of each sum separately and adding them up, as follows (cash flows listed in reverse order):

$$
\begin{array}{rcl}
\$2,000 \times 1.0000 &=& \$\ 2,000 \\
2,000 \times 1.1000 &=& 2,200 \\
2,000 \times 1.2100 &=& 2,420 \\
2,000 \times 1.3310 &=& 2,662 \\
2,000 \times 1.4641 &=& \underline{\ 2,928} \\
&& \$12,210
\end{array}
$$

The last cash flow occurs at the end of the fifth period. It earns no interest; it is already at its future value. The next-to-last cash flow occurs at the end of the fourth period; it earns one period of interest. The factor of 1.1000 is for 10% and one period of interest. The third cash flow earns two periods of interest, thus the factor of 1.2100. And so on. Why does it work? Add up the five interest factors, $1 + 1.1 + 1.21 + 1.331 + 1.4641$, and the sum is 6.1051, the interest factor in Table D-2. This summing process is true for all values in Table D-2.

Suppose now that the pension fund compounds interest semiannually and the rent is $1,000. (Both examples add $10,000 to the pension fund.) Look up the interest factor for 5% and 10 periods. It is 12.577. Ted would have $1,000 × 12.577, or $12,577. Why is there more money? Because more frequent compounding adds interest to the pool more quickly. In general, other things being equal, more frequent compounding yields higher future values. This is true for single sums and annuities.

Present Value of a Single Sum

A different type of problem is now cast. If money is paid or received in the future, how much is it worth today? This is referred to as present value. Tables D-3 and D-4 contain the interest factors for the present value of a single sum and an annuity.

Edith is entitled to receive $1,000,000 ten years from now. If the interest rate is 15%, what is its value today? Look up the interest factor in Table D-3, pages 532–33, since this situation is a *present value of a single sum*. The interest factor for 10 periods at 15% is .2472, thus the present value is $1,000,000 × .2472, or $247,200. An explanation for this is that if the organization that owes $1,000,000 to Edith would take $247,200 and put it in the bank at 15% for 10 years, they would have the $1,000,000 to pay Edith.

Given the alternative explanation, you should be able to recognize that the future value of a single sum and the present value of a single sum are inverse problems. Indeed, the interest factors in one of these tables are the reciprocals of the respective interest factors in the other table. For example, consider the interest factor for 9%, five periods is 1.5386 in Table D-1 and .6499 in Table D-3. Take the reciprocal of 1.5386: $1/1.5386 = .6499$ (approximately).

The higher the interest rate, the lower the present value. If the interest rate is lower, the present value is higher. Here are the present values to Edith at different interest rates:

Interest Rate	Present Value of $1,000,000 10 Years from Now
4%	$675,600
8%	463,200
12%	322,000
16%	226,700
20%	161,500

What is the impact of the compounding period? The more frequent the compounding, the less the present value. The less frequent the compounding, the greater the present value. To illustrate this, here are some present values to Edith for an interest rate of 12% with various compounding schemes.

Compounding Period	Present Value of $1,000,000 10 Years from Now at 12%
Monthly	$303,000
Quarterly	306,500
Semiannually	311,800
Annually	322,000

Present Value of an Annuity

If there are several cash flows and we wish to determine the present value, we can always compute the present value for each cash flow separately and then sum them. For example, to determine the present value of an annuity of $5,000 each year for four years at 7% compounded annually, we would get the following:

$$\begin{aligned}
\$5,000 \times .9346 &= \$\ 4,673 \\
5,000 \times .8734 &= \ 4,367 \\
5,000 \times .8163 &= \ 4,081 \\
5,000 \times .7629 &= \underline{\ 3,814} \\
&\quad \underline{\$16,935}
\end{aligned}$$

An easier way is to look up the interest factor for an annuity in Table D-4, pages 534–35. At 7% and four periods, the factor is 3.3872. The present value of the annuity is $5,000 × 3.3872, or $16,936. Similar to the previous discussion about future values, this result occurs because the numbers in the Table D-4 are related to the relevant numbers in Table D-3. Thus, 3.3872 = .9346 + .8734 + .8163 + .7629. Each factor in Table D-4 is equal to the sum of the factors in Table D-3 for the same interest rate of each of the periods.

As is true of the present values of single sums, for annuities, higher interest rates lead to lower present values and vice versa. In addition, the more frequent the compounding, the lower the present value and vice versa.

Unlike single sums, the annuity interest factors for future and present values are not reciprocals. This is easy to see, since most numbers in Tables D-2 and D-4 are greater than one.

Using Present Value Tables to Solve Problems

Before leaving this section, one more point should be made. The calculations involving the time value of money are a function of the interest rate, the period or the number of periods, and the cash flow. If any three of these are known, the other can be found. Suppose John buys a car costing $20,000. He has 24 monthly payments to make of $1,057.42 each. What is the interest rate? Since $20,000 is the value today, the problem is one of the present value of an annuity. Obtain the interest factor by dividing $20,000 by $1,057.42. The interest factor is 18.9139. Look in Table D-4 across the row for 24 periods. The interest factor found is in the "2%" column. Therefore, the answer is that the interest rate is 24% compounded monthly.

METHODS FOR EVALUATING PROPOSED PROJECTS

CHAPTER OBJECTIVE 4
Advantages and disadvantages of proposed evaluation methods

There are a variety of ways to evaluate capital projects, as mentioned earlier. Five popular methods are: (1) the *payback method,* which estimates the time to recoup the investment; (2) the *accounting rate of return,* which estimates the accounting profits divided by the investment base; (3) the *net present value* method, which compares the cash flows using the time value of money; (4) the *discounted payback method,* which estimates the time to recover the investment in discounted dollars; and (5) the *internal rate of return,* which gives a return percentage of the cash flows in terms of their time value.

To illustrate these five techniques, the data for Grail, Inc., in Exhibit 14-3 will be used throughout this section. Assume that there are two projects, X and Y. Both cost $20,000. The annual cash inflows from Project X are $10,000, $9,000, $6,000, and $4,000, respectively. Cash inflows for Project Y are $7,435 per year for four years (it is

EXHIBIT 14-3

ILLUSTRATION OF CAPITAL BUDGETING TECHNIQUES

Year	Project X	Project Y
0	$(20,000)	$(20,000)
1	10,000	7,435
2	9,000	7,435
3	6,000	7,435
4	4,000	7,435
Payback	2.17 years	2.69 years
Accounting rate of return	22%	24%
Net present value	$1,733	$1,227
Discounted payback	3.24 years	3.71 years
Internal rate of return	20%	18%

an annuity). The question before us is whether Grail should accept the proposed project. Another possible question is which project should be accepted if only one can be approved (that is, if they are alternative projects to accomplish the same task).

Payback Method

The first method is the payback method. The payback period is the number of years it takes to return the cost of the investment. For Project X, it takes longer than two years, since only $19,000 is returned after two years. In Year 3, $6,000 is returned, on which $1,000 is a recovery of the investment. The payback period is 2⅙, or 2.17 years. Project Y has a payback of two years plus 5,130/7,435 or 2.69 years.

The way it is applied is for the management to set some benchmark, such as a payback of three years. Accordingly, projects whose payback is less than three are accepted; those whose payback is greater than three are rejected. If three years is the standard for Grail, Inc., both X and Y are accepted. If only one can be accepted (if they are mutually exclusive), then Grail would choose the one with the shorter payback period. For this example, Grail would choose X.

The payback method is easy to use. It also provides an index of the riskiness of the project—assuming that the later the cash flow, the riskier is the measurement of the cash flow and the riskier it is that the cash will actually be received. This method is also an index of liquidity. That is, the larger the payback, the longer the period is in which the cash is tied up in the project.

Problems with the payback period are that it ignores the time value of money—it gives equal weight to a dollar received in Years 1, 2, 3, and 4. The payback method also has the disadvantage of ignoring cash flows beyond the payback period. For example, if another Project Z existed with cash flows as follows:

Year	Amount
1	$ 10,000
2	9,000
3	6,000
4	1,000,000

that project would be evaluated as equivalent to Project X.

Accounting Rate of Return

The second method is the accounting rate of return. Though popular, it has little conceptual support. First, the average profit for the project is computed. Temporarily we will assume that for Grail, Inc.'s two project proposals the cash flows are equal to the profits. Project X earns profits of $9,000, net of depreciation, over four years for an average profit of $2,250. Project Y earns net profits of $9,740 over four years for an average profit of $2,435. Next we compute the average investment bases for the projects. The *average investment base* is the value of the investment at the beginning plus the value of the investment at the end, divided by two. For now it is assumed that there is no terminal value (to be explained later), so Projects X and Y each have an average base of ($0 + $20,000)/2, or $10,000. The accounting rate of return is equal to the average profits divided by the average investment base. For X, it is $2,250/$10,000, or 22%. For Y it is $2,435/$10,000, or 24%.

The corporation—here Grail, Inc.—usually sets a benchmark for evaluation purposes. If 30% is the minimum accounting rate of return, for example, both of these projects are rejected even though Project Y is ranked higher than Project X.

The accounting rate of return has no redeeming feature. Disadvantages are that it ignores the time value of money, in practice it includes noncash items such as depreciation expense, and it is easy to manipulate. For example, by increasing the salvage value, a manager could decrease depreciation expense and so increase profits.

Net Present Value

The third method for evaluating capital projects is the **net present value** method. It gets its name because the present values for the cash flows are computed. If the present value of the cash inflows exceed the present value of the investment, then the project is accepted. Otherwise, the project is rejected. If the projects are mutually exclusive, the project with the higher net present value is selected.

In our example, assume that Grail, Inc.'s cost of capital is 15%. (*Cost of capital*, discussed on pages 506–509, is the cost of raising funds.) The present value of Project X is computed in Exhibit 14-4. The present value of Project Y is also computed. Note that the inflows for Y form an annuity. Factors for Project X are taken from Table D-3 and for Y from Table D-4. The present values are computed for the outflows and for the inflows. The net amount is obtained. Since the net present values are positive, both projects would be accepted. If only one can be accepted, choose Project X since it has the higher net present value.

The net present value method has many advantages. It incorporates the time value of money. It considers all of the project's cash flows. And the net present value is the increment to stockholders' wealth. The method has no disadvantages. A practical concern is that it requires the corporation to know its cost of capital.

Discounted Payback

A fourth method is the **discounted payback** method. This method basically follows the spirit of the payback method except that it uses the present values of the cash flows instead of the cash flows themselves. This technique indicates the amount of time to recover the investment in terms of discounted dollars. The method is a hybrid of the payback method and the net present value method. Criteria for application are similar to the payback method.

Project X has discounted cash flows of $19,446 through the first three years ($8,696 + $6,805 + $3,945). An additional $554 is needed to reach the payback point. In year 4, $2,287 discounted dollars are received. Thus, the discounted payback for X is 3.24, or [3 + (554/2,287)]. The discounted payback for Project Y is 3.71 [3 + (3,024/4,251)].

Advantages of this technique are that it provides an index of risk and an index of liquidity, and it considers the time value of money. The disadvantage is that it ignores cash flows beyond the discounted payback period.

EXHIBIT 14-4

PRESENT VALUE CALCULATIONS

Project X

Cash Flow	Interest Factor (15%)	Present Value
(20,000)	1.0000	(20,000)
10,000	.8696	8,696
9,000	.7561	6,805
6,000	.6575	3,945
4,000	.5718	2,287
		1,733

Project Y

Cash Flow	Interest Factor (15%)	Present Value
(20,000)	1.0000	(20,000)
7,435	2.8550	21,227
		1,227

or:

Cash Flow	Interest Factor (15%)	Present Value
(20,000)	1.0000	(20,000)
7,435	.8696	6,465
7,435	.7561	5,622
7,435	.6575	4,889
7,435	.5718	4,251
		1,227

Internal Rate of Return

The last method described here is the internal rate of return. The **internal rate of return** is the rate that would make the net present value equal to zero.

If the cash inflows are an annuity, the internal rate of return can be found in a straightforward manner. Divide the investment amount by the yearly cash inflow. This number is the interest factor. Go to Table D-4, interest factor for present values of annuities, and look across the row for a given number of periods. The interest rate that yields the factor closest the calculated number is the internal rate of return.

Consider Grail, Inc.'s Project Y. Divide the investment of $20,000 by the yearly cash flows of $7,435. The number is 2.6900. Look in Table D-4 across the row for four periods, the number of periods of cash flows projected for Project X. This number is almost the same as 2.6901, interest factor for 18% and four periods. We conclude that the internal rate of Project Y is approximately 18%.

EXHIBIT 14-5

FINDING THE INTERNAL RATE OF RETURN FOR PROJECT X

	16%		18%	
Cash Flow	Interest Factor	Present Value	Interest Factor	Present Value
(20,000)	1.0000	(20,000)	1.0000	(20,000)
10,000	.8621	8,621	.8475	8,475
9,000	.7432	6,689	.7182	6,464
6,000	.6407	3,844	.6086	3,652
4,000	.5523	2,209	.5158	2,063
		1,363		654

	20%		24%	
Cash Flow	Interest Factor	Present Value	Interest Factor	Present Value
(20,000)	1.0000	(20,000)	1.0000	(20,000)
10,000	.8333	8,333	.8065	8,065
9,000	.6944	6,250	.6504	5,854
6,000	.5787	3,472	.5245	3,147
4,000	.4823	1,929	.4230	1,692
		(16)		(1,242)

It is much more difficult to obtain the internal rate of return for Project X. By hand, the best one can do is use trial and error. Several computations are shown in Exhibit 14-5 for a variety of interest rates. The interest rate of 20% yields a net present value of $(16), which we take as approximately equal to zero. Thus Project X has an internal rate of return of approximately 20%.

To evaluate a project using internal rate of return, one compares the cost of capital to the internal rate of return. If the internal rate of return is higher than the cost of capital, accept the project. Otherwise, reject it. If the projects are mutually exclusive, choose the one with the higher internal rate of return. In our example, if the cost of capital is 15%, both projects are accepted. If only one can be taken on, it is Project X because its internal rate of return is higher.

The internal rate of return has the advantages of considering the time value of money and considering all cash flows. It has the disadvantage of sometimes yielding multiple rates of return.

It should also be pointed out that the net present value method and the internal rate of return method generally give the same accept-or-reject evaluation (see Problem 14-77 for an exception). However, if the projects are ranked, these two measures can give conflicting signals. (This does not occur in the present illustration.)

	EXHIBIT 14-6	

ADVANTAGES AND DISADVANTAGES OF THE METHODS OF EVALUATING PROPOSED CAPITAL PROJECTS

Method	Advantage	Disadvantage
1. Payback	Easy to use.	Ignores time value of money.
	Index of risk.	
	Index of liquidity.	Ignores cash flows beyond payback period.
2. Accounting rate of return		Ignores time value of money.
		Includes noncash items in calculation
		Easy to manipulate
3. Net present value	Considers time value of money.	
	Considers all cash flows.	
	Measures increment to stockholders' wealth.	
4. Discounted payback	Index of risk.	Ignores cash flows beyond discount payback period.
	Index of liquidity.	
	Considers time value of money.	
5. Internal rate of return	Considers time value of money.	Sometimes gives multiple answers.
	Considers all cash flows.	

The advantages and disadvantages of the five evaluative methods are summarized in Exhibit 14-6. Using a decision support system, Grail, Inc., can include multiple evaluative methods as a routine part of the analysis to provide comparative results, as a review of Exhibit 14-3 makes clear.

CHANGES IN THE COST OF CAPITAL

CHAPTER
OBJECTIVE 5
*Impact of changes in
the cost of capital*

The net present value method and the internal rate of return are generally considered superior to the other methods of evaluating proposed projects. This priority is due to their incorporating the time value of money and considering all cash flows. The net present value method depends directly on the cost of capital. The internal rate of return method indirectly depends on it for evaluating whether to accept a project. Two questions emerge: (1) What is the cost of capital? (2) What happens when it changes in value?

Briefly, the cost of capital is the cost of raising funds. The two sources of funds used by almost every firm are debt and common stock. The cost of capital is an average of the cost of debt and the cost of common stock or common equity. The *cost of debt* to the firm is the expected interest to be paid to creditors less any tax advantages. The federal government allows interest charges to be tax deductible. The *cost of equity* to the firm is the expected rate of return the stockholders of the corporation desire. It is composed of the expected dividend yield plus the expected capital gains on the stock. There is no subtraction for taxes, since the federal government does not allow the firm to deduct dividends or capital gains of individual shareholders. These two costs, the cost of debt and the cost of equity, are *combined in proportion* to their contribution to the capital structure of the firm. That is, the cost of capital is composed of a *weighted average* of these two costs.

Consider Alpha Corporation, which has 40% debt and 60% common stock. The expected interest charges are 12% and the expected return desired by common stockholders is 15%. The firm's marginal tax rate is 30%. What is Alpha's cost of debt? It is the interest rate times one minus the tax rate. The cost of debt is 12% × (1 − 30%) = 12%(70%) = 8.4%. In effect, the tax benefit of 3.6% (30% × 12%) is deducted because the federal government allows it to be. The cost of common stock is 15%; there is no tax deduction here. The cost of capital is the weighted average of the cost of debt and the cost of common stock where the weights are their proportion to the capital structure. Thus, the cost of capital to Alpha Corporation is:

$$(8.4\% \times 40\%) + (15\% \times 60\%) = 3.36\% + 9.0\%$$
$$= 12.36\%$$

Now we return to the Grail, Inc., example in the previous section and described in Exhibit 14-3. Assume all the data is the same except that the cost of capital is now 8%. What changes? Recall that the payback method and the accounting rate of return are completely divorced of the cost of capital and so do not change in any way. Computation of the internal rate of return is not modified either, although for accept-or-reject decisions it is compared with 8%, the new cost of capital. The only methods that change the results are the net present value method and the discounted payback method. At 8% the net present value for Project X is $4,678 and for Project Y is $4,625. The discounted payback period is 2.63 years for Project X and 3.15 years for Project Y. Calculations are left for the reader to verify.

Net Present Value Profile

A useful tool for analyzing the impact of a changing cost of capital on the net present value is to prepare a **net present value profile.** This profile is a graph of the cost of capital against the net present value. Generally the cost of capital is assigned to the X

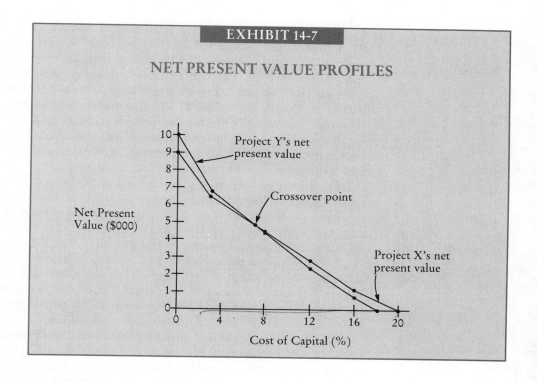

EXHIBIT 14-7

NET PRESENT VALUE PROFILES

axis and the net present value is plotted along the Y axis. Net present value profiles are prepared for Grail, Inc.'s Projects X and Y and shown in Exhibit 14-7.

The sensitivity of the net present value to changes in the cost of capital is clearly shown in the profile. The graphs are downward-sloping, which indicates that increases in the cost of capital decreases the net present value and vice versa. Intersections on the Y axis are for the undiscounted dollar values because the interest rate is zero. An intersection on the X axis signals the internal rate of return of the project since it is a present value of zero.

Note that in Exhibit 14-7 the two profiles cross each other somewhere between 7% and 8%. Below the crossover point Project Y dominates but above it Project X dominates. This means that any cost of capital below the crossover point will rank Project Y above Project X. It also means that any cost of capital above the crossover point will rank Project X as better than Project Y. Above the crossover point, the net present value method and the internal rate of return are always consistent. That is, they rank projects the same way. Below the crossover point, however, the net present value method and the internal rate of return are not consistent. They rank Projects X and Y differently.

IMPACT OF TAXES AND DEPRECIATION ON CAPITAL BUDGETING

CHAPTER OBJECTIVE 6
Role of taxes in capital budgeting

In practice, one of the cash outflows that must be considered is the tax bill. Taxes require complex calculations and tend to be a major factor in the decisions of managers. They should, of course, be incorporated into any analysis of capital budgeting. The treatment of taxes in this section is illustrative and conceptual, not comprehensive.

Recall that the cash inflows of Grail, Inc.'s Project X are $10,000, $9,000, $6,000, and $4,000, respectively. These profits are taxable; they increase the taxes payable by the firm. In capital budgeting, the tax outlays must be recognized for the budget to be realistic. The increase in taxes is estimated by multiplying the profits by the corporation's marginal tax rate. If the marginal tax rate is 40%, then the taxes from Project X are $4,000, $3,600, $2,400, and $1,600. The net cash inflows are equal to the profits less the taxes. For Project X, the net cash inflows are $6,000, $5,400, $3,600, and $2,400. An alternative way of computing these numbers is to multiply the revenues by one minus the tax rate (1 − tax rate)—in this case, by 60%, because 60% represents the portion of incremental profits retained by the investor.

The federal government goes further and allows firms to deduct depreciation as an expense. In other words, income taxes are paid on the revenues less expenses including the depreciation expense. This is referred to as the depreciation tax shield. Keep in mind that depreciation itself is not a cash flow; instead, it enters the analysis only because it affects the measurement of taxes payable, which does require a cash outflow.

We will illustrate the impact of taxes and depreciation with three types of financial accounting depreciation: straight line, sum-of-the-years' digits, and double-declining balance. Tax depreciation is actually computed in a different and more complex way. We use financial accounting methods of depreciation only to illustrate the concept. See a tax accounting textbook for the actual tax depreciation rules.

Another tax consideration arises in some years when the U.S. Congress allows firms to take an investment tax credit (ITC). (At this writing Congress does not allow the ITC. We still cover the material since we feel that Congress might reinstate it when it deems that there is a need to stimulate the economy.) Companies are allowed to subtract a certain proportion of the investment from their tax bill in the first year. The purpose of this tax rule is to spur investment.

Straight-line Depreciation

We return to Grail, Inc.'s Project X, which has a cost of $20,000. If it is depreciated according to the straight-line method, the depreciation is equal to

$$\frac{\text{Cost} - \text{Salvage Value}}{\text{Life of the Asset}}$$

The cost is how much it takes to acquire the asset. In this case, the cost is $20,000. The salvage value is the estimated value of the asset at the end of its economic life. Assume it is zero. The life of the asset is its projected economic life to the business. Project X has a life of four years. The annual straight-line depreciation is then $5,000, or ($20,000 − $0)/4.

If the rate of the investment tax credit is 10%, then the ITC is 10% of $20,000, or $2,000. The tax bill in the first year can be lowered by this $2,000.

Analysis of the tax impact on a project's cash flows is given in part A of Exhibit 14-8. Income before depreciation and taxes is just the cash inflows from the project. Depreciation is computed using the straight-line method and is $5,000 each year. Subtracting out depreciation yields income. Taxes are computed on the income at a marginal rate of 40%. The investment tax credit of $2,000 lowers the tax bill in year 1. The sixth line gives the net tax cash outflows.

EXHIBIT 14-8

CASH FLOW EFFECTS OF DEPRECIATION AND TAXES

A. Straight-line Depreciation

	Year 1	Year 2	Year 3	Year 4	Total
Income before depr., taxes	$10,000	$9,000	$6,000	$ 4,000	$29,000
Depreciation	5,000	5,000	5,000	5,000	20,000
Income before taxes	$ 5,000	$4,000	$1,000	$(1,000)	$ 9,000
Taxes (40%)	$ 2,000	$1,600	$ 400	$ (400)	$ 3,600
Investment tax credit*	2,000				2,000
Tax cash outflows	$ –0–	$1,600	$ 400	$ (400)	$ 1,600
Operating cash flows	$10,000	$9,000	$6,000	$ 4,000	$29,000
Tax cash flows	–0–	1,600	400	(400)	1,600
Project cash flows	$10,000	$7,400	$5,600	$ 4,400	$27,400

B. Sum-of-the-years' Digits

	Year 1	Year 2	Year 3	Year 4	Total
Income before depr., taxes	$10,000	$9,000	$6,000	$ 4,000	$29,000
Depreciation	8,000	6,000	4,000	2,000	20,000
Income	$ 2,000	$3,000	$2,000	$ 2,000	$ 9,000
Taxes (40%)	$ 800	$1,200	$ 800	$ 800	$ 3,600
Investment tax credit*	2,000				2,000
Tax cash outflows	$(1,200)	$1,200	$ 800	$ 800	$ 1,600
Operating cash flows	$10,000	$9,000	$6,000	$ 4,000	$29,000
Tax cash flows	(1,200)	1,200	800	800	1,600
Project cash flows	$11,200	$7,800	$5,200	$ 3,200	$27,400

C. Double-declining Balance

	Year 1	Year 2	Year 3	Year 4	Total
Income before depr., taxes	$10,000	$9,000	$6,000	$ 4,000	$29,000
Depreciation	10,000	5,000	2,500	2,500	20,000
Income	$ –0–	$4,000	$3,500	$ 1,500	$ 9,000
Taxes (40%)	$ –0–	$1,600	$1,400	$ 600	$ 3,600
Investment tax credit*	2,000				2,000
Tax cash outflows	$(2,000)	$1,600	$1,400	$ 600	$ 1,600
Operating cash flows	$10,000	$9,000	$6,000	$ 4,000	$29,000
Tax cash flows	(2,000)	1,600	1,400	600	1,600
Project cash flows	$12,000	$7,400	$4,600	$ 3,400	$27,400

*10% of $20,000.

The negative tax flow in year 4 arises because of the negative income of year 4. Assuming that Grail, Inc., has other income in year 4 to match against this loss in year 4, the effect is to reduce the tax bill for Project X plus the offsetting income. Thus, the tax outlay is shown as a negative number.

The next three lines show the cash flows themselves. The first one repeats the operating cash flows. The second line repeats the tax cash outflows. Subtracting the second line from the first line gives the last line, the *project cash flows*. These are the cash flows the firm will receive from the project—on an after-tax basis.

The five methods for evaluating proposed projects are not calculated in Exhibit 14-8. This is because the tax impact of the depreciation tax shield and the investment tax credit affect the determination of the project cash flows. They do not change how to compute payback or net present value.

Accelerated Depreciation

Straight-line is only one of many different types of depreciation schemes. Two additional types are called *accelerated methods of depreciation*. They are the *sum-of-the-years' digits* and *double-declining balance* methods. While they do not change the tax bills over the life of the asset, they do rearrange the tax outlays. Specifically, they have higher depreciation charges in the early years and lower depreciation charges in the latter years of the project's life, relative to the straight-line method. This fact implies that the accelerated forms of depreciation have lower taxes in the early years than the straight-line method and so higher cash flows. This is reversed in the later years. By delaying the timing of the tax payments, the accelerated depreciation forms increase the net present value of the project.

Sum-of-the-Years' Digits.   Depreciation under the **sum-of-the-years' digits'** rule proceeds as follows. Each period the depreciation expense is equal to

$$\frac{\text{Number of Periods Remaining}}{\text{Sum-of-the-Years' Digits}} \times \text{Depreciable Cost}$$

The *depreciable cost* is the cost of the asset minus its salvage value. For Project X, the depreciable cost is $20,000 − $0, or $20,000. The sum-of-the-years' digits is obtained by taking the life of the asset, in this example four years, and adding up the integers from 1 to 4. So the sum-of-the-years' digits is 10 (1 + 2 + 3 + 4). The numerator is the number of periods remaining as of the beginning of the year. For the first year the numerator is 4; for the second year it is 3; for the third 2; and for the last year 1. Thus, the depreciation expense for Project X is:

Year 1: 4/10 × $20,000 = $8,000
Year 2: 3/10 × $20,000 = $6,000
Year 3: 2/10 × $20,000 = $4,000
Year 4: 1/10 × $20,000 = $2,000

In part B of Exhibit 14-8, the cash flows for the project are determined if the sum-of-the-years' method is used for tax purposes. The arrangement is the same as in part A.

Note that the investment tax credit is unaffected by the depreciation method used. Note also that the taxes over the four years are $1,600 for both straight-line and sum-of-the-years' digits methods. Similarly, the project cash flows are the same, $27,400. What changes is the timing of the cash flows.

Double-declining Balance.   The **double-declining balance** method is still a third way to depreciate an asset. According to this technique, annual depreciation is:

$$\frac{2}{\text{Life of the Asset}} \times \text{Remaining Book Value of the Asset}$$

2 × straight line [handwritten note]

Do Not consider salvage value [handwritten note]

where the book value of the asset is its cost less its accumulated depreciation. The method gets its name because it takes the straight-line rate of depreciation (1/life) and doubles it (2/life). In the last year, the depreciation is such that it reduces the book value to the salvage value. For Project X, which has a life of four years, the double-declining balance method produces these numbers:

$$
\begin{aligned}
&\text{Year 1: } 2/4 \times (\$20{,}000 - \$0) &&= \$10{,}000 \\
&\text{Year 2: } 2/4 \times (\$20{,}000 - \$10{,}000) &&= \$5{,}000 \\
&\text{Year 3: } 2/4 \times (\$20{,}000 - \$15{,}000) &&= \$2{,}500 \\
&\text{Year 4: Plug} &&= \$2{,}500
\end{aligned}
$$

The $20,000 represents the cost of the asset. The $0, $10,000, and $15,000 represent the accumulated depreciation for the first three years. Year 4's depreciation fully depreciates the asset, so that its book value is equal to the salvage value. In this case $0.

Panel C of Exhibit 14-8 contains the cash flows of Project X if double-declining balance is used for tax purposes. Again, the investment tax credit is unaffected by the choice of depreciation method. Also the taxes over the four-year period are unchanged at $1,600 and the project cash flows are still $27,400. The only thing that changes is the timing of the cash flows.

Accelerated Cost Recovery System

The depreciation method generally used in practice at this writing is called the Accelerated Cost Recovery System (ACRS). Initiated by Congress in 1981, it has been modified several times, most significantly by the Tax Reform Act of 1986, and is now called the Modified Accelerated Cost Recovery System (MACRS). Under this method assets are partitioned into eight property classes. A table for each class indicates the amount of depreciation that can be taken in a particular year. The approximate percentages for three-year property class assets are 33% for the first year, 45% for the second year, 15% for the third year, and 7% for the fourth year. Multiply the appropriate percentage by the cost of the asset to obtain the amount of depreciation. Further discussion can be found in any tax accounting textbook.

Why should management accountants be concerned about which depreciation method to use in capital budgeting? Because the net present value of the project is affected. The accelerated methods are better for the firm because they delay the tax payment. This gives additional cash to the firm in the earlier years. Managers could invest this cash and later pay the additional taxes. If the cost of capital is 15%, the project has a net present value of $489 if the straight-line method is used, $886 if sum-of-the-years' digits is used, and $999 if the double-declining balance method is used. Double-declining balance does not always beat sum-of-the-years' digits, but both always yield higher net present values than the straight-line method. In many cases, MACRS depreciation is the best. Decision support system models permit multiple depreciation methods to be included in the project proposal analysis.

DECISION SUPPORT SYSTEMS AND CAPITAL BUDGETING

CHAPTER
OBJECTIVE 7
How decision support systems aid in capital budgeting

In practice, the computations for capital budgeting are generally computerized. Many software packages exist that perform the computations and speed up proposal evaluation. While the computer carries out the work in practice, management and management accountants still should understand what the program is doing, the assumptions behind the techniques, and the advantages and disadvantages of various methods of depreciation and evaluation.

People are obviously the ones who input data and the quality of the data is related to the quality of the solutions. In the corporate world, the data are seldom as precise as in textbook illustrations. That is certainly true in capital budgeting, primarily because most of the data consists of forecasts and projections. The manager must predict future cash flows and the cost of capital facing the firm in the future. The predictive nature of capital budgeting makes it a hazardous process.

Five methods were presented to evaluate proposed projects. The accounting rate of return has no merit so it should never be used. The two payback methods are useful since they provide an index of risk. They are also helpful when considering the liquidity of the enterprise. The two discounted cash flow methods are useful since they include the time value of money and they analyze all cash flows. In essence, they provide an index of profitability. We suggest that managers use some or all of these four methods since each has something to offer. Each method provides a perspective useful for the manager as a point of comparison. If they provide conflicting signals, the manager should use good business sense in deciding which one to use. He or she should do that even if the signals are in agreement.

Cash flows and costs of capital are only estimates. Computerized what-if analysis can be used to assess the impact of the estimates on the results. A manager can change one or more of the estimated numbers and view the result, then insert other numbers to examine yet other results. By doing this, a manager can determine the sensitivity of the results to the estimates of the cash flows and of the cost of capital.

Goal-seeking can also be used in drawing up and evaluating capital budgets. For example, a manager could set a goal of a certain net present value or internal rate of return and find out what cash flows are needed to achieve that goal. Or the manager might find out what cash flows are needed to achieve a given payback goal. The manager is then in a position to appraise the likelihood of obtaining those cash flows.

Another form of evaluation concerns analysis of the relationships among the variables and of the assumptions. For example, the proposed cash flows might be conditioned on some economic assumptions. The manager is advised to examine those economic assumptions and try different ones. He or she should see how sensitive the results are to different sets of assumptions.

For example, capital budgeting decisions depend on analyses of at least two different options—such as "invest" or "do not invest." Often the alternative action is

BEYOND "WHAT IF": A RISK-ORIENTED CAPITAL BUDGETING MODEL

Spreadsheet software has become one of the more popular tools used by decision makers and business planners. There are a number of reasons for this, including the low cost of the spreadsheet software, the relatively low cost of the computer that uses the software, and the ease with which users can alter the problem parameters. This last characteristic is the "what if" capability which is universally a part of spreadsheet software. Spreadsheet literature usually hails this as a powerful feature since it allows the user, for example, to quickly determine the net present value of an income stream if the cost of capital were eight percent instead of, say, nine percent.

There can be no question about the convenience of the "what if" capability. Anyone who has performed present value analysis with only paper, pencil, and a set of tables can attest to the reduction in computational burden and therefore the convenience afforded by the feature. However, the contention here is that the mere convenience of changing and recalculating is not necessarily beneficial to the user in terms of the quality of decision that results from the use of "what if." The "what if" values are only helpful if they bear some resemblance to future reality. Unfortunately, decision makers are usually inaccurate in the prediction of future income and expenses.

In a classic paper, David B. Hertz described the idea of associating future financial values with a measure of the likelihood that they will occur.[1] There has been low utilization of these ideas by small firms, probably because they involve Monte Carlo simulation. Monte Carlo is a technique for selecting numbers randomly from a probability distribution for use in a simulation trial.[2] Most spreadsheet software does not have the capability for such simulation and many users are unfamiliar with this technique. The modeling software that is capable of simulation is often expensive and requires relatively expensive hardware.

[Some] integrated software tools on the market . . . [have] a spreadsheet and language capability sufficient to use risk simulation at very affordable cost.

There are several steps in constructing the capital budgeting model with risk incorporated. First, the decision maker must identify the factors involved in the decision. Second, a risk or likelihood distribution for each factor must be developed. Third, after the model is developed, it must be executed repeatedly and the resulting NPVs noted. Finally, the NPVs must be sorted and displayed in such a manner that the risk associated with the various outcomes is indicated.

[1]David B. Hertz, "Risk Analysis in Capital Investment," *Harvard Business Review* (January/February 1964), pp. 95–106.

[2]Sang M. Lee, Laurence J. Moore, and Bernard W. Taylor, *Management Science* (Dubuque, IA: William C. Brown Co., 1981), p. 464.

SOURCE: Adapted from Charles W. Golden and Mary Golden (Auburn University), "Beyond 'What If': A Risk-Oriented Capital Budgeting Model," *Journal of Information Systems* (Spring 1987), pp. 53–64. Adapted by permission of the authors.

assumed to be the status quo. That is why the benchmark is a net present value of zero. When a corporation investigates investment decisions regarding high-tech items (such as computer integrated manufacturing or computer assisted design), however, the alternative usually is *not* the status quo. Managers should assume that at least some of their competitors will invest in the high-tech items and so erode the company's position. Not to invest might mean the decline of market share or lost sales. The manager should assess these different scenarios carefully.

Finally, the cash flows might be viewed in a probabilistic fashion. Some firms will assign probabilistic properties to the variables and then study the results. This can be done by trying to determine the mean and the standard deviation of the net present value through a simulation study. Alternatively, with appropriate distributional assumptions, one could analytically derive the probabilistic properties of the net present value. Computer programs are available to carry out such analysis.

BEHAVIORAL ASPECTS OF CAPITAL BUDGETING

CHAPTER
OBJECTIVE 8
*How behavioral issues
affect capital budgeting*

Six behavioral issues are relevant for the topic of capital budgeting. The first is the need to foster creativity. Although corporations generally do not need creativity to produce literary or musical compositions, they do need sufficient creativity to search for new products, new markets, and new uses for existing products. They need creativity to search and design for new assets to help in the production process. Corporations might try to formalize this creativity through a research and development staff. Or they might try to reward creativity through raises, bonuses, and even sharing royalties.

Another important organizational aspect of capital budgeting is that the numbers generated in the capital budgeting process are meant to be used as aids in the decision-making about capital projects. Often, however, the numbers are used as weapons in intraorganizational disputes. With appropriate changes in the estimates and the assumptions, one side could argue for the project while another group argues against it. Holding managers responsible for their estimates, for example through *post-audits*, might help alleviate this. Keep in mind that the numbers are not gospel, nor are they a substitute for thinking.

As implied above, manipulation of the numbers is always possible. If a sponsor or evaluator really wants a project, he or she can inflate the estimated cash inflows. If the evaluator dislikes the project, he or she can deflate the numbers. Top management should be aware of this possibility and scrutinize the estimates carefully.

Decisions about proposed projects are generally group decisions. Individuals in a group bring to it different levels of knowledge, different risk perceptions and risk tolerances, different goals and objectives, different levels of analytical and forensic ability, and different commitments to the firm. In a few companies, the group is led by an autocrat who makes the decisions. In most firms, the individuals bargain with each other and must make compromises. The decision is based in part on their negotiating skills.

The capital budgeting of technology presents interesting issues to managers and management accountants. For example, a drawback of capital budgeting in practice is the reluctance to include items in the analysis which are difficult to quantify. A technological improvement might lead to higher quality and thus lower production costs; but if it is hard to verify, for example by an engineering report, managers might not want it included in a capital budget analysis. Firms that ignore hard-to-quantify items might not invest in technological improvements, and as a result find themselves in a poorer competitive position with firms that address these factors, such as Japanese corporations. Firms are encouraged to include such items in the analysis because they are important even if difficult to measure. They can then use what-if analysis and other tools of decision support systems to assess the estimates.

Finally, the implicit alternative in capital budgeting is that nothing happens. In the net present value method, we compare the net present value to zero because of this assumption. In reality this may not be true. The firm may choose not to invest, for example, in robotics, but its competitors might. Their investment could lead to a declining market share for the firm. Thus, it is not always appropriate to compare a net present value calculation to a zero base. (On the other hand, it is very difficult to determine a different benchmark since it depends on what the competitors do.)

Demonstration Problem

Sandy Hurtubise is trying to decide whether to go to college or not. If she does not go to college, she could teach ice skating for the next 30 years at an estimated salary of $30,000 per year. If she does go to college and obtains a bachelor's degree in sports psychology, she would pay $10,000 per year for four years and then earn an estimated salary of $40,000 per year for the next 26 years. A third alternative is to get a master's degree as well. In this case, Sandy would pay $10,000 per year for four years and (assuming she gets an assistantship) $5,000 per year for years five and six and then earn an estimated salary of $60,000 per year for the next 24 years.

REQUIRED

Analyze the cash flows in Sandy's alternatives, assuming everything else remains constant and a cost of capital of 8%.

SOLUTION TO DEMONSTRATION PROBLEM

The present value of the first option is:

$$\$30,000 \times 11.2578 = \underline{\$\,337,734}$$

The present value of the second option is:

$$\$(10,000) \times 3.3121 \qquad\qquad = \$\,(33,121)$$
$$\$40,000 \times 10.8100 \times .7350 = \underline{\$317,814}$$
$$\underline{\$284,693}$$

The last term was obtained by finding the present value of an annuity over 26 years, which is the present value at the end of four years. Then it is multiplied by .735 to obtain the result in today's present value terms.

The third alternative is as follows:

$$\$(10,000) \times 3.3121 \qquad\qquad \$\,(33,121)$$
$$\$(5,000) \times 1.7833 \times .7350 \qquad (6,554)$$
$$\$60,000 \times 10.5288 \times .6302 \qquad \underline{398,115}$$
$$\underline{\$358,440}$$

Thus, Sandy Hurtubise should plan to go to college and obtain both a bachelor's degree and a master's degree.

Review of Chapter Objectives

1. Describe the process of capital budgeting (pp. 491–95).

   ■ The first step is the development of the ideas. The second step is to classify the project by its type, for example, new project, replacement, cost reduction, safety or environmental, and other. The third step is the formal project request. The fourth step is the estimation of the cash flows. The fifth step is the evaluation of the project, using such techniques as payback, accounting rate of return, net present value, discounted payback, and internal rate of return. Step six is to carry out a project audit.

2. Define *time value of money* and distinguish between simple and compound interest (pp. 495–97).

   ■ The time value of money refers to the concept that one dollar today is worth more than one dollar received in the future since interest can be earned on to-day's dollar. Interest is the amount paid or received for the borrowing or the lending of money. Simple interest determines the amount of the interest as a function of the principal. Compound interest is computed not only on the princi-pal but also on any interest earned but not yet paid or received.

3. Explain and compute future value and present value for single sums and annuities (pp. 497–500).

   ■ *Single sums* simply means that there is but one cash flow. An annuity is a series of cash flows of the same amount and paid or received on a periodic basis. Future value is the amount a cash flow made today is worth at some future date. Present value is the worth today of a cash flow made in the future. Tables are usually used when dealing with annuities.

4. Calculate and explain the advantages and disadvantages of the methods used to evaluate proposed capital projects (payback, accounting rate of return, net present value, discounted payback, and internal rate of return) (pp. 500–505).

   ■ The payback period is the number of years it takes to return the cost of the in-vestment. The accounting rate of return is the average profit of the project di-vided by the average investment base. The net present value method computes the present value of the cash inflows and subtracts the present value of the cash out-flows (the investment). The discounted payback method combines the payback and the net present value methods. It computes the payback period, but it uses the discounted cash flows. The internal rate of return is that rate at which the net present value is zero.

   ■ The advantages and disadvantages of these five methods of evaluating proposed capital projects are described in Exhibit 14-6. The key points from that exhibit are that: (a) the net present value, the discounted payback, and the internal rate of return consider the time value of money; (b) the payback period is easy to use and to explain; and (c) the net present value and internal rate of return methods consider all the cash flows and do not contaminate the calculations with arbitrary allocations.

5. Determine the impact of changes in the cost of capital on the various methods of capital budgeting (pp. 506–507).

   ■ The cost of capital is the cost of raising funds. It includes the cost of debt and the cost of common stock. Changes in the cost of capital indicate whether it is easier or harder to raise funds. Changes in the cost of capital do not affect the payback method and the accounting rate of return (which helps to pinpoint a weakness in these methods). It does not affect the calculation of the internal rate of return, though it changes the benchmark when deciding whether to accept or reject a project. Changes in the cost of capital do change the computation of net present value and the discounted payback period.

6. Indicate the role of taxes in capital budgeting (pp. 507–512).

   ■ Taxes affect the determination of the future cash flows since they add an additional tax outflow that is a consequence of the project. The tax outflow, however, is lowered by the existence of depreciation tax shields. Though it is not a cash flow, depreciation enters the capital budgeting assessment process because of its effect on income taxes. Three depreciation techniques were discussed: the straight line, the sum-of-the-years' digits, and double-declining balance. Usually the accelerated forms (the latter two) provide better benefit to the taxpayer.

7. Explain how decision support systems help managers perform capital budgeting (pp. 512–14).

   ■ Because of the many estimates in the process of capital budgeting, a decision support systems approach is advisable. Managers can probe the proposal with what-if questions and goal-seeking. A probabilistic analysis may be taken.

8. State how behavioral issues affect capital budgeting (p. 514).

   ■ Behavioral aspects are important because creativity should be encouraged. Top management also needs to be aware of possible manipulation and intraorganizational disputes in the capital budgeting process.

   ■ Capital budgeting of technology is difficult because many of the benefits of technology are nonquantifiable. Nevertheless, the management accountant should not ignore them because the benefits are quite real even if difficult to measure.

Glossary of Key Terms

accounting rate of return A capital budgeting technique in which the project's accounting profits are divided by the average investment base.

annuity A set of equal cash flows paid or received in equal time intervals.

capital budgeting The process of financial planning that examines the cash flows of proposed long-term assets.

compound interest An interest method that adds unpaid interest to the old principal to get a new principal. Thus additional interest is computed on the old principal plus any unpaid interest.

cost of capital The future cost of raising capital. It is the weighted average of the cost of debt and the cost of common stock. Weights are the proportions of debt and common stock in the capital structure.

depreciation tax shield A reduction of taxes due to the allowance of depreciation as a tax deduction.

discounted payback A capital budgeting technique that indicates the amount of time to recoup the investment in terms of discounted dollars.

double-declining balance   An accelerated form of depreciation. Annual depreciation is equal to (2/life of the asset) × book value. The last year's depreciation is whatever is necessary to reduce the book value to the salvage value.

future value   The value at a future time of a cash flow made today.

interest   The amount paid or received for the borrowing or lending of money.

internal rate of return   A capital budgeting technique that determines the rate at which the investment has a net present value of zero.

investment tax credit   A tax method sometimes allowed by Congress to spur investment. It is a percentage of the investment in specified assets and is directly subtracted from the tax bill.

net present value   A capital budgeting technique in which the present value of the cash inflows is netted against the present value of the cash outflows.

net present value profile   A graph of the net present values as a function of the cost of capital.

ordinary annuity   An annuity whose cash flows occur at the end of the period.

payback period   A capital budgeting technique that indicates the amount of time required to recover the investment from the budgeted cash inflows.

present value   The value today of a cash flow made in the future.

project audit   An examination of the results of a capital project. This examination is carried out to assess the accuracy of the estimates and to decide whether the correct decision was made.

simple interest   Interest computed only on the original principal.

single sum   Only one cash flow.

straight line   A form of depreciation. Annual depreciation is equal to (cost - salvage value)/life of the asset.

sum-of-the-years' digits   An accelerated form of depreciation. Annual depreciation is equal to the product of the number of periods remaining divided by the sum-of-the-years' digits times the depreciable cost (cost minus salvage value).

time value of money   The concept that one dollar received today is not equivalent to one dollar received in the future because of interest.

APPENDIX D

| Future and Present Value Tables | Future and present value tables D-1 to D-4 are located at the end of this chapter (pages 528–35) rather than at this point, due to their length and their integral use in solving many of the exercises and problems in the following pages. For easier reference, large black tabs have been printed at the tops of the pages on which these tables occur. |

Review Questions

14-1   What is capital budgeting? What is its purpose?

14-2   Name the six steps in the capital budgeting process.

14-3   Why is creativity important in capital budgeting?

14-4   Where can ideas for capital projects arise?

14-5   How may capital projects be classified?

14-6   What data is included in a formal capital budget project request?

14-7   What cash flows are to be analyzed in capital budgeting?

14-8   Name five common techniques used to evaluate proposed projects?

14-9   Why might an uneconomical project be accepted?

14-10   What is the purpose of a project audit?

14-11   What is the time value of money?

14-12   What is interest?

14-13   What is simple interest? How is it measured?

14-14   What is compound interest? How is it measured?

14-15   What is future value? What is present value?

14-16   What is a single sum?

14-17   What is an annuity? What is an ordinary annuity?

14-18   How are future and present value tables such as in Appendix D used to compute future and present values of single sums and annuities?

14-19   What types of adjustment are made to the interest rate and the period when using the compound interest tables?

14-20   (a) Are the interest factors for the future and present value of single sums reciprocals? (b) Are they for the future and present value of annuities?

14-21   If the interest rate increases, what is the impact on the future and present value of single sums and annuities? What is the impact if the interest rate declines?

14-22   What is the impact of the compounding frequency on the future and present value of single sums and annuities?

14-23   How is the payback period computed? What are the advantages and the disadvantages of the payback method?

14-24   How is the accounting rate of return computed? What are its advantages and disadvantages?

14-25   How is the net present value computed? What are its advantages and disadvantages?

14-26   How is the discounted payback period computed? What are the advantages and the disadvantages of the method?

14-27   How is the internal rate of return computed? What are its advantages and disadvantages?

14-28   What is the cost of capital?

14-29   Suppose an analysis of a proposal has been made and all five techniques have been used. Someone wants to try a different cost of capital. What changes?

14-30   What is a net present value profile? What is the significance of the intersection on the X-axis?

14-31   Why are taxes included in the evaluation of proposed capital projects?

14-32   Why is depreciation a tax shield?

14-33   Why are accelerated forms of depreciation better to use for tax purposes than the straight-line method?

14-34   What is the investment tax credit? How is it computed?

14-35   Give the formulas for straight-line depreciation, sum-of-the-years' digits depreciation, and double-declining balance.

14-36   What are the decision support system aspects of capital budgeting?

14-37   What are the behavioral aspects of capital budgeting?

Discussion Questions

14-38　Illustrate the interrelationships among the tables in Appendix D by deriving the values in the four tables for the first five years for 11%. Do not use a calculator or a computer that has functions that can do this.

14-39　A Japanese firm and an American firm are considering the same project. The Japanese firm decides that the project is a worthwhile investment but the American firm turns it down. Why?

14-40　A project costs $100 million and has no cash inflows for 19 years. In the 20th year the project is expected to return $10 billion. Is a manager likely to fund the project? The cost of capital is 15% and the internal rate of return is 25.8%.

14-41　If a capital project requires the firm to hold extra inventories or extra receivables, how should these facts be incorporated into the capital budgeting analysis.

14-42　How does inflation affect the net present value analysis? Hint: inflation could affect two items, the cash flows and the cost of capital.

14-43　A manager at Grail, Inc., decides to approve Project X, presented in Exhibit 14-3. Assume no taxes. An audit four years later reveals the following results:

Year	Predicted Cash Flow	Actual Cash Flow	Variance
0	$(20,000)	$(21,000)	(1,000)
1	10,000	8,000	(2,000)
2	9,000	8,000	(1,000)
3	6,000	4,000	(2,000)
4	4,000	1,000	(3,000)

The actual present value is $(3,793), the payback is four years, there is no discounted payback, and the internal rate of return is negative. Should the manager be penalized?

Exercises

14-44　**SIMPLE AND COMPOUND INTEREST**　Allen obtains a $20,000 loan for three years. The interest rate is 12% and the loan is to be repaid at the end of the three years.

CO 2　a.　How much is to be paid if the interest is simple interest?

b.　How much is to be paid if the interest is compounded annually? Of this amount, how much is interest?

14-45　**FUTURE VALUE OF SINGLE SUM**　Karen puts $1,300 into a savings account paying 9% compounded annually. How much will she have after:

CO 2, 3　a.　Three years.

b.　Five years.

c.　Ten years.

d.　Fifteen years.

14-46 FUTURE VALUE OF SINGLE SUM Louise has $2,650 and wishes to put the amount in a savings account for five years. How much will she have if the interest rate is

CO 2, 3   a. 3%.

b. 6%.

c. 9%.

d. 12%.

e. 15%.

14-47 FUTURE VALUE OF SINGLE SUM Brian places $500 into a savings account at an interest rate of 12%. How much will he have after one year if the interest is compounded:

CO 2, 3   a. Monthly.

b. Quarterly.

c. Semiannually.

d. Annually.

14-48 FUTURE VALUE OF SINGLE SUM Brent has $1,000 and needs help with his savings options.

CO 2, 3   a. If he puts it into the bank at 8%, how long will it take to accumulate $2,000?

b. If he wants to have $2,000 after five years, what must the interest rate be?

14-49 FUTURE VALUE OF AN ANNUITY Andy puts $1,000 per year each year into a fund paying 6%. What will the fund be worth after:

CO 2, 3   a. Three years.

b. Five years.

c. Ten years.

d. Fifteen years.

14-50 FUTURE VALUE OF AN ANNUITY Sam and Dinah invest $3,000 into a fund annually and plan to withdraw it after five years. How much will they have if the interest rate is:

CO 2, 3   a. 3%.

b. 6%.

c. 9%.

d. 12%.

e. 15%.

14-51 FUTURE VALUE OF AN ANNUITY Joe puts $600 into a fund each year, though he may divide it up into several payments. The fund earns 12%. How much will he have after two years if the interest is compounded and Joe's payments are made:

CO 2, 3

a. Monthly.

b. Quarterly.

c. Semiannually.

d. Annually.

14-52   FUTURE VALUE OF AN ANNUITY Stephanie places $1,000 into the bank each year.

CO 2, 3   a. If the bank pays 8%, how long will it take Stephanie to earn $10,000?

b. If she wants $10,000 after six years, what must the interest rate be?

14-53   PRESENT VALUE OF SINGLE SUM David and Laura are to receive a $1,000 balance from a fund paying 6%. What is the fund worth today if they are to receive the cash in:

CO 2, 3   a. Three years.

b. Five years.

c. Ten years.

d. Fifteen years.

14-54   PRESENT VALUE OF SINGLE SUM Janet is saving for $10,000 for new furniture. She plans to buy the furniture in three years. How much must she invest today if the bank is paying:

CO 2, 3

a. 3%.

b. 6%.

c. 9%.

d. 12%.

e. 15%.

14-55   PRESENT VALUE OF SINGLE SUM Doug is saving $15,000 for a new car. He desires to purchase the car in one year. The bank is paying 12%. How much must he place into the savings account today if the interest is compounded:

CO 2, 3

a. Monthly.

b. Quarterly.

c. Semiannually.

d. Annually.

14-56   PRESENT VALUE OF SINGLE SUM John needs to save up $5,000. He only has $1,000 to put into a savings account.

CO 2, 3   a. How long does he need to wait if the bank is paying 9%?

b. If he wants to earn the money after ten years, what must the interest rate be?

14-57   PRESENT VALUE OF AN ANNUITY Kathleen is to receive $1,000 each year from a fund paying 8%. What is the present value of these cash flows if she is to receive them for

CO 2, 3   a. Three years.

b. Five years.

c. Ten years.

d. Fifteen years.

14-58   PRESENT VALUE OF AN ANNUITY Luke and Joyce obtained a loan and are repaying it at $1,200 per year for five years. How much did they borrow if the interest rate is

CO 2, 3   a. 3%.

b. 6%.

c. 9%.

d. 12%.

e. 15%.

14-59   PRESENT VALUE OF AN ANNUITY Sam and Nancy obtained a loan and are repaying it at $1,200 per year for two years, though it may be divided up into several payments. Their interest rate is 24%. How much did they borrow if the interest is compounded and payments are made

CO 2, 3

a. Monthly.

b. Quarterly.

c. Semiannually.

d. Annually.

14-60   PRESENT VALUE OF AN ANNUITY Elsie borrowed $25,000 and pays the bank $3,669 each year.

CO 2, 3

a. If the bank charges 10%, how long will it take to pay off the loan?

b. If she wants to pay it off in eight years, what must the interest rate be?

14-61   CAPITAL BUDGETING METHODS A project has a cost of $100,000. It is estimated to return $40,000 cash each year for three years. The cost of capital is 10%. Compute the:

CO 4

a. Payback period.

b. Accounting rate of return.

c. Net present value.

d. Internal rate of return.

14-62   CAPITAL BUDGETING METHODS A project has a cost of $2,000,000. It will generate cash revenues of $800,000 annually for six years. The cost of capital is 12%. Compute the:

CO 4

a. Payback period.

b. Net present value.

c. Internal rate of return.

14-63   CAPITAL BUDGETING METHODS Project Zeta costs $75,000. It promises to return cash flows as follows:

CO 4

Year	Cash Flow
1	$20,000
2	40,000
3	50,000
4	30,000

The cost of capital is 12%. Compute the:

a. Payback period.

b. Accounting rate of return.

c. Net present value.

d. Discounted payback period.

e. Internal rate of return.

14-64   CAPITAL BUDGETING METHODS Project Omega costs $100,000. It has expected cash flows as follows:

CO 4

Year	Cash Flow
1	$10,000
2	60,000
3	60,000

The cost of capital is 10%. Compute the following:

a. Payback period.

b. Net present value.

c. Discounted payback period.

d. Internal rate of return.

14-65   COST OF CAPITAL The cost of debt after taxes for Yuri Corp. is 8%. The cost of common stock is 16%. If the firm has 60% of debt in its capital structure, what is Yuri's cost of

CO 5   capital?

14-66   COST OF CAPITAL Zeina and Company has 70% debt and 30% common stock. The expected interest charges are 15% and the expected return desired by stockholders is 18%. The

CO 5   firm's marginal tax rate is 30%. What is Zeina's cost of capital?

14-67   DEPRECIATION An asset cost $30,000 and has no salvage value. It has an estimated life of five years. Compute the depreciation each year using the

CO 6   a. Straight-line method.

b. Sum-of-the-year's digits method.

c. Double-declining balance method.

14-68   DEPRECIATION An asset cost $42,000 and has no salvage value. It has an estimated life of six years.

CO 6   a. Compute the depreciation each year using the (1) straight-line, (2) sum-of-the-years' digits, and (3) double-declining balance methods.

b. If the asset qualifies for an 8% investment tax credit, how much is the credit?

Problems

14-69   NET PRESENT VALUE A project has a cost of $60,000 and will have an economic life of three years. The marginal tax rate is 40% and the cost of capital is 15%. The expected cash

CO 4, 6   inflows from the project are $40,000 each year.

REQUIRED

Find the net present value of the proposed project if:

a. Straight-line is used. *73,062,40*

b. Sum-of-the-years' digits is used. *73,910,80*

c. Double-declining balance depreciation is used. *73,910,80*

14-70   NET PRESENT VALUE A project has a cost of $100,000 and will have an economic life of four years. The marginal tax rate is 30% and the cost of capital is 18%. The expected cash inflows from the project are $40,000 each year.

CO 4, 6

REQUIRED

Find the net present value of the proposed project if:

a. Straight-line is used.

b. Sum-of-the-years' digits is used.

c. Double-declining balance depreciation is used.

14-71   CAPITAL BUDGETING METHODS A project has a cost of $60,000 and will have an economic life of three years. The marginal tax rate is 40% and the cost of capital is 15%. The expected cash inflows from the project are $40,000 each year. The investment tax credit is 10%. Straight-line depreciation is used.

CO 4, 6

REQUIRED

Find the following:

a. Payback period. *1.69 years*

b. Net present value. *$18,280*

c. Internal rate of return.

14-72   CAPITAL BUDGETING METHODS A project has a cost of $100,000 and will have an economic life of four years. The marginal tax rate is 30% and the cost of capital is 18%. The expected cash inflows from the project are $40,000 each year. The investment tax credit is 5%.

CO 4, 6

REQUIRED

Compute the payback period and the net present value for the following:

a. Straight-line.

b. Sum-of-the-years' digits.

c. Double-declining balance.

14-73   CAPITAL BUDGETING METHODS Yeagley Company is considering a new product that will require an investment of $100,000. The product would have a selling price of $12 per unit, a variable cost of $7 per unit, and fixed costs of $10,000 per year, not counting

CO 4, 6

depreciation. The sum-of-the-years' digits method will be used. The life of the project is five years. Expected units to be sold are as follows:

Year	Units
1	12,000
2	15,000
3	18,000
4	15,000
5	10,000

The tax rate is 40%, the cost of capital is 18%.

REQUIRED
Determine whether Yeagley should invest in this new product.

14-74   CAPITAL BUDGETING Todaro & Todaro is considering replacing a conveyor belt with a new design that will increase earnings before depreciation by $50,000 per year. The net asset has a cost of $125,000 and an estimated economic life of 10 years. The cost of capital is 15%. The investment tax credit is 10%. Straight-line depreciation is used. The tax rate is 40%. The old machine has been fully depreciated and has no exit value (i.e., it cannot be sold) but is still usable.

CO 4, 6

REQUIRED
Determine whether Todaro & Todaro should make the replacement.

14-75   CAPITAL BUDGETING Kanoff, Inc., is considering a new investment of $60,000 that would reduce labor costs by $15,000 and overhead costs by $8,000 per year. The project has a life of three years. Double-declining depreciation is used. Investment tax credit is 5%. The cost of capital is 12%. The tax rate is 30%.

CO 4, 6

REQUIRED
Determine whether Kanoff should invest in the project.

14-76   NET PRESENT VALUE PROFILE Fies & Son have a proposed project with cash inflows as follows:

CO 5

Year	Cash Inflows
1	$1,000
2	2,000
3	3,000
4	4,000

Cost of the project is $5,000.

REQUIRED
Present a net present value profile.

CO 5

14-77   NET PRESENT VALUE PROFILE Refer to the data in Problem 14-76 except assume that the cost of the project is $15,000 and it is paid in year 5.

REQUIRED

Explain what the net present value profile tells you about the relationship between the net present value method and the internal rate of return.

Business Decision Case

Passaeur, Inc., has been advised by its legal staff that it must install some antipollution equipment. It has three equipment choices:

	From Axel, Inc.	From Loop Co.	From Lutz Co.
Cost	$100,000	$200,000	$400,000
Operating cost per year	50,000	35,000	10,000

The economic life is 10 years for all possibilities. Straight-line depreciation is used. The marginal tax rate is 40%. The cost of capital is 18%.

REQUIRED

Determine which alternative Passaeur, Inc., should choose.

APPENDIX D

Future and Present Value Tables

TABLE D-1

Future Value of $1 at the End of *n* Periods

Period	1%	2%	3%	4%	5%	6%	7%	8%	9%	10%
1	1.0100	1.0200	1.0300	1.0400	1.0500	1.0600	1.0700	1.0800	1.0900	1.1000
2	1.0201	1.0404	1.0609	1.0816	1.1025	1.1236	1.1449	1.1664	1.1881	1.2100
3	1.0303	1.0612	1.0927	1.1249	1.1576	1.1910	1.2250	1.2597	1.2950	1.3310
4	1.0406	1.0824	1.1255	1.1699	1.2155	1.2625	1.3108	1.3605	1.4116	1.4641
5	1.0510	1.1041	1.1593	1.2167	1.2763	1.3382	1.4026	1.4693	1.5386	1.6105
6	1.0615	1.1262	1.1941	1.2653	1.3401	1.4185	1.5007	1.5869	1.6771	1.7716
7	1.0721	1.1487	1.2299	1.3159	1.4071	1.5036	1.6058	1.7138	1.8280	1.9487
8	1.0829	1.1717	1.2668	1.3686	1.4775	1.5938	1.7182	1.8509	1.9926	2.1436
9	1.0937	1.1951	1.3048	1.4233	1.5513	1.6895	1.8385	1.9990	2.1719	2.3579
10	1.1046	1.2190	1.3439	1.4802	1.6289	1.7908	1.9672	2.1589	2.3674	2.5937
11	1.1157	1.2434	1.3842	1.5395	1.7103	1.8983	2.1049	2.3316	2.5804	2.8531
12	1.1268	1.2682	1.4258	1.6010	1.7959	2.0122	2.2522	2.5182	2.8127	3.1384
13	1.1381	1.2936	1.4685	1.6651	1.8856	2.1329	2.4098	2.7196	3.0658	3.4523
14	1.1495	1.3195	1.5126	1.7317	1.9799	2.2609	2.5785	2.9372	3.3417	3.7975
15	1.1610	1.3459	1.5580	1.8009	2.0789	2.3966	2.7590	3.1722	3.6425	4.1772
16	1.1726	1.3728	1.6047	1.8730	2.1829	2.5404	2.9522	3.4259	3.9703	4.5950
17	1.1843	1.4002	1.6528	1.9479	2.2920	2.6928	3.1588	3.7000	4.3276	5.0545
18	1.1961	1.4282	1.7024	2.0258	2.4066	2.8543	3.3799	3.9960	4.7171	5.5598
19	1.2081	1.4568	1.7535	2.1068	2.5270	3.0256	3.6165	4.3157	5.1417	6.1159
20	1.2202	1.4859	1.8061	2.1911	2.6533	3.2071	3.8697	4.6610	5.6044	6.7275
21	1.2324	1.5157	1.8603	2.2788	2.7860	3.3996	4.1406	5.0338	6.1088	7.4002
22	1.2447	1.5460	1.9161	2.3699	2.9253	3.6035	4.4304	5.4365	6.6586	8.1403
23	1.2572	1.5769	1.9736	2.4647	3.0715	3.8197	4.7405	5.8715	7.2579	8.9543
24	1.2697	1.6084	2.0328	2.5633	3.2251	4.0489	5.0724	6.3412	7.9111	9.8497
25	1.2824	1.6406	2.0938	2.6658	3.3864	4.2919	5.4274	6.8485	8.6231	10.834
26	1.2953	1.6734	2.1566	2.7725	3.5557	4.5494	5.8074	7.3964	9.3992	11.918
27	1.3082	1.7069	2.2213	2.8834	3.7335	4.8223	6.2139	7.9881	10.245	13.110
28	1.3213	1.7410	2.2879	2.9987	3.9201	5.1117	6.6488	8.6271	11.167	14.421
29	1.3345	1.7758	2.3566	3.1187	4.1161	5.4184	7.1143	9.3173	12.172	15.863
30	1.3478	1.8114	2.4273	3.2434	4.3219	5.7435	7.6123	10.062	13.267	17.449

Period	12%	14%	15%	16%	18%	20%	24%	28%	32%	36%
1	1.1200	1.1400	1.1500	1.1600	1.1800	1.2000	1.2400	1.2800	1.3200	1.3600
2	1.2544	1.2996	1.3225	1.3456	1.3924	1.4400	1.5376	1.6384	1.7424	1.8496
3	1.4049	1.4815	1.5209	1.5609	1.6430	1.7280	1.9066	2.0972	2.3000	2.5155
4	1.5735	1.6890	1.7490	1.8106	1.9388	2.0736	2.3642	2.6844	3.0360	3.4210
5	1.7623	1.9254	2.0114	2.1003	2.2878	2.4883	2.9316	3.4360	4.0075	4.6526
6	1.9738	2.1950	2.3131	2.4364	2.6996	2.9860	3.6352	4.3980	5.2899	6.3275
7	2.2107	2.5023	2.6600	2.8262	3.1855	3.5832	4.5077	5.6295	6.9826	8.6054
8	2.4760	2.8526	3.0590	3.2784	3.7589	4.2998	5.5895	7.2058	9.2170	11.703
9	2.7731	3.2519	3.5179	3.8030	4.4355	5.1598	6.9310	9.2234	12.166	15.916
10	3.1058	3.7072	4.0456	4.4114	5.2338	6.1917	8.5944	11.805	16.059	21.646
11	3.4785	4.2262	4.6524	5.1173	6.1759	7.4301	10.657	15.111	21.198	29.439
12	3.8960	4.8179	5.3502	5.9360	7.2876	8.9161	13.214	19.342	27.982	40.037
13	4.3635	5.4924	6.1528	6.8858	8.5994	10.699	16.386	24.758	36.937	54.451
14	4.8871	6.2613	7.0757	7.9875	10.147	12.839	20.319	31.691	48.756	74.053
15	5.4736	7.1379	8.1371	9.2655	11.973	15.407	25.195	40.564	64.358	100.71
16	6.1304	8.1372	9.3576	10.748	14.129	18.488	31.242	51.923	84.953	136.96
17	6.8660	9.2765	10.761	12.467	16.672	22.186	38.740	66.461	112.13	186.27
18	7.6900	10.575	12.375	14.462	19.673	26.623	48.038	85.070	148.02	253.33
19	8.6128	12.055	14.231	16.776	23.214	31.948	59.567	108.89	195.39	344.53
20	9.6463	13.743	16.366	19.460	27.393	38.337	73.864	13.37	257.91	468.57
21	10.803	15.667	18.821	22.574	32.323	46.005	91.591	178.40	340.44	637.26
22	12.100	17.861	21.644	26.186	38.142	55.206	113.57	228.35	449.39	866.67
23	13.552	20.361	24.891	30.376	45.007	66.247	140.83	292.30	593.19	1178.6
24	15.178	23.212	28.625	35.236	53.108	79.496	174.63	374.14	783.02	1602.9
25	17.000	26.461	32.918	40.874	62.668	95.396	216.54	478.90	1033.5	2180.0
26	19.040	30.166	37.856	47.414	73.948	114.47	268.51	612.99	1364.3	2964.9
27	21.324	34.389	43.535	55.000	87.259	137.37	332.95	784.63	1800.9	4032.2
28	23.883	39.204	50.065	63.800	102.96	164.84	412.86	1004.3	2377.2	5483.8
29	26.749	44.693	57.575	74.008	121.50	197.81	511.95	1285.5	3137.9	7458.0
30	29.959	50.950	66.211	85.849	143.37	237.37	634.81	1645.5	4142.0	10143.

TABLE D-2

Sum of an Annuity of $1 per Period for *n* Periods

Period	1%	2%	3%	4%	5%	6%	7%	8%	9%	10%
1	1.0000	1.0000	1.0000	1.0000	1.0000	1.0000	1.0000	1.0000	1.0000	1.0000
2	2.0100	2.0200	2.0300	2.0400	2.0500	2.0600	2.0700	2.0800	2.0900	2.1000
3	3.0301	3.0604	3.0909	3.1216	3.1525	3.1836	3.2149	3.2464	3.2781	3.3100
4	4.0604	4.1216	4.1836	4.2465	4.3101	4.3746	4.4399	4.5061	4.5731	4.6410
5	5.1010	5.2040	5.3091	5.4163	5.5256	5.6371	5.7507	5.8666	5.9847	6.1051
6	6.1520	6.3081	6.4684	6.6330	6.8019	6.9753	7.1533	7.3359	7.5233	7.7156
7	7.2135	7.4343	7.6625	7.8983	8.1420	8.3938	8.6540	8.9228	9.2004	9.4872
8	8.2857	8.5830	8.8923	9.2142	9.5491	9.8975	10.259	10.636	11.028	11.435
9	9.3685	9.7546	10.159	10.582	11.026	11.491	11.978	12.487	13.021	13.579
10	10.462	10.949	11.463	12.006	12.577	13.180	13.816	14.486	15.192	15.937
11	11.566	12.168	12.807	13.486	14.206	14.971	15.783	16.645	17.560	18.531
12	12.682	13.412	14.192	15.025	15.917	16.869	17.888	18.977	20.140	21.384
13	13.809	14.680	15.617	16.626	17.713	18.882	20.140	21.495	22.953	24.522
14	14.947	15.973	17.086	18.291	19.598	21.015	22.550	24.214	26.019	27.975
15	16.096	17.293	18.598	20.023	21.578	23.276	25.129	27.152	29.360	31.772
16	17.257	18.639	20.156	21.824	23.657	25.672	27.888	30.324	33.003	35.949
17	18.430	20.012	21.761	23.697	25.840	28.212	30.840	33.750	36.973	40.544
18	19.614	21.412	23.414	25.645	28.132	30.905	33.999	37.450	41.301	45.599
19	20.810	22.840	25.116	27.671	30.539	33.760	37.379	41.446	46.018	51.159
20	22.019	24.297	26.870	29.778	33.066	36.785	40.995	45.762	51.160	57.275
21	23.239	25.783	28.676	31.969	35.719	39.992	44.865	50.422	56.764	64.002
22	24.471	27.299	30.536	34.248	38.505	43.392	49.005	55.456	62.873	71.402
23	25.716	28.845	32.452	36.617	41.430	46.995	53.436	60.893	69.531	79.543
24	26.973	30.421	34.426	39.082	44.502	50.815	58.176	66.764	76.789	88.497
25	28.243	32.030	36.459	41.645	47.727	54.864	63.249	73.105	84.700	98.347
26	29.525	33.670	38.553	44.311	51.113	59.156	68.676	79.954	93.323	109.18
27	30.820	35.344	40.709	47.084	54.669	63.705	74.483	87.350	102.72	121.09
28	32.129	37.051	42.930	49.967	58.402	68.528	80.697	95.338	112.96	134.20
29	33.450	38.792	45.218	52.966	62.322	73.639	87.346	103.96	124.13	148.63
30	34.784	40.568	47.575	56.084	66.438	79.058	94.460	113.28	136.30	164.49

Period	12%	14%	15%	16%	18%	20%	24%	28%	32%	36%
1	1.0000	1.0000	1.0000	1.0000	1.0000	1.0000	1.0000	1.0000	1.0000	1.0000
2	2.1200	2.1400	2.1500	2.1600	2.1800	2.2000	2.2400	2.2800	2.3200	2.3600
3	3.3744	3.4396	3.4725	3.5056	3.5724	3.6400	3.7776	3.9184	4.0624	4.2096
4	4.7793	4.9211	4.9934	5.0665	5.2154	5.3680	5.6842	6.0156	6.3624	6.7251
5	6.3528	6.6101	6.7424	6.8771	7.1542	7.4416	8.0484	8.6999	9.3983	10.146
6	8.1152	8.5355	8.7537	8.9775	9.4420	9.9299	10.980	12.135	13.405	14.798
7	10.089	10.730	11.066	11.413	12.141	12.915	14.615	16.533	18.695	21.126
8	12.299	13.232	13.726	14.240	15.327	16.499	19.122	22.163	25.678	29.731
9	14.775	16.085	16.785	17.518	19.085	20.798	24.712	29.369	34.895	41.435
10	17.548	19.337	20.303	21.321	23.521	25.958	31.643	38.592	47.061	57.351
11	20.654	23.044	24.349	25.732	28.755	32.150	40.237	50.398	63.121	78.998
12	24.133	27.270	29.001	30.850	34.931	39.580	50.894	65.510	84.320	108.43
13	28.029	32.088	34.351	36.786	42.218	48.496	64.109	84.852	112.30	148.47
14	32.392	37.581	40.504	43.672	50.818	59.195	80.496	109.61	149.23	202.92
15	37.279	43.842	47.580	51.659	60.965	72.035	100.81	141.30	197.99	276.97
16	42.753	50.980	55.717	60.925	72.939	87.442	126.01	181.86	262.35	377.69
17	48.883	59.117	65.075	71.673	87.068	105.93	157.25	233.79	347.30	514.66
18	55.749	68.394	75.836	84.140	103.74	128.11	195.99	300.25	459.44	700.93
19	63.439	78.969	88.211	98.603	123.41	154.74	244.03	385.32	607.47	954.27
20	72.052	91.024	102.44	115.37	146.62	186.68	303.60	494.21	802.86	1298.8
21	81.698	104.76	118.81	134.84	174.02	225.02	377.46	633.59	1060.7	1767.3
22	92.502	120.43	137.63	157.41	206.34	271.03	469.05	811.99	1401.2	2404.6
23	104.60	138.29	159.27	183.60	244.48	326.23	582.62	1040.3	1850.6	3271.3
24	118.15	158.65	184.16	213.97	289.49	392.48	723.46	1332.6	2443.8	4449.9
25	133.33	181.87	212.79	249.21	342.60	471.98	898.09	1706.8	3226.8	6052.9
26	150.33	208.33	245.71	290.08	405.27	567.37	1114.6	2185.7	4260.4	8233.0
27	169.37	238.49	283.56	337.50	479.22	681.85	1383.1	2798.7	5624.7	11197.9
28	190.69	272.88	327.10	392.50	566.48	819.22	1716.0	3583.3	7425.6	15230.2
29	214.58	312.09	377.16	456.30	669.44	984.06	2128.9	4587.6	9802.9	20714.1
30	241.33	356.78	434.74	530.31	790.94	1181.8	2640.9	5873.2	12940.	28172.2

TABLE D-3

Present Value of $1 at the End of n Periods

Period	1%	2%	3%	4%	5%	6%	7%	8%	9%	10%
1	.9901	.9804	.9709	.9615	.9524	.9434	.9346	.9259	.9174	.9091
2	.9803	.9612	.9426	.9246	.9070	.8900	.8734	.8573	.8417	.8264
3	.9706	.9423	.9151	.8890	.8638	.8396	.8163	.7938	.7722	.7513
4	.9610	.9238	.8885	.8548	.8227	.7921	.7629	.7350	.7084	.6830
5	.9515	.9057	.8626	.8219	.7835	.7473	.7130	.6806	.6499	.6209
6	.9420	.8880	.8375	.7903	.7462	.7050	.6663	.6302	.5963	.5645
7	.9327	.8706	.8131	.7599	.7107	.6651	.6227	.5835	.5470	.5132
8	.9235	.8535	.7894	.7307	.6768	.6274	.5820	.5403	.5019	.4665
9	.9143	.8368	.7664	.7026	.6446	.5919	.5439	.5002	.4604	.4241
10	.9053	.8203	.7441	.6756	.6139	.5584	.5083	.4632	.4224	.3855
11	.8963	.8043	.7224	.6496	.5847	.5286	.4751	.4289	.3875	.3505
12	.8874	.7885	.7014	.6246	.5568	.4970	.4440	.3971	.3555	.3186
13	.8787	.7730	.6810	.6006	.5303	.4688	.4150	.3677	.3262	.2897
14	.8700	.7579	.6611	.5775	.5051	.4423	.3878	.3405	.2992	.2633
15	.8613	.7430	.6419	.5553	.4810	.4173	.3624	.3152	.2745	.2394
16	.8528	.7284	.6232	.5339	.4581	.3936	.3387	.2919	.2519	.2176
17	.8444	.7142	.6050	.5134	.4363	.3714	.3166	.2703	.2311	.1978
18	.8360	.7002	.5874	.4936	.4155	.3503	.2959	.2502	.2120	.1799
19	.8277	.6864	.5703	.4746	.3957	.3305	.2765	.2317	.1945	.1635
20	.8195	.6730	.5537	.4564	.3769	.3118	.2584	.2145	.1784	.1486
21	.8114	.6598	.5375	.4388	.3589	.2942	.2415	.1987	.1637	.1351
22	.8034	.6468	.5219	.4220	.3418	.2775	.2257	.1839	.1502	.1228
23	.7954	.6342	.5067	.4057	.3256	.2618	.2109	.1703	.1378	.1117
24	.7876	.6217	.4919	.3901	.3101	.2470	.1971	.1577	.1264	.1015
25	.7798	.6095	.4776	.3751	.2953	.2330	.1842	.1460	.1160	.0923
26	.7720	.5976	.4637	.3607	.2812	.2198	.1722	.1352	.1064	.0839
27	.7644	.5859	.4502	.3468	.2678	.2074	.1609	.1252	.0976	.0763
28	.7568	.5744	.4371	.3335	.2551	.1956	.1504	.1159	.0895	.0693
29	.7493	.5631	.4243	.3207	.2429	.1846	.1406	.1073	.0822	.0630
30	.7419	.5521	.4120	.3083	.2314	.1741	.1314	.0994	.0754	.0573

Period	12%	14%	15%	16%	18%	20%	24%	28%	32%	36%
1	.8929	.8772	.8696	.8621	.8475	.8333	.8065	.7813	.7576	.7353
2	.7972	.7695	.7561	.7432	.7182	.6944	.6504	.6104	.5739	.5407
3	.7118	.6750	.6575	.6407	.6086	.5787	.5245	.4768	.4348	.3975
4	.6355	.5921	.5718	.5523	.5158	.4823	.4230	.3725	.3294	.2923
5	.5674	.5194	.4972	.4761	.4371	.4019	.3411	.2910	.2495	.2149
6	.5066	.4556	.4323	.4104	.3704	.3349	.2751	.2274	.1890	.1580
7	.4523	.3996	.3759	.3538	.3139	.2791	.2218	.1776	.1432	.1162
8	.4039	.3506	.3269	.3050	.2660	.2326	.1789	.1388	.1085	.0854
9	.3606	.3075	.2843	.2630	.2255	.1938	.1443	.1084	.0822	.0628
10	.3220	.2697	.2472	.2267	.1911	.1615	.1164	.0847	.0623	.0462
11	.2875	.2366	.2149	.1954	.1619	.1346	.0938	.0662	.0472	.0340
12	.2567	.2076	.1869	.1685	.1372	.1122	.0757	.0517	.0357	.0250
13	.2292	.1821	.1625	.1452	.1163	.0935	.0610	.0404	.0271	.0184
14	.2046	.1597	.1413	.1252	.0985	.0779	.0492	.0316	.0205	.0135
15	.1827	.1401	.1229	.1079	.0835	.0649	.0397	.0247	.0155	.0099
16	.1631	.1229	.1069	.0930	.0708	.0541	.0320	.0193	.0118	.0073
17	.1456	.1078	.0929	.0802	.0600	.0451	.0258	.0150	.0089	.0054
18	.1300	.0946	.0808	.0691	.0508	.0376	.0208	.0118	.0068	.0039
19	.1161	.0829	.0703	.0596	.0431	.0313	.0168	.0092	.0051	.0029
20	.1037	.0728	.0611	.0514	.0365	.0261	.0135	.0072	.0039	.0021
21	.0926	.0638	.0531	.0443	.0309	.0217	.0109	.0056	.0029	.0016
22	.0826	.0560	.0462	.0382	.0262	.0181	.0088	.0044	.0022	.0012
23	.0738	.0491	.0402	.0329	.0222	.0151	.0071	.0034	.0017	.0008
24	.0659	.0431	.0349	.0284	.0188	.0126	.0057	.0027	.0013	.0006
25	.0588	.0378	.0304	.0245	.0160	.0105	.0046	.0021	.0010	.0005
26	.0525	.0331	.0264	.0211	.0135	.0087	.0037	.0016	.0007	.0003
27	.0469	.0291	.0230	.0182	.0115	.0073	.0030	.0013	.0006	.0002
28	.0419	.0255	.0200	.0157	.0097	.0061	.0024	.0010	.0004	.0002
29	.0374	.0224	.0174	.0135	.0082	.0051	.0020	.0008	.0003	.0001
30	.0334	.0196	.0151	.0116	.0070	.0042	.0016	.0006	.0002	.0001

TABLE D-4

Present Value of an Annuity of $1 per Period for *n* Periods

Period	1%	2%	3%	4%	5%	6%	7%	8%	9%
1	0.9901	0.9804	0.9709	0.9615	0.9524	0.9434	0.9346	0.9259	0.9174
2	1.9704	1.9416	1.9135	1.8861	1.8594	1.8334	1.8080	1.7833	1.7591
3	2.9410	2.8839	2.8286	2.7751	2.7232	2.6730	2.6243	2.5771	2.5313
4	3.9020	3.8077	3.7171	3.6299	3.5460	3.4651	3.3872	3.3121	3.2397
5	4.8534	4.7135	4.5797	4.4518	4.3295	4.2124	4.1002	3.9927	3.8897
6	5.7955	5.6014	5.4172	5.2421	5.0757	4.9173	4.7665	4.6229	4.4859
7	6.7282	6.4720	6.2303	6.0021	5.7864	5.5824	5.3893	5.2064	5.0330
8	7.6517	7.3255	7.0197	6.7327	6.4632	6.2098	5.9713	5.7466	5.5348
9	8.5660	8.1622	7.7861	7.4353	7.1078	6.8017	6.5152	6.2469	5.9952
10	9.4713	8.9826	8.5302	8.1109	7.7217	7.3601	7.0236	6.7100	6.4177
11	10.3676	9.7868	9.2526	8.7605	8.3064	7.8869	7.4987	7.1390	6.8052
12	11.2551	10.5753	9.9540	9.3851	8.8633	8.3838	7.9427	7.5361	7.1607
13	12.1337	11.3484	10.6350	9.9856	9.3936	8.8527	8.2577	7.9038	7.4869
14	13.0037	12.1062	11.2961	10.5631	9.8986	9.2950	8.7455	8.2442	7.7862
15	13.8651	12.8493	11.9379	11.1184	10.3797	9.7122	9.1079	8.5595	8.0607
16	14.7179	13.5777	12.5611	11.6523	10.8378	10.1059	9.4466	8.8514	8.3126
17	15.5623	14.2919	13.1661	12.1657	11.2741	10.4773	9.7632	9.1216	8.5436
18	16.3983	14.9920	13.7535	12.6593	11.6896	10.8276	10.0591	9.3719	8.7556
19	17.2260	15.6785	14.3238	13.1339	12.0853	11.1581	10.3356	9.6036	8.9501
20	18.0456	16.3514	14.8775	13.5903	12.4622	11.4699	10.5940	9.8181	9.1285
21	18.8570	17.0112	15.4150	14.0292	12.8212	11.7641	10.8355	10.0168	9.2922
22	19.6604	17.6580	15.9369	14.4511	13.1630	12.0416	11.0612	10.2007	9.4424
23	20.4558	18.2922	16.4436	14.8568	13.4886	12.3034	11.2722	10.3711	9.5802
24	21.2434	18.9139	16.9355	15.2470	13.7986	12.5504	11.4693	10.5288	9.7066
25	22.0232	19.5235	17.4131	15.6221	14.0939	12.7834	11.6536	10.6748	9.8226
26	22.7952	20.1210	17.8768	15.9828	14.3752	13.0032	11.8258	10.8100	9.9290
27	23.5596	20.7069	18.3270	16.3296	14.6430	13.2105	11.9867	10.9352	10.0266
28	24.3164	21.2813	18.7641	16.6631	14.8981	13.4062	12.1371	11.0511	10.1161
29	25.0658	21.8444	19.1885	16.9837	15.1411	13.5907	12.2777	11.1584	10.1983
30	25.8077	22.3965	19.6004	17.2920	15.3725	13.7648	12.4090	11.2578	10.2737

Period	10%	12%	14%	15%	16%	18%	20%	24%	28%	32%
1	0.9091	0.8929	0.8772	0.8696	0.8621	0.8475	0.8333	0.8065	0.7813	0.7576
2	1.7355	1.6901	1.6467	1.6257	1.6052	1.5656	1.5278	1.4568	1.3916	1.3315
3	2.4869	2.4018	2.3216	2.2832	2.2459	2.1743	2.1065	1.9813	1.8684	1.7663
4	3.1699	3.0373	2.9137	2.8550	2.7982	2.6901	2.5887	2.4043	2.2410	2.0957
5	3.7908	3.6048	3.4331	3.3522	3.2743	3.1272	2.9906	2.7454	2.5320	2.3452
6	4.3553	4.1114	3.8887	3.7845	3.6847	3.4976	3.3255	3.0205	2.7594	2.5342
7	4.8684	4.5638	4.2883	4.1604	4.0386	3.8115	3.6046	3.2423	2.9370	2.6775
8	5.3349	4.9676	4.6389	4.4873	4.3436	4.0776	3.8372	3.4212	3.0758	2.7860
9	5.7590	5.3282	4.9464	4.7716	4.6065	4.3030	4.0310	3.5655	3.1842	2.8681
10	6.1446	5.6502	5.2161	5.0188	4.8332	4.4941	4.1925	3.6819	3.2689	2.9304
11	6.4951	5.9377	5.4527	5.2337	5.0286	4.6560	4.3271	3.7757	3.3351	2.9776
12	6.8137	6.1944	5.6603	5.4206	5.1971	4.7932	4.4392	3.8514	3.3868	3.0133
13	7.1034	6.4235	5.8424	5.5831	5.3423	4.9095	4.5327	3.9124	3.4272	3.0404
14	7.3667	6.6282	6.0021	5.7245	5.4675	5.0081	4.6106	3.9616	3.4587	3.0609
15	7.6061	6.8109	6.1422	5.8474	5.5755	5.0916	4.6755	4.0013	3.4834	3.0764
16	7.8237	6.9740	6.2651	5.9542	5.6685	5.1624	4.7296	4.0333	3.5026	3.0882
17	8.0216	7.1196	6.3729	6.0472	5.7487	5.2223	4.7746	4.0591	3.5177	3.0971
18	8.2014	7.2497	6.4674	6.1280	5.8178	5.2732	4.8122	4.0799	3.5294	3.1039
19	8.3649	7.3658	6.5504	6.1982	5.8775	5.3162	4.8435	4.0967	3.5386	3.1090
20	8.5136	7.4694	6.6231	6.2593	5.9288	5.3527	4.8696	4.1103	3.5458	3.1129
21	8.6487	7.5620	6.6870	6.3125	5.9731	5.3837	4.8913	4.1212	3.5514	3.1158
22	8.7715	7.6446	6.7429	6.3587	6.0113	5.4099	4.9094	4.1300	3.5558	3.1180
23	8.8832	7.7184	6.7921	6.3988	6.0442	5.4321	4.9245	4.1371	3.5592	3.1197
24	8.9847	7.7843	6.8351	6.4338	6.0726	5.4510	4.9371	4.1428	3.5619	3.1210
25	9.0770	7.8431	6.8729	6.4642	6.0971	5.4669	4.9476	4.1474	3.5640	3.1220
26	9.1609	7.8957	6.9061	6.4906	6.1182	5.4804	4.9563	4.1511	3.5656	3.1227
27	9.2372	7.9426	6.9352	6.5135	6.1364	5.4919	4.9636	4.1542	3.5669	3.1233
28	9.3066	7.9844	6.9607	6.5335	6.1520	5.5016	4.9697	4.1566	3.5679	3.1237
29	9.3696	8.0218	6.9830	6.5509	6.1656	5.5098	4.9747	4.1585	3.5687	3.1240
30	9.4269	8.0552	7.0027	6.5660	6.1772	5.5168	4.9789	4.1601	3.5693	3.1242

15

Financial Statement Analysis

CHAPTER
OBJECTIVES

After reading Chapter 15, you should be able to do the following:

1. Identify the objectives of financial statement analysis (pp. 537–39).

2. State the importance and the limitations of accounting data (pp. 539–40).

3. Describe time-series analysis, including percentage analysis and trend analysis (pp. 540–43).

4. Explain cross-sectional analysis, including common-size statements and financial ratios (pp. 543–45).

5. Name major classifications of financial ratios and the purpose of each group (pp. 547–55).

6. Discuss financial statement analysis in the context of decision support systems and its behavioral aspects (p. 556).

*T*he financial statements of an organization are the balance sheet, the income statement, and the statement of cash flows. Financial statement analysis consists of reading, interpreting, and drawing inferences from data in a company's financial report in order to make decisions. These decisions include whether to invest or sell stock, whether one corporation might acquire another, whether to reward managers for their corporate performance, and whether to spin off a part of the corporation. It can be seen that financial statement analysis is useful for many different people, including managers, investors, creditors, government agencies, labor unions, suppliers, and auditors. Our focus remains on managers in this chapter.

The heart of financial statement analysis is the accounting numbers. These data are important because they quantify various financial dimensions of the enterprise such as profitability, solvency, and debt structure. The data do have limitations for management, however; they are historical data, they are not perfectly measured, and other important factors influence decision making that are not quantifiable.

There are two basic techniques in financial statement analysis. *Time-series analysis* consists of analyzing one firm across time. Popular time-series tools include *percentage analysis* and *trend analysis*. *Cross-sectional analysis* consists of analyzing several firms at one point in time. *Common-size statements* and *ratio analysis* are popular cross-sectional techniques.

OBJECTIVES OF FINANCIAL STATEMENT ANALYSIS

CHAPTER OBJECTIVE 1
Objectives of financial statement analysis

Financial statement analysis is the process of analyzing corporate financial statements. The purpose of the analysis is to determine meaningful relationships among the accounting numbers and to draw accurate conclusions about what they imply. How a user interprets the numbers and makes deductions about them depends on the decision context. An investor, for example, is looking for different information than is a manager. The objectives of financial statement analysis depend on the decision maker's objectives.

An investor in the common stock of a corporation makes the investment in hopes of obtaining a good return. Return to the investor is in the form of cash dividends and appreciation in the price of the common stock. These cash flows are, of course, future cash flows and therefore subject to uncertainty about their amounts and when they would be received. Theoretically, the value of the stock investment is the discounted present value of the cash dividends and the discounted value of the stock when sold. However, this theoretical value is extremely difficult to calculate, so investors look for other evidence to help them make their investment decisions. Accounting numbers are one form of evidence. By examining profitability ratios, for example, an investor could make some assessments about the amounts of the future cash flows. By analyzing the firm's debt structure and short-term liquidity ratios, he or she could estimate the riskiness of the investment.

Creditors and investors in the bonds of a corporation also hope to earn a good return on their investment. Return to creditors is in the form of cash interest and principal. A lender, such as a mortgagee, typically receives monthly payments that include interest and reduction of the principal. The payments continue until the principal is completely repaid. A bond issuer usually makes interest payments every six months. Then at a preset time, for example at the end of 20 years, the entire principal is received by the bond owner. Either way, the cash flows are contractually set. Unless there is a default, both creditor and borrower know the amounts and timing of the future cash flows. This is in contrast to the investors in the equity of a company—stockholders—who must estimate future cash flows. The only major unknown to a creditor is the probability that the borrower will default on the loan and, if so, how much could be collected and when. Theoretically, the value of the credit or bond investment is the discounted present value of the interest and the principal repayment. However, the theoretical value would have to account for the risk of default. Such a theoretical value is very hard to measure, so creditors look to accounting numbers to signal the chance of default. Profitability ratios and cash flow ratios could signal the ability of the borrower to generate cash flow from operations. The company's debt structure might signal the degree of credit commitments already made by the borrower.

Creditors typically require borrowers to sign a *debt covenant*. The contract contains clauses designed to protect the creditor such as limits on how much the firm may borrow, restrictions on dividends, and perhaps a provision to set aside money (called a *sinking fund*) to pay off the debt. Debt covenants often include financial ratio requirements such as a minimum amount for the *current ratio* and a maximum *debt/equity ratio* (these terms are defined later).

Managers can use financial statement analysis for both planning and control purposes. Financial planning often uses projected financial statements. As well as restating them in common-size form and calculating their financial ratios, managers can apply *time-series analysis* to these projected statements. Managers use these numbers, especially financial ratios, to identify areas of strength and weakness. Managers can then better plan on exploiting those strengths and alleviating the weak spots. They can also compute the ratios of their competitors to assess how well their own company is doing relative to others in the industry. If managers are considering a merger or acquisition, or if they are contemplating a disinvestment of part of the present business, they can use financial statement analysis to inform themselves of the relative strengths and weaknesses of the proposition.

Managers often use financial statement analysis on their own present and past company data. Such data can be aggregated for the firm as a whole, or it can be presented by division, by product, or by geographical area. By focusing on the analysis of the accounting numbers, managers can better assess how well the firm or parts of the firm are doing. The numbers could also be used to reward those doing well or punish those who are performing poorly. Some bonus plans are based in part on financial statement analysis. For example, if earnings per share surpasses some threshold, a certain bonus might be paid.

While investors, creditors, and managers are the major users of financial statement analysis, other decision makers might also benefit from it. Government agencies might look at accounting numbers in order to set and administer public policy. For example, public utility commissions set utility rates for consumers in part on the basis of accounting numbers. By observing several ratios, the commission ascertains the profitability and the riskiness of the utility and determines a fair rate of return. Labor unions are obviously interested in keeping the jobs of their members and in negotiating for raises and benefits. Labor unions are interested in such things as profitability ratios and earnings per share to determine whether they believe corporations are capable of giving raises and benefits and in what amounts. Suppliers use financial statement analysis to assess whether their customers are capable of paying for credit sales. Auditors use financial statement analysis to assess the reasonableness of the audited financial statements.

The common point of all these users is the financial health of the company under observation. They all look to the financial statements to give indications of how healthy the corporation is. Since the users have different orientations, they emphasize different aspects of the corporate health. Nonetheless, financial statement analysis is helpful to meet the objectives of all these various users.

IMPORTANCE AND LIMITATIONS OF ACCOUNTING DATA

CHAPTER OBJECTIVE 2
Importance and limitations of accounting data

Since financial statements rely on accounting data, it is necessary to realize the importance and the limitations of the data. Accounting data quantify several financial dimensions of the enterprise. *Quantification* means assigning numbers on the basis of that dimension. This measurement process allows the user to assess whether a company has a lot or a little of some financial variable and to compare and contrast one firm against another. It also allows the user to combine the data and to perform mathematical manipulations on them.

Accounting data have several limitations, however. One weak point is that they are overwhelmingly historical in nature. Many decision makers would rather have future-oriented data so that they can make decisions with some knowledge about future events. Predicting the future is quite hazardous; it is fraught with many errors. So users frequently rely on historical numbers such as accounting data. Although not as relevant to upcoming decisions as future-oriented data, historical accounting numbers are more reliable than projections. Once quantified and understood, data can be used as indicators of future events.

Another limitation is that accounting data are not completely accurate. The process of data collection, classification, and summarization is very involved, and it is unrealistic to think that no errors are made in the process. The accounting process also involves several arbitrary decisions. For example, some firms might expense any item costing less than $1,000. The choice of a cutoff is arbitrary. Estimation is sometimes necessary, for example, in determining the depreciable life of an asset. Deciding whether a cost is a period cost or a product cost is sometimes ambiguous. In addition there are several accounting alternatives that a firm may choose from to account for some event. For example, a corporation may choose to use first-in, first out (FIFO), last-in, first out (LIFO), or the weighted average method in inventory accounting. The resulting accounting numbers are somewhat ambiguous. In these and other ways, the measurement process is not completely accurate.

A further limitation is that some important factors for users are not quantifiable. Marketing strategies can be important to stock investors; trustworthiness is of prime concern to creditors; consumer preferences must be known by managers; in setting utility rates, government agencies need to know the public opinion about nuclear power plants; labor unions would like to know how safe the workers' tools and operating environment is; suppliers would like to be aware of any change in their customers' long-range goals; and auditors need to assess the internal control of their clients. All of these factors are overwhelmingly qualitative in nature. Accounting data cannot help very much for evaluating these factors.

Even with these deficiencies, accounting data can be helpful. The numbers can signal how profitable the firm may be, its liquidity, its degree of risk, and its ability to sell inventory and collect on its receivables. Accounting numbers and ratios can be inputs for several different models such as credit scoring (deciding whether to grant credit to a firm), predicting bankruptcy, and predicting merger candidates. Although not perfect, accounting data and financial statement analysis based on that data can prove beneficial to decision makers.

TIME-SERIES ANALYSIS

CHAPTER OBJECTIVE 3
Time-series analysis: percentage and trend analysis

The tools and techniques of financial statement analysis can be classified as either time-series analysis or cross-sectional analysis. They can be combined as will be shown later. Time-series analysis consists of analyzing one firm across time. *Cross-sectional analysis*, discussed in the next section, consists of analyzing several firms at one point in time.

Before continuing, it should be pointed out that financial statement analysis is an art and requires judgment to interpret the data. Entire courses are offered to teach one how to interpret the results. In this chapter the most popular techniques of financial statement analysis are illustrated. These techniques provide only the foundation of the analysis; the analyst must still make them meaningful. One way to do this is to compare the numbers of all the firms in the industry. In this context, the numbers themselves are not critical, but the relative position of the firm within the industry is.

EXHIBIT 15-1			
PERCENTAGE ANALYSIS			
	19X0	**19X1**	**Percentage Change**
INCOME STATEMENT			
Sales	$50	$55	10%
Cost of Sales	20	25	25%
Gross Margin	$30	$30	0%
Expenses	10	12	20%
Net Income	$20	$18	(10)%
BALANCE SHEET			
Assets			
Current Assets	$ 5	$ 7	40%
Long-term Assets	5	5	0%
Total Assets	$10	$12	20%
Liabilities and Stockholders' Equity			
Current Debts	$ 2	$ 3	50%
Long-term Debts	4	4	0%
Stockholders' Equity	4	5	25%
Total Liabilities and Stockholders' Equity	$10	$12	20%

Percentage analysis is one type of time-series analysis. Very simply, this form of analysis is a list of the percentage change in selected accounts. The change equals the balance in one year minus the balance in the earlier year; therefore, the percentage change is the change divided by the balance in the earlier year times 100. An illustration is contained in Exhibit 15-1. This table contains selected items from the income statements and balance sheets of 19X0 and 19X1. The percentage change is given for each account selected. For example, consider sales. In 19X1, sales is $55 and in 19X0 it is $50. The change is $5. The percentage change is:

$$\frac{\$55 - \$50}{\$50} \times 100 = 10\%$$

Another example is net income. The change is $18 − $20 = ($2). The percentage change is ($2)/$20 × 100, or (10%).

Percentage analysis can help differentiate large changes from small changes. One exception is if the denominator is small in comparison to those of other accounts. From only a $1 change, current debts in the illustration changes 50%. The problem is the small denominator, $2. Another exception is if either number is negative. No meaningful percentage change can be computed in this case. Except for these problems, percentage analysis helps to identify the amount of change and to highlight the major changes. As a demonstration of this, consider again the abbreviated income statement in

---

EXHIBIT 15-2

TREND ANALYSIS: INCOME STATEMENT

A. Abbreviated Income Statements

	19X0	19X1	19X2	19X3	19X4	19X5	19X6	19X7
Sales	$50	$55	$62	$30	$55	$60	$65	$100
Cost of Sales	20	25	27	10	27	28	30	50
Gross Margin	$30	$30	$35	$20	$28	$32	$35	$ 50
Expenses	10	12	13	10	15	12	14	18
Net Income	$20	$18	$22	$10	$13	$20	$21	$ 32

B. Time-series Trends

	19X0	19X1	19X2	19X3	19X4	19X5	19X6	19X7
Sales	1.00	1.10	1.24	0.60	1.10	1.20	1.30	2.00
Cost of Sales	1.00	1.25	1.35	0.50	1.35	1.40	1.50	2.50
Gross Margin	1.00	1.00	1.17	0.67	0.93	1.07	1.17	1.67
Expenses	1.00	1.20	1.30	1.00	1.50	1.20	1.40	1.80
Net Income	1.00	0.90	1.10	0.50	0.65	1.00	1.05	1.60

EXHIBIT 15-3

TREND ANALYSIS: BALANCE SHEET

A. Abbreviated Balance Sheets

	19X0	19X1	19X2	19X3	19X4	19X5	19X6	19X7
Assets								
Current Assets	$ 5	$ 7	$ 7	$4	$ 5	$ 7	$ 9	$11
Long-term Assets	5	5	6	5	5	5	6	14
Total Assets	$10	$12	$13	$9	$10	$12	$15	$25
Liabilities and Stockholders' Equity								
Current Debts	$ 2	$ 3	$ 3	$2	$ 2	$ 3	$ 4	$ 6
Long-term Debts	4	4	4	3	3	3	4	9
Stockholders' Equity	4	5	6	4	5	6	7	10
Total Liabilities and Stockholders' Equity	$10	$12	$13	$9	$10	$12	$15	$25

B. Time-series Trends

	19X0	19X1	19X2	19X3	19X4	19X5	19X6	19X7
Assets								
Current Assets	1.00	1.40	1.40	0.80	1.00	1.40	1.80	2.20
Long-term Assets	1.00	1.00	1.20	1.00	1.00	1.00	1.20	2.80
Total Assets	1.00	1.20	1.30	0.90	1.00	1.20	1.50	2.50
Liabilities and Stockholders' Equity								
Current Debts	1.00	1.50	1.50	1.00	1.00	1.50	2.00	3.00
Long-term Debts	1.00	1.00	1.00	0.75	0.75	0.75	1.00	2.25
Stockholders' Equity	1.00	1.25	1.50	1.00	1.25	1.50	1.75	2.50
Total Liabilities and Stockholders' Equity	1.00	1.20	1.30	0.90	1.00	1.20	1.50	2.50

Exhibit 15-1. By viewing the percentage changes, we can understand that the 10% decline in income came about because costs rose faster than sales, 25% to 10%.

To inquire about more than two periods, **trend analysis** is available. Selected accounts are chosen for a period of several years. The first year is called the *base year*. The trend numbers are created by dividing the account in a given year by the account in the base year. An example is provided in Exhibit 15-2 (p. 541). Part A contains abbreviated income statements for an eight-year period, 19X0–19X7. Part B yields the trends in the accounts. For example, look at the Sales account. Sales in the base year (19X0) is $50. The sales of all years are divided by $50 to give the trend numbers for sales in Part B. For example in 19X1, sales of $55 divided by base year sales of $50 is equal to 1.10. Trend analysis can also be performed on balance sheets. Exhibit 15-3 illustrates trend analysis for balance sheets. Trend calculations are performed in a similar manner. Trend analysis can also be carried out on statements of cash flows.

Trend analysis can help to pinpoint periods of unusual activity. From Exhibits 15-2 and 15-3 we can see that 19X3 was a disastrous year and 19X7 was an excellent year for the subject company. The analyst should follow up on these numbers and try to determine why 19X3 was so bad and 19X7 so good. For example, a major strike may have occurred in 19X3, or possibly a severe recession in the local market took place. In 19X7 a merger or an acquisition may have been made.

Using trend analysis requires caution. One needs to be alert to any accounting changes that may have occurred (such as a change from FIFO to LIFO). This, of course, disrupts the analysis. If the data are available, the analyst may adjust the numbers as though the corporation used the same accounting method for all periods. Care must also be used in selecting the base year. The analyst or manager should choose a year that does not have any unusual activities so the subsequent years do not look out of line in relation to it, when in fact it is the base year itself that is out of line.

COMMON-SIZE STATEMENTS

CHAPTER OBJECTIVE 4
Explain cross-sectional analysis: common-size statements

Cross-sectional analysis consists of analyzing several firms at one point in time. Common-size statements and financial ratio analysis are two types of cross-sectional analysis. These computations will be shown here, but remember that in practice the numbers would be compared with other firms, industry averages, or averages for the economy as a whole.

Common-size statements basically break down a financial statement by the proportion contributed by each account. These proportions frequently are reported in percentage form. Line items in the income statement are shown as a percentage of sales. Net income is not used, because it could be negative and thus give meaningless results. Items in the balance sheet are shown as a percentage of the total assets (which equals total equities). To prepare a common-size statement of cash flows, one might put the statement in balanced form—that is, display an increase in cash as a "use" and a decrease in cash as a "source." Then sources of cash equal uses of cash. Items in the statement of cash flows then are shown as a percentage of the total sources of cash (which is also the total uses of cash). (The activities format of the cash flow statement, as presented in Chapter 6, is not amenable to common-size statements.)

Exhibit 15-4 illustrates common-size statements for 19X0 using the data in Exhibits 15-2 and 15-3. For the income statement, the sales number is used as the basis; it is considered 100%. The rest of the items are shown as percentages of the $50 sales. Net income, for example, is $20; thus in the common-size statement it is calculated as 40% ($20/$50 × 100). Total assets and total liabilities and stockholders' equity are the basis in the balance sheet. Thus, the base figure is $10. The other accounts are shown as percentages of the $10 total assets (or liabilities and stockholders' equity). Look at long-term debts, valued at $4. In the common-size income statement it is indexed at 40%, which is calculated as $4/$10 × 100.

Common-size statements are often revealing if presented over time. The data in Parts A and B of Exhibits 15-2 and 15-3 are recast into common-size income statements and balance sheets. These can be seen in Exhibits 15-5 and 15-6 (pp. 544, 545).

Why are common-size statements helpful? The principal reason is that they provide an easy and quick idea of the financial structure of the organization. In our hypothetical example, cost of sales generally range from 40% to 50% and the other expenses generally range from 20% to 30%. It is obvious that if managers want to control costs, they

---

EXHIBIT 15-4

COMMON-SIZE STATEMENTS

	19X0	
INCOME STATEMENT	$	Common-size
Sales	$50	100%
Cost of Sales	20	40
Gross Margin	$30	60%
Expenses	10	20
Net Income	$20	40%

BALANCE SHEET

Assets

Current Assets	$ 5	50%
Long-term Assets	5	50
Total Assets	$10	100%

Liabilities and Stockholders' Equity

Current Debts	$ 2	20%
Long-term Debts	4	40
Stockholders' Equity	4	40
Total Liabilities and Stockholders' Equity	$10	100%

EXHIBIT 15-5

COMMON-SIZE INCOME STATEMENTS OVER TIME

	19X0	19X1	19X2	19X3	19X4	19X5	19X6	19X7
Sales	100%	100%	100%	100%	100%	100%	100%	100%
Cost of Sales	40	45	44	33	49	47	46	50
Gross Margin	60%	55%	56%	67%	51%	53%	54%	50%
Expenses	20	22	21	33	27	20	22	18
Net Income	40%	33%	35%	34%	24%	33%	32%	32%

---

should concentrate on controlling cost of sales. In the balance sheet, short-term assets approximately equal long-term assets. Also, the capital structure is about 50%–60% debt and 40%–50% stockholders' equity. This type of analysis is especially useful over time since it helps to detect changes in revenue and expense relationships, asset structure, and debt structure. It is also quite revealing when comparing one firm against another, for it helps to detect any structural differences.

	EXHIBIT 15-6							

COMMON-SIZE BALANCE SHEETS OVER TIME

	19X0	19X1	19X2	19X3	19X4	19X5	19X6	19X7
Assets								
Current Assets	50%	58%	54%	44%	50%	58%	60%	44%
Long-term Assets	50	42	46	55	50	42	40	56
Total Assets	100%	100%	100%	100%	100%	100%	100%	100%
Liabilities and Stockholders' Equity								
Current Debts	20%	25%	23%	22%	20%	25%	27%	24%
Long-term Debts	40	33	31	33	30	25	27	36
Stockholders' Equity	40	42	46	44	50	50	47	40
Total Liabilities and Stockholders' Equity	100%	100%	100%	100%	100%	100%	100%	100%

RATIO ANALYSIS

CHAPTER OBJECTIVE 4
Explain cross-sectional analysis: ratios

Perhaps the most popular tool in financial statement analysis is the analysis of financial ratios. They are called *ratios* because most of the statistics are computed by dividing one number by another one. The rationale for dividing one account by another is to put different companies on the same footing. If two firms have different amounts of assets and everything else is the same, no one would expect them to produce the same earnings. Larger companies generally have larger earnings. To enhance comparison between the firms, we would compute a ratio, such as net income/total assets. The ratio reduces the effect of the size differential, providing a better comparison between or among the organizations.

Be aware that no standards exist in the preparation of ratios. By that it is meant that there is no theory indicating which ratios to compute or how to calculate them. Different textbooks present different ratios, different terminology, and different ways to calculate them. Various financial monitoring organizations, such as Dun and Bradstreet, Standard and Poor's, and stockbrokers also use different ratios, different terminology, and different ways of measurement.

The ratios discussed in this section are grouped into five categories, reflecting five different measures of a company's health: profitability, solvency, structure, operating cycle, and market ratios. All the ratios will be illustrated with the data contained in Exhibit 15-7. In this table are the financial statements for Charitou Cargo, Inc. Throughout the rest of this chapter, we assume that the market price of Charitou's common stock is $40 per share.

It should again be pointed out that the numbers do not mean anything by themselves. There is no "optimum" ratio, no theoretical value that we know is either good or bad. The ratios are meaningful in conjunction with the company's ratios for prior years, the ratios of other corporations, or industry averages of ratios.

EXHIBIT 15-7

FINANCIAL REPORT FOR RATIO ANALYSIS

Charitou Cargo, Inc.
Income Statement
For the Year Ended June 30, 19X1

Sales	$500,000
Cost of Goods Sold	210,000
Gross Margin	$290,000
Wages and Salaries	72,000
Rent	60,000
Utilities	24,000
Interest	14,000
Depreciation	8,000
Miscellaneous	13,000
Operating Expenses	$191,000
Income before Taxes	$ 99,000
Taxes	42,000
Net Income	$ 57,000

Charitou Cargo, Inc.
Statement of Cash Flows
For the Year Ended June 30, 19X1

Cash Flows from Operating Activities

Cash Collections from Customers	$525,000	
Cash Paid out for Inventory	(230,000)	
Gross Margin	$295,000	
Cash Paid out for Expenses	(150,000)	
Cash Flows before Taxes	$145,000	
Cash Paid out for Taxes	(40,000)	
Net Cash Provided by Operating Activities		$105,000

Cash Flows from Investing Activities

Purchase of Equipment	$ (80,000)	
Net Cash Used by Investing Activities		(80,000)

Cash Flows from Financing Activities

Proceeds from Issuance of Long-term Debt	$ 50,000	
Dividends Paid to Preferred Stock	(10,000)	
Dividends Paid to Common Stock	(30,000)	
Net Cash Provided by Financing Activities		10,000
Net Increase in Cash		$ 35,000

(continued)

EXHIBIT 15-7 *(continued)*

Charitou Cargo, Inc.
Balance Sheet
June 30, 19X1

ASSETS

Current Assets

Cash		$ 50,000
Receivables (beginning, $80,000)		90,000
Inventory (beginning, $100,000)		220,000
Prepaid Expenses		55,000
Total Current Assets		$415,000

Property, Plant, and Equipment

Equipment	$600,000	
Less: Accumulated Depreciation	250,000	$350,000
Land		100,000
Total Property, Plant, and Equipment		$450,000
Total Assets		$865,000

LIABILITIES AND STOCKHOLDERS' EQUITY

Current Debts

Accounts Payable	$180,000
Taxes Payable	20,000
Total Current Debts	$200,000

Long-term Debts

Bonds Payable	$100,000
Mortgage Payable	250,000
Total Long-term Debts	$350,000
Total Debts	$550,000

Stockholders' Equity

Preferred Stock (1,000 shares)	$100,000
Common Stock (10,000 shares)	150,000
Retained Earnings	65,000
Total Stockholders' Equity	$315,000
Total Liabilities and Stockholders' Equity	$865,000

Profitability Ratios

CHAPTER
OBJECTIVE 5
*Classifications and
purposes of financial
ratios*

Profitability ratios are designed to indicate how well the corporation is generating profits. Accounting profits are important because they can signal (imperfectly) future cash flows of the enterprise. Profitability ratios can be further partitioned into return ratios and earnings per share.

The focus of these ratios is not on net income but on operating income. The difference between them pivots on what are called "extraordinary items." An extraordinary event is one which is *both* unusual in nature and infrequent in occurrence. The environment of the business must be considered before classifying an event as ordinary or extraordinary. Examples of extraordinary items are losses from earthquakes, hailstorms, and tornadoes in areas where such activity is rare. The analyst desires to remove extraordinary events from consideration because they are unlikely to happen again. The analyst, however, is also trying to determine events that are likely to recur.

Return ratios are basically income from operations divided by some base of activity. Common denominators include total assets, sales, and stockholders' equity. Return ratios indicate how efficient management has been in the generation of profits. *Return on total assets* (income/total assets) tells how efficiently management has utilized its assets. *Return on sales* (income/sales) tells how well management has been able to generate profit out of its sales. *Return on equity* (income/stockholders' equity) shows how well management has been able to use the capital provided by the stockholders of the corporation.

Solving for these in using Charitou Cargo, Inc., we obtain:

$$\text{Income/Total Assets} = \$57{,}000/\$865{,}000 = .066$$
$$\text{Income/Sales} = \$57{,}000/\$500{,}000 = .114$$
$$\text{Income/Stockholders' Equity} = \$57{,}000/\$315{,}000 = .181$$

Some common variations are to use income before taxes, income before interest and taxes, income minus preferred dividends, and common stockholders' equity. Whatever variation is selected, the analyst must be consistent in applying it to all the bases of activity chosen.

Another signal of profitability is *earnings per share*. This number is probably the most popular ratio and it is defined as:

$$\text{Earnings per Share} = \frac{\text{Income} - \text{Preferred Dividends}}{\text{Number of Common Shares}}$$

For Charitou Cargo, Inc., the value is:

$$\text{Earnings per Share} = \frac{\$57{,}000 - \$10{,}000}{10{,}000} = \$4.70$$

Earnings per share should show how much of the earnings can be distributed per share of common stock. That is why preferred dividends are subtracted; doing so yields income available for common stockholders. So earnings per common share is income available for common stockholders divided by the number of common shares outstanding. If extraordinary items have occurred, it is typical to show two earnings-per-share ratios: one based on operating income and one based on net income.

Solvency Ratios

CHAPTER
OBJECTIVE 5
*Classification and
purposes of financial
ratios*

Profitability refers to a company's ability to produce earnings which can translate into cash inflows. *Solvency* refers to the ability to pay off one's debts. Profitability ratios are important because they signal the company's ability to generate cash flows on a long-range basis. To assess solvency, however, we need to know about the cash available today and the company's ability to generate cash flows on a short-term basis.

RATIO ANALYSIS: TIPS FOR BETTER MANAGEMENT REPORTS

Most financial reports have become tailored over time to accommodate changing responsibility centers, product lines, corporate objectives, and real or perceived problems. Unfortunately, this often results in an internal reporting system that is confusing, fragmented, and ultimately overwhelming.

At times, little consideration is given to the needs or expertise of the user. Although accounting supposedly recognizes that not all managers' needs are the same, it continues to send "uniform" reports, expecting each recipient (and his operation) to adjust accordingly. The reports often require extensive recalculations before they yield meaningful information.

At other times, multiple reports provide only fragmentary information. For example, when someone identifies a piece of data that is considered important, finance will often send an entire report full of data that obscures the one bit of needed information. This can create a great deal of work and confusion. One vice president complained about having to scour over twenty different reports for the few relevant bits of data he needed to put together one meaningful operational report, and his plight is not uncommon.

Reports that require users to recompile, manipulate, and recalculate information before it meets their needs are inefficient. It takes away from the user's primary focus, which is managing his own operation. These people should not have to reprocess reports. Recipients of a report should be able to use the information—as received—to aid them in analysis and decision making.

Ratio Analysis

Ratio analysis is a simple—but powerful—tool for analysis. The ability to reduce different-sized and changing dollar (or unit) amounts to a common denominator greatly aids in making evaluations and comparisons. Managers should take the following steps to make their ratio analyses more meaningful:

● *Relate financial reports to the manager's operation.* Most managers relate better to quantities of activity than to dollar amounts, because they work daily with quantities and activities. At times, dollars (used to "keep score") may be perceived as one step removed from the manager's primary activity or responsibility.

For example, miles per gallon is a ratio commonly used to relate two different, nonmonetary units. Miles per gallon is often far more meaningful to us than either number of miles or gallons of fuel alone.

Quantities and dollars are both important, and both have to be managed. By integrating them in management reports, financial managers will aid operational managers to make the connection between dollars and activities, help provide another perspective, and also encourage better understanding and management.

● *Use graphics.* Graphics provide an excellent method for sending a message. Readers can better relate to a graphic display than they can to rows and columns of numbers.

Many managers now use data on a spreadsheet to develop their own graphs. This not only aids their own analysis but helps in conveying information both to their own employees and to other managers.

● *Communicate.* To work well, accountants and users of information must keep the lines of communication open. A healthy, open dialogue will promote increased effectiveness on everyone's part. Not only will the user feel more involved and get better information but he will also understand his or her operation better than anyone else. Likewise, with the user providing insight to the accountant, financial activities (analysis and budgeting, for example) related to that operation will also be improved.

SOURCE: Adapted from Charles A. Krueger, "Ratio Analysis: Using Spreadsheets for Better Management Reports," *Corporate Accounting* (Spring 1987), pp. 17–26. Adapted by permission.

One set of solvency ratios are the *cash flow ratios.* They are like return ratios except that they replace earnings with cash flow. The ratios are equal to cash flow divided either by total assets (*cash flow to total assets*), sales (*cash flow to sales*), or stockholders' equity (*cash flow to equity*). For Charitou Cargo, Inc., they are as follows:

$$\text{Cash Flow/Total Assets} = \$105,000/\$865,000 = .121$$
$$\text{Cash Flow/Sales} = \$105,000/\$500,000 = .210$$
$$\text{Cash Flow/Stockholders' Equity} = \$105,000/\$315,000 = .333$$

The cash flow ratios demonstrate management's ability to generate cash flow from operations efficiently from total assets, sales, and stockholders' equity.

Another group of solvency ratios are called *cash position ratios.* These ratios look at the amount of cash on hand relative to certain attributes of the company. Some common denominators used for these ratios are current debts, total debts, and sales. These ratios should indicate the adequacy of the cash available to pay debts. *Cash to current debts* shows the sufficiency of the cash on hand to meet the current obligations of the firm. *Cash to total debts* indicates the adequacy of the cash on hand to meet the total liabilities. Since the long-term portion of total liabilities does not mature until some time in the future, it is not expected that the current cash balance is sufficient to pay off these debts today. It is not even expected that there is enough cash to pay off the current debts. This is because cash inflows continue on a day-to-day basis. *Cash to sales* shows the firm's ability to provide cash on hand from its sales activities.

Measurement of these ratios for Charitou Cargo, Inc., is as follows:

$$\text{Cash/Current Debts} = \$50,000/\$200,000 = .250$$
$$\text{Cash/Total Debts} = \$50,000/\$550,000 = .091$$
$$\text{Cash/Sales} = \$50,000/\$500,000 = .100$$

Short-term liquidity ratios comprise the third set of solvency ratios. The rationale behind these two ratios is that certain assets can be turned into cash quickly if cash is needed to pay off debts. Current assets include all assets that are consumed or converted into cash within one year or the operating cycle if longer. The length of the operating cycle is the time it takes to invest cash in inventory, to sell the inventory, and to receive the cash from the receivable. Common current assets are cash, marketable securities, receivables, inventories, supplies, and prepaid expenses. Charitou Cargo, Inc.'s current assets are $415,000. Some of these current assets are not as quickly converted into cash as others. To focus on the accounts that can be converted quickly one would look only at Cash, Marketable Securities, and Receivables. These items are referred to as *quick assets.* For Charitou, quick assets total $140,000 ($50,000 Cash + $0 Marketable Securities + $90,000 Receivables).

The common short-term liquidity ratios are the current ratio and the quick ratio. The *current ratio* is defined as current assets divided by current debts. The *quick ratio* (sometimes called the acid-test ratio) is equal to quick assets divided by current debts. For Charitou Cargo, Inc., these ratios are:

$$\text{Current Ratio} = \$415,000/\$200,000 = 2.075$$
$$\text{Quick Ratio} = \$140,000/\$200,000 = 0.700$$

The current ratio shows how much coverage the current assets have to meet the current obligations; the quick ratio tells how much coverage the quick assets have to meet them.

> ## EXHIBIT 15-8
>
> ### DEMONSTRATION OF LEVERAGE EFFECTS
>
> | | Percentage of Debt of Stockholders' Equity | | | |
> |---|---|---|---|---|
> | | 0% | 25% | 50% | 75% |
> | **Capital Structure** | | | | |
> | Debt (@ 10% interest) | $ –0– | $ 2,500 | $ 5,000 | $ 7,500 |
> | Stockholders' equity | | | | |
> | ($100 per share) | 10,000 | 7,500 | 5,000 | 2,500 |
> | Total capital | $10,000 | $10,000 | $10,000 | $10,000 |
> | | | | | |
> | **Earnings before interest and taxes** | $ 500 | $ 500 | $ 500 | $ 500 |
> | Interest (10% of debt) | –0– | 250 | 500 | 750 |
> | Earnings before taxes | $ 500 | $ 250 | $ –0– | $ (250) |
> | Taxes (40% rate) | 200 | 100 | –0– | (100) |
> | Earnings | $ 300 | $ 150 | $ –0– | $ (150) |
> | Earnings per share | $3 | $2 | $ –0– | $(6) |
> | | | | | |
> | **Earnings before interest and taxes** | $2,000 | $2,000 | $2,000 | $2,000 |
> | Interest (10% of debt) | 0 | 250 | 500 | 750 |
> | Earnings before taxes | $2,000 | $1,750 | $1,500 | $1,250 |
> | Taxes (40% rate) | 800 | 700 | 600 | 500 |
> | Earnings | $1,200 | $1,050 | $ 900 | $ 750 |
> | Earnings per share | $12 | $14 | $18 | $30 |

Structure Ratios

CHAPTER
OBJECTIVE 5
*Classification and
purposes of financial
ratios*

Besides profitability and solvency, users must also be able to evaluate the financial structure of the corporation. Users would like to assess the capital structure, the asset structure, and the debt structure of the firm. These are analyzed using the **structure ratios**.

Capital structure refers to the relative amount of debt and stockholders' equity in the company. It can be measured as total debts to total assets (*debt to assets*) or as total debts to stockholders' equity (*debt to equity*).

Adding debt to the capital structure can add to the expected return of common stockholders, but it also adds risk. This concept is referred to as *financial leverage*. Refer to Exhibit 15-8 to see how it works. Assume that there is a company with total capital of $10,000. It can be structured as 0%, 25%, 50%, or 75% debt and the rest as common stock. The debt carries an interest charge of 10%. The stock is sold in shares valued at $100 each. If earnings before interest and taxes (EBIT) are only $500, then the negative effects of leverage are seen. The interest on the debt must be paid. The greater the debt, the lower the earnings per share. However, if earnings before interest and taxes are $2,000, then the positive effects of leverage are felt. In this case the greater the leverage, the higher the earnings per share. Thus, financial leverage is a double-edged sword depending on the level of the earnings before interest and taxes.

Following are the calculations of the structure ratios for Charitou Cargo, Inc.:

$$\text{Total Debts/Total Assets} = \$550,000/865,000 = .636$$
$$\text{Total Debts/Stockholders' Equity} = \$550,000/\$315,000 = 1.746$$

The first ratio for Charitou Cargo, Inc., indicates the proportion of total assets supported by debt; the rest of the debt $(1 - .636 = .364)$ is supplied by the stockholders. The debt-to-equity ratio (the second ratio) is an alternative way of expressing the relation.

Asset structure indicates the amount of current assets in relation to long-term assets. Typical ratios are *current assets to total assets* and *long-term assets to total assets.* They are computed for Charitou Cargo, Inc., as follows:

$$\text{Current Assets/Total Assets} = \$415,000/\$865,000 = .480$$
$$\text{Long-term Assets/Total Assets} = \$450,000/\$865,000 = .520$$

These ratios show the proportional amount of the current assets and the property, plant, and equipment.

Debt structure refers to the relative amount of current and long-term debt. So the ratios are *current debts to total debts* and *long-term debts to total debts.* Charitou Cargo's ratios are:

$$\text{Current Debts/Total Debts} = \$200,000/\$550,000 = .364$$
$$\text{Long-term Debts/Total Debts} = \$350,000/\$550,000 = .636$$

These ratios indicate the relative amounts of liabilities that mature in the short run and in the long run.

Operating-cycle Ratios

CHAPTER
OBJECTIVE 5
*Classification and
purposes of financial
ratios*

Operating-cycle ratios capture data concerning the operating cycle of a firm (discussed below), the length of time from obtaining inventory to sell to collecting debts from sales of that inventory. *Accounts receivable turnover* is measured as sales divided by the average accounts receivable balance. The average balance of the receivables is equal to the beginning balance in accounts receivable plus the ending balance in accounts receivable divided by two. For Charitou Cargo, Inc., the computation is:

$$\text{Accounts Receivable Turnover} = \frac{\$500,000}{\frac{\$80,000 + \$90,000}{2}} = 5.882$$

This ratio says that during the year Charitou's Accounts Receivable balance is collected about 5.882 times.

Interpretation of this turnover ratio is frequently enhanced by converting it into the days for collection. The average number of days taken to collect accounts receivable is 365 divided by the accounts receivable turnover. For Charitou, the calculation is:

$$\text{Collection Period} = \frac{365}{5.882} = 62.054 \text{ days}$$

This statistic says that it takes about 62 days to collect an average receivable. Depending on the industry, this may be considered a long period or short period and may need the attention of management.

The *inventory turnover ratio* is measured in an analogous way. It is the cost of goods sold divided by the average inventory balance. The average inventory balance is the beginning inventory plus the ending inventory divided by two. For Charitou, this ratio is calculated as:

$$\text{Inventory Turnover} = \frac{\$210,000}{\dfrac{\$100,000 + \$220,000}{2}} = 1.312$$

This ratio tells us that Charitou Cargo's inventory in stock is turned over about 1.312 times per year.

As was true for the accounts receivable turnover ratio, this analysis can be improved by transforming the inventory turnover into the number of days it takes to sell the inventory. Accordingly for Charitou:

$$\text{Days to Sell Inventory} = \frac{365}{1.312} = 278.201 \text{ days}$$

This number indicates that it takes about 278 days to sell Charitou's entire inventory. This may be an acceptable number for the furniture industry or hardware stores but is obviously unacceptable for grocery stores.

The *operating cycle* is the amount of time it takes to invest cash in the inventory of the business, sell it to the customers, and collect the accounts receivable. To use this concept in financial analysis, we may simply add the days to sell inventory and the collection period. For Charitou Cargo, Inc., this is:

$$\text{Length of Operating Cycle} = 62.054 + 278.201 = 340.255 \text{ days}$$

Thus, it takes an average of 340 days for Charitou to invest cash in the inventory of the business and to collect cash from its customers.

Market Ratios

CHAPTER OBJECTIVE 5
Classification and purposes of financial ratios

Cash dividends and common stock prices are of major concern to common stockholders. Several ratios have been devised to capture these aspects of the firm and are referred to as **market ratios**.

Two popular dividend ratios are dividend yield and dividend payout. *Dividend yield* equals the dividends per share divided by the market price per share. It indicates the return to the common stockholder from the cash dividends. *Dividend payout* is the dividends per share divided by earnings per share. It shows the proportion of the earnings that is distributed as dividends. The rest of the earnings are retained in the business. Calculations for Charitou Cargo, Inc., are as follows:

$$\text{Dividend Yield} = \$3/\$40 \quad = .075$$
$$\text{Dividend Payout} = \$3/\$4.70 = .638$$

Perhaps it should be mentioned that the dividends per share of $3 is obtained by taking the number of common shares, 10,000, shown on the balance sheet and dividing this into the cash dividends paid to the common stockholders, $30,000, which is given in Charitou's statement of cash flows in Exhibit 15-7.

There are two commonly used market ratios. The *price-to-earnings ratio* (or price/earnings) is computed as the stock market price per share divided by the earnings per share. This is also seen in its reciprocal form, called the *earnings yield*. Basically, these ratios indicate the market value placed on a dollar of earnings of the corporation. For Charitou Cargo, Inc., these ratios are as follows:

$$\text{Price/Earnings Ratio} = \$40/\$4.70 = 8.511 \text{ times}$$
$$\text{Earnings Yield} = \$4.70/\$40 = .117$$

EXHIBIT 15-9

SUMMARY OF FINANCIAL RATIOS

Group	Ratio Name	Calculation
Profitability	*Return ratios:*	
	Return on total assets	Income/Total Assets
	Return on sales	Income/Sales
	Return on equity	Income/Stockholders' Equity
	Earnings per share	(Income − Preferred Dividends)/Number of Common Shares
Solvency	*Cash flow ratios:*	
	Cash flow to total assets	Cash Flow/Total Assets
	Cash flow to sales	Cash Flow/Sales
	Cash flow to equity	Cash Flow/Stockholders' Equity
	Cash position ratios:	
	Cash to current debts	Cash/Current Debts
	Cash to total debts	Cash/Total Debts
	Cash to sales	Cash/Sales
	Short-term liquidity ratios:	
	Current ratio	Current Assets/Current Debts
	Quick ratio	Quick Assets/Current Debts

EXHIBIT 15-9 *(continued)*

Structure	*Capital structure ratios:*	
	Debt to assets	Total Debts/Total Assets
	Debt to equity	Total Debts/Total Stockholders' Equity
	Asset structure ratios:	
	Current assets to total assets	Current Assets/Total Assets
	Long-term assets to total assets	Long-term Assets/Total Assets
	Debt structure ratios:	
	Current debts to total debts	Current Debts/Total Debts
	Long-term debts to total debts	Long-term Debts/Total Debts
Operating Cycle	Accounts receivable turnover	Sales/Average Accounts Receivable
	Collection period	365/Accounts Receivable Turnover
	Inventory turnover	Cost of Goods Sold/Average Inventory Balance
	Days to sell inventory	365/Inventory Turnover
	Length of operating cycle	Collection Period + Days to Sell Inventory
Market	Dividend yield	Dividends per Share/Market Price per Share
	Dividend payout	Dividends per Share/Earnings per Share
	Price to earnings	Market Price per Share/Earnings per Share
	Earnings Yield	Earnings per Share/Market Price per Share

Summary

In the latter half of this chapter, 27 financial ratios have been presented. These ratios are summarized for your convenience in Exhibit 15-9. These ratios are important because they are indexes of several attributes of the entity's financial character. Keep in mind that they frequently do not have much meaning in themselves, but they acquire meaning when compared with the ratios of other firms. A time-series analysis can be performed on ratios as well as on selected financial statement numbers.

In using these ratios to compare firms, part of any differences might be attributed to differences in accounting methods. Where this is the case, the analyst has two choices. He or she may leave the differences unadjusted and simply keep them in mind when making a decision. Alternatively, the analyst may try to adjust one of the firm's accounting numbers and recompute the financial ratios.

DECISION SUPPORT SYSTEMS AND BEHAVIORAL ASPECTS OF FINANCIAL STATEMENT ANALYSIS

Financial planning models look at the financial variables of the corporation in the future. Such models frequently estimate the forecasted financial statements, especially the forecasted income statement. These financial planning models can be augmented by financial statement analysis as discussed in this chapter. Most popular in these settings are the financial ratios.

Decision support systems are affected by the inclusion of the appropriate variables of interest. DSS models can be improved by calling managers' attention to critical financial ratios such as the profitability ratios. What-if analysis can also be carried out. Thus, when different scenarios are examined, as illustrated in the demonstration problem, the decision maker can observe the financial ratios as well as the components of the forecasted financial statements.

A prevalent management use of financial statement analysis is to assess the effect of a possible transaction on the financial report that the corporation will send to stockholders and creditors. Managers know that these users will evaluate their performance and that of the company in part by the financial statements. Managers can include this perspective in their planning to determine the effects of a proposed transaction. If the proposed transaction is felicitous, then management can engage in the transaction. If the proposal has deleterious effects, then management can decide against it. Of course, it is best for the manager to take a long-term strategic viewpoint. This might mean that he or she will have to accept financial effects that are not attractive in the short run but will reap their benefits several years later. (Some financial economists believe that one reason for the success of Japanese firms is their adoption of long-term strategic viewpoints.)

Demonstration Problem

Recall the data in Exhibit 15-7 for Charitou Cargo, Inc., for fiscal year ending June 30, 19X1, on pages 546–47. Assume that operations for the fiscal year ending June 30, 19X2, are like those for year-end 19X1 except that there is no purchase of equipment. Also assume that additional assets are all cash.

Charitou Cargo, Inc., is considering trading all of its preferred stock for an additional $100,000 bonds payable. Annual interest charges would increase by $14,000 and income taxes would decrease by $5,600.

REQUIRED
Compute the profitability ratios for Charitou Cargo, Inc., assuming (a) that the preferred stock/bonds payable transaction is consummated and (b) that it is not.

SOLUTION TO DEMONSTRATION PROBLEM
The net income of $57,000 for 19X1 would decline to $48,600 for 19X2 ($57,000 − $14,000 incremental interest + $5,600 decrease in taxes).

The cash flows from operations for 19X1 was $105,000. The cash flows from operations for 19X2 would be $96,600 ($105,000 − $14,000 additional interest + $5,600 decrease in taxes).

Charitou's total assets ($865,000 for 19X1) would increase for 19X2 by the amount of net income less the dividends paid out, or $18,600 ($48,600 − $30,000). Thus for 19X2 cash is $68,600 ($50,000 + $18,600); current assets are $433,600 ($415,000 + $18,600); and total assets are $883,600 ($865,000 + $18,600).

Current debts for 19X2 remain unchanged from 19X1 at $200,000. Long-term debts become $450,000 ($350,000 + $100,000). Thus, total debts for 19X2 are $650,000 ($200,000 + $450,000).

Stockholders' equity for 19X2 consists of common stock of $150,000 plus retained earnings of $83,600 ($65,000 + $48,600 − $30,000), or $233,600.

Given these data, the ratios can now be computed. The raw data and the profitability ratios are tabulated as follows. The proposed transaction would improve return on equity and earnings per share but worsen return on total assets and return on sales. (The reader should think about the impact on the other ratios as well.)

Data and Ratios	Without Transaction	With Transaction
Income	$ 57,000	$ 48,600
Total assets	$892,000	$883,600
Sales	$500,000	$500,000
Stockholders' equity	$332,000	$233,600
Preferred dividends	$ 10,000	$ −0−
Number of common shares	10,000	10,000
Return on total assets	.064	.055
Return on sales	.114	.097
Return on equity	.172	.208
Earnings per share	$4.70	$4.86

Review of Chapter Objectives

1. Identify the objectives of financial statement analysis (pp. 537–39).

   ■ Financial statement analysis is the process of examining corporate financial statements. It is the process of reading the reports, computing various summary indicators, and interpreting what they mean. Based on these interpretations, the user would make decisions such as buying or not buying stock and issuing or not issuing a loan. The purpose of financial statement analysis is to assist the manager in making a decision. Financial statement analysis is helpful because it provides summary indicators of how well the firm has done with respect to financial factors such as profitability and solvency.

2. State the importance and the limitations of accounting data (pp. 539–40).

   ■ Financial data are important since they can be combined in useful fashions to obtain percentages, trends, and ratios that can be interpreted to explain various corporate phenomena. The analysis is limited, however, because accounting data are historical, they are measured with error, and some important qualitative factors are not captured in the accounting data.

3. Describe time-series analysis, including percentage analysis and trend analysis (pp. 540–43).

   ■ Time-series analysis consists of analyzing one firm across time. Popular time-series methods are percentage analysis and trend analysis. Percentage analysis deals with the percentage change in selected accounts. Trend analysis concentrates on the values of selected accounts across time in terms of base-year values that are frequently assigned a value of 1.00.

4. Explain cross-sectional analysis, including common-size statements and financial ratios (pp. 543–45).

   ■ Cross-sectional analysis consists of analyzing several firms at one point in time. Popular cross-sectional techniques include common-size statements and financial ratio analysis. Common-size statements put the line items in the statement on a proportional basis relative to some total. The income statement places the line items in relation to total sales, the balance sheet places them in relation to total assets and total equities, and the cash flow statement places them as a proportion of total source and total uses. (One must make the cash flow statement balance, sources and uses, if one wishes to use a common-size approach.) Ratio analysis looks at one number divided by another. This puts the firms on a comparable basis and allows a better analysis.

5. Name major classifications of financial ratios and the purpose of each group (pp. 547–55).

   ■ We presented 27 financial ratios, which are summarized in Exhibit 15-9. To make them easier to remember, the ratios are also categorized into groups. Profitability ratios look at the profit-generating activities of the firm. Solvency ratios focus on its ability to pay its debts. Structure ratios concentrate on the composition of the firm's capital, assets, and liabilities. Operating-cycle ratios analyze the length of the operating cycle and its components. Finally, market ratios consist of the dividend-paying activities of the firm as well as the stock market prices.

6. Discuss financial statement analysis in the context of decision support systems and its behavioral aspects (p. 556).

   ■ There are many ways in which to conduct financial statement analysis. Decision support systems allow a user to enter the data into models and perform a variety of analyses, such as ratio analysis, then to make decisions based on both the model and on professional judgment. Models can be used and analyzed in a variety of ways. (Some models are illustrated in the discussion questions.) What-if analysis is a major aspect of this analysis. By examining various scenarios, the user can have a better idea of how to proceed.

   ■ A potential problem is that a manager might engage (or not engage) in a project solely because of its financial effects. Although this may help his or her career (especially if not caught), it is harmful to the firm especially in the long run. Competition from Japanese companies vividly demonstrates that long-term success can be achieved by concentrating on economic fundamentals. Companies that look at financial effects and not at the economic fundamentals usually lose out in the long run.

Glossary of Key Terms

common-size statements   Financial statements that report the line items by their proportion to the total sales on the income statement, to total assets (equities) on the balance sheet, and to total uses (sources) of cash on the cash-flow statement. This is also referred to as vertical analysis.

cross-sectional analysis   Analysis of several firms at one point in time. Popular cross-sectional methods include common-size statements and ratio analysis.

market ratios A group of ratios that focus on the cash dividends paid out and on the market price of the common stock.

operating cycle ratios A group of ratios that concentrate on accounts receivable, inventory, and estimating the length of the operating cycle.

percentage analysis A type of time-series analysis that focuses on the percentage change in selected accounts.

profitability ratios A group of ratios that indicate the profit-making capabilities of the company.

ratio analysis A type of cross-sectional examination that typically looks at one number divided by another. Five categories of ratios are: profitability, solvency, structure, operating cycle, and market ratios.

solvency ratios A group of ratios that indicate the firm's ability to pay its debts.

structure ratios A group of ratios that examine the firm's composition of its capital, assets, and liabilities.

time-series analysis Analysis of one firm across time. Popular time-series methods include percentage analysis and trend analysis. This is also referred to as horizontal analysis.

trend analysis A type of time-series analysis that focuses on the values of selected variables across time in terms of base-year values.

Review Questions

15-1 What is financial statement analysis and what is its purpose?

15-2 How might financial statement analysis help investors?

15-3 How might financial statement analysis assist creditors?

15-4 How might financial statement analysis be used by managers?

15-5 What is the importance of accounting data in performing financial statement analysis?

15-6 What are the limitations of accounting data?

15-7 What is time-series analysis?

15-8 What is percentage analysis?

15-9 What is trend analysis?

15-10 How are percentage analysis and trend analysis related?

15-11 What is cross-sectional analysis?

15-12 What are common-size statements and how are they created?

15-13 What is ratio analysis? What is the rationale for ratio analysis?

15-14 What are the five basic categories of ratios?

15-15 What is the purpose of profitability ratios? Name the ratios.

15-16 What are extraordinary items? Why are they ignored when computing profitability ratios?

15-17 What is the purpose of solvency ratios? What are the subgroups of the solvency ratios? Name the ratios.

15-18 What is the purpose of structure ratios? What are the subgroups of the structure ratios? Name the ratios.

15-19 What is financial leverage? What is its benefits? What is its cost?

15-20   What is the purpose of operating cycle ratios? Name them. How can the length of the operating cycle be measured?

15-21   What is the purpose of the market ratios? Name them.

15-22   Do financial ratios standing alone have meaning? How do they acquire meaning?

15-23   How does the selection of accounting methods affect ratio analysis?

Discussion Questions

The following two questions refer to data from Charitou Cargo, Inc., on pages 546–47.

15-24   One practical way of using financial ratios is to assess the financial health of a corporation such as predicting whether or not the enterprise will go bankrupt. Altman developed the following model to discriminate between failing and nonfailing firms[1]:

$$Z = .012X_1 + .014X_2 + .033X_3 + .006X_4 + .999X_5$$

where

X_1 = working capital/total assets
X_2 = retained earnings/total assets
X_3 = earnings before interest and taxes/total assets
X_4 = market value of equity/book value of total debt
X_5 = sales/total assets

When computing the "Z-score" for an enterprise, ratios X_1 through X_4 should be expressed in percentage form but X_5 should be expressed as a decimal fraction.

The cutoff point is 2.675. This means that the model predicts bankruptcy if the score falls below 2.675 and it predicts a going concern if the score exceeds 2.675. Altman recommends that a "grey zone" be constructed around that number in which the Z-score indicates that the prediction is too close to call. He suggests that firms having a Z-score over 2.99 be classified as nonfailing, firms with a Z-score below 1.81 be classified as failing, and other firms be classified as too close to call.

a. Compute the Z-score for Charitou Cargo, Inc.

b. What does the model predict?

c. What are the limitations of using a model such as this to predict bankruptcy?

Note: Answers to this discussion question are also used in the Business Decision Case for this chapter, on page 573.

15-25   Modern portfolio theory claims that assets are priced according to some rational model. One very popular model is the capital asset pricing model. This model claims that expected returns are a linear function of risk. This risk is often referred to as β. To get some idea of expected return, an investor would want to investigate the risk of his or her portfolio.

---

[1]Altman, E. I., "Financial Ratios, Discriminant Analysis and the Prediction of Corporate Bankruptcy." *The Journal of Finance* (September 1968): 589–609.

A β of 1 is said to have the same risk as an individual would have by investing all of the securities in the stock market. A β of 0 has no risk, such as an investment in a government bond. Other values of β can be interpreted in relation to the market risk ($\beta = 1$). A β of, say, 0.80 has 80% of the risk the market has. A model to predict β was developed by Beaver, Kettler, and Scholes.[2] It is:

$$\beta = 1.016 - .584X_1 + .835X_2 + 3.027X_3$$

where

X_1 = average dividend payout
X_2 = average growth rate in total assets
X_3 = standard deviation (variability) of earnings yield

a. Compute the estimated β for Charitou Cargo, Inc. Use the dividend payout for X_1. Assume total assets in the previous year were $700,000. Then use the percentage change in total assets for X_2. Assume X_3 equals .036.

b. What is the advantage of using averages of ratios?

c. What is the advantage of using standard deviations of ratios?

Exercises

15-26 PERCENTAGE ANALYSIS Compute the percentage change in the following selected accounts:

CO 3

	19X0	19X1
Current Assets	$120,000	$140,000
Total Assets	275,000	290,000
Total Debts	180,000	185,000
Sales	500,000	550,000
Cost of Sales	210,000	225,000
Net Income	75,000	80,000
Cash Flow	65,000	85,000

15-27 PERCENTAGE ANALYSIS Compute the percentage change in the following selected accounts and comment on any problems.

CO 3

	19X0	19X1
Total Assets	$ 500,000	$ 510,000
Stockholders' Equity	225,000	200,000
Sales	1,000,000	1,000,000
Cost of Sales	455,000	490,000
Net Income	30,000	(10,000)
Cash Flow	100	12,000

[2]Beaver, W. H., P. Kettler, and M. Scholes, "The Association Between Market-Determined and Accounting-Determined Risk Measures." *The Accounting Review* (October 1970): 654–82.

15-28 TREND ANALYSIS The following is a series of balance sheets. Prepare a trend analysis of the balance sheet accounts.

CO 3

Hussein's Restaurant
Balance Sheets
June 30, 19X0, 19X1, 19X2

Assets	19X0	19X1	19X2
Cash	$ 10	$ 20	$ 30
Accounts Receivable	90	80	100
Inventory	200	300	370
Property	500	500	600
Equipment (net)	600	700	750
Total Assets	$1,400	$1,600	$1,850
Liabilities and Stockholders' Equity			
Accounts Payable	$ 50	$ 100	$ 150
Notes Payable	100	200	250
Bonds Payable	250	250	250
Common Stock	400	400	500
Retained Earnings	600	650	700
Total Liabilities and Stockholders' Equity	$1,400	$1,600	$1,850

15-29 TREND ANALYSIS The following is a series of income statements. Prepare a trend analysis of the income statement accounts.

CO 3

Wyman and Company
Income Statements
For the Years Ended June 30, 19X0, 19X1, 19X2

	19X0	19X1	19X2
Sales	$1,000	$1,200	$1,300
Cost of Sales	400	500	500
Gross Margin	$ 600	$ 700	$ 800
Wages and Salaries	$ 150	$ 160	$ 180
Utilities	125	120	140
Rent	100	100	100
Depreciation	75	80	100
Interest	25	20	15
Operating Expenses	$ 475	$ 480	$ 535
Income before Taxes	$ 125	$ 220	$ 265
Taxes	25	70	100
Net Income	$ 100	$ 150	$ 165

15-30 TREND ANALYSIS The following is a series of statements of cash flows. Prepare a trend analysis of these statements.

CO 3

Bullfrogs and Butterflies
Statements of Cash Flows
For the Years Ended June 30, 19X0, 19X1, 19X2

	19X0	19X1	19X2
Cash Flows from Operating Activities	$ 120	$ 125	$ 100
Cash Flows from Investing Activities			
Purchase of Property, Plant, and Equipment	$(275)	$(125)	$(200)
Sale of Property, Plant, and Equipment	$ 20	$ 75	$ 50
Cash Flows from Financing Activities			
Issuance of Bonds Payable	$ 100	$–0–	$ 100
Issuance of Common Stock	$ 100	$ 100	$ –0–
Cash Paid out as Dividends	$ (25)	$ (25)	$ (25)
Net Increase in Cash	$ 40	$ 150	$ 25

15-31   COMMON-SIZE ANALYSIS Put the balance sheets in Exercise 15-28 on a common-size basis.

CO 4

15-32   COMMON-SIZE ANALYSIS Put the income statements in Exercise 15-29 on a common-size basis.

CO 4

15-33   COMMON-SIZE ANALYSIS Put the statements of cash flows in Exercise 15-30 on a common-size basis. *Hint:* You cannot do this with the FASB activities format. Rewrite the statement in a cash inflows and cash outflows format and then solve it.

CO 4

15-34   RATIO ANALYSIS ABC Corporation has net income for 19X2 of $20,000. This includes a deduction of $5,000 for an extraordinary flood loss. The corporation has sales of $100,000, stockholders' equity of $60,000, and total equities of $80,000. Preferred dividends amount to $5,000 and the firm has 10,000 common shares outstanding. Compute the profitability ratios.

CO 4, 5

15-35   RATIO ANALYSIS JEK and Associates has cash of $10,000, cash flows from operations of $30,000, current assets of $60,000, current liabilities of $30,000, quick assets of $24,000, sales of $100,000, stockholders' equity of $125,000, and total assets of $200,000. Calculate the solvency ratios.

CO 4, 5

15-36   RATIO ANALYSIS Dirsmith, Inc., has current assets of $400,000 and long-term assets of $600,000. It also has current liabilities of $175,000 and long-term liabilities of $400,000. From these accounts determine the structure ratios.

CO 4, 5

15-37   RATIO ANALYSIS Jablonsky, Inc., has $100,000 of debt with an interest rate of 10% and stockholders' equity of $100,000 (with a price per share of $10). The tax rate is 40%. Calculate the earnings per share if earnings before interest and taxes is:

CO 4, 5

a. $10,000.

b. $20,000.

c. $30,000.

d. $40,000.

15-38 RATIO ANALYSIS The Milliron Partnership has sales of $10,000,000 and cost of goods sold of $6,000,000. Average accounts receivable are $2,500,000 and average inventory is CO 4, 5 $3,000,000. Compute the operating cycle ratios.

15-39 RATIO ANALYSIS Schrader, Ltd., has earnings per share of $5, dividends per share of CO 4, 5 $2, and market price per share of $40. Calculate the market ratios for Schrader, Ltd.

Problems

15-40 TIME-SERIES ANALYSIS Carpenter & Company has the following comparative balance sheets and income statements:

CO 3, 4

Carpenter & Company
Balance Sheets
December 31, 19X1 and 19X2

	19X1	19X2
ASSETS		
Current Assets		
Cash	$ 25	$ 40
Receivables	150	160
Inventory	375	400
Current Assets	$ 550	$ 600
Long-term Assets		
Land	$1,000	$1,000
Property and Equipment (net)	2,000	2,400
Long-term Assets	$3,000	$3,400
Total Assets	$3,550	$4,000
LIABILITIES AND STOCKHOLDERS' EQUITY		
Accounts Payable	$ 200	$ 300
Notes Payable	200	150
Current Debts	$ 400	$ 450
Preferred Stock	$1,500	$1,500
Common Stock	1,000	1,000
Retained Earnings	650	1,050
Stockholders' Equity	$3,150	$3,550
Total Liabilities and Stockholders' Equity	$3,550	$4,000

Carpenter & Company
Income Statements
For the Years Ended December 31, 19X1 and 19X2

	19X1	19X2
Sales	$5,000	$6,000
Cost of Goods Sold	2,500	3,000
Gross Margin	$2,500	$3,000
Wages	$ 600	$ 650
Depreciation	300	400
Taxes	500	400
Operating Expenses	$1,400	$1,450
Net Income	$1,100	$1,550

REQUIRED

a. Prepare a percentage analysis of all accounts of Carpenter & Company.

b. Prepare common-size balance sheets and income statements of the company for both 19X1 and 19X2.

15-41   **TREND ANALYSIS** Following are the balance sheets and income statements of Gupta, Inc., over the five-year period 19X4–19X8:

CO 3, 4

Gupta, Inc.
Balance Sheets
June 30, 19X4–19X8

	19X4	19X5	19X6	19X7	19X8
Current Assets	$ 40	$ 45	$ 35	$ 50	$ 45
Long-term Assets	60	75	70	80	95
Total Assets	$100	$120	$105	$130	$140
Current Debts	$ 20	$ 25	$ 15	$ 30	$ 25
Long-term Debts	40	45	45	50	45
Total Debts	$ 60	$ 70	$ 60	$ 80	$ 70
Stockholders' Equity	$ 40	$ 50	$ 45	$ 50	$ 70
Total Equities	$100	$120	$105	$130	$140

Gupta, Inc.
Income Statements
For the Years Ended June 30, 19X4–19X8

	19X4	19X5	19X6	19X7	19X8
Sales	$400	$500	$450	$200	$500
Cost of Sales	200	240	200	120	230
Gross Margin	$200	$260	$250	$ 80	$270
Operating Expenses	190	245	240	80	230
Net Income	$ 10	$ 15	$ 10	$ 0	$ 40

REQUIRED

Prepare a trend analysis of the preceding statements for the five years shown.

15-42   RATIO ANALYSIS Largay, Inc., reported the following balance sheet and income statement for its fiscal year-end. There are 100 common shares outstanding valued at $5 each and receiving $1.50 dividends each.

CO 4, 5

Largay, Inc.
Balance Sheet
October 31, 19X2

Assets	
Cash	$ 25
Accounts Receivable (beginning balance $200)	250
Inventory (beginning balance $520)	600
Current Assets	$ 875
Long-term Assets	1,125
Total Assets	$2,000
Liabilities and Stockholders' Equity	
Current Debts (beginning balance $300)	$ 375
Long-term Debts	475
Stockholders' Equity	1,150
Total Liabilities and Stockholders' Equity	$2,000

Largay, Inc.
Income Statement
For the Year Ended October 31, 19X2

Sales	$720
Cost of Goods Sold	300
Gross Margin	$420
Depreciation	$ 60
Other Operating Expenses	235
Total Operating Expenses	$295
Net Income	$125

REQUIRED

a. Prepare the common-size balance sheet and income statement.

b. Compute all 27 financial ratios.

15-43   RATIO ANALYSIS Buckmaster Manufacturing issues the following statements at its year-end. There are 100 common shares outstanding valued at $12 each and receiving $0.50 dividends each.

CO 4, 5

Buckmaster Manufacturing
Balance Sheet
December 31, 19X1

Assets

Cash	$ 100
Accounts Receivable (beginning balance $350)	300
Inventory (beginning balance $250)	300
Current Assets	$ 700
Long-term Assets	2,300
Total Assets	$3,000

Liabilities and Stockholders' Equity

Current Debts (beginning balance $300)	$ 400
Long-term Debts	1,600
Stockholders' Equity	1,000
Total Liabilities and Stockholders' Equity	$3,000

Buckmaster Manufacturing
Income Statement
For the Year Ended December 31, 19X1

Sales	$1,800
Cost of Goods Sold	1,000
Gross Margin	$ 800
Depreciation	$ 100
Other Operating Expenses	350
Total Operating Expenses	$ 450
Income before Extraordinary Item	$ 350
Extraordinary Hurricane Loss	50
Net Income	$ 300

REQUIRED

a. Prepare the common-size balance sheet and income statement for the dates shown.

b. Compute all 27 financial ratios.

15-44 RATIO ANALYSIS Following are the financial statements of Maher Systems at year-end. Its common stock is selling for $24.50 per share. Cash flows from operations are $95,000. Preferred stockholders receive $12 dividends per share; common stockholders receive $2 per share.

CO 4, 5

Maher Systems
Income Statement
For the Year Ended December 31, 19X2

Sales	$600,000
Cost of Goods Sold	250,000
Gross Margin	$350,000

(continued)

Wages and Salaries	$ 80,000
Rent	50,000
Utilities	12,000
Interest	11,000
Depreciation	9,500
Miscellaneous	4,000
Operating Expenses	$166,500
Income before Taxes	$183,500
Taxes	41,000
Income before Extraordinary Items	$142,500
Extraordinary Tornado Loss	20,250
Net Income	$122,250

Maher Systems
Balance Sheet
December 31, 19X2

ASSETS

Current Assets

Cash		$ 60,000
Receivables (beginning, $100,000)		90,000
Inventory (beginning, $90,000)		150,000
Prepaid Expenses		65,000
Total Current Assets		$365,000

Long-term Assets

Equipment	$500,000	
Less: Accumulated Depreciation	65,000	$435,000
Land		130,000
Total Long-term Assets		$565,000
Total Assets		$930,000

LIABILITIES AND STOCKHOLDERS' EQUITY

Current Liabilities

Accounts Payable	$200,000
Taxes Payable	15,000
Total Current Liabilities	$215,000

Long-term Liabilities

Bonds Payable	$100,000
Mortgage Payable	200,000
Long-term Liabilities	$300,000
Total Liabilities	$515,000

(continued)

Stockholders' Equity

Preferred Stock (1,000 shares)	$100,000
Common Stock (10,000 shares)	100,000
Retained Earnings	215,000
Total Stockholders' Equity	$415,000
Total Liabilities and Stockholders' Equity	$930,000

REQUIRED

Compute the 27 ratios for Maher Systems from the preceding statements.

15-45 RATIO ANALYSIS Killough, Inc., has issued the following balance sheet and income statement at its fiscal year-end. Its common stock is selling for $58 per share at this date. Cash from operating activities is $220,000.

CO 4, 5

Killough, Inc.
Income Statement
For the Year Ended March 31, 19X1

Sales	$1,000,000
Cost of Goods Sold	325,000
Gross Margin	$ 675,000
Wages and salaries	$ 200,000
Rent	60,000
Utilities	22,000
Interest	21,000
Depreciation	16,000
Miscellaneous	9,000
Operating Expenses	$ 328,000
Income before Taxes	$ 347,000
Taxes	102,000
Income before Extraordinary Loss	$ 245,000
Extraordinary Loss	30,000
Net Income	$ 215,000

Killough, Inc.
Balance Sheet
March 31, 19X1
ASSETS

Current Assets

Cash	$125,000
Marketable Securities	30,000
Receivables (beginning, $80,000)	100,000
Inventory (beginning, $31,000)	32,000
Prepaid Expenses	40,000
Total Current Assets	$327,000

(continued)

Long-term Assets

Land		$250,000
Equipment	$600,000	
Less: Accumulated Depreciation	205,000	395,000
Total Long-term Assets		$645,000
Total Assets		$972,000

LIABILITIES AND STOCKHOLDERS' EQUITY

Current Liabilities

Accounts Payable	$ 20,000
Notes Payable	45,000
Taxes Payable	12,000
Total Current Liabilities	$ 77,000

Long-term Liabilities

Bonds Payable	$255,000
Total Liabilities	$332,000

Stockholders' Equity

Preferred Stock (10,000 shares; dividends are $2 per share)	$100,000
Common Stock (10,000 shares; dividends are $2.50 per share)	200,000
Retained Earnings	340,000
Stockholders' Equity	$640,000
Total Liabilities and Stockholders' Equity	$972,000

REQUIRED

Compute the 27 ratios for Killough, Inc., from the preceding statements.

15-46   LEVERAGE EFFECTS Managers at Brown & Richardson Company are involved in yearly corporate planning. They anticipate total capital to be $1,000,000 and are trying to determine what the capital structure should be. They ask you to show them the effects of leverage. Interest rates are expected to be 15%. Stock is sold at $100 per share. The tax rate is 30%.

CO 5, 6

REQUIRED

Show the leverage effects for debt/total assets of 0%, 25%, 50%, and 75%. Assume that earnings are $50,000, $100,000, $150,000, and $200,000.

15-47   RATIO ANALYSIS Following are 10 transactions:

CO 5

a. Sell goods for cash.
b. Sell goods on credit.
c. Purchase inventory for cash.
d. Purchase inventory on account.
e. Declare and issue a cash dividend to common stockholders.
f. Issue common stock.

g. Issue bonds payable.
h. Buy equipment with cash.
i. Sell equipment at a gain.
j. Sell equipment at a loss.

REQUIRED

For each transaction, note the effect on each of the 27 financial ratios. Note whether the ratio increases (I), decreases (D), stays the same (S), or it cannot be determined what the effect is (unknown = U).

CO 3

15-48 COMMON-SIZE ANALYSIS The common-size balance sheet and income statement are displayed below for Beams, Inc. Earnings per share equal $3. There is no preferred stock, and common stock has a par value of $4 per share. One hundred shares are outstanding.

Beams, Inc.
Common-size Income Statement
For the Year Ended April 30, 19X2

Sales	99.8%
Interest Revenue	0.2
Total Revenue	100.0%
Wages	40.0
Utilities	24.0
Depreciation	12.0
Taxes	8.0
Miscellaneous	4.0
Total Expenses	88.0%
Net Income	12.0%

Beams, Inc.
Common-size Balance Sheet
April 30, 19X2
ASSETS

Current Assets

Cash		0.50%
Marketable Securities		1.00
Accounts Receivable		1.50
Inventory		2.00
Prepaid Expenses		2.50
Total Current Assets		7.50%

Long-term Assets

Land		50.00
Equipment	50.00%	
Less: Accumulated Depreciation	26.25	23.75
Building	95.00	
Less: Accumulated Depreciation	76.25	18.75
Total Long-term Assets		92.50%
Total Assets		100.00%

(continued)

LIABILITIES AND STOCKHOLDERS' EQUITY

Current Liabilities

Accounts Payable	.75%
Notes Payable	1.25
Total Current Liabilities	2.00%

Long-term Liabilities

Mortgage Payable	38.00%
Total Liabilities	40.00%

Stockholders' Equity

Common Stock	20.00
Retained Earnings	40.00
Stockholders' Equity	60.00%
Total Liabilities and Stockholders' Equity	100.00%

REQUIRED

Prepare the balance sheet and the income statement for Beams, Inc., for the above dates.

CO 5   15-49 **RATIO ANALYSIS** Cranor Company has the following values for selected ratios for 19X1.

Return on total assets	.08	Current assets to total assets	.20
Return on sales	.20	Long-term assets to total assets	.80
Return on equity	.10	Current debts to total debts	.40
Earnings per share	$ 2.00	Long-term debts to total debts	.60
Cash flow to total assets	.06	Accounts receivable turnover	20.00
Cash flow to sales	.15	Collection period	18.25
Cash flow to equity	.075	Inventory turnover	8.00
Cash to current debts	.25	Days to sell inventory	45.625
Cash to total debts	.10	Length of operating cycle	63.875
Cash to sales	.05	Dividend yield	.20
Current ratio	2.50	Dividend payout	.50
Quick ratio	1.50	Price to earnings	2.50
Debt to assets	.20	Earnings yield	.40
Debt to equity	.25		

This is the first year of operations for Cranor Company. The common stock is selling at $5 each. Cash flows from operations equals $150. Gross margin is 60% of sales.

REQUIRED

Prepare the balance sheet and the income statement for Cranor Company as of the year ending December 31, 19X1.

Business Decision Case

Several agencies rate the bonds issued by corporations. Two well-known agencies are Moody's and Standard and Poor's. These agencies rate the bonds on the basis of the probability that the issuer will default. In other words, they rate the bonds on the likelihood of the corporation's ability to make the interest payments and to repay the principal.

Standard and Poor's gives a rating of AAA to the bonds with the lowest default risk. AA is considered very good, A is upper-medium quality, and BBB is medium-grade quality. BB and B bonds are considered speculative. CCC and CC bonds are considered highly speculative. C, DDD, DD, and D bonds are the issues with interest not regularly paid or bonds in default.

Horrigan built a model to predict a corporation's bond rating.[3] The model is:

$$Z = 1.197X_1 + .034X_2 + .272X_3 - .501X_4 + 4.519X_5 - .203X_6$$

where

$$X_1 = 0 \text{ if bond is subordinated; 1 otherwise}$$
$$X_2 = \text{total assets}$$
$$X_3 = \text{stockholders' equity/total debts}$$
$$X_4 = \text{working capital/sales}$$
$$X_5 = \text{operating income/sales}$$
$$X_6 = \text{sales/stockholders' equity}$$

The financial ratios, however, are divided by the industry averages before using the model. Thus, X_2 through X_6 are computed as the company's ratio value divided by the industry ratio average. The Z-score would then be used to predict the bond rating as follows:

Interval	Predicted Bond Rating
$2.855 < Z$	AAA
$2.094 < Z < 2.855$	AA
$1.602 < Z < 2.094$	A
$0.838 < Z < 1.602$	BBB
$0.360 < Z < 0.838$	BB
$Z < 0.360$	B or lower

REQUIRED

a. Using data from Charitou Cargo, Inc., predict its bond rating. Assume the bonds are not subordinated. The industry averages are:

$$X_2: \$5,000,000$$
$$X_3: 0.712$$
$$X_4: 0.455$$
$$X_5: 0.105$$
$$X_6: 1.319$$

b. State whether these results can be reconciled with those in Discussion Question 15-24.

c. Describe the advantage of dividing ratios by industry averages.

[3]Horrigan, J., "The Determination of Long-Term Credit Standing with Financial Ratios." *Journal of Accounting Research* (Supplement, 1966): 44–62.

16

Impact of Changing Prices on Management Accounting

CHAPTER OBJECTIVES

After reading Chapter 16, you should be able to:

1. Differentiate between general and specific price-level changes and define and contrast entry and exit values (pp. 575–77).

2. Prepare price-level-adjusted financial statements (pp. 577–84).

3. Understand the management of financial assets and liabilities, including the effect of purchasing power gains and losses (pp. 584–85).

4. Explain how to manage productive assets such as inventory and property, plant, and equipment (pp. 585–86).

5. Show the impact of changing prices on standard costing, breakeven analysis, cash budgeting, and capital budgeting (pp. 586–91).

6. Discuss decision support systems and describe the behavioral aspects of managing in a world of changing prices (pp. 591–92).

Costs, selling prices, and values are not static; they are always changing. Managers must be aware of these changing prices and of the impact that they have on the corporation and the accounting information. Changing prices affect the management of financial assets and liabilities and influence the management of productive assets. They change the way in which managers apply such techniques as breakeven analysis, cash budgeting, standard costing, and capital budgeting. Managers and management accountants should know the effects of changing prices and must be able to incorporate them in the planning and control aspects of their jobs.

This chapter describes how changing prices affect management accounting and how managers can adjust their tools and concepts so that the accounting information can remain useful even in an environment of changing prices.

GENERAL AND SPECIFIC PRICE LEVELS

CHAPTER
OBJECTIVE 1
*General vs. specific
price-level changes*

Prices of goods and services change for a variety of reasons, but these reasons can be reduced to two types. Prices might change because of declines or increases in the value of the dollar, or because of commodity-specific reasons such as shifts in the demand or supply curve of the good or service. Accounting makes a distinction between these two basic causes. We will refer to price changes due to fluctuations in the value of the dollar as **general price-level changes.** These changes affect all the economic resources of a society. We will refer to price changes due to the economic resource itself as **specific price-level changes.** These changes are caused by changes in the supply and demand of the specific good or service. Sometimes both general and specific price-level changes are called inflation, but strictly speaking *inflation* refers only to the change in the value of the dollar or a general price-level change. Further, we often will use the term "inflation" to mean rising prices and "deflation" to mean falling prices.

Historical cost accounting enumerates the assets of the firm at their original cost less any accumulated depreciation (or depletion or amortization). Land bought 20 years ago would still be presented on the balance sheet at the cost of the land when it was purchased. Costs incurred by the firm are determined and matched either with the revenues they are associated with (*product matching*) or with the period in which they occur (*period matching*). Costs that are carried forward on the balance sheet are not adjusted for subsequent changes in value. Advocates of historical cost accounting defend it on the basis that: (1) it logically matches costs with their associated revenues; (2) it maintains the integrity of a cost system; (3) it follows an events approach, in which the financial reports highlight actual events involving the entity rather than hypothetical events; (4) managers cannot easily distort earnings under historical cost accounting; (5) it is relatively more objective than the other alternatives; and (6) it is cost effective.

CHAPTER
OBJECTIVE 1
Entry vs. exit values

Current value accounting, on the other hand, shows the assets at their market value as of the balance sheet date. In this scheme, land bought 20 years ago would be displayed on the balance sheet with its market value today. Notice that current value accounting deals primarily with specific price-level changes.

Current value accounting actually has two major alternatives. They are distinguished from each other in that one emphasizes input prices and the other output prices. The first type is referred to as **current entry value accounting,** or *current cost*

MANAGING IN A HIGHLY INFLATIONARY ENVIRONMENT

This article, although clearly written before the recent rise in oil prices, is a useful look at how management must work within an inflationary environment.

Inflation has been less of an issue for U.S. corporations at home, but it is a continuing problem in planning, managing, and measuring their businesses in other countries. U.S. and other multinational companies continue to invest in hyperinflationary countries, sometimes profitably, but in many cases without the tools necessary to earn real money commensurate with the risk involved.

Because the inflation problem seems to have "gone away" here at home, however, executives may be less motivated to recognize its importance, particularly when setting targets for managers and when trying to track results against such targets. Techniques designed for a noninflationary environment just do not work. Management must recognize inflation and plan and measure its entities differently when they are located in high inflationary economies.

There are several key characteristics of successful operations in a hyperinflationary environment that management needs to understand and address. For example:

● Operating decisions have larger financial implications. Receivables, inventories, and monetary assets have significant impact on results because of the higher cost of money and inflationary losses.

● These inflationary losses are not reflected in "reported results" but have a direct impact on cash flows.

● Economic conditions are subject to significant fluctuations to which the company must react quickly.

There are three fundamental requirements that must be met in order to implement an effective measurement system in an inflationary environment.

1. *Understanding how inflation impacts the business.* This understanding would start with an assessment of how the unique characteristics of the company are impacted by inflation (examples might include material sourcing, labor, sales, distribution, seasonality, geography, and the like), and how operating decisions affect "real profits" and cash flows.

2. *Obtaining top managements' commitment and conviction.* Management must be convinced that inflation should be treated as a real factor in performance measurement, incentive compensation, and overall portfolio evaluation. Without such top management support, use of information may not go beyond the controller's organization.

3. *Being able to match responsibility with the ability to control results.* The measurement system must be able to identify and track the impact that inflation has on those elements of the P&L statement, balance sheet, and cash flows influenced by local operating management separately from those elements influenced by financial management.

SOURCE: Adapted from Edward H. Schwallie and Alonso Martinez, "Managing in a High Inflationary Environment," *Management Accounting* (October 1987), pp. 21–24. Adapted by permission.

accounting or *replacement cost accounting.* (Although some authors make a distinction among these terms, for our purposes we will assume that they are synonymous and will use the first term for the sake of consistency.) The second type is called *current exit value accounting,* to be discussed shortly.

The distinguishing feature of current entry value accounting is that assets are valued at the balance sheet date at their current input prices—that is, at the price to *make or buy* the asset today. (Keep in mind that historical or original cost was the current input price on the date of acquisition.) Income under this proposal is essentially computed as sales less the current cost of providing sales. The differences between current entry values and original costs are called *holding gains and losses*. Some advocates think holding gains and losses enter the calculation of earnings; others advocate reporting them as direct adjustments of stockholders' equity. Proponents defend current entry value accounting because (1) it approximates economic earnings, (2) it accounts for specific price-level changes, (3) it may be more relevant for decision making, (4) it separates operating profits from holding gains, and (5) it recognizes the gains of the enterprises as they occur.

Under **current exit value accounting**, all assets are reported in the balance sheet at their current output price, the amount for which they can be *sold*. Income is equal to the difference between the selling price of the asset at the date of sale if sold during the period, or at the balance sheet date if not sold, and the selling price of the asset at the date of acquisition if acquired during the period or at the previous balance sheet date if acquired earlier. The advantages of current exit value accounting, according to its proponents, are that (1) it allows a user to know what cash would be obtained if an asset were sold, (2) it avoids arbitrary depreciation methods, (3) it recognizes the gains of the enterprise as they accrue, and (4) it may be more relevant for decision-making.

Constant-dollar accounting or general price-level accounting adjusts the assets' value for inflation. It is therefore fundamentally related to general price-level changes. Such adjustments could be applied either to historical cost accounting or to current value accounting. These are frequently referred to as *price-level-adjusted historical cost accounting* and *price-level-adjusted current value accounting*. The major advantage of constant-dollar accounting is that it puts all accounts into dollars of the same purchasing power.

FINANCIAL STATEMENTS UNDER VARIOUS ACCOUNTING ALTERNATIVES

CHAPTER OBJECTIVE 2
Price-level-adjusted financial statements

This section contains a comprehensive example to illustrate the alternatives defined in the previous section. As described above, there are three major methods of accounting and financial reporting for price changes: historical cost, current entry value, and current exit value. For the following example, the financial statements are prepared under each of these three methods. The statements are the balance sheet, the income statement, and the statement of cash flows. The statement of cash flows is the same under the three alternatives, so it will be shown only once.

The example actually consists of two parts. The first will assume no inflation, and the second does have some general price-level changes. We do this to emphasize that the two current value methods pertain to specific price-level changes and to show how to fuse general price-level adjustments to the three accounting alternatives.

Example of Alternatives with No Inflation

Assume Stalwart Company started operations with $20,000 cash on January 1, 19X1. On that date it acquired for cash 600 units of inventory for $15 each and a building costing $10,000 with an expected life of 10 years and no salvage value. Assume straight-line depreciation. The firm sells 300 units during the period at $20 each. At mid-year the current entry, or wholesale, value of each unit is $21. On December 31,

19X1, the current entry value of the inventory is $22 per unit while the current exit value is $26 per unit. On the same date, the current entry value of the building is $12,000 and the current exit value is $9,500. Assume no inflation.

Statement of Cash Flows.   The only items of relevance to the statement of cash flows are the actual cash flows of the firm, primarily the determination of cash flows from operating activities. For this example, the only operating flows are sales and the purchase of inventory:

Cash Flows from Operating Activities	
Cash Generated by Sales (300 × $20)	$ 6,000
Cash Expended for Inventory (600 × $15)	(9,000)
Net Cash Used by Operating Activities	$(3,000)

The entire statement of cash flows would appear as follows in condensed form:

Cash Flows from Operating Activities	$(3,000)
Cash Flows from Investing Activities:	
Acquisition of Building	(10,000)
Cash Flows from Financing Activities:	
Cash from Stockholders	20,000
Net Increase in Cash	$ 7,000

The final number, of course, agrees with the net change in cash—that is, the final balance of cash—$7,000 less the $0 initial balance of cash (remember, this is a new company).

Historical Cost Accounting.   The income statement consists of the revenue less the cost of sales and depreciation:

Sales		$6,000
Cost of sales (300 × $15)	$4,500	
Depreciation ($10,000/10)	1,000	5,500
Net Income		$ 500

The balance sheet consists of the assets at their original cost, modified by any accumulated depreciation:

Assets	
Cash	$ 7,000
Inventory (300 × $15)	4,500
Building ($10,000 − $1,000)	9,000
Total Assets	$20,500

Stockholders' Equity	
Invested Capital	$20,000
Retained Earnings	500
Total Stockholders' Equity	$20,500

Current Entry Value Accounting.   The income statement also consists of revenue less the cost of sales and depreciation. In this case, however, the cost of sales is based on the current entry value of the inventory. It is equal to the 300 units sold times the $21 current entry value when the units were sold. Similarly, depreciation is computed on the current entry value of the building: $12,000/10, or $1,200. The income from operations is calculated in this manner:

Sales		$ 6,000
Cost of sales (300 × $21)	$6,300	
Depreciation ($12,000/10)	1,200	7,500
Income from operations		$(1,500)

Also to consider are the **holding gains** on inventory and property, plant, and equipment. The **realized holding gain** on the inventory is the amount due to the units sold. It is 300 × ($21 − $15), or $1,800. Note that we are using the current entry value of $21 on the date the inventory was sold. In general, the current entry value on the date sold is different from the current entry value at the end of the period. The **unrealized holding gain** on the inventory is the amount due to the units still in inventory (those that are not yet sold). It is 300 × ($22 − $15), or $2,100. The **realizable holding gain** on the inventory is the sum of the realized holding gain, $1,800, and the unrealized holding gain, $2,100. We thus obtain $3,900.

The realizable holding gain on the building is the difference between the current entry value of the building and its acquisition cost, $2,000 ($12,000 − $10,000). The realized holding gain on the building is the amount of the realizable holding gain recognized through the depreciation process. It is equal to $2,000/10, or $200. The unrealized holding gain on the building is the remaining portion, $1,800 ($2,000 − $200). It is also equal to the amount of the excess depreciation per year multiplied by the number of remaining years. Thus, it is $200 × 9, or $1,800.

Note that current entry value income from operations plus the realized holding gain is equal to historical cost net income [($1,500) + $1,800 + $200 = $500]. This will always be true. It pinpoints the essential differences between historical cost accounting and current entry value accounting. First, historical cost accounting admits realized holding gains into income whereas current entry value accounting admits both realized and unrealized holding gains. (A number of advocates of current entry value claim that holding gains should be handled in other ways. These debates are beyond the scope of this text.) The income statement is therefore as follows:

Sales		$ 6,000
Cost of Sales	$6,300	
Depreciation	1,200	7,500
Income from Operations		$(1,500)
Holding Gains:		
From Inventory	$3,900	
From Building	2,000	5,900
Earned Income		$ 4,400

A second difference between the two is that current entry value accounting separates operating activities from holding gains whereas historical cost accounting intermingles them. Proponents of current entry value accounting claim this is an advantage because managers are responsible for the income from operations, but they cannot control (and thus should not be given credit for) holding gains, nor should they be held responsible for holding losses. This is consistent with our discussions of responsibility accounting in Chapters 1 and 12.

The balance sheet states the assets at their current entry value less any amortization:

Assets

Cash	$ 7,000
Inventory (300 × $22)	6,600
Building ($12,000 − $1,200)	10,800
Total Assets	$24,400

Stockholders' Equity

Invested Capital	$20,000
Retained Earnings	4,400
Total Stockholders' Equity	$24,400

Current Exit Value Accounting. The income statement consists of the increments in current exit value of the various assets. There are three items to include: (1) the gain from the inventory sold during the period, (2) the gain from the ending inventory, and (3) the gain from the building. The income statement is thus:

Gain from Sold Inventory	
[300 × ($20 − $15)]	$1,500
Gain from Unsold Inventory	
[300 × ($26 − $15)]	3,300
Loss from Building	
($10,000 − $9,500)	(500)
Net Income	$4,300

The balance sheet, as follows, lists the assets at their current exit value. Note that there is no depreciation, so there is no accumulated depreciation.

Assets

Cash	$ 7,000
Inventory (300 × $26)	7,800
Building	9,500
Total Assets	$24,300

Stockholders' Equity

Invested Capital	$20,000
Retained Earnings	4,300
Total Stockholders' Equity	$24,300

Example of Alternatives with Inflation

If inflation exists, all three of the accounting alternatives would be adjusted. The essential differences among the choices are illustrated in the previous example. There are no new conceptual differences to present in this section. The set of illustrations that follow have the more modest goal of showing how each of the accounting methods can be adjusted for general price-level changes.

Assume the same facts for Stalwart Company as in the previous section, except that there is inflation, as reflected in the Consumer Price Index (CPI) issued by the U.S. government. The Consumer Price Index was 100 for January 1, 19X1, 105 for June 30, 19X1, and 110 for December 31, 19X1. Thus, there is 10% (110/100 − 1) inflation during the year.

Purchasing power gains and losses, also called *monetary gains and losses,* must be calculated for all three methods. These are the gains and losses that arise from holding monetary debts and monetary assets during inflationary times. Monetary items are accounts stated in fixed dollar amounts regardless of the inflation rate. For example, cash, accounts and notes receivable, and investments in bonds are monetary items. Nonmonetary items are accounts that are not monetary, such as inventory, land, buildings, and common stock. A monetary gain arises from holding monetary debts during a period of inflation, because the fixed debts are paid off with dollars of less value than those dollars initially borrowed. In like manner, a monetary loss arises from holding monetary assets during a period of inflation, because they have less purchasing power than they had before. During a period of deflation, the reverse holds true.

For this example, cash is the only monetary item. The monetary loss for holding cash during the period is $386. It is computed as follows. On the first day of the year, Stalwart Company obtains $20,000 cash and expends $19,000 for inventory and a building. The remaining $1,000 is held for the year. The loss for holding this $1,000 is equal to ($1,000 × 110/100 − $1,000), or $100. The other cash flow is from sales. We assume that sales occur evenly during the year so we will "average" the flows as occurring at the midpoint of the year. The loss from holding this cash is thus only a half-year's loss equal to ($6,000 × 110/105 − $6,000), or $286. The total monetary loss is $386 ($100 + $286). Note that the index used in the denominator is the one on the date the cash flow occurs. Also notice that the adjustment puts the accounts into December 31, 19X1, dollars (because the numerator index is 110).

Statement of Cash Flows.   We recompute the calculations of the cash flows so that they are all measured in December 31, 19X1, dollars. Cash flows from operating activities is obtained in this way:

Cash Flows from Operating Activities

Cash Generated by Sales (300 × $20 × 110/105)	$ 6,286
Cash Expended for Inventory (600 × $15 × 110/100)	(9,900)
Net Cash Used by Operating Activities	$(3,614)

Again notice that the index numbers are chosen to correspond to the general price level on the appropriate date. The index 110 is in the numerator to restate the numbers to year-end dollars; the index 100 is in the denominator when the original dollars are stated in January 1, 19X1, dollars; and index 105 is in the denominator when the dollars are stated in average-year (mid-year) dollars. The statement of cash flows would appear as follows in condensed form:

Cash Flows from Operating Activities	$ (3,614)
Cash Flows from Investing Activities:	
Acquisition of Building ($10,000 × 110/100)	(11,000)
Cash Flows from Financing Activities:	
Cash from Stockholders ($20,000 × 110/100)	22,000
Monetary Loss	(386)
Net Increase in Cash	$ 7,000

Historical Cost Accounting.   Constant-dollar accounting adjusts the accounts into constant dollars. In other words, the accounts are measured in dollars of the same value whatever the period. Monetary items are already in constant dollars, so this additional conversion is unnecessary for them. In general, nonmonetary items are stated in historical dollars. We must adjust nonmonetary items to put them in the same purchasing-power units as the monetary items. The dollar value of the nonmonetary items is converted by the following formula:

$$\text{Constant-dollar Amount} = \text{Dated-dollar Amount} \times \frac{\text{Numerator Index}}{\text{Denominator Index}}$$

The *numerator index* is the CPI on the desired date of conversion. The *denominator index* is the CPI on the date the item was acquired or the transaction took place. These index numbers are prepared by the federal government. Essentially the government determines the price of various goods and services in the United States and obtains their average. This average is compared to the average price in some base year and the result is the general price-level index.

Continually occurring accounts, such as sales, are adjusted by averaging the sales over the period, such as using the half-year's inflation index. Cost of sales and depreciation are adjusted with denominator indexes on the dates that the assets were acquired. The adjusted historical cost income statement is:

Sales ($6,000 × 110/105)		$6,286	
Cost of Sales ($4,500 × 110/100)	$4,950		
Depreciation ($1,000 × 110/100)	1,100	6,050	$ 236
Monetary Loss			(386)
Net Income			$(150)

Monetary items are not adjusted for the balance sheet, given that their dollar amounts are fixed. The nonmonetary items are adjusted using indexes of the dates on which the items were obtained. The adjusted balance sheet for Stalwart Company would be as follows:

Assets

Cash	$ 7,000
Inventory ($4,500 × 110/100)	4,950
Building ($9,000 × 110/100)	9,900
Total Assets	$21,850

Stockholders' Equity

Invested Capital ($20,000 × 110/100)	$22,000
Retained Earnings	(150)
Total Stockholders' Equity	$21,850

Current Entry Value Accounting. The mechanics of handling inflation using current entry value accounting are similar to those for historical cost accounting, except that certain items are already stated in December 31, 19X1, dollars. No adjustment is made for depreciation because it is already stated in year-end dollars. Accordingly, the adjusted income statement is as follows:

Sales ($6,000 × 110/105)		$6,286	
Cost of Sales ($6,300 × 110/105)	$6,600		
Depreciation	1,200	7,800	$(1,514)
Monetary Loss			(386)
Loss from Operations			$(1,900)

The realized holding gain on the sold inventory is equal to [(300 × $21 × 110/105) − (300 × $15 × 110/100)], or $1,650. The unrealized holding gain on the unsold inventory is [(300 × $22 × 110/110) − (300 × $15 × 110/100)], or $1,650. Total holding gain on inventory is $1,650 + $1,650, or $3,300. The holding gain on the building is its $12,000 current entry value at December 31 minus the $11,000 historical cost adjusted to current dollars. It is $12,000 − ($10,000 × 110/100), or $1,000. The total holding gain is $4,300 ($3,300 + $1,000) and may be included in income. Net income becomes $2,400.

The balance sheet is as follows:

Assets

Cash	$ 7,000
Inventory	6,600
Building	10,800
Total Assets	$24,400

Stockholders' Equity

Invested Capital ($20,000 × 110/100)	$22,000
Retained Earnings	2,400
Total Stockholders' Equity	$24,400

Current Exit Value Accounting. The mechanics for current exit value accounting are very similar to those of the previous alternative. Therefore, we obtain the following income statement and balance sheet.

Gain from sold inventory
[(300 × $20 × 110/105) − (300 × $15 × 110/100)] $1,336
Gain from unsold inventory
[(300 × $26 × 110/110) − (300 × $15 × 110/100)]   2,850
Loss from building
[$9,500 − ($10,000 × 110/100)]   (1,500) $2,686
Monetary Loss   (386)
Net Income $2,300

Assets

Cash	$ 7,000
Inventory	7,800
Building	9,500
Total Assets	$24,300

Stockholders' Equity

Invested Capital ($20,000 × 110/100)	$22,000
Retained Earnings	2,300
Total Stockholders' Equity	$24,300

MANAGEMENT OF FINANCIAL ASSETS AND LIABILITIES

CHAPTER OBJECTIVE 3
Management of financial assets and liabilities

The previous discussion indicates how a manager can prepare financial statements to assess the effects of general or specific price-level changes. In the next two sections, two applications are introduced that use those adjusted numbers. In this section, the management of financial assets and liabilities is briefly described. The following section focuses on the management of productive assets.

A *financial asset* is an asset in which the firm invests in order (at least in part) to receive interest. This includes cash, receivables, and investments in bonds. A *financial liability* is a liability in which the firm receives cash and must repay it with interest. Most liabilities are financial in nature. Financial assets and liabilities tend to be fixed in their dollar amount and so are considered monetary items.

In a world without inflation, the interest rate is a function of a risk-free rate (such as for deposits insured by the federal government) and the riskiness of the borrower. Let us call this the real interest rate and denote it by r. If Company A lends $1,000 to Company B at an interest rate of 8% to be repaid in one year, the amount of interest is $80 (8% × $1,000) and the amount repaid is $1,080 ($1,000 + $80).

Let us change the example by assuming that inflation occurs at 5%. Then the purchasing power loss to Company A and the purchasing power gain to Company B is $50. The reason for this is that the $1,000 loan must grow at 5% per year just to maintain its same value in purchasing power. In other words, it must be valued at $1,050 in year-end dollars. Since money maintains its *nominal* (or face) value, it remains redeemable at $1,000. This situation leads to a loss for A and a gain for B. A useful way to show this fact is by netting the purchase power gain or loss against the interest:

Interest	$80
Less: Purchasing power gain or loss	50
Net interest	$30

But we have oversimplified the scenario in one very important respect. Lenders generally are aware of inflation and its detrimental consequences to their net interest. Lenders therefore raise the interest rates to adjust for the expected inflation rate. Denote the inflation rate with i and the **nominal interest rate** with n. Then the nominal rate of interest can be approximated by adding the real rate of interest and the inflation rate:

$$n = r + i$$

In the example of Companies A and B, if the lender expected a rate of inflation of 5%, then it would charge an interest rate of 13% (8% + 5%). The nominal interest would then be $130 ($1,000 × 13%). The purchasing power loss is still $50 and is computed in the same way. The net interest is now $80:

Interest	$130
Less: Purchasing power loss	50
Net interest	$ 80

In general, the purchasing power gain or loss is the financial market's adjustment for the expected impact of inflation on interest-bearing assets and debts.

One further complication can be mentioned. Suppose that the lender does not correctly predict the inflation rate. In our example, suppose the actual inflation rate is 6% instead of the anticipated 5%. The interest is still $130, but now the purchasing power loss is $60 ($1000 × 6%).

Interest	$130
Less: Purchasing power loss	60
Net interest	$ 70

The net interest is only $70. The lender has lost $10 because it has underestimated the future inflation.

Some financial managers break the problem into expected and unexpected components:

Interest	$130
Less: Purchasing power loss (expected)	50
Expected net interest	$ 80
Less: Purchasing power loss (unexpected)	10
Actual net interest	$ 70

Such an analysis helps financial managers set interest rates on loans and provides a basis on which to evaluate whether financial managers are obtaining suitable returns.

MANAGEMENT OF PRODUCTIVE ASSETS

CHAPTER OBJECTIVE 4
How to manage productive assets

When managing inventory and property, plant, and equipment in a period of price changes, the manager should know the present value of all remaining future cash flows (PV), the entry value (EV), and the exit value (XV). Historical cost is not considered very important for decision making because its valuation is generally out of date. There are a total of six possible relationships among these terms (ignoring equalities). These ordering combinations are:

1. $EV > PV > XV$ 4. $PV > XV > EV$
2. $EV > XV > PV$ 5. $XV > EV > PV$
3. $PV > EV > XV$ 6. $XV > PV > EV$

Decisions to Sell or Hold the Asset

Managers have basically two types of decisions for which these data can be useful. The first is whether the asset should be sold or whether it should be held for use by the firm. *The asset should be held if the present value exceeds the exit value,* because the organization gains greater value through using the asset. On the other hand, *the asset should be sold if the exit value is greater than the present value.* In that case, the firm maximizes its value by selling the asset and obtaining the proceeds. So situations 1, 3, and 4 imply that the corporation should hold the asset, whereas situations 2, 5, and 6 imply that it should sell the asset.

Situations 1, 3, and 4 are probably realistic scenarios for property, plant, and equipment, because the company gets more value from the productive use of these types of assets. Situations 2, 5, and 6 seem to be likely ones for inventory. In these situations, the firm makes or buys the inventory and then sells the items to its customers. This selling activity is the more profitable one only if the exit value is greater than the present value.

Decisions to Replace the Asset Once Sold or Used

Another decision is whether or not to replace an asset after it has been sold or used. That is, once the asset is used up, either by selling it or through productive use, should the firm get another one? Generally, *the asset should be replaced as long as either the present value or the exit value is greater than the entry value.* This scenario occurs in situations 3, 4, 5, and 6. The asset should not be replaced otherwise, because the asset costs more than the value it could provide.

We can combine these considerations as follows. For long-term assets, situations 3 and 4 tell the manager to replace the asset and to hold it for use. Situation 1 says to use the asset as long as it is useful but not to replace it. Situation 3 seems to be the most likely one for fixed assets used by the firm. For inventory, situations 5 and 6 indicate that the asset should be replaced and that it should be sold. Situation 2 says that the manager should sell the existing assets but should not replace them. If situation 2 occurs, management should look for other product lines to enter.

CHANGING PRICES AND STANDARD COSTING

CHAPTER OBJECTIVE 5
Changing prices and standard costing

The impact of changing prices is more pervasive than the analysis so far reflects. The rest of the chapter provides some additional examples and is consistent in its approach with that of the earlier part.

Recall from Chapters 7 and 8 that a *standard cost system* is one in which standard quantities and standard prices are set for a variety of costs, generally direct materials, direct labor, and overhead. A *variance analysis* consists of comparing the actual costs against the standard costs. In particular, the actual quantity multiplied by the actual price is compared to the standard quantity times the standard price.

In an environment with changing prices, the management team must be careful when setting standard prices. In essence, the standard price reflects management's expected inflation rate. This fact is not too critical for the quantity variances (materials quantity variance, labor efficiency variance, and variable overhead efficiency variance) because they depend primarily on the actual versus the standard use of inputs. Specifically, the quantity measures determine whether the variance is favorable or not. If the actual quantity of inputs is greater (less) than the standard quantity allowed for production, then the variance is unfavorable (favorable). The standard price will affect the measurement of the variance, but not whether it is plus or minus. (Note: we are assuming that the quantities are not affected by the prices. If they are, then the analysis should include these facts, but the analysis becomes very difficult.)

However, the expected inflation rate does affect the price variances (material price variance, labor rate variance, and variable overhead spending variance), which are fundamentally equal to the actual quantity of inputs times the difference between the actual and the standard input price. If the actual input price, the cost, exceeds (is less than) the standard input price, the standard cost, then the variance is unfavorable (favorable). A mistake in specifying the standard can affect whether the variance is favorable or not. Since changes in input prices are caused by inflation in the environment, the manager should not be held responsible for them. He or she has no control over inflationary factors. Accordingly, the manager should not be accountable for unexpected inflation.

Firms have two basic ways of handling this problem. First, they assume no price changes when setting the standard, or they set the standard based on the expected price change. In either case, it is best to adjust the standard for the price changes at the *end* of the period. It is important to make this adjustment only for externally related price changes, so that the difference between actual and standard prices can reflect the abilities of those being evaluated. A second way is not to make a formal adjustment of the standard for the price change, but to calculate the variances with the predetermined standards. The manager can then make informal adjustments when evaluating the workers.

CHANGING PRICES AND BREAKEVEN ANALYSIS

CHAPTER OBJECTIVE 5
Changing prices and breakeven analysis

As Chapter 3 explained, *breakeven analysis* is a managerial tool for assessing the number of units it takes to sell in order to achieve an income of zero. It is significant in that it helps to determine how achievable that number of sales is and indicates to some degree the risk of incurring a loss. Additional sales beyond the breakeven point add to income by the contribution margin, since fixed costs are already covered.

As discussed in Chapter 3, the formula for finding the breakeven point (in units) is:

$$\text{Breakeven} = \frac{FC}{SP - VC}$$

where

FC = fixed costs
SP = selling price per unit
VC = variable cost per unit

For example, if a widget has a selling price of $200 per unit, a variable cost of $150 per unit, and fixed costs of $50,000, then the breakeven point is 1,000 units.

What happens when price changes are introduced in breakeven analysis? Price changes can affect both fixed and variable costs. The two major questions in such analyses are whether the price changes affect the fixed and variable costs to the same degree and whether the cost increases can be passed on to the customer. The simplest case is when the price changes are the same for both types of costs and when the price increases can be passed on to the customer. Then the breakeven point is not affected. If the price increase is i, then we have:

$$\text{Breakeven} = \frac{\text{FC} \times (1 + i)}{[\text{SP} \times (1 + i)] - [\text{VC} \times (1 + i)]}$$

$$= \frac{\text{FC} \times (1 + i)}{(\text{SP} - \text{VC}) \times (1 + i)}$$

$$= \frac{\text{FC}}{\text{SP} - \text{VC}}$$

For example, we change the widget example just given by introducing a 10% price change. Fixed costs become $55,000, selling price per unit is $220, and variable cost per unit is $165. The breakeven point is still 1,000 units.

If the price effects are differential, then they are simply handled separately. Thus, we have the following formula:

$$\text{Breakeven} = \frac{\text{FC} \times (1 + i_{fc})}{[\text{SP} \times (1 + i_{sp})] - [\text{VC} \times (1 + i_{vc})]}$$

where

i_{fc} = price-level change of fixed costs
i_{sp} = price-level change in selling price per unit
i_{vc} = price-level change of variable cost per unit

For the widget example, assume that $i_{fc} = .10$, $i_{sp} = .08$, and $i_{vc} = .10$. Then the breakeven point is

$$\text{Breakeven} = \frac{50,000 \times (1 + .10)}{[200 \times (1 + .08)] - [150 \times (1 + .10)]}$$

$$= \frac{55,000}{216 - 165} = \underline{\underline{1,078}} \text{ units}$$

EXHIBIT 16-1

CASH BUDGET ADJUSTED FOR INFLATION

	0% Inflation	10% Inflation
Beginning cash	$ 10,000	$ 10,000
Receipts from customers	150,000	165,000
	$160,000	$175,000
Disbursements		
Direct materials	$ 30,000	$ 33,000
Direct labor	80,000	88,000
Overhead	20,000	22,000
Total disbursements	$130,000	$143,000
Ending cash	$ 30,000	$ 32,000

In this case, the inability to pass on fully the price increases requires an additional 78 units to be sold in order to reach the breakeven point.

CHANGING PRICES AND CASH BUDGETING

CHAPTER OBJECTIVE 5
Changing prices and cash budgeting

Cash budgets are prepared by corporations to help them plan for the future operations and activities. Cash budgets were explained in Chapter 5. It helps them project the cash receipts and disbursements and determine the need for financing or the opportunity to invest extra funds.

An example of an abbreviated cash budget is found in Exhibit 16-1. Under the column for 0% inflation are the various projected cash flows and balances. To the beginning cash balance of $10,000 is added the cash receipts of $150,000 and subtracted from that are the cash disbursements of $130,000. The ending cash balance is $30,000.

If price changes are expected, then the manager should adjust the cash flows for the price increase or decrease. Suppose that a 10% inflation is expected for the year. Then cash receipts become $165,000 and cash disbursement $143,000. Since beginning cash is still $10,000, these facts mean that the ending cash position is anticipated to be $32,000.

The management team should realize that the $32,000 balance at the end of the inflationary year is actually worse than the $30,000 balance at the end of the noninflationary year. To maintain purchasing power, the ending balance should have increased by at least $3,000 (10% of $30,000). The ending balance is $1,000 less. Why? The answer is simply that the original cash balance was not used in some sense to get a return that could match the effects of the price changes. Thus, there is a purchasing power loss of $1,000 (10% × $10,000). This fact accounts for the lack of keeping up. Managers should be aware that they must get a return from their beginning financial assets or balance them with financial liabilities.

Of course, the economy's price changes could affect various sectors differently. If so, the budget should simply use different adjustments for the different accounts.

CHANGING PRICES AND CAPITAL BUDGETING

Capital budgeting, discussed in Chapter 14, is the management activity of examining whether to accept or reject a project. There are a variety of tools by which to help managers to make this decision. This section focuses only on the net present value method. Recall that in the net present value method, the cash inflows are discounted at an appropriate cost of capital and then the investment is subtracted from it. If the net present value (NPV) is less than zero, reject the project; otherwise, accept it. A formula for this is:

$$NPV = (-\text{Cost}) + \frac{CF_1}{(1+c)} + \frac{CF_2}{(1+c)^2} + \frac{CF_3}{(1+c)^3} + \cdots$$

where

$$\text{Cost} = \text{the investment cost of the project}$$
$$CF_i = \text{cash inflow in year } i$$
$$c = \text{cost of capital}$$

Consider a project with cash flows of $4,000, $5,000, and $3,000 in years 1, 2, and 3, respectively. The project costs $9,000 and the cost of capital is 10%. Should management accept this project?

The answer is yes, as can be seen in the following arithmetic:

$$
\begin{aligned}
NPV &= -\$9,000 + \frac{\$4,000}{1.1} + \frac{\$5,000}{(1.1)^2} + \frac{\$3,000}{(1.1)^3} \\
&= -\$9,000 + \$3,636 + \$4,132 + \$2,254 \\
&= \underline{\$1,022}
\end{aligned}
$$

If present value tables are used, we obtain the same answer:

$$
\begin{aligned}
NPV &= -\$9,000 + \$4,000(.909) + \$5,000(.826) + \$3,000(.751) \\
&= \underline{\$1,022}
\end{aligned}
$$

Now we assume that price changes are added to the project budget. As in the problem for the previous breakeven, the answer is unaffected if inflation affects the cash flows and the cost of capital the same way. The cash flows would be adjusted for the inflation factor, but so would the discounting factor. Therefore, a particular term would look like this (for some time period t):

$$\frac{CF_t \times (1+i)^t}{(1+c)^t \times (1+i)^t} = \frac{CF_t}{(1+c)^t}$$

In other words, the impact of inflation cancels out and the net present value number is unchanged. As an illustration, assume an inflation of 4% per year in the preceding example. Then the cash flows become:

Year	Amount
1	$\$4,000 \times 1.04 = \$4,160$
2	$\$5,000 \times 1.04 \times 1.04 = \$5,408$
3	$\$3,000 \times 1.04 \times 1.04 \times 1.04 = \$3,375$

The cost of capital becomes 14.4%, shown as follows:

$$c = (1 + .10)(1 + .04) - 1 = .144$$

Then the inflation-adjusted net present value can be computed as follows:

$$
\begin{aligned}
\text{NPV} &= -\$9,000 + \frac{\$4,160}{1.144} + \frac{\$5,408}{(1.144)^2} + \frac{\$3,375}{(1.144)^3} \\
&= -\$9,000 + \$3,636 + \$4,132 + \$2,254 \\
&= \underline{\$1,022}
\end{aligned}
$$

Because inflation affects both cash flows (now $4,160, $5,408, and $3,375) and the cost of capital (now 14.4%), the impact of inflation cancels out and the net present value of $1,022 is the same as previously calculated without the inflation adjustment.

Inflation could affect the variables at different rates. Then the nice result above is no longer true. Each of the units—the cash flows and the cost of capital—would be adjusted separately. The formula for the net present value becomes:

$$\text{NPV} = -\text{Cost} + \frac{\text{CF}_1 \times (1 + i)}{(1 + c) \times (1 + k)} + \frac{\text{CF}_2 \times (1 + i)^2}{(1 + c)^2 \times (1 + k)^2} + \cdots$$

where

$$i = \text{price-level change on cash flows}$$
$$k = \text{price-level change on cost of capital}$$

To complicate things even more, one could view the price-level changes to be different in different years. This difficulty, however, is beyond the scope of this text.

DECISION SUPPORT SYSTEMS AND INFLATION

CHAPTER OBJECTIVE 6
DSS in a world of changing prices

It is clear by now that the firm must be able to anticipate an inflation rate and adjust its planning accordingly. This expected price change cannot be predicted accurately. Consistent with the decision support systems philosophy, the manager should perform what-if analysis and assess the effects of different inflation rates on the decisions ahead.

When preparing a cash budget, for example, the manager should try a variety of rates. This gives the decision maker realistic answers for several scenarios. More importantly, inflation-adjusted analyses pinpoint variables that are sensitive to the chosen rate. The manager then knows which costs need greater attention and perhaps additional fact finding.

For example, when doing breakeven analysis, the manager and the management accountant should ask, "What is the impact of changing prices on this analysis? What if inflation affects the fixed costs? What if inflation affects the selling price per unit? What if inflation affects the variable costs per unit?" These questions may be asked singly or jointly. On a computer the accountant could try various inflation rates to assess the impact of changing prices on the project under consideration. Similar processes may be carried out with other tools and techniques.

More importantly, the DSS philosophy and models permit an examination of many alternative scenarios. These multiple scenarios enable management to examine its goals, assumptions, and interpretations of results.

BEHAVIORAL ASPECTS OF MANAGING WITH INFLATION

CHAPTER OBJECTIVE 6
Behavioral aspects of changing prices

Managing the impact of inflation on the organization depends on two factors. First, management should include possible price changes in its *planning process*. Although certain decisions may not be greatly affected (such as capital budgeting, when the effects of price changes are the same on cash flows as on the cost of capital), other planning aspects are critically dependent on planning for the impact of inflation. Whether a corporation should use an asset or sell it and whether the firm should replace an asset depends on inclusion of these price-level effects in the analysis of the available choices. Therefore, management should not only be concerned about the impact of price changes on its decisions but also should place some department or group in charge of monitoring and evaluating these changes and then factoring them into the relevant proposals, decision support, and information system available. Usually the accounting or finance group performs these activities.

The second factor in managing the effects of inflation is the proper *evaluation* of managers. Management accounting principles indicate that managers should be accountable only for costs that they can control. Their responsibility should not extend to items they cannot control or influence, such as inflation. Evaluations should adjust for these price effects and remove them from the manager's responsibility. An illustration of this was discussed in the section on standard costing concerning input costs.

Demonstration Problem

John and Barbara First start a firm on January 1 with $50,000 cash. On that date they bought 10,000 units of inventory at $2 each. John and Barbara sell 9,000 units over the year for $10 each. At mid-year the current entry value is $2.50. At year-end the current entry value is $3 and the current exit value is $12. Assume no inflation.

REQUIRED
Prepare (a) a statement of cash flows, (b) a historical cost income statement, (c) a current entry value income statement, and (d) a current exit value income statement at the First's year-end.

SOLUTION TO DEMONSTRATION PROBLEM

a. The statement of cash flows is as follows:

Cash Flows from Operating Activities

Cash Generated from Sales (9,000 × $10)	$90,000	
Cash Expended for Inventory (10,000 × $2)	(20,000)	
Net Cash Generated by Operating Activities		$ 70,000

Cash Flows from Financing Activities

Owner's Investment		50,000
Net Increase in Cash		$120,000

b. The historical cost income statement is prepared in the following manner:

Sales	$90,000
Cost of Sales (9,000 × $2)	18,000
Net Income	$72,000

c. The current entry value income statement is prepared as follows:

Sales	$ 90,000
Cost of sales (9,000 × $2.50)	22,500
Income from Operations	$ 67,500
Holding Gain on Inventory [(9,000 × [$2.50 − $2]) + (1,000 × [$3 − $2])]	5,500
Net Income	$ 73,000

d. The current exit value income statement is presented as follows:

Gain from Sold Inventory [9,000 × ($10 − $2)]	$72,000
Gain from Unsold Inventory [1,000 × ($12 − $2)]	10,000
Net Income	$82,000

Review of Chapter Objectives

1. Differentiate between general and specific price-level changes and define and contrast entry and exit values (pp. 575–77).

   ■ Price changes due to fluctuations in the value of the dollar are called general price-level changes. Price changes due to the economic resource itself are called specific price-level changes.

   ■ Historical cost accounting lists the assets of the firm at their original cost less any accumulated depreciation. There is no adjustment for price changes. Specific price-level changes can be accounted for in two ways, both referred to as current value accounting. One is current entry value accounting, which values assets at their input prices. The other is current exit value accounting, which values assets at their output prices. The first values assets at how much a company will have to pay to obtain them, the second at for how much the company can sell them.

2. Prepare price-level-adjusted financial statements (pp. 577–84).

   ■ Constant dollar accounting or general price-level accounting adjusts the assets' value for the general price-level changes. These adjustments can be overlaid on any of the three major methods: historical cost, current entry value, and current exit value.

   ■ The purchasing power gain or loss is the gain or loss from holding monetary items during a period of inflation (that is, general price-level changes). This gain or loss is calculated for all three methods.

   ■ The student should pay careful attention to the financial statement preparation under all six methods. Look at the illustration, with and without inflation, and understand it thoroughly.

3. Understand the management of financial assets and liabilities, including the effect of purchasing power gains and losses (pp. 584–85).

   ■ In a world without inflation, the real interest rate is a function of a risk-free rate due to the time value of money and the riskiness of the borrower. In a world of inflation, however, an inflationary component is added to the interest rate. The nominal interest rate is equal to the real rate of interest plus the expected inflation rate.

4. Explain how to manage productive assets such as inventory and property, plant, and equipment (pp. 585–86).

   ■ Six possible combinations are possible among the three variables: entry value, exit value, and present value. The six possibilities are not equally likely, but they indicate the decision rules available in the management of productive assets.

   ■ An asset should be held if the present value exceeds the exit value, because the corporation gains greater value through the use of the asset. On the other hand, the asset should be sold if the exit value is greater than the present value.

   ■ Should an asset be replaced after it has been sold or used? This question may be answered by looking at the entry value. The asset should be replaced if either the present value or the exit value is greater than the entry value. Otherwise, the firm should not replace the asset.

5. Show the impact of changing prices on standard costing, breakeven analysis, cash budgeting, and capital budgeting (pp. 586–91).

   ■ Before this chapter, we implicitly assumed that inflation did not exist. The various tools of the management accountant were then developed. Now that we are admitting the influence of changing prices, the tools need to be reanalyzed to determine how to amend them so that the influence of changing prices is accounted for. The student should notice that sometimes no change needs to be made. This follows typically when one can assume that the prices of all items are changing in the same proportion. At other times, the formulas or algorithms must be modified to account for changing prices.

6. Discuss decision support systems and describe the behavioral aspects of managing a firm in a world of changing prices (pp. 591–92).

- In the real world, managers must ask what price changes will occur and what effects will they have on the organization. No one can predict the future, so a decision support systems approach is called for. For example, budgets might be prepared under a number of scenarios that make various assumptions about inflation and its effects on the firm.

- The behavioral issues dealing with inflation center on planning and evaluation. Proper planning necessitates the examination of the potential changing prices and then determining a course of action for the corporation. In terms of the evaluation process, managers do not cause inflation, thus they should not be held accountable for its effects. Managers are responsible for the items under their control, not for uncontrollable factors such as inflation.

Glossary of Key Terms

constant-dollar accounting   A set of adjustments to show the effects of general price-level changes. It can be applied to current entry value accounting, current exit value accounting, and historical cost accounting.

current entry value accounting   A system of accounting that assigns the assets on the balance sheet their current input prices—that is, the current price to make or buy the asset.

current exit value accounting   A system of accounting that assigns the assets on the balance sheet their current output prices—that is, the current price at which the asset can be sold.

general price-level changes   Changes in the value of an asset or liability stemming from changes in the value of the dollar.

historical cost accounting   A system of accounting that assigns the assets on the balance sheet their original cost less any accumulated depreciation.

holding gains (or losses)   The increase (or decrease) of the asset's current entry value over a period.

monetary items   Assets and liabilities that represent claims or obligations in fixed dollar amounts regardless of the inflation rate. Monetary items include cash, accounts receivable, accounts payable, and notes payable.

nominal interest rate   An interest rate that includes an expected inflation rate component. It is equal to the real interest rate plus the inflation rate.

purchasing power gain or loss   Gain (or loss) that arises from holding liabilities (or assets) during a period of inflation or that arise from holding assets (or liabilities) during a period of deflation. They arise because later cash flows are made with dollars of lesser value during a period of inflation or greater value during a period of deflation.

real interest rate   An interest rate that does not include an expected inflation rate component.

realizable holding gain   A holding gain due to the sale or use of an asset or to an unsold or unused asset. Thus, realizable holding gains are equal to realized holding gains plus unrealized holding gains.

realized holding gain   A holding gain due to the sale or use of an asset. Commonly, realized holding gains are attributable to sold units of inventory and to the current depreciable amount of long-term assets.

specific price-level changes   Changes in the value of an asset or liability due to the economic conditions of a specific resource or group of resources.

unrealized holding gain   A holding gain due to an unsold or unused asset. Commonly, unrealized holding gains are attributable to unsold units of inventory and to the undepreciated amount of long-term assets.

Review
Questions

16-1   What are general price-level changes? What causes them?

16-2   What are specific price level changes? What causes them?

16-3   Why is it important to distinguish between general and specific price-level changes?

16-4   Distinguish between historical cost accounting and current value accounting.

16-5   What are the two major types of current value accounting?

16-6   What are the arguments for historical cost accounting?

16-7   What are the arguments for current entry value accounting?

16-8   What are the arguments for current exit value accounting?

16-9   What is constant-dollar accounting? What are its advantages?

16-10   How is income from operations calculated under current entry value accounting?

16-11   What are holding gains?

16-12   Define realizable, unrealized, and realized holding gains. How are they related?

16-13   What is the advantage of separating operating income from holding gains?

16-14   Are holding gains part of income?

16-15   How are historical cost accounting and current entry value accounting related? What are their fundamental differences?

16-16   What is income under current exit value accounting?

16-17   What are monetary assets and liabilities? Give some examples.

16-18   What are purchasing power gains and losses?

16-19   Why is there a purchasing power gain from holding monetary debts during a period of inflation?

16-20   How are accounts adjusted in constant-dollar accounting?

16-21   What is a nominal rate of interest? A real rate of interest? How do these concepts help us interpret purchasing power gains and losses?

16-22   When should a productive asset be sold and when should it be held for use?

16-23   When should a productive asset be replaced?

16-24   How does inflation affect standard cost systems? Variance analysis?

16-25   When does inflation change the result of a breakeven analysis?

16-26   How does inflation affect cash budgets?

16-27   When does inflation change the net present value of a capital budgeting project?

16-28   In a decision support context how does management deal with inflation?

16-29   Inflation affects the planning and control aspects of management. How?

Discussion
Questions

16-30   One criticism of historical cost accounting is that it presents distorted numbers when there are price changes. Consider the following. Daley's, Inc., has sales of $1,000 in year 1 and labor expenses of $200. The only other expense is depreciation on an asset that cost $5,000, has a 10-year life, and has zero salvage value. The firm faces 10% inflation in years 2 and 3. Sales and labor expenses change from year 1 only in the amount of the inflationary pressure.

a. Prepare the historical cost income statements for years 1, 2, and 3.

b. Prepare the constant-dollar historical cost income statements for years 1, 2, and 3. Assume all cash is distributed as dividends so there is no purchasing power gain or loss.

c. Adjust the numbers in requirement b into year 3 year-end dollars.

d. Compare the numbers you get in requirements a and c. What do they tell you about the firm?

16-31 One advantage of current entry value accounting, according to proponents, is that it approximates economic earnings. *Economic earnings* are the cash flows plus the changes in the present values of the assets. For this approximation to work, however, current entry value accounting must use present value depreciation.

Present value depreciation is the year-to-year change in present value of the asset using the forecasted cash flows at the beginning of the asset's life. Changes in the forecasts are part of the holding gains.

Consider the following example. At year 0, Black Co. acquires an asset for $10,000. It has expected cash flows of $5,400 at year 1 and $5,832 at year 2. All cash flows occur at the end of the year. At year 1, however, the cash flow at year 2 is changed to $5,940. Actual cash flows are $5,400 and $5,940, respectively. The cost of capital is 8%.

a. What is the present value of the asset at years 0, 1, and 2?

b. What are the economic earnings in years 1 and 2?

c. What is the present value of the asset at year 1 using the original forecast of cash flows?

d. What is the present value depreciation in years 1 and 2?

e. What is the holding gain in years 1 and 2?

f. Prepare a current entry value income statement assuming holding gains are part of income.

16-32 Financial statement analysis can be performed with the various alternatives of accounting. Although the analysis and interpretation is beyond the scope of this book, it is still instructive to examine these ratios and compare them with the traditional ratios.

Compute the financial ratios for all six accounting alternatives using the Stalwart Company example presented in the chapter. Consider holding gains to be part of current entry value income. The ratios to calculate are: return on assets, equity, and sales; cash flow to assets, equity and sales; cash to assets, equity, and sales; current assets to total assets, and long-term assets to total assets.

16-33 The primary way for a creditor to lose from the impact of inflation is if there is unexpected inflation. This is true because creditors add the expected inflation into the interest rates they charge; creditors are still exposed to unexpected inflation. Specifically, if actual inflation is greater than anticipated, creditors lose since they did not add enough to the interest rate. On the other hand, they could gain if actual inflation is less than expected.

This exposure to unexpected inflation is sometimes called *inflation risk*. Creditors can reduce this risk by having monetary liabilities as well as monetary assets. Purchasing power gains on monetary debt offset any purchasing power losses on monetary assets. Structuring the assets and debts of the firm this way in order to reduce inflation risk is called *hedging*. A perfect hedge exists if monetary assets equal monetary liabilities.

Consider the following example. Perkins Company has beginning monetary assets of $100,000 and monetary liabilities of the same amount. Expected inflation is 0%. All inflows of monetary assets are immediately paid out in dividends. Now consider unexpected inflation of 4%, 8%, and 12%. What are the purchasing power gains or losses on debt? On assets? What is the net purchasing power gain or loss?

Exercises

16-34 CURRENT ENTRY VALUE Kelvin Corp. bought 1,000 units of inventory at the beginning of 19X1 at $10 each. It also bought a building for $100,000. The building has a life of 40 years and no salvage value. The firm sells 600 units at $40 when the entry value is $12 each. The entry value of the inventory is $15 per unit at the end of the year. The entry value of the building is $120,000 at year end.

CO 1, 2

Prepare the year-end income statement under current entry value accounting. Include holding gains.

16-35   CURRENT ENTRY VALUE Jackson Company bought 500 units of inventory at the beginning of 19X1 at $10 each. It also bought a building for $100,000. The firm sells 400 units at $40 when the entry value is $9. The entry value of the inventory is $8 per unit at the end of the year. The entry value of the building is $95,000. The building has a life of 20 years and no salvage value.

CO 1, 2

Prepare the income statement at year-end under current entry value accounting. Include holding gains.

16-36   CURRENT EXIT VALUE Ricky Jones and Company bought 1,000 units of inventory at the beginning of 19X1 at $10. It also bought a building for $100,000. The building has a life of 40 years and no salvage value. The firm sells 700 units at $30. The exit value of the inventory is $35 per unit at the end of the year and the exit value of the building is $110,000 at the end of the year.

CO 1, 2

Prepare the year-end income statement under current exit value accounting.

16-37   CURRENT EXIT VALUE Adam Wetzel and Company bought 1,000 units of inventory at the beginning of 19X1 at $10. It also bought a building for $100,000. The firm sells 600 units at $12 each. The exit value of the inventory is $9 per unit at the end of the year. The exit value of the building is $95,000 at the end of the year.

CO 1, 2

Prepare the year-end income statement under current exit value accounting.

16-38   PURCHASING POWER GAIN OR LOSS Christy and Associates had a cash balance of $100,000 at the beginning of 19X1. Operating cash flows for the period are $250,000. The general price level index is 100 at the beginning of the year; 104 at mid-year; and 109 at the end of the year.

CO 1, 2

Compute the purchasing power gain or loss for 19X1.

16-39   PURCHASING POWER GAIN OR LOSS Alexa and Suzanne Digging Company had monetary assets of $100,000 at the beginning of 19X1. Operating increases in the monetary assets for the year are $200,000. Monetary liabilities at the beginning of the year are $150,000. Operating increases in the monetary liabilities for the year are $200,000. The general price-level index is 100 at the beginning of the year; 104 at mid-year; and 109 at the end of the year.

CO 1, 2

Compute the purchasing power gain or loss for 19X1. (*Hint:* Net the monetary items.)

DATA FOR EXERCISES 16-40, 16-41, 16-42

For Exercises 16-40, 16-41, and 16-42, use the following general price-level indexes: 100 at the beginning of the year; 110 at mid-year; and 121 at the end of the year.

16-40   CONSTANT DOLLAR HISTORICAL COST Harveywebster, Inc., started operation with $10,000 at the beginning of 19X1. On that date the firm acquired 400 units of inventory at $20 each. During the year 300 units were sold at $50 each. Prepare the price-level-adjusted historical cost income statement for the year-end.

CO 1, 2

16-41   CONSTANT DOLLAR CURRENT ENTRY VALUE Use the data in Exercise 16-34 for Kelvin Corp. to obtain a price-level-adjusted current entry value income statement. Assume the firm began with $200,000 cash. Ignore holding gains.

CO 1, 2

16-42   CONSTANT DOLLAR CURRENT EXIT VALUE Use Exercise 16-36 for Ricky Jones and Company to obtain a price-level-adjusted current exit value income statement. Assume the firm began with $200,000 cash.

CO 1, 2

16-43 CURRENT ENTRY VALUE Hastings, Inc., is a merchandising firm. Its inventory transactions and events for 19X0 and 19X1 are as follows:

CO 1, 2

Date	Purchase	Sell	Current Entry Value
January 1, 19X0	500 @ $15		
June 30, 19X0		300 @ $50	$18
January 1, 19X1	600 @ $20		
June 30, 19X1		700 @ $60	$22
December 31, 19X1			$25

a. Compute the historical cost income for 19X0 and 19X1. Use the first-in, first-out (FIFO) method.

b. Compute current entry value income from operations for 19X0 and 19X1.

c. Compute realized and unrealized holding gains in 19X0 and 19X1.

d. For each year show that historical cost income equals current entry value income from operations plus realized holding gains.

16-44 CURRENT ENTRY VALUE The relationship between historical cost accounting and current entry value accounting also exists if both are general price-level adjusted. As an example of this, perform the price level adjustment for both income statements and the holding gains in Exercise 16-43. Use the following general price-level indexes:

CO 2

Date	Index
January 1, 19X0	100
June 30, 19X0	120
January 1, 19X1	144
June 30, 19X1	168
December 31, 19X1	216

Assume that the firm began with $10,000 cash.

16-45 REAL AND NORMAL INTEREST Thiel Bank charges 12% interest on one year loans of $10,000 if there is no inflation. What rate is charged if Thiel anticipates an inflation rate of 2%? 4%? 6%? Show why Thiel does not lose during inflationary times as long as it correctly forecasts inflation. How can a creditor lose during inflationary times?

CO 3

16-46 PRODUCTIVE ASSETS Blackledge, Inc., has several assets. Their entry values, exit values, and present values are as follows:

CO 4

Asset	Entry Value	Exit Value	Present Value
CP10	$ 1,000	$ 600	$ 500
CP20	40	50	35
CP30	4,800	4,000	5,000
CP40	90	100	95
CP50	10,000	7,000	9,000
CP60	35	40	50

What advice would you offer Blackledge concerning these productive assets?

16-47   **STANDARD COSTS** Strang and Associates has a standard cost card that reveals the following:

CO 5

Materials	(4 pieces of Xadox @ $100 per piece)	$400
Labor	(10 hours @ $25 per hour)	250
Variable overhead	(10 hours @ $15 per hour)	150
		$800

Suppose, however, that the corporate economist says that the costs will go up by 8%. Reset the standards.

16-48   **BREAKEVEN POINT** Shaffer, Inc., is considering the production of a new type of football. The fixed costs would be $2,000; the selling price, $25 per football; the variable cost, $20 per football.

CO 5

a. What is the breakeven point?

b. Suppose that all factors are affected by 12% price changes. What is the breakeven point?

16-49   **CASH BUDGETS** Knizer, Inc., produces the following cash budgets depending on the inflation rate.

CO 5

	0%	8%
Beginning cash	$ 25,000	$ 25,000
Cash from customers	200,000	216,000
	$225,000	$241,000
Cash disbursements	150,000	162,000
Ending cash	$ 75,000	$ 79,000

Is the firm better off with inflation?

16-50   **CAPITAL BUDGETING** Darrell Roberts, Inc., is considering a project having a cost of $8,000 and cash flows of $3,000, $4,000, and $3,000 in years 1, 2, and 3, respectively. The cost of capital is 15%.

CO 5

a. What is the net present value of the project? Should the firm accept or reject the project?

b. Suppose the inflation rate will be 5% for both the cash flows and the cost of capital. What is the net present value? Should the firm accept or reject the project?

Problems

16-51   **GENERAL AND SPECIFIC PRICE LEVELS** Michelle Frank starts a firm with $50,000 cash on January 1, 19X0. On that date she acquires for cash 1,000 units of inventory for $20 each and a building costing $25,000. The building has an expected life of 25 years and no

CO 2

salvage value. Frank uses straight-line depreciation. The firm sells 600 units during the period at $50 each. The current entry value of the inventory is $22 at mid-year and $25 at the end of the year. The exit value of the inventory is $60 at the end of the year. The building has an entry value of $30,000 and an exit value of $35,000 at the end of the year. The general price level index is 100 at the beginning of the year, 110 at mid-year, and 121 at the end of the year.

REQUIRED

Prepare the statement of cash flows, the income statement, and the balance sheet for Michelle Frank at December 31, 19X0, under:

a. Historical costing.

b. Current entry value.

c. Current exit value.

d. Price-level-adjusted historical cost.

e. Price-level-adjusted current entry value.

f. Price-level-adjusted current exit value accounting.

Assume that holding gains are part of current entry value net income.

Note: Prepare only two statements of cash flows, one for requirements a, b, and c, and one for requirements d, e, and f. Also, compute only one purchasing power gain or loss for requirements d, e, and f.

16-52 GENERAL AND SPECIFIC PRICE LEVELS Rose Wells starts a firm with $40,000 cash on January 1, 19X1. On that date she acquires for cash 1,000 units of inventory for $20 each and a building costing $10,000. The building has an expected life of 10 years and no salvage value. Use straight-line depreciation. The firm sells 800 units during the period at $40 each. The current entry value is $18 at mid-year and $16 at the end of the year. The exit value of the inventory is $35 at the end of the year. The building has an entry and exit value of $9,000 at the end of the year. The general price level index is 100 at the beginning of the year, 96 at mid-year, and 90 at the end of the year.

CO 2

REQUIRED

Prepare the cash flow statement, the income statement, and the balance sheet under the following:

a. Historical cost.

b. Current entry value.

c. Current exit value.

d. Price-level-adjusted historical cost.

e. Price-level-adjusted current entry value.

f. Price-level-adjusted current exit value accounting.

Assume that holding gains are part of current entry value net income.

Note: Prepare only two statements of cash flows, one for requirements a, b, and c, and one for requirements d, e, and f. Also compute only one purchasing power gain or loss for requirements d, e, and f.

16-53 PURCHASING POWER GAIN OR LOSS Tolkien and Associates requires your assistance in the computation of its purchasing power gain or loss. Records for Tolkien uncover the following events:

CO 2

Cash, beginning balance	$ 10,000
Accounts receivable, beginning balance	60,000
Notes payable, beginning balance	40,000
Sales on account, made evenly through year	400,000
Cash collections of receivables, occurring evenly through year	360,000
Cash expenses, paid evenly through year	275,000
Cash payment on notes payable, July 1	5,000

The general price-level indexes are 100 at the beginning of the year, 110 at mid-year, and 121 at the end of the year.

REQUIRED
Compute the purchasing power gain or loss. (*Hint:* Aggregate monetary items of the same time dimension.)

16-54   STANDARD COSTS David Hume and Sons has a standard cost card that reveals the following:

CO 2

Materials	(3 pieces @ $10 per piece)	$ 30
Labor	(5 hours @ $20 per hour)	100
Variable overhead	(3 hours @ $6 per hour)	18
		$148

Hume starts and completes 10,000 units during the month. At the end of the month the following data are obtained:

Actual material purchased and used	31,000 pieces
Actual material cost	$12 per piece
Actual labor hours	48,000 hours
Actual labor cost	$22 per hour
Actual variable overhead used	30,500 hours
Actual variable overhead cost	$6 per hour

REQUIRED
a. Compute the variances.

b. Suppose there is 10% inflation that affects materials, labor, and variable overhead. Reset the standards and revise the variance analysis.

16-55   BREAKEVEN POINT Hamilton, Inc., has plans to produce a new ice skating boot. It anticipates fixed costs of $60,000, selling price of $500 per pair of boots, and variable costs of $200 per pair. The company, however, is trying to plan for inflation. Fixed costs will be unaffected because they can be contractually set with a contractor.

CO 4

REQUIRED
a. Calculate the effect of 4%, 8%, 12%, and 16% price increases assuming that these increases can be passed on to the consumer.

b. Assess the impact if the selling price cannot be increased.

Compute the breakeven point under these various scenarios.

16-56 CASH BUDGETING Sam Malone is examining his cash budget for the next year. The cash budget unadjusted for price changes is:

CO 4

Beginning cash	$ 5,000
Cash from customers	200,000
	$205,000
Cash disbursements	175,000
Ending cash	$ 30,000

He thinks that cash from customers might be increased by 8%. Cash disbursement impact increases by 8% or 10%.

REQUIRED

Prepare cash budgets for Malone under the various combinations (including 0%).

Business Decision Case

Short & Co. is considering a project having a cost of $7,000 and cash flows of $3,000, $4,000, and $3,000 in years 1, 2, and 3, respectively. The cost of capital is 15%. Price increases are expected, however, of either 0%, 1%, 2%, 3%, 4%, or 5%. Unfortunately, the cash flows are not expected to increase because of these inflationary changes.

REQUIRED

a. Compute the net present value at 0%, 1%, 2%, 3%, 4%, and 5% inflation.

b. Determine the project's internal rate of return.

c. Explain how the internal rate of return can help in assessing the impact of inflation on the accept-reject decision of capital budgeting.

IMPACT OF TECHNOLOGY

Emerging Issues in Management Accounting

CHAPTER OBJECTIVES

After reading Chapter 17, you should be able to:

1. Describe the impact of structural changes on cost drivers and activity-based costing (pp. 607–608).

2. Define *flexible manufacturing systems* and *just-in-time production* (pp. 608–609).

3. Discuss the impact of flexible manufacturing systems and just-in-time production on cost accounting systems (pp. 609–612).

4. Explain the likely effects of changes in service industries, globalization, and Japanese management practices on management accounting (pp. 612–17).

5. Define *computer integrated manufacturing* and *manufacturing (or materials) resource planning* (pp. 617–18).

6. Describe office automation, expert systems, and executive information systems (pp. 618–21).

7. Explain how human behavior is affected by changes in the environment and in technologies (pp. 621–22).

8. Indicate the future role of management accounting (pp. 622–23).

$\mathcal{M}$anagers with a view to success in the twenty-first century must be aware of the full range of the environment in which they operate and make decisions. They should not only understand the critical importance of management accounting to their success, but must be able to weave its concepts and practices into the fabric of their work. Therefore, in contrast to those who hold that most management accounting textbooks can only be a collection of disjointed topics, we argue that the diversity of topics reflects the broad range of decisions managers face daily. This chapter integrates the topics presented throughout the textbook into a look at the spectrum of issues ahead for managers and their companies.

Each of these topics, and the chapters that have introduced them, has a role in the decision process. Given their importance and the volatility of any business environment, managers should assess these developing and future issues and their likely impact on management accounting.

Selected topics will be examined for their possible impact on management accounting based on emerging trends. We encourage you to explore alternative scenarios in order to recognize the vitality of management accounting now and in the future.

There are many important issues facing management accounting, including the contemporary ones of advanced manufacturing technology. We have certainly not identified all current or future ones. This chapter focuses on future issues and their possible impact on management accounting and on management. The issues identified in this chapter are the most important ones for management accountants.

STRUCTURAL CHANGES

The emerging issues in management accounting may be divided into two categories: structural changes and technological changes. By *structural changes* we mean changes due to new ways of doing business, presumably improvements in business practices and in management accounting. By *technological changes* we mean changes due to scientific breakthroughs. They include changes in manufacturing, for example, due to automation and robotics, and changes in computers and software that allow new ways of data processing and reaching business decisions.

This section describes the impact of structural changes on management accounting. The next section explains the impact of technological changes on management accounting. In this section we discuss cost drivers, flexible manufacturing systems and just-in-time production, and their impact on cost accounting systems, service industries, globalization, and Japanese management practices.

Cost Drivers

CHAPTER
OBJECTIVE 1
Impact of structural changes on cost drivers

Numerous academic and professional writers have suggested many changes to management accounting concepts. Some of these suggestions have centered on the *cost drivers* or production divisors (the variables used to set the predetermined overhead rates, as discussed in Chapter 8) in product costing and profitability analysis.

Traditionally, direct labor hours have been used as cost drivers. The rationale was that most of a product's cost was labor cost or related to it. However, for many firms today this is no longer true. Due to the increasing prevalence of factory automation, labor costs may be a very small proportion of a product's costs. Sixty years ago it was not unusual for direct labor costs to be 60–70% of the product's total cost. Some were even higher. Today direct labor costs may account for less than 5% of the total cost, as at Hewlett-Packard, for example. In addition, overhead costs may not be closely related to direct labor hours. When this situation occurs, the firm should not use direct labor hours as its cost driver. It should use some measure such as machine hours, which provides a better explanation or prediction of a product's costs.

Throughout the text we have used several different cost drivers. The best one in any given situation is the one that best explains that product's costs. One way of assessing this was illustrated in Appendix A, in Chapter 3: regression analysis. An accountant might regress several different candidates for cost driver against product costs. Other possibilities for cost drivers are number of parts, number of vendors, number of labor transactions, and use of space. The management accountant should choose the candidate that gives the best regression equation (for example, as measured by R^2). It is also possible to use more than one cost driver. The use of diverse cost drivers in conjunction with an activity-based accounting system was also discussed in Chapter 8.

Flexible Manufacturing Systems and Just-in-Time Production

Both job and process costing systems will need revisions based on changes in the underlying technologies and cost relationships. These changes do not mitigate the need for cost accounting; they simply draw attention to the need for understanding the entire range of management accounting objectives.

Job costing and process costing are and will continue to be influenced by the changing manufacturing environment. Flexible manufacturing systems, just-in-time production, and other such changes will affect the cost accounting by changing the relationships among materials, labor, and overhead.

CHAPTER
OBJECTIVE 2
Define FMS *and* JIT
production

A flexible manufacturing system (FMS) is a group of machines or other equipment that can make a number of different products. After producing one type of good, the machines can be altered quickly to manufacture a different product. Often FMSs use robots and other technologies to make these products. Also, a computer often directs and controls the manufacturing processes. The advantage of an FMS is the ability to produce a large number of products without a lot of down time for setups.

An FMS would link a number of machines and a materials handling system, using a computer to coordinate the manufacturing activities. The computer would decide which machine would do what work, provide for the proper materials as input, and direct the finished product to the proper location. Consider the FMS used by General Electric. In one of its plants, the FMS produces diesel engines of different sizes and different types. The FMS allows these various types of diesel engines to be made with little retooling and with only a small amount of down time.

Just-in-time (JIT) production is a philosophy about doing business. The idea is to manufacture products only when it is necessary—when customers order them. Even then, the company should manufacture only the number necessary to fill the customer's order. This philosophy also extends to buying raw materials. The idea is to buy the materials only as needed and only in the quantity necessary. The advantages of using JIT are the reduction of raw materials, work in process, and finished goods inventories, reduction of waste and spoilage, and shorter production time. JIT works something like this. Raw materials arrive from the vendor just in time for the production run. (In practice there would be a raw materials inventory, but it would be very small.) The production run is started and the raw materials are introduced into the process. Each worker along the assembly line does his or her work and the unit continues down the assembly line when the next worker is ready for it.

If some defect is noticed, the assembly line is stopped and the defect is analyzed and corrected. This inquiry leads to high quality, as no worker wants to be the one responsible for the defect too often.

The unit on the production line is not automatically passed to the next worker. Rather than "pushing" items through the production process, in JIT the goods are "pulled" through. When a worker has finished one unit and is ready for the next one, he or she indicates this to the appropriate worker in the assembly line. This process continues until the product is finished.

JIT has two potential drawbacks: lost materials discounts and stockouts. Materials discounts are often granted by a supplier when a firm buys a large order of materials. Small purchase sizes, typical in JIT, might mean no discounts. This problem is mitigated by having a long-term contract to cover a period such as a year. A discount could be negotiated for the annual purchase of materials.

A *stockout* could arise when the goods are not manufactured in time. This in turn could stem from down time on the assembly line or from the lack of raw materials. To curb the down time in the assembly line, the JIT firm must place a premium on quality and assure that the machinery is working as necessary and is properly maintained. To attenuate the lack of raw materials, the firm could have more than one supplier or it could negotiate penalty clauses for late deliveries.

JIT has been introduced in a number of American enterprises, including IBM, Hewlett-Packard, General Motors, and General Electric. They have employed variations of the general pattern we have described, but the essence of each of these JIT processes is the emphasis on quality, making the manufacturing a "pull" system, and the reduction of inventories. All of these companies have noted improvements.

Impact of FMS and JIT on Cost Accounting Systems

CHAPTER OBJECTIVE 3
Changes in cost accounting systems

The changes we have already discussed have had and will continue to have an impact on cost accounting systems. Five of these changes are discussed in this section and are summarized in Exhibit 17-1 (page 610).

As we have mentioned, direct labor becomes less important in the new and advanced manufacturing systems; it can even sometimes become insignificant. Thus it is necessary for a company to use a more informative cost driver, perhaps machine hours. Firms are also discovering that there may be more than one factor driving the cost of a product. This recognition by managers that multiple factors drive the cost of a product means that the accounting system must use more than one cost driver. Firms are beginning to employ multiple bases of allocating costs to a product. This leads to more accurate product costs and it helps managers focus the firm's attention on all of the major factors that influence the cost of the product.

Let us illustrate this concept by considering a firm with two products, A and B. Suppose that the firm expects to produce and sell 300,000 units of A and 100,000 units of B. Suppose further that the overhead costs are estimated to be $600,000, so that the overhead rate is $1.50 per unit (assuming the simple allocation scheme of $600,000/ 400,000).

EXHIBIT 17–1

CHANGES IN COST ACCOUNTING SYSTEMS

Changes in Manufacturing	**Changes in Cost Accounting Systems**
Multiple factors in the cost of a product (not just direct labor).	Multiple bases of allocating costs to a product; increased attention to all of these factors.
Decreases in inventories, especially work in process inventory.	Decreased attention to allocation of cost between inventories and cost of goods sold; decreased attention to equivalent units calculation.
Emphasis on quality.	Development of measures to assess quality and to assess the cost of quality.
Increased concern with productivity.	Development of measures of productivity.
Mass production of several items.	Replacement of job costing with process costing.

On further analysis, management determines that a better way to cost the product is to break it into the two components of overhead, electricity and indirect materials. Electricity costs $2 per kilowatt hour and product A requires one-half kilowatt hour per unit produced, while product B needs one kilowatt hour per unit. Indirect materials cost $.10 per unit of A and $.70 per unit of B. The management accountant ascertains that the overhead was calculated as follows:

Product	Number Produced	Electricity	Indirect Materials
A	300,000	300,000 × (1/2 × $2) = $300,000	300,000 × $.10 = $ 30,000
B	100,000	100,000 × (1 × $2) = 200,000	100,000 × $.70 = 70,000
		$500,000	$100,000

Therefore, each unit of A has overhead costs of $1.10 ($1 of electricity plus $.10 for indirect materials) and each unit of B has overhead costs of $2.70 ($2 + $.70). Notice that this investigation reveals more accurate costs because it determines the costs based on each of the factors in the production process.

A second aspect of this advanced manufacturing environment is that there is a decrease in inventories, especially work in process inventory. One implication for accounting is that there is less concern about the allocation of the cost of goods manufactured into cost of goods sold and inventory cost. If inventory is approximately zero,

APPLYING COST ACCOUNTING TO FACTORY AUTOMATION

How are American manufacturing companies relating their cost accounting practices to the automation of their factories? More companies are automating every day so they can deliver customized products on a timely basis, improve quality, increase manufacturing flexibility, and reduce costs.

The increase in factory automation has exposed and magnified cost accounting problems related to investment justification, product costing, and performance measurement. The solution to these problems lies in the use of cost accounting practices appropriate for automated machine environments.

A CHALLENGE FOR COST ACCOUNTANTS

Cost accounting practices related to factory automation need to be improved. In the area of investment justification, this implies the expanded use of DCF [discounted cash flow] techniques,

better efforts to quantify the more intangible benefits and costs, the expanded use of probabilities or other risk analysis techniques, and the use of realistic hurdle rates. In regard to product costing, companies need to establish overhead application rates for individual departments, work cells within departments, or individual machines rather than for individual or multiple plants. They should use machine-based overhead rates instead of labor-based rates and should consider the use of multiple overhead bases. Performance measures in automated environments need to focus on quality, material control, delivery, inventory, and machine performance. If cost accounting practices related to factory automation are improved, the ability of American manufacturing firms to compete in world markets should improve.

SOURCE: Adapted from James A. Hendricks, "Applying Cost Accounting to Factory Automation, *Management Accounting* (December 1988), pp. 24–30. Adapted by permission.

then cost of goods manufactured is approximately equal to cost of goods sold. As described in Chapter 8, this type of accounting is called *activity-based costing*. It is generally appropriate when the firm has multiple factors that drive overhead costs.

Process costing is further affected by the decrease in inventory levels. In particular, there will be decreased attention to the computation of equivalent units. If work in process inventory is approximately zero, then the equivalent units may be estimated simply as the number of units produced.

A third feature of the modern changes in manufacturing is the emphasis on quality. This affects management accounting in a simple way: the accountant must be able to measure quality and its cost. Some ways of doing this are to measure defects, warranty adjustments, amount of rework, amount of scrap, amount of spoilage, and amount of down time. Such statistics were typically not maintained in the past, but they are critical for managing in today's environment. Such statistics help pinpoint the firm's ability to produce goods with a high degree of quality.

Finally, new ways of manufacturing increase concern for productivity. By *productivity* we mean the amount of output given the amount of input. The more productive a segment is, the greater the proportion of output to input there is—a measure of its efficiency. The increased emphasis on productivity is due to the necessity of controlling costs of production and to becoming ever more efficient in order to compete in today's business world. As was true of quality, accounting traditionally did not measure productivity. Management accountants can be helpful to managers by developing measures of the firm's productivity. For example, managers would be aided by knowing the output effects from changes in the volume. Managers would also be helped by knowing the effects of substitution among materials, electricity, labor, and so on.

One last change in cost accounting systems arises from the change in how goods are produced. Recall from Chapters 10 and 11 that different production schemes lead to use of either job costing or process costing. In an advanced manufacturing setup, such as with FMS, several goods are made. In other words, the firm is mass producing a variety of items. When this is done it is difficult to cost each individual job; thus, job costing becomes obsolete. Job costing cannot be carried out because it requires that costs be accumulated by job. Instead, under FMS costs are accumulated by department or work station, and this implies a process cost system.

Service Industries

CHAPTER
OBJECTIVE 4
Service industries

Forty years ago, the U.S. economy was mostly manufacturing operations. Today it consists mostly of service-oriented activities, and this proportion is continuing to grow. As the economy continues to move even further toward an information- and service-based environment, management accounting will have to move with it. Previous management accounting efforts in service industries have been either nonexistent or simplistic and not necessarily oriented to providing information to management. Today, managers in the service industries face the same need for consistent and timely management accounting information as do all managers.

In the past, accounting for a service firm focused on its financial accounting. Management accounting played a minimal role in the service industries. Yet managers in these companies would benefit from a greater role by the management accountant. Information needs of managers that can be satisfied by management accounting include cost analyses of "products," profitability analysis by service and by customer, asking whether a new service should be offered, and assessing customer satisfaction with the service provided. These details are summarized in Exhibit 17-2.

The first emerging trend is the growth in costing techniques. This is easily conceptualized simply by thinking of the service as a product. Then the various services can be costed just as are the various products in a manufacturing concern.

EXHIBIT 17-2

MANAGEMENT ACCOUNTING ASPECTS OF SERVICE INDUSTRIES

New Concepts for the Service Industries	Related Concept in Management Accounting
Considering the service as the "product"	Cost services as if they were products; use job or process costing.
Determining profitability by service	Perform segment analysis with the services as segments.
Determining profitability by customer	Perform segment analysis with the customers as segments.
Asking whether a new service is worth offering	Perform a capital budgeting analysis on the new service.
Striving for customer satisfaction	Develop measures of quality.

In most service industries, the key costing approach was to sum all costs and divide by a denominator to arrive at some estimate of unit cost. Note that this is somewhat analogous to the use of direct labor to estimate unit overhead costs. Service industries recognize the inherent shortcomings in estimating costs under this approach and have moved to establish costing systems that recognize the multiple factors driving the costs for the company. This too is somewhat analogous to the manufacturing concept of cost drivers, as discussed earlier in this chapter. Job costing may also be applied to service firms. This is illustrated by Problem 10-39 (in Chapter 10).

Given the increased attention paid to costs in service industries, management may now assess the profitability of each customer and service (or "product"). This is achieved by segment analysis, as described in Chapter 13. Costs are accumulated for the particular service or for the particular customer. Revenues are also gathered. Then, remembering not to assign common costs to any segment, a segment margin can be computed in the same manner as it is for industrial firms. An example of this process is contained in Problem 13-37 of Chapter 13. This segment analysis will permit management to adjust prices as needed, to assess profitable and unprofitable segments, and to reward or punish segment managers as indicated.

Managers in service firms might also inquire whether it is profitable to engage in a new service. This question can be answered by capital budgeting, as explained in Chapter 14. The technique of capital budgeting is applied in the usual way. The future cash inflows and outflows are estimated and discounted. One can then compute the payback period, the net present value, and the internal rate of return.

Finally, managers of service firms are placing more emphasis on customer satisfaction. This is akin to manufacturers' rising concerns about quality. Traditionally, accounting did not measure customer satisfaction because it was not a transaction to be accounted for. Nonetheless, customer satisfaction is important to managers because dissatisfied customers might take their business elsewhere. The management accountant will create measures of customer satisfaction so that this factor can be tracked. Some possible measures are number of complaints, number of compliments, and number of reworked services. Marketing questionnaires might also be distributed so that interested customers may rate the services received.

Thus many of the concepts and methods discussed throughout this text are applicable to service-oriented businesses. We expect to see more firms in the service industries using them.

Globalization

CHAPTER
OBJECTIVE 4
Globalization

There was a time when managers could ask how a decision would affect or be affected by others in the United States, ignoring the rest of world. Managers can no longer afford to overlook the extent to which the global marketplace affects their companies. Clearly, not every organization becomes a global marketer; however, every manager in every firm must make a conscious decision to evaluate the potential of international markets and competition, as the very existence of these outside forces will have increasing impact on his or her job. The media coverage of the Japanese influence on management practices, including management accounting, is minor compared to the global influences of international production and foreign markets that will continue to affect U.S. managers and their firms.

For example, the opportunity that the 1992 European Community situation presents is most challenging to the rest of the world. By December 31, 1992, the European Economic Community (EEC) plans to remove economic barriers among the member nations. This creates an economy of 300 million people. Will this economic integration, as it is proposed, actually materialize? If it does, will it "freeze out" U.S. firms that do not establish themselves in Europe before then? How can firms take advantage of this opportunity? What are the costs and benefits to U.S. firms of adapting their operations to the different environment of Europe? These questions and others may be answered only with a good understanding of both the strategic situation and the capabilities of management accounting.

Another example concerns the opening of various command economies, such as the Soviet Union and Eastern Europe, to a more free-market orientation. How do managers reconcile these opportunities with the apparent facts that these countries remain burdened with central-planning ministries with their entrenched bureaucracies? Can managers determine a way to barter with countries that have no hard currency? What hurdle rates are necessary for capital budgeting projects in such countries? Will there be a societal backlash if the projects fail or the country turns from free markets to a command economy again?

The Persian Gulf Crisis of 1990 serves a third example of how global events affect U.S. businesses. Oil is a commodity whose supply is uncertain and whose price is subject to international politics. Since all firms in every economy worldwide rely directly or indirectly on oil, every company must assess the future risks of oil's availability and include those assessments and price estimates in its plans.

What about Third World countries, which are just emerging into the twentieth century, not the twenty-first century? These countries may or may not have significant natural or human resources. They want to enter the world marketplace in order to better the economic conditions of their citizens and yet not become hostage to more industrialized countries. Yet these countries raise many of the same queries as above. Can management assess a profitable opportunity in such a country? What political and economic variables interact to create a positive or negative business and economic environment?

These globalization issues do not imply new concepts or new methods. Rather, they require the management accountant to apply proven concepts and techniques in these new areas. We have introduced this subject so that the management accounting student can be sensitized to the topic. In addition, globalization requires the management accountant to tailor his or her methods to the particular country involved. For example, when Pepsico was considering whether to enter into a contract with the Soviet Union, it had to adjust the usual capital budgeting procedures because the Soviet Union, lacking a hard currency, wanted a barter arrangement. In other words, Pepsico did not receive any direct cash inflows from the arrangement. Instead it received such Soviet staples as vodka and caviar. Pepsico could resell these items and obtain cash that way (or it could consume the goods!). The point is that Pepsico had to value the goods received from the Soviet Union before a net present value could be calculated. While the concepts and techniques that have been described in this book do not change, the management accountant needs to be creative and flexible in applying the tools of the trade to global situations.

Japanese Management Practices

CHAPTER
OBJECTIVE 4
*Japanese management
practices*

Whether or not Japanese management practices are the standard by which management should be measured is debatable. What is certain is that Japanese enterprises have been able to cultivate a competitive performance on a global basis. The key is to examine this phenomenon and decide what can be learned and applied, then attempt to extrapolate to other possible scenarios. For example, might there be another country or countries, such as South Korea, that will be the next century's version of the Japanese miracle? With that thought in mind, let's examine some of the Japanese management practices.

Strategic Planning and Human Resources: The Long Term.   Japan happens to dominate discussion now and may well continue to do so toward the twenty-first century. After all, Japan recovered from its defeat in the Second World War to become a financial miracle. Looking carefully, one finds that many variables worked together for Japan. Its highly structured culture, the scarcity of natural resources, and the clean slate that its defeat and devastation caused permitted Japan to develop high productivity compared to other countries. In other words, the Japanese knew they had to be competitive in external markets and operated accordingly. The two areas in which they best developed and refined their advantages are human resource management and taking the long-term perspective. This assertion does not denigrate their commitment to technology but rather views it as an outcome of these two main advantages.

The longer view taken be Japanese firms allows them to cultivate relative job security. Increased job security leads to a desire for more consensus in the decision-making process, because the participants will likely be in the organization for an extended period, thus making it disadvantageous to engage in short-term "stopgap" measures and internal politics. This longevity in turn leads to extensive job rotation at all levels. Managers must rotate through a variety of peer-level positions rather than engage in "fast-tracking" to top management. This process in turn mitigates the need to identify superstars—and for managers to groom themselves as stars by inflating their segment's performance for the short-term—as self-selection and emergent leaders are revealed for eventual promotion. Given this environment, it should be no surprise that the performance system is oriented to both qualitative and quantitative measurements.

One outcome of this philosophy is that the management accountant is rotated to other jobs—for example, to the marketing department or to the manufacturing department. The idea is that when he or she is rotated back to the accounting department, he or she will have a broader view of the firm. As accounting tasks are carried out, the management accountant will not think only as an accountant, but will think also in terms of what information is needed by the marketing department and by the manufacturing department. American firms might consider rotating management accountants so that they will not become too provincial. This is an idea suggested by many authors, among them Peters and Waterman in their book *In Search of Excellence.*[1]

This style of management does not eliminate quantitative, financial evaluation. Instead, financial measures are integrated in the performance system. That is, financial goals must still be met, but they are subject to a variety of other variables. Previous chapters have emphasized that financial analysis is insufficient by itself for decisions. The Japanese approach has simply integrated the performance appraisal system in such a way as to be consistent with U.S. definitions. For example, since the Japanese firms are strongly committed to quality, they make quality measures a part of the evaluation package. For example, a Japanese manager might earn a bonus only if he or she earns, say, 12% return on investment and if he or she has no more defects than one product in every 10,000 products built.

---

[1]Thomas J. Peters and Robert H. Waterman, Jr., *In Search of Excellence: Lessons from America's Best-Run Companies* (New York: Macmillan Publishing Co., 1982.).

The long-term view taken by Japanese companies is clearly evident in their treatment of human resources, but what motivates their long-range strategy in financial analysis? It is almost impossible to obtain internal decision criteria from any Japanese firm. However, we know of some cases in which the long-term perspective seems to be in evidence. The most well documented case is the Caterpillar–Komatsu heavy equipment war. Caterpillar Inc. was the dominant force in heavy equipment for 50 years until Komatsu Ltd. came along in the 1980s. The arrival of Komatsu as a major competitor did not occur overnight. Apparently Komatsu engaged in a long-term plan that permitted it to operate with a lower profit margin to gain competitive advantage and to build market share. Of course, Komatsu may have had a cost advantage for some of its products; but overall, it priced its products lower than Caterpillar for the long term to gain market share. The key is that Komatsu's management accounting information system supported its decision-making process and behavioral intent by providing analyses of market share and long-term profits.

Just-in-Time Production.   Advanced manufacturing technology has received attention in this textbook as well as in the press. Given global competitiveness as a goal, most firms have little choice than to engage a constant need to lower costs and improve quality. Out of these precepts comes JIT production. As explained earlier, the ultimate goal of such a production system is to order, deliver, and produce "just in time" for delivery to the next process or to the customer. What is not so clear is whether JIT should be the evolving operational concept for all firms at all levels of production—by virtue of its success—or should be reserved as a strategy to guide decision making and operationalized to the extent possible. We believe that many, but not all, U.S. firms can benefit by adopting a JIT philosophy.

The JIT concept does not stop with the production process that we described earlier but extends into the purchasing, work force management, supplier relationship, and financial strategies. Because the factory ceases to produce when purchasing is miscalculated or out of step with the production demands, purchasing must be integrally linked to the concept and its performance measured accordingly. Work force training, recruiting, and retention is dictated by the concept. Job redesign, rotation of employees among a variety of jobs, quality circles, and other resource development programs become the way to create a flexible work force. This approach differs from the more traditional specialization approach. Clearly, employee absenteeism becomes critical when a work group is responsible for output levels. Supplier relationships must be carefully developed and nurtured, since any supplier can effectively shut down a factory with late deliveries or defective parts. Financial strategies become complex when they become more oriented to managing fixed investments in production and personnel than inventories. But the ability to produce cost effectively becomes a function of having the proper infrastructure relative to market needs. Thus, financial strategies are inextricably linked to the entire JIT concept, as it will be impossible to operationalize this concept without proper financial planning involving all the elements of management accounting discussed in this text and elsewhere. The JIT philosophy is compared with the conventional means of production in Exhibit 17-3.

In summary, the Japanese economic impact on global competitiveness has been substantial. The impact was made possible by a confluence of variables including Japan's highly regulated culture, a scarcity of natural resources, a long-term perspective, and a "clean slate" due to Japan's loss in World War II. The ability of the rest of the world to compete is substantially determined by the ability of each country, firm, and individual to operate at the level of competition Japan has introduced. No one country will be able

---

EXHIBIT 17-3

CONVENTIONAL VS. JUST-IN-TIME MANUFACTURING

Conventional Production	Just-in-Time Production
Mass-production assembly line.	Focus on smaller lots in a work (group) of machines.
Substantial inventories.	Reduced inventories.
Incurs setup and changeover time.	Minimizes (eliminates) setup and changeover time.
Overhead allocation via one or two cost pools.	Overhead allocation via as many cost pools as necessary to reveal economics of production.
Quality control after the fact.	Continuous quality control.
Normal and abnormal scrap is produced.	All scrap is abnormal.
Single-skilled workers.	Multi-skilled workers.

---

to dominate the world economy in such a way as to prevent competitive responses. It will not be easy to compete, but it *is* possible—as the newly industrialized countries such as Korea, Singapore, and others demonstrate.

TECHNOLOGICAL CHANGES

Technological changes have affected and will continue to affect management accounting. These changes include manufacturing changes, office automation, expert systems, and executive information systems. As we discuss each of these changes, consider the extent to which they are currently occurring as well as the extent to which they are likely to continue to occur.

Manufacturing Methods

CHAPTER OBJECTIVE 5
CIM and MRP

Manufacturing processes have been revolutionized by technology in the recent past. Scale economies have changed to such an extent that managers now speak of "mass-produced customized products." These products have the characteristics desired by the customer at a price that reflects mass production. JIT concepts, often using FMS, interact in this environment to keep inventories lower than previously thought possible. Such an environment is highly dependent on information technology as well as on manufacturing technology. In fact, the ultimate goal is to have a fully integrated system referred to as **computer integrated manufacturing** (CIM). CIM is the philosophy that all of the technologies in a firm must be linked together and work as a whole. The manufacturing technology, including the design and engineering phases and the functions of raw materials acquisition and scheduling, and the information technology are to become one system. The importance of the management accounting process is critical to the development and implementation of such systems because of the financial evaluations that need to be done at each stage. Management accounting will be needed to evaluate the present situation, propose alternatives, and constantly reevaluate decisions over time.

As integration becomes the normal situation, management will continue to strive for the ultimate manufacturing environment, whether it is called CIM or something else. One subset of CIM is FMS, as described on page 608. FMS is an integrated set of computerized machines designed to automate a set of production operations. These FMSs have elements of the CIM but are not completely integrated with all other management systems. One rationale for FMS has been to provide the opportunity to phase in the ultimate CIM. The advantages of CIM/FMS are that they provide a flexible manufacturing environment, reduce labor and inventory costs, and improve the overall quality of the products and operations.

These automated environments require a common database from which to operate the integrated systems. One common term for such a database is **manufacturing resource planning** or **materials resource planning** (MRP). MRP systems are computer systems focusing on inventory control and production planning for a manufacturing process. The essence of MRP is the integration of production, marketing, purchasing, engineering, accounting, finance, forecasting, and other relevant functions. Such an environment provides an opportunity to manage the organization using an integrated system.

Two factors that might impede the company's phasing in of such systems are resistance to change and an inability to justify the investment from the standpoint of capital budgeting. Resistance to change is a problem when employees think that they might lose their jobs or if they are fearful that they cannot learn the new technology. Japanese firms overcome these potential problems by guaranteeing jobs to their employees even if the position is eliminated. That is, they guarantee that they will create another position for the individual. American companies can reduce the workers' fear of losing their jobs by attempting to do the same. The second potential problem, fear of inability to learn the new technology, can be overcome by educational programs that are stimulating and encouraging and that provide the knowledge and reassurance needed for employees to carry out the new tasks.

Capital budgeting for CIM and related parts of it are difficult to implement in practice. Conceptually, nothing is new. The firm wants to generate at least enough cash inflows to justify the cash outflows. The problem in practice is that many companies, at least in the recent past, did not allow any estimates of cash inflows due to higher quality, lower inventory costs, or increases in productivity. Their thought was that these factors are too difficult to measure. Such firms must change because they may be missing out on great opportunities. Just because it may be difficult to measure the cost savings from higher quality or from higher productivity does not mean that these factors are unimportant or that they are small in magnitude. Management accountants can assist managers by pointing out that these cost savings may be large and by attempting to measure them for their corporation.

Office Automation

CHAPTER OBJECTIVE 6
Office automation, expert systems, and executive information systems

Materials resource planning involves automating not only the manufacturing environment but the office as well. Marketing, finance, accounting, purchasing, and other functions are integrated under MRP, thus mandating the automation of the office whether in the factory or in the general administrative area. **Office automation** (OA) is the computerization and interconnection of office activities. Management is inextricably connected to information systems for decision making in this environment.

This does not mean the manager does not interact with others, but simply that the combination of information and interaction is critical to his or her decision making.

Several examples will allow us to understand this idea. Spreadsheets were first computerized only recently. Yet, now a manager would not consider performing spreadsheet analysis manually. In fact, the reliance on spreadsheet automation is virtually complete in most classroom assignments as well as in the real world. Moving beyond spreadsheets, we find the increasing use of modeling languages such as *Interactive Financial Planning Systems* (IFPS), in which the spreadsheet cells are defined in an English-like language. These languages usually permit significant manipulation and interrogation, even including some "expert system" queries (discussed next). More importantly, they allow managers to interact with the information system in a natural decision-making mode as necessary without extensive training. Office automation also includes word processing and electronic mail.

With an integrated system, a firm can link to customers in a substantial way to maintain customer relations. This is referred to as *electronic data interchange*. The customer can be given access codes to query the system for order status. This provides a closer relationship between customer and supplier for increased profitability; conversely, it offers immediate information that otherwise might not be given out to customers. For example, if a customer makes an on-line change to the needed delivery date of its order, the MRP/CIM/OA system could reveal the impact of such a change immediately. Other customers may find their own delivery dates affected by the change.

As an example of such a system, consider American Hospital Supply. This corporation installed terminals in the clients' hospitals. These terminals were connected directly to American Hospital Supply. When a doctor, nurse, or administrator noted that something was needed, he or she could simply enter the item on this terminal. American Hospital Supply would then receive the request on its terminal and fill the order right away. This allowed the hospital to obtain its supplies in a minimal amount of time. They also found that errors (wrong amounts or wrong items) were reduced since the order was written down only once and on the computer of American Hospital Supply. Because of the fast delivery and the reduction of errors, American Hospital Supply and the hospitals were happy with the computerized ordering system.

Expert Systems

As automation becomes pervasive, management will find it impossible to manage without developing some type of automated decision system. Several names have been given to these systems: expert systems, artificial intelligence, knowledge systems, and expert support systems, among others. Whatever the name attached to it, the proposed benefits are the same: automating elements of the decision-making process based on the expertise of management. We want to emphasize that the approach is to automate elements of management expertise, not to replace all managers.

An **expert system** is a computer program that captures the knowledge of a human expert generally as a set of related rules. The rules focus on some particular activity such as if and when to buy or sell stock. The expert system examines the data available and makes a decision. Of course, humans can overrule the expert system's decision.

Decision support systems (DSS), discussed throughout the textbook, and expert systems are very much alike. They both use databases and focus on decision making. The two types of programs differ in two respects, however. First, the expert system explicitly attempts to capture and codify human expertise; decision support systems use models and statistical techniques. Second, the expert system can be asked to explain how it reached its conclusion. An illustration of this EXPLAIN function is contained in Exhibit 17-4. The user can accept the explanation, ask for further explanation, or reject the recommendation. In the latter case the user should know why he or she is rejecting the recommendation.

By automating elements of expertise we can provide the opportunity for management to concentrate on the more complex and seemingly unanswerable questions. Such questions include the strategic decisions for the organization. For example, an expert management accounting system can help analyze budget requests and perform the initial variance investigations for a performance analysis. Budgets prepared under and with such a system can be evaluated without physical and mental exhaustion playing a part. The budget may be subjected to a complete scrutiny as needed without conflicts with the time pressures of individual managers. (We assume that the budget is prepared on time and in an appropriate format for the expert system to perform its analysis. Thus, the routine part, the automated elements, are done by the system and the difficult parts, the interpretation and decision making, are carried out by a human decision maker. As the system and manager learn more about automated budget analysis, the expert system may be refined. Note that the issue here is not the technical components of an expert system but rather the managerial use of such systems as explained in Chapter 5.

The Impact of Expert Systems on Management and the Firm. The rate of growth in the number of managers slows in an expert systems environment, but managers become even more critical to the decision process than ever before. Due to the automation of fairly routine analyses, fewer managers are needed. (Redundancies in managers would be discovered anyway if the firm were to critically ascertain their value. The automation process simply reveals their relatively small contribution to decision making.) The remaining managers become increasingly important in two ways. One, their expertise is what must be captured in the expert system. Two, their ability to interpret the results of the expert system are vital to the success of the organization.

EXHIBIT 17-4

SAMPLE DIALOGUE WITH AN EXPERT SYSTEM

Computer: Sell the stock of XYZ Corporation.
User: Explain.
Computer: There is high probability that XYZ Corporation will go bankrupt.
User: Explain.
Computer: 1. Profit potential is low.
  2. Cash flow potential is low.
  3. XYZ Corporation has a lot of debt.
  4. There is high probability that XYZ Corporation will not generate enough cash to pay its debts.

Most of the routine decisions will be made by the system and most of the analyses requiring a decision will be performed by the system; the manager's tasks are to validate the system for the routine decisions and to make decisions in the more complex scenarios. The manager will not have the luxury of being able to switch back and forth between the simple and complex, nor to concentrate on the analysis part; he or she must concentrate continually on the interpretation and decision-making aspects. What we do not yet understand is the impact that making only complex decisions on a regular basis will have on the manager.

Executive Information Systems

Executive information systems (EIS) are computer systems designed to provide executives at varying levels with the information necessary for decision making. Executive information systems are special types of decision support systems designed to meet the specific needs and desires of the top executives of a firm. Executive information systems often focus on retrieving and processing data needed by the executive and on supporting human communications.

The major differences between EISs and other systems are that the EIS is future-oriented, links internal and external databases as necessary, and has a graphical and icon-based interface that allows executives with no technical computer training to access information and input decisions easily. Most systems are said to be future oriented, but the EIS is clearly designed to look at the past as a basis to predict the future. Historical databases are used to analyze the past to give insight to the future. External databases are accessible to provide information relative to trends and other queries of executives as they consider decisions, usually strategic decisions. We do not mean to imply that only strategic decisions are undertaken with an EIS, but they do form a significant portion of the decisions made by executives.

GenRad Inc. developed an executive information system. This EIS scans both internal and external information. Internal information includes financial statements, financial forecasts, performance reports, statistics on quality control, and segment information. External information includes access to stock prices, news services, business and economic news, and information about competitors. Features of the system allowed the data to be analyzed statistically and with what-if analysis and to be displayed graphically. It also provided for electronic mail.

BEHAVIORAL ASPECTS OF CHANGE

CHAPTER OBJECTIVE 7
Behavioral aspects of change

Changes in the way we do business and changes in technology will affect human behavior. These effects can be classified as *individual responses* and *organizational issues*.

The old adage, "All is change; only change is changeless," certainly applies to today's society. However, many people are resistant to change. After learning to perform a task one way, they keep on doing it and perfecting it and making that way as efficient as possible. A change in the tasks to be performed or in the way they must be carried out may cause stress in humans. Some people embrace change and grow; others blockade or sabotage it. Managers and management accountants must not only advocate change but must be able to convince others in the organization why change is needed and why it is good for them and for the firm. Someone may even be put in charge of the change—he or she is called a *change agent*. The duty of a change agent is to describe the change to others, obtain support for it, and reduce or eliminate resistance to implementing it.

At the organizational level change can also be a major issue. Not only will people change, but the organization itself will change. The organization needs to learn how to cope and, more fundamentally, should try to understand *how* it learns. This **organizational learning** focuses on challenges to assumptions and to traditional modes of operation. Because of this examination, the organization will be able to modify some of its operating rules and philosophies. In doing so the organization should become healthier and stronger.

Change is often painful and uncomfortable. Nonetheless, it gives people and organizations the opportunity to adapt and provides them a better chance to compete.

THE CHANGING ROLE OF THE MANAGEMENT ACCOUNTANT

CHAPTER
OBJECTIVE 8
*Future role of
management
accounting*

The role of the management accountant has changed over time and will continue to do so. What seems clear is that management and management accounting must become more closely linked. That is, management accounting has always been allied with management and decision making; we now argue that the alliance must become even closer.

Controllership

Controllership or management control systems have always been the focus of management accounting. Elements include budgeting, cash flow analysis, profitability reviews, and other such matters. These elements are even more critical in a competitive, fast-moving, highly automated environment. Is it possible for a manager to decide on product line profitability without proper use of management accounting? A quick review of some of the issues discussed in this chapter includes changeovers to advanced manufacturing technologies, global operations, and Japanese management practices. Decisions involving all of these issues consist of alternatives: invest or do not invest; phase in the system gradually or try to change "overnight"; integrate new JIT concepts into the planning process, or wait until the MIS is on line. If alternatives are present, there is a necessity for selection; if selection is necessary, evaluation tools are vital. Management accounting has those tools.

One area of concern is performance evaluation. Managers and management accountants will need to determine the appropriate measures for evaluating performance of individuals and groups. Meeting budgets will no longer suffice; increasingly, qualitative measures will be included. To accomplish this, management accounting will have to determine measures that are linked with the goals of the organization and understandable to managers. This is far simpler to say than to do.

Treasurership

Treasury functions are oriented to the external aspects of an organization such as financing, international currency management, and other such tasks. (These functions exist in a similar and no less volatile environment as controllership.) The automation of expertise in these functions is and has been continuing; supercomputers are being used increasingly for some of these functions. Given the rising need to operate globally and instantaneously, it seems likely that treasury functions will increase in importance.

Management Accountants

Management accountants of the future will likely be more integrally involved in planning and decision making than ever before. The trend to automation will continue, requiring significant involvement by management accountants in selection and implementation of these systems.

Management accountants of the future will be both technologically and interpersonally qualified. They will be technologically qualified in order to manage and work in technologically rich environments. They will be interpersonally qualified because of the necessity of working in groups composed of people from many different backgrounds and perspectives. Ultimately, they should be qualified for the more demanding executive positions.

Review of Chapter Objectives

1. Describe the impact of structural changes on cost drivers and activity-based costing (pp. 607–608).

   ■ In the past, labor cost was the largest component of manufacturing costs. Naturally, direct labor cost was employed as a cost driver to estimate product costs, especially for applying an overhead rate. In today's world, and in the foreseeable future, labor costs are becoming a much smaller portion of product cost. Also labor cost is often not a good estimator of overhead. Thus, it is necessary to try different, and multiple, measures for cost drivers. One alternative is machine hours.

2. Define *flexible manufacturing systems* and *just-in-time production* (pp. 608–609).

   ■ A flexible manufacturing system is a group of machines or other equipment that can make a number of different products. Often it uses robots and is directed by a computer. Such systems can produce a variety of products easily because much of the down time for setups is unnecessary.

   ■ Just-in-time production is the philosophy to manufacture products only when customers order them and make only the number ordered. The idea is to reduce inventory costs, reduce waste and spoilage, and shorten the production time.

3. Discuss the impact of flexible manufacturing systems and just-in-time production on cost accounting systems (pp. 609–612).

   ■ The changing manufacturing environment, characterized by flexible manufacturing systems and just-in-time production, leads to smaller inventory levels. Work in process inventory in particular is reduced to an almost zero level, eliminating the need in process costing to compute equivalent units. Practically speaking, the number of equivalent units will simply be the number of units produced during the period.

■ Job costing no longer exists in flexible manufacturing environments. Given that many jobs are small in size, since the corporation produces only the amount ordered by the customer, it becomes impractical to track costs by jobs. Rather, costs are accumulated with a process cost system.

4. Explain the likely effects of changes in service industries, globalization, and Japanese management practices on management accounting (pp. 612–17).

■ Service industries have grown considerably in the United States during the recent past. With the large size of the service industry firms, management accountants have become aware that many of the concepts in management accounting are applicable to these companies. By thinking of a service, such as a hairstyling, a consultation, or an aerobics class, as a product, it is readily seen that these services can be analyzed by management accounting tools.

■ Globalization means that firms should consider internationalizing their business, selling products to any market in the world, and producing goods in factories in any country having a competitive wage structure and available shipping facilities. Conversely, what happens politically, economically, or militarily in the world might have an impact on the corporation. Managers need to take a broad perspective of their business and management accountants need to assist them.

■ Many Japanese firms use just-in-time production with great success. Because of this success, a number of American corporations have followed suit. More fundamentally, many Japanese companies also stress human resource management and taking a long-term perspective. It is likely that these practices will also be adopted by some U.S. corporations.

5. Define *computer integrated manufacturing* and *manufacturing* (or *materials*) *resources planning* (pp. 617–18).

■ Computer integrated manufacturing is the philosophy that all of the technologies involved in manufacturing must be linked together and work as a whole. This includes the technical manufacturing and information technology alike.

■ Manufacturing (materials) resource planning, a step or component of computer integrated manufacturing, is a type of computer system that focuses on inventory control and on production planning for a manufacturing process.

6. Describe office automation, expert systems, and executive information systems (pp. 618–21).

■ Office automation is the computerization and interconnection of office activities. This includes spreadsheets, word processing, and electronic mail.

■ An expert system is a computer system that captures the knowledge of a human expert generally as a set of rules. It is like a decision support system in that they both use databases and both focus on decision-making. Expert systems differ from decision support systems in that they explicitly codify human expertise on some issue and can explain its recommendations.

■ Executive information systems are a type of decision support system that is designed to meet the specific needs of the top executives of the firm. They often focus on the data needs of these executives and on supporting human communications.

7. Explain how human behavior is affected by changes in the environment and in technologies. (pp. 621–22).

- People tend to resist change. Managers and management accountants need to be aware of this and educate employees on why the change is needed. The idea is to obtain support for the change and attempt to eliminate resistance to the change.
- Organizations also change. It is helpful to assess how change occurs in the firm and how the firm learns. Such organizational learning will assist the firm in becoming better and stronger.

8. Indicate the future role of management accounting (pp. 622–23).

- Both the controllership and the treasurership aspects of management accounting will become more important because of the introduction of new manufacturing technologies, global operations, and Japanese management practices. It will also become more streamlined with the help of information technology.

Glossary of Key Terms

computer integrated manufacturing   The philosophy that all of the manufacturing technologies must be linked together and work as a whole.

executive information systems   Special types of decision support systems designed to meet the specific needs and desires of top executives.

expert system   Computer system that captures the knowledge of a human expert generally as a set of rules.

flexible manufacturing system   A group of machines or other equipment that can make a number of different products. They often use robots and computers in the manufacturing process.

just-in-time production   A manufacturing philosophy in which the product should be made only after a customer has ordered it and only for the amount ordered. The idea is to reduce inventory costs and to create a more efficient manufacturing system.

manufacturing (or materials) resource planning   Computer systems focusing on inventory control and production planning for a manufacturing process.

office automation   The computerization and interconnection of office activities.

organizational learning   The process of an organization learning about its environment and learning how to learn.

Review Questions

17-1   Describe the argument surrounding the issue of cost drivers and product costing.

17-2   What is a flexible manufacturing system?

17-3   What is just-in-time production?

17-4   Describe revisions needed in process costing systems based on changes in technology.

17-5   Describe revisions needed in job order costing systems based on changes in technology.

17-6   Describe some likely uses of management accounting information in service industries.

17-7   Describe the globalization of the economy and its impact on management accounting.

17-8   Describe some Japanese management practices and how they were able to use these practices to achieve economic success.

17-9   How are financial aspects integrated into the decision process within Japanese management practices?

17-10   Discuss the concepts of computer integrated manufacturing.

17-11   What is manufacturing (materials) resource planning?

17-12   Explain the term *office automation.*

17-13   What is meant by expert systems?

17-14   What is an executive information system?

17-15   Explain how human behavior can be managed in the face of technological changes.

17-16   What is the future of management accountants given the technology changes in society?

Discussion Questions

Note: All of these questions require the reader to integrate the material in this chapter with the rest of the book.

17-17   What impact do technological changes have on the income statement (including the cost of goods manufactured), the balance sheet, cash flow analysis, and financial statement analysis?

17-18   How do technological changes affect breakeven analysis and flexible budgeting?

17-19   How do technological changes affect decision making and the criterion of relevant costs?

17-20   What impact do technological changes have on the master budget?

17-21   What is new in the analysis of direct materials, direct labor, variable overhead, and fixed overhead in a world of technological changes?

17-22   Do technological changes have any affect on variance analysis?

17-23   How can a process costing system be implemented in an advanced manufacturing plant?

17-24   How do technological changes affect performance measurement and segment analysis?

17-25   What influence do technological changes have on capital budgeting?

Appendix E

Operating Instructions for MicroStudy+ ®

INTRODUCTION

These brief operating instructions let you start using MicroStudy+®, the software study aid. After you study a chapter in the textbook, use MicroStudy+ to reinforce your understanding. The program is as flexible and comprehensive as possible to speed the learning process. More complete operating instructions are available from within the program itself.

HARDWARE AND SOFTWARE REQUIREMENTS

MicroStudy+ is available on both 5¼-inch and 3½-inch disks for use with most DOS-based microcomputers, such as the IBM PC® or PS/2®. Use PC-DOS or MS-DOS version 2.1 or higher.

Your instructor will tell you how to obtain or make a copy of the MicroStudy+ software. Typically the publisher gives each school a master disk for these purposes. You may run the software from an individual floppy disk or you can copy it onto a hard disk drive.

GETTING STARTED

These instructions assume that you know how to start your computer and obtain a DOS prompt, such as

A>

The instructions also assume that you will be running the software from the A drive.

1. At the A> prompt, type **STUDY** (in either upper or lower case) and then press the <**Return**> key.
2. Next you will see one or more introductory screens. Typically a screen will display for several seconds and then the next screen will replace it automatically, until the Main Menu appears.
3. At the Main Menu, take a minute to review your menu choices:

```
1. Select Chapter in Textbook for Review
2. Study Chapter Preview Questions
```

3. List Key Terms in the Chapter
4. Vocabulary Building with Matching Exercises
5. True/False Statement Drill
6. Multiple Choice Question Drill
7. Review Instructions for Using MICROSTUDY
8. Set or Change the Operating Environment
                    <ESC> to Exit

For more detailed operating instructions, choose menu option 7 by obtaining the Main Menu and then pressing the <7> key.

Appendix F

What if? Electronic Spreadsheet Templates for Decision Making

The electronic spreadsheet templates accompanying *Management Accounting* by Ketz, Campbell, and Baxendale give the student an opportunity to practice the construction of electronic worksheets in the context of management accounting problems. One problem is selected from each chapter (except Chapter 17) to permit the student to gain an appreciation of the use of computer models in dealing with management accounting issues.

These partially completed electronic spreadsheet templates presuppose that the student has completed the electronic spreadsheet portion of the Lotus® 1-2-3® tutorial that comes with the Lotus 1-2-3 software. Many of the concepts learned in that tutorial will be used in completing the spreadsheets associated with the problems from the textbook.

In addition to completing the spreadsheets, the students will be asked to use the models they construct to evaluate the impact of changes in assumptions. This evaluation of the impact of changes in assumptions is called *what-if analysis*. It is used to gain insight into business situations in which there is uncertainty. This "what-if" approach to management accounting analysis is particularly important in complex business situations that involve many variables.

The electronic spreadsheet problems for the first two chapters do not require the student to do any spreadsheet programming. Those first two problems are already completely developed in order to give the student an example of electronic spreadsheets used for what-if analysis. They only require the student to evaluate changes in assumptions through the use of what-if analysis.

The selected problems associated with the remaining chapters require the students to use the skills learned in the Lotus 1-2-3 tutorial to complete the spreadsheet. Once the spreadsheet has been completed, the student will then be requested to use what-if analysis in analyzing the business situation. The instructions for each of the problems are the same ones shown in the textbook; however, there are instances in which additional instructions are given to the student. The additional instructions are shown at the top of the file for each of the problems.

The student disk has sixteen files on it, one file for each problem in Chapters 1 through 16. The file name is constructed in a way that will help you select the file for the related problem in the textbook. For example, in Chapter 1, the Business Decision Case in Chapter 1 is included among the computerized problems. Thus the file name is 1_BDC.WKS to indicate that the computerized problem is the Business Decision Case in Chapter 1. Similarly, the file name 7_33.WKS refers to problem 33 in Chapter 7.

These problems and their related solutions were created using the original version of Lotus 1-2-3 (Version 1A). They may be accessed by all later versions of Lotus 1-2-3 and compatible spreadsheet applications. If you are using a spreadsheet other than Lotus 1-2-3, it may be the case that the templates must be converted to an acceptable format and that the menu keystrokes will differ to some small degree. Please consult the spreadsheet's user's manual for the proper routines.

If you are not an experienced spreadsheet user, brief instructions on how to start and work in Lotus 1-2-3 are available on your student template disk. To view these instructions, simply place the disk in the "A" drive of your computer, then type:

A:<**return**>

The A> prompt should appear onscreen. Now type:

readme<**return**>

The instructions will appear onscreen. If you wish, you may print the instructions. To do this, turn on your printer and make sure it is on-line. Then type:

copy readme.doc prn<**return**>

Glossary

The number at the end of each entry indicates the chapter in which the main discussion of the term may be found.

absorbed overhead   The portion of factory indirect cost that has been allocated to a specific product. The allocation process is usually carried out by the application of an appropriate overhead rate to specific units of production. (Ch. 8)

accounting rate of return   A capital budgeting technique in which the project's accounting profits are divided by the average investment base. (Ch. 14)

activity-based costing   A cost system that traces costs to activities and then traces costs to products. (Ch. 8)

activity level   The operating level or volume chosen for examination, stated in either units or dollars. (Ch. 3)

activity variance   The difference between the income projected by the master budget and the income projected by the flexible budget. (Ch. 9)

administrative cost   Cost associated with the general management of the organization. (Ch. 2)

analysis of the variables   With respect to decision support systems, a request to know how a variable is calculated. (Ch. 1)

annuity   A set of equal cash flows paid or received in equal time intervals. (Ch. 14)

avoidable cost   An ongoing cost that may be eliminated by ceasing to perform some economic activity or segment thereof or by improving the efficiency by which such activity is accomplished. (Ch. 4)

breakeven analysis   Analysis of sales, variable costs, and fixed costs to determine the breakeven point. (Ch. 3)

breakeven point   The point at which total revenues equal total costs. (The formula can be amended to include target net income.) (Ch. 3)

budget   A financial plan that provides the basis for performance appraisal as well as a blueprint for future resource, organization, and general management decisions (Ch. 1); quantification of a plan (Ch. 5).

budget committee   A steering committee to advise the chief management accountant or chief financial officer and coordinate the overall budget process. (Ch. 5)

budget slack   Padding in the budget, usually by lowering revenues or increasing expenses, to make budgeted levels easier to achieve. (Ch. 5)

budget variance   The difference between budgeted fixed manufacturing overhead and actual fixed manufacturing overhead. (Ch. 8)

budgetary control   The actions necessary to ensure that budget objectives, plans, policies, and standards are attained or revised. (Ch. 5)

budgeted balance sheet   Balance sheet prepared as a result of predicted operations linking the previous balance sheet to the budgeted income statements. (Ch. 5)

budgeted income statement   Income statement prepared as a result of predicted operations. (Ch. 5)

budgeting The process of planning all flows of financial resources into, within, and from an entity during some specified future period. It includes providing for the detailed allocation of expected available future resources to projects, functions, responsibilities, and time periods. (Ch. 5)

capacity cost The fixed cost of an entity resulting from the need to provide operating facilities to process material and services. (Ch. 3)

capital budgeting The process of financial planning that examines the cash flows of proposed long-term assets. (Ch. 14)

capital charge Controllable investment times the minimum required rate of return. Used in calculating residual income. (Ch. 12)

cash budget A period-by-period statement of cash on hand at the start of a budget period; expected cash receipts classified by source; expected cash disbursements classified by function, responsibility, and form; and the resulting cash balance at the end of the budget period. (Ch. 5)

cash inflow An activity that increases cash. (Ch. 6)

cash outflow An activity that decreases cash. (Ch. 6)

centralization An organizational approach in which a supervising function maintains significant direction and authority over operations and policies relating to a number of identifiable, separate activities and operations. (Ch. 1)

Certified Management Accountant (CMA) A professional designation awarded by the Institute of Management Accounting to an accountant who has met the requirements of the institute, including satisfactory completion of a comprehensive examination. (Ch. 1)

chief financial officer (CFO) Usually the chief management accountant, in some organizations referred to as the chief information officer, controller (or comptroller), or management accountant. (Ch. 1)

common cost A cost of resources used jointly in the production of two or more outputs; the cost cannot be directly assigned to those outputs. Customarily, assignment is made through a series of consistent allocation procedures. Also called joint cost. (Ch. 4)

common-size statements Financial statements that report the line items by their proportion to the total sales on the income statement, to total assets (equities) on the balance sheet, and to total uses (sources) of cash on the cash-flow statement. This is also referred to as vertical analysis. (Ch. 15)

composite unit A production cost unit that describes the fixed proportions of a sales mix in a multiple-product organization. (Ch. 3)

compound interest An interest method that adds unpaid interest to the old principal to get a new principal. Thus additional interest is computed on the old principal plus any unpaid interest. (Ch. 14)

computer integrated manufacturing The philosophy that all of the manufacturing technologies must be linked together and work as a whole. (Ch. 17)

constant-dollar accounting A set of adjustments to show the effects of general price-level changes. It can be applied to current entry value accounting, current exit value accounting, and historical cost accounting. (Ch. 16)

constraint An activity, resource, or policy that limits or bounds the attainment of an objective. (Ch. 4)

continuous budget A budget that adds a time period in the future as the time period just ended is dropped. (Ch. 5)

contribution margin Sales price minus variable cost; also referred to as marginal income. It may be expressed as a total, as a ratio, or on a per-unit basis. (Ch. 3)

contribution margin ratio   The contribution margin divided by the sales price. (Ch. 3)

control   The review of performance and progress toward goals, and reinforcing or taking corrective action where necessary. (Ch. 1)

controllable cost   Cost that managers can influence and for which they are responsible. (Ch. 2)

controllable investment   The net of assets and liabilities that can be significantly influenced by the decisions of the responsibility center managers. (Ch. 12)

controllable revenues   Revenues that can be significantly influenced by the decisions of the responsibility center manager. (Ch. 12)

conversion cost   Direct labor cost plus manufacturing overhead costs. (Ch. 2)

cost   The amount paid or charged for something. Usually "paid or charged" means that the firm has given up or will give up cash or some other asset. Sometimes "paid or charged" means the sacrifice of other potentially good courses of action. In all cases, *cost* refers to the firm's sacrifice of something to obtain something else. (Ch. 2)

cost accounting   The process of accumulating and determining the cost of a project, process, or activity. (Ch. 1)

cost center   A group of operating activities having some common characteristics for the measurement of performance and the assignment of responsibility for the incurrence of costs. (Ch. 12)

cost driver   The divisor used in calculating the predetermined variable manufacturing overhead rate. This divisor is the estimate of the expected level of production. It is often expressed in terms of machine hours or direct labor hours. (Activity-based costing treats any activity that causes overhead as a cost driver.) (Chs. 7, 8)

cost of capital   The future cost of raising capital. It is the weighted average of the cost of debt and the cost of common stock. Weights are the proportions of debt and common stock in the capital structure. (Ch. 14)

cost of goods manufactured   The cost of the product made by the manufacturing firm. It is equal to direct materials plus direct labor plus overhead plus beginning work in process inventory minus ending work in process inventory. (Ch. 2)

cost of goods sold   The cost of the product sold to the firm's customers. For a merchandiser, it is equal to beginning merchandise inventory plus net purchases minus ending merchandise inventory. For a manufacturer, it is equal to beginning finished goods inventory plus cost of goods manufactured minus ending finished goods inventory. (Ch. 2)

cost of raw materials used in production   The cost of direct materials placed in the production process. It is equal to beginning raw materials inventory plus net purchases minus ending raw materials inventory. (Ch. 2)

cost pool   A group of factors, as nearly homogeneous as possible, that cause resources to be used in making a product. Cost pools are used in activity-based costing. (Ch. 8)

cost–volume–profit analysis   The study of the effects of changes in fixed costs, variable costs, sales quantities, sales prices, and sales mix on profit. (Ch. 3)

cost–volume–profit graph   A graph depicting the relationships between variable costs, fixed costs, total costs, and total revenue. (Ch. 3)

cross-sectional analysis   Analysis of several firms at one point in time. Popular cross-sectional methods include common-size statements and ratio analysis. (Ch. 15)

current entry value accounting   A system of accounting that assigns the assets on the balance sheet their current input prices—that is, the current price to make or buy the asset. (Ch. 16)

current exit value accounting   A system of accounting that assigns the assets on the balance sheet their current output prices—that is, the current price at which the asset can be sold. (Ch. 16) data   Symbols that represent something. (Ch. 1)

decentralization   An organizational approach in which a supervising function does not maintain significant direction and authority over operations and policies relating to a number of identifiable, separate activities and operations. Rather, it allows decentralized divisions to have that authority. (Ch. 1)

decision   A choice among alternatives on a given issue. (Ch. 1)

decision support systems (DSS)   Computer systems designed to support the decision-making process of managers by providing information from data and models. (Ch. 1)

denominator activity level   The value of the cost driver. It is the denominator of the fraction comprising the predetermined fixed manufacturing overhead rate. (Ch. 8)

depreciation tax shield   A reduction of taxes due to the allowance of depreciation as a tax deduction. (Ch. 14)

direct cost   Given a particular activity, product, or organizational unit, a cost that can be traced easily and unambiguously to it. (Ch. 2)

direct labor   The workers who make a product; the cost in wages of these workers. (Ch. 2)

direct labor budget   A budget that estimates the cost of direct labor for the future production process. (Ch. 5)

direct materials   Raw materials that are used in the manufacture of a product; the cost of these materials. (Ch. 2)

direct materials budget   A budget that estimates the purchases of direct or raw materials. (Ch. 5)

directing   Leading the organization toward the achievement of its goals. (Ch. 1)

discounted payback   A capital budgeting technique that indicates the amount of time to recoup the investment in terms of discounted dollars. (Ch. 14)

double-declining balance   An accelerated form of depreciation. Annual depreciation is equal to (2/life of the asset) × book value. The last year's depreciation is whatever is necessary to reduce the book value to the salvage value. (Ch. 14)

effectiveness   The degree to which a goal or objective is accomplished. (Ch. 1)

efficiency   The degree to which a limited amount of resources (input) are expended to achieve a certain output. (Ch. 1)

equivalent units   The number of units that could have been completed if the entire effort were spent only on making whole units. (Ch. 11)

executive information systems   Special types of decision support systems designed to meet the specific needs and desires of top executives. (Ch. 17)

expert system   Computer system that captures the knowledge of a human expert generally as a set of rules. (Ch. 17)

factory overhead budget   A prediction of all production costs for a budget period, except direct material and direct labor costs, classified by responsibility, function, or form. (Ch. 5)

financial accounting   Accounting for purposes of financial reporting to external users via the financial statements. (Ch. 1)

financial planning languages   Programming languages that permit modeling of the financial interactions and simulation of the results. (Ch. 5)

financing activities   Activities relating to obtaining capital. They include borrowing debt and issuing preferred and common stock. They also include repayment of debt and reacquisition of stock. (Ch. 6)

finished goods inventory   Completed but unsold goods; the cost of such goods. (Ch. 2)

fixed costs   Cost that does not vary as the activity level changes. (Ch. 2)

flexible budget   A budget structure in which the budget amounts may be adjusted to any activity level. (Ch. 9)

flexible budget variance   The difference between the income predicted by the flexible budget and the actual income. (Ch. 9)

flexible manufacturing system   A group of machines or other equipment that can make a number of different products. They often use robots and computers in the manufacturing process. (Ch. 17)

full costing   A method of costing which allocates the fixed overhead to ending inventory and cost of goods sold. (Ch. 5)

fundamental funds equation   The equation that states that the net increase in cash is equal to cash inflows minus cash outflows. (Ch. 6)

future value   The value at a future time of a cash flow made today. (Ch. 14)

general price-level changes   Changes in the value of an asset or liability stemming from changes in the value of the dollar. (Ch. 16)

general variance model   A model that characterizes all variances to be equal to a price variance (which is actual cost minus input standard cost) plus a quantity variance (which is input standard cost minus output standard cost). (Ch. 7)

goal congruency   Various people in the organization working toward the organization's goals. (Ch. 4)

goal incongruency   People in the organization working to accomplish different and conflicting goals that are at odds with the organization's goals. (Ch. 4)

goal-seeking   With respect to decision support systems, setting some goal and specifying some variable to change in an attempt to reach the goal. (Ch. 1)

goals   An objective established to coordinate and direct a group in the pursuit of desired activities. (Ch. 5)

gross margin or **gross profit**   Sales minus cost of goods sold. (Ch. 2)

high–low method   A rudimentary approach to separating fixed and variable components of total cost by selecting a high and a low activity level and corresponding cost within the relevant range of activity, drawing the points on a cost–volume–profit graph, and extending a line through the points. (Ch. 3)

historical cost accounting   A system of accounting that assigns the assets on the balance sheet their original cost less any accumulated depreciation. (Ch. 16)

holding gains (or losses)   The increase (or decrease) of the asset's current entry value over a period. (Ch. 16)

ideal standard cost   The minimum cost that would result if all productive inputs were combined under ideal conditions to achieve a given output level. Due to its premise, such cost is meaningful only in a relative and not in a practical sense. (Ch. 7)

incremental analysis   The examination of only the cost and revenue items that differ among decision alternatives. (Also known as differential analysis.) (Ch. 3)

incremental cost   A cost that appears in one alternative but not in another in a particular decision-making context. (Ch. 2)

incremental revenue   The additional revenue, either as to amount or as to timing, that results from pursuing an alternative course of action. (Ch. 4)

indirect cost   Given a particular activity, product, or organizational unit, a cost that cannot be traced easily or unambiguously to it. (Ch. 2)

information Data processed to yield useful insights for a decision maker. (Ch. 1)

input standard cost A general term that refers to the actual quantity of input multiplied by the standard price. (Ch. 7)

interest The amount paid or received for the borrowing or lending of money. (Ch. 14)

internal rate of return A capital budgeting technique that determines the rate at which the investment has a net present value of zero. (Ch. 14)

investing activities Activities relating to obtaining long-term assets. They include the purchase and the sale of long-term assets such as stocks and bonds of other corporations, property, plant, and equipment. (Ch. 6)

investment center A unit headed by a manager responsible for costs, revenues, and long-term outlays. (Ch. 12)

investment tax credit A tax method sometimes allowed by Congress to spur investment. It is a percentage of the investment in specified assets and is directly subtracted from the tax bill. (Ch. 14)

job cost report The detailed record for the accumulation of job costs (that is, the material, labor, and overhead cost incurred on a job or specific production). (Ch. 10)

job costing A method of cost accounting in which costs for material, labor, and overhead (either actual or standard) are charged to a specific job or lot. The job or lot may consist of either a single unit or like units and pertains to either goods or services. (Ch. 10)

joint products Two or more products so related that one cannot be produced without producing the others, each having relatively high substantial value and being produced simultaneously by the same process up to a split-off point. (Ch. 4)

just-in-time production A manufacturing philosophy in which the product should be made only after a customer has ordered it and only for the amount ordered. The idea is to reduce inventory costs and to create a more efficient manufacturing system. (Ch. 17)

labor efficiency variance The difference between the actual direct labor cost at the standard wage rate and the standard direct labor hours times the standard wage rate. (Ch. 7)

labor rate variance The difference between actual wage rate and standard wage rate multiplied by the actual hours of direct labor used. (Ch. 7)

linear programming A mathematical technique for allocating limited resources among activities for the attainment of goals. The measure of performance is a linear function of the controllable variables, and restrictions on the use of resources may be expressed as linear equations or inequalities. (Ch. 4)

make-or-buy decision The decision whether to produce a component, product, or service internally versus purchasing it from an outside supplier. (Ch. 4)

management accounting "The process of identification, measurement, accumulation, analysis, preparation, interpretation, and communication of information used by management to plan, evaluate, and control within an organization and to assure appropriate use of and accountability for its resources." (*NAA Statement No. 1A*, 1981) (Ch. 1)

management planning and control The process of implementing the strategic goals of the firm effectively and efficiently. (Ch. 1)

manufacturing organization A firm that makes a product and sells it to its customers. (Ch. 2)

manufacturing (or materials) resource planning Computer systems focusing on inventory control and production planning for a manufacturing process. (Ch. 17)

market ratios A group of ratios that focus on the cash dividends paid out and on the market price of the common stock. (Ch. 15)

master budget A set of interrelated budgets depicting the interrelationships of all the subsidiary budgets. (Ch. 5)

master budget variance The difference between the income predicted by the master budget and the actual income. (Ch. 9)

material price variance The difference between actual cost per unit and standard cost per unit multiplied by the actual quantity of material purchased. (Ch. 7)

material quantity variance The difference between the actual unit usage of materials and the established standard unit usage, multiplied by the standard unit price for the material. (Ch. 7)

merchandise inventory Goods awaiting sale that were acquired from another organization; the cost of such goods. (Ch. 2)

merchandising organization A firm that buys a product and then sells it to its customers. (Ch. 2)

minimum required rate of return Used in computing residual income, it is the rate of return that reflects the company's estimated cost of capital and growth expectations. (Ch. 12)

mixed cost A cost composed of fixed and variable components over various relevant ranges of operation. (Ch. 3)

monetary items Assets and liabilities that represent claims or obligations in fixed dollar amounts regardless of the inflation rate. Monetary items include cash, accounts receivable, accounts payable, and notes payable. (Ch. 16)

net present value A capital budgeting technique in which the present value of the cash inflows is netted against the present value of the cash outflows. (Ch. 14)

net present value profile A graph of the net present values as a function of the cost of capital. (Ch. 14)

nominal interest rate An interest rate that includes an expected inflation rate component. It is equal to the real interest rate plus the inflation rate. (Ch. 16)

noncontrollable cost Cost that a manager cannot influence and for which he or she is not responsible. (Ch. 2)

office automation The computerization and interconnection of office activities. (Ch. 17)

operating activities Activities relating to the profit-making aspects of the firm. They include the sale of goods and services, the purchase of raw materials and supplies, the conversion of these raw materials into finished goods inventory, and the administrative and selling tasks of the firm. (Ch. 6)

operating cycle ratios A group of ratios that concentrate on accounts receivable, inventory, and estimating the length of the operating cycle. (Ch. 15)

operating expense budget A schedule of the various production, administration, and distribution expenses, classified by the nature of the expense, of an organizational unit or subunit required to attain unit objectives during a period. (Ch. 5)

operational control The process of carrying out specific tasks effectively and efficiently. (Ch. 1)

opportunity cost The potential benefits sacrificed by the selection of one particular action over another. (Ch. 2)

ordinary annuity An annuity whose cash flows occur at the end of the period. (Ch. 14)

organization A group of individuals united to achieve common goals. (Ch. 1)

organizational learning The process of an organization learning about its environment and learning how to learn. (Ch. 17)

organizing   The determination of the structure needed to achieve a goal. (Ch. 1)

output standard cost   A general term that refers to the standard quantity of inputs for the actual output multiplied by the standard price. (Ch. 7)

overabsorbed overhead   The excess of manufacturing overhead applied to production over the actual expenses incurred. Synonymous with *overapplied overhead.* (Ch. 8)

overhead   Any production cost except direct materials and direct labor. (Ch. 2)

overhead rate   The ratio of overhead costs for a period of time to the amount of some measurable associated causal factor in the same period of time. For example, the expected or standard overhead costs divided by the expected or standard productive output. (Ch. 7)

participative budgeting   A budgeting approach in which subordinates and supervisors work together to establish the budget. (Ch. 5)

payback period   A capital budgeting technique that indicates the amount of time required to recover the investment from the budgeted cash inflows. (Ch. 14)

percentage analysis   A type of time-series analysis that focuses on the percentage change in selected accounts. (Ch. 15)

period cost   Cost matched against revenues on a period basis. (Ch. 2)

planning   The identification of a future position or goal and the determination of the necessary steps to reaching it. (Ch. 1)

pool rate   The cost per unit of the cost driver for a given cost pool. It is equal to the estimated costs of the cost pool divided by the estimated measure of the cost driver. (Ch. 8)

practical standard cost   A realistic expectation of the cost that would result under typical operating conditions, in which there is unavoidable material waste and normal nonproductive labor hours. (Ch. 7)

predetermined fixed manufacturing overhead rate   The rate at which fixed manufacturing overhead is applied to production, based on the ratio of total budgeted fixed overhead costs for a period of time to the expected total of some measure of activity (cost driver) for the same period, such as machine hours or direct labor hours. (Ch. 8)

predetermined manufacturing overhead rate   The predetermined variable manufacturing overhead rate plus the predetermined fixed overhead rate. (Ch. 8)

predetermined variable manufacturing overhead rate   The rate at which variable manufacturing overhead is applied to production, based on the ratio of total budgeted variable overhead costs for a period of time to the expected total of some measure of activity (cost driver) for the same period, such as machine hours or direct labor hours. (Ch. 7)

present value   The value today of a cash flow made in the future. (Ch. 14)

price variance   A general term used to refer to the difference between actual input costs and their standard costs. The more specific terms are *material price variance, labor rate variance,* and *variable overhead spending variance.* (Ch. 7)

prime cost   A term for direct materials plus direct labor. (Ch. 2)

process costing   A method of cost accounting wherein costs (either actual or standard) are charged to processes, operations, or departments. This method of costing is used where there is continuous mass production of like units that usually pass in consecutive order through a series of production steps called operations or processes. Costs are accumulated by those operations or processes for a specified period of time; an average cost per unit of output is developed for costing purposes. (Ch. 11)

product cost   Cost associated with the purchase or manufacture of a product in whatever period the costs are incurred. (Ch. 2)

product costing   The use of a system of accounting to determine the cost of a unit of product or service. There are two basic systems of product costing: job costing (q.v.) and process costing (discussed in Chapter 11). (Ch. 10) product margin   The segment margin when the segment is a product. (Ch. 13)

production budget   A prediction of the cost of producing the goods needed to meet the sales budget and maintain suitable inventories. (Ch. 5)

profit center   A segment of a business for which revenues and costs are directly traceable to a segment manager and are accumulated in the accounts. Such data are then used to evaluate managerial performance and accountability. (Ch. 12)

profitability ratios   A group of ratios that indicate the profit-making capabilities of the company. (Ch. 15)

program, planning, budgeting systems   Budgets classified by programs. Used by some non-profit organizations. (Ch. 5)

project audit   An examination of the results of a capital project. This examination is carried out to assess the accuracy of the estimates and to decide whether the correct decision was made. (Ch. 14)

purchases budget   A prediction, by types of material, of the cost and time needed to provide budgeted material requirements. (Ch. 5)

purchasing power gain or loss   Gain (or loss) that arises from holding liabilities (or assets) during a period of inflation or that arise from holding assets (or liabilities) during a period of deflation. They arise because later cash flows are made with dollars of lesser value during a period of inflation or greater value during a period of deflation. (Ch. 16)

quantity variance   A general term used to refer to the difference between input standard cost and output standard cost. The more specific terms are *material quantity variance, labor efficiency variance,* and *variable overhead efficiency variance.* (Ch. 7)

ratio analysis   A type of cross-sectional examination that typically looks at one number divided by another. Five categories of ratios are: profitability, solvency, structure, operating cycle, and market ratios. (Ch. 15)

raw materials inventory   The stock of raw materials that will be used in the production process; the cost of these materials. (Ch. 2)

real interest rate   An interest rate that does not include an expected inflation rate component. (Ch. 16)

realizable holding gain   A holding gain due to the sale or use of an asset or to an unsold or unused asset. Thus, realizable holding gains are equal to realized holding gains plus unrealized holding gains. (Ch. 16)

realized holding gain   A holding gain due to the sale or use of an asset. Commonly, realized holding gains are attributable to sold units of inventory and to the current depreciable amount of long-term assets. (Ch. 16)

regression analysis   A statistical method that determines the best straight line that represents a data set. (Appendix A)

relevant cost   A cost that should be considered when choosing among alternatives. Only those costs yet to be incurred (future costs) that will differ among the alternatives (the differential costs) are relevant in decision making. (Ch. 4)

relevant range   The range of economic activity within which estimates and predictions are valid. The range of activity levels (volume) over which fixed costs remain fixed in total and variable costs are proportional in total to the volume. Cost–volume–profit analysis assumptions are valid within the relevant range. (Ch. 3)

reporting   Receiving and transmitting information about performance and progress toward goals. (Ch. 1)

residual income (controllable)   The net income that the investment center manager is able to earn above the capital charge. The capital charge is based on the controllable investment. (Ch. 12)

responsibility accounting   A reporting system in which costs and revenues are assigned to the level of the organization having responsibility for them. (Chs. 1, 12)

return on investment (controllable)   The ratio of controllable profit to controllable investment. (Ch. 12)

sales budget   A prediction, classified by responsibility, product, and area, of the net revenue from sales expected to be available to an organization in a period of time. (Ch. 5)

sales forecasting   A prediction of the sales for the budget period using various data and methods such as trend projections, correlation analysis, operations research techniques, and computer simulation, or less rigorous prediction procedures. (Ch. 5)

sales mix   The relative combination of quantities of the various products that make up the total sales of a company. (Ch. 3)

sales variance   The differences between the sales revenues predicted by the flexible budget and the actual sales revenues. (Ch. 9)

scarce resources   Resources limited in some way that hinders unlimited production and sales. (Ch. 4)

segment   An identifiable collection of related resources and activities. Operationally it is a significant strategic or organizational component of an entity enterprise—a subsidiary, division, department, the entity itself, or other units—having distinctive resources and activities that can be treated as an entity for planning and control purposes. (Ch. 4)

segment analysis   The examination of a portion of an entity, a product line, or any other subdivision of an entity. (Ch. 4)

segment margin   The contribution margin for each segment of a business less all separable fixed costs. (Ch. 13)

segment reporting   The process of presenting financial and other information for components of a business entity. (Ch. 13)

selling cost   Cost incurred in order to sell a service or a product. (Ch. 2)

sell-or-process-further decision   The decision regarding joint products that may be sold or processed further at the split-off point. (Ch. 4)

separable cost   The cost or resource uniquely associated with an organizational unit. (Ch. 13)

service department   Departments that do not produce goods but provide services to producing departments. (Ch. 13)

service organization   A firm that sells a service (as opposed to a product) to its customers. (Ch. 2)

simple interest   Interest computed only on the original principal. (Ch. 14)

single sum   Only one cash flow. (Ch. 14)

solvency   A firm's ability to pay its debts. (Ch. 6)

solvency ratios   A group of ratios that indicate the firm's ability to pay its debts. (Ch. 15)

span of control   The number of subordinates directly answering to one manager. (Ch. 12)

specific price-level changes   Changes in the value of an asset or liability due to the economic conditions of a specific resource or group of resources. (Ch. 16)

split-off point   The point in the production process for with joint products, at which common inputs become separable, individual products become identifiable, and beyond which separate costs are recognized. (Ch. 4)

staffing   The selection of personnel to perform the organization's tasks. (Ch. 1)

standard cost   A predetermined cost of the product that management sets as the goal to be attained under projected conditions. (Ch. 7)

standard cost system   An accounting technique whereby costs are recorded on the basis of predetermined standards while deviations (variances) from such standards are identified separately for analysis and control. (Ch. 7)

standard quantity expected   The standard quantity of inputs that is allowed given the actual quantity produced. (Ch. 7)

statement of cash flows   A financial statement that shows the cash inflows and outflows of the entity. (Ch. 6)

static budget   Master budget made for only one activity level. (Ch. 9)

step method   A method for allocating costs of service departments. (Ch. 13)

straight line   A form of depreciation. Annual depreciation is equal to (cost - salvage value)/life of the asset. (Ch. 14)

strategic planning   The process of summarizing and articulating the basic objectives and goals for the organization. (Ch. 1)

structure ratios   A group of ratios that examine the firm's composition of its capital, assets, and liabilities. (Ch. 15)

sum-of-the-years' digits   An accelerated form of depreciation. Annual depreciation is equal to the product of the number of periods remaining divided by the sum-of-the-years' digits times the depreciable cost (cost minus salvage value). (Ch. 14)

sunk cost   A cost that has already been incurred. (Ch. 2)

T-account approach   A method that helps one to prepare statements of cash flow. It consists of a series of account entries such that the debit side of the cash accounts indicates a cash inflow and the credit side shows cash outflows. (Appendix B)

target net income   A desired level of profit or contribution management establishes as a goal. (Ch. 3)

time-series analysis   Analysis of one firm across time. Popular time-series methods include percentage analysis and trend analysis. This is also referred to as horizontal analysis. (Ch. 15)

time value of money   The concept that one dollar received today is not equivalent to one dollar received in the future because of interest. (Ch. 14)

transfer price   The price charged on a good transferred between divisions of the same company. (Ch. 12)

trend analysis   A type of time-series analysis that focuses on the values of selected variables across time in terms of base-year values. (Ch. 15)

unavoidable costs   Sunk costs that have been incurred and thus cannot be changed; future costs that do not differ among alternatives. (Ch. 4)

underabsorbed overhead   The excess of actual manufacturing expenses incurred over the amount of manufacturing overhead applied to production. Synonymous with *underapplied overhead*. (Ch. 8)

unrealized holding gain   A holding gain due to an unsold or unused asset. Commonly, unrealized holding gains are attributable to unsold units of inventory and to the undepreciated amount of long-term assets. (Ch. 16)

variable cost   A cost that varies in proportion with changes in activity level. (Ch. 2)

variable costing   A method of costing that does not allocate fixed overhead to ending inventory and cost of goods sold. Instead, fixed overhead is kept as a separate expense on the income statement. (Ch. 5)

variable manufacturing overhead efficiency variance The difference between actual direct labor hours incurred and the standard direct labor hours of actual production, multiplied by the standard variable overhead rate per direct labor hour, where direct labor hours is the basis for applying overhead (other appropriate bases could be used). (Ch. 7)

variable manufacturing overhead spending variance The difference between actual variable overhead costs incurred and the actual number of units of input (direct labor hours or machine hours) multiplied by the actual variable overhead rate per unit of input. (Ch. 7)

variance The difference between actual and planned results (Ch. 1); the difference between actual cost and standard cost (Ch. 7).

volume variance The difference between fixed cost assigned to products in a specified time period and budgeted fixed manufacturing overhead. (Ch. 8)

what-if analysis With respect to decision support systems, the altering of certain parameters and variable relationships to assess the sensitivity of the solution to these changes. (Ch. 1)

work in process inventory Goods that have been placed in production but are not yet complete; the cost of such goods. (Ch. 2)

zero-based budgeting The process of developing a periodic budget on the assumption that the enterprise is initiating operations at the beginning of the budget period; thus a total budget must be developed anew for each successive period rather than relying on budgets based on incremental changes from period to period. (Ch. 5)

Index

Page numbers in boldface indicate main discussions of glossary terms.